ESSENTIAL SKILLS FOR BUSINESS

ESSENTIAL SKILLS FOR BUSINESS

Lee Perlitz

National Library of Australia Cataloguing-in-Publication Data

Author: Lee Perlitz
Title: *Essential Skills for Business*
ISBN: 9781760427221 (paperback)

NATIONAL LIBRARY OF AUSTRALIA

A catalogue record for this work is available from the National Library of Australia

---

Published in Australia by

McGraw-Hill Education (Australia) Pty Ltd
Level 33, 680 George St, Sydney, NSW 2000

Publisher: Sarah Cook
Content developer: Caroline Hunter
Production editor: Elmandi Du Toit
Digital specialist: Bethany Ng
Copy editor: Robyn Flemming
Proofreader: Sue Jamieson
Permissions cleared by: Straive, India
Indexer: Straive, India
Cover design: Sarah Cook
Cover image: Goodstudio/Shutterstock
Internal design: Simon Rattray, Squirt Creative
Typeset by Straive, India
Printed in Singapore by Markono Print Media Pte Ltd

Foreword

Without business, and business skills, nothing happens.

A good idea, product or service is not enough. Each must be developed to the point where it is useful for a client or customer. It then has to be promoted and sold.

Geoff Bezos would own a small web company instead of Amazon if he could not work effectively with customers, staff and colleagues. He would not be successful if he did not understand finance, time management, documentation and all the other aspects of business.

My career has focused on using technology to enhance education and other processes. I have met people who think that they can easily find the knowledge they need now that we have search engines and information available on the internet.

Yet, I have discovered that you can't Google wisdom.

It is essential to get the necessary knowledge and information from *experts*. This information needs to be condensed and sequenced appropriately so that it can be understood and absorbed easily. Good luck finding that through random search results.

Instead, clever people go to a reliable, expert source. It may cost a little up front, but in the long term, it is much more effective and efficient, and much likelier to lead to success.

Hence, Lee's business book has been in print since 2007. It is a proven solution.

In my more than twenty-five years at the forefront of education and technology, I have found that "low-hanging fruit" and "quick wins" are not effective. Technology, even in the amazing world we live in, doesn't change the fundamentals.

- Build on the basics.
- Learn from experts.
- Become knowledgeable.
- Study effectively.

Learn the skills of effective business and success will follow, whether you are working for a small business, a large company or starting your own business.

Welcome to a proven pathway. Good luck—use it to help create a successful future.

Peter N West
Emerging Technologies Manager, TAFE NSW, Australia

Peter West is an educational technology specialist and organisational leader with more than 25 years' experience. He is credited for successfully elevating Australian schools to leading positions by orchestrating and delivering education ecosystems that generated significant outcomes and improved learning experiences for students, educators, administrators and parents.

Peter has published over 80 articles on organisational change, professional development and modern educational practices that leverage technology. He has presented at many conferences nationally and internationally and has received many awards and recognitions.

In 2018, Peter's industry and peer recognition saw him approached to lead the Learning Technologies team in the then newly created Digital Learning Lab at TAFE NSW. Peter's small team of specialists focuses on researching and developing a wide range of cutting-edge technologies to enhance education and provide strategic advantage to TAFE NSW.

Brief contents

PART 1	The business core	1
Chapter 1	Engage in workplace communication	2
Chapter 2	Use inclusive work practices	24
Chapter 3	Support personal wellbeing in the workplace	44
Chapter 4	Apply critical thinking skills in a team environment	60
Chapter 5	Assist with maintaining workplace safety	73
Chapter 6	Participate in sustainable work practices	101
PART 2	**In the office**	**117**
Chapter 7	Maintain business resources	118
Chapter 8	Organise workplace information	134
Chapter 9	Organise schedules	152
Chapter 10	Purchase goods and services	172
Chapter 11	Write simple documents	183
Chapter 12	Design and produce business documents	203
Chapter 13	Design and produce spreadsheets	229
Chapter 14	Create electronic presentations	261
Chapter 15	Maintain financial records	281
PART 3	**Working with customers and colleagues**	**311**
Chapter 16	Deliver and monitor a service to customers	312
Chapter 17	Advise on products and services	337
Chapter 18	Process customer complaints	352
Chapter 19	Organise personal work priorities	366
Chapter 20	Work in a team	386
Chapter 21	Support effective workplace relationships	405

Contents

Preface ix
About the author xvi
Text at a glance xvii

PART 1
The business core

CHAPTER 1
Engage in workplace communication 2
1.1 Planning workplace communication 3
1.2 Undertaking routine communication 9
1.3 Participating in workplace communication 15

CHAPTER 2
Use inclusive work practices 24
2.1 Establishing practices that support individual differences in the workplace 25
2.2 Working effectively with individual differences 34
2.3 Assessing the use of inclusive practices 39

CHAPTER 3
Support personal wellbeing in the workplace 44
3.1 Recognising factors that impact personal wellbeing 45
3.2 Planning communication with a supervisor 48
3.3 Communicating with a supervisor 52
3.4 Investigating available wellbeing resources 54

CHAPTER 4
Apply critical thinking skills in a team environment 60
4.1 Preparing to address workplace problems 60
4.2 Evaluating solutions for workplace problems 64
4.3 Finalising and reviewing solution development 68

CHAPTER 5
Assist with maintaining workplace safety 73
5.1 Assisting to incorporate WHS policies and procedures into work team processes 74
5.2 Contributing to consultative arrangements for managing WHS 80
5.3 Contributing to organisational procedures for providing WHS training 84
5.4 Participating in identifying hazards, and assessing and controlling risks for the work area 88

CHAPTER 6
Participate in sustainable work practices 101
6.1 Measuring sustainable work practices 102
6.2 Supporting sustainable work practices 107
6.3 Seeking opportunities to improve sustainable work practices 113

PART 2
In the office

CHAPTER 7
Maintain business resources 118
7.1 Advising on resource requirements 119
7.2 Acquiring resources 124
7.3 Monitoring resource usage and maintenance 128

CHAPTER 8
Organise workplace information 134
8.1 Receiving, acquiring and assessing information 135
8.2 Organising information 141
8.3 Reviewing information needs 148

CHAPTER 9
Organise schedules 152
9.1 Establishing schedule requirements 153
9.2 Managing schedules 164
9.3 Evaluating the effectiveness of schedules 169

CHAPTER 10
Purchase goods and services 172
10.1 Understanding purchasing and your own requirements 173
10.2 Making purchases 175
10.3 Receiving purchases 180

CHAPTER 11
Write simple documents 183
11.1 Planning a simple document 184
11.2 Drafting a simple document 194
11.3 Finalising a simple document 197

CHAPTER 12

Design and produce business documents 203

12.1 Selecting and preparing resources 204
12.2 Designing a document 210
12.3 Producing a document 223
12.4 Finalising a document 225

CHAPTER 13

Design and produce spreadsheets 229

13.1 Selecting and preparing resources 230
13.2 Planning spreadsheet design 234
13.3 Creating a spreadsheet 236
13.4 Producing charts 252
13.5 Finalising and presenting spreadsheets 258

CHAPTER 14

Create electronic presentations 261

14.1 Preparing to create a presentation 262
14.2 Creating a presentation 266
14.3 Finalising a presentation 278

CHAPTER 15

Maintain financial records 281

15.1 Recognising the key components of organisational accounting systems and procedures 282
15.2 Preparing journals required for posting to the general ledger 288
15.3 Posting journal entries and reconciling discrepancies 294
15.4 Maintaining the general ledger 303
15.5 Understanding legislation, codes of practice and national standards 306

PART 3
Working with customers and colleagues

CHAPTER 16

Deliver and monitor a service to customers 312

16.1 Identifying customer needs 313
16.2 Delivering a service to customers 319
16.3 Evaluating customer service delivery 330

CHAPTER 17

Advise on products and services 337

17.1 Developing product and service knowledge 338
17.2 Responding to customer requests 344
17.3 Enhancing the information provided 348

CHAPTER 18

Process customer complaints 352

18.1 Receiving complaints 353
18.2 Processing complaints 357
18.3 Resolving complaints 360

CHAPTER 19

Organise personal work priorities 366

19.1 Organising and completing your own work schedule 367
19.2 Evaluating your own work performance 376
19.3 Coordinating personal skills development and learning 381

CHAPTER 20

Work in a team 386

20.1 Identifying individual work tasks within a team 387
20.2 Contributing effectively to team goals 392
20.3 Working effectively with team members 396
20.4 Communicating effectively with the team 401

CHAPTER 21

Support effective workplace relationships 405

21.1 Gathering information and ideas 406
21.2 Developing team relationships and networks 414
21.3 Contributing to positive team outcomes 419

Glossary 425
Index 431

Preface

Life can present many opportunities, but the most rewarding and valuable ones are those you make for yourself. Your career, like your life, will be shaped by the commitment you make to developing these opportunities, as well as by the goals you set and the decisions you make.

Working towards a qualification—particularly a business qualification—is the first step in developing such opportunities. All industries must use basic business principles in order to succeed. By gaining a business qualification, you will be able to find work along many different pathways in many different industries.

In this text, you will learn about common business practices such as communicating effectively, using critical thinking skills in a team environment, working with customers and colleagues, and performing administration duties such as organising schedules and workplace information.

Legal and industry obligations

Each chapter addresses a different aspect of the business world. Some chapters may have overlapping elements, while other areas will require a unique perspective. However, all areas of business, regardless of industry, have legislative requirements and industry codes of practice.

While some of these, along with organisational policies and procedures, will be covered in individual chapters, we will look at the general legal obligations and considerations of doing business, as they are essential elements in your everyday work.

Ethical principles

Ethical principles are designed to guide you in your dealings with other people, whether they are customers, colleagues, suppliers or anyone else you work with. They include many of the following ideals:

- *Honesty in your dealings with others.* This is the cornerstone of trust, and trust is essential in developing good working relationships. You should be truthful in all your dealings and not deliberately mislead or deceive others by misrepresenting or overstating issues, telling partial truths or selectively omitting facts.
- *Respect for other people.* This is demonstrated by treating others with dignity and as equals, and by showing interest in them regardless of their background.
- *Integrity and impartiality.* This refers to the "wholeness" of a person's character, which is demonstrated by their being principled, reliable, scrupulous, and consistent in their thoughts, words and actions.
- *Reputation and morale.* This refers to understanding the importance of your organisation's standing in the business community and the pride and morale of the people who work within it and ensuring that nothing is done to undermine its reputation or morale.
- *Accountability and transparency.* This is demonstrated by taking responsibility in your work teams, sharing information and being open about your methods of working.

Industry codes of practice

A code of practice is a written guideline generally issued by a professional association. It is based on the ethical standards for a profession, trade, occupation, organisation or union. Codes of practice don't usually carry the same legal obligations as legislation. Often, they consist of rules crafted in response to actual or potential dangers observed on the job. For example, work health and safety (WHS) codes of practice are issued for various industries in order to encourage safer working conditions, and WHS professionals are expected to work within the codes that are applicable to their activities and industries.

An industry's code of practice is therefore generally based on principles, values and behaviours that are specific to that industry's particular needs, as outlined in its code of ethics. A code of practice sets out:

- the rights of employees to be treated fairly and equitably in the workplace
- avenues for resolving complaints or breaches of policies and codes
- the legal and ethical obligations and expectations of all staff to act in accordance with the expressed standards of conduct, integrity and accountability contained in relevant legislation, work policies and agreements.

Its objectives are to:

- provide direction to staff on expected behavioural standards while working within their industry or individual organisation
- assist staff in dealing with ethical issues in ways that reflect the organisation's values and standards
- promote professionalism and excellence within its industry
- showcase the organisation's social responsibilities.

It is important to remember that codes of practice differ for every organisation and that they don't and can't cover every possible situation. Some industries offer national codes of practice that provide standards of behaviour for their specific industries.

Bullying and harassment

Workplace bullying and/or harassment is a repeated and unreasonable behaviour directed towards an individual or a group of people. It is a risk to health and safety, as it may affect the mental and physical health of workers.

Bullying can be psychological, physical or even indirect (e.g. when a person is deliberately excluded from work-related activities). It might be obvious, but it can also be subtle and not always easy to spot. Examples of workplace bullying include:

- abusive or offensive language or comments
- aggressive and intimidating behaviour
- belittling or humiliating comments
- practical jokes or demeaning initiation rituals
- unjustified criticism or complaints.

Failure to take steps to manage the risk of workplace bullying can result in a breach of WHS laws (dealt with shortly). Organisations can minimise the risk of workplace bullying by taking a proactive approach. They can do this through early identification of unreasonable behaviours and situations likely to increase the risk of workplace bullying, and by implementing control measures to manage these risks. A proactive approach include activities such as:

- regularly consulting with workers and WHS representatives to determine if bullying is occurring or whether there are factors likely to increase the risk of workplace bullying
- setting the standard of workplace behaviour, for example through a code of conduct or workplace bullying policy
- designing safe systems of work by clearly defining jobs and providing workers with the resources, information and training they need to carry out their work safely
- implementing workplace bullying reporting and response procedures
- developing productive and respectful workplace relationships through good management practices and effective communication
- providing information and training on workplace bullying policies and procedures, available support and assistance, and how to prevent and respond to workplace bullying
- prioritising measures that foster and protect the psychological health of employees.

Work health and safety

The *Work Health and Safety Act 2011* (Cth) sets out the laws about health and safety requirements affecting most workplaces, work activities and specified high-risk plants, and must be followed by all people in the workforce. Full details on this important issue will be given in Chapter 5.

Organisational requirements for a safe work environment

All organisations are, by law, required to ensure the health and safety of their staff and customers entering their premises. Most will have policies and procedures in place to ensure this and, as an employee, you have an obligation to follow all of them. Where these relate to WHS issues, you may need to look at the ergonomic requirements of your specific work area to ensure that you are working in the best possible environment.

Setting up your work area

A well set-up work area should not only allow easy access to the resources and equipment that you need in the course of your normal working day, but it should also be set up with WHS and ergonomics in mind. Although it isn't always possible, your computer monitor and keyboard should ideally be placed directly in front of you, rather than off to one side. This kind of set-up avoids you having to twist in your seat and thereby possibly injuring your spine over time. In the workplace set-up, items such as in/out trays, paper, letterheads, envelopes, pens and files should all be within easy reach, making the area an efficient and productive place to work. Here are some other factors to consider:

- *Desk.*
  - The top of your desk should be at elbow height when sitting down. To achieve this, you may need to adjust the height of your chair.
  - Avoid a cluttered workspace. Give yourself plenty of room to work. Keep items such as paper, pens, paperclips and hole punches in drawers or on shelving around your desk so that they are easily accessible.
  - The desk surface should be large enough to accommodate input devices such as a keyboard and mouse. Ensure they are easily accessible and can be moved out of the way when you aren't using the computer and need extra work space.
  - The work surface should be high enough underneath so that you don't continually bump your legs against it when sitting down.
  - Use a document holder when you are typing to avoid bending your head forward over a flat document for long periods of time.
- *Lighting and glare.*
  - Use blinds or curtains over windows to reduce glare.
  - Use natural lighting wherever possible.
  - Position your computer monitor so that direct light doesn't reflect off the monitor or into your eyes. The best way to organise this is to position the monitor at right angles to any light source.
  - Use an anti-glare screen if possible. This looks very much like a window screen in the home.
  - Ensure sufficient lighting to work without strain. Too much or too little light can cause headaches, which not only affects your efficiency but also your general health.
- *Chair.*
  - Your chair height should be set so that your feet are flat on the floor and your thighs horizontal.
  - Make sure your chair is adjustable for height and tilt of the seat and backrest.
  - Avoid chairs with armrests, as they restrict movement.
  - Use a lumbar support cushion if the seat doesn't have adequate back support.
  - If necessary, use a footrest to ensure a comfortable sitting position and ensure your legs are bent at a 90- to 110-degree angle.

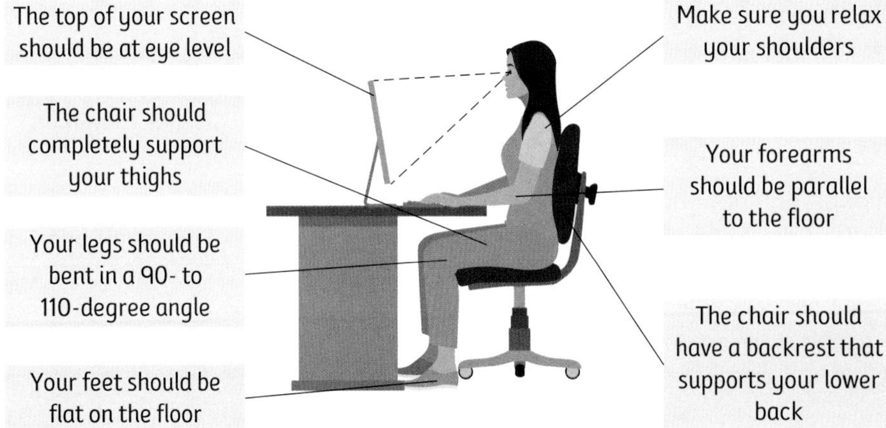
The top of your screen should be at eye level
The chair should completely support your thighs
Your legs should be bent in a 90- to 110-degree angle
Your feet should be flat on the floor
Make sure you relax your shoulders
Your forearms should be parallel to the floor
The chair should have a backrest that supports your lower back

- *Noise reduction.* Noise at work can cause hearing damage that is permanent and disabling. This can be minimised, for example, by housing a noisy machine where it cannot be heard by workers. If this isn't possible, investigate:
  - using screens, barriers, enclosures and absorbent materials to reduce the noise to the people exposed
  - designing and organising the workplace to create quiet workstations
  - improving work techniques to reduce noise levels
  - limiting the time people spend in noisy areas.
- *Repetitive work.* If your job involves sitting at your desk typing for much of the day, you should take regular breaks from this task and do other work. You could do some filing, take care of the mail or run any errands that need to be taken care of. In other words, break up your day into varied tasks. This will avoid putting undue strain on your back, hands or legs due to long periods of repetitive actions.

Work health and safety requirements

In addition to all the requirements already mentioned, most organisations should have policies and procedures in place to deal with:

- inspections (or audits) that should be carried out on a regular basis to ensure the workplace and its equipment and machinery are safe and well maintained
- organisational procedures regarding incidents, accidents, fire and emergencies
- workplace meetings to ensure all staff are consulted and included in WHS issues
- general workplace safety procedures that provide staff with guidance on regulations specific to their industry (e.g. food hygiene or tobacco and alcohol regulations in the hospitality industry).

State and federal legislation and inclusivity

With an eye to ensuring equality for all people, the Commonwealth Government has put in place legislation to safeguard a person's rights to fair treatment, not only in the workplace but also in their personal lives. This means that everyone has the right to live and work in an environment that is free of discrimination and promotes equal employment opportunity (EEO). It is very important to be aware of, and to comply with, the policies and procedures set by your organisation when working with clients and colleagues, as many of these protocols will be based on legislative requirements. Penalties can be very high, both for organisations and for individuals, when in breach of any legislative requirements.

Equal Employment Opportunity Act 1987 (Cth)

Discrimination is any practice that makes distinctions between individuals or groups in order to disadvantage some and advantage others. People can also be discriminated against indirectly if certain attributes, such as parental status, religion, race or impairment make them less able, or even unable, to participate in an activity. Each state has its own specific requirements for EEO and it is important that you are familiar with them. For example, Queensland's anti-discrimination laws require employers to treat people on their merits at every stage of their employment—from the recruitment and interview process through to their daily duties, promotion, training and development opportunities, and their resignation, retrenchment or redundancy.

Further legislation

The following very basic information from the Australian Human Rights Commission website (https://humanrights.gov.au/) provides an overview of further relevant legislation.

- *Age Discrimination Act 2004* (Cth). The Act helps to ensure that people are not treated less favourably on the ground of age in various areas of public life, including:
  - employment
  - provision of goods and services
  - education
  - administration of Commonwealth laws and programs.

  The Act also provides for positive discrimination—that is, actions that assist people of a particular age who experience a disadvantage because of their age. Exemptions apply in the following areas:
  - superannuation
  - migration, taxation and social security laws
  - state laws and other Commonwealth laws
  - some health programs.
- *Disability Discrimination Act 1992* (Cth). The Act's major objectives are to:
  - eliminate discrimination against people with disability
  - promote community acceptance of the principle that people with disability have the same fundamental rights as all members of the community
  - ensure, as far as practicable, that people with disability have the same rights to equality before the law as other people in the community.
- *Australian Human Rights Commission Act 1986* (Cth) (the AHRC Act). The Act established the Human Rights and Equal Opportunity Commission (now known as the "Australian Human Rights Commission") and gives it functions in relation to the following international instruments:
  - *International Covenant on Civil and Political Rights*
  - *Convention Concerning Discrimination in Respect of Employment and Occupation*
  - *Convention on the Rights of Persons with Disabilities*
  - *Convention on the Rights of the Child*
  - *Declaration of the Rights of the Child*
  - *Declaration on the Rights of Disabled Persons*
  - *Declaration on the Rights of Mentally Retarded Persons*
  - *Declaration on the Elimination of All Forms of Intolerance and of Discrimination Based on Religion or Belief.*

  In addition, the Aboriginal and Torres Strait Islander Social Justice Commissioner has specific functions under the AHRC Act and the *Native Title Act 1993* (Cth) to monitor the human rights of Indigenous people.

- *Racial Discrimination Act 1975* (Cth). The Act relates to Australia's obligations under the *International Convention on the Elimination of All Forms of Racial Discrimination.* Its major objectives are to:
  - promote equality before the law for all persons, regardless of their race, colour or national or ethnic origin
  - make it unlawful to discriminate against people on the basis of their race, colour, descent, or national or ethnic origin.
- *Sex Discrimination Act 1984* (Cth). The Act relates to Australia's obligations under the *Convention on the Elimination of All Forms of Discrimination against Women* and certain aspects of the *International Labour Organization Convention 156.* Its major objectives are to:
  - promote equality between men and women
  - eliminate discrimination on the basis of sex, marital status or pregnancy and, with respect to dismissals, family responsibilities
  - eliminate sexual harassment at work, in educational institutions, in the provision of goods and services, in the provision of accommodation and in the delivery of Commonwealth programs.

Further information can be found at http://www.hreoc.gov.au/about/legislation/index.html

Privacy

Respecting privacy is an important element in any business and aligns with ethical principles. Customers will trust you with personal information and they have a right to expect you to protect that information. The *Privacy Act 1988* (Cth) was introduced to regulate, and give individuals greater control over, the way personal information is handled. It allows a person to:

- know why their personal information is being collected, how it will be used and who it will be disclosed to
- choose not to identify themselves, or to use a pseudonym, in certain circumstances
- ask for access to their personal information (including health information)
- stop receiving unwanted direct marketing
- ask for their personal information that is incorrect to be corrected
- make a complaint about an organisation or agency the *Privacy Act* covers if they think their personal information has been mishandled.

The following are examples of privacy policies:

- Services Australia Privacy Policy
- Office of the Australian Information Commissioner Privacy Policy
- The Smith Family WHS Policy
- Southern Cross University WHS Policy.

Principles of fairness and equity

What all of this means is that it is an employer's duty to ensure that all staff are treated fairly, equally and in line with legal obligations. While there is no definitive measure of what the "principles of fairness and equity" are, the Oxford Dictionary interprets these terms as follows:

Fair:

(a) treating people equally; without favouritism or discrimination

(b) just or appropriate in the circumstances

Equity:

(a) the quality of being fair and impartial

Social and cultural sensitivity means that we should behave in a courteous and respectful way towards all our customers and colleagues. We should be impartial, committed to service, accountable and ethical in all our dealings.

As you can see, legislative issues are an important part of any workplace operation. It is essential that you familiarise yourself with the legal obligations they represent to ensure compliance and a harmonious and safe working environment.

Assessment and practice opportunities

In each chapter, you will be able to review the things you are required to have learnt (the "Think about" feature) or to put theory into practice (the "Try this now" feature). At the end of each main section, you will also find review questions (the "Knowledge check" feature). These questions represent elements of your formal assessment in your studies and must be successfully completed in order for you to gain your qualification. Your trainer will provide you with exact details of what you need to do to answer these questions successfully. Don't hesitate to ask them to clarify anything you don't fully understand. All questions are based on information provided in this text, so you should have everything you need to answer each one successfully. As you move through each chapter, however, you may find that some questions relate to the information provided in this Preface and you may need to refresh your knowledge here.

About the author

Lee Perlitz has more than 35 years' experience in the sales, marketing and training fields. In her corporate career, she has been part of the national senior management team of British Airways and held senior sales positions with the Telstra Corporation and the ANA Hotel Group.

Seventeen years ago, Lee turned her hand to corporate and vocational training and has worked as a trainer and RTO manager. In 2006, she founded the Coomera Training College, the RTO arm of Coomera Anglican College. With this experience, Lee is well aware of the issues facing trainers and RTO administrators. For some years now, Lee has owned and operated an RTO consultancy, which offers assistance and compliance services to RTOs Australia-wide.

Lee is a regular and award-winning author for McGraw Hill and other publishers. She has written sixteen educational textbooks covering business, tourism, retail and TAE studies.

Text at a glance

▾ **Learning elements** Learning elements map out the important topics and learning goals to help guide you through the chapter. These Learning elements are mapped against the relevant heading level.

Learning outcomes

1.1 Plan workplace communication

1.2 Undertake routine communication

1.3 Participate in workplace communication

1.1 Planning workplace communication

It could be said that communicating is a self-evident and simple skill; after all, you talk to friends and family all the time, don't you? In the workplace, however, communication takes on very different aspects and needs to be more considered. Much depends, for example, on:

- why you need to communicate
- who you will be communicating with
- how this communication needs to take place
- what needs to be said.

▾ **Think about** Scattered throughout chapters, this feature encourages further thinking.

Think about

1. What type of information do you need to do your work? What type of information does your supervisor need to do their work? What type of information does your organisation's general manager need to run a successful business? How do these types of information vary?

▾ **Try this now** These are practical group/individual activities for students to complete to gain and reflect on knowledge.

Try this now

1. Hold a five-minute conversation with someone in your class or workplace and reflect on your own style of communication. How well do you communicate with others? Is there anything you could do to adjust your style of communication to better accommodate others?

▾ **Boxed example** Included in relevant chapters, these are practical examples to demonstrate key topics and to embed knowledge.

Example

An organisation's website is dated and unable to handle new methods of online sales. This is potentially a big problem for the organisation; however, introducing a new system can be complex and costly and involve long time frames. On the other hand, the organisation is missing out on online sales that would help to pay for system improvements.

When the team meets to discuss the problem, Amar, the sales manager, suggests that the task "upgrading the website" should be placed in Quadrant 1. He feels it is urgent and important, as the business is missing out on sales as customers move increasingly online. The finance manager, Kamala, feels it should be in Quadrant 2—while it is certainly important, it isn't a matter of great urgency and is a project that needs to be properly planned. She also felt it would be very costly and hadn't been budgeted for.

▼ **Knowledge check** Found at the end of each section, these formal assessment questions test student knowledge and must be completed successfully in order to gain the qualification.

Knowledge check

1. Explain why it is important to establish who is the audience for your workplace communication.
2. List at least five reasons why workplace communication might take place.
3. Give at least four examples of how communication needs might vary between different audiences and purposes.
4. When determining the audience for and the purpose of a communication, you should ask yourself a range of questions. List three of these.

▼ **Summary** Each chapter contains a summary of the key points and topics.

Summary

The importance of communication, not only in the workplace but in your personal life, should never be underestimated. The way you present yourself, and your ideas, skills and knowledge, is the foundation upon which you can build your future career and life prospects. One of the best ways of achieving this is by communicating as effectively as possible, and this means being *aware* of what you are saying and doing at all times.

▼ **Key terms** Within each chapter key terms are presented in bold. The definition of these terms can be found in the Glossary at the end of the book.

1.1.5 Planning content of message or communication

When communicating in a **business environment**, it is important to be clear, succinct and not to waste other people's time. When planning your message, consider the following:

- Is the structure of the message logical? Aim for a structure that flows well. Set out what you want to say in a logical manner: step 1, then step 2, and so on.

yet been received.

adjusted entries accounting journal entries that are made at the end of an accounting period after a trial

business environment all the internal and external factors that influence business operations.

business strategies sets of guidelines and action

▼ **QR codes** Wherever you see a QR code, scan it with your phone or tablet to view a short video that demonstrates the practical steps outlined in the book.

Video: Formulas and functions in Excel

Creating basic formulas in Excel isn't difficult. It is a matter of combining the cell references of your data with the correct mathematical operator. **Mathematical operators** are instructions that specify what type of calculation you want to perform on the numbers: are you adding, subtracting, dividing or multiplying? The mathematical operators used in Excel formulas are similar to those used in mathematics:

- Subtraction: minus sign −
- Addition: plus sign +

1

PART 1

The business core

CHAPTER 1

Engage in workplace communication

Learning outcomes

1.1 Plan workplace communication

1.2 Undertake routine communication

1.3 Participate in workplace communication

In the workplace, we are constantly communicating with colleagues and customers. **Communication** can be on the phone, in writing (often emails or short messages on apps such as Teams) or face to face. Good communication skills help us to respond promptly to instructions and enquiries. This is important not only for our own work but also for other people's job performance, which may depend on how effectively we respond to them. Effective communication therefore improves an organisation's efficiency and productivity.

Communication is arguably the single most important component in a successful business. Your organisation can have qualified and reliable staff, clear policies and procedures, and a great location, but none of that matters if the communication process doesn't work. Poor communication in the workplace can result in frustrated employees or customers and misunderstandings that waste time and resources. All of this can lead to an unhappy, incohesive workplace.

The difference between a successful organisation and an unsuccessful one is the ability of its staff to communicate at an appropriate level, using the best possible methods, to achieve the organisation's desired outcomes.

1.1 Planning workplace communication

It could be said that communicating is a self-evident and simple skill; after all, you talk to friends and family all the time, don't you? In the workplace, however, communication takes on very different aspects and needs to be more considered. Much depends, for example, on:

- why you need to communicate
- who you will be communicating with
- how this communication needs to take place
- what needs to be said.

In smaller organisations, people often work together in a small group and in a small space. Communication can be very simple and informal, even between employees and managers. People might use first names and relate to each other in a casual, familiar way. In larger, multinational companies, on the other hand, you are less likely to speak often with a senior manager, the group chief executive officer (CEO) or the chairperson. On those occasions when you need to, you would be expected to communicate in a more formal way or even to follow certain protocols.

An organisation's **productivity** depends on work being done efficiently. Time, as they say, is money. People in the business world are generally very busy and don't have time to waste on irrelevancies or trying to understand confused messages. This means that the time that's available to you to communicate with people in the workplace may be limited, so you need to know exactly what you want to say, how it relates to your audience, and why it is important for them to have this information.

1.1.1 Establishing the audience and purpose of workplace communication

Who is the audience?

When communicating in a business environment, the first thing you need to consider is who your audience is. These people may include:

- colleagues, with whom you might discuss day-to-day issues related to your specific jobs
- supervisors or senior managers, with whom you might need to communicate to:
  - report on any issues or problems
  - receive instructions
  - pass on customer complaints
  - request authority for something you want to do that may need approval
  - discuss reviews, training or any other business-related issues
- customers, who might need assistance with, or information about, products or services
- suppliers, to order stock or other necessary supplies or to chase up deliveries.

Your audience will determine the level of formality you use. When passing information on to a colleague or team leader, you won't need to be as formal as if you were addressing the organisation's CEO or a customer.

What is the purpose of the communication?

The many types of interactions that take place on a daily basis in a work environment may have very different purposes and require different communication methods. For example, the purpose of the communication may be to:

- gather information that you need to complete a task or project
- share information with colleagues or supervisors
- provide training

- update others on the progress of a work project
- research information to meet a specific work need
- sell a product or service to customers
- lodge a complaint
- suggest improvements.

Who you are addressing, and the reason for the communication, will determine the appropriate communication method and style.

1.1.2 Identifying information needs and communication requirements

Depending on what is to be communicated and its intended recipient, information needs will vary, as will the frequency of that communication and the method used. For example:

- The sales and marketing department needs information relating to:
  - competitor brochures or product information
  - results of customer feedback on your products and services
  - latest trends and fashions within your organisation's industry.
- The accounts department needs information about:
  - financial reports
  - sales figures
  - banking records and paperwork
  - receipts for sales made
  - invoices received
  - stocktakes, inventories, and so on.
- Customers want to know about:
  - the features and benefits of your products or services
  - refund policies
  - sales and special promotions
  - events.
- Operations managers will need information about:
  - customer orders to be fulfilled
  - delivery schedules for incoming and outgoing goods
  - the state of the organisation's inventory, so that supplies can be replenished
  - maintenance of equipment or premises.
- Senior managers will need to know about:
  - sales reports
  - staff performance
  - work health and safety (WHS) issues
  - legal matters and **codes of practice**.

These are just a few examples of the information needs within an organisation. Some of this information will be communicated in written form (either on paper or in electronic format). For example:

- brochures or articles you have found
- bank statements, receipts and invoices to accounts
- customer order forms and delivery schedules to the operations staff.

Customer feedback, on the other hand, could be passed on verbally, and products or services would often be sold in a face-to-face encounter. How often such communication takes place will be guided by the nature of the information, its importance and/or urgency to your organisation, and the needs of the people who are receiving it. For example:

- Customer complaints or serious workplace problems should be communicated to relevant supervisors *as soon as they occur*.
- Individual teams or departments within a business might share information *each day* on what work is to be done that day and any particular issues that might be relevant.
- Management teams might hold *weekly* staff meetings to consider important business information that potentially affects the entire organisation.
- *Monthly* reports to senior management, or the board of directors, provide an overall picture of how the organisation is doing.

In summary, the method and style of communication you use will depend on the specific audience and purpose. For example:

- How quickly or urgently does the information need to be passed on?
- Does there need to be a written record of the communication?
- What is the audience preference? Do they prefer to discuss issues face to face, or to talk on the phone, or do they generally like to see things in writing?

Think about

1. What type of information do you need to do your work? What type of information does your supervisor need to do their work? What type of information does your organisation's general manager need to run a successful business? How do these types of information vary?

1.1.3 Establishing and selecting methods of communication

It isn't unusual in today's business world not to meet a customer face to face and for all communication with them to take place via the internet. And, thanks to online communications, people working for the same organisation don't necessarily need to work in the same building, city or even country. This changing nature of business means that organisations use many different methods of communicating.

How you communicate with others in the workplace will vary depending on organisational protocols, the urgency of the communication and the preferences of the people involved. Communication methods suited to audience and workplace requirements can include verbal means, written means and the Internet of Things.

Verbal communication

Verbal communication allows for efficient interaction between people. It enables them to ask and answer questions, examine a topic and debate an issue, so that they can quickly solve a problem or make a decision. Verbal communication, in the traditional sense, means actually speaking with someone. This can be done in a number of ways:

- *By face-to-face communication*. This occurs when you speak to, for example, a colleague, supervisor or customer directly.
- *By telephone*. Most larger organisations use landlines for their telecommunication systems. A number of lines are routed via a switchboard, with calls answered by a receptionist who then passes them on, or via direct extension numbers. Companies that use landlines may have FreeCall numbers for customers to call them, such as 13 or 1300 numbers.

GoodStudio/Shutterstock

- *By mobile devices and videoconferencing.* More and more employees are being offered flexible work-from-home arrangements. The recent pandemic, COVID-19, has had a significant impact on such workplace arrangements and it is expected that these will remain in place for the foreseeable future. This means that devices and laptop computers that allow users to communicate both verbally and visually are increasingly popular. Many organisations now use **apps** such as Google Meet, Zoom, GoToMeeting and Microsoft Teams to facilitate remote communication with employees and customers.

Written communication

Written communication between colleagues can be formal (e.g. official documents) or informal (e.g. quick, short messages). Written communication also allows you to document a conversation or a process. This may be important for compliance issues or future audits, or when you want to share information with colleagues. Written documents can be used as proof of what was said or not said during a dispute. If a "paper trail" is necessary as part of an improvement process or a conflict resolution, then written communication is the best option. Written communication includes:

- *Letters.* While sending printed letters via the post is less common these days, there are still cases where a traditional letter is needed—for example, for more formal or official documentation such as legal matters, reference letters and job offers that require signatures. These letters can also be sent and signed electronically with programs such as DocuSign.
- *Reports.* Business reports contain facts and research that help businesses to plan and make decisions. Reports use headings to organise information and often are based on an organisational template.
- *Emails.* One of the most widely used written communication methods, emails allow you to send attachments such as documents and images. They also provide an excellent written pathway, as they are date and time stamped, so you can track exactly when an email was sent or received.
- *SMS (Short Message Service).* Similar to sending an email, text messaging has the added advantage of being totally mobile. By providing "on the go" access, it enables quick responses.
- *Social media.* A great deal of business communication today takes place via social media. It is an excellent way of staying in touch with customers, and of promoting your organisation and its products to potential consumers.
- *Intranet.* Many organisations have an **intranet**, where information can be shared internally. They may also have administration or operational systems that collect information from data that you enter. This data can then be used to:
  - understand and take advantage of any trends in product or service sales that might be occurring
  - control stock or material inventories, allowing the organisation to better manage and control its finances
  - communicate with staff, customers or suppliers in an automated manner, sending information that is of interest as and when required.

GoodStudio/Shutterstock

Internet of Things

Internet of Things (IoT) is a catch-all term used for the increasing number of electronics that aren't traditional computing devices but are connected to the internet to send information and/or receive instructions. Almost every aspect of our lives now generates data. Smartwatches track each step we take and sense each beat of our heart. The smartphones in our pockets know our location at any moment, our hobbies, where we're going on holiday, and what we're considering buying.

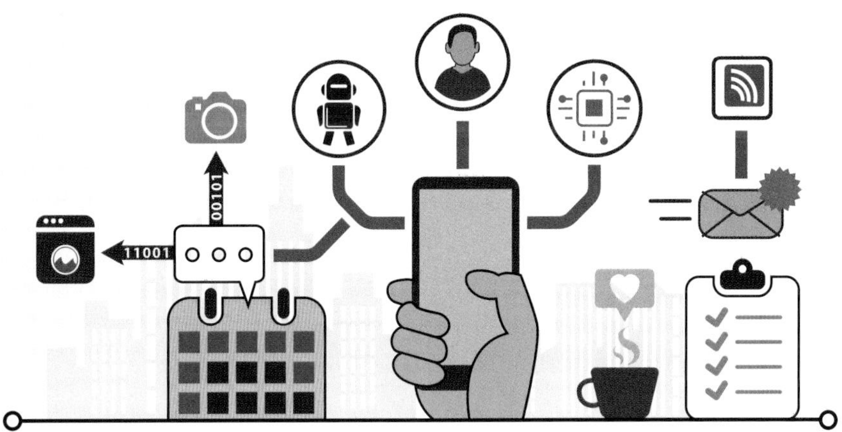

a-image/Shutterstock

The IoT brings the power of the internet, data processing and analytics to the real world of physical objects. In the same way that you can ask "Alexa" to play your favourite songs or turn on the air conditioner, you can ask IoT systems to run specific programs on computers that control manufacturing, administration or reporting processes. For example, the IoT can be used in the workplace for these purposes:

- Tracking maintenance with connected printers or copiers. Many offices are already using internet-connected office equipment, but a new generation of smart alternatives has become available that allows the organisation to monitor paper, ink and toner usage and warns when they are getting low. They can also connect to inventory systems and make orders without human involvement.
- Enabling intelligent lighting with smart bulbs. Such lighting can be used in a number of ways to improve business office efficiency; for example, it can be set to adjust brightness or colour balance throughout the day, thereby helping to minimise eye strain, stress and discomfort.
- Enabling smart assistants such as "Alexa" or "Cortana" to sync whole offices, track meetings and control all manner of customer-related settings.
- Controlling the office climate. Smart thermostats can be used to adjust the temperature and keep staff comfortable.

The age of digital communication has made it much easier and more convenient to undertake a whole range of work processes. It is allowing us to cast a wide, global, net when dealing with customers or working with staff and other business network partners—no matter where they are.

Think about

2. When choosing the most appropriate communication method, think about the message being delivered, who it is being delivered to, and its purpose. Which method would you choose when asking a friend to meet up for coffee? When applying for a job? There are no right or wrong answers, but it's unlikely you would choose the same method for both examples. One is a casual communication; the other is more formal.

1.1.4 Communication styles

Your communication style is the way in which you interact with others. It determines how you speak, act and react in various situations. It has also been found that efficiency, innovation and team spirit in the workplace can increase when you better understand the characteristics and tendencies of the different communication styles, and how to effectively interact with someone of a different style. There are four primary approaches to communication, as outlined in Figure 1.1.

Figure 1.1 The four primary approaches to communication

Passive communication style

The passive communicator often blends into their background, taking little part in team discussions or debates and tending to remain fairly quiet. They rarely take a strong point of view on any workplace subject, which can make it difficult for other team members to communicate with them or draw out any issues they may be having.

Aggressive communication style

Team members with this communication style will often dominate any conversations they are part of and express their thoughts and feelings both freely and strongly. This often comes at the expense of other members of the team, who may feel intimidated by them. Aggressive communicators do, however, have the makings of good leaders but would need to take a calmer and more reasoned approach when communicating.

Passive–aggressive communication style

People who display this communication style often appear to be calm and passive on the surface but may have strong motivations behind their actions. Initially, they can sound as if they are in agreement while discussions take place; however, their actions may not always align with what they have said. It is said that passive–aggressive communicators can be manipulative in order to achieve their preferred outcome.

Assertive communication style

This communication style is perhaps the most productive of the different styles. The assertive communicator is respectful towards others while sharing their thoughts and ideas in a confident manner. They have the ability to make others in the team feel confident, but they are also aware of their own limitations and know when to ask for help. They are ready to take on challenges but have the confidence to say "no" when necessary. These are people you will look to include in a team because you know they can help to achieve an effective outcome.

Try this now

1. Hold a five-minute conversation with someone in your class or workplace and reflect on your own style of communication. How well do you communicate with others? Is there anything you could do to adjust your style of communication to better accommodate others?

1.1.5 Planning content of message or communication

When communicating in a **business environment**, it is important to be clear, succinct and not to waste other people's time. When planning your message, consider the following:

- Is the structure of the message logical? Aim for a structure that flows well. Set out what you want to say in a logical manner: step 1, then step 2, and so on.
- Is the information appropriate? Are you sending this information to the right audience, using the right method? Have you provided enough information to capture the audience's attention without overloading them?
- Is the key message clear? Irrelevancies cloud the issue and create confusion. Use illustrations, examples or facts that strengthen your key message.
- Is the message free of errors, factual and up to date? Make sure you use reliable information from trustworthy sources. You should never damage your, or your organisation's, credibility by communicating unverified facts.
- Have you included all the key points—that is, the information that is most important to the communication?
- Always check spelling and grammar in any written communication. Accuracy isn't only about using the correct information; it is also about using proper language skills.

Knowledge check

1. Explain why it is important to establish who is the audience for your workplace communication.
2. List at least five reasons why workplace communication might take place.
3. Give at least four examples of how communication needs might vary between different audiences and purposes.
4. When determining the audience for and the purpose of a communication, you should ask yourself a range of questions. List three of these.
5. Briefly describe the following communication methods:
   - verbal methods
   - written methods
   - Internet of Things (IoT).
6. Which method of communication would be most appropriate for each of the following examples? Briefly explain why you chose each method.
   - Passing on a telephone message to a colleague.
   - Sharing the outcomes of research your boss has asked you to undertake.
   - Advising your boss of sensitive personal information.
7. List the four recognised communication styles and give a brief description of each.
8. When planning your message, you need to consider a number of questions. List at least four of these.

1.2 Undertaking routine communication

Communication can be complex, as it needs to be relevant and tailored to specific audiences, methods and needs. It can also be relatively simple, such as when sharing information with colleagues or talking to customers. Whatever the case, communication takes place routinely in the workplace and it must fulfil its purpose.

1.2.1 Communicating your message or information

When communicating in the workplace, as always, you need to keep organisational requirements in mind, such as making sure you don't go against any organisational policies or procedures or breach any laws. As detailed in the preface to this text, legislative and organisational requirements relevant to workplace communication may relate to abiding by legal obligations, ethical behaviour and industry codes of conduct.

There will also be policies and procedures put in place by your own organisation to guide staff on the standards they are expected to work to and the manner in which tasks should be completed. These policies and procedures may relate to your organisation's:

- reputation and culture
- style guides and templates.

Organisational reputation and culture

Organisational culture is a collection of values, expectations and practices that will guide employees' actions and behaviour while in the workplace. While each organisation will develop its own specific culture, the following qualities are generally expected:

- Organisational objectives and the motivation of the team to achieve them are aligned, so that everyone is pulling in the same direction.
- Appreciation is shown to all team members.
- Trust and integrity is built on effective communication, consistency and reliability.
- All team members should be motivated to perform to the best of their abilities and talents to ensure the success of the business.

A great deal of time, effort and money has likely been spent in establishing the organisation's reputation and building its unique culture. It should not be undermined by employees making careless or thoughtless comments or sending out messages inconsistent with the organisation's mission and values.

Style guides and templates

Many organisations will also have invested time and resources in developing an "organisational image", or **brand**. This might include its logos, mission statements, and colours and visual identity. The same may be true of the way the organisation expects communications to be carried out on its behalf. It is important, therefore, that all staff comply with organisational requirements relating to style guides and templates. These requirements may include the following:

- *House style*. An organisation's **house style** will dictate how all correspondence is to be produced. The format of a letter will vary according to individual organisational policies and preferences. It involves such things as:
  - Margins. The organisation may specify how many spaces to leave between the head of the letter and the body or the ending, and how wide the margins should be on each side, as well as the position of the text on the page (e.g. centred, with equal margins on each side).
  - Font. Most organisations use a standard font in all their written communications. The font determines what the writing looks like. Examples of fonts include **Times New Roman**, **Arial** and **Verdana**. Fonts like *brush script* and Comic Sans are not considered professional and are unlikely to be used in a business setting.
  - Font size. Font sizes are measured in points. Sometimes an organisation's written communications may vary (increase or decrease) the font sizes used to fulfil different purposes. For example:

    This text is written in 14 point font size.

    This text is written in 9 point font size.
  - Alignment. This determines the appearance of the paragraph edges in relation to the margins. A paragraph may have the straight edge of text aligned to the left, middle or right of the page, or it can be aligned evenly along both sides of the page (as in this text). This alignment is known as "justified".

- *Use of templates and forms.* Many organisations have set templates or forms that must be used for specific purposes. These could include using "standard" letters such as standard replies to job application letters or product enquiries. Forms could include applications for annual leave, a car allowance, and so on.

Adjusting communication methods for those from diverse backgrounds or special needs

As we discuss in Chapter 2, the term "diverse" relates to all the ways in which people are different from one another. Recognising social and cultural diversity is an important part of the world of work. With such diversity in our daily working lives, effective communication skills have become ever more important. When communicating with people from backgrounds different from our own, it is important not to make any assumptions. Even when a language barrier doesn't exist, cross-cultural communication can be challenging so we may need to adjust our methods of communication. Here are some useful tips:

- *Respect other cultures' conventions regarding etiquette.* Before you meet, research the target culture, or if time allows, do some cross-cultural training. Many cultures have specific rules of **etiquette** around the way they communicate, such as expecting a degree of formality when individuals first start to communicate. For example, in Germany, a person will be addressed initially as "Herr" or "Frau". Other cultural differences include putting the person's family name first, before their given name, in China, and using "san" in Japan for both men and women. Be aware of these conventions around using familiar forms of address and don't call someone by their given name until you receive a cue from them that it's okay to do so.
- *Avoid using slang terms.* Not even the most educated non-native English speaker will have a comprehensive understanding of English slang, idioms and sayings. They may understand the individual words you have said, but not the context or the meaning. As a result, you could confuse them or, at worst, offend them. Misunderstandings can also occur between different generations of native English speakers who may use different slang terms or phrases.

GoodStudio/Shutterstock

- *Speak slowly.* Speak clearly and pronounce your words properly. Use short sentences and give your listener time to translate and digest your words as you go. But don't slow down too much, as this might seem patronising. If the person you are speaking to is talking too quickly or their accent is making it difficult for you to understand them, don't be afraid to politely ask them to slow down, too.
- *Keep it simple.* In a cross-cultural conversation, there is no need to make it harder for both of you by using long, complex words.
- *Practise active listening.* Active listening is a very effective strategy for improving cross-cultural communication. Restate or summarise what the other person has said, to ensure that you have understood them correctly, and ask frequent questions. This helps to build rapport and ensures that you don't miss or misunderstand important information.
- *Take it in turns to talk.* The conversation will flow more freely if you take it in turns to speak. Make a point, and then listen to the other person's response. Particularly when people are speaking English as their second language, it is better to communicate in short exchanges rather than deliver a long monologue that might be difficult for them to follow.
- *Avoid asking "closed" questions.* Don't phrase a question that needs a "Yes" or "No" answer. In many cultures, it is considered humiliating to answer in the negative, so you will always get a "yes" even if the real answer is "no". Instead, ask open-ended questions that require information as a response.

- *Be careful with humour.* Many cultures take business very seriously and believe in behaving professionally and following protocol at all times. Consequently, they don't appreciate the use of humour and jokes in a business context. If you do decide to use humour, ensure that it will be understood and appreciated by the other person and won't cause offence in their culture.
- *Be supportive.* Effective cross-cultural communication is about all parties feeling comfortable. In any conversation with a non-native English speaker, treat them with respect, do your best to communicate clearly and encourage them when they respond. This will help to build their confidence and trust in you.

You may also need to adjust your communication style and methods in the work environment to accommodate people with special needs. For example:

- If a person has a hearing disability, adjust your rate and volume of speech to ensure they can hear and understand you. In cases where the person is fully deaf, you could write or use sign language to pass on information to them.
- If a person has a vision impairment, ensure that they are aware of where you are when speaking to them so as not to disorientate them.

Making these adjustments takes very little effort but contributes greatly to team spirit and good working relationships.

1.2.2 Receiving and responding to workplace information and instruction

In your work role, you will be required to perform specific tasks. In smaller organisations, with small teams, it is easier to discuss various tasks and to clarify instructions you receive so that the work can get done. In larger work environments, however, doing your job correctly and in a timely manner may be a matter of greater complexity.

It is essential that you thoroughly understand any information passed on to you or any instructions you receive. Always make sure you know what is expected of you and clarify anything you don't fully understand.

Team leaders and supervisors provide instructions so that workplace policies and procedures are followed correctly. This ensures that:

- legal obligations are met
- no breaches of WHS regulations occur
- productivity is efficient
- budgets are kept to
- products and services are of a consistently high quality.

It is equally important that you respond to any instructions or communications you receive so that others involved with your work know:

- that you have understood what is required of you
- when you are likely to complete your work, so that the next task or phase of work can begin, ensuring efficiency
- if any issues have arisen that you, or a supervisor, might need to deal with.

Think about

3. How do you receive work instructions in your job? Do you have the opportunity to ask questions to clarify anything you don't understand? What do you think might happen if you don't understand your instructions clearly and go ahead with the work—and make mistakes?

1.2.3 Identifying and reporting any communication challenges

No workplace is completely harmonious at all times. From time to time, issues might arise because of miscommunication. This is particularly true now that remote teams have become more common, where a lot of communication is done via email or videoconferencing and some colleagues might never meet face to face. When challenges do arise, they must be dealt with in order to maintain a smooth and efficient work operation. The communication challenges you face might include:

- conflicts with clients or team members
- unethical or inappropriate communication
- potential risks or safety hazards.

Conflicts with clients or team members

Conflict between colleagues has the potential to completely disrupt the workplace and the team spirit. Conflict in the workplace is corrosive; if left unchecked, it can weaken an organisation and perhaps even destroy it. To prevent what may start out as a relatively minor issue escalating into a major one, conflict situations need to be identified and dealt with quickly and effectively.

Good conflict resolution skills include a willingness to meet the needs of others, whether they are team members or clients. The issues involved in the situation must certainly be discussed and addressed, but what about a person's human needs—their need, for example, to be a recognised and valued member of the team? These are important aspects of dealing with conflict situations and require good communication skills.

Possible causes of workplace conflict are outlined in Figure 1.2. All of these issues can cause dissatisfaction and a lowering of staff morale. If acted upon sensitively and quickly, however, they can be resolved without disrupting the work environment.

Figure 1.2 Possible causes of workplace conflict

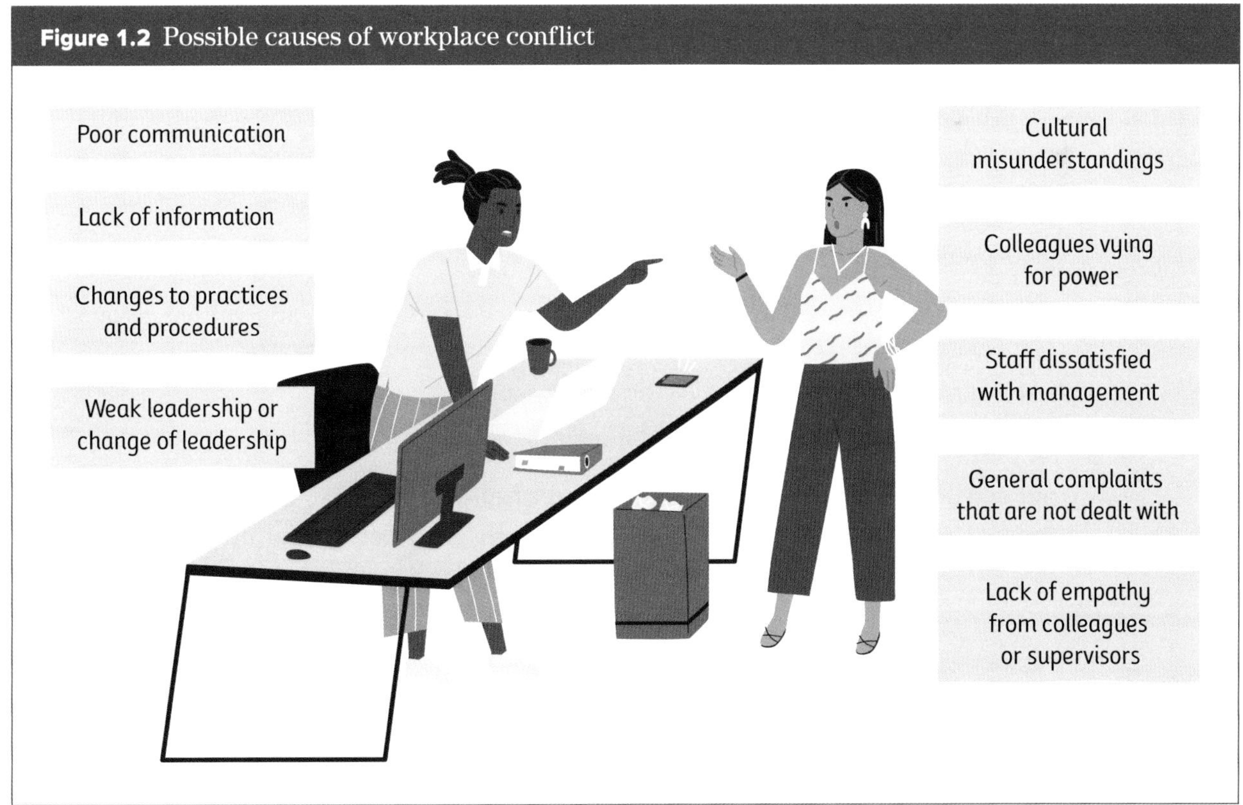

GoodStudio/Shutterstock

If potential causes of conflict are ignored, then what may have started out as minor problems can completely disrupt harmony within the workforce. This, in turn, can affect an organisation's productivity as staff become de-motivated. Poor productivity then affects the organisation's revenue earnings, which in extreme cases could result in failure of the business.

Unethical or inappropriate communication

Much of your working day will involve interactions with other people, be they colleagues or customers. All of these interactions should be professional and **ethical**. Report any instances where you notice unethical or inappropriate language being used. The following are examples of such behaviours:

- *Lies.* Lying is a trait that is detested in and outside the workplace. It kills trust and affects relationships between staff, customers and suppliers.
- *Taking credit for another person's work.* By doing this, you may be denying another person a promotion, a bonus or commendation for a job well done, which may discourage them from contributing and sharing ideas in the future.
- *Verbal harassment or abuse.* There is no excuse for such behaviour in any environment. In fact, it could lead to legal action being taken against the person doing this.
- *Violence.* Similar to verbal harassment, employees should never resort to violent behaviour when dealing with co-workers or customers.
- *Theft or embezzlement.* This behaviour attracts criminal penalties. It includes diverting organisational funds into your own bank account, padding project quotations and falsifying expense claims to deceive the organisation.
- *Sexual harassment.* This offence isn't limited to the workplace alone. An employee accused of sexual harassment will not only have to face workplace consequences but may also be charged under the law.

Such behaviours can seriously damage an organisation's reputation and could potentially lead to legal action being taken.

Potential risks or safety hazards

Some workplaces are higher risk environments than others. For example, a chemical plant or an engineering business would have more risk and **hazard** factors than an accountancy firm or a law office. However, all workplaces have areas where a person might come to harm.

It is the employer's duty to ensure the workplace is safe and as risk free as possible. It is every employee's duty to work within the organisation's policies and procedures, and to report any potential breaches of those procedures to the appropriate manager.

In terms of communication, all WHS information should be provided in such a way that all staff can follow directions, regardless of their language levels. This means ensuring the following:

- WHS instructions and information about risks and hazards are clearly written, using simple statements and sentences and, where possible, illustrations and diagrams.
- Signage in hazardous areas is clear.
- Exits are clearly marked.

Techniques to resolve communication challenges

Should you find yourself in a conflict, or if you are aware of general dissatisfaction, in the workplace, there are steps you can take to help calm and resolve the situation. For example:

- *Avoid jumping to conclusions.* Let the other person have their say, without interrupting or imposing your own thoughts or ideas on them.
- *Find some common ground with the other person.* Look for something you can agree on. This will keep the process on a positive footing.
- *Make sure you keep to the facts.* Don't let your emotions get in the way. When emotions surface, communication can often break down, as tempers heat up and people become agitated.
- *Avoid placing blame.* The purpose of a conflict resolution isn't to determine who is right or wrong, or who is at fault, when a problem exists. What you are trying to do is to find a solution to the problem that will be satisfactory to everyone concerned. Finding someone to blame isn't going to resolve the situation.

- *Consider cultural differences.* Perhaps the conflict has arisen due to a misunderstanding over different beliefs or customs. In this case, an effort could be made to gain this understanding and perhaps even to learn something new.
- *Check to see if anything has been left unsaid.* Issues, even minor ones, that haven't been dealt with, or that haven't been resolved satisfactorily, can fester and spring up again without warning. A situation that you thought was resolved may not be! To be sure, ask questions. For example: "I believe that the main thing you're concerned about is [issue]. Now that we've discussed it, how do you feel about the situation now?" In doing this, we check to make sure that the other person is satisfied with the resolution, or if there are still issues that need to be addressed.
- *Be courteous and respectful.* Allow the other person to state their case without interruption or interference.

Reporting communication challenges

If you are faced with a communication challenge or conflict, you should speak to your supervisor or manager. They will be able to guide you through some possible resolutions. This might, for example, involve having a constructive conversation with a colleague you are experiencing issues with.

If you don't feel comfortable talking to your manager, then many companies have a human resources manager (HRM) who can assist. The HRM is there for all staff and will be able to help and advise you. Many companies will have policies and procedures in place to ensure that any conflicts are handled confidentially and with the best interests of all parties in mind.

You should try to avoid talking about any issues or conflicts with other colleagues. Gossiping about issues can lead to even more conflict, which may start to affect your colleagues and lead to a less productive and happy workplace.

Knowledge check

9. It is essential to be familiar with and comply with legislative and organisational requirements in the workplace. List at least five legal or organisational areas that you need to comply with.
10. Give a brief example of what the following policies and procedures might include:
    - WHS procedures
    - ethical behaviour
    - code of conduct
    - anti-discrimination.
11. Explain the value of diversity in a workplace and why adjustments might need to be made in communication methods and styles.
12. When working in an "inclusive" work environment, you may need to adjust your methods of communicating. Give at least six examples of how you could do this.
13. Explain why it is important to ensure you understand the instructions you receive and how your understanding of them might impact on your organisation.
14. It is equally important that you respond to instructions you have received. Why?
15. No workplace is always free of friction or completely safe, so there will inevitably be communication challenges. Identify four possible challenges.
16. Identify at least six techniques you could use to resolve communication challenges.

1.3 Participating in workplace communication

We know that working as part of a team means being able to communicate with many different people, at many different levels. We have also learnt that good communication skills allow you to interact with others in a harmonious way. Avoiding misunderstandings, and thereby conflicts, is a matter of making sure you fully understand what others are saying—and clarifying anything you don't. This means developing an understanding of body language (or **non-verbal communication**), speaking clearly and concisely so that misunderstandings don't occur, and listening carefully to what a customer or colleague is saying to you.

1.3.1 Using active listening and questioning techniques

A good communicator is able to gain information in a respectful and friendly manner by:

- asking questions effectively
- adopting a positive listening attitude
- understanding non-verbal language.

Asking questions effectively

Gaining information in the most efficient manner is the main purpose of any interaction between people, regardless of whether they are your customers or your colleagues. Gaining this information means asking questions.

There is an art to asking questions that makes the difference between conducting an interrogation and having a conversation. The art is in knowing the different types of questions, and how and when to use them. They can be of the following types:

- *Open questions.* An **open question** should be asked at the beginning of any conversation when you are gathering initial information. An open question generally begins with the words: *What*, *Why*, *Which*, *Where*, *When* or *How* and can rarely be answered in just a word or two. For example, if you were working in a computer shop, a customer will usually give you a fairly detailed answer if you ask them "What kind of computer did you have in mind?", as opposed to "Do you want to buy a computer?" (where they might simply answer "Yes"). Or if you are communicating with a colleague who seems upset, you could get a better idea of what is bothering them by asking "How can I be of help?" rather than "Are you okay?"
- *Clarifying questions.* A **clarifying question** can be useful during the initial conversation, or at the end of the conversation as a way to summarise your understanding of what has been discussed. It is used to ensure that you and your colleague or customer are in agreement or to get additional information. An example of clarifying to summarise is: "So, what you're saying is that you would like [repeat your understanding of the person's needs]. Is that correct?" They will then either confirm your understanding or correct you. An example of clarifying to get additional information is: "You mentioned that you would like your computer to have desktop publishing software. Will you be using this to produce promotional materials?" The answer to this question may give you a better understanding of how the customer will be using the computer and you can then provide them with more detailed and tailored information. Clarifying questions are extremely useful in ensuring that your response to the other person is on the mark in terms of their needs.
- *Leading questions.* A **leading question** is mostly used by salespeople; they lead a customer into making a purchasing decision and, potentially, influence them to buy one of your organisation's preferred products. For example: "So, you agree that the iPhone is a better option for you than the Galaxy?" or, "The Toshiba laptop suits what you are looking for better than the HP, don't you agree?" The response to a leading question will generally be much shorter than to an open question. Leading questions also provide an opportunity to influence a customer so that they choose one product over another—preferably one of your preferred products. In the two examples above, specific companies were highlighted for agreement. The iPhone was put forward as the better option, as was the Toshiba laptop. Both options are still available to the customer and the ultimate choice is, of course, theirs. By asking leading questions, you can often influence a person to make the choice or decision that you want them to.
- *Closed questions.* A **closed question** should be asked when you have enough information, or are ready to wind up a conversation, or you only need a short answer or confirmation. A closed

question will generally get you a "Yes" or "No" answer—or a very short response. Closed questions usually start with the words: *Do*, *Can*, *Is*, *Will* or *Are*. Use this type of question when you are summarising the conversation. For example:

- "Is this what you had in mind?"
- "Can I do anything else for you?"
- "Will you be paying for that by credit card or cash?"

Adopting a positive listening attitude

There are four basic types of communication:

- reading
- writing
- speaking
- listening.

Which type do you think is the most important? Communication is one of the most essential skills we will learn in life. We spend most of our time communicating in some form or other. It begins from the moment we wake up. Dealing with our partners and our children, we discuss what to eat, what to wear and what we plan to do today. It continues all day long: we talk to colleagues and customers, read reports and emails, come home and talk about our day, and so on. It goes on our entire lives.

Here is something for you to think about: You've spent years at school, where you were taught to read and write. Your parents and teachers spent years teaching you how to speak. How long have you spent learning how to listen?

Listening is, arguably, the most important of the communication methods. If it is done correctly, it allows us to understand completely what is being said to us. If we understand completely, then there is little room for conflict due to misunderstanding. Therefore, equally as important as knowing how to ask effective questions is being able to focus on a person and really listen to what they are saying. More often than not, when someone is talking to you, you are already thinking of what you are going to say to them in reply, or you're thinking about what you are going to do this afternoon when you get home. You are doing anything except really listening to them. This can lead not only to misunderstanding (because you haven't been paying attention) but also to a possible conflict, because they feel you haven't taken them seriously. It is important, therefore, that you develop a positive listening attitude. Here is how to be a positive listener:

- Focus your attention on the person.
- Don't be distracted by other staff or events happening around you.
- Maintain eye contact with the person and use open body language to show you're interested in them.
- Ask clarifying questions to ensure you have understood them correctly.

Understanding non-verbal language

In addition to developing your questioning and listening skills, it is important to learn to understand non-verbal language. It is entirely possible for a person to *say* one thing while *thinking* something completely different. For example, a work colleague might say they think a suggestion you've made is good but actually think it isn't. Learning to read a person's non-verbal language is an essential skill of an effective communicator.

Non-verbal communication sends signals that can be interpreted subconsciously as *positive* (e.g. they indicate the sender is open, honest and sincere) or *negative* (the sender is insincere and untrustworthy). You may not even be aware that you are sending these signals and that you could potentially be undermining your own efforts by coming across as being dishonest or that you are hiding something.

How non-verbal communication works

From the time we are born, we are subject to a wide range of influences. The person we become is the sum total of all of these influences (Figure 1.3). Starting with our genetic make-up—that is, the qualities we have inherited from our parents and that we have no control over—we learn and adapt as we grow. Our upbringing, level of education and cultural background then contribute to making us the person that we are. The environment in which we live will also have a strong influence on the way we look at things.

Figure 1.3 Factors that contribute to making us who we are

When we communicate with other people, the thoughts and feelings we express are based on our accumulated personal history to date. This is an important point to keep in mind when seeking to communicate effectively. A person's feelings and opinions are very real and valid to them. If your feelings and opinions are different from theirs, it doesn't make theirs invalid or wrong—just *different*!

Is the communication process really just a simple matter of speaking to someone, and of having them speak back to you? True communication is a composite not only of the words that are spoken, but also of the many forms of non-verbal communication that take place. Some of these are:

- the way the voice is used—tone, pitch and rate of speech
- physical gestures and body language
- facial expressions.

If communication consisted only of words, then most conversations would be boring and it would be very difficult for the "listener" to read the other person correctly. Notice that I used the words "*read* the other person", not "*hear* the other person". It's the things that are *not* being said that give us a true picture of what is actually going on. We also need to "*read* between the lines".

Think about

4. Look at the non-verbal cues of the characters in Figure 1.4. What messages do you get from their body language—for example, their facial expressions or the way they are standing?

Figure 1.4 Non-verbal cues

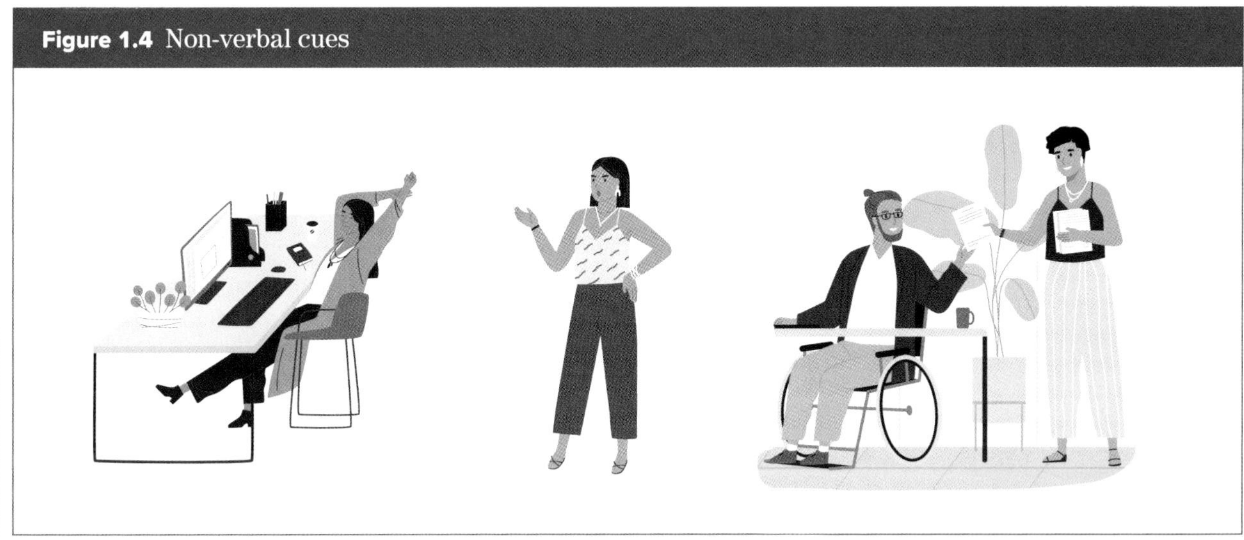

GoodStudio/Shutterstock

It is entirely possible to say one thing and mean another! If our intention is to reach a solid understanding of what another person is trying to convey to us, we need to consider a number of things. Experts have designed a model that explains the communications process. The communications model technically looks something like the conversation between Kai and Aleyah shown in Figure 1.5.

Figure 1.5 The communications model

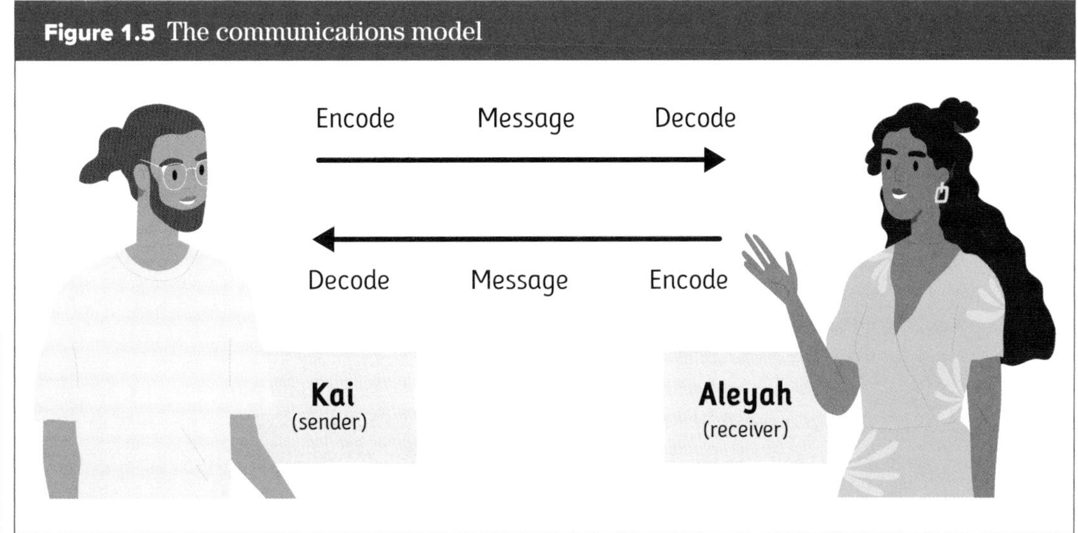

GoodStudio/Shutterstock

Kai is speaking to Aleyah. To *transmit* his message, he *encodes* it with a number of non-verbal signals such as eye contact, tone/pitch/rate of speech, body language, and so on. Aleyah *receives* the message Kai is sending, but she is also watching Kai to *decode* his non-verbal signals. Aleyah will then respond to Kai based on what she has heard *and* seen. In other words: "I *hear* what you're saying and I *see* what you're saying, and the way in which I will respond to you will depend entirely on whether what I heard and what I saw *match up*."

For example, if Kai was telling Aleyah that he liked her new hairstyle, but he wasn't making eye contact with her and was covering his mouth while he spoke, it is likely that he isn't telling the truth. Not looking a person in the eye and touching one's mouth while talking to someone are non-verbal gestures that indicate the speaker is nervous and defensive. In this case, what Aleyah hears and what she sees don't match up. Her response to Kai will be based on the fact that she now feels uncomfortable and believes that Kai's comment isn't sincere. Had Kai maintained eye contact and smiled at her while telling her he liked her new hairstyle, she would have had good reason to feel flattered!

Communications experts estimate that only 10 per cent of communication is in the spoken word, 30 per cent is in the sound (tone, pitch and rate of speech) and 60 per cent is in body language!

Non-verbal communication can be demonstrated in a number of ways:

- *Eye contact.* Maintaining eye contact with a person you are talking to indicates that you are interested in what they are saying. It is a good sign of positive listening skills. When someone won't look you in the eye when you are talking to them, it makes you feel uncomfortable and could lead to misunderstandings and conflict.
- *Gestures.* Your gestures can indicate what you are really thinking. For example, a person who covers their mouth while speaking may not be being entirely truthful, while a person who crosses their arms and leans away from you is indicating they are uncomfortable in your presence or have something to hide. However, gestures in isolation can be misread. A person who crosses their arms may simply be feeling cold! You should therefore look for groups, or "clusters", of gestures. For example, a person who scratches the back of their neck *and* doesn't look you in the eye is probably hiding something or not telling the truth.
- *Handshakes.* As another common form of non-verbal communication, handshakes can be dominant, subservient or neutral, depending on how the hands are clasped—hand twisted to clasp on top is dominant, hand on bottom is subservient, while hands that are clasped side by side are neutral.
- *Facial expressions.* While usually easy to read, facial expressions can also be misunderstood. A smile isn't really a smile if the person's eyes aren't involved in the process. If a person looks interested but their eyes are glazed over—are they really as interested as you think?
- *Tone and pitch of voice.* The tone and pitch of a person's voice can be excellent indicators of their true state of mind and real thoughts and feelings. Their tone can indicate enthusiasm, arrogance, dissatisfaction, desperation, and so on, even if their words don't. Pitch is equally as telling. The higher the pitch (compared to their normal speaking voice), the more emotional the person is. This can be positive—with enthusiasm and excitement, for example—or it can be negative—when a voice is raised in annoyance or anger.
- *Rate of speech.* A person's rate of speech is also a good way of gauging their actual feelings. The faster the rate of speech, the more emotion is involved. Once again, this can indicate either enthusiasm or anger, so we need to look for clusters of gestures. A person might speak quickly naturally, but if their fast rate of speech is accompanied by a high pitch and aggressive body language such as sweeping arm movements—then they are probably upset!
- *Physical presentation.* The way in which you present yourself physically can also say a lot without you speaking a word. It has been estimated that we have only *three seconds* in which to make a first impression. That impression is consolidated by whatever happens during the following three minutes. When communicating, to make a good impression it's important to pay attention to your:
  - cleanliness
  - hair
  - clothes
  - confidence
  - smile
  - posture.
- *Culturally specific communications and customs.* In today's world, we deal with people from other countries and cultures on an almost daily basis. It is important to understand that certain behaviours and gestures that you find acceptable might not necessarily be acceptable to people from other cultures. If you are interacting regularly with customers or colleagues from other cultures, be aware of their customs around communication (e.g. polite forms of address), which may differ from your own, to make them feel more comfortable. Also consider their level of English—don't use difficult words and use short sentences that are easily understood. If you are aware that someone has a physical or mental disability, adapt your communication style accordingly.

Using appropriate language and levels of formality

Good communication skills will also depend on your ability to use the appropriate language and level of formality when dealing with colleagues and customers. You will need to consider the following factors:

- *Your familiarity with the person.* Communication will differ greatly depending on how well you know the person you are talking to. With someone you know well, you can be less formal in the way you address them and talk to them; for example, you might call them by their first name, use an informal, casual tone and language, and even joke around. With a person you know less well, you may need to be more formal and professional. While it might be fine to call a younger person by their first name and to adopt a friendly tone, it is probably not acceptable to address a senior person in this manner. You should address them by their title and surname—for example, "Good morning, Mr Smith"—unless they invite you to be less formal.
- *Your relationship with them.* Once again, depending on the nature of your relationship, it is acceptable to communicate in a friendly and relaxed manner with colleagues, suppliers and well-known customers. Always remember, however, that your reputation, and that of your organisation, depends on your level of professionalism. Therefore, you should always adopt a courteous and professional manner when dealing with all staff (particularly senior staff) and customers.
- *Your surroundings.* It is also important to be aware of your surroundings when talking to customers or colleagues. It is unprofessional to joke and banter overly much with other staff or long-term customers when you are within earshot or view of new visitors to your organisation.

Try this now

2. Once again, hold a five-minute conversation with a colleague or someone in your class. Be aware of what their non-verbal language is saying to you—and be aware of what yours is saying to them. Do they seem interested in what you are saying? Are you showing that you are interested in what they are saying? Afterwards, summarise what the other person said to you to show that you have listened to them.

1.3.2 Contributing clear ideas and information to workplace discussions

As an employee, you are part of a team; as such, you are in a position to contribute ideas that can be of value. Within your role or your department, you will have gained an insight as to how the work you do fits into the organisation's operation. You may, therefore, have ideas on how things in your area might be improved so that the operation could function more efficiently. For example, you might have ideas about:

- competitors' activities
- new trends in your industry that you are aware of
- possible improvements to work systems, policies and procedures
- inadequacies of the WHS systems or other areas of concern.

How you say something is as important as *what* you are saying. Even the best message can fall on deaf ears if you don't format your message in a clear manner. The ideas or information you want to communicate may be about minor issues, but sometimes it might be about something very important. In either case, when contributing your ideas to a workplace discussion, you should:

- speak clearly and concisely
- explain, in a logical manner, how your suggestion can benefit the organisation

- be ready to answer any questions that others may have
- ensure that you have fully thought your suggestion through in terms of:
  - how it could be implemented
  - what resources might be needed
  - any cost factors, and so on.

1.3.3 Supporting others to communicate in workplace discussions

A willingness to support each other is important in a team environment, where everyone on the team should be working towards the same goal and have the opportunity to contribute. Sometimes, however, a person might have a good idea but lacks the confidence to talk about it during a group discussion. You can help and support them to put their idea forward by:

- smiling at them encouragingly
- using open body language
- listening actively when they are speaking
- asking them questions during the discussion to draw them out
- not interrupting them while they are speaking
- helping them with problem solving
- providing feedback about their ideas and suggestions.

1.3.4 Seeking feedback from others on the effectiveness of communication

One of the most important aspects of any business environment is **continuous improvement**. There is always room to make changes for the better, whether this relates to administrative tasks, business operations, customer service—or communication.

The best way to determine areas for improvement is to ask for feedback. You can get this from customers, colleagues, managers or any other person with whom you regularly communicate. Feedback can be provided in a number of ways, including:

- *Survey forms or questionnaires*—where you ask set questions about the effectiveness of your communication.
- *Face-to-face discussions (or forums)*—where you meet with a group of colleagues (or customers) and ask similar questions to those you might have on a questionnaire. The advantage here, however, is that unlike with a written question sheet, you can ask further questions on why the group answered as they did. Why did they think that? What improvements would they suggest?

Questions you might ask when looking for feedback about the effectiveness of your communication may include:

- Did the information you provided flow logically?
- Was it easily understood?
- Did it include all the necessary key points?
- Was the language level appropriate?
- Was the method of communication used appropriate? If not, why not, and what method would have been better?
- Did it achieve the desired results?
  - Did it lead to action being taken?
  - Did it provide sufficient information upon which to base a decision?

- Was it accurate and relevant?
- Was it of sufficient quality and quantity to be useful?

These and many other questions can help you understand the communication process as it currently exists and allow you to make improvements accordingly.

Communication is the basis for everything we do. We are communicating with people constantly. The more effort we put into communicating effectively and respectfully, the better we become at understanding the world around us.

It is essential to your life objectives that you communicate your ideas clearly and precisely and that you clarify anything you don't fully understand. Tailoring your message to suit the person you want to communicate with and using appropriate communication styles and methods can go a long way towards helping you achieve what you set out to do. Listening carefully to what is being said to you, and asking relevant questions, will help you to fully understand what is expected of you, as will understanding non-verbal language.

Communication, then, is a key element in your future success.

Knowledge check

17. Describe at least four signs of unethical or inappropriate communication.

18. Good communication means being able to ask questions effectively. Identify the four types of questions and give an example of how to use each one in a conversation.

19. Explain why it is important to develop good listening skills. Describe ways in which you can do this.

20. When contributing ideas to the work team, you need to ensure that you are heard and that your suggestions are listened to. Explain how you can ensure this.

21. Explain why it is important to support others in the workplace. What methods can you use to show that support?

22. Explain why gathering feedback on the effectiveness of communication is important.

23. When seeking feedback about communication, what five questions might you ask?

Summary

The importance of communication, not only in the workplace but in your personal life, should never be underestimated. The way you present yourself, and your ideas, skills and knowledge, is the foundation upon which you can build your future career and life prospects. One of the best ways of achieving this is by communicating as effectively as possible, and this means being *aware* of what you are saying and doing at all times.

CHAPTER 2

Use inclusive work practices

Learning outcomes

2.1 Establish practices that support individual differences in the workplace

2.2 Work effectively with individual differences

2.3 Assess the use of inclusive practices

Since the introduction of mass transport by Thomas Cook in the late 19th century, people have taken advantage of every opportunity to move about the globe. As a result, our world has become a place of great cultural diversity—a rich cultural tapestry that filters through all aspects of our lives. People also differ from each other in many other ways, including age, ability, wellness, gender identity, religion, ethnicity, opinions and associations. When communities and human organisations act to embrace and welcome everyone as equally valuable, they are participating in **inclusive practices**.

Building inclusive practices into workplaces requires an understanding of the diversity that exists within both the workforce and the general community. Recognising diversity is an important issue. In our everyday lives, it is unlikely that we will deal only with people of similar nature, background, abilities and ideals as ourselves. We come into daily contact with many different people among our customers and colleagues, and we need to recognise and accept this diversity as a strength while adjusting our practices to welcome and accommodate people with additional needs.

2.1 Establishing practices that support individual differences in the workplace

Inclusive work opportunities have enabled many people to gain employment who may have previously been excluded from the workforce. Although more needs to be done, many more women participate in work today than in 1980. The Australian Bureau of Statistics has found that only 45 per cent of women were employed in 1980, compared to 63 per cent in 2022 (Gustafsson 2021). Changing attitudes and values, political movements, and changes in work practices, leave provisions, laws and policies over this period have resulted in women increasingly sharing in the benefits of paid work in Australia. Similarly, the World Health Organization (WHO) has found that great progress has been made in recent decades in making the world more accessible for people experiencing disability (World Health Organization 2022a).

Inclusive practices provide great benefits to some individuals, but they also offer great opportunities to businesses and other organisations. The Australian Government has identified the following benefits for businesses that embrace diversity and inclusive practice:

- better business performance and productivity from employees
- more creative and innovative thinking among staff
- improved staff health and wellbeing
- lower risk of discrimination and harassment in the workplace. (Australian Government 2021)

Conversely, ignoring diversity and inclusive practice poses a serious legal risk to businesses, as federal, state and territory laws in Australia require businesses to act in ways that protect people from exclusion or discrimination. Currently, it is illegal in Australia for an employer to discriminate against someone on the basis of their:

- colour
- gender
- sexual orientation
- age
- physical or mental disability
- marital status
- family or carer's responsibilities
- pregnancy
- religion
- political opinion
- national extraction (place of birth or ancestry)
- social origin (class, caste or socio-occupational category)
- industrial activities (such as belonging to a trade union). (Adapted from Australian Government 2021)

Given that our workplaces offer such rich diversity, it is important for organisations to establish practices that take account of individual differences and provide guidance on inclusive practices and policies. Organisational codes of ethics, policies and procedures manuals, and government legislation may assist in supporting workers to positively embrace individual differences in the workplace.

2.1.1 Identifying individual differences in colleagues, clients and customers

Australia is a multicultural nation. As well as being the home of the world's oldest continuous Indigenous cultures, Australians can trace their heritage back to over 270 different countries of origin. Figure 2.1, from the Australian Human Rights Commission, provides some interesting statistics and facts about cultural diversity in Australia.

Figure 2.1 Australian Human Rights Commission fact sheet

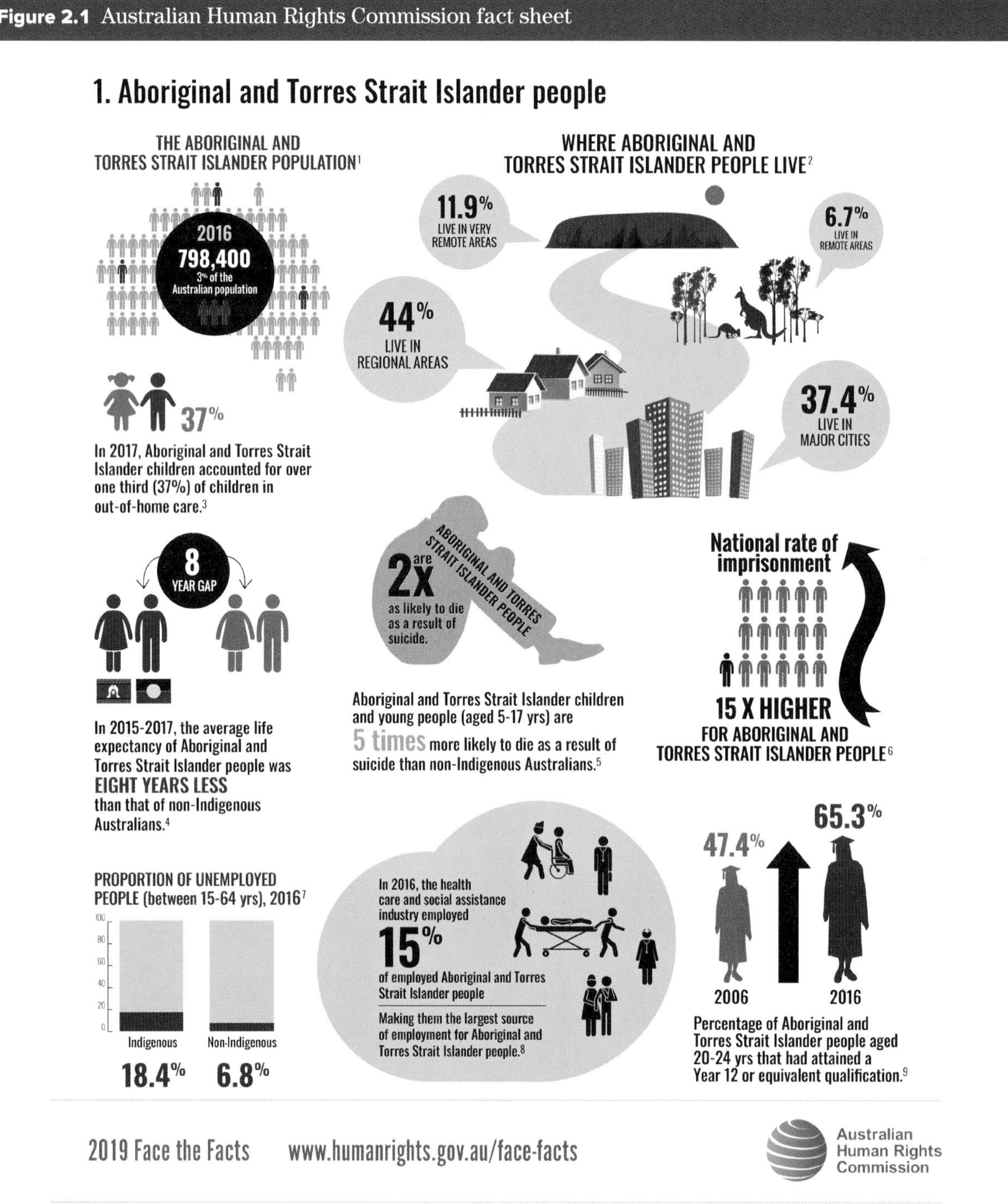

Source: https://humanrights.gov.au/our-work/education/face-facts-cultural-diversity/

Because of this diversity, it would be very difficult for anyone to understand the complex and vast range of backgrounds, needs, beliefs and practices that exist in Australia, or even within a single workplace. Although it can be helpful to research information about particular nationalities, religions and ethnic groups, it is usually more effective in a workplace simply to ask people about their culture and if any particular considerations should be made at work to accommodate their needs. Similarly, it is helpful to ask everyone if there are any adjustments or flexible arrangements that need to be made to a workplace or to workplace conditions that will help them to perform to the best of their abilities.

Stereotypes

Falsely held beliefs about any group of people may be referred to as "stereotypes". **Stereotypes** are beliefs that are based on a very small amount of information and are falsely thought to apply to everyone who fits with a particular label or grouping. Australians are occasionally stereotyped when they travel overseas when it is believed they ride kangaroos, live with venomous snakes and spiders, own surfboards and live at Summer Bay.

It is discriminatory to make workplace decisions based on stereotypes or on what you assume a person may need or about how they will perform. The Australian Public Service Commission found that four common assumptions or stereotypes were made regarding people with a disability in decisions regarding staff selection. These were:

- People with disability are best suited to unskilled work.
- Insurance costs will increase if I hire someone with disability.
- People with disability are less productive.
- People with disability will not fit in. (Australian Public Service Commission 2021)

Although each of these assumptions has been shown to be completely false, they may influence hiring decisions and may lead to someone being treated unfairly. The best approach to overcoming stereotyping in the workplace is to listen to each individual and get to know their particular needs and requirements. It is also the most respectful and courteous way to embrace diversity.

What is social diversity?

In order to fully understand the value of a socially diverse workforce, however, we must first understand the meaning of the terms "social" and "diverse" in a workplace context. "Social" relates to the way in which society is organised and the way in which people interact with one another. "Diversity" relates to the many ways in which people differ from one another. **Social diversity**, at its simplest, therefore refers to how we interact and work with people regardless of who they are, what they believe in, what their capabilities might be, or where they come from.

Regular/Shutterstock

Cultural background

Culture is made up of the values, beliefs, systems of language, communication styles, and practices that people share in common and that can be used to define them as a group. Culture is in a constant state of change: as conditions change and new generations are born, cultural groups adapt and grow. Culture has many layers; what you see, on the surface of a person, may only be a small part of the complex whole person, so generalisations never tell the full story. This is why there is no substitute for building respectful, supportive personal relationships with the individuals you work with.

Religious background

Although religion is becoming less popular across the world, it still forms a significant part of most national identities, with 84 per cent of the world's population identifying with a religion. The world's major religions represent the following numbers of people worldwide:

- Christianity: 2.38 billion
- Islam: 1.91 billion

- Hinduism: 1.16 billion
- Buddhism: 507 million
- Folk religions: 430 million
- Other religions: 61 million
- Judaism: 14.6 million
- Unaffiliated: 1.19 billion. (World Population Review 2022)

In Australia, there has been a pronounced shift away from religion, particularly since 1971. Although 43.9 per cent of Australians continue to identify with Christianity, a similar number (38.9 per cent) report having no religious affiliation at all. Other world religions are also represented in Australia, including Islam (3.2 per cent), Hinduism (2.7 per cent) and Buddhism (2.4 per cent) (Australian Bureau of Statistics 2022).

Some followers may adhere to the customs, practices and traditions of their religion, while others may not. Religious practices are very diverse, but they might include rituals for prayer or worship, celebration of festivals and holy days, fasting and dietary restrictions, wearing particular styles of clothing or headwear, refraining from some activities on certain days, attending funerals, or partaking in "sorry" business. Being able to listen openly to, and to develop an understanding of, others' religious beliefs and practices is an important step toward working harmoniously with customers and colleagues.

In all Australian workplaces, religious understanding and tolerance is supported by **anti-discrimination** law. However, it is the attitudes, values and actions of individuals that really make inclusivity happen at the workplace level. It is important to understand that being tolerant of people of different faiths doesn't require anyone to compromise or question their own religious beliefs. The opportunity to learn about different cultures, religions and beliefs at work enables us to broaden our own world view and to develop a more diverse social network. Displaying an attitude of understanding and tolerance is also beneficial for business, as it communicates acceptance of and interest in the lives of clients and colleagues.

Family structure

Not all families are the same. The traditional family with two parents, where the father works and the mother looks after the home and family, is no longer the norm. There are a number of possible family structures and situations, including:

- *Families where one or both parents return to work after spending many years raising their family.* Some mothers and, increasingly, some fathers will choose to step away from work to raise their children or to search for a more satisfying work–life balance. Whatever the reason, after spending time away from a work environment, some people may feel unsure of their abilities and might need extra assistance and understanding from their colleagues. People who return to work after a period of raising children usually have a great deal of practical knowledge and experience that can be helpful in organising and improving working conditions and work relationships.
- *Single-parent families, where there is only one parent to look after children and also provide an income.* This type of family can often be a struggle for the parent involved. Juggling school timetables, and supervising and caring for children, can have an impact on their ability to work.
- *Families where both parents work while still raising their family.* There are many families where both parents work either full time or part time. This could be for financial reasons, or because both parents enjoy their work and wish to continue their careers. Again, this can involve a lot of juggling of timetables.
- *Family situations influenced by cultural considerations and norms.* People from other cultures place varying degrees of importance on family, which may affect the way they work. Some cultures have an "all hands on deck" attitude, with every family member working for the good of the whole clan, while other cultures don't allow women to work while their children are still young—if at all.

Flexible work is on the increase—and not only for workers with families. Many single or child-free people enjoy working from home, or working reduced hours, in order to better manage their work–life balance. These workers still contribute effectively to the workforce and may even be more productive because of the flexibility the arrangement offers them.

Age

People in today's society can be categorised into generations by their birth years. These categories are:

- *baby boomers*—those born between 1946 and 1964
- *generation X*—those born between 1965 and 1979
- *generation Y*—those born between 1980 and 1994
- *generation Z*—those born between 1995 and 2012
- *generation alpha*—those born between 2013 and 2025.

Certain behavioural characteristics have been attributed to members of the baby boomer, X, Y and Z generations, as shown in Figure 2.2. Remember that these are generalisations—not everyone fits neatly into these categories!

Figure 2.2 Characteristics of different generations

- *Baby boomers.* The term "career" is associated mostly with baby boomers, who expected to stay in one job or with one employer for many years.
- *Generation X.* Said to be generally more interested in a series of work-related experiences interspersed with "lifestyle" events such as cross-cultural learning.
- *Generation Y.* These employees begin and may stay with part-time employment. They see their working life as an ongoing process of balancing their personal priorities and their work experience.
- *Generation Z.* These employees are keen to avoid burnout and being time poor, like their parents have been. Gen Z is said to be more interested in flexibility and social and environmental responsibility than big pay packets. They are more willing than older generations to walk away from a job that doesn't meet these needs.

We can also see that, as people age, their values and participation levels in society change. How the generations interact with each other and balance their participation in the workforce will determine the workplace of the future, especially given that the youngest baby boomers are entering their sixties in 2024.

We often hear of the "generation gap" and of how people of different age groups have difficulty communicating with each other. However, with a little effort, some understanding of the other person can be achieved. Every generation has a lot to contribute if they each recognise the opportunities, constraints and unique experiences of the other. For example, young people have:

- the vitality, drive and high energy levels to work productively within a team or enthuse a customer
- an eagerness to learn
- a fresh perspective
- a working knowledge of the latest trends and fads.

More mature people have:

- experience and expertise that other members of the team can draw on
- the ability to help nurture and educate younger people in their respective industries and jobs
- the confidence that comes from having years of experience to handle most crises calmly and professionally.

Through speaking and listening to each other, all generations can work towards a common understanding and appreciation of their different and diverse experiences and perspectives.

Gender

Workplaces also need to be gender inclusive. Historically, women have faced many barriers in the workplace simply because of their gender. Females are still typically paid 15.3 per cent less than their male counterparts for the same job (Australian Government 2018).

People often subconsciously apply stereotypes to genders. Figure 2.3 provides examples of these. Stereotypes can be both positive and negative. For example, even today it is often not as acceptable for a man to take extended leave on the birth of his child as it is for a woman. Women who are strong and assertive can be viewed as bossy and aggressive, while men who display these same traits are seen as natural leaders.

Figure 2.3 Stereotypical characteristics of men and women in the workplace

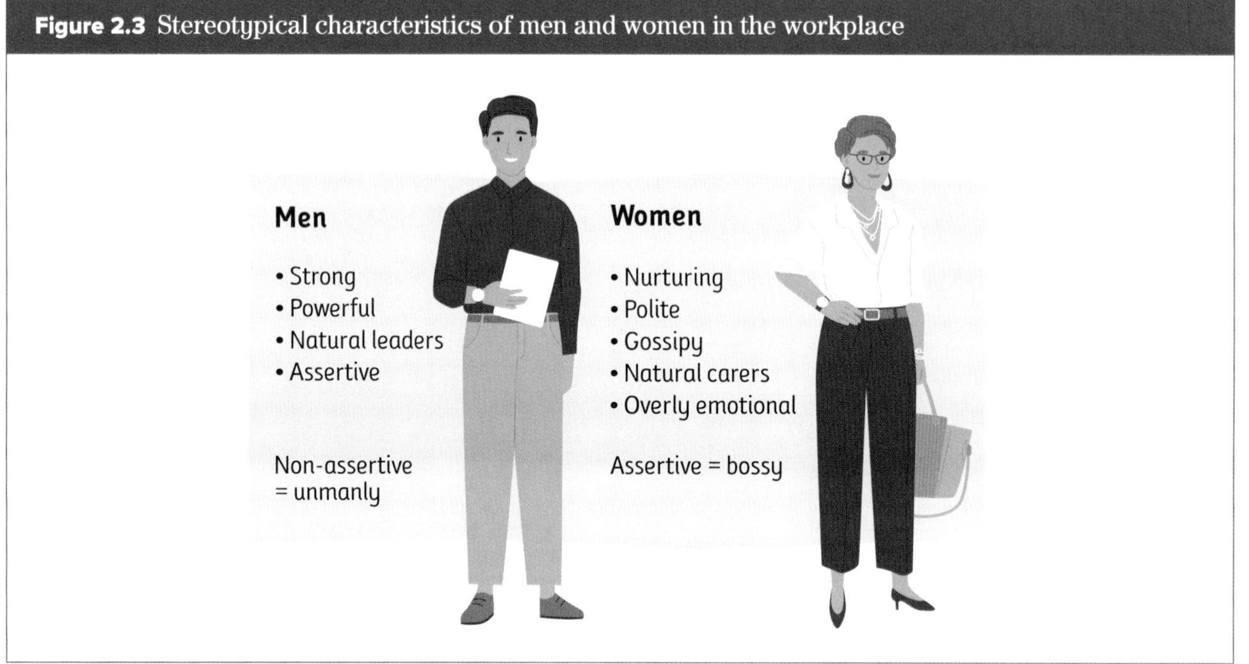

GoodStudio/Shutterstock

While things are changing in the workplace, there is still a lot of catching up to do. One of the main things you personally can do to help create a more inclusive environment for all genders is to be aware of your own stereotypes or beliefs.

Transgender and non-binary

The WHO refers to gender as "the characteristics of women, men, girls and boys that are socially constructed" (World Health Organization 2022b). This is distinct from biological sex, which is generally assigned at birth and based on physical characteristics such as genitalia. "Transgender" is a commonly used term for people whose gender identity doesn't conform with the sex they were assigned at birth. "Non-binary" is a term that is used by people who don't identify exclusively as a man or a woman.

As with gender stereotypes, the first step to inclusivity is to reflect on your own stereotypes or the beliefs you have about transgender and non-binary people. Some other suggestions include:

- *Educate yourself.* There are lots of great resources, including readings and videos, that can help you learn more and dispel any myths or preconceptions you might have.
- *Use the personal pronouns a person prefers.* A transgender or non-binary person might specify that you should address them as she/her or he/him, or they may prefer the neutral they/them. If you are unsure, you can respectfully ask a person which pronoun they prefer.
- *Advocate for non-binary friendly policies.* It's important for *all* people to be able to live, dress and have their gender respected at work, at school and in public spaces.

To foster gender inclusivity, workplaces can also put in a range of measures, including:

- instituting flexible work arrangements, so that both men and women can meet parenting demands
- avoiding gendered language in job descriptions, proactively hiring women to do jobs traditionally given to men, and including a diverse interview team
- providing training for staff on bias.

Intellectual or physical ability

It is against the law to discriminate against people because of a disability in some situations. Anti-Discrimination NSW sets out these situations, and also provides guidance on the types of disability that are covered by discrimination laws.

Disability discrimination is when you have been treated unfairly because:

- you have a disability
- people think you have a disability
- you used to have a disability
- you may acquire a disability in the future
- you are the friend, relative or colleague of a person with a disability.

Disability discrimination is against the law in certain public places, including:

- workplaces, such as when you apply for a job or while you are at work
- employment agencies, such as when you use recruitment companies
- when you access goods and services, such as when you go shopping, do your banking or access medical services
- state education, such as when you apply for study and during your studies
- accommodation, such as when you rent accommodation
- industrial organisations, such as membership of a union
- qualifying bodies, such as an institute that issues qualifications
- at registered clubs (clubs that sell alcohol or have gambling machines), such as when you try to enter or join a club.

The law protects a wide range of disabilities and illnesses, including:

- physical disabilities
- diseases that make a part of the body or brain work differently
- mental illness or psychiatric disabilities
- behavioural disorders
- intellectual disabilities
- learning or cognitive disabilities
- adverse changes to the body or brain following an accident or surgery
- a different formation of a body part
- diseases or illnesses caused by a virus or bacteria.

(Anti-Discrimination NSW 2022.)

Sometimes, modifications may need to be made to the way a person with a disability performs work. These modifications are the responsibility of an employer and are termed "reasonable adjustments". Anti-Discrimination NSW provides some examples of reasonable adjustments:

- flexible working hours
- remote work options

- changes to work premises
- specialised hardware, software and equipment
- use of an assistance dog
- use of specific equipment such as a mobility aid
- regular breaks
- adaptive equipment.

The word “reasonable” is included in the law to protect employers from encountering excessive costs or burdens as a result of employing a person who has a disability. In New South Wales, the law requires that when employing a person who has a disability, employers must provide any services or facilities that are needed for the employee to do their job—unless it would cause them unjustifiable hardship to do so. The NSW Anti-Discrimination Board can determine what is reasonable on a case-by-case basis and generally aims to find solutions that suit employees and employers equally.

Think about

1. Think about people you know in your workplace or community. Have you been told of any difficulties or barriers that they experience in their workplace or community? What could you, as an individual, do to help with any difficulties they have? What adjustments could be made to a workplace or community facility to make it easier for this person to participate more fully?

2.1.2 Organisational policies and procedures relating to inclusive work practices

At the start of this chapter, we saw that it is against the law to disadvantage employees and job seekers on the basis of individual difference. All organisations should therefore have in place policies and procedures that comply with workplace inclusivity regulations, standards and codes of practice. These policies and procedures might also include:

- developing workplace training programs that promote cultural awareness
- holding events that celebrate diversity and encourage employees to share their experiences and different cultures when requested by colleagues and co-workers
- modifying workplace procedures to allow for people with disability to participate fully in work duties
- supporting flexible working arrangements, and more.

2.1.3 Developing plans for incorporating inclusive practices

With the above in mind, as well as legal and industry-wide considerations, a plan for incorporating inclusive practices into the workplace should be designed and tailored to suit your specific organisation, around specific work areas and in cooperation with relevant personnel, including:

- diversity champions
- employee representatives
- human resources (HR) officers
- line or team manager
- colleagues within the organisation.

All of these people, and perhaps others, should have an input into the design of an inclusivity policy.

While having all staff in the workplace understand their procedural and legal obligations is a step in the right direction, organisations should take a structured or planned approach to ensure both consistent behaviour and compliance with policies and procedure. A policy should consider how an organisation commits to, and takes responsibility for, inclusion. It should state how you, the organisation and its stakeholders are held accountable for inclusion. The policy should say: "Inclusion is important". But more than that, it should say: "This is how we're going to address it and this is what it means for us". It should then provide mechanisms for actually delivering on those statements.

A policy should, ideally, consider the following issues:

- *Access*. **Access** revolves around the importance of generating a welcoming environment and the habits that create it. This lays the foundations of what people experience when they come to your organisation and includes not only the atmosphere of the workplace but also the culture that is evident throughout it. It also means looking at the physical aspects of the organisation to ensure that all people, regardless of their physical abilities or disabilities, can gain access. It is important, therefore, to explore what access really means in both the physical and non-physical sense and making whatever adjustments are necessary to provide an inclusive environment.
- *Attitude*. This looks at how willing people within the organisation are to actually embrace inclusion and diversity, and therefore to take meaningful action. Attitude isn't simply about being positive about inclusivity; it means having a willingness to take real action.
- *Communication*. This is perhaps one of the most important aspects of any business environment (refer to Chapter 1). You will need to examine the way people learn about the inclusivity within the organisation and how they can get involved with and learn about the culture. In communicating, we need to think about *who* we are addressing and *how* the message will be communicated, ensuring that it is inclusive and easy for others to understand.
- *Opportunity*. This relates to exploring what options are available for all people within a workplace to progress toward new opportunities. Regular performance reviews or capability planning meetings can provide opportunities for managers and supervisors to ask their employees: "What do you want to do, and what do you need to be able to do it?" This policy explores what opportunities are actually available in the workplace and, if required, makes any necessary adjustments to accommodate the stated needs. For example, a structured plan for inclusivity could include such things as:
  - developing standards on which tasks must be performed, so that all staff understand exactly what to do and what is required of them
  - valuing the ideas and knowledge of all team members and incorporating these into policies and procedures
  - developing inclusive communication methods that will help all staff understand what is required of them, and making all staff feel a part of the team by providing training and information materials in various languages and using a range of presentation types when demonstrating procedures and processes.

Examples of inclusivity policies and procedures

The following are examples of inclusivity policies:

- Department of Social Services Policy (https://www.dss.gov.au/sites/default/files/documents/01_2015/access_and_equity_policy_23_jan_15.pdf)
- Queensland Government Diversity and Inclusion Policy (https://ppr.qed.qld.gov.au/pp/diversity-and-inclusion-policy)
- CPA Australia Inclusion and Diversity Policy (https://www.cpaaustralia.com.au/about-cpa-australia/corporate-responsibility/inclusion-and-diversity-policy).

Knowledge check

1. Diversity can take many forms and have many aspects. List at least seven ways in which people might differ from each other.
2. Briefly describe the diverse nature of at least four of the aspects you listed.
3. Give a brief description of the following organisational policies:
   - ethical principles
   - codes of practice.
4. With an eye to ensuring equality for all people, the Commonwealth government has passed various Acts to safeguard a person's right to receive fair treatment. List at least four of these Acts.
5. Describe what is meant by "fairness and equity".
6. List at least three things that you should consider when developing a structured plan for inclusivity.

2.2 Working effectively with individual differences

No matter what industry you work in, you will come into contact with a range of different people each day. If we don't recognise and acknowledge the cultural differences between people, we could create disharmony and distrust in the workforce. People you encounter in the workplace will have different ideas and opinions; they will come from diverse backgrounds; and they will come from other regions of the world and different social and economic backgrounds. All of them will offer the opportunity for personal growth and the enhancement of the work team.

2.2.1 The value of cultural and social diversity

The value of diversity in business is enormous; it can improve not only the level of teamwork but also the organisation's overall performance and customer service through a broadened base of knowledge and experience. An inclusive workforce is creative and flexible. It exposes customers and colleagues to new ideas, and different ways of working and of reaching decisions. Learning from customers and colleagues from other backgrounds also broadens our own personal horizons and expands our own knowledge base, making us more efficient and tolerant as individuals.

An organisation that is known for its inclusive practices is more likely to attract a broader range of talent to its workforce, due to its greater flexibility and larger range of options. Such an organisation is also more likely to provide increased employee satisfaction—and when employees are happy in their work environment, this can lead to greater creativity and innovation in the way work is carried out. This, in turn, can have a positive impact on the organisation's financial performance, as employees' productivity increases and they are less likely to take "sick days", which can be very costly.

2.2.2 Supporting colleagues and sharing skills

GoodStudio/Shutterstock

Workplace difficulties and conflicts can sometimes arise simply because a colleague feels overwhelmed by work (or, perhaps, personal) pressures. In these cases, it is important to offer support and help them to resolve any difficulties they may be having. It is also important to support colleagues for the good of the entire team. Small issues that aren't resolved can—and do—have a habit of blowing up out of proportion, so that a situation that could have been fixed easily and quietly has suddenly become a major problem for the entire organisation.

Effective workplace relationships can only be built and maintained when there is trust among colleagues and they have confidence that they will be supported in performing their tasks. This doesn't mean that you have to be best friends with all of the people you work with—but you must be able to work with them in a professional and courteous manner. In extreme cases, tension among team members in the workplace can bring an organisation to its knees. Such an atmosphere must be avoided, or dealt with immediately if it arises, if the business is to be successful.

The set of skills required for resolving conflicts can be acquired and practised by everyone in the organisation, so that conflict situations can be transformed into opportunities for people to grow and learn from each other. Table 2.1 outlines the main skills involved in **conflict resolution**. Working through the questions for a particular problem may help to elicit the skills or tools you need to address the issue.

Table 2.1 Conflict resolution checklist

Question to ask yourself	Skill or strategy required
Can you see the whole picture and not just your own point of view?	Broaden your outlook
What are the needs and concerns of everyone involved?	Write them down
How can we make this fair?	Negotiate
What are the possibilities?	Think up many solutions Pick ones that give everyone more of what they want
Can you work it out together?	Treat each other as equals
What are you feeling?	Could you get more facts, take time out to calm down, tell them how you feel? Are you too emotional?
What do you want to change?	Be clear. Attack the problem, not the person
What opportunity does this situation present?	Work on the positives, not the negatives
What is it like to be in the other person's shoes?	Do they know that you understand them?
Do you need a neutral third person?	Could this person help you to understand each other, yet build your own solutions?
How can you both win?	Work toward solutions where everyone's needs are respected

Source: Adapted from https://crnhq.org/files/Handouts%20and%20Posters/ResolveTheConflictGuideposter.pdf

Treat people with integrity, respect and empathy

In establishing a trusting and confident relationship with colleagues, we need to look at, and understand, the key terms used in building and maintaining such relationships. These terms are integrity, respect and empathy.

Having *integrity* means being open and honest with the people you work with (whether they are colleagues, customers or suppliers) and living up to any workplace commitments you have made. It also means completing tasks allocated to you conscientiously, to the required standard and within the required time frame. This ensures that people know that they can trust you.

When you share your knowledge and abilities freely with colleagues, you gain their *respect*. Respect can also be shown by acknowledging the achievements, abilities and qualities of others and tapping into these skills.

No two people are alike; therefore, others may not view or react to given situations in the same way that you would. This doesn't mean that you are right in your views and they are wrong; it just means that they see things differently from you. Understanding this and respecting their ideas and feelings—having *empathy*—will allow them to feel confident in contributing to the workplace without fear of rejection or ridicule. Empathy has also been shown to increase collaboration, increase productivity and competitiveness, and improve customer and staff satisfaction (Alonsagay 2022).

You cannot possibly know everything there is to know about everything. Synergy within the workplace can often reveal "just the thing" you need; it doesn't matter where or who it comes from. In simple terms, **synergy** means that the *whole* is greater than the *sum* of the individual parts. In a business sense, this means that teamwork will produce a much better result than if each person in the organisation was working toward the same goal individually.

Sharing information with other staff members enriches the pool of information the entire staff is able to draw from. Your organisation's customers will never cease to amaze you with the requests and demands they make. Then, too, sharing information about different cultures, backgrounds, and work and life experiences, as well as specific skills, can lead to a more unified team where everyone has something to teach—and to learn.

Information can be shared in a number of ways, including:

- one-on-one discussions with colleagues
- general staff meetings at which a range of issues are discussed
- special staff meetings to discuss a particular piece of news or event
- training sessions
- written emails or internal memos.

2.2.3 Identifying and implementing inclusive work practices

When employees come from diverse backgrounds, their differing talents and experiences and wide variety of viewpoints and ideas invariably contribute to an organisation's overall growth. Embracing employees with different skills and cultural viewpoints helps in understanding the needs and requirements of an organisation's customers on a global scale and in formulating the best business strategy.

In summary, the following are some of the advantages of diversity in the workplace:

- *Increased creativity.* When people with different ways of solving problems work together towards a common solution or improvement, they can offer insightful alternatives you might not have considered. There is no one best answer to any question. The more ideas you can obtain from different people, the more likely you are to develop a workable answer.
- *Increased productivity.* Productivity increases when people of all cultures pull together to achieve a single inspiring goal (Alonsagay 2022).
- *Increased language skills.* In today's increasingly global economy, being able to utilise the language skills of colleagues from diverse backgrounds can lead to the organisation working in a broader, worldwide marketplace. This can mean greater success for the organisation, as well as a sense of accomplishment for the staff involved.
- *Increased understanding of how our country fits into the world picture.* This understanding is crucial. By relating to people of all backgrounds, we will gain a more sophisticated perspective on how different cultures operate, which can result in greater success both in the local community and in global business.
- *Increased efficiency.* New, more efficient processes can result when people with different ideas come together and collaborate. In today's fast-moving world, there is no longer room for thinking, "We've always done things this way. There's no need to change." For optimal efficiency, workers must bring multiple skills to the environment, think cross-culturally and adapt quickly to new situations.

Workplace inclusivity can make organisations more productive and profitable, but it also brings differences that we must understand and trust if those benefits are to be realised. Trust develops from consistent actions that show colleagues you are reliable, cooperative and committed to team success. Research has shown that trust is a significant factor in fostering:

- better teamwork and collaboration
- higher morale and lower stress
- increased productivity
- better acceptance of change
- improved employee performance
- improved ethical decision making.

In general, inclusive work practices might include ensuring that all behaviour is consistent with legislative requirements and enterprise guidelines. Methods by which this can be accomplished will be guided by the organisation's policies and procedures, which will be based on relevant laws. As discussed in the preface to this text, the organisation will have a legal obligation to observe these laws; any breaches could result in heavy penalties or fines, or even in legal action being taken against it. These organisational guidelines might also involve policies and procedures being developed internally to cover such HR issues as the recruitment, selection, induction and monitoring of staff.

Think about

2. Think again about the diverse people you know in your workplace or community. How have they made a positive contribution to the organisation? What have you learnt from them that has broadened your own point of view or added to your skills?

2.2.4 Modifying verbal and non-verbal communication to accommodate individual differences

A **communication barrier** is anything that prevents someone from understanding what you are trying to convey. There are many communication barriers that can occur in the workplace between colleagues or with customers. If someone doesn't understand you or misinterprets what you say, it can result in confusion or wasted time and resources. It is important, therefore, to be aware of some of these barriers and to have some strategies to help overcome them.

Examples of communication barriers

Communication barriers can include language barriers and cultural barriers.

- *Language barriers*. Language can be a common barrier in a diverse workforce. A colleague with a non-English speaking background may have difficulty understanding a native speaker if they speak too quickly or use too much slang. Alternatively, a person with a strong accent might be misunderstood by native speakers. Some workplaces also use organisation-specific language or industry jargon that new employees, or colleagues from different departments, might not understand. Even when two native speakers are communicating, misunderstandings can occur if the person giving the message isn't clear.
- *Cultural barriers*. Social norms differ among different cultures. For example, in some cultures it is polite to look someone in the eye when speaking with them, while in others this can be seen as rude, particularly when speaking to a superior.

GoodStudio/Shutterstock

Strategies to overcome barriers

There are many strategies available to help overcome communication barriers. Small adjustments can help to ensure you are understood by the people you are communicating with.

- *Use plain language*. When speaking or writing, be mindful of the language you are using and of your audience. Try to avoid using jargon or industry terms if you are speaking with a new colleague or a customer who may not have the same understanding as you.
- *Use visual methods of communication*. Having visual aids can help your message be understood more quickly. Using graphs, images, or even just sketches, makes it easier for native and non-native speakers alike to quickly grasp what you are trying to communicate.

- *Be respectful.* Communications barriers can be frustrating, but it is important to be patient and understanding when they do occur. If someone appears not to understand what you are saying, speak more slowly and clearly. Don't do what many people do and raise your voice.
- *Take an interest.* Read about different cultures and, while you are reading, think about how their cultural norms might be different from your own.
- *Don't jump to conclusions or make assumptions.* If you don't understand a message, ask questions to clarify the meaning. If you assume you have understood something, it can lead to mistakes or further misunderstandings.
- *Practise self-reflection.* If someone doesn't understand you or has language difficulties, it doesn't mean they aren't intelligent. Think about how you are communicating and how you might be able to adjust your message to help the other person better understand you.

Communication barriers can be frustrating. However, by taking the time to overcome these, you will see that culturally diverse teams can be very creative and successful, with lots of different points of view helping to create unique solutions.

2.2.5 Sharing and documenting knowledge, skills and experience

Sir Francis Bacon, in the 1500s, said: "Knowledge is power". His statement is as true today as it was then. The world runs on information. Any good business operator understands that sharing knowledge, skills and experience among teams provides a solid foundation for future success and inclusivity. Acknowledging the contributions to the team of colleagues from diverse backgrounds can be effective in encouraging them to use and share their specific qualities, skills or backgrounds with other team members and clients in order to enhance work outcomes.

It may also be necessary at times in the workplace to bring together *formal* working teams. This might be to achieve a goal, to act as a committee, to develop a program, or to complete a large task. Participants should be chosen for what they can bring to the team—that is, qualities they have that can assist in getting the job done. In such cases, it is useful to have a record of the skills, knowledge and experience among your team so that the right people can be chosen for each given task.

Recognising others' knowledge, skills and expertise might be a matter of:

- reviewing documented evidence of their skills and experience, such as:
  - resumes
  - awards
  - letters of appreciation
  - certificates
- directly observing their skills and knowledge
- developing an understanding of diversity and how this diversity can be applied to best advantage.

Documenting the contribution that individual team members have made in achieving an objective can also be useful for future projects. If you are aware that specific staff members have talents or expertise in given areas, they can be called upon again should other similar opportunities arise. Documentation can take the form of notations in the staff member's personnel file, a certificate of appreciation for their contribution, or documentation of their participation in a project report.

To be truly useful, information needs to be shared with colleagues to ensure that all staff are working toward the same goals and making the team that much stronger and more inclusive.

- Sharing *knowledge* means providing your team with information you have that they might not have, and which might be useful in the workplace.
- Sharing *skills* means showing others how to undertake a task, whether it is technical, administrative, manual or mental.

- Sharing *experience* means advising others of ways in which you have successfully applied knowledge and/or skills in a previous role or situation.

All of this goes toward building a well-rounded and inclusive workforce. When sharing information, there are a number of things to consider.

- Is the information of a confidential nature? If it is confidential, you need to be aware of who this information can be shared with.
- What is the best method of distributing information so that all staff can access it? Distribution methods can include:
  - regular staff meetings
  - meetings held specifically to share information
  - training sessions held to share detailed information
  - emails or memos to staff
  - reading distribution lists, where staff are required to read the material supplied and to check off that they have read and understood it.

You also need to consider the audience you are sharing information with. Adjust the method used to share it to accommodate the diverse range of people with whom you work.

Diversity in the workplace might relate to people with specific social, cultural and other needs that require a range of strategies and approaches which will impact on the way you communicate with them. For example, people with language difficulties may appreciate information when it is provided in a number of ways, such as visually (using pictures or diagrams), via video or live demonstration, as well as in the form of verbal and written instructions in a variety of languages. By providing a variety of communication channels, it is likely that more people will be able to understand the communication and feel included in the interaction.

Knowledge check

7. In your own words, describe the value of inclusivity in the workforce and the impact this has on the organisation's ability to attract staff, promote employee satisfaction and achieve its financial performance goals.
8. Describe methods by which you can gain the trust of your colleagues.
9. Describe why it is important to share information with other staff. List at least four methods you could use to do this.
10. Describe at least three general inclusive work practices that could be put in place in the average workplace.
11. Explain why it may be necessary to modify verbal and non-verbal communication when working with people from diverse backgrounds.
12. List at least four methods you can use to overcome language barriers.
13. In addition to verbal communication, you may also need to be aware of non-verbal language. What does "non-verbal communication" mean? Give examples of at least four ways in which people might communicate non-verbally.
14. Explain why it is important to document the developed knowledge, skills and experience of an organisation's workforce.
15. Describe what things you should consider when sharing information.

2.3 Assessing the use of inclusive practices

All successful organisations and teams will communicate on a regular basis to monitor their progress and offer support where needed. Part of this communication process involves evaluating the organisation's performance, reflecting on activities undertaken and identifying opportunities for improvement.

As information is only as good as the use to which it is put, at some point it is necessary to evaluate how well it was used and whether it led to any actual improvement. This means asking for feedback from workers, customers and community members in order to identify any practices or activities that could operate in more inclusive ways.

2.3.1 Seeking feedback on inclusive practices from a supervisor

In order for an organisation to remain successful, its focus should be on increasing employee engagement, decreasing employee turnover, and fostering a positive, nurturing, employee-focused culture. This is where feedback culture comes in. By creating a culture where feedback and honesty are valued, employee morale can be increased, which, in turn, can lead to improved job performance. A **feedback culture** is an environment in which every employee feels they have the right to give feedback to another person in the organisation—no matter where they may fall on the organisational chart. Creating a feedback culture in the workplace might mean:

- *Encouraging employees to provide feedback.* This might mean providing feedback between colleagues or between staff and management.
- *Providing feedback training.* All employees should take part in feedback training. Some people may be better at giving constructive feedback than others. Those who don't have much experience in this, or who can be blunt and somewhat rude, will benefit (and avoid hurting others' feelings) by being shown sensitive ways to provide feedback.
- *Using continuous feedback rather than periodic feedback.* The annual **performance review** is no longer the best way to ensure that a team member is working to the best of their ability and in line with organisational policies and procedures. Rather, providing and receiving feedback on an ongoing basis enables issues to be recognised quickly and improvements implemented as needed.
- *Emphasising openness and trust.* For feedback culture to succeed, everyone must feel able to speak their mind. Because of this, openness and trust are critical. Employees should feel free to share feedback with one another—and with the organisation—without any fear of reprisals or punishment.
- *Balancing critical feedback with positive feedback.* Feedback needs to walk the fine line between being honest and being negative. It must address any shortcomings in team behaviour, but it should never discourage or humiliate the person concerned. It should outline what they have done well and provide guidance on where they need to improve.
- *Using multiple feedback channels.* Not everyone feels comfortable with a one-on-one, face-to-face feedback session. Different ways to give feedback include online feedback platforms and small-group feedback sessions. By providing employees with flexibility when it comes to giving feedback, the organisation can cater to those who may not be as comfortable interacting with their peers, thereby increasing their engagement with your program.

Try this now

1. Ask a colleague or your supervisor to give you feedback on your work practices.
2. Observe how work is being carried out around you and think about the feedback you might give those you have observed.

2.3.2 Evaluating feedback and identifying opportunities for improvement

The world is changing constantly and rapidly, so it is important to ensure that you keep pace with the changes that impact on the workplace. You can do this by monitoring your organisation's policies and procedures on a regular and ongoing basis, through collecting feedback, to ensure they remain effective and still achieve their purpose. Having gathered feedback, however, you need to examine what it is telling you, where you are performing well, and where improvements may be needed.

To gauge how effective your organisation's various strategies and solutions are, ask yourself the following questions:

- What did we do well? For example, which of our inclusive activities and opportunities produced the best results (and why)?
- What issues did we encounter that caused issues or problems?
- Why did these issues happen in the first place? A close examination of the circumstances surrounding the matter can show up problems in procedure or policy. Issues to look at could include:
    - Was there a breakdown in communication?
    - Are the organisation's inclusivity policies and procedures as effective as they could be?
- Did we effectively resolve any issues that arose? When looking at how the problem was resolved:
    - Ask critical questions about the outcome. Was it the best possible option for everyone concerned?
    - Evaluate the customer's reaction to your proposal. Were they happy with it? Were they prepared to be reasonable?
    - Compare the situation to any previous incidents of this nature. How was it handled last time? Is there a pattern emerging that should be addressed?
- What can we do to prevent it happening in the future? By looking at how the problem occurred in the first place, and how effectively you resolved it, you can then take any necessary steps to prevent the same thing happening again. This might mean:
    - a change in policy or procedure
    - training staff in inclusivity practices
    - training staff in conflict handling.

By asking these and other relevant questions, you can make improvements to the organisation. This could lead to greater staff satisfaction which, in turn, will have a positive impact on the organisation's continued success and prosperity.

2.3.3 Incorporating feedback to make improvements

The evaluation process, and the questions asked, should provide the foundation for future planning and continuous improvement and result in a list of future tasks outlining areas that have been identified as having:

- worked well but that could still be improved upon
- issues or problems that can be properly dissected and discussed in terms of how these issues can be resolved.

The cycle of innovation and improvement then begins again, with tasks being allocated to relevant, qualified team members, schedules and time frames set, and progress monitored on a regular basis. This cycle forms the basis of the organisation's continuous improvement program, where small, ongoing changes are made over time (Figure 2.4). Continuous improvement has two main advantages:

- The recognition that processes must be improved before performance can be enhanced fosters process-oriented thinking in the team. Focusing on ways to constantly improve the process becomes part of a workplace movement in which those closest to the problem, usually frontline staff, become involved in and responsible for getting things right. A "can do" attitude becomes a way of workplace life.
- A continuous improvement culture can and does complement innovative leaps and breakthroughs. In order to have a long-lasting effect, leaps and breakthroughs need to be followed up with continuous improvement activities.

Figure 2.4 Cycle of innovation and improvement

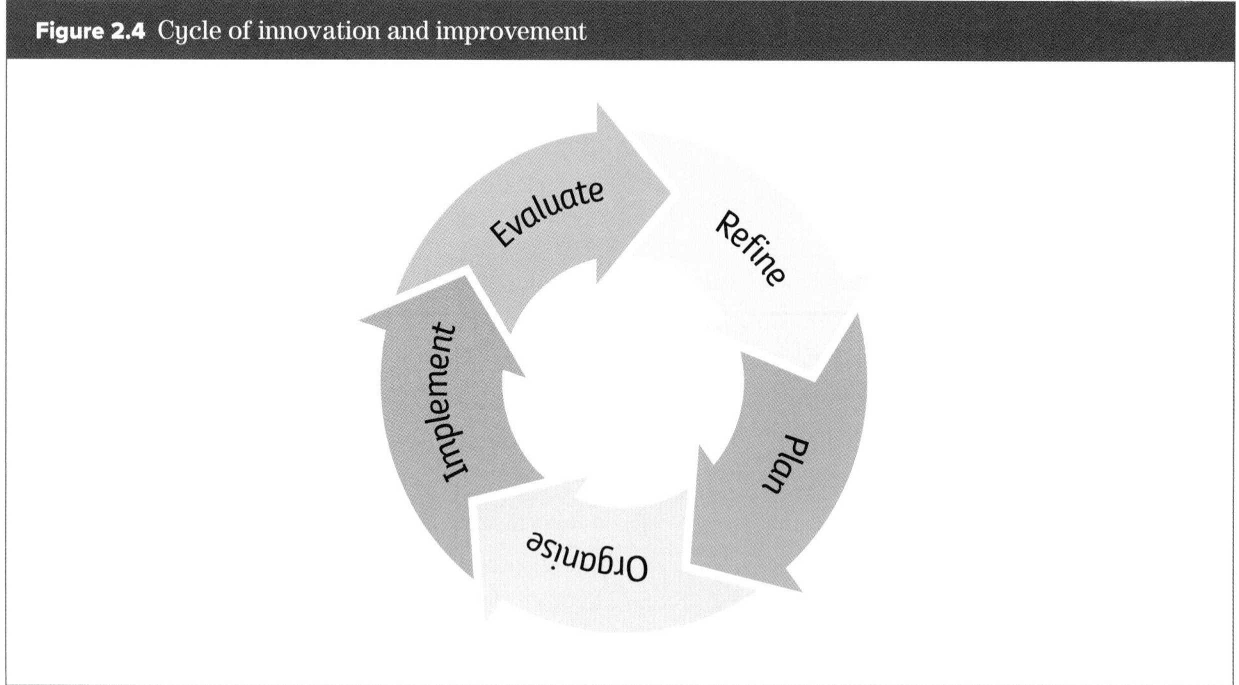

Documenting feedback, and then making continuous improvements based on that feedback, is important for a number of reasons:

- It shows compliance with legislative requirements, which might require both internal and external audits to be undertaken at regular intervals.
- It keeps track of changes made through the years—showing what worked or what didn't work, and why. This, in itself, provides valuable information about possible future trends and needed improvements.

A continuous improvement log should be an ongoing, "living" document that outlines what issues were identified, when they were identified, and what action was taken. Table 2.2 is an example of such a log. It was developed for a department store to show how it improved both WHS obligations as well as productivity issues.

Table 2.2 Example of a continuous improvement log

Continuous improvement log				
Issue	**Date identified on/by**	**Recommendation or action taken**	**Who is responsible?**	**Date actioned**
Staff evacuation drill took too long, and some staff didn't know where the "meeting point" is located.	12.6.23	1. Undertake evacuation drill every quarter. 2. Develop an evacuation and emergency procedures manual.	1. Department supervisors 2. WHS warden and HR manager	1. Every quarter in line with attached schedule. 2. Must be completed by 12.7.23.
Sales are declining, as more people are shopping online.	19.7.23	1. Investigate an online shopping app for our business. 2. Re-examine our social media policies.	1. Hannika (IT department) 2. Jillian (marketing coordinator)	Both steps to be researched by 1.8.24, ready to make recommendations to the board.
Review recommendations on online shopping and social media opportunities.		Board to review recommendations and take appropriate decisions.	Board members, CEO	15.8.23

16. Describe the advantages of a feedback culture. What methods could you use to create a feedback culture in your workplace?

17. List at least five questions you should ask when evaluating feedback and identifying opportunities.

18. Incorporating feedback received should result in a cycle of continuous improvement. Explain why this is important.

Summary

An inclusive workplace is one where all employees can work together in harmony and where everyone feels their contributions are welcome. Inevitably, issues and conflicts will occur, but inclusive work practices and policies will provide a pathway by which these can be overcome effectively and workplace relationships can stay true and intact.

References

Alonsagay, A.I. 2022. "Why empathy may be the most important business skill", https://www.upskilled.edu.au/skillstalk/empathy-important-business-skill, accessed September 2022.

Anti-Discrimination NSW, 2022. "Disability discrimination", https://antidiscrimination.nsw.gov.au/anti-discrimination-nsw/discrimination/types-of-discrimination/disability-discrimination.html, accessed September 2022.

Australian Bureau of Statistics, 2022. "Census shows changes in Australia's religious diversity", media release, 28 June, https://www.abs.gov.au/media-centre/media-releases/2021-census-shows-changes-australias-religious-diversity, accessed September 2022.

Australian Government, 2018. "Face the facts: Gender equality 2018", https://humanrights.gov.au/our-work/education/face-facts-gender-equality-2018, accessed September 2022.

Australian Government, 2021. "Equal opportunity and diversity", *Business.gov.au*, last updated 7 April, https://business.gov.au/people/employees/equal-opportunity-and-diversity#:~:text=All%20employees%20have%20a%20right,and%20harassment%20in%20the%20workplace, accessed September 2022.

Australian Public Service Commission, 2021. "Disability myths and stereotypes", 2 June, https://www.apsc.gov.au/working-aps/diversity-and-inclusion/disability/disability-myths-and-stereotypes, accessed September 2022.

Gustafsson, L., 2021, "Australian labour force participation: Historical trends and future prospects", Treasury Working Paper 2 2021–22, ACT: The Treasury, modified April 2021, https://treasury.gov.au/sites/default/files/2021-04/p2021-164860_australian_labour_force_participation.pdf, accessed September 2022.

World Health Organization, 2022a, "Disability", https://www.who.int/health-topics/disability, accessed September 2022.

World Health Organization, 2022b. "Gender and health", https://www.who.int/health-topics/gender#tab=tab_1, accessed September 2022.

World Population Review, 2022. "World population by religion", https://worldpopulationreview.com/country-rankings/religion-by-country, accessed September 2022.

CHAPTER 3

Support personal wellbeing in the workplace

Learning outcomes

3.1 Recognise factors that impact personal wellbeing

3.2 Plan communication with a supervisor

3.3 Communicate with a supervisor

3.4 Investigate available wellbeing resources

Wellbeing is something that everyone should be concerned with and is associated with numerous health, job, family and economic benefits. For example, higher levels of wellbeing can result in a decreased risk of disease, illness and injury; better immune functioning; speedier recovery; and increased longevity. Individuals with high levels of wellbeing are more productive at work and are also more likely to contribute to their communities.

There is no consensus around a single definition of wellbeing, but there is general agreement that at minimum, it includes:

- the presence of positive emotions and moods such as contentment and happiness
- the absence of negative emotions such as depression or anxiety
- satisfaction with life
- a sense of fulfilment and positive functioning.

In simple terms, **wellbeing** can be described as having a positive life attitude and feeling good. Even though happiness is an integral part of your personal wellbeing, it includes other things, such as the fulfilment of long-term goals, your sense of purpose and how in control you feel in life.

3.1 Recognising factors that impact personal wellbeing

An overall sense of wellbeing can rarely be achieved without having a balance in the following key areas:

- *Physical wellbeing.* This includes lifestyle choices that affect the functioning of our bodies. What we eat and how active we are will affect our physical wellbeing.
- *Emotional or psychological wellbeing.* This is our ability to cope with everyday life and reflects how we think and feel about ourselves.
- *Social wellbeing.* This is the extent to which we feel a sense of belonging and social inclusion. The way we communicate with others, our relationships, values, beliefs, lifestyles and traditions, are all important factors of social wellbeing.
- *Spiritual wellbeing.* This is the ability to experience and integrate meaning and purpose in life. It is achieved through being connected to our inner self, to nature or even to a greater power.
- *Intellectual wellbeing.* Gaining and maintaining intellectual wellbeing helps us to expand our knowledge and skills in order to live an enjoyable and successful life.
- *Economic wellbeing.* This is our ability to meet our basic needs and to feel a sense of security.

The world we live in is complex. Understanding the factors that influence wellbeing, whether as an individual, community or nation, helps us to work together to improve our quality of life. Although genetics and personal behaviour play a large part in determining an individual's health, our wellbeing starts with where we live, where we work and learn, and where we play.

3.1.1 Identifying personal and workplace factors that may impact on wellbeing

Wellbeing isn't just the absence of illness or of feeling bad. As we have seen, it is a complex combination of physical, mental, emotional and social health factors and is strongly linked to happiness and life satisfaction. It doesn't simply "happen", though. Personal and workplace factors all impact on your state of wellness (as shown in Figure 3.1).

Personal factors can include:

- *Culture.* Your cultural upbringing may influence what foods you can and cannot eat, how you dress, how you relate to people of other cultures, and what cultural customs you must observe whether you are at work or not.
- *Education.* Your education level may be a factor in your social interactions, influencing who you socialise with and the types of activities you participate in. It will also be a factor in determining the type of job you can get.
- *Environment.* This includes not only environmental factors that impact on your health, such as air and water quality, but also things such as the quality of your home life or your neighbourhood environment.
- *Family life.* Family influences include your responsibilities towards your family, whether you have enough private space and time, and how pressured you feel to do well.
- *Finances.* Your financial state impacts on what you can and cannot afford to do. It influences where you can live, and how much **disposable income** you have to spend on doing things you enjoy.
- *Psychological state.* All these personal factors influence the amount of pressure a person feels to work harder in order to succeed.

Figure 3.1 Personal and workplace factors that affect personal wellbeing

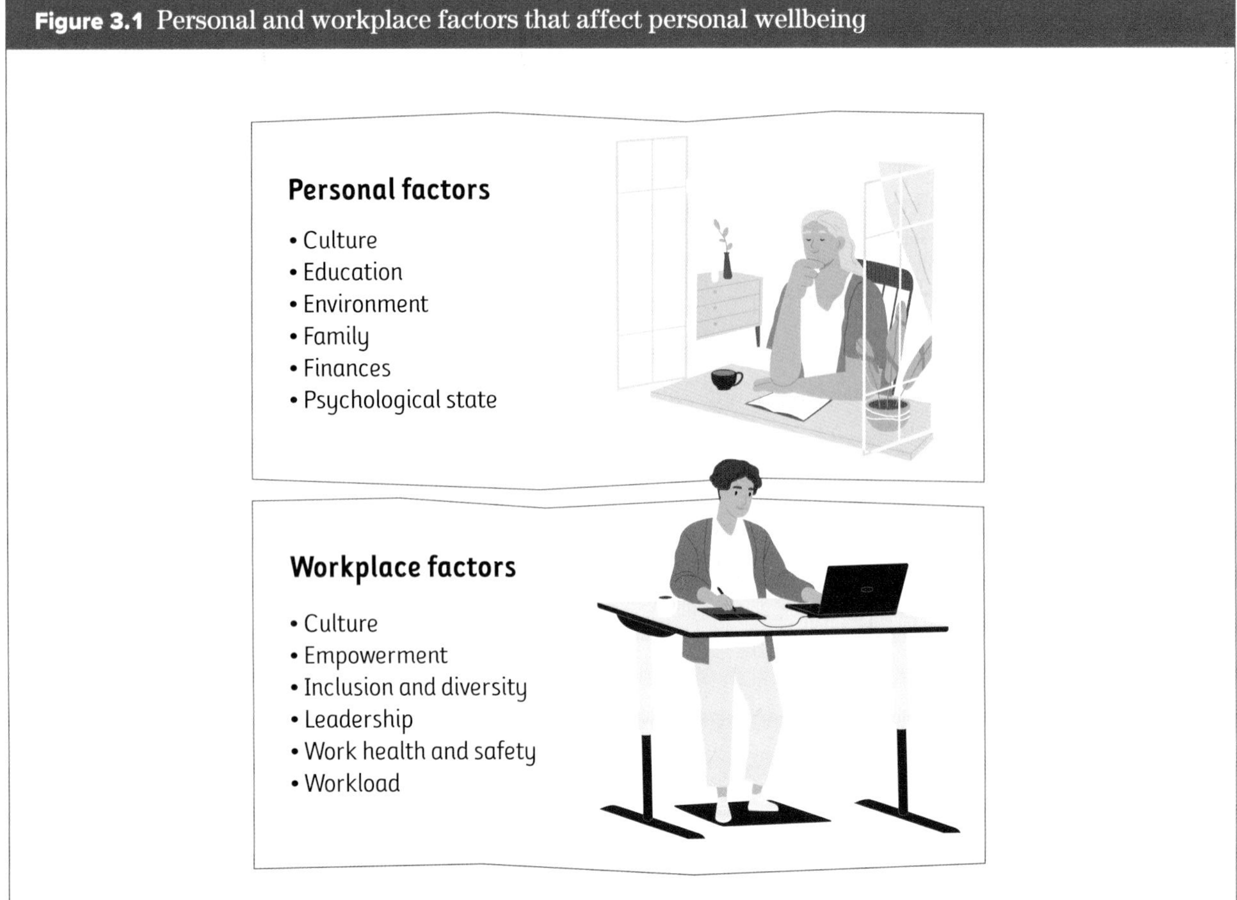

Personal factors
• Culture
• Education
• Environment
• Family
• Finances
• Psychological state
Workplace factors
• Culture
• Empowerment
• Inclusion and diversity
• Leadership
• Work health and safety
• Workload

GoodStudio/Shutterstock

Workplace factors can include:

- *Culture*. **Workplace culture** is different from your personal cultural background. It describes an organisation's general view of its work operations and its team of employees. This might relate to:
  - how social the organisation is in terms of relationships with its staff
  - whether there is an "open door" policy between staff and management
  - its environmental policies and views on "green" workplace operations
  - its work ethics (e.g. the organisation might have a "no nonsense" approach to work processes and discourage social interaction among staff).
- *Empowerment and psychological safety*. Factors here might include:
  - possibilities for promotion
  - praise and recognition
  - the feeling that you are secure in your job.
- *Inclusion and diversity*. While it is against the law to discriminate against people because of their culture, religion, physical or mental abilities, and gender, among other things, it does still happen that people from diverse backgrounds feel excluded from workplace teams or social activities.
- *Leadership*. It could be said that strong leadership within an organisation creates a strong team, while weak leadership might lead to an environment in which everyone works to their own agenda and there is a lack of team spirit. This, in turn, can lead to job dissatisfaction and resentment. Strong leadership:
  - provides motivational strategies designed to build a cohesive team, so that members work together for the good of the organisation and its people as a whole

- creates an organisational structure that has clear lines of responsibility
- provides policies and procedures that ensure a safe, smooth and consistent mode of business operation
- allows team members to offer suggestions and ideas
- allows team members to approach their supervisors about any concerns they might have
- offers wellbeing programs as part of the organisational culture and ensures that the workplace is a safe and healthy environment.

- *Work health and safety (WHS)*. WHS programs are a legislative requirement in all workplaces. They ensure that workers (or anyone visiting business premises) have a safe and risk-free environment in which to work. Some workplaces are hazardous by their very nature, which puts additional pressure and stress on workers. Inadequate WHS policies and procedures can lead to sickness, serious illness, accidents, or even deaths, in the workplace.
- *Workloads*. In an effort to maximise profits, some organisations expect more work to be done by fewer people, causing stress from the pressure of getting work done.

It is easy to become overwhelmed by pressures, so it is important to take steps to maintain your wellbeing both at home and in the workplace.

Think about

1. Think about your own work or study environment. How do the factors identified in this section impact on your sense of wellbeing?

3.1.2 The relationship between personal wellbeing and workplace factors

In order to support and increase your own wellbeing, you first need to understand the relationship between personal wellbeing and the identified workplace factors that are relevant to your own role. The factors that influence wellbeing are interrelated, so they should not be considered in isolation. In your own case, for example, you might find the following:

- Your education level influences the type of job you can get or your job security.
- Your cultural heritage may have an impact on:
  - the type of work you are allowed to do
  - the hours you are allowed to work
  - workplace social activities you can take part in
  - how you are perceived by work colleagues
  - the extent to which you are accepted as part of "the team".

  A job provides not just money, but also a sense of purpose, goals, friendships and a feeling of belonging.

- Your family culture around using resources wisely or wastefully may have an impact in a work environment where wastefulness is frowned upon and is a matter of organisational culture.

Wellbeing in the workplace can also be negatively affected by a lack of understanding of your role and responsibilities in the organisation. Remedies for this might include:

- Read your job description, which will set out exactly what your particular role and responsibilities are within the organisation.
- Discuss with human resource (HR) staff and/or your supervisor anything you don't understand about how your work fits into the organisation as a whole.

- Establish relationships with colleagues to gain a better understanding of your work environment and to have people you can seek help from when needed.

Knowledge check

1. List at least five personal factors that can impact on your wellbeing.
2. List at least five workplace factors that can impact on your wellbeing.
3. Describe how personal and workplace factors are interrelated. Give an example of how this might impact on your wellbeing.

3.2 Planning communication with a supervisor

Not all workplaces will have, or may even have heard of, wellness programs. Nor may they have an understanding of work–life balance. In the absence of an existing program, you could discuss with your supervisor any factors that are impacting on your ability to do your job. However, supervisors and managers are generally very busy overseeing teams of staff and various workplace operations, so be fully prepared before making your approach to them in order to get the most out of your meeting with them.

3.2.1 Selecting the appropriate communication approach

Chapter 1 explains that business takes place on many different levels and uses many different communication methods. In a small organisation, your approach might be very casual. In a medium-size or large organisation, a more formal approach might be needed, with specific communication protocols to be observed. For example:

- It may be the organisation's policy to make formal appointments with the people who have the authority to assist you with your concerns.
- Organisational policy may require you to send an initial email request for a meeting, describing what it will be about.
- Supervisors may routinely only make time available to deal with matters that are urgent or important. If your request isn't urgent but you feel it is important to you, then you will need to give them a reason to agree to meet with you.

How you communicate with others in the workplace will also depend on company protocols and how urgent the matter is, but your approach to them might also vary depending on the preferences of the people concerned. Ask yourself questions such as:

- What, exactly, is it that I want to say?
- Should I be tentative or firm in my approach?
- What communication style should I use?
- Will I need to communicate verbally and in person, or will written or electronic communication be the best approach?

These and other questions tailored to your specific purpose can help you to decide the best way to get your message across in order to achieve a successful outcome.

Advantages and disadvantages of different communication styles

In selecting your communication approach, you might also consider your own communication style as well as that of your supervisor. Communication is all about interacting with others, so the approach you take might be influenced by your particular communication style. This determines how you speak, act and react in various situations, and how you might react to people with communication styles different from your own.

As Figure 1.1 in Chapter 1 shows, there are four common communication styles that you are likely to encounter in the workplace: passive, aggressive, passive–aggressive, and assertive. Each of these styles has certain advantages and disadvantages.

- *Passive communication style.* Passive communicators tend to avoid conflict and are perceived by others as patient and easygoing but somewhat aloof. They avoid eye contact and extended conversations. Though passive, they may nevertheless be prone to explosive outbursts after prolonged disappointment, frustration or criticism. The advantage of passive communication is that the individual is viewed as amiable and always concerned with others. Co-workers like to be around colleagues who don't constantly make waves and who agree to take on tasks without complaint. This type of communicator regularly gives in to others' ideas and projects low self-esteem and low self-worth.
- *Aggressive communication style.* The aggressive communicator is always advocating their own opinions, ideas and needs. Whether in email, memos or other work communication mediums, this communicator is telling others what to do and is argumentative if there is no buy-in. A leader who uses an aggressive communication style might overwhelm subordinates in the work environment and can create tension among team members. On the positive side, aggressive communicators know what they want and are willing to push forward regardless of adversity.
- *Passive–aggressive communication style.* Passive–aggressive individuals aren't truthful about their feelings and opinions: they appear to be passive, but inside they are angry at others. You can recognise this communication style by the person's sarcastic remarks, mutterings and whispered complaints, and disruptive behaviours, such as using chat software to gossip about co-workers who are often in the same room. This is a toxic communication style that needs to be dealt with quickly in a business environment to prevent strife in the team and with clients or consumers.
- *Assertive communication style.* Assertive communication is the opposite of passive communication. This style of communicator states their opinions effectively (e.g. when leading a team) and is their own advocate (e.g. when asking for a raise). Assertive communicators look you in the eye and are confident about conveying ideas. Because an assertive communication style considers others' opinions and values both parties, it is the preferred communication style in business, especially among managers and sales staff.

Creating a rapport

In addition to recognising the communication style of the person you are talking to, creating a rapport and a good relationship with them can improve the chances of a successful outcome. For example:

- Before going into the meeting, check your appearance to ensure you are neat and tidy.
- Rather than launch straight into your purpose, it sometimes helps to spend a couple of minutes easing into the conversation.
- Remember the basics of good communication.
- Find some common ground.
- Be empathic.

Another aspect of good communication skills is the art of "mirroring". Subtly matching the actions, gestures and mode of communication of the person you are talking to helps them to feel relaxed and comfortable in your company. For example:

- If the person you are meeting with is soft spoken, then don't speak to them in a loud voice. Match their tone.
- If they rest their arms on the table or desk, gradually adopt a similar position.

GoodStudio/Shutterstock

- If they speak slowly, then don't chatter away at a rapid pace. Slow you own speech pace down to match theirs.

By matching a person's behaviour, you can help create an atmosphere that allows for comfortable, friendly and open communication.

Try this now

1. Hold a conversation with someone you don't know very well from your class or workplace in which you want to ask them a favour. Use the tips discussed to build a rapport with them.

3.2.2 Identifying appropriate methods for communicating about wellbeing

The method you use to communicate issues about wellbeing in the workplace can vary. For example, an appropriate means of communication might include one of the following:

- *Newsletters.* An in-house newsletter is an excellent way to distribute or collect information throughout the entire organisation. You could start by providing your own general information about the nature of wellbeing and follow this up by asking for opinions from others. You can then use the results of your research during your discussions with your supervisor.
- *One-on-one meetings with peers and supervisors.* Having done some research, you could meet with your supervisor for initial discussions about wellbeing in the workplace.
- *Online assessments.* The internet is an excellent source of all kinds of information, including online reviews and assessments. Other people will have had issues and, perhaps, introduced wellbeing programs into their workplace. You can research how they went about this, find out what went well, what pitfalls they may have found, and learn from their experience.
- *Safety shares.* A **safety share** is when a colleague shares lessons learnt from personal experience in terms of any WHS issues. The idea is that the information is shared so that others don't make the same mistakes or can find out about how to access assistance.
- *Team meetings.* Discussing your initial thoughts and ideas with your colleagues allows you to put ideas out in the open and ask your colleagues for their input. They may be affected by wellbeing issues, too, so they will have their own thoughts about what needs to be done.
- *Toolbox talks.* A **toolbox talk** is defined as a team meeting or gathering with a workplace team. It almost always revolves around a specific WHS issue. Typical topics might include:
  - the relationship between the workplace and mental health
  - anxiety and depression in the workplace
  - taking action to support someone at work.

All of these forms of communication, and the information you collect, add weight to, and provide a foundation for, discussions with your supervisor. The more facts you can gather, and the more methods of communication you can make use of, the better your approach can be.

3.2.3 Planning relevant content for communication

At this point, you may have amassed a great deal of information. Some of it will be relevant and some of it less so. When communicating in a business environment, always remember that it is important to be clear and succinct so as not to waste the other person's time. You may therefore need to review all the information you have compiled, along with its sources, and select only that which will be most useful in planning your discussion.

When planning your message, consider the following:

- What outcome are you hoping to achieve?
- Is there a time limit to consider? If so, what is it?
- Is your key message clear? Irrelevancies cloud the issue and confuse the message, so use only illustrations, examples and facts that strengthen the key message.
- Is the message logical and coherent? Does the structure flow well? Set out what you have to say in a step-by-step manner (step 1, step 2, and so on).
- Is the information appropriate? Are you sending this message to the right audience, using the right method? Provide enough information to capture the audience's attention without overloading them.
- Is the information accurate? Make sure you use reliable sources. Far-reaching organisational decisions might be made based on the information you provide, so it is important to check your facts for accuracy and currency. You should never damage your credibility by putting forward unverified facts.
- Have you included all the key points—the information that is most important to the communication?
- Always check your spelling and grammar. Accuracy isn't just about using the correct information; it's also about using proper language.

Strategies for dealing with a negative response

The issues you raise, and the possible introduction of a **wellbeing program**, may have an impact on your organisation. It could affect the way in which managers typically deal with staff issues, and it might require a significant investment of time, effort, resources and money to establish. You should therefore expect that the response to your initial approach might be negative, due to an unwillingness to change. This is something you can prepare for by:

- anticipating the hard questions that may be asked or problems that might surface
- fully researching all aspects of the subject you wish to discuss
- being ready to defend your point of view with verifiable facts.

Here are some strategies you can use:

- Outline your issues, explaining in general terms what they are, what you have in mind, and how you came to assess the need for a solution.
- Cite sources for the information and data you include. These underpin the legitimacy of your research and are therefore the foundation of any solution you present.
- Address the advantages of your solution for both the organisation and the staff. For example, explain how a wellbeing program can help to increase productivity and staff efficiency.
- Explain what resources might be needed. For example:
  - physical resources
  - cost budgets
  - time frames.
- Provide information on outside sources of assistance and/or funding that can be accessed for advice or help.

These and other industry-relevant strategies will help in addressing any issues or challenges you might face during the presentation of your proposal.

Knowledge check

4. List four questions you might ask when determining which communication approach to take.
5. List the four main communication styles. Briefly describe their advantages and disadvantages.
6. Describe methods you could use when developing a relationship or establishing a rapport with someone.
7. List at least five means of communication you could use in the workplace. Briefly describe them.
8. List at least five issues you might consider when planning a communication message.
9. List at least six strategies and/or problem-solving skills you can use to deal with negative responses.

3.3 Communicating with a supervisor

Once you have done your initial research and determined the best approach to take, you should arrange a meeting with your supervisor to discuss the health and wellbeing issues in the workplace that concern you.

3.3.1 Arranging to communicate with the supervisor

Everyone has different preferences when it comes to communication. Some supervisors have an "open door" policy and don't mind being interrupted for a quick chat, while others prefer you to make an appointment. Some would rather receive written notification about what you want before actually meeting face to face. Taking all of this into consideration will give you a good indication of the best time and method for an approach. Having said that, senior staff are busy people so, depending on protocols and the seriousness of your intentions, you should always try to book a formal, face-to-face appointment with your supervisor. This will ensure they will have sufficient time set aside for you and will be able to pay attention.

Using communication skills effectively

You will also need good, basic **communication skills**, such as questioning techniques and listening skills, to help you. As Chapter 1 explains, asking questions effectively and listening carefully are important skills that can make the difference between having a conversation with a person—or interrogating them. Refer to section 1.3.1 and review the basic question types: open, clarifying, leading and closed.

Positive listening skills require paying attention to what is being said to you and not being distracted by others or what is going on around you. These skills are essential in order to fully understand what is expected of you. Good listening skills are also a vital component in any negotiation you may be involved in when putting your ideas and thoughts to a supervisor or manager. Listening, and responding appropriately, to their own thoughts, ideas or objections can help you to further your cause.

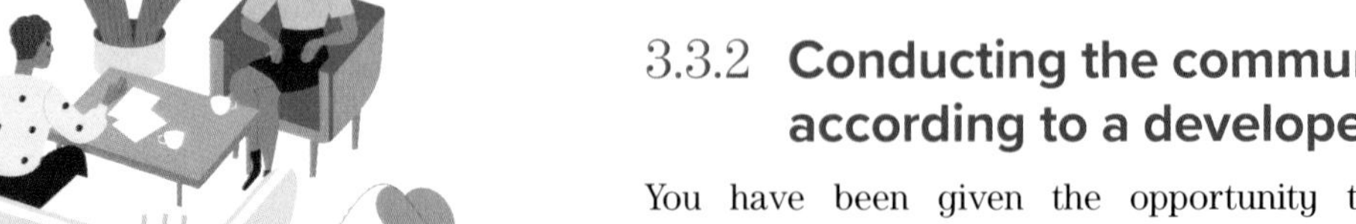

GoodStudio/Shutterstock

3.3.2 Conducting the communication according to a developed plan

You have been given the opportunity to discuss your concerns; don't waste it. Make sure you have all the necessary documentation with you for the appointment and that you know what you want to say to, or to raise with, your supervisor.

- *Clearly state what you need.* Your supervisor won't have time to waste on things that are irrelevant to what you are asking for. Clearly state what it is you are hoping for so they can make a decision in a timely manner. Start the conversation with an overview and then fill in the details once you have put forward the main points.

- *Show value.* You were hired because of your qualifications, experience and personality, so don't be afraid to make your suggestions or to voice your opinion. It is in the long-term interests of the organisation to make improvements to their operation and management procedures, so putting forward proposals to make such improvements can only be a good thing.
- *Be aware of your body language.* When you are talking to your supervisor, make sure you use confident body language. For example:
    - maintain an upright posture (i.e. don't slouch)
    - avoid fidgeting
    - maintain eye contact.
- *Get your facts straight.* As mentioned earlier, ensure you have thoroughly researched your subject and that your information is accurate, up to date and relevant. Presenting material that has no factual basis can mean the end of your suggestion before it has even been properly heard.
- *Be solution oriented.* You are going to your supervisor with a problem, so be sure also to have a solution. This shows that you are proactive and can be trusted to get on with your work. You are bringing an issue to their attention and saying that you have a solution.
- *Don't take criticism personally.* Your proposal may initially be met with resistance, so you must be prepared to answer hard questions, to deal with scepticism and to defend your idea. What you are proposing might be a new idea to the supervisor, who may have a great many other things to do. It may therefore take time for the idea to fix in their minds and for them to take a serious look at it. Be patient.

Try this now

2. You are planning to ask your supervisor for permission to work from home two days a week. Using the information in this chapter, plan what you will say, what challenges you should anticipate, and how you will go about stating your case. Role play the conversation with a friend or colleague to practise this skill.

3.3.3 Reviewing the effectiveness of communication

Have you ever come out of a meeting or interview and thought, "I wish I'd said ..." or "Why did I do that?" Reviewing the effectiveness of your communication is the best way to improve, so that next time, perhaps, you *will* say that, or do something better.

You can learn from mistakes, or gain a better understanding of the communication process, by asking yourself questions such as:

- Did the meeting go as well as I expected? If not, why not?
- Did communication flow logically and naturally?
- Did I include all the points I wanted to make?
- What did I miss or leave out? Why?
- Was the language level I used appropriate?
- Was the method of communication I used appropriate? If not, why not? What method would have been better?
- Was my information accurate and relevant?
- Did I achieve the desired results?
- Did it lead to any action being taken?

GoodStudio/Shutterstock

These and other similar questions can help you to understand the effectiveness of the meeting and your communication skills, allowing you to make any necessary improvements.

Communication is the basis for everything we do. We are communicating with people constantly. The more effort we put into doing this effectively and respectfully, the better we will become at understanding the world around us.

Knowledge check

10. Explain what issues you might face when arranging to communicate with your supervisor. Why is it important to consider these?
11. When conducting a conversation with your supervisor, there are a range of things you should bear in mind in order to gain the best possible outcome. List at least five of these.
12. Explain why it is important to review the effectiveness of your communication style and methods.
13. When reviewing your communication, what questions could you ask yourself? List at least six questions.

3.4 Investigating available wellbeing resources

Employers are now beginning to see the value of supporting their employees' sense of wellbeing and there are significant advantages for organisations that are able to do this. Many of them have included employee wellbeing in their HR strategies and have gone so far as to implement ongoing wellbeing initiatives. Figure 3.2 identifies some of the most common such initiatives, which can be

Figure 3.2 Some common wellbeing initiatives in the workplace

GoodStudio/Shutterstock

offered to employees with relative ease, at low cost, and have far-reaching impacts on staff. The benefits of wellbeing initiatives include:

- improved productivity and quality of work being produced
- improved overall morale and culture of the organisation
- higher staff retention rates
- the ability to attract quality candidates who can see that the organisation values employees' health and wellbeing, care about employees as individuals and fulfils its social corporate responsibilities
- avoidance of high costs associated with absenteeism, injury and illness.

Not all wellbeing programs are equal, however. While they may have similar components, they may not all be practical in all workplaces. An office environment will have very different working conditions from a construction site. Some jobs can be considered more stressful than others; for example, firefighters, police officers, nurses and doctors are subjected to levels of stress and trauma that far exceed what a typical office worker faces. Choosing the appropriate wellbeing resource is a matter of identifying and then examining the proposed program or activities in detail, and determining if its recommendations and requirements are practical in your specific work environment.

3.4.1 Identifying and reviewing wellbeing resources

One of the most important parts of understanding, and introducing, wellbeing practices into the workplace is to find credible sources of information. Some of these will be resources provided by external organisations and some might come from internal sources.

External resources, for example, can include the Australian HR Institute (AHRI) (https://www.ahri.com.au/resources/ahriassist/health-and-wellbeing), which is the professional body that sets the industry standard for HR practitioners in Australia. The AHRI ensures that HR practitioners:

- hold to a professional code of conduct that is supported by governance requirements and disciplinary procedures
- are effectively supported in their continuing professional development to ensure the currency of their skills and knowledge is maintained.

The AHRI also provides a wide range of learning and development opportunities in human resources, people management and business skills, and offers advice on wellbeing programs. (For more information on AHRI, see www.ahri.com.au.)

Online resources

We begin with a note of caution. Vast quantities of information on all manner of subjects are freely available on the web at the press of a key. However, it is important to be careful about *where* you get your information—just because you found it on the internet doesn't mean it is accurate. Sources on the internet are not all official, and anyone can upload information outlining their personal views and understandings on any given subject. While the internet is an excellent and freely available source of information, for business purposes you should use only credible sites approved of by product or service operators and suppliers, government bodies, regional councils, and so on.

Examples of online resources on wellbeing subjects include:

- Head to Health—a division of the Department of Health (https://www.headtohealth.gov.au)
- Australian Institute of Health and Welfare (https://www.aihw.gov.au)
- The Employee Assistance Professional Association of Australasia (EAPAA) (https://eapaa.org.au/site/)—the peak Australasian body representing provider and user members that supply employee assistance programs in the workplace. In cooperation with employees and

management, the primary objective of EAPAA members is to provide the most effective employee assistance services to individuals and their families suffering from personal or work-related problems that negatively affect their work and wellbeing.

The internet also provides information on wellness program providers who can work with an organisation to improve employee wellbeing. Some of these providers are:

- Ford Health (https://fordhealth.com.au)
- Healthworks (https://www.healthworks.com.au)
- Corporate Wellness Australia (https://corporatewellness.com.au)
- EapAssist (https://eapassist.com.au/about-eapassist).

Other external resources

Other external sources of information and assistance include government payment options and welfare services.

- *Government payments*, such as income support payments, family assistance payments and supplementary payments, aim to support people who cannot fully support themselves. They do so by providing sustainable social security payments and assistance. Payments can be available short or long term, or for a transitional period, and the eligibility requirements and amounts received vary. Payments are available to eligible people at different stages of life with differing needs.
- *Welfare services* are provided to people and families of widely differing ages and social and economic circumstances. Services aim to encourage participation and independence and can help enhance a person's wellbeing. As well as helping people and families directly, welfare services help indirectly by, for example, developing community networks and infrastructure.

Services respond to need across a person's life. The need and demand for welfare services are mediated by informal supports and the availability of other services at community or individual levels. Examples of welfare services that aid in wellbeing can include:

- employment services—to help people secure and maintain stable employment
- disability services—to help people with disability and their carers participate in society
- aged care services—to help elderly people with their living arrangements
- child protection services—to assist vulnerable children
- youth justice services—to support young people to rehabilitate and reintegrate into the community
- family support services—to support families with domestic and sexual violence circumstances
- homelessness services—to provide people who are homeless or at risk of homelessness with support and accommodation
- social housing—to provide people with low incomes and housing need with affordable and secure housing.

Internal resources

Internal resources offered in the workplace might include:

- *Support staff such as HR personnel.* These staff can be approached to help with any workplace concerns you have. They can:
  - provide learning and development programs that can assist you in your job
  - sort out any issues that affect your wellbeing in the workplace.
- *WHS wardens and officers.* These people look after, and are responsible for, the health and safety aspects of a workplace. You can approach them if you have any issues that affect your health.

- ***Employee assistance programs (EAP)*** *and* ***employee assistance schemes (EAS)***. An EAP is a work-based intervention program designed to enhance the emotional, mental and general psychological wellbeing of all employees and includes services for immediate family members. Its key purpose is to provide preventive and proactive interventions for the early detection, identification and/or resolution of both work and personal problems that may adversely affect performance and wellbeing. These problems and issues may include: relationships, health, trauma, substance abuse, gambling and other addictions, financial problems, depression, anxiety disorders, psychiatric disorders, communication problems, legal matters and coping with change.

3.4.2 Selecting appropriate wellbeing resources

When selecting a provider of a wellbeing program for your organisation, there are a number of things to consider:

- *Do they focus on health behaviours*? Health behaviours are those things that are directly responsible for elevated health risks. Employees who have elevated health risks are more likely to have a chronic disease and high health-care costs. Successful wellness programs are focused on helping employees to modify health behaviours. Therefore, if the goal of a wellness program is to reduce health-care costs and improve employee health, then the focus of the wellness program should be on helping employees to adopt and maintain new, healthy behaviours. Healthy behaviours are the key to most wellness outcomes.
- *Do they provide valid, independent references*? The most unbiased advice you can get is from existing users of the wellness program provider you are considering. Ask existing users what they like and don't like about their provider. These person-to-person reviews are more valuable than online reviews, blog posts or even company testimonials.
- *Do they use benefits-based incentives*? Employee health behaviours probably won't improve if the employees don't actually participate in the wellness program. This is why incentives can be important. Leadership support, healthy cultures, effective wellness committees, and even small gift cards or awards may be helpful incentives.
- *Do they interact with employees*? Every wellness provider should have a website. Effective work health promotion programs have real people that you can talk to—people who plan, administer and evaluate a wellness program, and who will help to organise and participate in meetings with the wellness committee.
- *Do they support culture change*? Adopting healthy behaviours is relatively easy. The challenge is to maintain these behaviours into the future. Workplaces that create health-promoting environments and a culture that supports healthy living can experience a variety of positive outcomes.
- *Do they customise programming to each workplace*? Every workplace is different. Each one has unique characteristics and challenges that make it hard to use a wellness program that takes a one-size-fits-all approach. Ask the wellness provider if they are willing to:
  - build special campaigns or challenges specific to your workplace
  - have their coders and engineers design and implement changes to the program from your specifications
  - offer their wellness programming in the languages that are used at your workplace.

3.4.3 Documenting methods for accessing resources

A great deal of effort can be put into researching and implementing a workplace wellness program. In order that the program can then be followed easily by employees, the process for accessing the service should be written down in a procedure that generally outlines the steps necessary to complete a task or process. Any business process (including participation in wellbeing programs) is, essentially, a group of interrelated procedures; if these aren't recorded somewhere, breakdowns

GoodStudio/Shutterstock

can occur. Wellbeing programs, for example, have repeatable processes that are fundamental to their success, and a process document can serve as a guide for employees and managers to refer to, as necessary, to ensure they are getting the most out of the program.

The method you use for documenting access to your wellbeing resources can vary, depending on the organisation and its capabilities. Options include:

- paper-based documents that form a "user manual"
- a mobile app or website provided by your wellbeing program provider
- a company intranet that only employees of the company can access.

Whatever method is used, the document should record such things as:

- any access codes needed, including:
  - website address or location of the program if it has been downloaded to the organisation's systems
  - username
  - password
- instructions on how to:
  - navigate the program once you have accessed it
  - check on your progress through the program
  - raise issues of health and wellbeing concern
  - contact the provider of the service in case of system issues
  - contact the person within your own organisation with any issues you might have.

Knowledge check

14. There are a number of common initiatives available for dealing with wellbeing. List at least six initiatives.

15. Using your own research skills, identify and access one internal and one external source of wellbeing information. Briefly describe each and provide a bibliography of your sources.

16. List at least three external sources of wellbeing information and briefly describe each.

17. Describe the key features of an employee assistance program (EAP).

18. Describe what internal resources may be offered in the workplace.

19. When selecting appropriate wellbeing resources, there are a number of things to consider. List five considerations and give a brief explanation of each.

20. Describe methods that an organisation can use to access and store wellbeing resources they have chosen to use.

Summary

Because work plays such a significant role in our lives, it is important to recognise its impact on our mental health and wellbeing. If a workplace isn't a "happy place", a large part of life is spent desperately waiting for 5 pm—and Fridays—to roll around. This is a scenario that is likely to make a person feel trapped and miserable way beyond Monday morning.

On the other hand, when employees enjoy a happy, healthy work environment, they are more productive and more likely to generate exciting innovations in the way their organisation conducts its business. It can be the difference between an organisation that is simply functioning and one that is capable of making huge leaps. In the end, it comes down to the people who are working within it.

Employees aren't just paid workers—they are also people in our communities. They are our siblings, our parents, our neighbours. If we can make organisations healthy, then we can help make our communities healthy. And that leads to a healthy environment where *everyone* can flourish.

CHAPTER 4

Apply critical thinking skills in a team environment

Learning outcomes

4.1 Prepare to address workplace problems

4.2 Evaluate solutions for workplace problems

4.3 Finalise and review solution development

No matter what industry you are in, methods of "doing business" are common across most of them. There are certain skills and knowledge elements that are useful and, indeed, necessary in order to be successful.

One of these skills is the ability to think clearly and with a critical mind. Much time and effort can be wasted by jumping enthusiastically into an idea, or by exercising a strategy without thinking through the ramifications or exploring all the options available to you. There are always choices in every situation, and the choices you make can lead to success or (if they aren't based on solid foundations) to problems or even failure.

Critical thinking, then, is the ability to stop and think before acting. It involves questioning, analysing and evaluating information to help you make decisions.

4.1 Preparing to address workplace problems

There is no such thing as a workplace that is problem free. There will always be issues, whether they are related to staff, administration, or the organisation's services or products. How serious these problems are, or become, depends on *what* action is taken about them and *when* that action is taken.

Problems left unaddressed can fester and cause significant damage to an organisation and its relationships with its staff and customers. They must therefore be addressed effectively, and as soon as they are noticed.

4.1.1 Identifying and selecting workplace problems to be addressed

There are a range of issues to be considered when dealing with problems that you feel need to be resolved. You may, for example, need to consider if the issue affects others in the organisation, or just yourself. If it affects only you, you should be able to find a solution quickly and without impacting on the organisation too much, if at all.

You may also need to consider if the problem is a **systemic** one or is localised within a small area of the company. If it is a systemic problem, then it is a larger issue that needs to be investigated and resolved at management levels. If it is a localised problem, then it may, again, be within the scope of your role and your team to find a solution within your department.

Then, too, when identifying problems that need to be addressed you should view them in terms of priority: Which problem is the most important and will have the biggest negative impact on your team or organisation? You might also look at problems in terms of urgency. A big problem may not always be urgent, just as an urgent problem may not always be big. The Eisenhower matrix is useful in properly identifying the level of urgency and importance of a task.

- *Urgent tasks* demand immediate attention and have clear consequences if they are not satisfied or completed on time.
- *Important tasks* contribute to longer-term objectives and goals that sometimes require planning in order to complete.

The matrix is divided into four quadrants (Figure 4.1). Assess the urgency and importance of individual activities, and sort them into the appropriate quadrants. Each quadrant has a specific call to action: *do*, *schedule*, *delegate* or *eliminate*. Each quadrant also has its own priority level: quadrant 1 tasks should be done first, while quadrant 4 tasks should be done last or eliminated.

Figure 4.1 The Eisenhower matrix

	Urgent	Not urgent
Important	**Quadrant 1: Do first** These tasks are both urgent and important, demanding immediate attention and action. Quadrant 1 activities are the highest priority group, with clear deadlines and consequences for not meeting the deadline.	**Quadrant 2: Schedule it** These tasks are important but not urgent. They may or may not have defined deadlines but are still critical for long-term goals. Quadrant 2 activities should have the second-highest priority after Quadrant 1 activities.
Not important	**Quadrant 3: Delegate if possible** These tasks are urgent but not important. Although there is a level of time sensitivity, the tasks don't necessarily contribute significantly to long-term goals. This is where the ability to distinguish between urgency and importance comes into play.	**Quadrant 4: Eliminate or do last** These tasks are neither urgent nor important. Tasks in this quadrant are not really necessary and don't contribute to long-term goals or interests. It is recommended to either do these activities last or eliminate them altogether.

Example

An organisation's website is dated and unable to handle new methods of online sales. This is potentially a big problem for the organisation; however, introducing a new system can be complex and costly and involve long time frames. On the other hand, the organisation is missing out on online sales that would help to pay for system improvements.

When the team meets to discuss the problem, Amar, the sales manager, suggests that the task "upgrading the website" should be placed in Quadrant 1. He feels it is urgent and important, as the business is missing out on sales as customers move increasingly online. The finance manager, Kamala, feels it should be in Quadrant 2—while it is certainly important, it isn't a matter of great urgency and is a project that needs to be properly planned. She also felt it would be very costly and hadn't been budgeted for.

4.1.2 Identifying organisational and legislative frameworks

Before looking at how to address problems, however, you may need to consider if there are any organisational policies or procedures, or legal aspects that need to be taken into account when developing solutions. For example, when working in an office environment you will need to ensure that all work health and safety (WHS) regulations are observed. This legislation covers matters such as ventilation and temperature in the office, access to toilet and eating facilities, and emergency exit plans.

If changes are made to staffing levels or conditions, you will need to be aware of **equal employment opportunity** and **fair work legislation** to ensure you are not discriminating against anyone. (This also applies to diversity regulations.) These and other industry-related legislation and codes of practice, as well as organisational standards, should be considered when addressing issues and developing solutions to avoid creating further problems.

4.1.3 Developing questions to identify key issues and challenges

Making changes to address workplace problems can often be a complex matter, sometimes impacting on several layers of an organisation's operations. It can also be time consuming and expensive, so changes shouldn't be made without first asking certain important and relevant questions—and being sure that you have all the answers necessary to make informed decisions.

Questions that might need to be asked and reflected upon include:

- What is the exact nature of the problem?
- Why has it become a problem?
- What impact does this problem have on:
  - staff
  - customers
  - products and services
  - efficiency
  - general organisational wellbeing?
- Can we fix the problem?
- How can we fix it?
- Where do we get help if we can't fix it internally?
- Do we need to get approval?
- Where do we get that approval?
- Are there any legal or ethical ramifications?
- What resources will we need?

- What are the cost factors? For example:
  - financial
  - resources
  - time frames to implement any changes
  - customer impact
  - staff impact
  - organisational reputation.

Try this now

1. Think of an area of your personal life, a workplace situation, or a task that you do regularly that could be improved upon. Apply these questions to that issue.

Consulting key stakeholders to gather information

Finding answers to these and other questions may mean discussing the issue with other people and getting their perspective on it. By gaining a variety of viewpoints, you can get a deeper understanding of the problem from different angles.

GoodStudio/Shutterstock

People in other areas of the organisation will have differing ideas on why something is—or isn't—a problem, as the issue may impact on them in specific ways unique to their job roles. As you saw in the previous Example, Amar and Kamala placed the problem of needing a website upgrade in two different quadrants of the Eisenhower matrix because they were thinking of how the issue applied to their specific roles.

In addition to consulting with others on your team, you may need to consult with people from outside of your team, such as other employees or even external experts, depending on the nature of the issue. They may have a "big picture" perspective that can provide insights into why something will or won't work. In summary, **key stakeholders** might include:

- colleagues from your own department or organisation
- supervisors or managers who might need to be made aware of issues and may need to approve any proposed solutions
- specialists in fields such as financial or legal issues
- government authorities who can provide information about legislation and compliance issues
- industry associations or governing bodies that can provide insights into your specific industry and offer advice on industry-related issues, technology and many other things.

During the consultation process, all of your key questions should be asked and answered accurately so that any solution you come up with is viable and based on known facts. You may also ask further questions of subject experts that had, perhaps, not occurred to any of the team previously. For example: "What might be the legal ramifications of making specific changes to company policies?" and "What can be done to legally mitigate or eliminate the issues surrounding these ramifications?" or "What new policies or procedures would we be obliged to put in place to ensure legal compliance?"

All of the information you gather can provide a solid foundation upon which to hold a stakeholder consultation and ensure that you have a sound understanding of the problem so that options and solutions can be assessed for effectiveness.

Knowledge check

1. When identifying and selecting a workplace problem to resolve, there are a number of issues to consider. Explain what they are.
2. Identifying workplace problems may involve addressing organisational and legislative issues. Give at least one example of how procedural or legal issues might affect problem resolution.
3. It is useful to develop a set of questions to identify any key issues or challenges you might face in resolving workplace problems. List at least six questions that might be relevant to ask.
4. Explain why it is important to consult with other stakeholders.
5. List at least four stakeholders who might need to be consulted in problem resolution.

4.2 Evaluating solutions for workplace problems

As will almost always be the case when consulting with others on workplace issues, there will be differing ideas and opinions on how to solve a problem. Some people will agree with the suggestions made, while others won't. For an issue to be resolved successfully, it is essential that the team stays focused on the problem at hand. To do this effectively, a thoughtful process of working through the key questions should be followed. For example, you could begin the consultation process by discussing the individual solutions generated with team members. This includes explaining and being able to apply critical thinking methods.

4.2.1 Identifying a range of critical thinking techniques to generate solutions

Critical thinking is the ability to stop and think before acting. It involves questioning, analysing and evaluating information to help you make decisions. Critical thinking involves the following steps (as summarised in Figure 4.2):

- *Step 1: Identify the problem.* What is the issue? Why do we need to resolve it?
- *Step 2: Understand the problem.* Gather information—research, data, feedback from colleagues—to help you better understand the problem.
- *Step 3: Analyse and evaluate the information gathered.* Check that it is reliable and determine whether you have enough information to help find a solution.
- *Step 4: Identify possible solutions.* In this step, you begin to develop possible solutions and discard irrelevant ones. Think through the effects your solution might have on other areas of the business.
- *Step 5: Communicate the solution.* Share your findings with your colleagues and anyone who will be affected by the changes being made.

Figure 4.2 Common steps in critical thinking

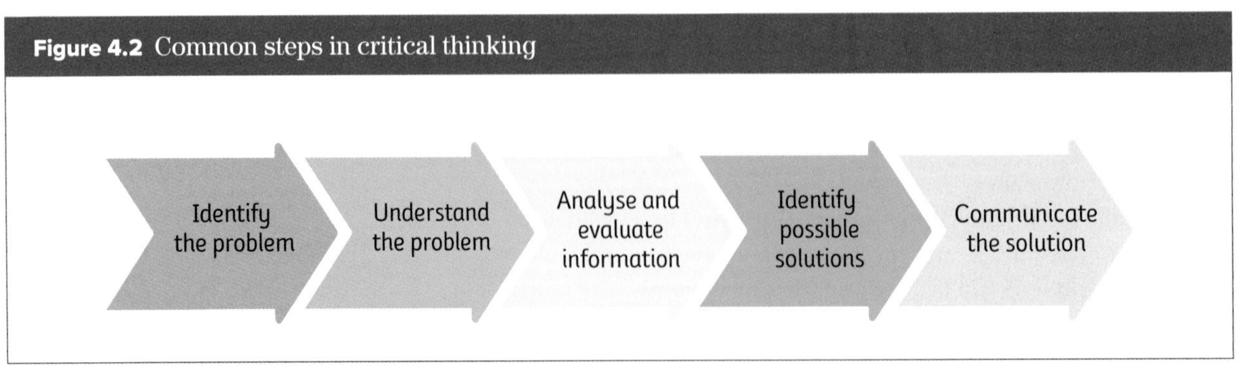

These steps, in themselves, will give a general overview of the issue at hand and possible ways in which it may be solved. Critical thinking, however, looks for more than a "quick fix" and should be focused on continuous improvement of processes and the future-proofing of the organisation. A deeper application of critical thinking might therefore involve:

- understanding the links between ideas
- determining the importance and relevance of arguments and ideas
- recognising, building and appraising arguments
- identifying inconsistencies and errors in reasoning
- approaching problems in a consistent and systematic way
- reflecting on the justification of your own assumptions, beliefs and values.

Skills of a critical thinker

The ability to think critically is an important skill to have at every career level, from an entry-level position to senior management, and across all industries. Those with such skills can work both independently and with groups to solve problems and generate ideas that will be of benefit not only to their organisation but also to their own career prospects. The skills needed are varied but generally include the ability to observe, analyse, infer, communicate and problem solve.

- *Observation skills*. The first thing a critical thinker does is *observe* what is going on around them. Where are problems occurring, and where are they likely to occur? A critical thinker often understands the reason why a work process has become a problem and may even be able, through observation, to predict where an issue might arise.
- *Analytical skills*. Having observed where issues are occurring (or where they might occur), a critical thinker can analyse all the known facts about the issue, as well as consider not only their workplace but the general business environment in order to form a full understanding of the problem.
- *Inference skills*. With facts, figures and a thorough knowledge of the issue at hand, a critical thinker should be able to infer a meaning from all of this information and draw logical conclusions that can be used to eventually solve the problem.
- *Communication skills*. Good communication skills are essential, whatever industry you are in. Having drawn conclusions from your observation, analysis and inferences, you will need to explain your thinking to other stakeholders and gain their cooperation and assistance in completing the work that needs to be done.
- *Problem-solving skills*. All of these skills inevitably lead to the need to actually solve the problem. A critical thinker will look for a range of options to deal with the issue(s) at hand and determine which of these will be the best workable solution.

Think about

1. Reflect on your own critical thinking skills. Which of these skills do you have? What could you do to improve, or gain, these skills?

4.2.2 Developing solutions using knowledge and experience of team members

As mentioned earlier, different people will have different ideas on how to solve a problem. To ensure the best possible outcome in what could potentially become a heated exchange of views, it is important for maintaining team morale and team spirit to ensure that everyone involved in the consultation process has the opportunity to have their ideas heard.

Not everyone in the consultation group may be working in the same department or area of the organisation as you. They may not even work for your organisation at all. The advantage of this is that they will bring a wealth of knowledge and expertise to the team that will provide an in-depth and well-rounded understanding of the matter under discussion.

Developing, agreeing on and applying criteria to assess potential solutions to issues

Solutions should *solve* a problem and not cause a whole new one or make the current situation worse than it already is. To ensure the team's efforts are effective and efficient, you might need to develop a set of criteria or conditions that an acceptable solution must meet. For example, questions the team can ask in considering a specific solution might include:

- Will this proposed solution solve the problem?
- Is it realistic?
- Is it fair and ethical?
- Is it economical?
- Will it provide more benefits than disadvantages?
- Are the benefits significant?
- Will it be harmful in any way?
- Is it in line with the organisation's mission statement and/or standards?

Brainstorming for ideas

Having determined some criteria, the team can begin to look at ideas for solving the problem, keeping these criteria in mind. The focus at this point, however, is on generating ideas, not on evaluating them. The following tips might help during brainstorming of ideas:

- Ideas are to be expressed freely, without evaluation from others.
- All ideas, however wild, are accepted by the team. (Rejection of ideas would create negativity and slow the process of producing ideas.)

Team members should try to think of as many ideas for solving the problem as possible. At this stage, it is about quantity over quality. If criteria questions can be answered positively for a proposed idea, then this idea could be short-listed for later evaluation and consideration. If the answers to any or all of those questions are negative, then the idea can be discarded.

Professional boundaries

In working together in a team, certain professional boundaries also need to be considered. For example, when sharing ideas in the group, ensure that:

- diversity issues are observed and no one is discriminated against
- no one is harassed or bullied
- any joking doesn't cross professional boundaries
- formalities are observed between staff at different levels
- organisational codes of conduct and ethics are observed
- the organisation's reputation is kept in mind at all times
- the process is conducted in a professional manner so that no one is left out or made to feel uncomfortable.

4.2.3 Critically evaluating and selecting solutions

Once satisfied that *all* questions have been answered and the criteria for choosing potential solutions have been met, the team can begin to evaluate and select the best options. Before evaluating those solutions, however, you first need to establish further criteria for judging those solutions. Questions you could ask at this stage to determine these criteria might include:

- Does it have acceptable **tradeoffs**? A proposed solution's potential negative side-effects must also be considered:
  - What are the downsides to this solution?
  - Can we live with them?
- Does the solution work within stated constraints?
  - Can it be achieved within a given time frame?
  - Does it meet specifications?
  - Is it within the cost budget?
  - Do we have the necessary resources on hand?
- Will the solution be acceptable by all users? Acceptance is a perceptual, emotional and psychological issue, as well as an intellectual one. If a change being made is significant, then those people who will be affected by it must be "on board" to ensure a successful transition between the old and new ways of doing things.
- Is the solution economical?
  - Can we afford it?
  - Is it worth the effort and/or money?
- Is the solution practical?
  - Is it logical, useful, systematic, understandable and not overly difficult or complex?
  - Is it a simple and direct way of achieving the desired outcome?
- Is the solution reliable and dependable? (Dependability is at the core of satisfaction.) Will it continue to work over time with a high degree of reliability, consistency and effectiveness?

Depending on the nature of the problem, and the industry you are in, there may be a range of other industry-specific questions that you need to ask to determine the suitability and effectiveness of your proposal.

In addition to the criteria-based method outlined, there are other methods of determining the best solution. They include:

- *Group consensus*—all members come to an agreement.
- *Majority vote*—a decision is based on the majority's preference.
- *Averaging individual opinion*—the opinions of all members are considered, with the most averagely agreed-upon solution selected.
- *Expert decision*—an expert opinion is sought on the matter.
- *Decision by authority*—the group leader, committee or board of directors decides.

Knowledge check

6. List at least eight steps used in critical thinking to generate solutions.
7. Describe the skills of a critical thinker.
8. Explain the advantages of a team approach in developing ideas for problem resolution.
9. List at least six questions a team might develop and agree upon to assess potential solutions to problems.
10. One method of reviewing an organisational process is to map that process. Describe what steps this might include.
11. One method of using critical thinking skills in problem resolution is brainstorming. List two tips that can help in generating ideas during a brainstorming session.
12. List at least six questions you could ask when critically evaluating solutions that have been generated by the team.

4.3 Finalising and reviewing solution development

As we have learnt, the solution to a problem can be complex, time consuming and costly. It is essential, therefore, to review whatever solution was decided upon before presenting it to all the relevant stakeholders for their final approval and to discuss any final issues.

Although the attitude of "Don't bring me problems, bring me solutions" is somewhat discounted today, due to the complexity of living in the modern world, many managers do still think this way. Therefore, when developing a solution to an organisational problem, it is important to ensure your final solution has been well thought through, with every aspect carefully researched, considered and mapped out.

4.3.1 Presenting a solution to relevant stakeholders

At some point, you might be asked to present the solution to a range of stakeholders different from those involved in developing the proposed solution. If this is the case, you should explain not only the solution you are putting forward but also the process you followed in arriving at it, so that those stakeholders who will be making the final decisions and giving approvals have a proper understanding of the proposal and its background. Tell them:

GoodStudio/Shutterstock

- how you identified the issue in the first place and how it impacted on the organisation
- who was involved in the resolution process
- the criteria used to find and evaluate the solution
- the critical thinking process that led to the final proposal.

Responding to challenges and questions from stakeholders

Depending on the complexity and cost of the solution being proposed, you may need to defend your ideas against objections and questions. You can prepare for this by having a detailed understanding of the solution you are presenting and anticipating any likely challenges and questions so that you can respond to them appropriately. Challenges you are likely to face, and should therefore be ready to answer questions about, might involve:

- exactly how the solution fixes the problem
- any negotiations you entered into and what (if any) concessions you had to make
- what costs are involved in terms of:
  - money to be spent
  - resources needed
  - time frames, and so on.

By being fully prepared, you can explain the **features** and **benefits** of your proposed idea and how it will fit into the organisation's culture and standards.

The presentation itself might take a number of formats, including:

- a personal, face-to-face presentation during a meeting with stakeholders
- an online presentation using an online meeting forum
- a paper-based presentation, with a written report or proposal
- a combination of any of these.

Whatever method is chosen, make sure you have all the necessary reports, equipment and resources needed to present the information accurately and professionally. How well prepared you are can influence whether your proposal is accepted.

4.3.2 Evaluating critical thinking processes with team members

Evaluating organisational processes and gaining feedback is one of the most important aspects of doing business, whether it relates to service or product issues, administrative tasks, policies and procedures, production methods, or any number of other business-related operations. It is vital for the continued success of the organisation that the consultation group uses the best possible resources and processes available, whether tangible or intangible.

In the **multimedia** world of today, ways of doing business change quickly and the organisation must be prepared to adapt. With this in mind, it is useful to get feedback from the consultation group on the way in which the current, or previous, issues were resolved, with an eye to improving the necessary processes.

Despite all efforts that can be made to streamline business operations, there may still be a great many activities that involve more than one department or team. This can mean connections, communications and handoffs between different sets of people. These handoffs create the risk of gaps, inefficiencies or duplications in the process, which can have a negative effect on performance or increase costs. Even well-designed processes and interactions run the risk of inefficiency creeping in. This is a fact of human nature and, as such, is something that needs to be managed.

Any workplace process can be improved upon. Depending on the size of the organisation and the complexity of a given process, a review might be a simple matter of discussing the latest project, and the manner in which it was handled, during a short meeting with relevant stakeholders. Larger, more complicated, processes might need a more formal review and structure and might include the steps discussed next.

Mapping the process

One of the first steps in reviewing and documenting an organisational process is to map that process as it currently exists. For example:

- Assemble a team to work on the project.
- Define the objectives of the project, stating *exactly* what it is you want to achieve.
- Define the scope of the project, what it should and shouldn't include, what constraints you will have to work within (budget, resources, time, etc.).
- Construct an initial plan or develop a range of ideas to be evaluated.

The mapping process may be fairly simple (Figure 4.3), or it could be a cross-functional one that takes into account various departments within the organisation and how they interact with each other on separate or joint tasks (Figure 4.4).

Analysing the process

With a process clearly mapped, the team can move on to discussing the pros and cons of each step.

1. *Assemble a team to work on the project.*
    - How did we go about choosing team members?
    - Did we choose the most effective people for the team?
    - Did we allocate individual tasks of the project effectively and make best use of team members' talents and experience?
    - Were there any issues in working together?
        - What were they?
        - What can we do to avoid personality issues within a team in future?
    - Should a formal criterion be used to choose team members?
        - What would that criterion need to be?
    - Which department(s) contributed the most/least to the project?
2. *Define the project objectives.*
    - Did we receive accurate instructions and objectives from management?
    - Did we define the objectives of the project accurately and in detail?

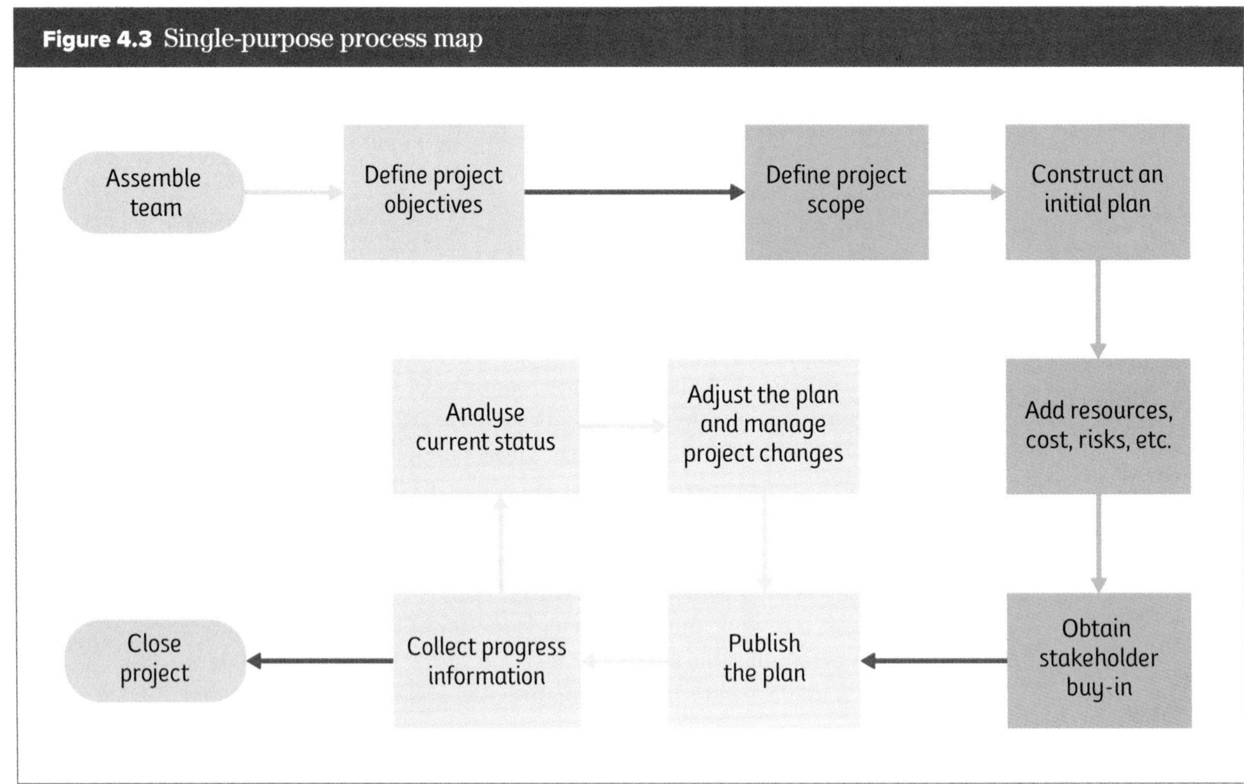

Figure 4.3 Single-purpose process map

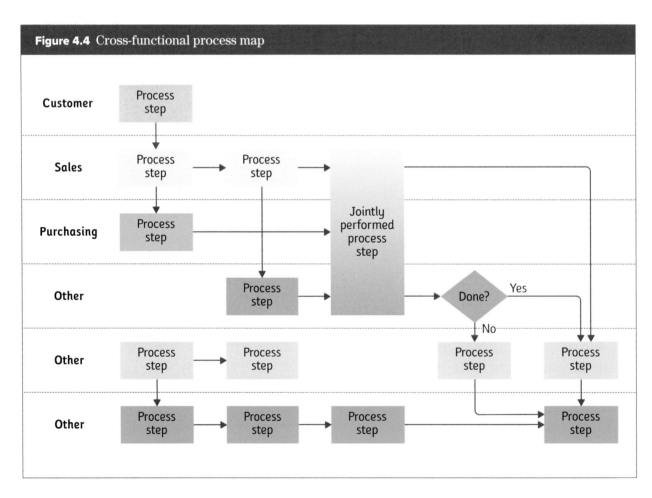

Figure 4.4 Cross-functional process map

Customer
Process step
Sales
Process step
Process step
Purchasing
Process step
Jointly performed process step
Other
Process step
Done?
Yes
No
Other
Process step
Process step
Process step
Process step
Other
Process step
Process step
Process step
Process step

- What did we miss?
- Should there be formal criteria for defining objectives?
- Was the objective achieved at the end of the project?
  - If not, why not? ... and so on.

Redesigning, implementing and communicating the new process

By using review questions such as these, you can begin to build a picture of what the team did well, and what areas didn't quite work. As each deficiency in the current process becomes clear, team members take note and put forward ideas and suggestions for improvement. These ideas and suggestions can then be evaluated by the review team, making sure that you aren't replacing one procedure for another equally ineffective one. A new process can then be designed with any new steps clearly outlined. Upon approval from relevant managers, this new process can then be implemented and communicated to all necessary staff members. Communication might take place:

- in a training session
- during a staff meeting
- by way of written instructions.

Written procedures are an excellent way of ensuring a consistent approach to completing work tasks. Consider this statement: "In the absence of any clearly stated instructions, whatever the worker does is right". The important point here is: "In the absence of clearly stated instructions". If staff aren't told what is expected of them, then work processes and tasks could be completed incorrectly, leading to a decrease in productivity and job satisfaction.

Documenting the review process

It should be noted that there are a great many industries that are subject to both internal and external audits. These might be conducted by the company's accountants or compliance officers, or by government officials (depending on the exact nature of the business). Such audits are carried out to ensure the organisation is meeting its legal and ethical obligations.

It is important, therefore, to document the entire review process so that you can show:

- your organisation is continually improving
- the reasons why a procedure or policy was changed
- how you went about reviewing the change
- what those changes were, and how you implemented and communicated them.

Identifying critical thinking learnings to apply to individual and team situations

The result of any feedback received, and the review process itself, can be used to improve the way in which the organisation or the team solves problems or changes its policies or procedures. But it can also lead to a way in which *individuals* think about workplace issues.

Learning from critical thinking processes helps both individual staff members and the organisation as a whole to:

- understand the links between ideas
- determine the importance and relevance of arguments and ideas
- recognise, build and appraise arguments
- identify inconsistencies and errors in reasoning
- approach problems in a consistent and systematic way
- reflect on the justification of your own assumptions, beliefs and values.

Knowledge check

13. When presenting a solution to relevant stakeholders, there are a number of things they should be told. What are they?
14. Describe what challenges you might face when presenting a solution to stakeholders. How might you prepare for them?
15. Describe the steps involved in evaluating the critical thinking process with your team members.
16. Learning from critical thinking processes helps both individual staff members and the organisation as a whole. Explain why.
17. Explain why it is important to document the resolution process.
18. When working in teams, it is essential that professional boundaries are observed. Explain what this means.
19. Describe the advantage of having different perspectives when consulting with others.

Summary

Critical thinking means being objective. It means being able to identify workplace issues and to analyse these problems without allowing emotions or assumptions to influence how you or the team respond. By using critical thinking skills, you analyse a problem based only on its context and known facts. Critical thinking also means gaining a deeper understanding of the links between ideas and of how a workplace actually works, with each area and task flowing together to create a cohesive whole. This, in turn, leads to better, long-lasting and forward-thinking solutions to workplace processes.

CHAPTER 5

Assist with maintaining workplace safety

Learning outcomes

5.1 Assist with incorporating WHS policies and procedures into work team processes

5.2 Contribute to consultative arrangements for managing WHS

5.3 Contribute to organisational procedures for providing WHS training

5.4 Participate in identifying hazards, and assessing and controlling risks for the work area

One of the most important aspects of any business is to ensure the health, safety and security of everyone who enters, or works on, its premises. Businesses have not just a duty of care but a *legal obligation* to ensure that no harm is done to anyone in the workplace. The state and federal governments have very strict regulations regarding work health and safety (WHS) and impose stiff penalties for any breaches.

It may be part of your role to make those you work with aware of their obligations under WHS regulations and to help implement WHS policies and procedures. In order to undertake such tasks confidently, you will need to be aware of the primary components of relevant state or territory WHS legislation, and of actions the employer must take to comply with its legal and organisational obligations to provide a safe workplace. For example, employers (or managers) are required to have in place acceptable consultation mechanisms such as WHS representatives and committees, which must fulfil specific roles and responsibilities.

The primary components of legislation will also include requirements for hazard identification, risk assessment, risk control and record keeping. Employers are obliged to provide adequate information and training so that staff members understand their roles and responsibilities, in WHS terms, and can do their work to the required standards. All staff must understand the ramifications of failure to observe WHS legislation and organisational policies and procedures.

We will look at all of these aspects as we move through this chapter.

5.1 Assisting to incorporate WHS policies and procedures into work team processes

WHS policies and procedures are put in place to ensure the safety of everyone on the business premises—whether staff, customers, suppliers or contractors. Policies and procedures might relate to:

- evacuating staff and customers in case of emergencies
- ensuring the secure management of cash, documents, equipment, keys or people
- ensuring the correct handling of chemicals and hazardous substances
- following any hygiene procedures required by your organisation and/or its industry
- identifying and reporting any workplace hazards
- reporting on any incidents or accidents in the workplace
- undertaking and reporting on risk assessment.

It follows, then, that everyone working in the business has roles and responsibilities that ensure the workplace is safe and secure, as set out in Table 5.1.

Table 5.1 Employer and employee responsibilities in the workplace

Employer responsibilities	Employee responsibilities
■ Establishing detailed policies and procedures, in line with government legislation, for ensuring the health, safety and security of workers. ■ Ensuring the workplace is safe by minimising and/or controlling hazards. ■ Ensuring that chemical storage facilities are adequate. ■ Maintaining machinery and equipment at all times, and doing regular checks to ensure safety standards are met. ■ Providing information, instruction, training and supervision. ■ Providing personal protective equipment (PPE). ■ Providing adequate welfare facilities such as washrooms, lockers and dining areas. ■ Maintaining information and records relating to the health and safety of employees. ■ Nominating a person with the appropriate level of seniority to act as the employer's representative in WHS matters. ■ Consulting with staff in developing, reviewing and improving WHS policies and procedures. ■ Providing workers' rehabilitation and compensation insurance to cover an injured worker's loss of income, associated medical costs and, possibly, retraining.	■ Following safety instructions. Failure to do so could result in injury to the employee and/or others and denial of any claim for workers compensation. ■ Using equipment carefully and according to the manufacturer's instructions. Careless use of machinery and work equipment can result in serious injury. ■ Reporting any hazards and injuries. Good work health and safety depends on all staff ensuring that everything is operating correctly. If management or the relevant staff aren't made aware of any hazards or potential hazards, they can't fix them. ■ Not interfering with or misusing WHS items provided, such as safety signs or first aid equipment. ■ Attending all relevant training sessions. Employees who are fully informed about new procedures and equipment are less likely to make a serious mistake that could injure them or others. ■ Not deliberately putting the health and safety of others at risk through recklessness and/or misuse of equipment. ■ Working in accordance with any relevant government regulations. ■ Using PPE as required and/or instructed by supervisors.

5.1.1 Identifying the characteristics and composition of the work team

Incorporating WHS processes into daily work can be a complex matter requiring information on policies and procedures to be distributed to relevant personnel and, possibly, training to be provided. Depending on the size of the organisation, this can be a job too big for one person, so tasks might need to be allocated to individual members of the work team. But who exactly is the work team, and why is it important to understand their **characteristics**?

Regardless of whether the team you are bringing together is for short, intense projects or for longer, ongoing work, you need to ensure it includes people you can trust and rely on, who will perform well together, who represent a diverse range of outlooks, and who have the experience and characteristics to get the work done efficiently and effectively.

Creating a well-rounded team begins with understanding who each team member is, what skills and experience they bring to the table, their commitment and approach to the work, and the way in which they communicate. Characteristics of a good team include:

- *A common goal.* Effective teams have a common goal that is known to all team members, is motivating and has a clear path to achievement.

- *Open communication.* The foundation of effective teamwork is good communication. Without clear communication, goals can't be achieved. Good communication involves sharing knowledge and skills, and creating an environment where team members can freely express their thoughts and opinions.

GoodStudio/Shutterstock

- *Practical problem solving.* Many problems may be encountered on the way to achieving a goal. An effective team will quickly identify and solve these problems in a practical manner.
- *Bonding.* A happy team is an effective team. Team members must trust one another to perform and have each other's back when support is needed.

An effective team, therefore, is one whose members have a mix of talent and experience and work together efficiently to achieve the team's desired outcome.

Think about

1. Identify who, within your workplace, is part of the WHS team. What are their specific roles? What WHS issues in your work area might they need to be made aware of?

5.1.2 Identifying the health and safety requirements of a work team

In order for the team to do their work in a safe way, they first need to understand what the health and safety requirements of their workplace actually are. Some requirements will be the same across all types of business, and some will be specific to an industry or organisation. Staff who work at a tourist attraction such as a theme park, for example, will need access both to general WHS information and to information relevant to specific organisations or sectors of the tourism industry. As such, the WHS requirements of a theme park will be very different from those of a firm of lawyers or an accountancy business. A theme park may involve adventure rides, wild animals and large crowds, all of which need to be properly controlled to reduce the risk of harm occurring should anything go wrong. This wouldn't be the case in an office or retail outlet, which have their own types of potential hazards.

5.1.3 Explaining organisational WHS policies, procedures, programs and legislative requirements

The team will need to be aware of the WHS requirements specific to the place, and even the department, where they are working. They will also need to be aware of their legal obligations under the relevant WHS legislation. It is the responsibility of every employer to ensure that their staff have the necessary information to work within the organisation's policies and procedures, as well as to comply with all legislative requirements.

General information can be contextualised to the specific organisation, in line with industry standards and practices. For example, while general policies on staff training might address emergency evacuation procedures, in a theme park (which might see 10,000 or more visitors every day) evacuation is a very different prospect than it would be in an accountancy office (with only a small number of staff). Evacuation of a theme park has a real danger of injury occurring due to the number of people who need to be moved quickly and who may be panicking. Therefore, crowd control must be at the foundation of such an organisation's evacuation procedures and staff must receive appropriate training.

Contextualisation of WHS information, policies and procedures also extends to the organisation's overall approach to WHS and any specific regulations and codes of practice.

For example, in the hospitality industry, staff would need to be trained in hygiene regulations and procedures. Workers in a manufacturing plant would need training in the safe use of machinery, and staff in a high-rise office might need training in the use of fire extinguishers and to practise fire and evacuation drills on a regular basis. Each organisation will also have in-house WHS policies and procedures relating to hazard identification, risk assessment and reporting documents, and their own specific methods for involving staff in general WHS management practices.

mentalmind/Shutterstock

Aside from specific regulations, general WHS policies and procedures that apply to most industries might include:

- manual handling techniques, to ensure staff don't injure themselves when moving heavy or awkward loads
- hygiene regulations and procedures, especially relating to the preparation and/or delivery of food and beverage products
- incident and accident procedures and reporting processes
- location of a first aid kit, and emergency procedures such as how to evacuate the premises, or how to deal with fire, robbery and theft
- general employee roles and responsibilities in WHS management and consultation practices
- written records of any WHS issues, such as documents relating to hazard identification and risk assessment, incidents, accidents or emergencies
- ethical principles and codes of practice relating to bullying and harassment.

5.1.4 Ramifications of failing to comply with legal obligations

Many of an organisation's policies and procedures will be based upon legislative requirements. Failure to comply with these could result not only in fines being levied against the organisation, but in the real risk of harm or injury occurring to a person or even, in extreme cases, in their death. All employees of an organisation are therefore legally obliged to comply with WHS Acts and regulations, as outlined in Figure 5.1.

Work Health and Safety Act 2011 (Cth)

The *Work Health and Safety Act 2011* (the WHS Act) sets out the laws about health and safety requirements affecting most workplaces, work activities and specified high-risk plants. Division 2, section 3, states:

> The main object of this Act is to provide for a balanced and nationally consistent framework to secure the health and safety of workers and workplaces by:
>
> a. protecting workers and other persons against harm to their health, safety and welfare through the elimination or minimisation of risks arising from work; and

Figure 5.1 Legislative framework

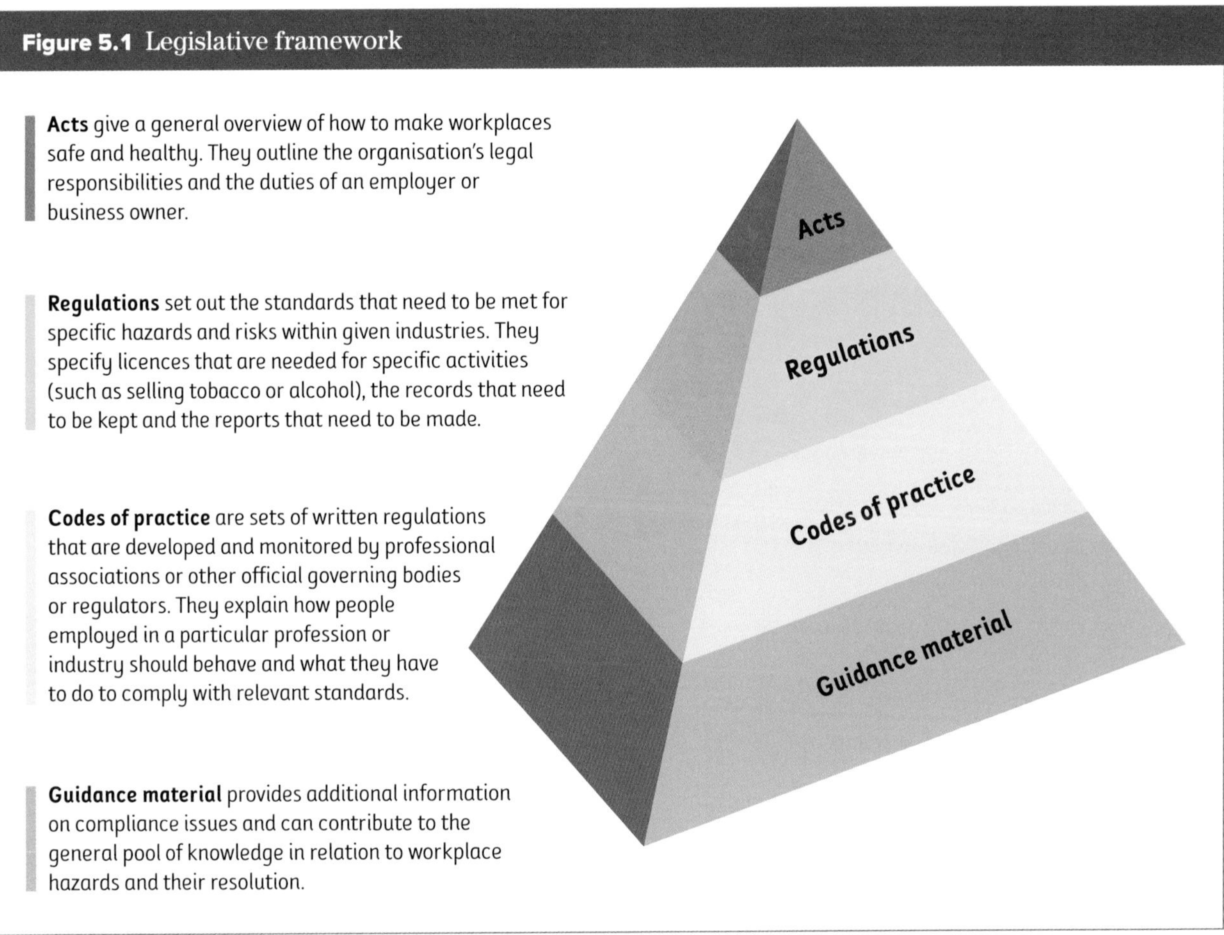

Acts give a general overview of how to make workplaces safe and healthy. They outline the organisation's legal responsibilities and the duties of an employer or business owner.
Regulations set out the standards that need to be met for specific hazards and risks within given industries. They specify licences that are needed for specific activities (such as selling tobacco or alcohol), the records that need to be kept and the reports that need to be made.
Codes of practice are sets of written regulations that are developed and monitored by professional associations or other official governing bodies or regulators. They explain how people employed in a particular profession or industry should behave and what they have to do to comply with relevant standards.
Guidance material provides additional information on compliance issues and can contribute to the general pool of knowledge in relation to workplace hazards and their resolution.
Acts
Regulations
Codes of practice
Guidance material

b. providing for fair and effective workplace representation, consultation, co-operation and issue resolution in relation to work health and safety; and
c. encouraging unions and employer organisations to take a constructive role in promoting improvements in work health and safety practices, and assisting persons conducting businesses or undertakings and workers to achieve a healthier and safer working environment; and
d. promoting the provision of advice, information, education and training in relation to work health and safety; and
e. securing compliance with this Act through effective and appropriate compliance and enforcement measures; and
f. ensuring appropriate scrutiny and review of actions taken by persons exercising powers and performing functions under this Act; and
g. providing a framework for continuous improvement and progressively higher standards of work health and safety; and
h. maintaining and strengthening the national harmonisation of laws relating to work health and safety and to facilitate a consistent national approach to work health and safety in this jurisdiction. (https://www.legislation.gov.au/Details/C2018C00293. Creative Commons Attribution 4.0 International (the CC BY 4.0 license), http://creativecommons.org/licenses/by/4.0.)

Whenever there is a new intake of staff, a change in WHS procedures or the introduction of new equipment or systems, employers must provide information and/or training as appropriate. Incoming staff normally go through an induction process that introduces them to their role and the organisation's policies and procedures. Relevant Acts and codes of practice are shown in Table 5.2.

Table 5.2 Examples of WHS Acts and codes of practice

State	Act/Regulation	URL
NSW	*Work Health and Safety Act 2011*	https://www.legislation.gov.au/Details/C2011A00137
	Work Health and Safety Regulations 2011	https://www.legislation.gov.au/Details/F2011L02664
	Codes of Practice	https://www.safeworkaustralia.gov.au/law-and-regulation/codes-practice
Qld	*Work Health and Safety Act 2011*	https://www.legislation.qld.gov.au/view/html/inforce/current/act-2011-018
	Work Health and Safety Regulations 2011	https://www.worksafe.qld.gov.au/licensing-and-registrations/licensing-index/hrw-licences?a=4659
	Codes of Practice	https://www.worksafe.qld.gov.au/laws-and-compliance/codes-of-practice
Vic	*Occupational Health and Safety Act 2004*	https://www.legislation.vic.gov.au/in-force/acts/occupational-health-and-safety-act-2004/041
	Occupational Health and Safety Regulations 2017	https://www.legislation.vic.gov.au/in-force/acts/occupational-health-and-safety-act-2004/043
	Compliance codes	https://www.worksafe.vic.gov.au/search?q=compliance
SA	*Work Health and Safety Act 2012*	https://www.legislation.sa.gov.au/lz?path=%2FC%2FA%2FWORK%20HEALTH%20AND%20SAFETY%20ACT%202012
	Work Health and Safety Regulations 2012	https://www.legislation.sa.gov.au/lz?path=%2FC%2FR%2FWORK%20HEALTH%20AND%20SAFETY%20REGULATIONS%202012
	SA Codes of Practice	https://www.safework.sa.gov.au/workplaces/codes-of-practice
WA	*Work Health and Safety Act 2020* Approved Codes of Practice	https://www.legislation.wa.gov.au/legislation/statutes.nsf/law_a147282.html https://www.commerce.wa.gov.au/worksafe/approved-codes-practice
	Work Health and Safety (General) Regulations 2022	https://www.legislation.wa.gov.au/legislation/statutes.nsf/law_s53267.html
Tas	*Work Health and Safety Act 2012*	https://www.legislation.tas.gov.au/view/whole/html/inforce/current/act-2012-001
	Work Health and Safety Regulations 2012	https://www.legislation.tas.gov.au/view/html/inforce/current/sr-2012-122
	Codes of Practice	https://www.worksafe.tas.gov.au/topics/laws-and-compliance/codes-of-practice
NT	*Work Health and Safety (National Uniform Legislation) Act 2011*	https://legislation.nt.gov.au/Legislation/WORK-HEALTH-AND-SAFETY-NATIONAL-UNIFORM-LEGISLATION-ACT-2011
	Work Health and Safety (National Uniform Legislation) Regulations 2011	https://legislation.nt.gov.au/Legislation/WORK-HEALTH-AND-SAFETY-NATIONAL-UNIFORM-LEGISLATION-REGULATIONS-2011
	Codes of Practice	https://worksafe.nt.gov.au/forms-and-resources/codes-of-practice
ACT	*Work Health and Safety Act 2011*	https://www.legislation.act.gov.au/a/2011-35/default.asp
	Work Health and Safety Regulations 2011	https://www.legislation.act.gov.au/sl/2011-36/
	Worksafe Codes of Practice	https://www.worksafe.act.gov.au/laws-and-compliance/codes-of-practice

Work-related injuries or illness impact on a workplace and the person concerned in a number of ways, including:

- personal anxiety due to loss of wages and/or lifestyle
- pain and suffering
- death or disfigurement
- decrease in productivity in the workplace due to shortage of staff
- loss of revenue directly linked to the decrease in productivity.

In accordance with the WHS Act, there are a range of actions that state or territory authorities and Safe Work Australia may enforce if WHS legislative obligations are not met. This means that all employers, employees and other parties are legally obliged to comply with WHS legislation, or risk incurring penalties for criminal breaches of the Act.

Areas of non-compliance can include:

- failure to meet legal requirements in WHS matters
- inadequate systems of information, instruction, training or supervision of staff
- poor or inadequate maintenance, or unsafe use or storage, of plant, equipment or substances
- poor consultation practices, where staff are not involved in the development or improvement of WHS practices within their workplace
- poor design of:
  - policies and procedures
  - workplace layout/set-up of machinery, so that staff and/or customers are endangered
  - lighting (e.g. inadequate illumination)
  - noise controls (e.g. inadequate noise guards or insulation against noise)
- inadequate identification or control of workplace hazards.

Think about

2. Look at your own work area. What hazards may be found there? What are the risks of harm or injury occurring? What could you do to prevent this?

5.1.5 Explaining hazard identification and risk assessment outcomes

All workplaces have hazards and risks to varying degrees. What is the difference between them?

- A hazard is any source or activity that has the potential to harm life, health, property or the environment.
- A **risk** is the likelihood that harm will occur as a result of a hazard.

In a theme park, for example, maintenance staff are exposed to considerable risks from working with toxic chemicals and climbing up very high structures for safety checks. Hospital workers are at risk of infection and disease. Working in an office environment might *seem* safe, but there are plenty of hazards there, too. Lifting heavy boxes (Figure 5.2) or sitting incorrectly at a desk can lead to back strain and injuries; computers and cords are electrical hazards; and stress, which can be difficult to identify, can cause health issues.

All relevant personnel should be made aware of the hazards and risks involved in their specific roles, and be advised how to identify them and how to work within WHS guidelines. The obligation to make others aware of these hazards and risks extends not only to the organisation's own staff but also to any contractors, or subcontractors, who may be visiting or working on the premises. They, too, will be exposed to any risks in the workplace and must therefore be given up-to-date information about any hazards they are likely to face.

Keeping a team motivated means maintaining open lines of communication, especially where health and safety are concerned. Business owners therefore have a duty of care to look into any identified hazards and to provide the team with information on the investigation's outcome. The team must be confident that their leaders will keep them safe by complying with WHS legislation. Leaders should report on:

- how hazards and risks are monitored
- the progress of investigation or evaluation of any identified hazard
- methods developed to mitigate or eliminate the identified risks.

Figure 5.2 The hazard and risk of incorrect lifting

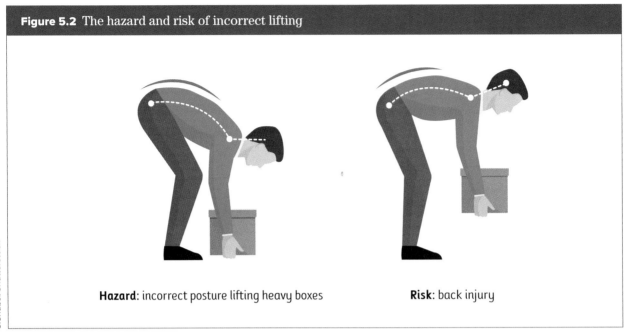

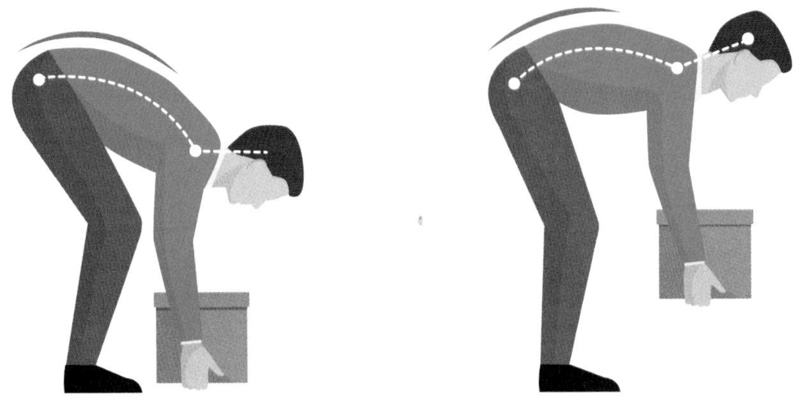

elenabsl/Shutterstock

It is essential for a safe and harmonious workplace that you understand your obligations under the WHS Act and the consequences of non-compliance. Following workplace policies and procedures will ensure that you, your colleagues and your customers can work in a safe environment.

We will look at hazards and risks in more detail later in the chapter.

Knowledge check

1. Explain how the identification of WHS requirements might differ among organisations and/or industries. Why is it important to recognise these differences?
2. When explaining WHS policies and procedures to other team members, there are a range of issues that might be classed as "general WHS policies". List at least six of these.
3. Give a brief explanation of the following organisational policies:
   - ethical principles
   - code of practice
   - anti-bullying/harassment policy.
4. Describe the ramifications of failure to comply with legal obligations.
5. List the main objectives of the *Work Health and Safety Act 2011*.
6. List at least four ways in which non-compliance with legal obligations can occur.
7. Explain why it is important to inform others of hazard identification and risk assessment.
8. Business owners/managers have a legal obligation to consult with others about management of WHS. Describe what is meant by "consultation" in this context, and explain when consultation is required.

5.2 Contributing to consultative arrangements for managing WHS

The process of managing WHS should be done in consultation with relevant stakeholders of the organisation. In fact, employers have a legal obligation to consult with and involve workers in the development and management of WHS matters within their organisation. The aim is that employers and employees tailor their consultative arrangements to best suit their organisation.

Consultation with stakeholders means:

- sharing relevant information with workers
- giving them a reasonable opportunity to express their views
- considering those views when making decisions
- advising all stakeholders of WHS-related decisions
- including the health and safety representatives (HSRs) or WHS committee in the process where they exist in a workplace.

Consultation is required when:

- identifying hazards and assessing risks
- making decisions about how to deal with hazards/risks
- making decisions about the adequacy of facilities for the welfare of workers
- proposing changes that may affect workers' health and safety
- making decisions about WHS procedures, which includes consultation, monitoring and dispute resolution
- providing information and training.

The main consultative obligations within a business relate to the use of HSRs and health and safety committees.

5.2.1 Health and safety representatives

Organisations can vary in size from relatively small, with only a few staff, to large, with hundreds (perhaps thousands) of staff members. Whatever the size, any member of an organisation should be able to ask management to arrange for the election of **health and safety representatives (HSRs)** to represent their best interests in WHS-related matters. The staff members can decide how elections will be conducted (provided they comply with any regulations on the matter), and a union can assist in the process if a majority of staff are in favour of involving it. Once elected, HSRs usually hold office for three years and are eligible for re-election.

The main functions of an HSR are to:

- represent the work group in matters relating to WHS
- monitor and review WHS measures undertaken by the **person conducting a business or undertaking (PCBU)** or their representatives
- investigate and attempt to resolve WHS-related complaints made by members of the work group, and if unable to do so, request an investigation by an inspector
- enquire into any matter that appears to be a WHS risk
- inspect the workplace where the work group works, either after giving reasonable notice to a PCBU or immediately if an incident or situation that poses a serious potential WHS risk arises
- accompany an inspector on a workplace inspection
- attend interviews between an inspector and/or PCBU and workers that the HSR represents
- receive information about WHS matters that may affect the work group, except if the information reveals personal or medical information about a worker without that worker's consent
- request the formation of a health and safety committee.

5.2.2 Health and safety committees

The WHS Act also makes provision for health and safety committees within the workplace. A number of regulations are involved in the formation and running of these committees.

- The PCBU must establish a committee within two months if requested to do so either by an HSR or at least five workers at the workplace. The PCBU may also establish a committee on their own initiative.

- The HSR must be a member of the committee. If there are more than two HSRs at the workplace, at least one must be on the committee. At least 50 per cent of the committee members must be people who were not appointed by the PCBU.
- In the event of any dispute over the formation or membership of a committee, any party may request the WHS authority in their state to appoint an inspector to deal with the matter.
- The functions of a committee are:
  - to facilitate cooperation between the PCBU and workers
  - to instigate, develop and implement measures to ensure health and safety at work
  - to assist in developing standards, rules and procedures relating to WHS
  - any functions agreed between the PCBU and committee or prescribed by regulations.

robuart/Shutterstock

- The committee must meet at least quarterly, and at any other reasonable time as requested by at least half its members.
- The PCBU must allow committee members sufficient paid time off work to attend meetings and to perform their committee functions. It must also provide them with WHS-related information on the same terms as for HSRs.

5.2.3 Implementing consultative processes

Effective communication between staff from across all levels of an organisation is the best way to achieve a safe workplace. It enables discussion of hazards and risks that have been identified, and identification of the best possible solutions to these problems. By cooperating with one another and drawing on the skills, knowledge and experience of the team, better decisions can be made about how work should be carried out safely. It is also important that managers give staff the opportunity to express their views or to voice their concerns. In this way, all relevant staff can have input into the safety and security of their work environment.

If implemented effectively, consultation can result in:

- informed decisions by management through gathering a wider and more reliable source of ideas about WHS
- greater employee commitment to WHS procedures, due to a better understanding of the decision-making process and of the reasons why decisions are made
- greater openness, respect and trust between management and employees as a result of better understanding each other's point of view
- higher employee morale and job satisfaction, with the employer demonstrating that employee views are encouraged, valued and considered
- healthier working environments and increased productivity
- greater opportunities for learning through the sharing of information, concepts and ideas
- reduced injury and disease, with consequent savings to the employer, employees and the general community.

Meaningful and effective consultation, then, involves drawing on the knowledge, experience and ideas of employees and encouraging their participation and input to improve the systems the employer has in place for managing WHS. It creates an inclusive work culture where employees feel they are valued and their opinions are respected. This, in turn, can lead to increased loyalty and support for organisational goals, which inevitably results in increased productivity.

5.2.4 Responding to WHS issues in a timely manner

No workplace will ever be completely free of hazards or risks. Accidents can and will happen. Most of these can be avoided, however, if staff are aware of any current or potential WHS issues. Such issues should be reported to relevant personnel, such their supervisor, a manager, or the WHS representative or committee (or other person responsible for WHS in the workplace).

Organisations with well thought-out WHS policies and procedures will have methods by which health and safety issues can be reported and actioned. This can mean the difference between maintaining a safe work environment and having an accident occur that could have been prevented, so it is essential to report any identified issues immediately.

Think about

3. Reflect on reporting procedures in your own organisation. Who is responsible for completing reports? What methods do they use to do this?

5.2.5 Encouraging others to participate in arrangements for managing WHS

While managing and controlling WHS policies and procedures is ultimately the responsibility of management, staff are involved in many ways. Every team member needs to participate in WHS within the scope of their roles and responsibilities. Being aware of what is going on around them and of the potential dangers in the workplace, raising WHS issues with the appropriate staff, and taking action to eliminate hazards and reduce risk are a large part of this process.

Employers need to inform all staff about their WHS rights and responsibilities by:

- distributing fact sheets
- including WHS information in the staff handbook
- holding WHS discussions as appropriate during the business day
- scheduling special staff meetings or workshops specifically to address WHS issues.
  In addition, employers need to provide opportunities for staff to put forward their views and suggestions on current and future WHS management practices. This may involve providing a suitable time, during work hours, for consultation with staff, and informing them of the different ways they can provide feedback or report issues of concern. For example, by:
  - writing in a diary or on a whiteboard, or placing a note in a suggestion box
  - attending formal meetings with agendas, minutes and action plans
  - convening informal meetings
  - completing surveys or questionnaires that invite staff feedback on WHS issues.

WHS consultations might revolve around a simple matter that can be dealt with quickly, or they could be complex and take days or even weeks to resolve. Questions that will determine who will be part of the consultation process, and how long it will take, include:

- How many people need to be consulted about the issue?
- How will the issue affect the business overall?
- What resources will be required to address the issue?
- What are the cost factors involved?
- What are the risks involved in solving this problem?

5.2.6 Identifying and implementing improvements in response to WHS feedback

Feedback is one of the most important aspects of any business: if you don't know what is wrong, how can you fix it? Feedback is always a priority with WHS, as ignoring safety issues could lead to serious harm or, in extreme cases, death.

Where feedback is received on WHS matters, the relevant personnel should:

- investigate the issue
- evaluate its impact on the organisation and team
- consult with relevant stakeholders to find a solution, such as:
  - management staff
  - workers
  - human resources (HR) staff
  - outside WHS consultants
- implement the solution and advise staff of outcomes and changes made
- record the issue, its solution and implementation in the organisation's continuous improvement log.

Knowledge check

9. Consulting with and encouraging the team to participate in WHS arrangements benefits both the organisation and its staff. List at least five benefits of consultation.
10. It is essential to respond to WHS issues in a timely manner. Explain why.
11. Explain what methods you could use to involve team members in managing WHS.
12. Explain what action should be taken in response to feedback about WHS issues.

5.3 Contributing to organisational procedures for providing WHS training

Managing WHS requires identifying all WHS risks within the organisation, assessing their potential to cause harm, and finding ways to minimise or mitigate these risks. For this to happen effectively, people must know what they are doing in their jobs and be able to perform them to the expected standards. WHS training, then, is an integral part of implementing the policies and procedures of a WHS management strategy. Training is required to ensure that staff have the appropriate skills and knowledge to perform their work safely and to the required standards, which in turn helps reduce the likelihood of an incident or accident in the workplace.

5.3.1 Identifying the WHS training needs of the work team

When determining the training needs of an organisation, you need to have an understanding both of the organisational procedures and standards that are to be met, and the current competencies of the staff involved in fulfilling the various workplace tasks. Any discrepancy found between the required standard and a staff member's ability is known as a **training gap**. This gap can be identified by:

- undertaking a time-consuming (and therefore expensive) formal WHS training needs analysis (TNA) of each staff member
- observing staff performance to identify areas of their performance that require attention and/or corrective action

- talking with staff and asking them to identify the areas in which they believe they need WHS training
- looking at staff HR records to determine their existing skill and competency levels with a view to identifying the areas where training is required
- employing the services of an outside consultant with specialist WHS knowledge and expertise to assess the competency levels of staff within the organisation, analyse the competencies needed and determine individual staff training requirements.

Think about

4. Are there any gaps in your WHS knowledge? For example, do you know the following:
    - What are your organisation's evacuation procedures?
    - How is PPE required to be used by your organisation?
    - Where are the emergency exits located?
    - Where is the fire-fighting equipment located?

5.3.2 Identifying strategies and opportunities for developing WHS competence

Training should be viewed as an essential tool in establishing a proactive approach to WHS in the workplace. The following questions can help to identify the strategies and opportunities for developing a team's WHS competence:

- What skills and knowledge are required to enable all employees to do their jobs safely and without risks to health?
- What is to be achieved by training, and who will ensure it takes place?
- What sort of training will be best for the workplace?
    - Is there a policy for health and safety training?
    - Is there a health and safety training program?
- What does existing WHS training cover?
    - Have all employees taken part in the required WHS training?
- Are WHS training records being kept?
    - What do they say about the level of WHS staff training delivered?
- Have all managers and supervisors had health and safety training?
- Is there an induction training program for all new and transferred employees?
    - Does the induction training program include training on health and safety legislation and venue/department health and safety policies and procedures?
- Is there workplace training on specific hazards, controls and health and safe work procedures?
    - Does this exist for every department and dangerous activity?
    - Is this training, including supporting information, sufficient, relevant and current?
- Does WHS training cater for employees with particular language, cultural or literacy needs?
- How does the organisation know, now and in the future, if the WHS training is effective?

Making arrangements for fulfilling training needs

Once training needs have been identified, relevant stakeholders should be informed and arrangements made to deliver the training. These stakeholders might include:

- *Managers*—who will need to approve the training program and sign off on resource and budget requirements.

- *HR staff*—who have overall responsibility for the staff, their development and wellbeing. Any training provided should be noted in that person's work file for future reference.
- *Trainers*—who will be delivering the training program. They might be internal trainers or external consultants.
- *Administrative staff*—who will be responsible for making all the necessary arrangements.

GoodStudio/Shutterstock

To facilitate the delivery of WHS training to staff, it may be necessary to:

- organise time release for staff so that they can attend training
- roster staff in a way that multiple training sessions can be run, ensuring that all staff can attend without too much disruption to the business
- conduct offsite training using external training providers
- close a department for a period while staff undertake training
- undertake training out of normal working hours, which may mean making overtime payments to staff.

The choice of strategy used to develop and implement the training will depend on the:

- trading hours of the organisation or training venue
- numbers of staff who require training
- urgency of the training need
- type of WHS training to be done
- general level of cooperation from all concerned.

A **training schedule** (or **lesson plan**) helps to ensure that a training program achieves the desired outcome and that all necessary points are covered. An example of a simple lesson plan developed for WHS training is shown in Figure 5.3.

Figure 5.3 Sample lesson plan for WHS training

Session title: Use of fire extinguishing equipment	**Session date(s):**
Venue: ABC Accountancy training rooms	**Duration:** 2 hours: 06.30–08.30 am
Purpose: In line with WHS policies of our organisation, this is an annual refresher course on how to use the office fire-fighting equipment for long-term staff and an induction for new staff.	
Learning outcomes **At the end of this session, the learner(s) will be able to do the following:**	
1. Identify different types of fire extinguishers.	
2. Confidently use an extinguisher to shut down a fire.	
3. Understand and use a range of other equipment such as fire blankets.	
Learner special needs: One of the staff has a hearing impairment and adjustments may need to be made to training styles to accommodate them.	
WHS issues: The training room isn't properly ventilated and becomes stuffy and hot. Air con to be fixed prior to training.	
Main points to include	**Topic details and activities**
Types of extinguishers	**Discussion on:** ■ differences between extinguisher types ■ different types of fires ■ which extinguisher to use for what kind of fire ■ how to successfully enable the extinguisher. **Activity:** Practice: Students to gather in car park where a fire has been started in the fire pit. Use extinguisher to put out the fire.
Other types of fire-fighting equipment and methods	**Discussion on:** ■ fire blankets and their use ■ smothering fires with any available and appropriate resources ■ ... and so on. **Activity:** Role play: Students to use resources at hand to smother a fire.
Assessment: Role plays and practice session	
Materials/resources: No special requirements.	
Session review: Upon completion of the training session, trainer to review effectiveness of the lesson plan and provide the results to ABC Accountancy for continuous improvement purposes.	
Trainer name:	

Training methods

Training can be delivered in a number of ways, which will be dictated by the type of industry, the size of the organisation, and constraints such as staff rostering, budgets and the space available. Training methods can include:

- *Workshops* on one or more specific WHS issues, using activities such as lectures, discussions, practical exercises and case studies (supplemented by guest speakers).
- *Information sessions*, including verbal delivery supported by:
  - handouts (notes, fact sheets and other literature prepared in-house or provided by manufacturers of equipment, suppliers of chemicals or the WHS authorities or agencies)
  - PowerPoint presentations.
- *Workplace mentoring and coaching*, where senior personnel with extensive experience develop a relationship with one or more staff for purposes of sharing information, providing advice and instruction, and discussing and solving workplace issues.
- *Lectures*, where trainers deliver formal talks on a nominated topic, supported by notes written on a smartboard, handouts and/or PowerPoint presentations.

- *Practical demonstrations* (either in a one-on-one or a group setting), where the training requires staff to learn how (and why) to do something. Opportunity for practice must be included.
- *Regular work health and safety meetings*, where the focus is on WHS issues such as new legislated or organisational requirements, operating procedures for new equipment, and so on.

In addition, work team members can be assisted and supported to develop their WHS competence by way of:

- *Peer or buddy systems*, where newly recruited staff can be paired with an existing team member who will work with them for a given period.
- *Safety committees*, which are responsible for all matters related to WHS.
- *Toolbox talks*, which are short safety meetings held just before a work shift begins to focus on a single aspect of WHS specific to your workplace.

Knowledge check

13. Describe how you would go about identifying the training needs of a work team.
14. List at least six questions you could ask when developing strategies and opportunities for supporting the work team's WHS competence.
15. List three methods of providing assistance to work team members to support their WHS competence.

5.4 Participating in identifying hazards, and assessing and controlling risks for the work area

While most industries have *common* hazards, specific industries will have hazards unique to them. For example, you may be working in the hospitality industry and be involved in a range of work activities such as food preparation where you would be dealing with hot oil, gas flames or sharp knives. Working as a tour guide, on the other hand, you may be dealing with large vehicles (such as coaches), road traffic issues, crowd control and security issues. As we have seen, all workplaces, regardless of industry or size, will have hazards and risks of some description. How do you control them?

5.4.1 Identifying hazards in the work area

Most accidents occur because of carelessness or lack of attention. Some common hazards found in most workplaces are shown in Figure 5.4.

Some other hazards that can contribute to workplace accidents include:

- high noise levels, which can cause industrial deafness or prevent you from hearing warnings about potential hazards
- heat (from heaters, machinery, ovens)
- lack of suitable signage about:
  - poisons and acids
  - emergency exits and evacuation procedures
  - fire-fighting equipment, such as hydrants, fire blankets and/or hoses
  - first aid kit locations
- lack of training on health and safety issues such as:
  - correct handling and storage of hazardous chemicals or equipment
  - hazardous work processes—for example, working with dangerous machinery or equipment.

Figure 5.4 Common hazards in the workplace

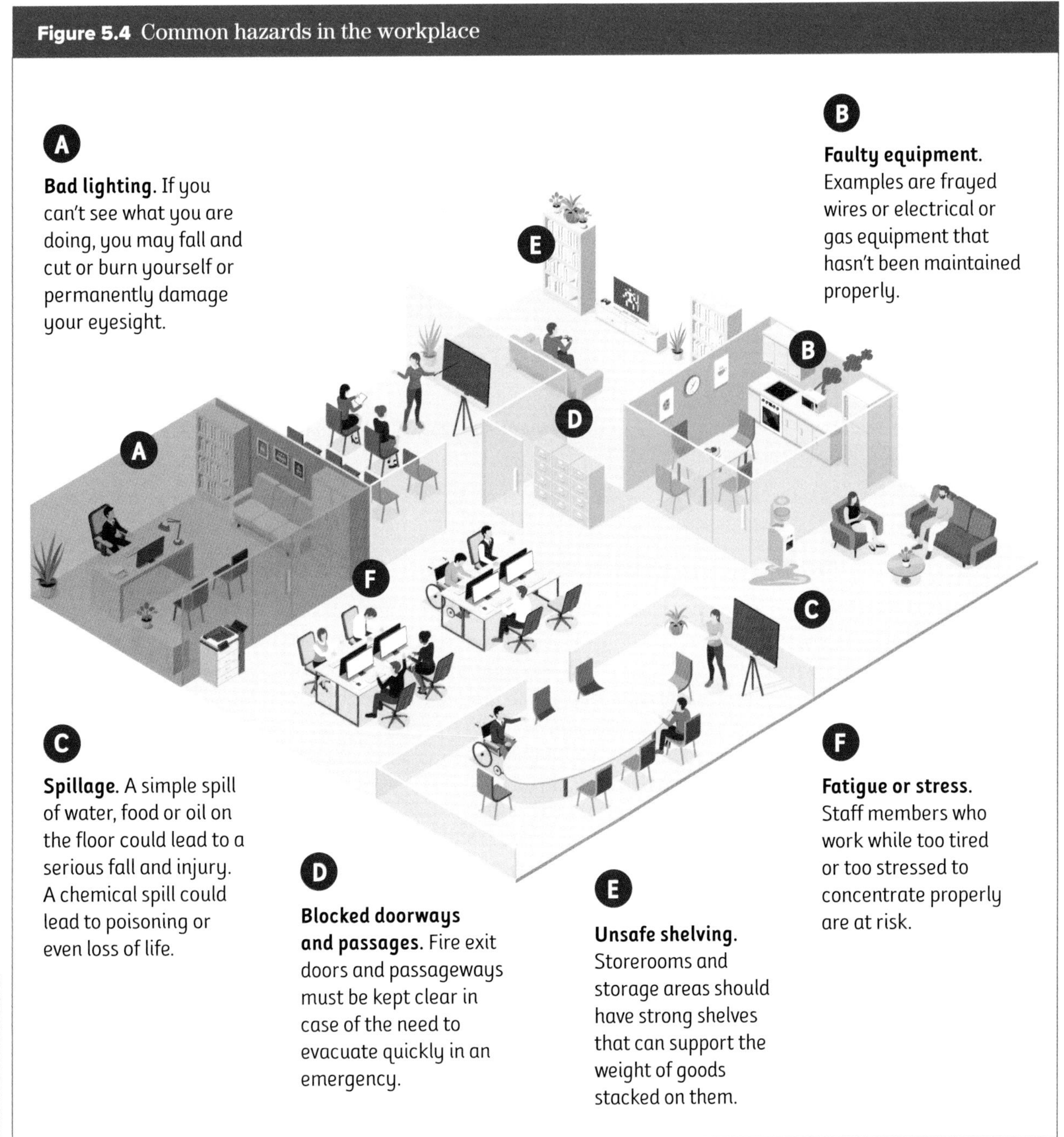

A
Bad lighting. If you can't see what you are doing, you may fall and cut or burn yourself or permanently damage your eyesight.
B
Faulty equipment. Examples are frayed wires or electrical or gas equipment that hasn't been maintained properly.
C
Spillage. A simple spill of water, food or oil on the floor could lead to a serious fall and injury. A chemical spill could lead to poisoning or even loss of life.
D
Blocked doorways and passages. Fire exit doors and passageways must be kept clear in case of the need to evacuate quickly in an emergency.
E
Unsafe shelving. Storerooms and storage areas should have strong shelves that can support the weight of goods stacked on them.
F
Fatigue or stress. Staff members who work while too tired or too stressed to concentrate properly are at risk.

Sensvector/Shutterstock

In addition to these obvious hazards, hidden hazards that may cause illness (physical or psychological) include poorly designed office furniture or lighting, toxic substances, and bullying or intimidation. Hidden hazards are often difficult to identify and may not be known until after the event. This might be the case, for example, with repetitive strain injury (RSI) from repeated keyboard operation or stress caused by badly designed jobs. When identifying hazards, then, attention should also be paid to risks that may not initially be obvious.

Workplaces aren't static; they change and evolve constantly. So, having gone through the hazard identification process once doesn't mean you can assume that nothing will change and new hazards and risks won't be introduced. For this reason, all staff should be encouraged, on an ongoing basis, to keep an eye on situations that could potentially prove hazardous.

Various methods can be used to identify hazards, including:

- casual observations during daily routine work
- formal inspections and surveys

- review of information provided by manufacturers, designers and suppliers
- review of past inspection records and comparison with current inspections
- review of previous incident, accident, injury and illness reports
- review of workers' compensation statistics
- conducting a plant, job or task safety analysis or audit.

Such hazards that are found should be reported to relevant stakeholders immediately. The greater the risk of harm, the more urgently a matter should be dealt with. Reports should be done in line with organisational procedures, which might include the use of a variety of forms. (Examples are provided at the end of the chapter.)

Try this now

1. Look around your own office or department and identify areas that are potential hazards. Who will you report these to?

5.4.2 Implementing processes designed to control risks

Effective risk management and control involves identifying all of the hazards in the workplace, and then assessing the severity of the associated risk and its priority for being dealt with. Safety inspections and audits are the main mechanisms used to identify hazards and to assess the likelihood that a hazard will cause harm, the type of exposure to it that might cause harm, and the degree of harm that might be caused by it.

Hazard identification should be conducted by managers and staff on an ongoing basis. However, it should be carried out, in particular, whenever:

- changes to the workplace are implemented before:
  - the premises are used for the first time
  - and during the installation or alteration of any machinery or equipment
  - changes to work practices are introduced
- any new information relating to health and safety risks becomes available.

Figure 5.5 Risk assessment

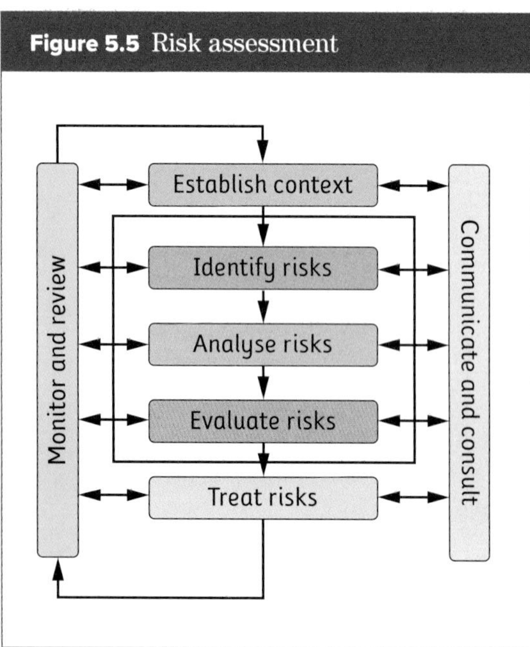

Conducting hazard identification

To be fully effective, hazard identification and risk assessment should follow a formal structure. Figure 5.5 outlines a typical risk assessment process and is designed to be applicable for organisations of all sizes and across all sectors.

Establishing the context of a project such as hazard identification means setting the parameters and conditions under which the project will be conducted. This might include determining the project's overall objective, its scope, the resources required to complete the task(s) and the time frames involved. Let's continue to use a theme park as our example. To conduct a WHS audit of the entire park would be an enormous task and impractical in terms of park operations. Therefore, in this case, the context might be "to ensure guest safety within the park confines", with site inspections scheduled in successive "blocks" determined by the individual areas of operation so that there is minimal disruption to the business and to customers. These blocks could be prioritised in terms of greatest perceived risks.

At this point, you might also need to decide the criteria that will be used to identify hazards and to evaluate their associated risks. For example, as a supervisor in the food service area of the theme park your daily inspection might consist of a walk-through to determine if there are any clearly visible and identifiable issues. You may decide, however, that a more thorough inspection is required. The criteria for the inspection might now include checking that:

- heating and cooling equipment is functioning properly and within the temperature guidelines set out in the Food Safety Standards
- knives and other sharp implements are properly stored
- food preparation equipment has been thoroughly washed and sanitised
- benches have been wiped and sanitised
- floors have been mopped thoroughly, and so on.

With the context and criteria for the site inspection established, you can then move onto the identification phase.

The purpose of *identifying and assessing risk* is to determine whether there is any likelihood of injury, illness or disease associated with each of the potentially hazardous situations. Consider the following:

- Is any person (staff and/or members of the public) exposed to the identified situations in any possible scenario (e.g. during installation, commissioning, operation, inspection, maintenance, repair, and service and cleaning of plant, equipment or areas)?
- What measures are already in place to protect the health and safety of people who may be exposed to the identified risk or hazard?
- How adequate are the existing measures for protecting the health and safety of people who may be exposed?

If it is unlikely—or there is no chance—that anyone will be exposed to a situation, there is no risk. Therefore, no risk control measures other than those that are already in place need to be introduced. However, if there *is* a likelihood that an event could occur and that people may be exposed to harm, however minor, then the *consequences* of that event occurring also need to be considered. This means that after the list of hazards has been finalised, documented and agreed on by the WHS team and management, a judgement needs to be made about the seriousness of each hazard and which one(s) require the most urgent attention. The process for doing this is as follows:

- Take a close look at each item on the “hazard identification” list and consider:
    - What is the possible outcome if things go wrong?
    - Are you talking about cuts, scratches and bruises, or is there the potential for someone to be seriously injured or even killed?
- Is the hazard an everyday task, or is it something that comes up only every now and again, giving you more time to find a solution?
- Are there things you can do right now as a short-term fix while you work out a better, more permanent solution? Never wait for all risks to be assessed before you start fixing things. Make a start by addressing at least one identified risk or threat.
- Once you have worked out which hazards have the greatest potential to cause injury or disease, or are a risk to public safety, mark these as your high-priority hazards. The other hazards should be ranked in priority order.
- Review the hazard list regularly to ensure that every aspect of the workplace is monitored and any new hazards are immediately identified. Remember: workplace safety is a dynamic concept.

Table 5.3 can be used to determine and prioritise the likelihood and consequences of an event.

Table 5.3 Risk assessment chart

Likelihood	Consequence				
	Insignificant	Minor	Moderate	Major	Critical
Almost certain	Medium	Medium	High	Extreme	Extreme
Likely	Low	Medium	High	High	Extreme
Possible	Low	Medium	High	High	High
Unlikely	Low	Low	Medium	Medium	High
Rare	Low	Low	Low	Low	Medium

Try this now

2. Using the list of hazards you identified in your own area, apply the risk assessment in the chart to each hazard to determine its risk.

Evaluating risks

The risk from a hazard is a combination of the likelihood of an incident occurring, what could go wrong, and how badly someone could be hurt. You assess risks so that you can control them effectively. To assess and evaluate a risk, then, you need to examine all of the factors that affect it.

Assessment should involve consultation and be conducted publicly—for example, in a WHS meeting where staff who are impacted by the risk being discussed, as well as WHS representatives and management, consider and evaluate the issue in order to identify an effective and practical control or solution. Issues to consider during the evaluation process include:

- the number of people exposed to the risk
- who these people are (e.g. new workers, casual employees, visitors, contractors, members of the public, disabled workers and customers) and any special needs they may have
- how near these people are to the risk
- how often they are exposed and for how long
- the combination of hazards they are exposed to and how serious the resulting harm could be
- how easily someone could be hurt
- what the law says about risk control
- how common it is for the hazard to cause problems in other workplaces
- any factors that could increase the likelihood of illness and injury
- the work processes involved (i.e. the practices, procedures and protocols for performing the particular task under consideration)
- how well your current precautions work, and whether the hazard has already caused any problems.

The evaluation process should produce a description of the likely consequences and what actions might need to be taken, such as shown in Table 5.4.

Implementing risk control methods

Once a risk has been identified, assessed and evaluated, measures must be taken to control that risk. This is where the "hierarchy of controls" (Figure 5.6) comes in. The **hierarchy of control** looks at risks in terms of what must (or can) be done to eliminate or minimise risk to staff, customers and premises.

Table 5.4 Description of risk levels and actions to be taken

Assessed risk level		Description of risk level	Actions
☐	Low	If an incident were to occur, there would be little likelihood that an injury would result.	Undertake the activity with the existing controls in place.
☐	Medium	If an incident were to occur, there would be some chance that an injury requiring first aid would result.	Additional controls may be needed.
☐	High	If an incident were to occur, it would be likely that an injury requiring medical treatment would result.	Controls will need to be in place before the activity is undertaken.
☐	Extreme	If an incident were to occur, it would be likely that a permanent, debilitating injury or death would result.	Consider alternatives to doing the activity. Significant control measures will need to be implemented to ensure safety.

Figure 5.6 Hierarchy of control

Most effective (high level)	*Elimination*: Remove the hazard completely from the workplace or activity.
	Substitution: Replace a hazard with a less dangerous one (e.g. a less hazardous chemical).
	Redesign: Make a machine or work process safer (e.g. raise a bench to reduce bending).
	Isolation: Separate people from the hazard (e.g. safety barrier).
	Administration: Put rules, signage or training in place to make a workplace safer (e.g. induction training, highlighting trip hazards).
Least effective (low level)	*Personal protective equipment*: Require the use of appropriate protective clothing and equipment. (Construction crews will need hard hats and sturdy work boots. Hospital workers will need gloves and masks. Hospitality workers will need gloves, and sturdy shoes with non-slip soles for working in kitchens.)

5.4.3 Identifying, documenting and reporting on inadequacies in existing risk control measures

A work environment is safest when all staff are engaged in making it so. They should therefore be encouraged to report issues they come across and be assured that they will be followed up on. In addition to your own observations and inspections, then, you will also need to pay attention to comments and reports from staff and respond to them accordingly. If you are advised of a workplace hazard and fail to do anything about it, staff members or customers could potentially be harmed and you could be held personally responsible. It could mean legal action being taken against both you and the organisation, a loss of your job, a loss of the organisation's reputation, and/or severe health consequences for the injured or harmed person.

Such reports may come in the wake of formal WHS meetings or training sessions, but can also be informal by way of casual comments or conversations about working conditions or issues. Regardless of the level of formality, action will or may need to be taken and feedback provided as and when appropriate.

Any deficiencies identified can also provide the foundations for improvement. Continuous improvement is essentially a small, step-by-step, incremental improvement strategy and is important for a number of reasons, including:

- It shows compliance with legislative requirements, which might require both internal and external audits to be undertaken at regular intervals.

- It keeps track of changes made over the years, showing what worked, what didn't work, and why, and thus provides valuable information for determining future trends and improvements.
- It provides a written record of what issues were identified, by whom and when, and what actions were taken.

Table 5.5 shows an example of a continuous improvement register.

Table 5.5 Example of a continuous improvement register

Issue identified by/on	Issue	Recommendation or action taken	Date actioned	Follow-up
Chris Ferguson 20/9/23	Air conditioner in the photocopy room isn't working.	Admin to arrange service and repair.	20/9/23	ABC Aircon arrived 20/9 at 3.30 pm. Air con fixed.
Chris Ferguson 20/9/23	Carpet in hallway is coming loose near the bathroom door (trip hazard).	Building maintenance to glue down.	21/9/23	Walter fixed the issue.
Prasanna Venkat 22/9/23	Items in the stationery room are shelved too high. Difficult to reach items on top shelf. Staff are standing on boxes to reach them.	Admin supervisor to undertake a review of stationery storage procedures.	25/9/23	New shelving has been ordered. Will be installed by 2/10/23.
Kim Lee 10/10/23	Frayed electrical cords are plugged into leads that are lying across the workshop floor. As the floor is often wet, there is a danger of electrocution.	*Interim*: Leads to be checked and replaced where they are frayed. Leads to be held off the floor at all times.	10/10/23	Update procedures for dealing with electrical equipment. WHS training for all workshop staff.

5.4.4 Completing and maintaining WHS incident records in the work area

Management may put a lot of time and effort into running the business but fail to keep accurate and up-to-date records of any workplace incidents that occur. WHS records must be kept in order to:

- meet legally imposed compliance requirements as specified by WHS legislation
- help track and monitor work health and safety to assist with evaluating WHS performance, and with identifying problems, risks and WHS trends
- function as reference sources when investigating WHS events and making decisions about WHS issues
- demonstrate responsible management of WHS matters
- provide accurate reports on workplace incidents or accidents.

Legal obligations in reporting

Whenever a notifiable incident occurs in the workplace, the business owner or manager is legally obliged to notify their WHS regulator. Failing to report such an incident is an offence and penalties can apply. The WHS law states that:

> A "notifiable incident" is to be reported to the regulator immediately after becoming aware it has happened if the regulator asks—written notification should be submitted within 48 hours of the request, and the incident site is to be preserved until an inspector arrives or directs otherwise (subject to some exceptions). (Safe Work Australia; CC BY 4.0 https://creativecommons.org/licenses/by/4.0/.)

But what, exactly, is a "notifiable incident"?

A notifiable incident is an incident arising out of the conduct of a business or undertaking at a workplace. These are:

- the death of a person
- a "serious injury or illness", or a "dangerous incident". (Safe Work Australia; CC BY 4.0 https://creativecommons.org/licenses/by/4.0/.)

Notifiable incidents can apply to any person on the work premises regardless of whether they are a staff member, a contractor or a member of the public. It is only necessary to notify the authority of the most serious work-related health or safety incidents. Where such an incident has occurred, and been notified, it may also mean that the site of the incident may need to be preserved for the arrival of a WHS inspector, or pending further instruction from the WHS regulator.

A serious injury or illness must be reported if the person requires any of the types of treatment listed in Table 5.6.

Table 5.6 Notifiable incidents

Types of treatment	Example
Immediate treatment as an in-patient in a hospital	Admission into a hospital as an in-patient for any duration, even if the stay is not overnight or longer. *It does not include*: ■ out-patient treatment provided by the emergency section of a hospital (i.e. not requiring admission as an in-patient) ■ admission for corrective surgery which does not immediately follow the injury (e.g. to fix a fractured nose).
Immediate treatment for the amputation of any part of the body	Amputation of a limb such as arm or leg, body part such as hand, foot or the tip of a finger, toe, nose or ear.
Immediate treatment for a serious head injury	■ Fractured skull, loss of consciousness, blood clot or bleeding in the brain, damage to the skull to the extent that it is likely to affect organ/face function. ■ Head injuries resulting in temporary or permanent amnesia. *It does not include*: A bump to the head resulting in a minor contusion or headache.
Immediate treatment for a serious eye injury	■ Injury that results in or is likely to result in the loss of the eye or total or partial loss of vision. ■ Injury that involves an object penetrating the eye (e.g. metal fragment, wood chip). ■ Exposure of the eye to a substance which poses a risk of serious eye damage. *It does not include*: Eye exposure to a substance that merely causes irritation.
Immediate treatment for a serious burn	A burn requiring intensive care or critical care which could require a compression garment or a skin graft. *It does not include*: A burn that merely requires washing the wound and applying a dressing.
Immediate treatment for the separation of skin from an underlying tissue (such as de-gloving or scalping)	Separation of skin from an underlying tissue such that tendon, bone or muscles are exposed (de-gloving or scalping). *It does not include*: Minor lacerations.
Immediate treatment for a spinal injury	Injury to the cervical, thoracic, lumbar or sacral vertebrae, including the discs and spinal cord. *It does not include*: Acute back strain.
Immediate treatment for the loss of a bodily function	Loss of consciousness, loss of movement of a limb, or loss of the sense of smell, taste, sight or hearing, or loss of function of an internal organ. *It does not include*: ■ mere fainting ■ a sprain or strain.
Immediate treatment for serious lacerations	■ Deep or extensive cuts that cause muscle, tendon, nerve or blood vessel damage or permanent impairment. ■ Deep puncture wounds. ■ Tears or wounds to the flesh or tissues—this may include stitching to prevent loss of blood and/or other treatment to prevent loss of bodily function and/or infection.
Medical treatment within 48 hours of exposure to a substance	"Medical treatment" is treatment provided by a doctor. "Exposure to a substance" includes exposure to chemicals, airborne contaminants, and to human and/or animal blood and body substances.

Source: Safe Work Australia information sheet, "Incident Notification" (revised version, November 2015). See https://www.safeworkaustralia.gov.au/resources-and-publications/guidance-materials/incident-notification-information-sheet.

Notification is also required for any infection where a person's work is a significant contributing factor. This includes any infection related to carrying out work:

- with micro-organisms
- that involves providing treatment or care to a person

- that entails contact with human blood or body substances
- that involves handling or contact with animals, animal hides, skins, wool or hair, animal carcasses or animal waste products.

Try this now

3. Download a copy of the "Incident Notification" information sheet from the Safe Work Australia website and keep it in a portfolio of useful workplace information (https://www.safeworkaustralia.gov.au/resources-and-publications/guidance-materials/incident-notification-information-sheet).

As discussed, there are a range of records that an organisation is required, by law, to keep. However, there are also documents that the organisation itself will have introduced to manage and monitor its WHS systems. They may include the following:

- Information provided to employees as necessary to enable them to perform their work in a safe manner without risks to health. This information is required to be supplied in appropriate languages to meet the language needs of workers.
- Records relating to the health and safety of the employees, including the results of monitoring activities where legislation (or business policies) require such records to be kept. For example, some businesses may test the hearing and/or general health of staff.
- A Register of Injuries or an Injury Report Book maintained to keep track of all workplace injuries. This record must contain details of any accidents or injuries, including:
  - worker's name and job details
  - date and time of injury or illness
  - exact location where injury or illness occurred
  - how it happened
  - the nature of the injury or illness and the body parts affected
  - names of any witnesses
  - name of the person entering details in the register
  - date when the employer was notified.
- A **hazardous substances/dangerous goods**/chemicals register listing all the chemicals and hazardous substances used in the business.
- Training action plans, which set out the courses/WHS topics to be covered by workplace training, including when and where these courses will be conducted.
- Training records indicating the specific WHS training provided, when it was provided and who it was provided to.
- Incident notification. Where an accident or injury occurs in the workplace and is of a certain severity or type, such as a death or serious injury (sometimes referred to as a "notifiable incident" or similar term), there is a need to complete, forward to the authorities, and maintain official forms and records. Serious injury may be seen as anything requiring:
  - medical treatment within 48 hours of exposure to a substance
  - immediate treatment as an in-patient in a hospital
  - immediate medical treatment for such things as amputation, serious head injury, serious eye injury, separation of skin from underlying tissue, electric shock, spinal injury or loss of bodily function.
- Consultation records such as minutes of WHS committee meetings, diaries of meetings, agendas for meetings, names of committee members, consultation decisions and follow-up actions.
- Checklists completed when undertaking WHS inspections, such as Monitoring Inspection records and WHS Inspection checklists.

- Hazard identification and risk assessment reports and records—documents used to conduct an analysis of specific identified risks in the workplace such as Job Safety Analysis sheets, including details of actions/controls decided on.
- Results of investigations into WHS events (including "near misses"), which may include photographs, witness statements and medical reports.
- Documentation relating to the insurance of workers to cover them for workplace accidents, injury or illness, including details of claims made against that insurance company.
- Agreed Issue Resolution procedures. These are the protocols for addressing WHS issues/ grievances. They are established in the workplace and agreed to by management and workers as the most effective or practical way to address identified problems.
- Return to Work documentation detailing the plan devised to assist injured workers to return to work after an accident or incident.
- Records from suppliers stating that the products they supply are safe and compliant with all legislated requirements.

Most organisations will have their own specifically designed forms for many of the purposes outlined. Figures 5.7, 5.8 and 5.9 are examples of forms that an organisation might use regularly.

The information contained in incident reports and other forms will highlight areas of concern that will need to be addressed and will help to ensure that the organisation is continually improving its systems and procedures. Information gathered can be used to:

- identify hazards, assess risks, and initiate possible suitable risk control measures
- identify unsafe work practices or situations
- identify training needs
- suggest new or changed procedures
- provide evidence of steps taken in a given situation should an audit, or legal action, take place.

Records kept can also help when comparing past performance with the effectiveness of current preventative strategies in order to determine whether there is a need for a more detailed investigation of, for example, the causes of particular incidents.

Figure 5.7 Sample hazard identification form

<table>
<tr><th colspan="2">Positive action request form</th></tr>
<tr><td>Staff name: Lucy Wu</td><td>Date: 30/5/2023</td></tr>
<tr><td colspan="2">Department: Sales & Marketing</td></tr>
<tr><td colspan="2">Non-conformance/complaint:
■ In the corridor between the sales department and the accounts department, next to the Head of Accounts' office door, the carpet has come loose and staff are tripping over it.
■ On Monday, 30 May 2023, Alison French tripped over the carpet and sprained her ankle, which necessitated a visit to the doctor.</td></tr>
<tr><td colspan="2">Positive action taken by (company name): short-term solution
Carpet has been taped down with packing tape.</td></tr>
<tr><td colspan="2">Preventative action: long-term solution
Carpet in corridor to be replaced by 15 June 2023.</td></tr>
<tr><td colspan="2">Follow-up action
■ 31/5/2023: Alan Barker to phone Carpet Warehouse and order carpet.
■ 6/6/2023: Alan Barker to confirm order and installation date.
■ 15/6/2023: Carpet installation—Alan Barker to confirm installation to board.</td></tr>
<tr><td>Staff signature: Lucy Wu</td><td>Supervisor signature: Alan Barker</td></tr>
<tr><td>Director signature: Ken Ng</td><td></td></tr>
</table>

Figure 5.8 Sample incident investigation form

Incident investigation form

Incident details			
Name of person involved in the incident:		Date of incident:	
Location of incident:			
Incident investigation team:			
What task was being performed at the time of the incident?			
What happened? (e.g. "employee tripped over box" or "forklift hit wall")			
What factors contributed to the incident?			
Environment:		**Equipment/materials:**	
☐ Noise	☐ Layout/design	☐ Wrong equipment for the job	☐ Equipment failure
☐ Lighting	☐ Dust/fume	☐ Inadequate maintenance	☐ Material/equipment too heavy/awkward
☐ Vibration	☐ Slip/trip hazard	☐ Inadequate guarding	☐ Inadequate training provided
☐ Damaged/unstable floor	☐ Other	☐ Other	
Work systems:		**People:**	
☐ Hazard not identified	☐ No/inadequate risk assessment conducted	☐ Procedure not followed/no procedure exists	☐ Drugs/alcohol
☐ No/inadequate safe work procedure	☐ No/inadequate controls implemented	☐ Fatigue	☐ Time/production pressures
☐ Hazard not reported	☐ Inadequate training/supervision	☐ Change of routine	☐ Distraction/personal issues/stress
☐ Other		☐ Lack of communication	☐ Other

Corrective actions:

Contributing factor (from above list)	What are we going to do to fix the problem?	Who	When	Completion date

Issue fixed?		
Name	**Signature**	**Date**
Person involved in incident:		
Manager:		

Source: WorkSafe Queensland, https://www.worksafe.qld.gov.au/safety-fundamentals/reporting/template

Figure 5.9 Sample hazard/incident report

Hazard/incident report form

Use this form in your workplace to report health and safety hazards and incidents. To notify SafeWork NSW of an incident, call 13 10 50.

Hazard/Incident

Brief description of hazard/incident: (Describe the task, equipment, tools and people involved. Use sketches, if necessary. Include any action taken to ensure the safety of those who may be affected.)

____

____

____

____

Where is the hazard located in the workplace?

____

____

When was the hazard identified? Date: ____/____/____ Time: ________am/pm

Recommended action to fix hazard/incident: (List any suggestions you may have for reducing or eliminating the problem – for example re-design mechanical devices, update procedures, improve training, maintenance work)

____

____

____

____

Date submitted to manager: Date: ____/____/____ Time: ________am/pm

Action taken

Has the hazard/incident been acknowledged by management? Yes/No

Describe what has been done to resolve the hazard/incident:

____

____

____

____

Do you consider the hazard/incident fixed? Yes/No

Name: ________________ Position: ________________

Signature: ________________

Date: ____/____/____

SW09097 0918

Source: Safe Work NSW, https://www.safework.nsw.gov.au/_data/assets/pdf_file/0003/414192/Hazard-incident-report-SW09097.pdf.

Knowledge check

16. Most accidents occur because of carelessness or lack of attention. List at least eight hazards that could generally be encountered in most workplaces.

17. Hazard identification, in any organisation, is essential and should be conducted regularly. Explain when, in particular, hazard identification should take place.

18. Describe the hazard identification process.

19. Explain what a risk assessment chart is and describe how it is used.

20. What is a hierarchy of controls? Briefly describe each stage.

21. Explain why it is important to identify and report on inadequacies of existing control measures.

22. Any deficiencies identified can also provide the foundations for improvement. Explain how feedback on inadequacies could be used for continuous improvement and why it is important to document such feedback.

23. Explain why it is important to complete and maintain WHS records.

24. Describe the characteristics of a good work team.

Summary

Each year, many hundreds of people are injured in the workplace in Australia. Most of these injuries can be avoided by putting WHS procedures in place. Work health and safety, then, is one of the most important aspects of any business. The employer has the responsibility to create a safe working environment, and employees have the responsibility to follow company WHS procedures. Everyone in the workforce can assist with incorporating WHS into their work methods, contributing by way of discussions and by reporting any hazards or risks they observe.

CHAPTER 6
Participate in sustainable work practices

Learning outcomes

6.1 Measure sustainable work practices

6.2 Support sustainable work practices

6.3 Seek opportunities to improve sustainable work practices

While the natural environment provides us with resources, unfortunately it is also a dumping ground for waste and resources that we no longer require. Our use and misuse of the world's resources impacts not just our own quality of life but also the health of the natural environment. Sustainable work practices are ways of working that reduce the harm we do to the environment and help preserve it for future generations.

6.1 Measuring sustainable work practices

Establishing an environmentally friendly and sustainable workplace begins with looking at the way in which your organisation operates, to determine whether resources are used to their best advantage and there is no unnecessary (and costly) waste. Many organisations will have followed the same workplace procedures—or used the same resources, purchased from the same suppliers—for years, with the attitude: "It's always worked in the past. Why change now?"

Developing a sustainable workplace, however, isn't just about being more environmentally friendly. There are sound business reasons for changing to more sustainable practices—activities that will save an organisation time, effort and money. When exploring how best to integrate sustainability into the workplace, it is necessary to first look at current practices and the resources used. For example:

- *Are resources being used as effectively as possible?* Is your organisation using equipment or materials in accordance with the manufacturer's instructions or guidelines? Incorrect or inefficient use of resources can cause damage or injury, as well as being wasteful.
- *Are you using the best resources for each particular job?*
  - Are there "green" products that could do the job?
  - Are there alternative methods of completing the task?
  - Could you do without that resource altogether?
- *Are you wasting resources?* Are you reusing and recycling resources wherever possible?
- *Does your use of resources present hazards to people or the environment?* The use of chemicals and other toxic substances, and bad lighting and poor ventilation, are all areas of concern. Workplace conditions should be reviewed, and alternative products and methods used, where hazardous conditions are identified.

Sustainability terms explained

What is a "carbon footprint"?

A **carbon footprint** is the direct effect our actions and lifestyle have on the environment in terms of carbon dioxide emissions. The biggest contributors to carbon footprint today are travel needs and electricity demands. However, in some way, *all* our actions have an impact, whether directly or indirectly, including the:

- food we eat
- clothes we wear
- way we entertain ourselves
- way in which we move from place to place (cars, buses, planes).

All of these things need to be manufactured or produced in some way. Machinery requires energy; cars, buses and planes burn fuel; and in our homes and offices we use significant amounts of electricity that generally comes from power plants that burn fossil fuels. These all contribute to accelerating global warming and climate change, leaving behind a "carbon footprint". Many businesses are now looking closely at their work practices and the resources they use in an attempt to reduce their carbon footprint.

What are "greenhouse gas emissions"?

Greenhouse gases are gases in Earth's atmosphere that trap heat. They let sunlight pass through the atmosphere, but they prevent the heat that the sunlight brings from leaving the atmosphere. The main greenhouse gases are water vapour and carbon dioxide.

Human activities are responsible for almost all of the increase in greenhouse gases in the atmosphere over the last 150 years. The following are the largest sources of greenhouse gas emissions from human activities:

- *Transportation*. Transportation accounts for the largest share of greenhouse gas emissions and primarily comes from burning fossil fuels for cars, trucks, ships, trains and planes.
- *Electricity production*. The second-largest share of greenhouse gas emissions comes from burning fossil fuels such as coal and natural gas to produce electricity.
- *Industrial activity*. Industries burn fossil fuels to produce goods from raw materials.
- *Commercial and residential usage*. Homes and businesses burn fossil fuels, for heat or for handling waste, or use products the production of which emits greenhouse gases.
- *Agriculture*. Greenhouse gas emissions from this sector come mainly from livestock, such as cows, or from agricultural soils and rice production.

6.1.1 Identifying sustainable work practices in your own role

The best place, and the easiest way, to start the process of "greening" your workplace is to look at things that you personally can control. Look at how your work habits might affect the environment and at ways in which you could use resources more efficiently. Figure 6.1 includes some examples.

Figure 6.1 Energy-saving tips at work

OFF
Turn off all computers, monitors and other office machines when not in use.
Avoid printing documents if they can be sent electronically.
Turn off lights when not in use (especially overnight and on weekends) and put up signs to remind other people to turn them off too.
Switch to energy-efficient light bulbs.

elenabsl/Shutterstock

Some more energy-saving tips include:

- Activate the energy-saving function that is installed on most new computers. If your computer doesn't have this software installed, you can save energy by simply switching off the monitor when not in use. Monitors can consume three times the energy used by your PC.
- Set photocopiers and printers to default to double-sided printing.
- Always choose the low water consumption feature on dishwashers (i.e. the short-wash option, often called "Economy"). Put up a sign to this effect for all users, including cleaners.
- Be mindful of your water usage. Don't leave taps turned on needlessly, and ensure that washers are replaced regularly to avoid water dripping.
- Remove light bulbs from areas where light isn't needed or where there are more lights (e.g. ceiling lights) than necessary.
- Open windows where possible, instead of using air conditioners. Remember that most air-conditioning systems provide less than 10 per cent fresh air.

- Program your climate control systems to turn off at the end of each day and on weekends. There is no point in heating or cooling empty offices.
- Install a desk-side recycling bin for all paper products. You can either reuse a cardboard box or ask your waste paper collection contractor to provide a receptacle. Most waste collection companies can provide these for you.
- Use email wherever possible. Use online (versus hard copy) versions of documents such as annual reports, information memorandums, etc. Cut and paste necessary information and/or print needed pages only (rather than whole reports). Avoid using cover sheets when sending facsimiles and "With compliments" slips when sending physical mail.
- Reuse envelopes, bags, etc. Make a space in your stationery store area for people to recycle them.
- Reuse paper that is unprinted on one side for in-house drafts, fax machines, photocopies.
- Establish a "Green Office" team or committee to implement longer-term and ongoing energy efficiency initiatives.
- Walk or cycle to work, or use public transport if possible.

Think about

1. What are your personal work habits? Do you turn off lights or equipment when not in use? Do you recycle paper or other recyclable resources? Do you use paper unnecessarily?

An environmentally sustainable workplace, however, is bigger than just your own workspace. It requires the resources, support and commitment of the entire organisation to fully succeed.

6.1.2 Identifying, measuring and documenting resource use

Identifying the resources used

Resources are all the things you need to do your job on a regular basis. They are the little things that you often take for granted and don't give any thought to, such as:

- paper products
- plastic products
- business equipment
- machinery of any kind
- toner and ink cartridges
- office furniture
- electricity
- chemicals for cleaning
- water usage.

These items can make an enormous difference not only to your organisation's cost efficiency but also to its carbon footprint. The more of these products or services you use, the more of them must be produced, using up yet more energy and natural resources.

Setting up **sustainability policies and procedures** requires a great deal of consideration and planning. Key questions in the initial process might include:

- Which resources are being used? (What are the inputs in terms of energy, water and materials?)
- Where do the resources come from?
- How are they being used?
- How many types of resources are being used?
- Where do they end up after use?
- How much of them is used, and how much does this cost?
- How much is wasted? (How much doesn't end up in the final product?)
- What are the organisational and environmental impacts of using these resources?
- Why is so much used/wasted?
- How efficient and/or effective are the resources currently being used?

- Are there any issues with the current resources?
- Can current resources be replaced by eco-friendly products that do the same job?
- Can the processes and procedures be amended to reduce or eliminate the need to use certain products altogether?
- What can you do to reduce the quantities used, the waste produced and the resulting environmental impact?
- How will you do this? (What is your action plan?)
- Has your action plan made an impact?

Your answers to these (and other) questions will provide you with basic information about your organisation's current use of resources, and will help you to make informed decisions about what, if any, changes you need to make to help ensure a sustainable environment.

Try this now

1. Apply these sustainability questions to your own work practices. How is your performance in terms of resource usage? Are you using them efficiently? Could you do better?

Recording and measuring resource usage

An organisation can track and monitor its use of resources by various means. For example:

- Software programs such as Excel can be used to record and measure resource use.
- Depending on the industry you work in, specialised technology can be used to measure such things as noise emissions and the efficiency of electrical equipment. This data can then be evaluated in terms of usage.
- Invoices from suppliers can be analysed to identify wasteful use of materials.
- Resource usage under different conditions can be measured to identify those times when more and fewer resources are used. For example, use of air conditioning would be higher in summer than in winter, using more energy and costing more money.
- Checklists used for work health and safety (WHS) and environmental audits can provide useful information.

Table 6.1 shows how an organisation might manage its office resources on a daily basis and keep continual track of how and where items are being used. For smooth business operations, they may have a threshold of how many of each product they should have on hand at any one time. Once the balance reaches, or goes below, that threshold, new supplies will be ordered. It is also a good way of examining which areas of the organisation are using specific resources and of determining if better methods, suppliers or items should be considered.

Table 6.1 Example of a stationery inventory register

Item	Taken by	Photocopy paper (boxes)	Plastic covers	Envelopes	Notepads	Pens
Threshold		**10**	**100**	**500**	**20**	**50**
In stock		**8**	**80**	**400**	**18**	**46**
12/4	Marketing	–3				
15/4	Sales	–2	–20	–100		
20/4	Accounts	–1		–100	–2	–4
... and so on.						
Balance		**2**	**60**	**200**	**16**	**42**

Table 6.2 shows how the resources were used over a longer period of time and allows you to see trends in resource usage. This, in turn, enables you to make informed decisions on sustainability issues.

An organisation will find this type of information extremely useful when the time comes to consider its work practices and the way it currently uses resources and to identify eco-friendly methods of working. For example, the first line of the spreadsheet shows that this company's use of photocopy paper has increased from 100 boxes in 2021, to 115 boxes in 2022, to 130 boxes in 2023. Over the three-year period being tracked, this amounts to 345 boxes of paper and a total cost of $10,962.50. This isn't just a substantial amount of money; it's a substantial amount of paper that may be being used unnecessarily. A review of the organisation's printing needs may identify alternative means of communicating, thereby saving money by using less paper and becoming more environmentally sustainable.

Table 6.2 Example of how an organisation can keep track of its resource usage

Items	2021			2022			2023			Total qty	Total cost ($)
	Qty	Unit ($)	Cost ($)	Qty	Unit ($)	Cost ($)	Qty	Unit ($)	Cost ($)		
Photocopy paper (boxes)	**100**	**30.00**	**3,000.00**	**115**	**32.50**	**3,737.50**	**130**	**32.50**	**4,225.00**	**345**	**10,962.50**
Toner cartridges	10	85.00	850.00	12	85.00	1,020.00	20	92.50	1,850.00	42	3,720.00
Pens	65	0.55	35.75	69	0.56	38.64	80	0.56	44.80	214	119.19
Notepads	120	1.20	144.00	131	1.25	163.75	135	1.27	171.45	386	479.20
Staples (boxes)	50	2.50	125.00	55	2.55	140.25	57	2.75	156.75	162	422.00
Paperclips (boxes)	70	2.95	206.50	68	3.10	210.80	72	3.15	226.80	210	644.10
Post-it notepads	200	1.10	220.00	250	1.15	287.50	255	1.15	293.25	705	800.75
Sticky tape	25	0.85	21.25	20	0.95	19.00	28	0.95	26.60	73	66.85
Manila folders	350	0.20	70.00	400	0.22	88.00	415	0.24	99.60	1,165	257.60
Lever arch files	100	2.50	250.00	115	3.00	345.00	110	3.10	341.00	325	936.00
Hanging indent files	210	0.55	115.50	200	0.65	130.00	215	0.75	161.25	625	406.75
Plastic sleeves (boxes)	30	20.00	600.00	25	22.50	562.50	28	23.85	667.80	83	1,830.30
Mailing labels (boxes)	20	25.00	500.00	21	28.95	607.95	25	29.55	738.75	66	1,846.70
Totals			**6,138.00**			**7,350.89**			**9,003.05**		**22,491.94**

Water and electricity usage should also be measured and documented regularly. The simplest method of doing this is to look at water and electricity bills, which provide information about current usage as well as (usually) a graph showing whether usage has increased or decreased over a given period.

Recording and filing information on resource usage can therefore be useful in identifying areas where improvements could be made.

Identifying resource deficiencies: The environmental audit

When examining current processes, procedures and resource usage with sustainability in mind, you are in effect conducting an **environmental audit** of the organisation. The purpose of such an audit is to identify resource deficiencies and assess areas that can be improved, by determining where the organisation is now, where it would like to be (in terms of environmental sustainability) and how to close the gap between the two.

An audit can be as basic as members of the team walking through the office, observing and reporting on how work is currently being carried out. For example, as a team member you might check to see if staff are following instructions and ensuring that equipment is left switched off when it isn't being used for long periods of time or after they have gone home. Or you might check what type of waste is being put into rubbish bins, or how often paper is being used on only one side. You might also look at current purchasing policies or talk to other staff about their ideas on sustainability.

However, an audit should, ideally, involve in-depth reviews of each area of the workplace, as follows:

- Look at tasks performed and determine if they are being done in the most effective, energy-efficient way.
- Determine how the organisation's activities might be affecting not only the workplace, but the environment generally.
- Assess the significance of the environmental impact the organisation is having and look at options for making improvements.

When conducting such an audit, it is a good idea to develop a checklist so that all workplace tasks and processes are reviewed regularly. Such a checklist can provide a picture, over time, of good and bad trends. An environmental audit checklist might look like the example in Figure 6.2.

Figure 6.2 Sample environmental audit

Audit area	Yes	No	Comment
Lights			
Lights are turned off in non-essential areas.			
Energy-efficient light bulbs are used in all areas.			
Excess light bulbs have been removed.			
Ventilation			
Windows are working.			
Fans have been checked and maintained.			
Air vents are clear of obstruction.			
Air conditioners are set to room temperature.			
Water			
Taps are checked regularly to ensure no drips.			
Taps are not left running needlessly.			
Dishwasher is set to economy wash setting.			
... and so on.			

Knowledge check

1. When exploring how best to integrate sustainability into the workplace, it is necessary to look at current practices and the resources used. List at least four issues you should consider.
2. You are responsible for participating in sustainability in your own role and work area. List at least six ways in which you can do this.
3. Setting up sustainability policies and procedures requires a great deal of consideration and planning. List at least six key questions that will help in the initial planning process.
4. Explain what methods you could use to measure and document resource usage.
5. Look at the resource usage in Table 6.2. List the three resources that this company uses the most. What sustainable alternatives could they use? Estimate how much money the company would save per year if it replaced these three items with sustainable resources.
6. When conducting a resource usage audit, there are a number of things that need to be considered. List three of these.

6.2 Supporting sustainable work practices

It is in the best interests of the organisation, the team and the community as a whole to support sustainable workplaces. Using resources efficiently means less wastage, reduced costs and less reliance on primary resources that provide fuel, energy and paper products, and this means a healthier community.

6.2.1 Identifying and complying with sustainability procedures

As with all other aspects of business operations, the environmental sustainability of an organisation will involve complying with organisational policies and procedures, as well as government and industry ones (as will be outlined). For example, internal policies may require an organisation to do the following:

- Provide guidance on how staff can meet relevant laws, by-laws and regulations or best practice. This could relate to international, Commonwealth, state/territory, local government or industry policies or procedures covering a range of issues.
- Design work plans and strategies to minimise waste or to increase efficient use of resources.
- Address environmental and resource sustainability initiatives such as environmental management systems, action plans, green office programs, surveys and audits.
- Determine the most appropriate waste treatment methods for the specific organisation (and in line with hazardous waste regulations).
- Appoint a staff member, or committee, to oversee the design, implementation and monitoring of a "green office" strategy for the organisation.
- Prevent or minimise environmental risks and hazards.
- Establish regular schedules for:
  - maintaining equipment in good working order so as not to waste energy
  - conducting resource usage audits to ensure resources are being used efficiently
  - conducting environmental/hazard identification audits to ensure the health and safety of both people and the environment.

Environmental Protection Acts and codes of practice

In Australia, various agencies (such as the Environment Protection Authority, or EPA) are responsible for overseeing and controlling a range of environmental factors, including such things as reducing our carbon footprint by managing waste. An important consideration in developing a sustainable workplace, then, is to be aware of any legal requirements that you may have to comply with. Environmental authorities in Australia include federal, state/territory and industry bodies. For example:

- *Australian Government, Department of Climate Change, Energy, the Environment and Water.* This body provides information about the *Environment Protection and Biodiversity Conservation Act 1999* (Cth) (EPBC Act). For full details of this Act, see http://www.dcceew.gov.au/environment/epbc.
- *State/territory Environment Protection Authority.* The EPA in each state/territory is responsible for regulating a wide range of activities and monitoring compliance with legislation and statutory instruments covering air emissions, noise, waste, water quality, forestry, contaminated sites, dangerous goods, hazardous materials and pesticides. For further information see:
  - Qld: www.des.qld.gov.au
  - NSW: www.epa.nsw.gov.au
  - Vic: www.epa.vic.gov.au
  - WA: www.epa.wa.gov.au
  - SA: www.epa.sa.gov.au
- *Industry bodies.* Depending on the industry you are in, there may be more—or less—stringent requirements for environmental protection and sustainability. For example:
  - When working in an insurance or accounts office, you may be encouraged to recycle paper or use power and water more efficiently.
  - In the construction industry (or one where hazardous substances are in use), you will have to comply with waste management policies and procedures, at the very least.

- Tourism has the potential to leave its mark, in a negative way, on natural attractions such as parks, forests and nature reserves. There are specific regulations that tourism operators must follow in order to minimise the environmental impact of tourism.

Think about

2. Think about your organisation's procedures for dealing with hazardous substances and the disposal of waste. How are such substances stored on your premises? How are they disposed of?

6.2.2 Identifying environmental hazards

An **environmental hazard** is any hazard that presents a danger to a surrounding environment. These dangers come in many forms and often go unnoticed until an accident occurs. The organisation and its employees should be aware of the types of hazards that can cause pollution or waste in the environment. These are outlined in Table 6.3.

Table 6.3 Common types of environmental hazards

Type of hazard	Notes
Air contaminants	Pollution in the air affects all living things. Organisations should have policies in place to ensure that any activities they carry out, such as manufacturing, are in compliance with legislation to ensure contaminants are not released into the air.
Noise	Noise is a pollutant, which you will know if you have ever been kept awake by neighbours playing loud music into the early morning. It can disrupt people's sleep, which can affect their ability to concentrate at work. Organisations need to monitor that any noise they make doesn't impact on neighbouring businesses and residents.
Stormwater waste	The water in our street drains flows directly into our lakes and oceans. Anything that is washed from the street by rain can therefore pollute the water that we—and our wildlife—drink and swim in. At work, then, you should be aware of anything that might pollute our waterways, including rubbish such as plastic bottles or cigarettes in the street, chemicals being used to clean driveways, and chemicals used when landscaping and gardening.
Dust	Dust can be harmful to humans and animals, when breathed, as well as to plants. It is common for dust to be created on construction sites, and in drilling and mining operations.
Waste	Waste is one of the most common types of environmental hazard for office-based organisations. The correct disposal of waste will be covered in more detail.

Hazardous waste regulations

The *Environment Protection and Biodiversity Conservation Act 1999* (Cth) (EPBC Act) enables the Australian Government to work with the states and territories to provide a truly national scheme of environment and heritage protection and biodiversity conservation. The objectives of the EPBC Act are to:

- provide for the protection of the environment, especially in matters of national environmental significance
- conserve Australian biodiversity
- provide a streamlined national environmental assessment and approvals process
- enhance the protection and management of important natural and cultural places
- control the international movement of plants and animals (wildlife), wildlife specimens and products made or derived from wildlife
- promote ecologically sustainable development through the conservation and ecologically sustainable use of natural resources

- recognise the role of Indigenous people in the conservation and ecologically sustainable use of Australia's biodiversity
- promote the use of Indigenous peoples' knowledge of biodiversity with the involvement of, and in cooperation with, the owners of the knowledge
- regulate the export and import of hazardous waste to ensure it is disposed of safely. (Australian Government 2022)

The Act defines waste as hazardous if it has properties that make it harmful to human health or the environment. For example, it could have irritant properties or be explosive, flammable, corrosive, oxidising or carcinogenic. Hazardous waste includes such things as:

- lead-acid batteries
- electrical equipment containing hazardous components, such as the cathode ray tubes in television sets
- solvent-based inks and paints
- waste oils
- pesticides
- acids
- some prescription medicines.

Waste disposal

Having determined whether a material you are disposing of is, indeed, "waste" and is hazardous, it must be disposed of correctly and in line with legal obligations. If an organisation produces hazardous waste, it must:

- comply with any disposal legislation applicable to its business and/or industry
- provide storage in appropriate secure, accessible containers
- inspect containers at least once a week
- train staff in the correct procedures for handling hazardous waste
- keep an inventory of stored hazardous waste
- ensure that handling and transportation are carried out only by registered or exempt waste carriers
- use consignment notes when hazardous waste is transported, and keep a copy on file as evidence that they have disposed of the waste in a proper manner
- ensure that recovery or disposal of waste is only carried out by firms authorised to do so.

Many hazardous products and substances come with a safety data sheet (SDS). **Safety data sheets** (previously known as "material safety data sheets") outline the properties of hazardous chemicals and how these can affect work health and safety (Figure 6.3). WHS regulations require the manufacturer or importer of a hazardous chemical to provide an SDS for all chemicals they produce or supply. The SDS should always be referred to when assessing risks in the workplace, as it contains information on:

- the identity of the chemical
- health and physicochemical hazards
- safe handling and storage procedures
- emergency procedures
- disposal considerations.

Figure 6.3 Sample safety data sheet

Safety data sheet	
Product name—Washwell	Heavy duty detergent
SDS issue date	1 February 2022
Product ID	1234
Company name	Kleenwell Pty Ltd Chemical Drive Keysborough VIC 3122 Phone: (03) 9768 1234
Ingredient	Sodium hydroxide (caustic soda)
Health hazards data Effects of exposure: Signs and symptoms of overexposure: First aid:	 Skin: concentrated solutions can be destructive to tissues, producing burns. Ingestion: can cause severe injury. Burns: skin, lungs, respiratory system disorders. Wash affected areas of skin with copious amounts of water. Obtain medical attention in all cases.
Handling and disposal Waste disposal methods: Handling and storage precautions:	 Dilute with copious amounts of water and dispose of according to federal, state and local regulations. Store in a dry area: keep container closed when not in use.
Fire and explosion hazard information Firefighting procedures: Unusual fire/explosion hazard:	 None required. Neutralisation with acids produces heat, sometimes violently.
Control measures Respiratory protection: Ventilation: Protective gloves: Eye protection: Work hygiene practices:	 None required. Local exhaust sufficient. Use recommended. Use recommended. Remove clothing; rinse thoroughly with water.
Physical/chemical properties Appearance and odour:	 Purple liquid with neutral odour.
Reactive data Materials to avoid:	 Strong acids.

6.2.3 Reporting hazards to the appropriate personnel

Understanding and identifying the various environmental hazards in your work area and taking the appropriate precautions will help prevent accidents, so it is an important part of any job role to report hazards to the relevant personnel in your organisation. In fact, in most cases it is important to report *any* issues, areas of concern or suggestions for improvement to the relevant people. These people might include the following:

- *Business owner or manager*—who has overall responsibility for the organisation, its policies and procedures, and will need to approve any changes and their associated budgets.
- *First aid officer*—who will need to be informed immediately if a hazard has caused harm to any person.
- *Human resources personnel*—who keep track of individual personnel issues and concerns.
- *Supervisor*—who is in charge of your specific work area and is directly responsible for your welfare.
- *WHS officer*—who must always be informed of any inadequacies in the WHS procedures, or breaches of legislation (see the next section), so they can take the necessary action to avoid future issues.

Any reports you make should be clear and concise, and provide accurate information on the nature of the hazard and where/when it was identified.

6.2.4 Reporting breaches to appropriate personnel

As you have learnt, compliance with regulations isn't just a matter of working to your organisation's rules but could be a matter of legal obligation. No organisation is ever completely free of workplace hazards; things can—and do—go wrong. As such, it is in everyone's best interest to keep an eye on any issues or areas of concern, as breaches of legal and organisational obligations could result in:

- harm being done to a person or persons
- damage being done to property or premises
- damage being done to the environment and the surrounding community
- legal action being taken against you and/or your organisation for non-compliance.

For this reason, it is important to be aware of what is going on in the workplace around you and to report any breaches of policy or procedure to the relevant supervisor, manager or person responsible for a given area. A breach can be reported by:

- discussing it directly with the person responsible for dealing with the issue
- sending an email to the relevant person
- discussing the breach during staff meetings
- discussing it during a meeting set up specifically to deal with continuous improvement
- completing the relevant documentation, such as incident forms or risk/hazard identification forms (as shown in Figure 6.4).

Figure 6.4 Example of a risk/hazard identification and action form

Risk/hazard identification and action form	
Staff name: Sabreen Hussain	**Date:** 30/5/2023
Department: Administration	
Non-conformance/complaint: Cleaning liquids are not properly stored or labelled. Jill Anderson went into the storeroom this morning and was overcome by fumes. She subsequently had difficulty breathing and was taken to the local hospital. She is now in a satisfactory condition. Steps need to be taken to ensure that hazardous substances are handled and stored correctly in order to avoid similar future incidents.	
Positive action taken by (company name): Short-term solution The cleaning room door has been locked and no unauthorised personnel are to be admitted. Liquid cleaner has been properly stored.	
Preventative action: Long-term solution ■ Staff to be trained in risk and hazard identification and management. ■ All hazardous substances to be labelled on delivery and checked to ensure they are in appropriate containers. ■ No unauthorised (and untrained) staff to be admitted to areas where hazardous substances are kept.	
Follow-up action 31/5/2023 Alan Barker to set up training session. 5/6/2023 Alan Barker to run training session. 15/6/2023 WHS Committee to review and amend policies and procedures.	
Staff signature: Sabreen Hussain	**Supervisor signature:** Alan Barker
Director signature: Ken Ng	

Knowledge check

7. Give at least five examples of things that would be considered environmental hazards in a workplace.
8. List the steps in hazard identification and risk evaluation.
9. Explain the purpose of identifying and assessing risks in the workplace.
10. Describe the objectives of the *Environment Protection and Biodiversity Conservation Act 1999* (Cth).

11. If a company produces hazardous waste, explain the steps they must take in storing and disposing of it.
12. In establishing a sustainable workplace, an organisation must provide guidance to staff on what they are expected to do. List at least four organisational policies and/or procedures they might use to provide such guidance.
13. Explain why it is important to report any breaches of organisational procedures or legislative requirements to the appropriate personnel.
14. When reporting hazards in the workplace, it is very important to advise the appropriate personnel. List who these people might be and briefly describe why they need to be informed.
15. You are in your work lunch-break area and have just noticed that the cord to the coffee vending machine is frayed at the power point and the power point itself looks slightly blackened. Complete a risk and hazard identification form like that in Figure 6.3. Explain who you would report this to, and why.

6.3 Seeking opportunities to improve sustainable work practices

All businesses should strive to continually improve the way they operate. If systems and processes are reviewed on a regular basis, this leads to better efficiency, greater productivity, improved cost control and a more sustainable work environment.

6.3.1 Benefits of sustainable work practices

When sustainability practices are introduced into a workplace, there will be a range of benefits for the organisation. For example:

- Reusing and/or recycling materials can reduce its operating costs.

  Its image as an environmentally friendly business will attract customers who want to support, and buy products and services from enterprises that are actively trying to reduce their impact on the planet. Corporate social responsibility research by Cone Communications (2015) suggests that as many as 91 per cent of millennials (those born between 1981 and 1996) would switch to using a company or brand based on its commitment to values such as sustainability.
- It can create a culture that attracts and retains staff members who are also concerned about sustainability matters and are committed to reducing waste in all their work practices.

6.3.2 Identifying areas for improvement

In order for improvements to work policies and procedures to be fully effective, many organisations will put in place continuous improvement programs. These programs allow for the ongoing review and evaluation of the organisation and its work practices to ensure that it is functioning optimally. Plans such as these can take considerable time and effort to develop, so it is important that all staff follow all instructions given in the implementation of improved environmental practices.

Working with colleagues to identify and assess potential improvements

In any work environment, opportunities will exist for staff to contribute to the continuous improvement of the organisation. Often you will work with teams of people in specific departments or areas of the business, which will mean that you—and your colleagues—will have a very good idea of how procedures and processes *actually* work, as opposed to how management thinks they *should* work. Wherever an opportunity for improvement is identified, colleagues from different areas of the organisation should be consulted to ensure that any procedures or products introduced are considered from all angles.

Based on the results of resource usage and environmental audits, you and your colleagues may have come up with a range of ideas and suggestions that can help to:

- improve energy efficiency
- increase use of renewable, recyclable, reusable and recoverable resources
- maximise opportunities such as use of solar power or other alternative forms of energy, where appropriate
- prevent and minimise risks
- reduce emissions of greenhouse gases
- reduce the use of non-renewable resources
- develop policies and procedures that outline:
    - sustainability guidelines for staff to follow
    - improved work practices
    - changes in resource suppliers and how these should be used efficiently
- produce work plans that minimise waste or increase efficiency of resources. The following are examples of such a work plan:
    - A *Green Office program* (see next section) enables functions that previously required manual/paper handling to now be accomplished electronically. A regular review of work procedures can often highlight functions that could be carried out more efficiently.
    - A *supply chain program for purchasing alternative products* can be an excellent way to reduce expenditure and improve sustainability. An organisation can waste money and resources simply by continuing to use the same materials and suppliers they have always used, without researching if there are better services and products available.
    - An *environmental management framework*, which consists of taking institutional measures to mitigate and monitor sustainability practices within the organisation.

6.3.3 Suggesting improvements to work practices in your own area

Everyone within an organisation will have ideas on how the workplace can be improved. This applies equally to sustainability measures that could be introduced. One of the most effective methods is to initiate a "Green Office" program.

"Green Office" program

Another way to minimise waste and contribute to sustaining our natural resources is to follow the 5 Rs. The 5 Rs is a hierarchy of actions you can follow in the workplace and at home to significantly reduce waste in the environment. You should always start at the top of the hierarchy, *Refuse*, and work your way down, as shown in Figure 6.5. Recycling is the last resort after all the other steps have been taken.

Figure 6.5 The 5 Rs hierarchy

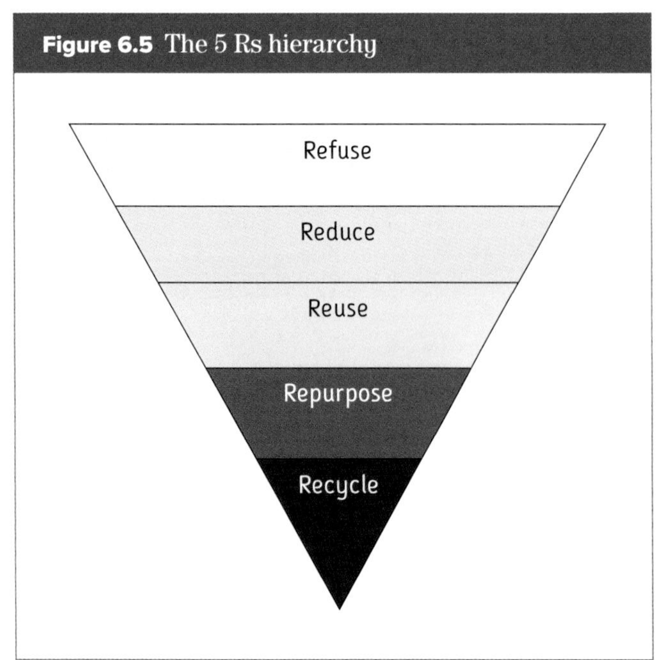

Step 1: Refuse

This step simply means refusing to use a product or material that will end up in the rubbish or recycling without having been of much use. A simple example of this at home is taking your own reusable bags to the shops and refusing the plastic bags offered by merchants. At work, for example, you can *refuse* by opting out of mailing lists so that you don't receive junk mail, or by stocking the staff kitchen with reusable cutlery and plates, instead of single-use plastic.

Step 2: Reduce

Reduce the amount of office waste by determining where the most paper is used. Practices that use a lot of paper include the production of numerous drafts of long documents or sending a personal copy of staff notices to each individual staff member, instead of circulating one copy to each section or work unit.

Before you print a document, consider whether it could be shared via email instead. Use online (versus hard copy) versions of documents such as annual reports and information memorandums. Cut and paste necessary information and/or print needed pages only (rather than whole reports).

Where a paper-based document *must* be presented, many organisations circulate one copy to a list of staff in order of priority. When the first person on the circulation list has read the document, they pass it on to the next person on the list. Figure 6.6 shows an example of a circulation slip, which is usually stapled to the front of the document to be circulated.

Figure 6.6 Example of a circulation slip that can be attached to a document

Circulate to:		
☐	Tariq Anwar	CEO
☐	Ji Hun Lee	Marketing
☐	Alan Clarke	Accounts
☐	Aaliyah Hassan	Sales
☐	Andrew Cole	Administration
☐	Mei Wong	Operations
Date received: 15/12/2023		

Step 3: Reuse

Reusing items in the office, rather than buying new ones, is another easy practice to introduce. The reverse side of paper that's already printed on can be used for writing drafts, as fax cover sheets or notepaper, and so on. You can also reuse old file folders, binders, bottles, envelopes, bags, and other items. Make a space in your stationery store area for people to place items that can be reused.

Other ways of reusing resources include:

- repairing broken items instead of buying new ones
- using refillable ink cartridges instead of disposable ones
- donating or reselling items the office no longer needs, instead of throwing them out.

Step 4: Repurpose

Also known as upcycling, "repurposing" means using an item for a different purpose than it was intended for. Examples of this at work include:

- using paper that is printed on one side for scrap paper or notes
- storing pens and pencils in tin cans or glass jars
- using binder clips to organise power cords and computer cables
- offering unused paper, pencils and pens to staff who have children, for use in craft projects.

Repurposing requires some creativity, but it can be fun!

Step 5: Recycle

If you have worked through the **hierarchy** and your item cannot be refused, reduced, reused or repurposed, recycling is your next best option. When a piece of paper or plastic can no longer be reused, it can be recycled. Many offices have recycling bins for cans, glass and paper products.

Every year, Australians throw away more than 18 million laser toner and inkjet cartridges, photocopier toner bottles and drums that will eventually end up in landfill. This amounts to more than 5,000 tonnes of material (Cartridge World 2022). Programs have been developed to help alleviate this problem—most notably "Planet Ark" (see www.planetark.org). By taking part in this program, you can make an enormous impact on our environment. All of these items are upcycled or reused in new applications. Even residue toner is reused as pigment for colouring plastic products.

Knowledge check

16. Describe the advantages of continuous improvement in the workplace.

17. Explain why consultation with colleagues is important when discussing potential improvements.

18. List at least three reasons why it is a good idea to introduce sustainable practices into the workplace.

Summary

Sustainability is an important issue in anyone's language. We all have a responsibility to ensure that the Earth's resources, both natural and man-made, will last and thrive into the future.

Sustainability in the workplace can begin by reviewing the type of resources you are currently using and looking for alternative products. It can also include looking at your actual work processes to see if there are better, more energy-efficient, means of carrying out the various tasks that need to be completed. Work practices that are sustainable can contribute not only to the natural environment but may also benefit the morale of an organisation's staff, its reputation and even its profitability.

By instigating just a few simple measures, we can all contribute to a better future.

References

Australian Government, 2022. Department of Climate Change, Energy, the Environment and Water, "About the EPBC Act", https://www.dcceew.gov.au/environment/epbc/about, accessed 11 October 2022.

Cartridge World, 2022. *Everything You Need to Know About Recycling Printer Cartridges*, https://www.cartridgeworld.com.au/blog/everything-you-need-to-know-about-recycling-printer-cartridges, accessed October 2022.

Cone Communications, 2015. *Cone Communications Millennial CSR Study*, https://www.conecomm.com/research-blog/2015-cone-communications-millennial-csr-study, accessed September 2022.

PART 2

CHAPTER 7

Maintain business resources

Learning outcomes

7.1 Advise on resource requirements

7.2 Acquire resources

7.3 Monitor resource usage and maintenance

In addition to looking after its customers and clients, an organisation needs to look after its resources in order to continue to run smoothly. Managing an organisation's resource needs means:

- monitoring resource usage
- managing budgets
- reviewing the need for resources
- controlling waste
- using technology effectively and safely
- obtaining the best value for money
- keeping stock levels under control.

Everyone in the organisation needs resources, and work can grind to a halt if insufficient stocks are on hand. This can decrease the organisation's efficiency, productivity and profit.

7.1 Advising on resource requirements

The resources that an organisation uses in its day-to-day operations are an expense that cannot be recovered directly through sales to customers. However, they are necessary so that the organisation can function efficiently.

As an administrator or receptionist, it may be part of your role to monitor the resource needs of your organisation. This will require you to ensure that the necessary resources are always on hand, while considering the cost involved in providing these items. This means you also need to ensure that the resources you purchase on behalf of your organisation are used as efficiently as possible and that there is minimal waste.

Depending on the size of the organisation you work for, and its processes, managing resources might be as simple as putting in a stationery request every so often when the stationery cupboard looks bare. In other instances, however, there may be budgetary considerations that make it necessary to monitor how resources are being used, in order to reduce costs, or to estimate the organisation's annual resource expenditure. It is this area of resource management that we will address in this chapter.

7.1.1 What are business resources?

Business resources are all those things that you need in order to conduct business—that is, to perform work tasks. They can take the following forms (see Figure 7.1):

- *Human resources*. No business can operate without people to perform the various tasks. People are an organisation's most valuable resource.
- *Capital resources*. These are normally large and/or very expensive items such as furniture, business vehicles, large items of machinery, and equipment such as photocopiers, telephone systems, and so on. Capital resources are items that don't need regular replacement and are expected to last for many years.
- *Business equipment*. These resources are less permanent than capital items and are often replaced annually, or at least within a few years. They include computers, printers, scanners, fax machines, computer software, digital cameras, and so on.
- *Consumables*. These are the items we use (and use up) on a daily basis. They can be of three types:
  - Raw materials, stocks and supplies, that is items used either to manufacture or to stock products sold by your organisation.
  - Equipment consumables, such as ink and toner cartridges for printers and photocopiers, batteries for small appliances such as digital cameras, USB drives and memory cards.
  - Stationery items, such as copy or printing paper, letterhead paper, envelopes, pens and pencils, staples/staplers and paperclips.

7.1.2 Calculating current and future resource requirements

Determining the resource needs of an organisation requires careful planning and an understanding of how, where and when those resources are used—and by whom. This means that a certain amount of research needs to be done in order to forecast, with any accuracy, what your needs might be for the foreseeable future. For the planning of business expense purposes, **forecasting** means predicting how many of each item you will need to buy for the coming year. This process enables the organisation's management to set its budgets by calculating its expenses in each area of the business and how much income it therefore needs to generate to cover those expenses.

A well-organised administration system will monitor and keep statistics on the use of resources over time. These statistics are a vital part of the forecast process, as they allow you to determine trends and patterns over time and can therefore give you a fairly accurate idea of what future needs might be. For example, Table 7.1 shows a number of columns listing various resource items. For each year shown, the table gives the quantity used, the cost per unit and the total cost. It also shows the total number of each item ordered and the amount spent over the period of the analysis, which in this case is three years but could be much longer.

Figure 7.1 Four types of business resources

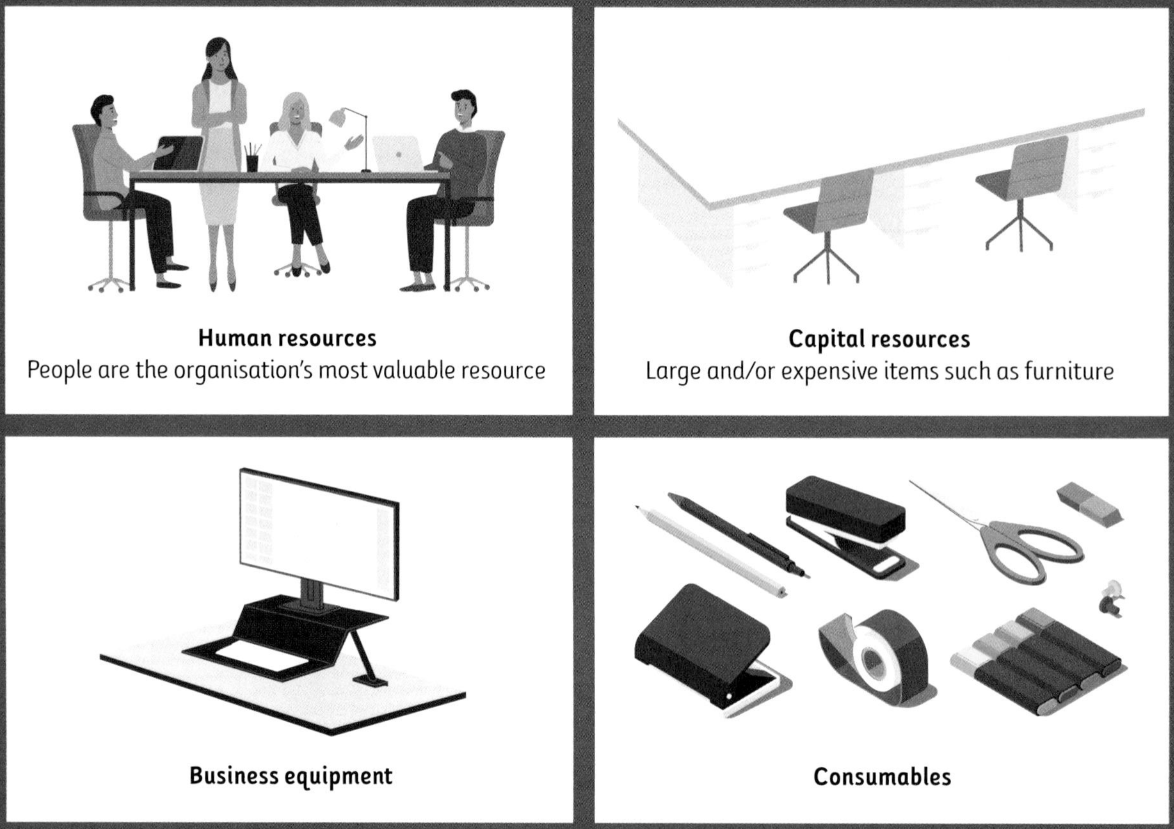

Human resources
People are the organisation's most valuable resource

Capital resources
Large and/or expensive items such as furniture

Business equipment

Consumables

robuart/Shutterstock

Table 7.1 Example of resource analysis sheet showing usage and costs

Items	2021			2022			2023			Total qty	Total cost ($)
	Qty	Unit ($)	Cost ($)	Qty	Unit ($)	Cost ($)	Qty	Unit ($)	Cost ($)		
Photocopy paper (boxes)	**100**	**30.00**	**3,000.00**	**115**	**32.50**	**3,737.50**	**130**	**32.50**	**4,225.00**	**345**	**10,962.50**
Toner cartridges	10	85.00	850.00	12	85.00	1,020.00	20	92.50	1,850.00	42	3,720.00
Pens	65	0.55	35.75	69	0.56	38.64	80	0.56	44.80	214	119.19
Notepads	120	1.20	144.00	131	1.25	163.75	135	1.27	171.45	386	479.20
Staples (boxes)	50	2.50	125.00	55	2.55	140.25	57	2.75	156.75	162	422.00
Paperclips (boxes)	70	2.95	206.50	68	3.10	210.80	72	3.15	226.80	210	644.10
Sticky notes	200	1.10	220.00	250	1.15	287.50	255	1.15	293.25	705	800.75
Sticky tape	25	0.85	21.25	20	0.95	19.00	28	0.95	26.60	73	66.85
Manila folders	**350**	**0.20**	**70.00**	**400**	**0.22**	**88.00**	**415**	**0.24**	**99.60**	**1,165**	**257.60**
Lever arch files	100	2.50	250.00	115	3.00	345.00	110	3.10	341.00	325	936.00
Hanging indent files	**210**	**0.55**	**115.50**	**200**	**0.65**	**130.00**	**215**	**0.75**	**161.25**	**625**	**406.75**
Plastic sleeves (boxes)	30	20.00	600.00	25	22.50	562.50	28	23.85	667.80	83	1,830.30
Mailing labels (boxes)	20	25.00	500.00	21	28.95	607.95	25	29.55	738.75	66	1,846.70
Totals			**6,138.00**			**7,350.89**			**9,003.05**		**22,491.94**

Let's take the photocopy paper figures from Table 7.1 as an example. The amount ordered and spent each year has increased. In the coming year, the organisation will be introducing a new procedure whereby promotional materials will be produced in-house by the marketing department rather than being sent out externally to be printed. This means that the quantity of copy paper used will increase considerably, which will need to be taken into consideration when setting the requirements and budgets for the year to come. The increase in paper use will also have a flow-on effect, as using more paper means using more toner, so this, too, will have to be factored into future budgets. On the other hand, the organisation is moving to an electronic document management system, which means that the majority of its files will be stored in computers rather than filing cabinets. This will reduce the need for manila folders and hanging indent files, so the quantity of these required to be purchased for the next year will decrease.

There are a number of things to consider when forecasting future resource needs. If the organisation has used more of certain items in some years, and less in others, you will need to look at the reasons for the shift in numbers. For example:

- Has the company grown?
- Are there more staff?
- Were there specific projects or campaigns that accounted for the fluctuation in numbers?
- Did the organisation change suppliers?
- Did the suppliers' cost structures change?
- Did the organisation's peaks and troughs change? If so, why?
- Did the organisation change or introduce new procedures?

The answers to these questions, among others, will give you a full understanding of the organisation's *past* resource requirements and help you to determine its *future* needs.

Having looked at past figures, you now need to estimate what you will need in the coming year. You do this by:

- taking past data into consideration
- looking at upcoming promotional campaigns and projects
- factoring in any changes the organisation is planning to make in the coming year that will affect its work output
- identifying any new industry trends that might affect peak and trough periods
- checking with suppliers about next year's prices.

When all of this is done, you should have sufficient information to estimate the coming year's requirements and can set up a budget accordingly.

Try this now

1. Make a list of the stationery items you use. For the next month, keep track of how many of each item you use, why you need to use it and how much it cost. Calculate the overall cost of what you used up during that month.

Organisational and legal requirements

Business resources can be more than just stationery items. Therefore, in addition to looking at all of the issues discussed, you have to consider internal organisational requirements that may extend to how business equipment is used, how organisational goals will be met through efficient use of resources, and communication channels and protocols. (**Protocols** are organisational guidelines that stipulate the manner in which communication should occur between staff members at different levels.) In addition, there will be legal requirements to consider.

Organisational and legal requirements could include the following:

- *Access and equity principles and practice*. It is against the law in Australia to discriminate against anyone due to their gender, religion, race and age (among other things). This means that all staff must have equal access to the resources provided. Allowances may therefore need to be made, when determining resource needs, for staff with language, literacy or numeracy difficulties, or who may have physical or mental impairments.

- *Business and performance plans.* Any decisions made about resource requirements must be in line with the organisation's overall **business strategies** for its future. This might mean ensuring that all expenses are kept to a minimum so as to reduce costs, and that all necessary resources are always available when needed, so that goals and objectives can be met and systems and processes can flow smoothly.
- *Defined resource parameters.* The organisation you work for may have set policies and procedures in place for dealing with resources. For example, there may be:
    - a given quality standard that will impact on the cost of the resource
    - a minimum threshold for each item which, when reached, will trigger an order for replacement items
    - minimum or maximum numbers allowed to be kept onsite at any one time
    - specified suppliers from whom you order resources
    - a sustainability requirement, where resources are to be ordered from environmentally friendly suppliers and used resources are to be recycled or reused.
- *Legal and organisational policies, guidelines and requirements.* The use and care of resources may have to comply with legislative or organisational policies or procedures. For example:
    - In some industries, it may be necessary to use chemicals or other substances that are toxic or otherwise hazardous to a person's health. In such cases, these resources must be handled and stored in strict accordance with the manufacturer's instructions and in line with legislative and organisational guidelines. Failure to do so could result in serious harm or injury to persons and could lead to legal prosecution.
    - The food industry is subject to strict hygiene regulations. As such, there will be specific legislation with regard to food storage. Again, failure to abide by these regulations could result in serious penalties and potential illness or harm to customers.
- *Work health and safety (WHS) policies, procedures and programs.* At all times, the health, safety and security of staff and customers must be considered. When determining resource requirements, you should therefore keep WHS issues in mind. This might include ensuring that:
    - harmful or hazardous items are transported, handled and stored correctly
    - resources are stored in such a way as not to cause harm due to slips, spills and falls
    - correct manual handling procedures are followed when moving heavy items into or out of storage areas.
- *Security and confidentiality issues.* Privacy and confidentiality is an extremely important issue. Information about what the organisation is doing, what its policies are, who its customers are, and so on, is considered to be confidential information and should not be discussed with people outside the organisation. All documents written and received by you and/or your organisation are also confidential and should not be shared with persons outside the organisation unless specifically designed for public information. A breach of an organisation's confidentiality policies could be grounds for instant dismissal from your position.
- *Management and accountability channels.* When determining your organisation's resource needs, you must also always bear **accountability** in mind. While you may be responsible for ordering and managing certain resources within the organisation, the authority to access budgets and make final decisions on the ordering process and resource requirements may, ultimately, rest with those in higher positions. You will need to liaise with these people throughout the forecasting and decision-making process to ensure that the best possible options and quantities are chosen for the future.
- *Quality and continuous improvement processes and standards.* Looking for ways in which to improve business processes should be standard operating procedure for all organisations. With technological changes happening almost daily and rising sustainability issues, it is in every organisation's interest to be continually reviewing its resource usage and business maintenance

systems and setting quality assurance standards for any resources it uses. While the cost of acquiring resources is certainly an important factor, so too is ensuring the best possible quality. While high-quality items may cost more than cheap items in the short term, they are more likely to last longer and so may prove more economical in the long term.

7.1.3 Providing advice on resources, equipment needs and supplier selection

Having researched and determined the organisation's resource requirements, you will need to provide this information to the relevant staff. Supervisors or managers will make decisions based on your information that will have an impact on the organisation as a whole. Therefore, your report should:

- be clear and concise, outlining exactly what resources are required and why
- show how your resource recommendations address organisational requirements and/or take into consideration new trends or organisational plans, goals or objectives
- provide comparisons to show which materials and suppliers are the most economical and effective choices.

Be sure that you are certain of your facts and recommendations, as you may be asked to justify them.

The impact of resource shortages

Ensuring that there is always an adequate supply of consumables or other resources on hand is extremely important. Often, in an organisation, there will be projects to complete in order for a business commitment to be met. For example, a large print or photocopy job may be called for where the copies are needed for a customer's upcoming event or meeting. If the copies aren't ready on time, this can lead not only to embarrassment on your organisation's part but also to a loss of reputation and the potential loss of business. This is particularly unfortunate if the deadline was missed due to the lack of necessary resources such as copy paper or toner cartridge, as such a situation is entirely avoidable with proper planning.

It is also very important to ensure that all equipment is maintained regularly, as breakdowns can seriously impact an organisation's workflow and productivity. Some industries and/or organisations rely completely on machines to manufacture or process their products, so breakdowns can mean serious financial losses and, potentially, a loss of reputation. Most organisations today rely on computers to capture information, process payments and much more; therefore, a breakdown in computer systems can stop an organisation in its tracks.

The failure of a computer or other piece of equipment in your workplace can cause problems that could take a substantial amount of time to fix, in the meantime halting work and decreasing productivity while staff wait for the problem to be resolved.

Knowledge check

1. Explain why it is important to accurately calculate organisational resource requirements.
2. List at least six things that are important to consider when calculating current, and estimating future, resource requirements.
3. Explain why it is important to observe organisational and legislative requirements when handling and storing resources. Give examples of when these requirements might apply.
4. Describe issues you should consider when providing advice on resources, equipment needs and supplier selection.
5. Describe how the shortage of necessary resources could impact on an organisation.
6. When providing advice on supplier selection, what specific things should you consider?

7.2 Acquiring resources

For a business to function smoothly and efficiently, it is important that resources are available when they are needed, that they represent the best value for money, and that they are in line with the organisation's actual requirements so that there is no wastage or loss of productivity. How resources are acquired will vary from one organisation to another; in general, however, all organisations follow a similar procedure, as we will see in this section.

7.2.1 Obtaining and storing resources

Depending on the size of an organisation, the acquisition of resources could be a fairly simple process, with individual staff members verbally letting the person who is responsible for ordering stocks know what they need. It could also be a more complex procedure that requires individuals or departments to complete an internal stationery order form that outlines what they require, their department name (or code), and their budget code (so that the goods can be charged to their budget). The form could be paper based or an online form that automatically calculates costs and tracks the individual items ordered and used. The information contained in the order form is transferred to whatever tracking method the organisation uses, whether a spreadsheet or a database. A paper copy of the order might be filed so that, in the event of an error or a dispute, the original is available for checking the exact details of the order.

Figure 7.2 shows an example of a typical in-house stationery order form. It indicates the department making the order, the name of the person requesting it and the date. It then notes the items requested, the cost per unit and the total cost (if known).

Many companies allocate specific budgets to individual departments. If this is the case, the stationery form, as indicated at the bottom of Figure 7.2, would have a space to show the department's budget code. This is important, as the value of the resources requested will be deducted from that department's budget once the goods have been handed over to them.

Figure 7.2 Example of a stationery order form

Stationery order form to be handed into Administration			
Department:	Marketing		
Requested by:	Asuka Sato		
Date:	20/6/23		
Qty	**Description**	**Per unit ($)**	**Total ($)**
1 box	Mailing labels	25.00	25.00
5 reams	Yellow copy paper	15.00	75.00
3 boxes	Large paperclips	2.50	7.50
	Total		**107.50**
Authorising officer: Ricky Lee Jones	**Budget allocation:** MKT 5820		
Signature: Ricky Lee Jones			

If the requested items are in stock, the stationery clerk disburses them to the department or individual and records the transaction accordingly. If stocks are low and an order must be placed with a supplier, many organisations will require a **purchase order** (as shown in Figure 7.3) to be issued.

Figure 7.3 Example of a purchase order

Purchase order				
		Acme Advertising Company PO Box 789 Springfield NSW 2888 Ph: (02) 9988 7766 Fax: (02) 99887755	**Date:** 24/6/23 **Purchase order:** 28762	
To:	Pacific Stationery Supplies			
Address	24/4567 Pacific Highway, Alstonville			
Phone:	(02) 9234 5678			
Fax:	(02) 9234 8765			
Email:	sales@pacificstationerysupplies.com.au			
Cat. no.	**Qty**	**Description**	**Per unit ($)**	**Total ($)**
001	4 boxes	Mailing labels	25.00	100.00
298	5 reams	Yellow copy paper	15.00	75.00
323	10 boxes	Large paperclips	2.50	25.00
7869	5 boxes	Plastic sleeves	10.00	50.00
541	3	Plastic in-trays	4.50	13.50
664	50	Manila folders	0.55	27.50
		Total		**291.00**

Order requested by: Gabriella Garcia **Department:** Administration	**Budget allocation** To be allocated upon disbursement to individual departments
Authorising officer: Janice Ian	**Signature:** Janice Ian

Organisational acquisition considerations

When ordering supplies, it is always important to keep in mind the organisation's set budget for these resources, the time frames involved in delivery, and how the items will then be stored.

Budgets

Organisational expenditure is carefully calculated for each area of the organisation, so adhering to these resource budgets is extremely important in ensuring its success. Should it become clear during the year that the budget is becoming "stretched", then the person responsible should take steps to ensure that it won't be exceeded. Methods of doing this could include:

- exerting tighter control over resource disbursement
- rationing the remaining budget over the number of months left in the year
- finding alternative products and procedures (e.g. recycling and reusing resources)
- finding cheaper products.

It is expected that, at the end of the year, this budget won't have been exceeded. If, however, you find yourself running short of funds early, there are a number of questions that management will ask:

- Was there any unnecessary ordering?
- Was there any waste?
- Did the organisation have any unanticipated usage issues, such as unexpected promotional opportunities that needed extra resources?
- Was the business equipment maintained according to schedule?

These are important questions, as any expenditure that exceeds the set budgets can upset the delicate balance between an organisation's income and expenses and can mean the difference between making a profit or suffering a loss.

Time frames

This is another extremely important aspect of managing resources. If a large photocopy job is to be undertaken and stocks of copy paper are low, it isn't practical to order the paper on the day it is required. The forecasting process discussed earlier involves looking at usage over the entire year and anticipating times of high and low use to ensure that sufficient supplies are in stock whenever they are needed.

Storing resources

After orders have been delivered by suppliers and checked against the delivery statement, they must be stored. Every organisation has its own way of doing this. Some have a central area where stocks are stored. Depending on the size of the organisation, this can consist of a stationery cupboard or shelf, a room or, indeed, a warehouse. In organisations where each individual department is responsible for ordering and storing its own stocks, each department would have a stationery cupboard or area.

A strict control needs to be exercised over access to and distribution of these stored resources. Providing general access to anyone who wishes to take things from the inventory will lead to a loss of control. This means that:

- stocks could run low without the responsible person being aware
- items are wasted
- **productivity** is reduced and revenue is lost while waiting for urgently needed items to be replaced
- there is no way to track who is using what, and when
- the budget is exceeded.

For these reasons, storage and distribution of resources must be strictly supervised. Depending on the nature of the organisation, you may also need to consider WHS and other issues when storing goods received. For example:

- Toxic chemicals used for cleaning, or for operational purposes, must be stored safely. They must be:
  - clearly labelled
  - stored in appropriate containers
  - kept out of general staff areas
  - carry warning signs where appropriate.
- Heavy items should be stored in such a way that they cannot fall and cause injury.
- Shelving systems need to be sturdy so they cannot topple and cause injury.
- Perishable items (such as food products) must be stored according to temperature and hygiene guidelines to avoid spoilage or contamination.

Think about

1. How does the ordering process happen in your organisation? Does each department have its own budget, or is there a central one? Is there only one person responsible for ordering resources, or are there many? What system is used for ordering—paper-based or electronic? Who has the authority to sign off on purchases?

7.2.2 Reviewing the acquisition process

At regular intervals, and at least annually, the purchasing procedures should be reviewed to ensure that:

- resources are being utilised effectively
- the process is working efficiently
- the organisation is getting the best value for its money
- the suppliers are living up to their agreement
- supplies are being delivered on time and in full
- after-sales service received from suppliers is of a consistently high standard.

As the world of business changes, so too should the processes and procedures that enable an organisation to operate. For example, the introduction of the internet has allowed purchases to be made online, saving time, effort and money. Therefore, it is important that an organisation's processes and procedures are reviewed on a regular basis.

In addition to experiencing peaks and troughs that impact on what items they need, and when, organisations are subject to major changes in trends, technologies used, and more. Changes of this nature may require a change in an organisation's procedure and in the resources needed to accommodate those changes. Discussions about new processes, and about their potential or actual impact on individual areas of the organisation, with the people directly involved will give an accurate picture of what resources might be needed in future. Relevant staff could include the following:

- *Colleagues*—the people who work with and on the same level as you. They are often the ones using the resources and they will know what works and what doesn't.
- *Supervisors*—the people who have an overall picture of their particular area of the organisation, whether they are responsible for an entire work team, section or department. They will have a good understanding not only of what resources are required to get the jobs within their area done, but also of budgetary requirements and restrictions.
- *Managers*—the people within the organisation who have a "big picture" view. They are aware of how each department fits within the entire group, and of how the requirements of each area impact on the whole. They will be the people who make the final decisions about what capital items are purchased, and what procedures and processes will be introduced. Therefore, they are responsible for setting the parameters of what the organisation should purchase and how much should be spent.

What should be reviewed?

Resource acquisition processes that may need to be reviewed can include the following:

- *Contracted supplier ordering.* Choosing a supplier is an extremely important part of resource acquisition and management. It is vital that your supplier:
  - carries all the items you need (or as many as practical)
  - can deliver supplies in a timely manner
  - is reliable
  - offers competitive pricing
  - offers excellent customer service, and so on.

  The period of time for the supply contract can vary from one to three years as a rule, but it could be longer. When choosing who will win an organisation's business, things to consider include:

  - price
  - quality
  - service

- product range
- ability to deliver on time
- payment terms, and so on.

The supplier who makes the best overall offer will normally win the contract.

- *Internal approvals.* This is a matter of assessing who has, or should have, authority to approve any purchases that are made. The decision will vary according to the nature of the resource to be acquired. For example, the recruitment of new staff may need to be approved by the company director and/or the human resource (HR) manager, whereas purchases of stationery items may need to be approved by the administration supervisor. This will depend entirely on the size and complexity of the organisation.
- *Tendered processes.* In the **tender** process, notification is sent out, by letter or open advertisement in the newspaper, that an organisation is looking for suppliers for certain aspects of its business. Interested suppliers will then submit their offer, which will outline:
  - what services or products they can offer the organisation
  - what discounts or bonuses they will provide
  - the terms and conditions under which the offer is made.

  In order to be able to make these offers, the amount of money an organisation expects to earn must be viable. For this reason, tenders are mostly restricted to large companies.
- *Non-tendered processes.* This is a much less formal process than opening the business to tender. In this instance, the organisation might approach, or be approached by, a local supplier. They might go to a trade show or see advertisements for services they require. The organisation will usually advise a supplier of their needs and negotiations then begin between the parties to secure the best outcome for both.

This section has highlighted that the acquisition of resources is a serious business that should be undertaken with due care paid to an organisation's budgets, needs and constraints.

7. List three things that you need to consider when storing resources.
8. List at least four reasons why it is important to review the resource acquisitions process.
9. Explain why it is important to consult with other people on staff when determining resource requirements.

7.3 Monitoring resource usage and maintenance

Monitoring resource usage, and ensuring that equipment is regularly maintained, helps to ensure that business operations run smoothly. By keeping track of who uses what resources, how many of each item are being used and how they are being used, you can ensure that there are always sufficient supplies on hand, without any wastage and therefore unnecessary expense. Keeping track of equipment maintenance schedules will also ensure that the resources staff need in order to do their work won't break down (unless the equipment develops an unforeseen fault).

7.3.1 Handling resources in line with organisational requirements

Bearing in mind that resources extend to more than just ordering paperclips, and may very well involve hiring staff, scheduling machinery or other major resources, or buying large and expensive items of equipment, it is important to ensure that organisational policies and procedures are complied with so that plans and objectives can be met and productivity isn't disrupted. Those policies and procedures might deal with issues such as the following:

- *Sustainability practices*. The use of alternative products can be an excellent way for an organisation to reduce its expenditure while at the same time contributing to global sustainability. An organisation can waste money and resources simply by using the same materials and suppliers it has always used without researching if there are better, more sustainable services and products available. Then, too, many functions that previously required manual/paper handling can now be accomplished electronically. A regular review of work procedures can often highlight areas that could be dealt with more efficiently.
- *Suppliers*. The suppliers used to purchase or source resources should be reviewed on a regular basis to check whether better materials might be available. You should also renegotiate pricing on a regular basis to ensure that you are receiving the best value for money. This can sometimes be done via a tendering process.
- *Storage and access to resources*. How will resources be stored, and how will staff access them? Depending on the size of the organisation and its procedures, there may be open access to materials via a stationery cupboard or room where all staff can go and take what they need. Or, one person or area might be responsible for distributing materials and keeping track and control of resource usage. You will also need to consider the health and safety aspects of storage:
    - Are correct manual handling techniques being used when moving heavy items?
    - Are items being stacked safely (where applicable) so that they don't fall and injure someone?
    - Are hazardous substances being handled and stored in accordance with the manufacturer's instructions and legislative requirements?
- *Scheduling resource usage*. In instances where important resources are in short supply but heavy demand, it may be necessary to schedule their use. This might be the case with:
    - reserving workplace spaces such as meeting rooms or boardrooms
    - booking time on specific pieces of equipment
    - making use of the company car.
- *Inventories and registers*. Keeping an eye on stock levels can be as simple as taking a look inside the stationery room or cupboard each week to see if anything needs to be replaced. Ideally, however, a register should be kept, not only to keep track of what is currently in stock, but also to capture this information for future reference and planning purposes. Remember: forecasting is based to a large degree on looking at *past* figures! While you can certainly use handwritten lists or registers to monitor and track your resource usage, there are many technological tools available to make this task easier. Depending on the size of your organisation, you can invest in software specifically developed for just this task, or you can use your organisation's existing software programs, such as word processing or spreadsheets, to do the same thing (as shown in Table 7.2).

Table 7.2 Example of an inventory register

Date: June	Copy paper	Pens	Manila folders	Staples	Paperclips
Open	**20**	**100**	**250**	**10**	**10**
7/6	1	5		1	2
8/6			10		
10/6		3	10		1
11/6				1	
12/6		10			3
20/6	1		10		
22/6		1			
25/6				1	1
Balance	**18**	**81**	**220**	**7**	**3**

- *Staff rosters.* Staff are a very real and very valuable resource within any organisation. Great care should therefore be taken in ensuring that there are always sufficient staff on hand to complete all the necessary tasks. Allocating the right staff, with the right qualifications, for the right task at the right time is all part of effective staff rostering. While this may not, normally, be a part of the administration role, it is important to understand the impact that this aspect of resource distribution has on the organisation.
- *Transport/travel policies.* Some staff may need to travel as part of their roles within an organisation. In order to do this, they may need to fly interstate or to drive around a given area using a company car. These work role requirements may fall within the parameter of workplace resources. For interstate travel, there will generally be specific policies to follow. For example, staff must fly with a specific airline, stay at specified hotels, and have a specified expenditure amount for meals while they are away. Use of a company car falls more readily into the process of managing resources. Cars, which are a resource, are allocated to specific staff either full time (as part of their salary package) or on a needs basis (they need to book the car for a given date and time). There will also be specific processes involved in using company cars, such as use of petrol cards, keeping a mileage log, and so on.
- *WHS requirements.* The management of workplace resources includes a number of health and safety issues. For example:
  - Equipment use—all company resources must be used correctly to ensure the safety of people, premises and equipment. This means ensuring that any item of equipment or resource that is potentially hazardous is used in accordance with the manufacturer's instructions and with WHS legislation in mind.
  - Manual handling procedures—it is extremely important to observe the correct procedures when moving heavy or awkward loads. Most workplace injuries happen when these procedures are not followed. The resulting severe back or muscle injuries can require many months of recuperation.
  - First aid kit—this is an essential resource that all organisations should have. In the case of an injury or accident, professional medical assistance should be called for, but immediate attention may be required to keep the injured person comfortable while waiting for help to arrive. A basic first aid kit should contain:
    - triangular bandages
    - crepe ("conforming" or elastic) bandages of varying widths
    - non-adhesive dressings in varying sizes
    - disposable gloves (medium and large), preferably non-latex ones
    - thermal blanket
    - notepad and pencil
    - plastic bags in varying sizes
    - adhesive tape (2.5 cm wide—preferably a permeable tape such as Micropore)
    - resuscitation mask or face shield.

While these policies and procedures may seem a little overwhelming written down here, they will become second nature to you as you grow into your role and develop the skills and knowledge to deal with them.

7.3.2 Monitoring effective resource usage

Choosing the right resource for the right job is a matter of determining what needs to be done and deciding how best to accomplish that task with the resources at your disposal. For example, you would not use an inkjet printer to make 200 copies of a 10-page document if a photocopier was available. Equally, you would probably not use a computer, word processing software and a printer to write a short note to a colleague, when a handwritten note or an email would do the job. Then, too, technology used effectively can help to monitor and keep track of resource usage, as shown in the tables in section 7.3.4.

7.3.3 Consulting with others to facilitate effective decision making

Keeping a resource register will tell you what resources are being used by the organisation. Depending on how the register has been set up, it may even tell you what departments, or individuals, are using certain resources. However, this only tells you *what* is being used, not *why* or *how* it is being used—which are important questions in the planning process.

Consulting with supervisors and/or colleagues will give you a better understanding of how and why specific resources are being used, which will enable you to make more informed decisions about the quality and quantity of the items you order. For example, the marketing department has designed drink bottles with the organisation's logo printed on them for promotional purposes. These are ordered by the thousands to be given out at trade fairs and other events to promote the organisation and generate sales. Unfortunately, the current supplier uses substandard printing processes and by the time the marketing staff have started giving away the bottles, the ink has come off and the logo can no longer be seen (which defeats the purpose of the giveaway). There is a substantial investment in buying these resources. By understanding why, where and how the marketing department uses these items, you can make a decision about changing suppliers or addressing the issue with the current supplier to ensure that this doesn't happen in future—thereby avoiding waste and unnecessary expenditure.

7.3.4 Monitoring and reporting on resource usage

Keeping statistics will help you to control your budget and resource usage in the short term. Keeping statistics over a number of years, however, will reveal trends, and show peaks and troughs, that allow you to accurately forecast budgets and resource requirements for the coming year.

- **Trends** tell us what items are being used, how many, by whom, and when they are using them.
- **Peaks** are times of high usage. Many industries are subject to seasonal fluctuations (e.g. the tourism industry) or have certain times of the year when they are busier than at other times (e.g. accountants during tax time). During these peak times, their use of resources will be higher than at other times of the year.
- **Troughs** are times of low usage. In the same way that some industries have peak times, they might also have low times when they are not very busy. For example, in the travel industry winter periods are generally slow times. So, too, is Christmas time a slow time for many businesses, which may even close over the holiday period. During these times, the number of resources used decreases considerably.

Monitoring the use of resources will not only help you to know what resources to order and when, but will also ensure that you have the right amount of resources available during peak usage times, and less on hand during slower times. This, in turn, means that you have better control over your budget. To be most effective, you can monitor the use of resources as follows:

- *Which department uses them?* Keeping a record of what each individual department uses is an excellent way of understanding the overall picture of how an organisation operates.
- *What items do they use?* Do all areas of the organisation use the same materials, or do they use materials appropriate to the work they carry out? For example, the marketing department may use different coloured and textured papers for promotional purposes, and toner for colour printers—items that other departments within the organisation have no use for. The IT department, on the other hand, would need supplies of cables and external hard drives for backup storage.
- *How often do they use them?* Are there times when some items are used more than others? If so, then supplies must be maintained during times of high usage so that work can carry on without interruption. In low usage times, the supplies on hand of these items can be allowed to decrease.
- *What do they use them for?* Are there alternative products that could do the job more effectively?
- *How much is wasted?* Could the introduction of new procedures or alternative products save material usage, and thereby save money?

All of this information, and more, is used to determine what stocks of resources need to be purchased in the coming year, how much it will cost and, if monitored accordingly, when these stocks must be available to the workforce.

When reporting on resource usage, you need to be as accurate and detailed as possible. Organisational budgets might be set company wide—where there is a central budget for certain expenditure areas across the company—or they could be set by department, with each area of the organisation having its own budget. The individual department might then break down its allocation into a variety of areas such as stationery, advertising, phone bills, and so on. The more information you can provide, the more accurate the budget forecasting can be.

Table 7.3 shows an example of a spreadsheet outlining stationery expenditure by the organisation's marketing department for the second half of the financial year ending 30 June 2023. This could be a spreadsheet that is updated each time the department requisitions stationery items and could potentially be very long.

Table 7.3 Spreadsheet showing stationery consumption and expenses for a given period of time

Marketing Department, 2023				
Date	**Item**	**Qty**	**Cost per item ($)**	**Total cost ($)**
1/1	Copy paper (reams)	10	5.55	55.50
25/1	Black pens	5	0.55	2.75
23/2	Staples (boxes)	2	1.50	3.00
14/3	Paperclips (boxes)	2	1.75	3.50
25/3	Sticky tape	1	0.65	0.65
16/4	Manila folders	50	1.00	50.00
19/4	Mailing labels (boxes)	2	25.00	50.00
30/4	Notepads	5	1.65	8.25
2/5	Lever arch files	2	2.50	5.00
17/5	Plastic sleeves (boxes)	1	20.00	20.00
Total				**198.65**

In Table 7.4, the information is collated, in a now familiar way, to reflect how many of each item was ordered each year, and how much was spent in total. This will give an accurate overview of usage trends, peaks and troughs in that department.

Table 7.4 Spreadsheet showing consumption of resources over several years

Marketing Department	2021	$	2022	$	2023	$
Copy paper (reams)	100	555.00	121	671.55	150	832.50
Black pens	55	30.25	66	36.30	45	24.75
Staples (boxes)	12	18.00	15	22.50	20	30.00
Paperclips (boxes)	15	26.25	19	33.25	21	36.75
Sticky tape	9	5.85	5	3.25	6	3.90
Manila folders	150	150.00	120	120.00	138	138.00
Mailing labels (boxes)	5	125.00	8	200.00	10	250.00
Notepads	25	41.25	30	49.50	28	46.20
Lever arch files	10	25.00	15	37.50	12	30.00
Plastic sleeves (boxes)	10	200.00	12	240.00	15	300.00
Total spent		**1,176.60**		**1,413.85**		**1,692.10**

This information can then be further refined into a graph that shows trends at a glance. For example, the graph in Figure 7.4 clearly shows that in 2021 and 2022 manila folders were the most used items, followed by copy paper. In 2023, the use of copy paper increased significantly. There may be a reason for this increase that will have an impact on future use, so you need to find out why it occurred. There may be valid reasons for many of the changes in usage shown in the graph—reasons that could apply to future planning. Only by keeping track of what is used, and when, can you build a solid picture of the organisation's requirements.

Figure 7.4 Graph outlining information from Table 7.4

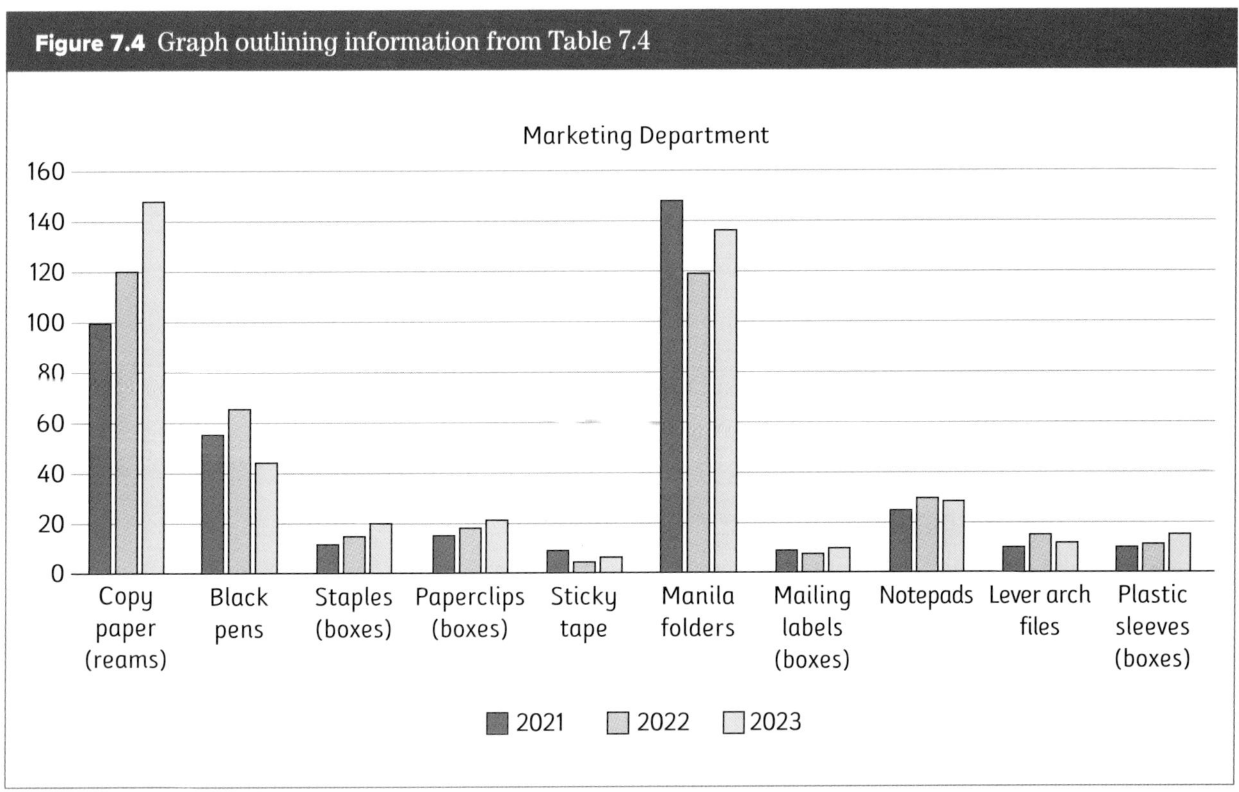

Knowledge check

10. List at least five items of technology you would use in an office environment. Briefly describe their use.
11. Describe why it is important to monitor and report on resource usage.
12. Describe what standard forms might typically be used for purchasing and storing resources.
13. Describe why it is necessary to review the organisation's purchasing procedures.
14. Explain what organisational considerations there are in acquiring resources.

Summary

Workplace resources are a vital part of your organisation's day-to-day operations. Without them, work could potentially come to a standstill. It is an important part of everyone's role, therefore, to ensure these resources are used effectively and with minimal wastage.

Each item, or piece of equipment, you use costs money and is therefore a drain on the organisation's financial resources. Proper research of available resources and their suppliers, the right choice of these suppliers, and the tracking and reviewing of resource usage all contribute to the organisation's success.

CHAPTER 8

Organise workplace information

Learning outcomes

8.1 Receive, acquire and assess information

8.2 Organise information

8.3 Review information needs

For an organisation to be successful, it requires information and in-depth knowledge to help management understand what is happening within their organisation, why it is happening, and what actions and decisions they might need to take. It is helpful, then, to understand the term "knowledge" in a business sense. Business knowledge is the culmination of a process that involves gathering *data*, developing useful *information* from this data, and then using this information to gain an in-depth insight into, or *knowledge* of, a given subject.

8.1 Receiving, acquiring and assessing information

Business knowledge is made up of a multitude of data and information gathered and stored by your organisation and is used for a variety of reasons. To clarify:

- *Data*—pieces of unrelated or linked information. For example, your organisation:
  - serves 50 customers a day
  - offers 120 different products
  - employs 25 staff.

  These are *pieces* of information that in themselves don't mean very much. The relevant question here is: "How does this data relate to my requirements?"
- *Information*—taking unrelated pieces of data and determining how they fit together to make a picture. For example: of the 50 customers you serve each day, 80 per cent buy only 10 different products. Of the 120 products you offer, 25 never sell. Of the 25 staff you employ, 10 work in sales and only five of those are actually good at their job. Information turns cold data, or facts, into useful information. You now have an overview of how your organisation actually operates. The question here is: "What can I learn from this information?"
- *Knowledge*—making intelligent decisions based on the meaningful information now to hand, to make the organisation more efficient and profitable. For example: if 25 of the products your organisation offers never sell, then a decision could be made to stop offering or producing these items, thereby saving time, effort and money. If only five of the salespeople are good at their job, then you may decide to transfer or train the remaining five, and so on.

As outlined, an organisation's success revolves around the quality of the information that it uses to base its business decisions on. However, not all information is useful or even relevant. It is essential, therefore, that an organisation develops a sound understanding of the knowledge it might need to stay successful. Most organisations will have specific, individual information needs. The information an architectural firm needs will, for example, be very different from the information needs of an insurance company or a hairdressing salon. However, there are certain information needs that will apply across all industries, as shown in Figure 8.1.

Other sources of information include:

- *Forms and templates*. These could include membership forms, incident reports (in the case of accidents or illness) and job application forms. Collating data from these forms and templates, over time, can show trends in performance. This trend information can then be used to make decisions on future actions and strategies.
- *Operational procedures*. These provide the organisation with information about, for example:
  - the standards to which tasks must be completed in order to deliver consistently high-quality service and products
  - how cash is to be handled
  - complaint-handling procedures
  - work health and safety (WHS) procedures
  - forms to be used for given tasks and situations.
- *Information about competitors*. This allows an organisation to remain in step with, if not ahead of, other organisations offering the same, or similar, products or services. Information about competitors can come from sources such as:
  - customer comments
  - media advertising
  - promotional flyers
  - window displays
  - personal visits or phone calls (ghost shopping)
  - internet—website
  - company reports.

Figure 8.1 Information that is commonly needed across all industries

Database information will include customers' contact details, purchasing history, account status and more.

Website or social media analytics provide information on how customers are engaging with you.

Sales and accounting records provide accurate records of the sales the organisation has made, its income and expenses, who owes it money, who it owes money to and more.

Invoices for goods received or supplied must be kept on file for a variety of reasons, including tax audits and financial planning.

Staff records provide information about job descriptions, pay scales, leave applications, performance appraisals, disciplinary actions, promotions and more.

Business plans and marketing strategies are the backbone of the organisation. They provide directions for it to follow to achieve future success.

General correspondence such as letters, memos, emails and faxes are often kept on file as a record of any transactions or deals made.

Minutes and agendas of meetings provide a written record of what is discussed at meetings and often form the basis for action plans.

Information about new legislation or other government issues ensures the organisation complies with its legal obligations.

vasabii/Shutterstock

- *Product information.* In order to be able to confidently recommend products and services to customers, you need to be fully conversant with what your organisation offers—whether it is insurance, real estate or cans of paint! Sources of this information could be:
  - inter-office memos on product information or changes
  - sales and marketing staff
  - operational staff
  - first-hand knowledge—trying it out for yourself!
  - interviews with colleagues to discuss operational or service issues.

All of these sources, and others, will provide information that an organisation can use to better understand its business and as a base for making business decisions. For example:

- Is the organisation offering its customers the best possible products or service?
- Is the organisation operating as cost efficiently as possible?
- Are there any new trends that the organisation should consider?

- Are there any new laws affecting the organisation's industry that it must take into consideration?
- What will be the organisation's future direction?
- How will the organisation improve the performance of its staff?

Think about

1. What kind of information does your organisation (or department) need in order to function effectively?

8.1.1 Methods of receiving and acquiring information

Information, as you have learnt, is vital to the success of an organisation. It may need to be created from scratch, or it may be extracted from existing sources. But where does the information come from? In general, information can be obtained through both external and internal sources (see Figure 8.2).

External sources are:

- *Federal, state and local government offices.* Governments can provide information about:
  - demographics (i.e. how the population in the country, state or local area live and work)
  - legislation and how it affects a variety of businesses and industries
  - industry regulations and standards that must be complied with.
- *Local libraries.* Libraries will often have back issues of magazines and newspapers containing stories or information about local events, etc.
- *Internet.* Through use of search engine facilities such as Google, there is almost nothing that cannot be found on the Web. Care should be taken, however, when sourcing information from the Web, as not all sites found there offer accurate, correct or up-to-date information.
- *Television.* News and lifestyle programs on television are an excellent source of general information.
- *Newspapers and trade magazines.* Printed publications and e-zines have information relating to the local community and industry-specific subjects.
- *Business networks and industry associations.* These bodies are an excellent source of information.
- *Competitor information.* It is important to know what direct competitors are doing as they, more than any other businesses, are likely to take customers away decreasing the organisation's sales and therefore profits.
- *Outside research.* Research provided by others outside of your organisation might include information provided by customers or suppliers.
- *Social media platforms.* Social media provide insights into who your customers are and what interests them. They are also a source of information by way of visitor comments.

Internal sources and methods of collecting information include existing documents that an organisation will have on file, as well as information that it creates for specific purposes. Sources will generally include:

- *Financial information.* This information tells an organisation how it is really doing in terms of profit and loss. Much of this type of information can be found in the form of spreadsheets or reports that are run from the organisation's accounting database. Financial information is normally restricted for use by management and the organisation's accountants.

Figure 8.2 (a) External information sources; (b) Internal information sources

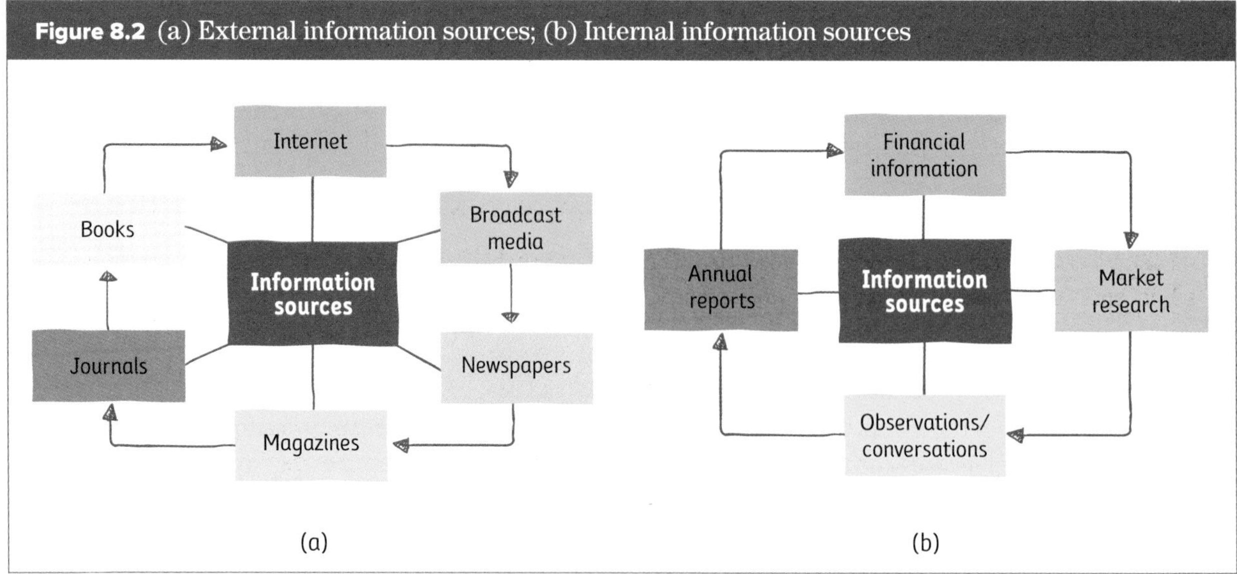

- *Market research*. Every business depends on customers. It is important, therefore, to know what customers are buying, who they are buying from, and why they are buying. This kind of information can be obtained from a wide variety of sources, including:
    - customer surveys and questionnaires (creating new information)
    - general conversation with customers (creating new information)
    - company sales reports (existing information)
    - customer information, the main sources of which are:
        - customer detail forms, which customers complete when they first open an account or do business with the organisation
        - customer survey forms, where the organisation asks customers questions specifically about its products and services
        - sales records and receipts, which capture information about what customers purchased, how much they paid, and on what date.
- *Observations and conversations*. Casual conversations or observations while in the workplace can often lead to interesting pieces of information that, if followed up on, can be used to improve the organisation.
- *Annual reports*. These internally generated reports provide a detailed view of the organisation's current position and future plans.

Try this now

1. Research information on one of your competitors. What sources of information did you use? How useful was this information? What conclusions could you draw from this information?

Organisational policies and procedures relating to receiving and acquiring information

To ensure that the information it acquires is useful and relevant to its needs, and that it meets all the legal requirements specific to its industry, an organisation may have certain policies and procedures in place. These might include:

- *Determining the purpose of the information to be collected*. With so much information available, the value and relevance of the information required needs to be determined before the cycle of information gathering can begin.

- *Determining when the information is needed by.* Often information is needed for a specific report or project, in which case time is of the essence.
- *Determining who will source the information.* Depending on the volume or type of information required, it may be necessary to allocate specific tasks to individuals within an organisation who have the necessary time and/or expertise to source the data most productively.
- *Setting limits as to how much information is collected.* Having too much information can be as damaging as having too little information. Too much data can lead to confusion over contradictory information. A great deal more research may be necessary to establish the facts.
- *Identifying gaps.* Once information on a required subject has been collected, it needs to be examined to determine if it meets the organisation's exact needs.
- *Determining the format the information should take.* Will it be paper based? Collated into a report? Made available only on the organisation's database software? And so on.
- *Deciding on management and accountability channels.* This may restrict who, within the organisation, has access to the information. Not all staff will be allowed access to all information. Some organisational documents may be confidential and should be distributed and stored strictly in accordance with organisational policies and privacy laws. Such information may include:
  - business strategies
  - financial information
  - staff personnel records
  - customers' private details
  - WHS policies and procedures to be observed when using equipment or storage facilities
  - security and confidentiality requirements for any information you collect.

When determining information needs, it is also important to consider your organisation's legal obligations, such as:

- *Code of conduct and code of ethics.* In terms of **information management**, this may relate to such issues as copyright and intellectual property and may restrict your rights to using any information you find. In the sense of gathering information, you should not claim, as your own, any information you didn't actually produce. This could lead to serious legal actions being taken against you.
- *Legal and organisational policies, guidelines and requirements.* This may relate to ensuring that information is stored safely and securely, or what information is to be stored and for how long. It may also be a matter of ensuring that you comply with all the necessary regulations. Legislative requirements are not optional; they are a legal obligation. Breaches of these requirements could result in your dismissal from your job, or even in legal action being taken against you.
- *Accuracy of sources.* This is particularly important when you are dealing with legislative issues. For example, if you are researching the requirements for obtaining a business licence from the government, the information will have to be accurate as your organisation's future could depend on the reliability of the information provided. Similarly, if you need to deal with a legislative issue surrounding work health and safety, the information you source must be accurate and complete.

8.1.2 Confirming that information is clear, accurate, current and relevant

While there are a great many sources of information, not all of them will be authoritative (correct or reliable), especially if the information is sourced from the internet. Anyone can post information on the web, on any subject, without actually knowing anything about it—they are merely offering their opinion. In order to reach well-founded decisions, you need to be sure that the information you have used is correct and up to date, so the sources you use must be trustworthy.

Decisions made are only as good as the information on which they are based, so once it has been collected it needs to be assessed. Questions to ask include:

- *Is the information relevant?* Gathering information merely for the sake of having it is pointless and time consuming. Any information collected should be relevant to the organisation's needs. Does this information answer the questions that have been asked? For example: "Is the organisation operating as cost efficiently as possible?" Relevant information in this case would include reports on its income and expenditure, and inventory reports showing which products are selling well and which are not. This type of information will help the organisation to make decisions on where it can save money, whereas information about current social trends, while interesting, might have little impact on the cost effectiveness of the organisation's operations.
- *Is the information clear and concise?* "Clear" means: is the information easy to understand, and does it flow logically? "Concise" means: is the information brief and to the point, without unnecessary words? Information fragments, such as loose pages from a larger document, can provide interesting information but could lead to decisions based on incomplete facts. Any reports compiled from a mass of information need to be clear, to the point and draw relevant conclusions.
- *Is the information of sufficient quantity?* A major business decision should never be based on a single fact. In most instances, these types of decisions need to be based on a range of information that views the situation or project from different viewpoints and aspects to minimise the risk of mistakes and pitfalls.
- *Has the information you are presenting been checked/proofread?* It is important to check that the information being gathered is correct. Information obtained from government sources, industry associations, corporate company reports, or directly from suppliers or manufacturers can usually be trusted to be correct. Information gathered from non-authorised sites or from comments made by customers or friends, however, should be properly verified to ensure it is correct. Proofreading also allows you to protect your organisation's professional image by checking that:
    - the spelling and grammar are correct
    - the facts are presented in a logical way that is easy to understand
    - the format of the information is in line with organisational policies and procedures and is appropriate for the type of material
    - all the necessary key points have been addressed.

8.1.3 Accessing additional required information

Your initial search will give you a certain amount of useful information. There will be times, however, when there are gaps in the total picture the organisation wants to create. In order to fill those gaps, or to draw on other sources of information, you may need to liaise with a range of stakeholders. These people will often know where you can find the information you are looking for, or they might even be the source of that information themselves. For example, your accounts department will have information about any missing financial information you need, or the marketing staff will be able to provide you with information about customer satisfaction levels, and so on.

The stakeholders you may need to work with can include:

- *Colleagues or employees*, who understand "on-the-job" information needs and may have thoughts and sources that will provide you with more in-depth knowledge of a given subject.
- *Supervisors or team leaders*, who will have a broader perspective on their department or specific work area and can provide information on how it fits in with the organisation as a whole.
- *Managers*, who have a full understanding of the organisation, its operational elements and its future plans, and can provide information that helps provides a well-rounded view of the organisation and its goals.

Knowledge check

1. List at least six specific information needs an organisation might have. Briefly describe each need.
2. List at least five external sources of information.
3. List at least five internal sources of information.
4. List at least six organisational and legislative issues that a business may consider when researching and collecting information for its specific needs.
5. Explain why it is important to confirm that information is clear, accurate, current and relevant.
6. In most cases, you will need to access information from a range of stakeholders. Describe who these stakeholders might be and how they contribute to information needs.
7. In assessing information, there are a range of questions you might ask. List at least three such questions.

8.2 Organising information

You now have a mountain of information. How you process and organise it will be a very important step in developing useful and meaningful knowledge on which to base decisions or complete tasks. Questions to ask include:

- How will you present the information?
- What technology can help you to collate and store it?
- How will you ensure that information is always up to date?

We will now consider these and other questions.

8.2.1 Organising information in a suitable format for analysis

Depending on the nature of the information you have collected and its intended purpose, you could end up with many different pieces of unconnected data that, by themselves, don't make much sense, or there may simply be too much of it to oversee comfortably. Before presenting the information to your colleagues, supervisors or managers, you will therefore need to put it all into some sort of logical order or context.

Analysis and interpretation

Data and information, on their own, may not give an organisation the knowledge it needs to make sound decisions. All the various pieces of data need to be collated and analysed so that information can be gained from it. For example, the marketing department of your organisation may have gathered data on how customers are finding out about the organisation. Figure 8.3 shows the forms of advertising the department used to attract customers over the period from January to June 2023. The numbers in themselves don't mean very much until you total up the columns.

The spreadsheet gives you information on trends; for example, more people responded that they saw your organisation's ads in May and June than in any other month. You could now take this information and find out why, to improve your knowledge of how these trends could be used to improve your organisation's advertising options. It also tells you that local businesses make up most of those surveyed, and that advertising on TV and at the cinema isn't working and should be discontinued. Information such as this can be collected over a number of years and, when collated and analysed, can give further insights into and knowledge of the organisation's marketing and advertising trends, as shown in Figure 8.4.

Sometimes data gathered on a specific subject by way of a survey, or from other sources, can take up many pages and come in different formats such as reports, spreadsheets and

Figure 8.3 Example of a spreadsheet summarising enquiry sources, from the various advertising methods, by month

Enquiry survey results, January–June 2023, by enquiry source

	Jan	Feb	Mar	Apr	May	Jun	Total Jan–Jun
TV	–	–	–	–	–	–	0
Cinema	–	–	–	–	–	–	0
Daily Bulletin	2	6	1	3	–	1	13
Daily Sun	–	–	–	–	–	6	6
Riverland Paper	–	–	–	–	–	–	0
Other newspaper	–	1	–	–	–	–	1
Radio	–	2	2	4	4	1	13
Live in the area	1	2	–	1	–	1	5
Local business	2	7	8	4	10	2	33
Website	–	4	3	–	8	4	19
Yellow Pages	–	2	–	–	1	–	3
Mail-outs	–	–	–	–	–	–	0
Other	3	5	2	9	10	21	50
Total	**8**	**29**	**16**	**21**	**33**	**36**	**143**

Figure 8.4 Example of a summary spreadsheet over a number of years

Enquiry survey comparisons, 2021–2023

	Jan			Feb			Mar			Apr			May			Jun			Totals Jan–Jun		
	21	22	23	21	22	23	21	22	23	21	22	23	21	22	23	21	22	23	21	22	23
TV	–	–	–	–	1	–	–	–	–	–	–	–	–	–	3	–	–	–	**0**	**1**	**3**
Cinema	–	–	–	–	–	–	–	–	–	–	–	–	–	–	–	–	–	–	**0**	**0**	**0**
Daily Bulletin	2	–	–	6	3	5	1	–	1	3	–	–	–	–	–	1	–	–	**13**	**3**	**6**
Daily Sun	–	–	–	–	–	–	–	–	–	–	–	–	–	–	–	6	–	–	**–**	**–**	**0**
Riverland Paper	–	–	–	–	–	–	–	–	–	–	–	–	–	–	–	–	–	–	**0**	**0**	**0**
Other newspaper	–	–	–	1	–	–	–	–	–	–	–	–	–	–	–	–	–	–	**1**	**0**	**0**
Radio	–	4	5	2	1	5	2	7	3	4	4	6	5	7	7	1	2	1	**–**	**25**	**27**
Live in the area	–	7	6	–	7	7	–	12	13	0	10	4	–	7	19	–	3	11	**0**	**46**	**60**
Local business	1	–	–	2	–	–	–	–	–	1	–	–	–	–	–	1	–	–	**5**	**0**	**0**
Website	4	2	–	6	2	1	7	6	1	1	1	2	10	4	7	5	1	3	**33**	**16**	**14**
Yellow Pages	2	–	–	7	–	–	8	–	–	1	–	–	10	–	–	3	–	–	**31**	**0**	**0**
Mail-outs	–	–	2	–	–	–	–	–	–	–	–	1	1	–	–	–	–	2	**1**	**0**	**5**
Other	–	3	2	4	3	4	6	4	4	1	2	4	8	5	5	4	3	–	**23**	**20**	**19**
Total	**9**	**16**	**15**	**28**	**17**	**22**	**24**	**29**	**22**	**11**	**17**	**17**	**34**	**23**	**41**	**21**	**9**	**17**	**127**	**111**	**134**

internet research. This can make the information difficult to read or to understand. Collating large amounts of information, as in Figures 8.3 and 8.4, means condensing the many pages and sources into a useful package where the information flows in a logical fashion, ideally with a summary attached. This information can be condensed still further by showing it in a graph. Figure 8.5 shows the number of enquiries made by month over a three-year period. It clearly shows that May and November are the busiest times of the year for enquiries coming into the organisation. Figure 8.6 summarises the same period in a graph, but by enquiry source.

Storing information using relevant systems and technology

The use of technology in information management and storage is commonplace in today's world. In most organisations, information is stored mainly in computer files, although paper-based filing systems still exist. The following types of technology are most used in information management:

- *Computers*. Computers provide an excellent method of storing large amounts of information. Depending on the size of the organisation, computers can be networked (i.e. connected to a large number of other computers via a server) and can share files. This means that staff can

Figure 8.5 Example showing the number of enquiries by month

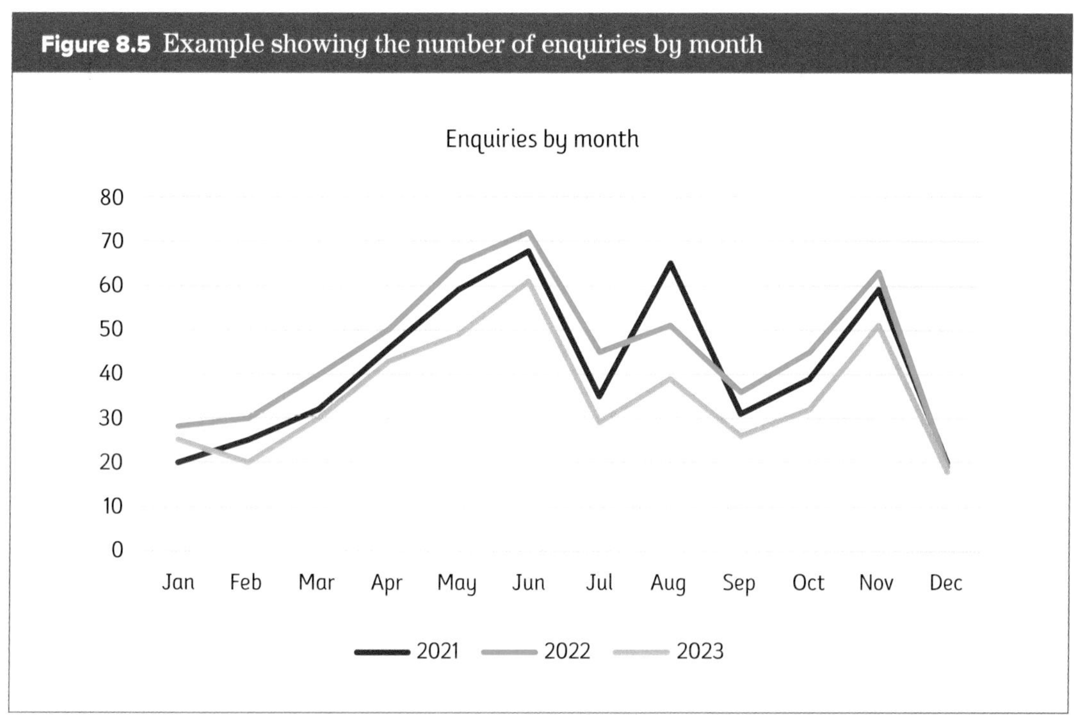

Figure 8.6 Example showing the number of enquiries by enquiry source

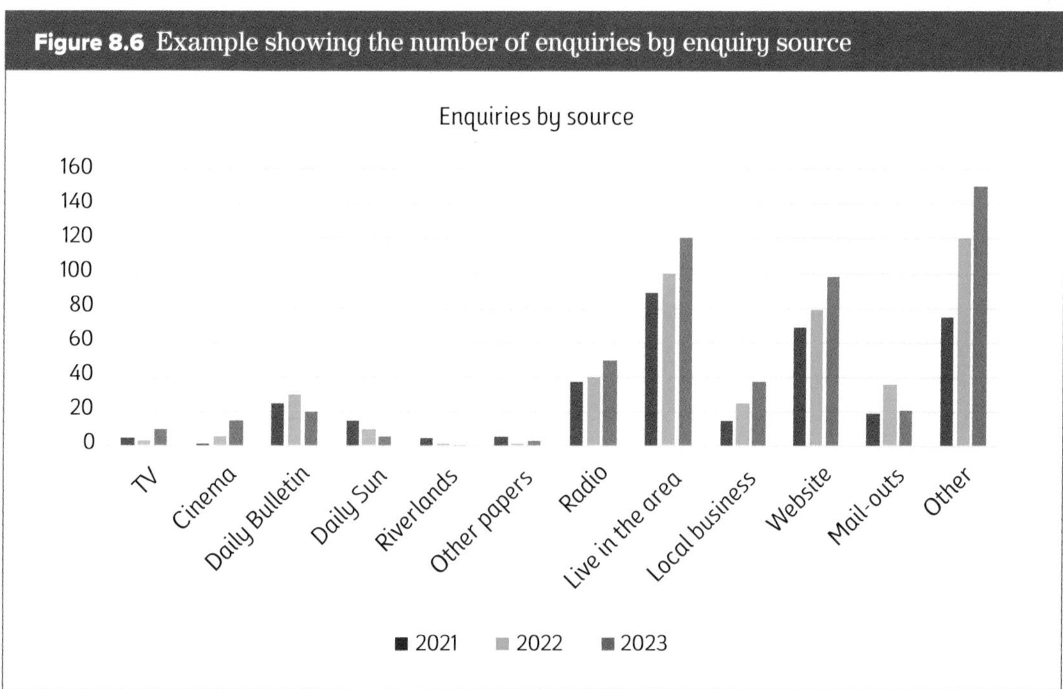

access all files on the network—or only those they have been authorised to access. Smaller organisations may only have one or two computers and may not be networked. This means that they would share their computer files via a disk or flash drive.

- **Cloud** digital platforms. For example:
  - Google Docs
  - Apple iCloud
  - Microsoft OneDrive
  - Dropbox.

These platforms allow you to save and store vast amounts of information securely offsite. Using such systems, you can easily share information and files with other relevant stakeholders such as colleagues, managers or even customers.

- *Software*. Computers are only good for storing information—the actual creation of information via a computer requires appropriate software, including the following:
  - Spreadsheets—used to collate large amounts of numeric information. A spreadsheet can be set up to calculate totals and percentages derived from a number of columns and/or other sources, thus collating a large amount of information into a summary.
  - Word processing—used to create documents such as letters, reports, contracts, manuals, and so on, that can be stored electronically for easy access and future use. Word-processed documents can also be easily retrieved and amended as and when needed.
  - Databases—there are many different styles of databases; some are generic and can be used across a wide variety of industries, and some are designed specifically for a given industry. Airline reservation systems are an excellent example of an industry-specific database. They contain large amounts of information about customers, products and services, operational issues, financial dealings, and much more.
  - Document retrieval and reference retrieval systems (dealt with shortly).

Think about

2. How does your organisation store information? Is it as efficient as it could be? Is the information easy to access?

Using business equipment and technology can ensure that the required information, regardless of its original formats, can be stored in a safe and easily accessible manner.

Electronic filing systems

Storing files within a computer is very similar to using an office file cabinet. A good filing system puts the organisation in control of its information resources, enhances its professional image and increases its productivity.

When saving files directly to a computer, there are a number of things to bear in mind, including ensuring that documents are saved into the correct folder (Figure 8.7). If attention isn't paid to where a file is being stored, it could end up anywhere within the system and may take a lot of effort to find.

Figure 8.7 Correct document storage in an electronic filing system

Main folder	Sub-folder	Document
Marketing	Newsletters/Blogs	Jan 2023 Feb 2023 Mar 2023 ...
	Client projects	Janson's Football campaign KP Printers' social media campaign ...
Accounts	Invoices	Jan 2023 Feb 2023 ...

Electronic document management systems

In addition to storing files in folders directly on the computer's hard drive, the emergence of **electronic document management systems** has made it possible to store all documents (whether paper based or electronic) received or sent by your organisation in your computer system or in a cloud-based storage system. These electronic systems allow you to:

- scan incoming items of mail and store them within the document management system, including faxes, letters, invoices, promotional flyers and materials, etc.

- store email messages in a central file according to a range of searchable criteria
- store all documents produced or received by your organisation in a central electronic system.

Unlike paper filing systems or normal files on a computer, where you must decide on one folder to store your file, the electronic document management systems are designed more as a database than a filing system. In a normal filing system, you must rely on memory and logic to find your files; if something has been incorrectly filed, it can prove difficult—or sometimes even impossible—to find.

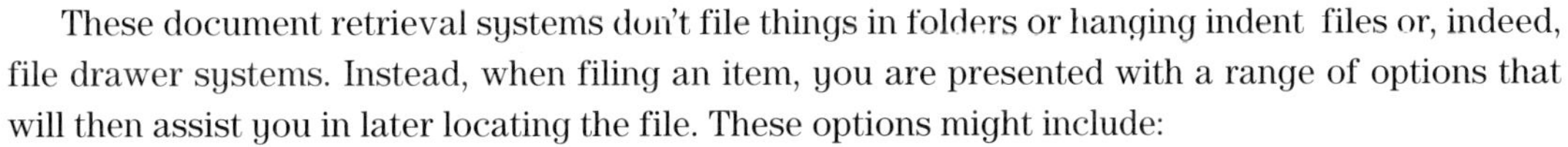

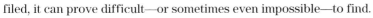

Andrew Krasovitckii/Shutterstock

These document retrieval systems don't file things in folders or hanging indent files or, indeed, file drawer systems. Instead, when filing an item, you are presented with a range of options that will then assist you in later locating the file. These options might include:

- *Name*—name of the person who sent the correspondence or to whom it was sent.
- *Category*—the area of business the correspondence deals with (e.g. marketing, operations, accounting, etc.).
- *Sub-categories*—for example, under the category "Marketing", you could sub-categorise "Newsletters" and "Advertising".
- *Calendar year.*
- *Document status*—this could be "Urgent Follow-up" or "Pending" or "Awaiting Reply" or similar—in other words, documents that require an action of some sort.
- *Document date*—the date the correspondence was received.
- *Index date*—the date the correspondence was filed.
- *Key words*—a number of words pertaining to the document subject that will allow it to be easily found.

When filing a document, you would then choose as many of the options as are relevant. Subsequently, you will be able to search for the file using any of these options. For example, you could search for any files sent to *John Dixon* in the *Sales Department* on *13 July*, about *Marketing and Advertising*. The system would search for these criteria, using those key words, and present you with all the files found.

Paper-based file storage systems

While paper-based systems are largely in decline, many companies do still use them. The actual file storage system used for paper-based files will depend entirely on the size of the organisation and the volume of paperwork that needs to be accommodated. Common paper-based file storage systems include:

- *Concertina files.* For use in very small offices or for home use, a concertina file can sit on your desk and be easily accessible. Separate pockets can be used to store files by subject, alphabetically or numerically, etc.
- *Portable hanging indent files.* This type of file system is basically a square stand on wheels, with a space in the top in which to store hanging indent files. It is mostly used in small offices.
- *One- to four-drawer file cabinets.* This is the most popular and widely used file system. File cabinets can be as small as one drawer or up to four drawers. Larger organisations may have several cabinets in rows, offering vast amounts of storage space.
- *Compactus.* This is an excellent storage system where maximum storage space is needed in a limited space. The compactus shelves are on rollers and can be moved left and right to reveal the shelves inside.
- *Specialist storage systems.* These are normally industry-specific filing systems that can store maps, blueprints, etc.

Monitoring and modifying information

Information that isn't kept up to date and relevant to the organisation will be of no use to it and is simply taking up valuable space. The decisions made by an organisation are only as good as the information on which they are based, so keeping information current is very important.

Maintenance of a knowledge management system can be as simple as throwing out old brochures or reports when new ones are produced, or it can be complicated and involve updating complete manuals or other important documents. Each organisation will have its own procedures for dealing with this. Most organisations, however, need constantly to replace, update or amend the following information to ensure it remains useful:

- *Customer details.* The customer may have moved, or they may have made a new purchase that needs to be recorded, and so on.
- *Organisational policies or procedures.* The company may have introduced new procedures or policies.
- *Staff details.* When staff are promoted, terminated, have moved, have received training, and so on, details must be recorded in their file.
- *Stock details.* Stock levels and locations need to be checked regularly.
- *Product profiles.* New enhancements to products, and changes in specifications or pricing, need to be recorded.
- *Legislation information.* New regulations and new licensing requirements must be noted.
- *Trend information.* Information on what are people are buying, and why, is useful.
- *Systems and software.* It is essential to keep the systems and procedures you use up to date, to ensure continual improvement and productivity.

Amendments to information held in the system should be made immediately. Leaving amendments, additions or changes until later can sometimes lead to errors, as they can easily be forgotten and records will therefore become incomplete. If this continues, what might initially be small problems could eventually become serious situations.

8.2.2 Distributing information to relevant stakeholders

Information is there to be used and will, at some point, need to be shared with other designated people. These people may include:

- *Clients*—who have contacted you and will need a reply to their query.
- *Colleagues*—who will need information set out in policy and procedure documents that detail how they are required to complete their work. They may also need access to:
  - general information about what the company is doing
  - meeting agendas, so they can prepare for meetings
  - minutes of meetings, so they can see what actions or tasks they have been allocated
  - information about WHS or legislative issues.
- *Committee members*—who will receive information and reports on how projects they are overseeing are progressing.
- *External agencies*—such as industry associations and clubs that might be interested in what your organisation is doing, or staff recruitment agencies that will need information about staff requirements.
- *Line management or supervisors*—who need information about how the various sections under their responsibility are doing and whether any action needs to be taken.
- *Statutory bodies or government organisations*—which may require an organisation to provide information about how they are complying with legislation.

In sharing information, you may need to follow the organisation's guidelines on distribution. As not all staff will be allowed access to certain types of information, you must treat information with respect and adhere to confidentiality requirements. Breaches of distribution policies could potentially lead to your dismissal.

You will also need to consider the distribution method. For example, information can be distributed via:

- email
- organisational intranet
- internal staff memo
- written report
- staff meeting or training session.

Think about

3. How does your organisation distribute important information?

Identifying issues in accessing, organising and storing information

There may be occasions when you are unable to gain access to, or find, an important piece of information. You may also have difficulty relating to information that is:

- contradictory, in that you have gathered several pieces of information about a subject and they each say something very different
- ambiguous, in that the information isn't clear and could be taken to mean different things
- inconsistent, in that some sources of information may address the given topic in a positive way, while others deal with it in a negative way—making it difficult to come to a conclusion about it
- outside your level of authority to access.

In these cases, it is always useful to discuss these issues with colleagues or supervisors who may have greater expertise, knowledge or access to the required information. Such discussions may help you to identify ways to solve the problem or to find alternatives to the information required. For example:

- Does anyone in your organisation know someone who can gain the specific information you require?
- Does anyone have any direct experience with the subject being researched who can then give you a first-hand report?
- Are there any other sources of information that you haven't thought of?
- Can you create the necessary information by conducting surveys?
- Will alternative information fulfil the same purpose as the specific information you've asked for?

Knowledge check

8. Explain why it is important to analyse and interpret information.
9. Technology offers a range of features and functions that help in organising and storing information. List at least four of these.
10. Describe at least two methods of storing information.
11. When creating a filing system for your information, there are a number of issues to consider. List at least four such issues and briefly describe each one.
12. Information is there to be used and will, at some point, need to be shared with other designated people. Identify five stakeholders who may need workplace information.
13. List at least four questions you might ask in order to identify and address issues in accessing, organising and storing information.

8.3 Reviewing information needs

You may well have found all the latest information when participating in organisational planning, but that may have been some time ago. In today's fast-paced business world, trends and the demands placed on an organisation change rapidly, so that what was relevant last year may not still be relevant this year. For this reason, it is extremely important to review the information needs of the organisation on a regular basis.

8.3.1 Seeking feedback on clarity, accuracy, relevancy and sufficiency of information

Everyone within an organisation needs information of some sort. They may use information specific to their role or department, or all staff may need access to general information such as policies and procedures. Whatever their needs, all staff will rely on having accurate, up-to-date knowledge so that they can perform to the best of their ability and should therefore have a say in reviewing the organisation's information needs.

There are a number of ways to get feedback on information needs:

- Seek feedback from the staff who actually use this information, and then follow up on their comments and requests.
- Check with suppliers, government bodies or industry bodies for any changes, and request updated information if necessary.
- Discuss with other relevant staff, such as supervisors or teammates, whether current information is still relevant.
- Discuss future information requirements with colleagues or supervisors. For example, management may be looking at a new project; or there may be a change of company direction, which may impact on the type of information required to build a solid knowledge base.
- Read newspapers and trade magazines for new trends and the latest information.
- Check appropriate websites for accurate and up-to-date statistics and legislative changes.
- Check audit and quality assurance documentation and reports, which can give an overview of whether the company is performing to the required standards.

8.3.2 Reviewing feedback and suggesting updates to receipt and acquisition processes

In the same way that staff, equipment, premises and products are all considered to be resources of an organisation, so too is information. How valuable this resource is depends on how useful it is, and how useful it is depends on its currency and relevance to the organisation. As we have seen, the information an organisation keeps on hand needs to be:

GoodStudio/Shutterstock

- the latest information available
- relevant to the work the organisation is currently doing
- reliable and accurate
- of sufficient quantity and quality for the organisation to make informed decisions about its current state and future plans.

Work policies and procedures may dictate how often a review of information should take place and who should carry it out. These policies will vary greatly among organisations. The review process can be an ongoing job carried out as part of a person's normal duties, or it could be a specific task given to a variety of staff members from different departments once or twice a year.

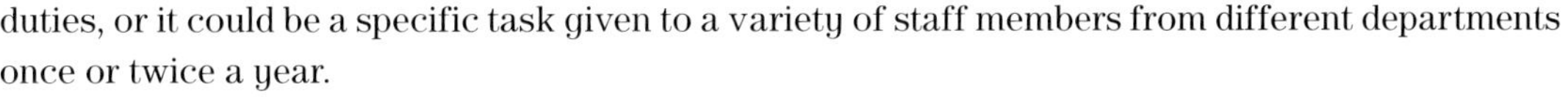

When reviewing information needs and determining what should be updated, kept as it is or discarded, it is sometimes necessary to take government regulations into consideration. Some government regulations dictate what information is to be stored and how long it should be kept. For example, an organisation's financial information must be kept for specified periods of time for audit purposes; while, in education, student records must be kept for 30 years.

All work practices can benefit from review and improvement—not least, the collection of information and the maintenance of the knowledge management system. When looking at how to improve organisational systems, the questions to be asked include: Does the current system work? Who uses it? The same is true of improving the use of knowledge within an organisation. Questions to ask can include:

- *What is the data used for?* It might be used for:
  - future planning
  - deciding on changes to products
  - deciding on changes to the product range
  - determining marketing strategies
  - developing promotional activities
  - determining customer satisfaction levels
  - reporting on the organisation's financial state, and much more.
- *Who uses it?* In essence, everyone uses business information—but for different reasons.
  - Marketing will look at information that relates to customers' buying trends.
  - Accounts will look at information that deals with incoming and outgoing money.
  - Administration will be concerned with resource stock levels, such as stationery and other consumables.
  - Operations might be interested in information about new manufacturing or production equipment.
  - Human resources will be interested in any information dealing with staffing issues, such as training, superannuation, taxation regulations, etc.
  - Management will be interested in all of the above and more, as they will be the ones setting the future direction for the organisation.
- *Was there sufficient information available upon which to base decisions*? As mentioned earlier, it isn't advisable to base a far-reaching and costly business decision on one simple fact or piece of information. There must be enough information to confirm that any decisions made are based on sound facts.

- *How often is it used?* How often information is used will largely determine how and where it is stored—or, indeed, whether it is stored at all. For example, if a piece of information is only used once a year, such as area demographics for business planning, then management might prefer to download this information directly from the appropriate website on the internet as they can then be sure it is up to date. Information that is used on a regular and frequent basis might be stored in the organisation's own computer system, where it is easily accessible by the relevant staff, or in a centrally located file cabinet (in the case of trade magazines, etc.).
- *How was the information useful in the decision-making process?* While facts that you gather might be very interesting in their own right, if they aren't used by the organisation, they are merely taking up space and "clogging" the information systems. If they aren't useful, discard them.
- *What can be archived?* Information that isn't used regularly but that still serves a useful purpose could be archived. This means that it can be removed from the day-to-day system and stored on a CD, USB, remote back-up drive or in a filing box, where it can be retrieved as and when necessary. In this way, the information is still available in case it is ever needed but isn't taking up valuable space. Some documentation, by law, must be kept for a certain amount of time—whether it is ever needed again or not. These types of documents, which the government may require be kept for reporting and audit purposes, include accountable documents (which often have a pre-printed number on them, such as cheques, receipts, invoices, etc. and usually deal with finance), other financial records, staff records, school records, and so on.
- *What can be discarded?* As discussed previously, old materials and items of information that are not accountable can and should be discarded on a regular basis.
- *Why should you do this?* The knowledge management system needs to be reviewed and cleaned out on a regular basis in order for it to remain efficient. Keeping outdated information on file could lead to confusion, and therefore to mistakes or poor decisions. It would also be time consuming to sort through in order to find exactly what you are looking for.

The more you know about your organisation, and about the way it operates and the environment in which it operates, the better it will function. Knowledge leads to understanding, and understanding can lead to improvements within the organisation that will make it a better, more efficient and more productive place to work.

Identifying and documenting future information needs

In going through the review process, you will be able to identify what gaps currently exist in the organisation's knowledge database and to start collecting more up-to-date and relevant information. Then, too, circumstances change frequently in the business world. New legislation may have been introduced, which may mean that an organisation's policies and procedures need to be changed. This, in turn, means that new information is needed. Or the company may decide to branch out in a new direction and will need information on which to base its future decisions. Or you may be aware of special projects or campaigns the organisation is planning to run and may need to do research related to these plans. This means that the cycle of collecting information begins anew.

- Determine what is needed by checking with relevant stakeholders.
- Find appropriate and authoritative sources for the information.
- Check any information collected for its accuracy and relevance.
- Organise and collate the information into a logical and concise package.
- Ensure that only those who are authorised to access that information receive a copy.
- Store the information securely, in line with organisational requirements.
- Review the information needs and usage as and when required.

Knowledge check

14. List at least four methods of gaining feedback on information needs.

15. When looking at improving organisational systems, there are issues to be considered in terms of information needs. List at least five of these and give examples of what each issue involves.

16. Describe some of the issues you need to consider when identifying future information needs.

17. Describe the advantages of electronic document management systems.

Summary

Information is the lifeblood of any business or organisation. It helps to dictate how a business will form its strategies, and how it will implement processes based on them. It is at the heart of business growth, which is why so much effort and resources should be put into developing efficient information management systems.

With access to vast amounts of information comes great responsibility; we share information both voluntarily and involuntarily with others every day. Organisations are under increasing pressure to handle information responsibly and ethically, and to comply with evolving legal regulations.

More transparency is being demanded by people and governments. Therefore, efficient, safe and effective management of an organisation's information about its people is more important than ever. Failure to comply with these regulations can land businesses in serious trouble, with huge fines potentially imposed, which is a further reason why organisations need to take information management so seriously.

CHAPTER 9
Organise schedules

Learning outcomes

9.1 Establish schedule requirements

9.2 Manage schedules

9.3 Evaluate the effectiveness of schedules

Time is one of the only things in life that can never be recovered; once it is gone, it is irretrievably gone. It should therefore be treated like the valuable resource it is, and not be needlessly wasted. Regardless of the industry you are in, or the organisation you work for, each person in the business will have to complete their work within a given time frame. Time must therefore be managed effectively if tasks are to be completed correctly and when required. Managing appointments and schedules is therefore a very important part of any business day. An **appointment** is a pre-allocated time in which two or more parties can meet; it is generally arranged in advance and relates to one meeting only. A **schedule**, on the other hand, relates to a series of events spread over an entire day, or a longer period, where activities and meetings are arranged in precise order and to set time frames.

9.1 Establishing schedule requirements

Managing schedules means that the day is organised into precisely timed activities. A full day for a marketing manager, for example, might include conducting a meeting with the marketing team or attending a meeting with printers or promotional companies. They might also need to conduct interviews with potential staff or complete office-based tasks that arise during the course of the day (e.g. returning or making phone calls). Without proper planning, it may be difficult to fit all of these tasks into the working day and to complete them effectively and efficiently in the time allocated.

An effective schedule must also consider work task priorities, by determining which tasks are more important or more urgent than others. It should outline how long each task will take and how much time should be left between each task or appointment so that follow-up work can be completed or notes made of the conversations held and agreements reached. In addition, it should describe what any scheduled meetings are about, where they will be held (with directions on how to get there if needed), and any items or files that may be needed to ensure the meetings are successful.

Many industries today work to very strict and tight timelines, as many tasks may need to be finished before other work can proceed. Time is such an important resource, businesses may charge their clients by the hour, by the quarter-hour, or even by the minute, for their services. Time must be allocated efficiently if a business is to remain efficient and financially sound.

9.1.1 Identifying organisational requirements and protocols for planning tools

In most cases, staff within an organisation will look after their own schedules. For example, salespeople spend a lot of their time out of their office and will update their schedules on an ongoing basis during the day. There will be times, however, when you will need to arrange appointments or schedules for other staff members, or when someone will share access to their diaries so the "team" can coordinate meetings or tasks more effectively. This might involve linking personal and executive diaries. Computer-based diaries should, ideally, be linked so that staff such as departmental secretaries or personal assistants can access all diaries and make appointments appropriately.

Being in control of someone else's time means that you will need to use appropriate scheduling tools. Care must be taken with this, as improper schedule management can lead to embarrassing and unprofessional situations. For example:

- Visitors arrive who are not expected because their appointment wasn't noted in the diary.
- Two or more visitors arrive at the same time. This can be very embarrassing and is potentially offensive to the visitors, as it indicates a lack of courtesy and is a waste of their time.
- An expected visitor may not arrive if they cancelled their appointment but the cancellation wasn't noted in the staff member's diary. This wastes the staff member's time while they wait, and it could lead to an embarrassing situation if they call the visitor to ask why they haven't arrived, only to learn that the appointment was cancelled several days before.

When managing other people's schedules, you need to understand how they prefer to allocate their time. However, it may not just be a matter of individual preference. Some industries may have specific requirements for how schedules are kept—for example, for accounting purposes. We will look at such requirements a little later in the chapter.

In addition to being aware of individuals' personal preferences, you will need to consider other factors:

- *What information needs to be available?* Ensure that any necessary information is available to the people attending the meeting, such as:
  - agendas
  - minutes of previous meetings

- reports
- client proposals.

- *Can the usual rules be bent?* Is the meeting with a high-priority client who expects direct and immediate access to staff, or is a close family member calling about a family matter that requires immediate attention?
- *What protocols must be followed when contacting people both within and outside your own organisation?* In the same way that people wanting access to the staff you support need to follow your organisation's usual protocols, you will have to follow the protocols of the organisations you contact to make appointments for your colleagues. This means you need to know who within the other organisation to contact to make appointments.
- *Has adequate time been allowed between appointments?* When making appointments or organising schedules, you need to allow enough time between each item so that the staff involved can make notes and discuss what occurred during the meeting before moving on to the next one. This is particularly important when interviewing potential staff.
- *Has sufficient time been scheduled to complete projects and meet deadlines?* In the same way as you need to leave time between appointments, staff need enough time to complete their projects or meet their deadlines without becoming stressed.

Diaries and planning tools

There are a large range of manual and electronic tools available to help in managing schedules. These can include:

- diaries
- wall planners
- electronic diaries
- mobile applications.

Manual tools

Most organisations today that use, or need to access and manage, diaries do so using computer programs or mobile applications. There may, however, be organisations that still use manual or paper-based methods. Examples of these include:

- *Desk diaries.* Desk diaries come in a variety of formats—from small booklets showing one week, to a double-page spread, to an A4-size book that can be divided into day allotments to suit a range of needs. Some of these diaries can be highly specialised and are designed for an entire industry. For example, medical diaries will often show time allocations of 15 minutes; hairdressing salon diaries are often divided into columns according to individual staff; and lawyers' diaries will allocate their time by the minute.
- *Planning wall charts.* A planning wall chart indicates when staff are away on leave or on a business trip, or for personal development training or another activity. It is important for managers to know where their staff are, and whether they need to bring in extra staff to cover for the periods of staff absence. This is particularly important in businesses that experience seasonal fluctuations. For example, in the finance industry, taking a leave of absence for whatever reason during tax time would leave the organisation seriously shorthanded during its busiest time of the year. A planning chart, drafted at the beginning of the year, indicates those periods of time when staff have planned to be away. It is, therefore, an excellent forward planning tool.

Think about

1. Does your organisation use manual scheduling tools? If so, how?

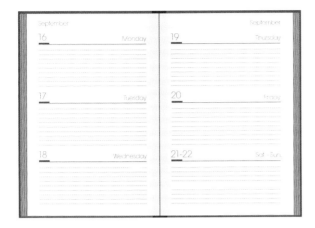

YEAR PLANNER 2023

Electronic tools

Most organisations will use electronic methods of booking appointments and keeping track of their schedules. Electronic tools include:

- computer software-based diaries
- customer contact database calendars
- personal organisers
- mobile telephone and tablet-based applications.

These electronic methods of managing schedules have many advantages, including their easy accessibility and the ability they provide users to reach large numbers of people almost instantly and with very little effort. Then, too, invitations to attend meetings can be accepted or declined by email, giving you written confirmation of people's ability to attend.

Some software programs are designed specifically for email, task and diary purposes. The most commonly used diary software programs include Microsoft Outlook and Google Calendar. It is relatively easy to book appointments and organise meetings using these programs. The Calendar application on a mobile phone or tablet produces similar results, is easy to use and provides a number of options, such as:

- *alerts*—to remind you of the appointment time
- *invitations*—so that you can invite others to a meeting and accept their confirmation (or decline)
- *address details*—which can also link to mapping programs that show means of getting to the meeting destination, and much more.

Video: Creating a new appointment or meeting in Outlook

Let's use Microsoft Outlook as an example of how to make a simple appointment. Using the desktop version of Outlook 365, click the *Calendar* icon on the bottom left of the window to access the *Calendar*, then click on the *New Appointment* option in the *New* tab in the *Home* ribbon at the top. (Figure 9.1). This will bring up a screen that allows you to make an appointment for the individual concerned and includes a range of options for you to add any necessary details (Figure 9.2). Clicking *Invite Attendees* in the *Attendees* tab in the *Home* ribbon will bring up additional contact information options to include in your invite (Figure 9.3). Complete each field in the same way you did for a simple appointment. The meeting invitation will then be sent to the people you have listed. This screen also gives you the option to attach documents, photos and a range of other things.

Microsoft Outlook allows add-ins for applications such as Skype, Microsoft Teams, Zoom and Cisco WebEx for conducting online, face-to-face meetings (Figure 9.4). You can set up your meeting by clicking on the icons in the relevant application tab in the *Meeting* ribbon. Outlook will schedule the meeting in the selected application and generate a link to the online meeting (Figure 9.5). This link will then be appended to the end of your invitation to send out to the invitees.

Google Calendar is another application that is particularly useful, as it syncs with a range of other Google applications, giving you access to your contact list, maps (so that you can input the

Figure 9.1 Outlook menu bar showing *New Appointment* option

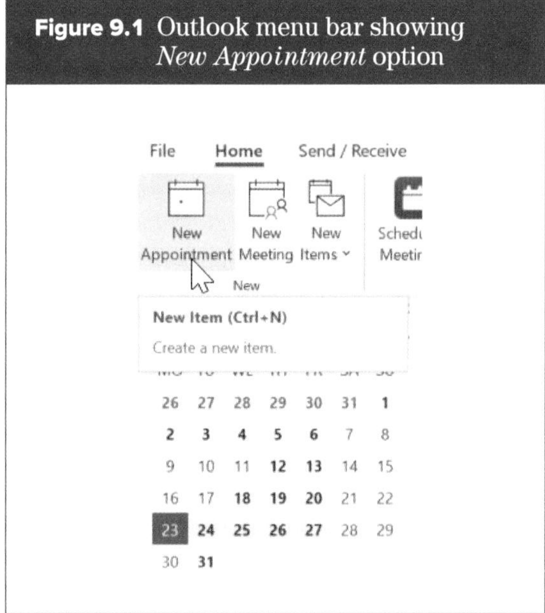

Figure 9.2 Outlook screen showing appointment options

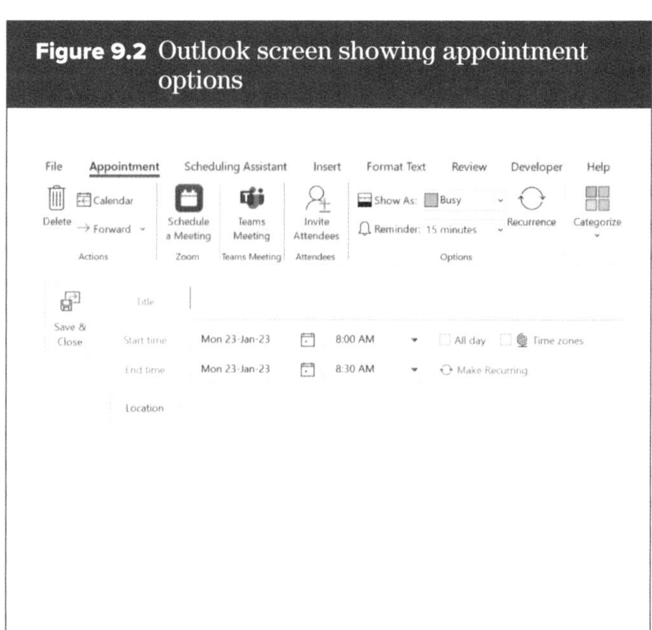

Figure 9.3 Outlook screen showing *Invite Attendees*

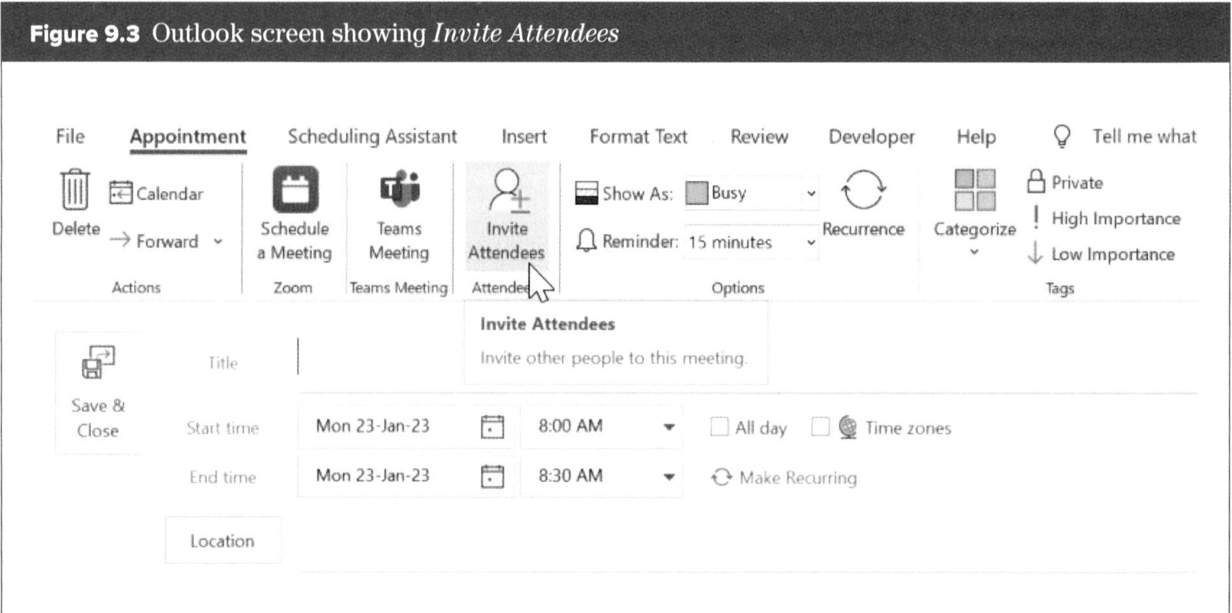

Figure 9.4 Outlook screen showing option to schedule a meeting

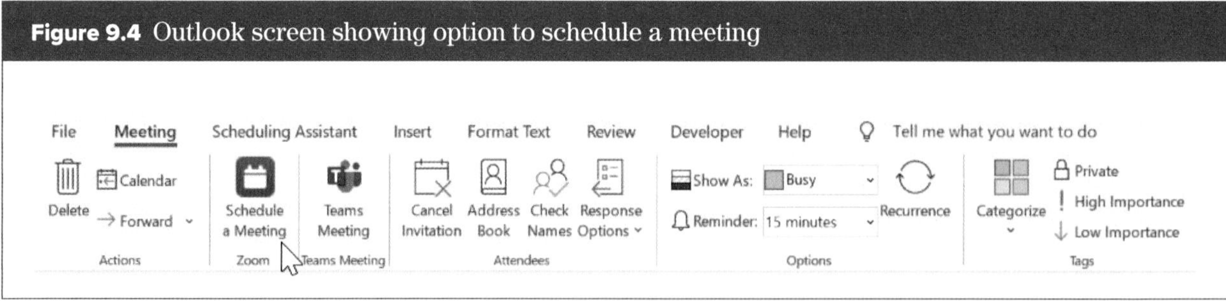

meeting address and use it to find the venue), documents, images, videoconferencing, and much more (Figure 9.6).

There are, of course, many other scheduling software programs and mobile applications. Some of these are designed specifically for certain industries, while others can be downloaded from the internet. Examples of other applications can include:

- Microfocus/Groupwise: https://www.microfocus.com/en-us/products/groupwise/overview

- Alloc8: https://www.alloc8.io/
- Connecteam: https://lp.connecteam.com/scheduling-app-aw/?utm_source=capterra.com&utm_medium=cpc&utm_campaign=scheduling&utm_adgroupname=capterra

Figure 9.5 Outlook options for scheduling a Zoom meeting

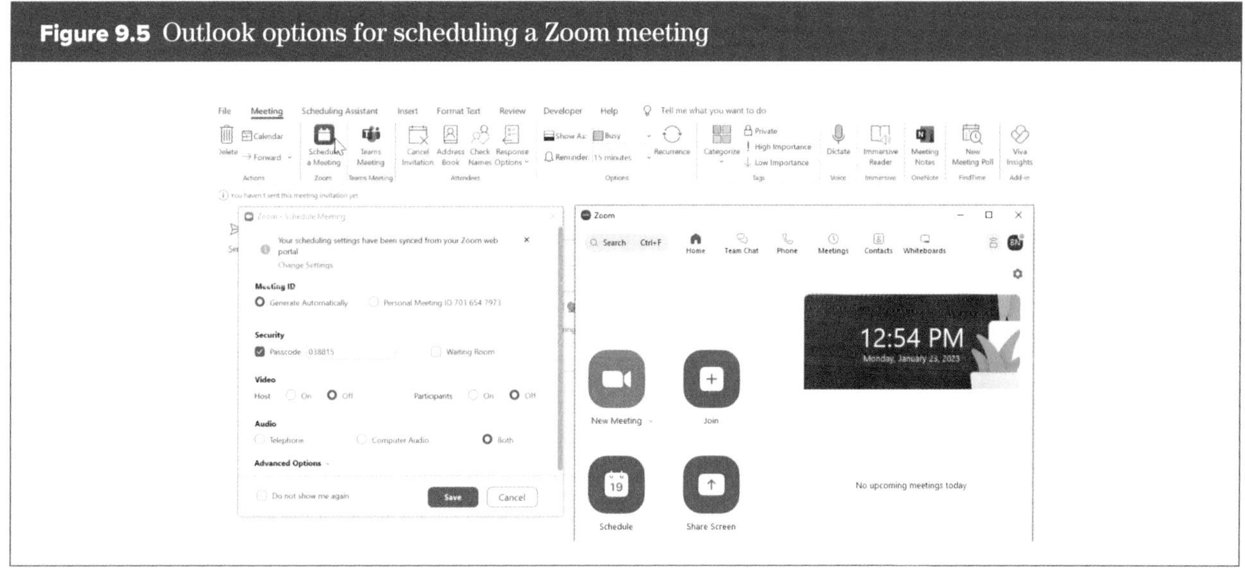

Figure 9.6 Meeting options in Google Calendar

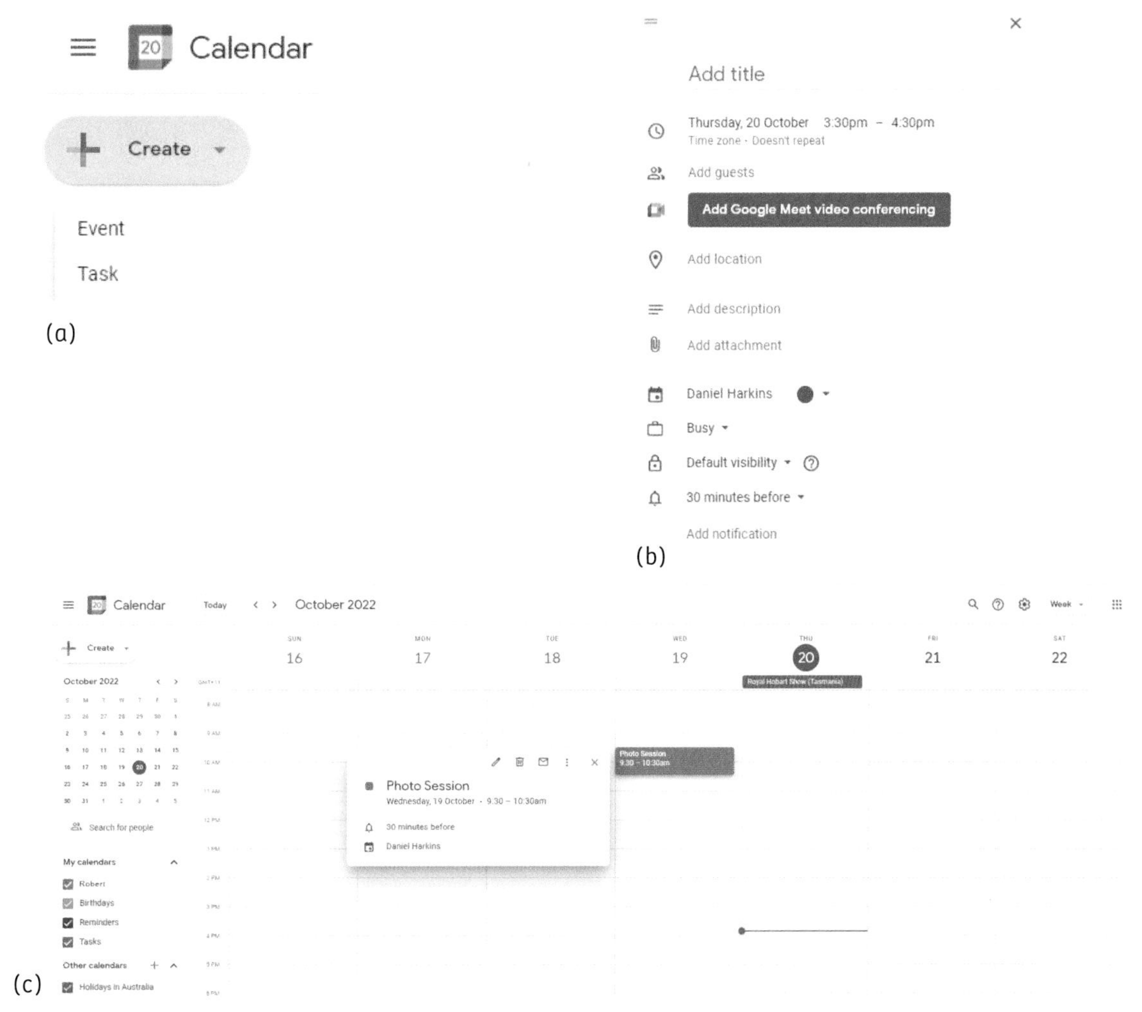

(a)

(b)

(c)

Try this now

1. Make an appointment and invite at least two other people. The appointment can be for any purpose you choose.

Customer contact database diaries

In addition to the purpose-built email and diary programs, other forms of computerised diaries include those that are part of a sales and marketing-based **customer contact database**. Again, you can choose to view the diary as a daily, weekly or monthly overview of appointments. The advantage of such diaries is that appointments and meetings are recorded in customer or supplier records and therefore can build a history of your dealings with a particular person or company.

Personal organisers

The increased use of mobile devices for business applications has seen paper-based personal organisers used less and less these days. These paper organisers look very much like a diary. The difference is that the organiser will also include the following sections:

- daily calendar
- contact details (address book)
- "to do" list
- financial information sheets, such as expenses and sales made
- notes pages
- business card holder.

Some electronic mobile apps now offer these same options.

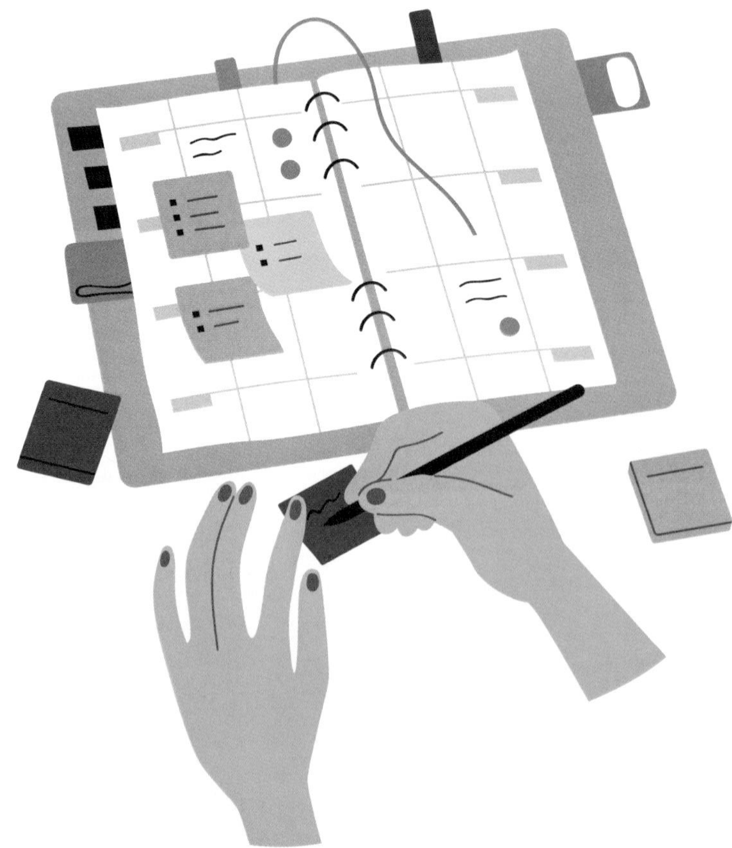

Today's smartphones and tablets also function as electronic organisers. They allow the user not only to make and receive phone calls, but also to keep a diary, write notes, send and receive emails, take photos and videos, and much more.

Both paper and digital (or electronic) organisers are generally personal methods of schedule management kept by individual staff members, although access to various sales or diary applications can be shared with other users who may have an interest in the diary details.

Time management software programs

As mentioned earlier, in some industries it is essential to allocate people's time exactly. This is because those people bill their clients for the number of hours and/or tasks the organisation is undertaking on the client's behalf. Businesses that operate in this way include law and accounting firms, project management consultancies and general consultancies, among others. Keeping track of the *exact* time and the *exact* tasks performed on a client's behalf can be complex; anything that you miss and, therefore, don't bill for means time, effort and revenue lost to the organisation. Fortunately, there are several software programs that allow you to track time and expenses expended on behalf of a client, project or task.

These programs help you to:

- track expenses and time spent
- keep a record of sub-contractor billing
- run reports on project progress
- invoice directly from the system
- keep records for audit purposes.

Think about

2. What are the advantages of being able to accurately track your time and how tasks were completed?

9.1.2 Understanding procedures for different types of appointments and schedules

Procedures used for managing schedules and appointments may differ depending on the size of the organisation. In a small organisation, for example, you may only be managing schedules for a handful of people and can talk to them all directly about their needs and preferences.

In a large corporation, however, it may be necessary to coordinate the schedules of several individuals from different departments, following a strict procedure. For example, when scheduling a meeting between department heads, time considerations of the most senior members may take priority over those of more junior members of staff. Then, too, the venue for a meeting may depend on the importance of the people involved. This will all take a great deal of coordination between those responsible for managing the individual schedules.

You may also be required to deal with or organise many different kinds of schedules. Some may be short, simple meetings or appointments, while others can be complex and take place over several days. There may also be specific time constraints that you will need to consider. Appointments and schedules can therefore include the following types:

- *Conferences.* A conference is an event normally held over several days and includes a variety of activities that participants can choose from. A schedule for a conference would include the times and dates of workshops, seminars and guest speakers. It would also include the dates and times of any social functions, such as dinners or "team-building" exercises. The cost of attending a conference can be substantial, with entry fees to the conference, hotel rooms, travel expenses and meals all needing to be paid for. All of the conference events and sessions therefore need to be properly scheduled so that attendees can make the most of the various opportunities offered. Figure 9.7 shows an example of a conference program. The person attending the conference would choose the topics most relevant to them and their organisation's needs and schedule the different talks accordingly.
- *Leave.* There will always be times when staff are away on annual leave, on business trips or are away from the office for an extended period of time. These absences can cause a decrease in productivity if they aren't scheduled into the organisation's staffing strategies. By scheduling these absences, you can ensure that there are sufficient staff available to cover the workload without a loss of productivity.
- *Meetings.* Meetings are held for a variety of reasons and between a variety of different people. You might need to meet with customers, suppliers, other staff from within your own organisation, as well as management and government representatives. As there may be more than one meeting on any given day, it is essential that they are diarised correctly to avoid embarrassment and wasted time.
- *Recurring appointments.* These are meetings that are held on a regular basis and could include board meetings, regular staff meetings and committee meetings. These types of appointments will generally be held around the same day and/or time at regular intervals—for example, each quarter, month or week.
- *Travel.* A business trip also requires proper scheduling (see Table 9.1). Business travel can be very expensive. The organisation will need to pay for the traveller's airfares (if applicable), hotel accommodation, meals and so on. In order for the trip to be as successful as possible, it is important for the traveller to know:
  - when and from where their flight, or other mode of transport, is leaving
  - where they will be staying in each city they may be visiting

Figure 9.7 Sample of a conference program outlining discussion topics and times

#2022NVC - DAY ONE

#2022NVC CONFERENCE PROGRAM DAY ONE
Thursday 3 November 2022

7.00am	Registration			
8.45am	Official Open and Welcome			
9.00am	Update from the Australian Skills Quality Authority Christina Bolger, Deputy Chief Executive Officer (ASQA)			
9.45am	Housekeeping and Message from our Platinum Sponsor			
10.00am	Morning Tea & Networking			
	Compliance	**Hands On/Hands Up (Training)**	**Deep Dive (Administration)**	**Digital/Online**
10.40am - 12.10pm	Arena 1B Working Towards Compliance: How to not be scared of audits **David Garner**	Central A Putting Creative Training Techniques into Practice **Marc Ratcliffe**	Arena 1A Planning and Managing Self-Assurance Activities **Angela McGregor**	Rooms 5, 6, 7 10 Quick-Fire Findings from Research **Dr Deniese Cox**
	Regulator/Government	**Digital/Online**	**Management**	**Assessment**
12.20pm - 1.05pm	Arena 1B Risk-Based Responsive Regulation – Our 2022-23 Program of Work **Sean Heffernan**	Central A Academic Integrity in Online Learning **Natalie Oostergo**	Arena 1A Help Your RTO Grow and Glow **Allison Miller**	Rooms 5, 6, 7 Implementing the Rules of Evidence: A close look at issues and how to avoid them **Coleen Rivas**
1.05pm	Networking Lunch			
	Administration	**Training/Student Engagement**	**Management**	**Digital/Online**
2.10pm - 3.05pm	Arena 1B Individual Support Needs: Identifying and responding **Angela McGregor**	Central A 10 Ways to Boost Your Facilitation Skills **Jason Ash**	Arena 1A Dynamic and Profitable Financials **David Jepsen**	Rooms 5, 6, 7 The Big Shift - Designing for Virtual Classrooms **Neil Von Heupt**
	Digital/Online	**Regulator/Government**	**Training/Student Engagement**	**Assessment**
3.15pm - 4.00pm	Arena 1B Top Trends in Digital Learning **Kerri Buttery**	Central A Self Assurance – Building Confidence in Quality Outcomes **Tracey Rees**	Arena 1A Ad-hoc Learning Design - Lessons from 12 Years in Instructional Design **Tony Kirton**	Rooms 5, 6, 7 Playing your Key Assessment Instruments ... the Right Way **Melanie Alexandra**
4.00pm	Afternoon Tea & Networking			
	Freestyle Facilitation	**Freestyle Facilitation**	**Freestyle Facilitation**	**Freestyle Facilitation**
4.30pm - 5.15pm	Arena 1B Let's talk about Compliance **David Garner**	Central A Let's Talk About Training **Marc Ratcliffe**	Arena 1A Let's Talk About Administration **Angela McGregor**	Rooms 5, 6, 7 Let's Talk About Assessment **Melanie Alexandra**
5.30pm - 8.30pm	WELCOME FUNCTION!			

Source: 2021 VELG Conference

- what companies they will be visiting, and when
- who they will be seeing
- how they will be getting around at their destination.

Table 9.1 Example of a travel itinerary showing daily schedule of events

Date	Time	Arrangement	Details
12 June	08:00	Flight QF123	Sydney–Melbourne. Arrive 09:00
	12:30	Meeting with Charles Li Managing Director	ACME Travel 123 Franklin St Melbourne Phone: (03) 9234 5678
	19:30	Dinner with Mr and Mrs Li	Windsor Hotel
13 June	10:45	Meeting with Alison Jenkins General Manager	Far Away Tours 15 Swanson St Melbourne Phone: (03) 9234 9876
	12:15	Meeting with Maaike De Vries Marketing Manager	ABC Airlines 15/987 Tullamarine Drive Tullamarine Phone: (03) 9254 7654
	15:30	Flight QF124	Melbourne–Sydney. Arrive 16:30

- *Deadlines.* Wherever specific projects are involved, the organisation may have given time frames in which sections of the project must be completed. In this case, a schedule may be drawn up at the beginning of the work project so that everyone involved knows what they have to do and when their part needs to be completed. This ensures that the next phase of the undertaking can proceed.
- *Agenda.* An agenda is used as a guideline in a meeting to ensure that all the necessary points are covered (Figure 9.8). Each participant in the meeting will be sent a copy of the agenda in advance, so that they know what will be discussed during the meeting and can prepare themselves accordingly. Agendas can be very simple, such as a bullet point list of topics, or they can be more complex and provide information on who will be attending, where the meeting is being held, how long each presentation is expected to last, and so on.

Figure 9.8 Example of an agenda outlining the topics of discussion during a meeting

Agenda

Date: 12/06/23
Time: 09:00

Purpose: Department monthly meeting

Venue: Boardroom

Participants: Dan Daly, Rui Yamamoto, Jackson Black, Veejay Dendijay

Time	Item	Presenter
09:00	Read minutes of last meeting and discuss any issues	Dan Daly
10:00	Results of customer service survey conducted last month	Rui Yamamoto
10:30	Allocation of action points resulting from survey results	Jackson Black
11:00 ... and so on.	Marketing initiatives for the coming quarter	Veejay Dendijay

9.1.3 Establishing schedule management requirements

No two people within an organisation will have the same requirements when it comes to allocating their time. They may have different priorities, different tasks to perform or different levels of authority. Apart from the actual time-keeping methods, then, you also need to consider how each individual might need to manage their time. For example, they may:

- prefer to restrict visitors or other appointments to specific times of the day
- choose to restrict the number of visitors they see each day

- have preferences in terms of days of the week when they will or won't see visitors
- be specific about the time allocated to each visit
- have certain visitors who take precedence over all others, so that you may need to rearrange existing appointments in order to fit such visitors in if necessary.

Developing appointment schedules and priorities

During the course of a normal working day, there will be people who make unsolicited calls and wish to speak to, or make appointments with, staff in your organisation. The purpose of these calls is often to sell your organisation something that may, or may not, prove useful to the organisation. It may become part of your role to sort out and decide who (if anyone) these calls should be passed on to.

You may also need to prioritise the time of the people whose diary you control. This might mean determining what is and isn't important, and how much of the person's time to allocate to given appointments in order to ensure their time is used effectively. Prior discussion with the people you look after will help you to determine how best to handle their calls and appointments.

Identifying task items

In prioritising appointments and schedules, you should consider the nature of the meeting. As discussed earlier, there are many different types of meetings and those attending them should be well prepared. When allocating time, consider the following:

- What type of meeting is it?
  - What information will the participants need in order to participate fully? For example:
    - profiles of the people who will be attending
    - any work files that may be required for the meeting
    - electronic equipment needed for communicating with participants who are attending online
    - presentation equipment and handouts.
  - What is on the meeting agenda?
    - How long will it take to go through each agenda item?
    - Should you allow extra time?
    - What else do participants have scheduled for that day that might impact on the length of this meeting?
- Who will be attending the meeting, and what are their specific needs? Participants will be responsible for a range of things within the organisation. Depending on their position in and importance to the organisation, you may need to discuss and clarify their needs. Individual personnel may include:
  - executive assistants
  - directors and managers
  - partners
  - supervisors.

By asking these and other relevant questions when developing appointments and schedules, you can ensure that participants have everything they need for conducting a successful meeting.

You might also need to consider the resources that you, yourself, may need to develop these schedules. For example:

- appropriate software and/or mobile applications used to manage schedules
- access to individual diaries, with permission from each person concerned
- contact details of other staff as well as external stakeholders such as:
  - board members
  - customers

   - suppliers
   - government agencies or industry bodies
- appropriate technology, such as:
   - computers and printers
   - mobile devices
   - email systems.

Knowledge check

1. There are a large range of both paper-based and electronic schedule planning tools available. List and briefly describe at least five of these tools.
2. Just as there are different software programs for organising schedules, there are different types of appointments and schedules. List and briefly describe at least five of these.
3. When establishing schedule management requirements for individuals, there are number of things to consider. List at least four of these.
4. Developing appointment schedules often means identifying task items. List at least five questions you could ask when considering these task items.
5. Identify the different types of individuals you might typically need to develop schedules for.
6. Task items might also include resources that you, yourself, might need for developing schedules. List at least three such resources.

9.2 Managing schedules

Dealing with initial appointments and schedules is only a small part of the process of managing time. Schedules aren't merely entries in a diary; people are involved. These people will have demands on their time which may, on occasion, conflict with meeting dates you need to set up. It may be part of your role to negotiate with the meeting participants to find a date that suits everyone.

9.2.1 Scheduling recurring appointments

Video: Scheduling meetings in Outlook

In addition to making general one-off appointments, you may be responsible for scheduling **recurring appointments** (i.e. that happen on a regular basis). You may need to manage the setting up of meetings by accessing a range of different staff member diaries and negotiating dates and times for meetings to be held.

Appointments that occur on a regular basis can include the following:

- *Sales meetings*. These meetings are often held weekly, on the same day and at a regular time. They are held so that sales staff can discuss the week's activities and their plans for the following week. Action points may be established and follow-ups discussed. To ensure that all necessary staff are in attendance, these meetings could be scheduled up to a year in advance. That way, unless there is a good reason, there is no excuse for staff not to attend.
- *Project management meetings*. These meetings will generally be held regularly for the duration of the project, be it weeks, months or even years. A schedule of dates could be set up, well in advance, so that all parties concerned can meet to discuss the project's progress and take whatever actions might be necessary.
- *Board or committee meetings*. These meetings will occur at regular intervals during the year. They may have specifically set days and times—for example: the first Thursday of every month at 7 am.

In all of these cases, electronic diaries can be set to show that these meetings are recurring at a given interval, and the system will automatically book all the relevant dates in the diary.

Example

The senior managers at Townhouse Marketing and Public Relations meet each month to discuss any issues that have arisen since the last meeting, as well as any upcoming events or promotions, and to examine how they are performing against the organisation's goals and objectives.

Up to now, there has been no set date or time, and the marketing director's personal assistant, Sally, has always had difficulty finding a day and time each month that suits everyone.

A decision was made last month to hold the meetings on the last Friday of every month and to diarise this for the entire year. Each department head would then know that they couldn't make any other appointment at that time on that day and would thus be available to attend this very important meeting.

Sally sets up a recurring meeting in the organisation's computerised diary and sends invitations to all managers. Once these staff members have "accepted" the meeting, the system diarises these dates and times so that they show up in everyone's computer diary, blocking that time and date slot from other appointments.

Diary systems should all offer the ability to book recurring meetings. In Outlook, for example, you can specify whether meetings are to take place daily, weekly, monthly or annually, and you can stipulate the day of the week on which the meetings will occur. You can also stipulate when the cycle of these recurring meetings is to start and when they should end. This is useful if, for example, a major work project is being undertaken and meetings need to be held on a regular basis to discuss progress.

To set up a recurring appointment in Outlook, create a new *Appointment* in your *Calendar*. Then do the following:

1. Click on the *Recurrence* icon in the *Options* tab to open the *Appointment Recurrence* window (Figure 9.9).
2. Select your preferences for the recurrence, including how often, on what day, and the range of dates affected. If you choose *Weekly*, for example, you will be given the option of choosing the day of the week, as well as selecting the date on which the recurring appointments should end (if necessary) (see Figure 9.10).
3. The invitation will be sent to all the listed participants. Once they accept the invitation, the recurring appointments will be marked in their diaries for all the relevant dates.

9.2.2 Scheduling appointments according to timelines and diary commitments

There will be times in everyone's working life when deadlines need to be met. This might, for example, be because special projects have been set up by the organisation, and staff rely on each other to get their work done so that they, in turn, can get on with their own tasks. When this happens, due dates for task completion or specific milestones should be entered into the diary or scheduling system to maintain control of all the tasks that need to be completed and to ensure they are on track. Scheduling these milestones allows all participants in the work being done to monitor progress and take corrective action if necessary.

Negotiating alternative arrangements

In setting up meetings, however, you may be faced with conflicting time requirements. Depending on the number of people required to attend, and their status and responsibility within the organisation, they may not always be able to accept the date or time set for a meeting. This may happen because of:

- clashing time schedules
- unexpected events that need to be dealt with urgently

Figure 9.9 Screen showing options for recurring appointments

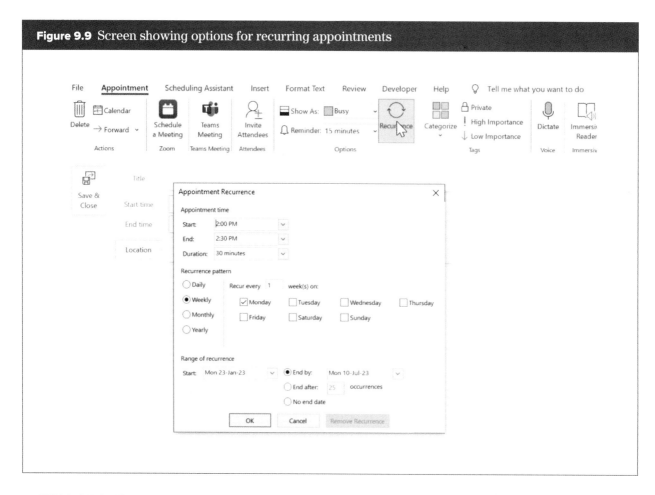

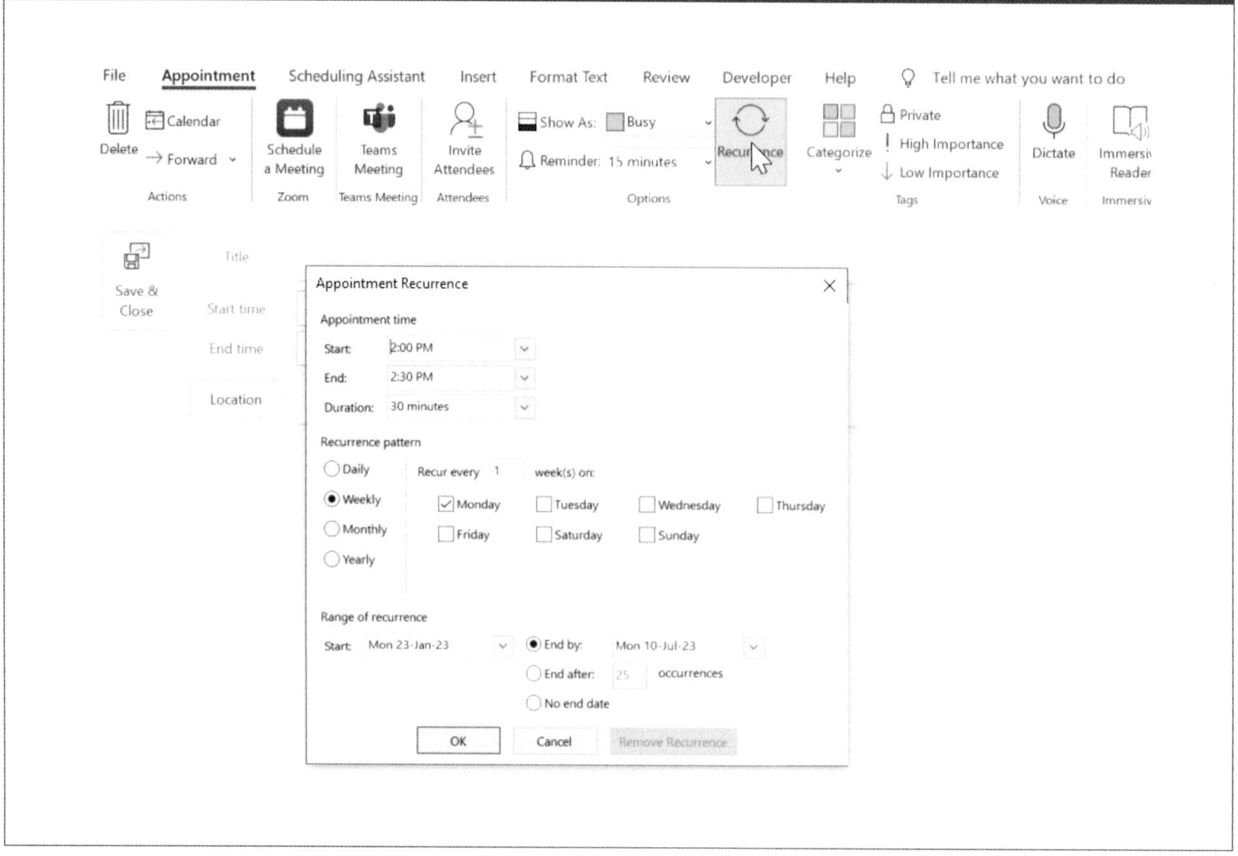

Figure 9.10 Screen showing further options for recurring appointments

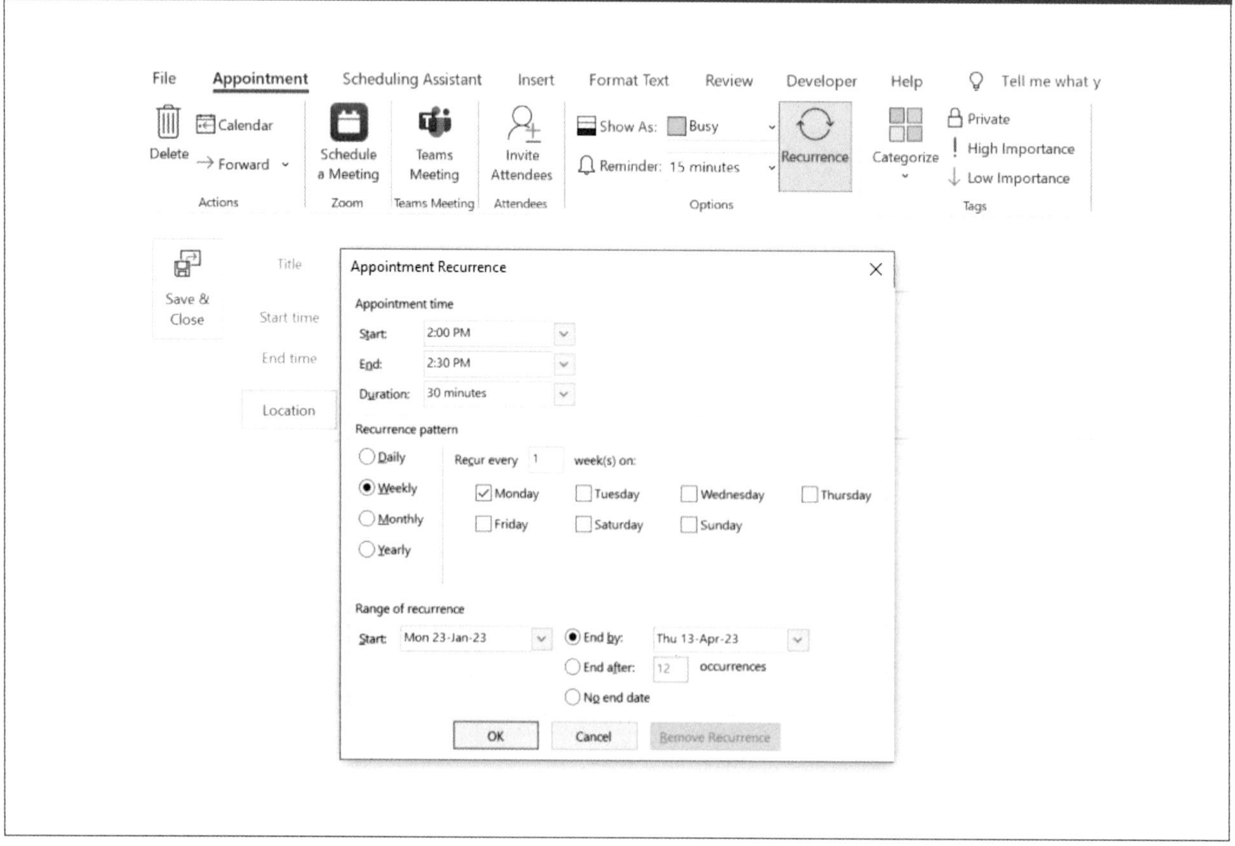

- superseding meetings of greater importance
- mistakes in diarising appointments, such as double bookings.

Depending on an attendee's specific role or importance, the planned meeting may have to be rescheduled, in which case it will be up to you to organise a date and time that will suit everyone involved. In these cases, you may need to liaise back and forth several times until another suitable date and time is found. When this is the case, steps will need to be taken to ensure maximum attendance. These steps might include determining what is the highest priority for the meeting: is it more important to have as *many* people as possible attend, or is it more important that *specific* people attend?

When arranging alternative dates and times, you may need to:

- call or email (via your computer diary) each individual and ascertain their availability on the new date/time
- continue to look for suitable dates/times until everyone who needs to be at the meeting is satisfied with the rescheduled date/time
- ensure that all parties are advised and have confirmed the new date/time.

Try this now

2. There needs to be a change to the appointment you previously made for yourself and the other two people. Change the appointment to a date that suits everyone by discussing alternative dates with them.

9.2.3 Recording and managing schedules

It is vital to accurately record details of the arrangements made so that the business can continue to run smoothly and no one is kept waiting or is embarrassed by misunderstandings around the schedule. Regardless of the diarising method used, you must make sure you have accurately recorded details such as:

- name of the person
- their contact details
- date and time of the arrangement
- purpose of the arrangement.

If changes are made to the arrangement, record these and notify immediately everyone affected by the changes. Also take note of the notification process: who you advised of the change, and when. Should a dispute arise, you will have a written record of when the change was made and who you spoke to about it.

Importantly, managing schedules also means working within the guidelines set by the organisation's policies and procedures. These may include the following:

- *A limit on the total number of appointments made for an individual on any one day.* Limiting appointments allows time for accurate processing of the information gained from each appointment, which leads to fewer mistakes and better organisation. Some organisations may specify that salespeople must see a minimum number of clients each day, so this also needs to be managed effectively.
- *The scheduling of breaks.* Consider the need for breaks when setting up a meeting, conference or other long work session. Sitting in a closed room for long periods of time can be stressful, so ensure there is a break every few hours. This might also mean organising refreshments or meals (lunch).

- *Work health and safety (WHS)*. For example:
  - Regular breaks keep participants alert and refreshed. They also give people a chance to get up and walk about, as sitting for extended periods of time can be harmful if the chair isn't comfortable or the person is unable to stretch and get their circulation going.
  - Ensure that the venue used for the meeting is well ventilated and well lit.
  - Check that all equipment is in good working order and doesn't pose a health risk.

9.2.4 Understanding any legislative requirements, codes and standards

Finally, in addition to observing your organisation's requirements, you may need to be aware of any legislative requirements and industry codes and standards of practice that may affect your business or industry. These may not necessarily have anything to do with time management itself, but it is necessary for you to understand their nature. To recap, they can include the following:

- *Anti-discrimination legislation*. It is against the law in Australia to discriminate against people because of their age, sex, religion, race or sexual orientation. Anti-discrimination legislation provides guidance on issues such as equal employment opportunity, harassment and bullying in the workplace, racial discrimination, and others.
- *Privacy laws*. These laws stipulate what information can and cannot be distributed or used by an organisation. When visitors to your workplace provide you with personal and private details, they trust that you will keep their information confidential. Australia's privacy laws outline people's rights and redress options in this regard.
- *WHS legislation*. It is vital that, whatever work you do, you do it in a safe and secure environment and in a safe and secure manner.
- *Ethical principles*. This relates to the way in which the organisation behaves towards its customers and suppliers and encompasses the actions all staff members on the organisation's behalf. An ethical company deals honestly and openly with its customers and suppliers.
- *Industry codes of practice*. These provide a set of guidelines and regulations that members of the relevant industry are expected to follow. They may not necessarily be mandatory, but it will nevertheless be recommended that all members of an industry follow these guidelines in order to provide quality service to their customers.

As mentioned, managing schedules is an important part of any business, as time must be used effectively if an organisation and its work teams are to achieve their goals. Ensuring that schedules flow logically, that no time is wasted, and that various task time frames have been considered is a role of great responsibility. For example: when developing a schedule for a specific project, all the necessary tasks must be ordered according to priority and the amount of time it will take to complete each one. This is very important as, often, the next step cannot be taken in a project until specific objectives have been met. If the tasks haven't been scheduled in the right order, or if there isn't enough time available to complete all the necessary steps, then this could hold up the entire project. In turn, this could cost the organisation a significant amount of money.

Knowledge check

7. Describe what is meant by the term "recurring appointments".
8. Give three examples of appointments that occur on a regular basis.
9. Sometimes not everyone who is required to attend a meeting will be available. Give at least three reasons why this might happen.
10. Describe what action you could take when arranging alternative dates.

11. Explain why schedules might need to be made according to timelines and diary commitments.
12. When recording and managing schedules, there are, at a minimum, four things you should take note of. What are they?
13. Managing schedules also means working within the guidelines set by the organisation's policies and procedures, as well as legislative requirements, codes and standards. Give at least four examples of what these might include.

9.3 Evaluating the effectiveness of schedules

Flexibility is a key element in the continued success of any business. While a set of procedures is an excellent source of guidance on business operations, they should be flexible enough to allow for changes and improvements when called for. Times change. For example, today's world is run on technology and new ways of thinking and doing business. The effectiveness of business practices should therefore be reviewed and evaluated on an ongoing basis. Does the current way we do things still work? Are there better, more efficient, methods of working now available? These and many other questions will help you to determine what, if anything, needs to be changed.

9.3.1 Seeking feedback and assessing the effectiveness of schedules

Evaluating work systems is important and should involve communication at every stage of the review process. Feedback can be sought in a number of ways:

- *Directly from the individuals who use the scheduling system*, that is, from those who understand how effective (or not) the process is.
- *Through planned reviews*, which can take the form of audits specifically designed to determine the effectiveness of the system. For example, a review could be made to determine how efficiently individual diaries can be accessed. Any issues identified during the review can then be discussed and rectified.
- *By means of team meetings*, which enable staff to bring issues and areas of concern to the attention of other team members and supervisors. Any concerns can then be discussed and a determination made about what, if anything, will be done.
- *By fully understanding organisational policies and procedures*, and how any changes in these could affect the organisation as a whole.

Feedback is one of the most effective and efficient methods of evaluating a process. It allows you to discuss, face to face with those using the system, the current methods used, any issues identified, and ideas for improvement, and to ask relevant questions to gain a deep understanding of any issues.

Questions to ask in a feedback session may include:

- Has anything changed in the way we do business?
- Does the current scheduling system do what we now need it to do?
- Did we encounter any problems with the system over the past year(s)?
- What was the impact (if any) of those problems on the business, or on the individuals concerned?
  - Was there a financial cost for the organisation?
  - Did we needlessly use up resources due to the error?
  - Did our reputation suffer as a result of the problem?
  - Did we lose business as a result of the problem?

- How did we resolve the problem?
  - Was there a cost factor involved in resolving the problem, in terms of expense, human resources, time and effort?
  - Was the resolution the best possible option?
  - Could it be further improved upon?
- What needs to happen in order to avoid such errors or problems in the future?

Asking questions and discussing feedback can provide a valuable insight into what is—or isn't—working efficiently and allows the organisation to proactively seek solutions or better methods of working.

Identifying areas for improvement

It should be clear, then, that identifying areas of improvement should be part of the organisation's regular continuous improvement program. An organisation that focuses on continuous improvement can remain successful and maintain its advantages in its industry.

In addition to gathering feedback from others, regularly reviewing and auditing work processes means:

- looking at existing processes to determine if they are still practical or in line with current business practices and market trends
- identifying what is, and isn't, working
- identifying opportunities for improvement
- determining what is needed in order to make the necessary changes:
  - What resources will you need?
  - How will this change affect the current capabilities of the organisation and its staff?
  - How can we ensure a smooth implementation?

Depending on the outcome of the feedback received and the review and evaluation process, you may end up with a list of areas that could be improved upon. An action plan can then be developed to initiate those improvements (Table 9.2).

Table 9.2 Areas for improvement

Issue	Action needed	By whom	By when
Diaries between Filippo and Julia (PA) don't sync properly.	Julia to contact IT to find and fix syncing error.	Julia and Jayleen from IT	25/6
Current system doesn't allow for online meetings, and most international customers now expect this.	Research new technology to replace current system.	IT staff	2/7
... and so on.			

The saying that "time is money" is certainly true in a business setting. Failure by employees to manage their time efficiently can have an enormous impact on their organisation's performance and productivity, which in turn affects its reputation and financial situation. Effective time management can help in:

- prioritising tasks so that important work is done on time
- improving efficiency and productivity
- producing better-quality work
- eliminating wasted time and procrastination
- reducing stress and anxiety caused by approaching deadlines
- making better decisions.

Knowledge check

14. List at least three ways in which feedback can be gathered.

15. List at least five questions you could ask when gathering feedback about a work process.

16. Describe the methods you could use when identifying areas for improvement.

Summary

Time is an important and valuable asset in every business; once spent, it can *never* be recalled. There are no "do-overs". As such, time should be handled with care and attention to ensure it is used in the most effective and efficient way. Understanding the nature of different types of appointments and schedules will help you to determine the best way to manage time. A key function of an administrative role is to understand the scheduling requirements of the people you work with, and to manage their time efficiently and effectively using the range of different tools that are available.

CHAPTER 10
Purchase goods and services

Learning outcomes

10.1 Understand purchasing and your own requirements

10.2 Make purchases

10.3 Receive purchases

Organisations need resources in order to function properly. From an administration perspective, you need pens, paper, staples, paperclips and so on. From an operations point of view, you would need computers, printers and copiers; and from a manufacturing perspective, you would need machinery, tools and raw materials with which to manufacture your goods. You may also need to pay for the services of people outside of your organisation, such as consultants and contractors.

All of these things, and many more, are resources that need to be purchased. While some purchases may be minor or are carried out regularly (such as replenishing stock or stationery items), others may occur less frequently or have a significant impact on the organisation's operations and ability to function efficiently. As such, purchasing goods and services is every bit as important as any other task you might be required to perform and should be undertaken with just as much care.

Then, too, every organisation works within a set **financial budget**. For example, money is allocated to such things as rent of premises, utility bills, staff wages, and the cost of other resources that need to be purchased, to name just a few. When making such purchases, you will therefore need to stay within the budget allocated.

You will also need to consider the organisation's purchasing procedures, which may include:

- obtaining quotes from prospective suppliers
- assessing the suppliers and their quotes, as well as the quality of the goods being offered
- selecting the appropriate purchasing methods
- receiving, checking and documenting purchases made into the organisation's inventory
- following organisational protocols in terms of:
  - getting purchase specifications
  - gaining approval for the purchase
  - completing the necessary documentation, and so on.

We will look at these procedures in more detail as we move through the chapter.

10.1 Understanding purchasing and your own requirements

Depending on the size of the organisation, the purchasing process can be relatively simple. In a small organisation, for example, purchasing needs might first be discussed by the relevant staff and the purchase then proceeds. In larger companies, however, the process can be very complex, requiring you to:

- follow strict protocols
- complete forms such as purchase orders
- get signed approvals from relevant supervisors or managers
- obtain quotes from suppliers
- make decisions about the best options, and so on.

Whatever the case, most organisations will have policies and procedures that provide guidance on a range of work tasks, and these must be considered and followed. Purchasing policies and procedures may relate to the following:

- *Record-keeping systems for purchases and assets.* This might involve such things as keeping track of the organisation's inventory. For example, some organisations will have thresholds below which new orders must be placed. This is to ensure that there is always a stock of given items available to keep operations running smoothly. It will also be important, for tax purposes, to keep a record of all purchases made that fall into the "capital resource" category, as these are considered to be "assets".
- *Standard contracting arrangements and templates.* Contracts are legally binding documents that detail the relationship between two parties. Supplier agreements or contracts would provide details on:
  - who is the supplier
  - what they have agreed to provide and at what price
  - time frames in which goods or services need to be supplied
  - the quantity and range of goods or services to be supplied
  - quality of the goods to be supplied
  - terms and conditions of doing business with each other.
- *Segregation of duties.* It is important that you understand not only your own role within the organisation, but that of others who will be relying on you to get work done and upon whom you will rely to complete their work. It also means knowing who is responsible for which work tasks and what your own limits are in terms of making workplace decisions.
- *Purchasing strategies.* These provide directions on how, when and from where goods and services may be purchased.

10.1.1 Understanding and clarifying an organisation's purchasing strategies

In order to achieve its objectives, an organisation will have plans and strategies in place covering a range of organisational elements such as sales, marketing, manufacturing and, possibly, purchasing. Why would it need a **purchasing strategy**? All items purchased by an organisation, whether it is a new stapler, a desk chair, a photocopier or a piece of heavy machinery, will cost money—money that is drawn from the organisation's financial accounts and allocated into budgets for specific purposes. Staying within the forecasted budget is essential for business success and growth; therefore, a strategy document can help to guide staff on what they can and cannot do in specific circumstances—such as spending money.

The purchasing process can include a number of steps. A basic strategy, for example, might involve the following stages (Figure 10.1):

1. *Conduct an internal needs analysis to understand the organisation's current performance levels.* This means looking at the resources currently being used, as well as the associated costs for all departments or functions within the organisation and current growth projections, and then identifying needs and targets so that a purchasing strategy can be developed.
2. *Research suppliers who can potentially provide the goods and services you need.* This might mean looking both nationally and internationally, initially casting a wide net to ensure you end up with the best possible options from which you can narrow your choice to a shortlist of best possibilities.
3. *Gather further information on likely suppliers.* Taking on a new supplier often means contracting with them for an extended period of time. This, in turn, means that you need to be able to trust that they are reliable and cost effective, and that their goods or services meet your exact needs. It is important, therefore, that you gather as much information about them as possible.
4. *Negotiate with potential suppliers.* The shortlist of potential suppliers can then be asked to "tender" for your business or, in the case of a smaller organisation, to submit their price lists. These can then be viewed by the relevant stakeholders within your organisation, who will select their preferred suppliers and, if necessary, enter into negotiations for better pricing or services. Whichever supplier offers the best overall service and pricing generally wins!
5. *Set up an ordering system for the chosen supplier(s).* These would include:
   - appropriate order forms (either paper-based or online)
   - a detailed lists of suppliers
   - methods of tracking orders placed
   - methods of forecasting future needs and expenditure
   - inventory management system to check and keep track of stock or assets
   - financial management of the supplier accounts
   - returns and refunds procedures, and more.

   We will look at many of these aspects as we move through the chapter.

Figure 10.1 Steps in the purchasing process

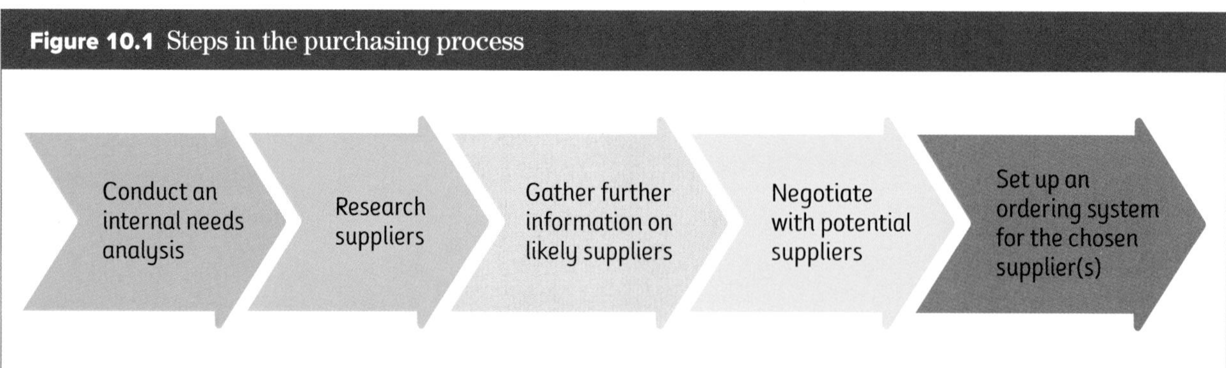

Think about

1. How does your organisation go about ordering goods and services? Is there a set procedure that you are required to follow? What are the advantages of having and following a set procedure?

10.1.2 Determining your own role and the limits of your authority

It is important to be clear on your own role, and the limits of your authority, in the purchasing process. Some items you will be asked to order may be very specific (such as particular machinery parts or software programs) or very expensive and may, therefore, be outside of what you are permitted to purchase on your own authority. What your personal budget limit is will depend on what has been discussed and approved by relevant personnel, such as:

- colleagues, with whom you can discuss current resource usage and needs
- heads of department or supervisors, who will be responsible for their departmental budget and may need to authorise any purchase you intend to make
- management and senior management, who have overall responsibility and financial control for the organisation.

Knowledge check

1. List at least three organisational policies and procedures that relate to the purchasing of goods and services.
2. Explain why it is important to have a purchasing strategy.
3. List the steps in a basic purchasing strategy.
4. Your own role and authority in purchasing goods and services may be limited. Explain why.
5. Describe the four principles generally applied to procurement.
6. List at least seven elements that are typically included in a purchase specification.

10.2 Making purchases

While it is important to understand your organisation's purchasing strategies, there are other policies and procedures around **procurement** that you must also be aware of. They include:

- *Accountability*. Who, within the organisation, is responsible for the various tasks around purchasing? For example:
  - Who makes the decision on what is to be purchased and why?
  - Who needs to give their approval?
  - Who is responsible for completing any necessary forms and paperwork?
  - Who looks after the relationship between the organisation and the suppliers?
  - Who is in charge of placing the actual orders and receiving and checking the goods received?
  - Who pays the bills?
- *Probity and transparency*. This refers to openness and honesty in your dealings with others, be they colleagues, customers or suppliers. This is an important aspect of a purchasing strategy, as the organisation may, at some point, need to show that it has behaved in an ethical way in terms of:
  - implementing processes and actions that are consistent, accountable, transparent and auditable
  - keeping track of inventory and maintaining good records
  - ensuring equity in decision making by consulting with relevant stakeholders in the purchasing process
  - monitoring and checking the processes that can identify probity issues
  - ensuring the security and confidentiality of information
  - identifying and managing conflicts of interest, whether actual, perceived or potential.

- *Risk management.* Depending on the industry you work in, some of your organisation's goods and services may represent hazards or risks. For example, toxic cleaning chemicals must be checked and stored correctly, and work health and safety (WHS) must be observed at all times when handling them. Systems must be put in place to ensure a safe, secure and healthy environment.
- *Inventory levels.* For a variety of reasons, such as budget or available floor space, the organisation may set a limit (or a threshold) for the number of goods to be kept on hand at any one time. Only when the inventory on hand reaches the stated threshold can new supplies be ordered.

10.2.1 Receiving purchase specifications from relevant personnel

Goods and services are purchased with a specific purpose in mind. It might be to replenish shop stock, to reorder necessary office stationery or to hire a business consultant. Whatever their purpose, the goods and services ordered *must* meet that need, so purchase specifications may be necessary.

A **purchase specification** is a detailed description of what goods or services you will buy and the conditions under which you will buy them. Developing specifications for the organisation will depend, to a large degree, on what the market offers. For example, while a white T-shirt may be offered by many suppliers, the required quality of the bulk order of T-shirts your organisation is planning to purchase will depend on whether it is needed for a weekend sales conference or is intended to be a durable work uniform. The specification for purchasing this item would therefore need to include details about the quality expected to ensure the correct product is ordered.

Purchase specifications should include not only a product description but also information about the suppliers who sell the products you need. In short, a purchase specification will, typically, include these elements:

- a description of the item to be purchased
- quantity of the item to be purchased
- physical specifications, such as size, weight and colour
- performance specifications, such as durability and the conditions under which the item is expected to perform
- the minimum acceptable quality of the item to be purchased
- documentation that is to be provided with the purchase
- services provided at delivery
- terms of acceptance of the purchase
- terms of payment
- shipping information
- warranty information.

Example

ABC Marketing Company uses many different types of paper stock—everything from fine silk paper through to cardboard and corrugated plastic (corflute). As these products are used for client advertising and marketing campaigns, quality is a major consideration. The company's purchasing specifications could therefore stipulate not only the quality of the paper, but the size and "weight" (or thickness) of each sheet, the ability of each type of paper product to absorb ink without "bleeding", and so on.

Specifications are a very important component of the purchasing process. Without them, there is no guidance on what is or isn't acceptable, and money, time and effort could be spent unnecessarily.

10.2.2 Selecting purchasing methods most appropriate to particular purchases

There are a number of different ways in which you can make purchases—in person, over the phone or online. Your organisation will have set up specific methods with the suppliers it uses. Beyond this, the methods used to purchase goods and services can also refer not only to *how* they are purchased, but *why*. Some methods for purchasing are outlined in Table 10.1.

Table 10.1 Purchasing methods

Purchasing method	Description
Purchasing by requirement	This applies to goods that are only purchased when needed and in the required quantity. Goods that are not needed regularly, such as a new desk or office chair, are generally purchased in this way. It can also refer to the purchase of emergency goods that may not necessarily be kept in stock but for which a sudden need has arisen.
Market purchasing	This refers to buying goods or services in order to take advantage of favourable market conditions. The purchase isn't made to meet an immediate need but in order to fulfil future requirements. This can be a useful tool, and can save the organisation substantial sums if future needs are estimated accurately and purchases are made whenever favourable market situations arise. It does mean, however, that the market should be constantly monitored for pricing trends.
Contract purchasing	This means that a specific quantity of goods or services is contracted to be purchased but delivery is taken in future. The goods are procured for future delivery, but the price and other terms and conditions are fixed at the time of the contract.
Scheduled purchasing	This involves negotiating specific delivery schedules with suppliers, who then provide their goods and services on the dates specified. Examples include: a cleaning service that is hired to come in and clean the office every Friday night; and having the office photocopier serviced and maintained once a month.
Cooperative purchasing	Small individual organisations may join together and pool their requirements, placing bulk orders with suppliers. This will help them to take advantage of rebates or cash discounts on large-quantity purchases which they would otherwise not be entitled to as individual businesses.

Think about

2. What purchasing method does your organisation use? Why does it use this method?

10.2.3 Obtaining approvals for purchases

As we have discussed, for some purchases, you will need to get the appropriate approval. This might apply to such things as a large piece of equipment, an expensive item, or something that isn't typically purchased by the organisation. In such cases, you will generally need to advise the relevant signing authority (supervisor or manager) of the identified need and provide justification for the purchase. For example:

- What will the good or service to be purchased be used for?
- How much will it cost?
- What value will it bring to the organisation to make it worth the expense?
- What might be the consequences of not making the purchase?

10.2.4 Obtaining quotations from suppliers

The relevant authority would then give their approval by signing a purchase request form. Once you have this approval, you can go ahead and make the purchase through your regular suppliers. For larger or expensive purchases, however, you may need to obtain quotes from at least three suppliers, for which you will need to know the purchase specifications. When asking for quotations from these suppliers, you would specify:

- what products or services are required
- the quality expected
- the quantity required (often, the larger the quantity the more you can negotiate with the supplier on final price)
- the terms under which the purchase will be made (this, too, is usually negotiable with the chosen supplier)
- when delivery of the goods or services is required
- the overall time frame in which the process of choosing suppliers and ordering the goods and services will be completed.

Each potential supplier would then submit their quote based on the criteria you have provided for them.

10.2.5 Selecting suppliers

Quotes received from suppliers can often be very similar and you may need to consider more than just who offers the cheapest price. Price isn't necessarily the best criterion on which to base your decision. Other factors to consider include:

- Which supplier is offering the best range of products or services?
- Do some items represent better value for money, even if they are a bit more expensive—for example, are they of a better quality and more durable than the cheaper options?
- Which supplier is able to supply the goods or services quickly?
- How reliable are the services each supplier is offering?
- How have the different suppliers' interactions with your organisation impressed you?

With these considerations in mind, you can compare the quotes you receive and make the best choice for your organisation. An **agreement** (or contract, if necessary) can then be drawn up, setting out the terms and conditions under which the goods and services will be supplied and received. As this is a legally binding document, care should be taken in setting out its terms. This is generally done at management level.

Try this now

1. **Research a range of products from at least two suppliers and compare them. Which one offers better value for money?**

10.2.6 Placing the order and making the purchase

With approvals in place and the best supplier chosen, you should then be able to go ahead and place an order for the goods or services required. Again, most organisations will have their own procedures for doing this. Generally, they will require a certain amount of paperwork (either paper-based or online) to be completed. For example:

- *Order form.* This is the request form that starts the purchase process. It lists the individual products or services to be purchased, the quantity to be ordered and the approximate cost, and is signed by whoever has the purchase authority for the organisation or individual department.
- *Purchase order.* This is an "accounting" document that is sent along to the supplier, along with the order form, and represents the actual—formal—authority to purchase. Sometimes the purchase order functions as both the order form and the formal purchase authority (Figure 10.2).

Figure 10.2 Sample purchase order

Greyson's Accounting			**Date: 10/07/23**
Purchase order 12148			
To:	Silverton's Stationery Store		
Address:	25 Old Coach Road, Oxenford QLD 4210		
Phone:	(07) 5550 1234		
Fax:	(07) 5550 5678		
Email:	pacstatsup@silvertons.com.au		
Qty	**Description**	**Per unit**	**Total**
1	Box photocopy paper	$24.00	$24.00
5	Writing pads	$15.00	$75.00
5	Black pens	$5.00	$25.00
	Total		$124.00
Order requested by: Katie Chan			
Department: Marketing Department			
Authorising officer: Lee Perlitz			
Signature: Lee Perlitz		**Budget code** 528	

- *Invoice*. This form is sent by the supplier, along with the ordered goods, and is their demand for payment (Figure 10.3).
- *Inventory register*. Depending on the organisation's own policies and procedures, as well as the nature of the goods ordered, the goods may need to be accepted into the organisation's inventory. This might apply to the following:
  - Stock ordered for a shop—as you would need to know exactly how many of each item you have, in order to undertake a stocktake. Stock represents a financial investment for the organisation and, as such, must be accounted for in the bookkeeping system.
  - Financial assets—that is, anything that isn't classed as a "consumable" (such as stationery) and may include computers, machinery, furniture and vehicles.

Figure 10.3 Sample tax invoice

Silverton's Stationery 25 Old Coach Road Oxenford Qld 4210	**Tax invoice** **No:** 0128 ABN 71 609 806 106
To: Greyson's Accounting ABN 89 123 456 789 **Address:** 29 Days Road Coomera QLD 4209 **Attention:** Alex Clifton **Purchase order:** 12148	
Description	**Amount**
1 box photocopy paper 5 writing pads 5 black pens GST	$24.00 $75.00 $25.00 $124.00 $12.40
Total:	$136.40
Due date: 30/7/2023	

Knowledge check

7. List and describe at least four formal methods of making a purchase.
8. Describe the issues you would need to address when getting approvals for a purchase.
9. List at least five things you would need to tell a supplier about the products and services you are asking them to quote on.
10. List at least five things that you should look for when determining which supplier you will choose from those who have quoted.
11. List, and give examples of, at least three forms that you may need to work with when ordering goods and services.

10.3 Receiving purchases

All purchases made represent a value to the organisation. They may be of a temporary nature, such as daily consumables, or they may be permanent fixtures and will become part of the organisation's assets. Whatever the case, all purchases must be "received" correctly and efficiently.

10.3.1 Receiving goods and checking for compliance with specifications

Receiving goods is, in its basic form, the process of checking the received goods against the purchase order and matching them up to ensure that everything that was ordered was, in fact, delivered and that it is received in good order (as per the purchase specifications).

The complexity of the steps followed in receiving goods will vary from one organisation to another. In general, however, the process will involve the following:

1. Receiving the goods.
2. Inspecting the goods in order to verify that they comply with the purchase specifications, as follows:
   - The goods delivered match those on the purchase order.
   - The correct quantity was delivered.
   - There is no breakage or damage to the goods and all seals (where applicable) are sound.
   - All unit measurements are correct. (For example, if a box of goods is meant to contain a dozen items, then all 12 should be present.)
   - All perishable items are in good condition and expiration dates have not been exceeded.
   - All items are in working order (if applicable).
   - No substitutions have been made. (That is, the supplier hasn't provided a product that is only similar to what was ordered, but isn't the exact item ordered.)
3. Signing the shipping order to acknowledge receipt.

Zouls/Shutterstock

Advising relevant personnel of receipt of purchase

Modern inventory systems often advise relevant personnel automatically of goods received, through an internal finance system. However, it is always advisable to speak to the relevant personnel and let them know their goods have been received, in case they are urgently required.

10.3.2 Taking action to resolve non-compliance with specifications

If, during your inspection of the goods, you find that an item is incorrect or missing, you will need to contact the supplier and negotiate a solution to the problem. This might involve a simple phone call for a replacement or exchange, or you might need to complete forms to arrange for refunds or credits.

Then, too, you should also open the actual packaging when you receive goods to check that the items inside haven't been damaged during shipping or delivery. When you sign the delivery slip, the shipment will be considered "accepted". If you simply pack away the box without checking the items, and then discover the breakage a few weeks or months later when the item is needed, the supplier might refuse to replace it.

10.3.3 Facilitating registration of new assets

Purchasing goods and services means you are acquiring business resources for the organisation. Business resources are all those things that you need in order to conduct business and to perform work tasks. For the most part, you will be involved in looking after **consumable resources**, such as:

- *raw materials, stocks and supplies*, which are used either to manufacture or to stock products for sale by your organisation
- *equipment consumables*, for example printer ink cartridges, toner cartridges for printers and photocopiers, batteries for small appliances such as digital cameras and memory cards
- *stationery items*, such as copier or printer paper, letterhead paper, envelopes, pens and pencils, staples/staplers and paperclips.

These resources are of a transitory nature. Aside from keeping a record of what has been ordered, you don't need to treat consumable resources as part of the organisation's formal assets. However, some purchases *do* need to be registered as assets. For example:

- *Capital resources.* **Capital resources** are normally large and/or very expensive items such as furniture, business vehicles, large machinery and equipment like photocopiers or telephone systems. They are items that don't need regular replacement and are expected to last for many years.
- *Business equipment.* This group is less permanent and is often replaced annually, or at the very least within a few years, and could include computers, printers, scanners, fax machines, computer software, digital cameras and other such items.

When business resources are received, they need to be entered into the organisation's **asset management system** and given an asset or **inventory number**. Keeping track of assets is important as they have actual value and add to the organisation's financial status. Managing its assets also means that the organisation:

- has a centralised system that stores data on its assets and where they are located
- can schedule maintenance of its assets where and when required
- can evaluate asset performance in order to understand how these assets are being used and thus gain maximum benefit from them.

10.3.4 Filing and storing purchase records

As you have learnt, another valuable business resource is information. Some of this information will be in the form of organisational records that can be used to examine the company's success or where it may need to improve. Purchasing records provide useful information on what goods and services have been purchased in the past, how they have been used, and whether their purchase was as cost effective as it could have been. This information, in turn, can be used to help create financial budgets for the coming year(s).

Therefore, filing records is an important element in business success.

- Balanced scorecards outline supplier performance in terms of their reliability, whether they have met purchasing criteria, and so on.
- Invoices, statements and payment requests provide information on how much money the organisation has spent, and on what.
- Purchase requests and orders provide information on what was ordered and how much it cost (as a comparison to invoices and statements).
- Supplier records provide contact details and information on supplier performance.

These records can be filed in either a paper-based format or in the organisation's electronic document management system (as discussed in Chapter 8).

Knowledge check

12. Describe the process you would undertake when receiving goods.
13. Explain why it is important to advise others of the delivery of goods and services.
14. The goods received haven't met your purchasing specifications. Describe what you will do.
15. Describe the type of purchases that will need to be registered as company assets.
16. List at least three types of purchase records that should be stored and filed.

Summary

When you are purchasing goods and services, you are representing your organisation and spending its money. It is important, therefore, that you understand its policies and procedures to ensure that you are receiving value for money and the best possible quality available for your budget.

Purchasing goods and services will also require you to communicate with stakeholders both from within and outside your organisation. You will need to consult with others within your organisation about what to buy, and when, and get the necessary approvals. You will also need to deal in a professional manner with outside suppliers in order to get quotes and to negotiate the best deals for your organisation.

Receiving the goods that have been ordered is an equally important task, ensuring that what you have received meets with the specified quality standards.

CHAPTER 11

Write simple documents

Learning outcomes

11.1 Plan a simple document

11.2 Draft a simple document

11.3 Finalise a simple document

Special note

This chapter deals primarily with the simple functions used to create basic business documents. More complex functions and document types are covered in Chapter 12. Software screenshots shown may be indicative only and not reflect the exact methods you will follow.

The fundamentals of any business enterprise are primarily concerned with building relationships, based on courtesy and politeness, between a business and its customers, staff and suppliers. The first contact you have with a customer or supplier might be by way of written communication, be it email, a social media platform or a formal letter. That being the case, it needs to set a positive tone for your future business relationship. Failure to observe the correct etiquette in your written communications can cause offence or lead to misunderstandings. Poorly constructed communications, complete with slang terms, spelling errors, poor grammar and sloppy formatting, can interfere with your efforts to establish a good business relationship. Furthermore, always keep in mind that words cannot be taken back once a letter or email has been sent, so any correspondence that leaves your organisation must be professional, accurate and to the point.

11.1 Planning a simple document

Communication experts tell us that it takes a mere three seconds to make a first impression on someone. The first contact you have with a customer or supplier is therefore extremely important. When communicating face to face, this first impression is easier to control as you can actually see and talk to the other person. However, the first contact may be in writing, so any document you send out must make that good first impression for you. Planning is therefore a very important step in establishing a good relationship with your customers.

11.1.1 Determining a document's audience and purpose

A crucial factor in planning the type and style of document you need to create is knowing who the document is aimed at and its intended purpose.

Who is the document aimed at?

It is important to determine who is the audience for the correspondence, as this sets the tone of the message. You may be communicating with people within your organisation, or externally with customers, suppliers or people making general enquiries. When corresponding with a new contact, it is appropriate to use a formal tone: make sure you address the person by their title, get quickly to the point of the communication, and avoid using industry jargon. When writing to a long-time, valued customer or a trusted supplier or employee, the tone of the letter can be somewhat friendlier with more personal content (if appropriate).

What is its purpose?

The purpose of the communication also determines how formal or informal it should be. A letter of congratulations, for example, will be much warmer in tone than a letter written in response to a complaint. A written communication's purpose may be to:

- *clarify an issue*—this might include responding to questions from a client about something your organisation has proposed, or to a request from a supplier for more information in order for them to provide you with a quotation. Requesting clarification in writing provides a written record of exactly what was (and wasn't) agreed to.
- *communicate about meetings or events*—a written memo, email or formal invitation to a meeting or other event is an effective way of keeping a record of the invitees and providing details of the event.
- *distribute the minutes or outcomes of a meeting*—the minutes or action items are a record of what was discussed during a meeting. It is important to distribute them to the people who attended a meeting as soon as possible after the event. Tasks may have been assigned during the meeting, and the minutes or action lists are a written record of who has been allocated a task and the time frame in which it is to be completed. The minutes are then used at subsequent meetings to review task progress.
- *report on staff or operational activities*—these might include product inventory, sales revenue earned over a given time frame, marketing activities, financial information and so on.
- *request information, advice or assistance*—requests for information, advice or assistance can come from customers as well as colleagues. Information or advice provided in written form for immediate use can also be kept on file for future reference.
- *keep historical records*—for example, information about customers, suppliers and product offerings can show trends over time in terms of purchasing habits, enquiry sources and so on.
- *provide proof of communication in legal issues*—there are situations in every business where a written record of a transaction or conversation may be needed as evidence of what was agreed to—and what wasn't. For example, if there is a dispute between the organisation and a customer about a product or service, written records of communication with the customer may clarify exactly what the purchase entailed.

What are the key points you need to get across?

When the purpose of a document is to outline key points of information, it is important to keep these points concise, to ensure their meaning is clear, and to arrange them in a logical, easy-to-follow order. If there are several points to be made, number them in order of importance, or list them in sequence if appropriate. For example, when providing instructions on how to use a product or service, list them in the order in which the steps need to be completed.

What method of communication is best suited to the audience and purpose?

The most suitable method of communication will depend on the intended audience and purpose. For example:

- *Is the matter urgent?* In this case, an email might be the best option.
- *How formal is the communication?* Does it involve a contract or an agreement that must be signed? In this case, a formal letter will need to accompany those documents.
- *How many people is the communication intended to reach?* If the communication is intended to reach a large number of people, you might consider using email or, in the case of a promotional activity, an online forum or social media platform.

11.1.2 What organisational requirements are relevant?

Your organisation's requirements relating to communication methods and styles also need to be considered. These might include:

- use of templates and forms
- response times
- budgets
- file usage and storage
- organisational and legislative policies (including work health and safety [WHS] and codes of conduct)
- house style.

We will look at each of these requirements in turn.

Use of templates and forms

Many organisations have templates or forms to be used for specific purposes. These could include "generic" letters, such as standard replies to job application letters or product enquiries. The use of these forms and templates ensures that information is collected and stored in a manner that maintains the integrity of any statistical data that is based on the collated information. Forms could include:

- sales report forms
- complaint forms
- refund forms
- hazard identification forms
- WHS incident report forms
- application forms
- order forms
- invoices and other financial documentation
- templates for producing a range of promotional materials
- style guides that outline how letters should be designed/formatted.

Response times

Good business etiquette calls for enquiries to be responded to promptly or within certain guidelines. Today's technology allows for instant communication, so response times should, ideally, never exceed 24 hours.

Budgets

Budgets may place restrictions on the number of copies of a document to be produced, the paper quality, whether the document will be printed in colour, whether the document should be printed out or emailed as a PDF file, and so on.

File usage and storage

Correct file storage might include following organisational requirements for:

- identifying and opening files
- saving and closing files
- file naming
- maintaining security and confidentiality of files and information.

Organisational and legislative policies, guidelines and requirements

Policies, guidelines and requirements are put in place to ensure that organisational standards will be met. Many organisations will have procedure manuals and/or quality assurance manuals that staff are required to access and to follow. Policies may cover the following matters:

- *Correct log-on procedures.* This might include ensuring that you shut down any equipment when it isn't in use, and not sharing your login details or password with others.
- *Manufacturers' guidelines.* These guidelines must be followed at all times to ensure that equipment and machinery are used correctly and that the warranty won't be voided should there be a fault or a breakdown. Manufacturers may not replace or repair equipment that breaks down as a result of incorrect use.
- *Internet usage and social media policies.* An organisation's guidelines might stipulate that, during working hours, staff should use the internet only for work purposes and not spend time chatting with friends on social media or browsing non-work-related websites. However, the internet is a useful method for quickly spreading word about a company's activities. To this end, most organisations will have policies that dictate such things as:
  - who is permitted to access the internet while at work
  - what types of websites staff members are permitted, or not permitted, to visit when researching information
  - how the organisation will use social media and the internet to promote its products/services
  - what information the organisation will post on the internet
  - who is responsible for creating online content.
- *WHS policies, procedures and programs.* Under the *Work Health and Safety Act 2011* (Cth) all employees (and employers) have rights and responsibilities while in the workplace. Briefly:
  - Employers are responsible for ensuring that all staff are properly trained in the use of machinery and equipment and, generally, for providing employees with a safe working environment.
  - Employees are responsible for working within the organisational and legislative guidelines and for not intentionally causing harm to persons, equipment or premises.
- *Industry codes of conduct.* These are generally rules or standards of conduct, set for an industry as a whole, that often include the relationship between industry participants or their customers. They provide the necessary regulatory support for a given industry and guard against misconduct and opportunistic behaviour, while encouraging long-term changes to business culture.

House style

Most organisations develop a "company image" or "house style", which might include its logo, corporate ID (including specific colours), and the design/layout of its letterhead, mission/value statements and other corporate communications. In some cases, an organisation may have spent considerable time, money and effort in establishing this corporate image. For this reason, management may expect communications carried out on the organisation's behalf at every level to comply with its "house style" requirements.

An in-house style guide will provide guidance on how all organisational correspondence is to be produced. It may include specifications relating to the following matters.

Margins

The guidelines may specify how many spaces to leave at the top and bottom of a letter (that is, between the masthead and the body, and between the body and the signoff), and in the margins on each side. For example, the house style of your organisation may be to left-align the text on the page, and to have equal margins at the top and bottom and on each side.

Font

Most companies have a standard font that is to be used in all its written communications. The font determines what the writing looks like. Examples of fonts include: **Times New Roman**, **Arial**, *brush script*, Comic Sans.

Font size

Font sizes are measured in points, which dictates the height of the font and how large it appears on the screen. Sometimes you may wish to highlight a specific portion of your text and you can do this by changing the font size. Figure 11.1 provides examples.

This text is written in 14 point font size.

This text is written in 9 point font size.

This text is written in 20 point font size.

To change the font and size, click on the drop-down menus available in the *Font* section of the *Home* tab and select the options you wish to use. In Figure 11.1, we have chosen Calibri font, size 11 point.

Figure 11.1 Menu options showing how to change font and size

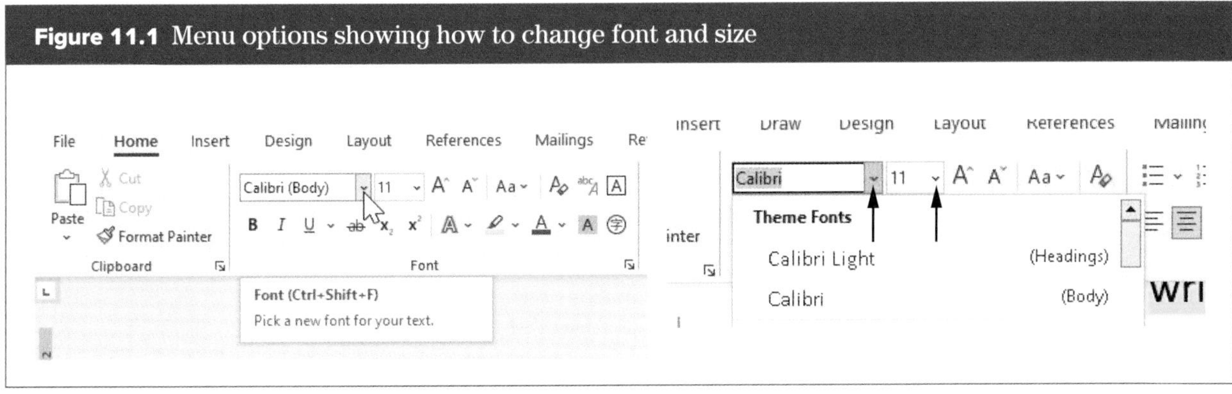

Alignment

This determines the appearance of the paragraph edges in relation to the margins (Figure 11.2). You can have the edge of your paragraph aligned to the left or right margins, centred in between the two, or aligned evenly along both (justified).

Figure 11.2 Alignment icons as used in word processing software

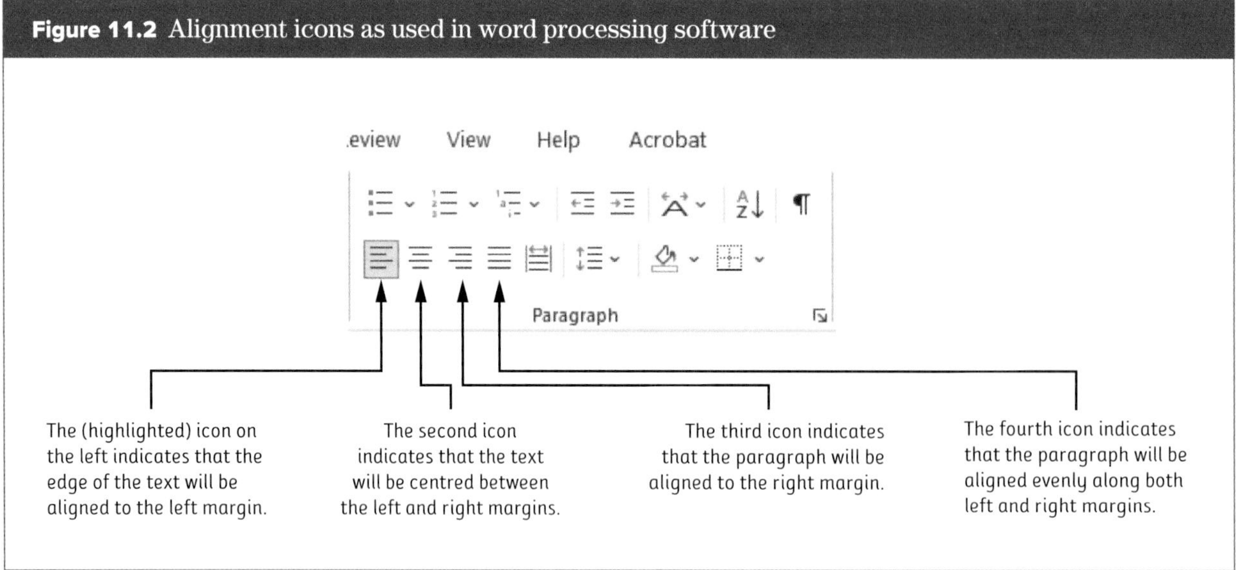

.eview
View
Help
Acrobat
Paragraph
The (highlighted) icon on the left indicates that the edge of the text will be aligned to the left margin.
The second icon indicates that the text will be centred between the left and right margins.
The third icon indicates that the paragraph will be aligned to the right margin.
The fourth icon indicates that the paragraph will be aligned evenly along both left and right margins.

Try this now

1. Type a half-page of text and try some of these functions for yourself.

11.1.3 What format, style and structure are appropriate?

You will also need to consider the format and structure of the communication. This goes hand in hand with its audience and purpose, but it will also be influenced by the urgency of the communication and organisational requirements in terms of style. Considerations might include:

- *Plain language and word choice.* Use simple language to make complex ideas easier to understand and to engage people quickly.
- *Sentence structure.* Long, complex sentences can be difficult for the reader to follow. Keep sentences short and to the point and eliminate any unnecessary words.
- *Use of paragraphs.* A paragraph should cover one specific topic. It is usually two to three sentences in length and can be used for various purposes, such as to clearly differentiate between separate topics, to break up large slabs of text by creating white space or adding headings—all of which make it easier for the reader to skim read the document.
- *Voice and tone.* This will depend on the message's audience and purpose.
- *Links to websites.* Links to further information are a useful addition to business communications. However, ensure that the link information is correct and that the website you are directing the reader to is relevant to and complements your organisation's products or services.
- *Lists.* Listed points make it easy for a reader to quickly scan a series of items.
- *Language and grammar specifications.* For example:
  - Are abbreviations and acronyms appropriate and useful?
  - Does the spelling conform to Australian English conventions?
  - How will you refer to numbers (e.g. use of "ten" rather than "10")?
- *Document specifications.* Such as:
  - title page and table of contents on longer documents
  - page numbering and how this should be formatted
  - punctuation

- use of graphics
- glossaries and references (in longer documents)
- inclusion and use of corporate branding
- use of the corporate colour schemes and graphics
- file naming standards in line with organisational standards.

- *Organisation of the material to suit the format.* This might, for example, mean looking at the quality of the documentation to be produced. Will it be sent by email and be meant for on-screen viewing only (in which case, the quality of any graphics may need to be higher than those printed on paper)? If images or graphics are to be used, will they be in colour or black and white? Is the document or image intended to be reproduced—say, for an advertising campaign (in which case, it should be of a sufficiently high quality so that any copies subsequently made will also be of a high quality)?
- *Use of visual signposting.* The use of headings, keywords and boxed text improves the flow of text in a document, enhancing its "readability".
- *Tables and charts/graphs.* These can be used very effectively to present numeric data and to demonstrate correlations and comparisons between specified values.

Many of these topics will be expanded in Chapter 12. Whatever its requirements and standards, the organisation will have set them for specific reasons. It is very important that all employees adhere to them, ensuring a consistently high level of service and maintenance of the company's "image".

11.1.4 Formatting a document using software functions and features

To produce professional-looking and useful documents, you will need to access a range of software functions and features, including:

Video: Inserting objects into Word: Part 1

- text boxes
- spelling and grammar checking
- styles
- bullets and numbered lists.

Text boxes

Text boxes can be used to highlight information that you particularly want to stand out from the rest of the text. There are a number of different types of text boxes (as shown in Figure 11.3), and they can be inserted at any place within a document. As they will shift any existing text around it to create space for it to sit, you must specify how the surrounding text should wrap around the text box in a way that suits your purpose.

Spelling and grammar checking

A very useful function is the ability to check your spelling and grammar. You can also look up a variety of different ways to word sentences using the *Synonyms* function or the program's built-in *Thesaurus*. (A thesaurus is a reference work that lists words in groups of similar meaning. Use it to help you find a word that best fits an idea that you are trying to convey.) Figure 11.4 shows the options found in the *Proofing* section in the *Review* tab. Take care when using the *Spelling* check option; it won't pick up words that are spelled correctly but used incorrectly. Examples include:

- *hear* instead of *here*
- *their* instead of *there*
- *see* instead of *sea*
- *two* instead of *too* or *to*.

Figure 11.3 Using text box options

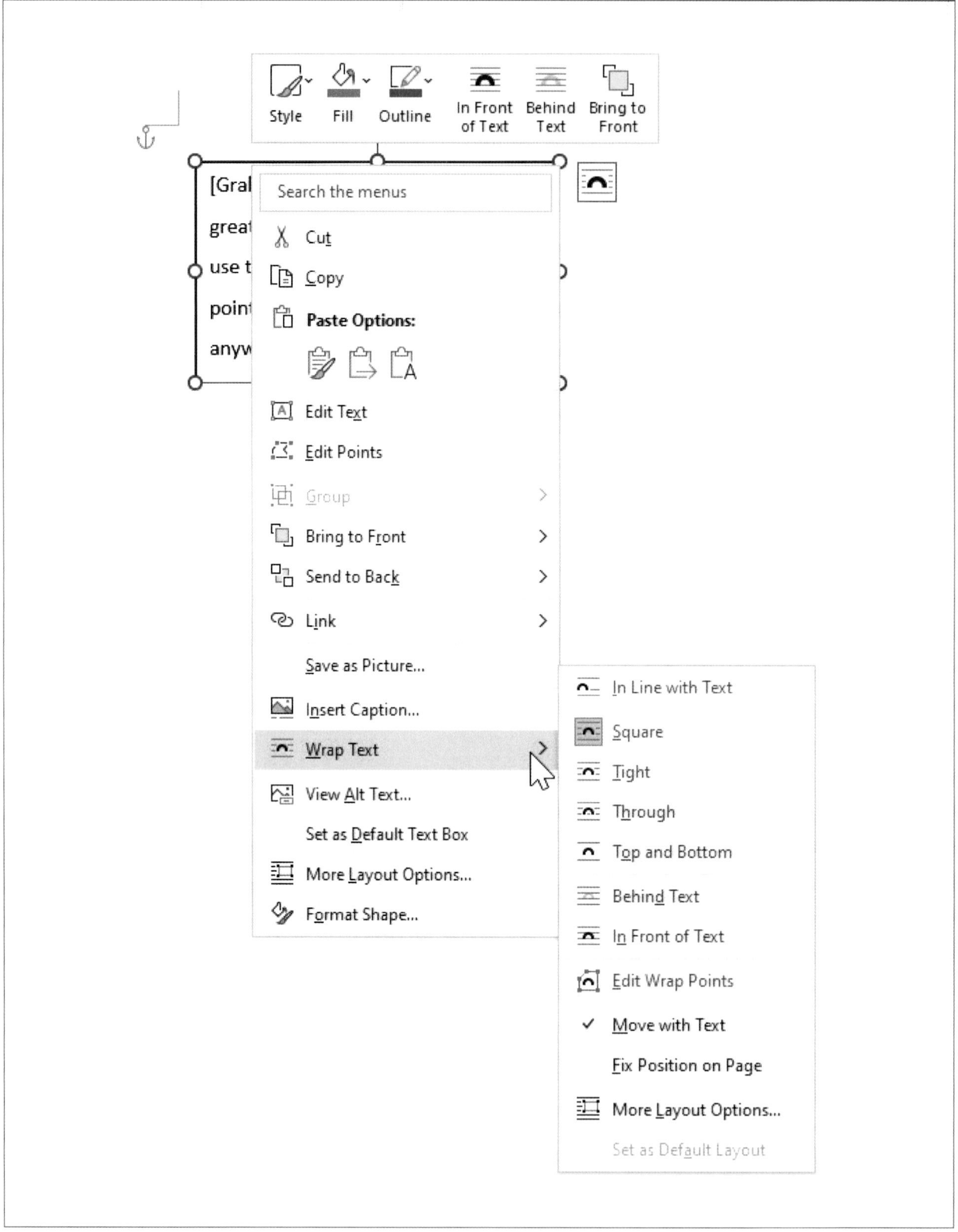

Style
Fill
Outline
In Front of Text
Behind Text
Bring to Front

[Gra
grea
use t
poin
anyw

Search the menus
Cut
Copy
Paste Options:
Edit Text
Edit Points
Group
Bring to Front
Send to Back
Link
Save as Picture...
Insert Caption...
Wrap Text
View Alt Text...
Set as Default Text Box
More Layout Options...
Format Shape...

In Line with Text
Square
Tight
Through
Top and Bottom
Behind Text
In Front of Text
Edit Wrap Points
✓ Move with Text
Fix Position on Page
More Layout Options...
Set as Default Layout

Figure 11.4 Options in the *Review* menu

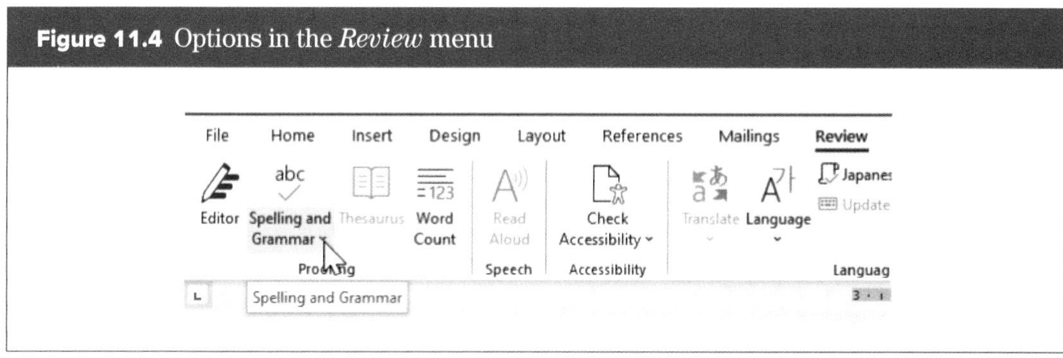

The *Grammar* check option will also help you to produce a professionally worded document. In the example shown in Figure 11.5, you will see that the word "or" is marked with a blue double underline. By right-clicking on the word, you will be provided with an explanation of the possible error and suggested solutions to correct it.

Figure 11.5 Highlighting a grammatical error

to produce an effect or change, to pretend

Grammar

Possible Word Choice Error

of

⊘ ···

Styles

An organisation that has developed a style guide for its documents may have set up a template with prescribed Styles in its word processing program to ensure staff actually use the correct fonts, sizes, numbered and bulleted list styles, line spacing and headings. In Microsoft Word, these can be found in the *Styles* section of the *Home* tab. Clicking on the arrow next to the box will expand the drop-down box shown in Figure 11.6.

Figure 11.6 Using *Styles*

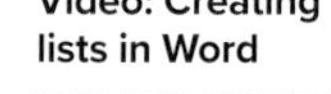
Video: Creating lists in Word

Bullets and numbered lists

Documents often include lists. To enhance the readability of these lists, it is a good idea to present them as either bullet points or numbered lists. In the *Paragraph* section of the *Home* tab, you will find the icons to insert bullets or numbering (Figure 11.7).

- *To insert bullets:* Click on the bulleted list icon and you will see a number of options, as shown in Figure 11.8. There are many different types and styles of bullet points. Go to *Define New Bullet* to choose from these options.
- *To insert numbering:* Click on the numbered list icon and you will be able to choose from a range of options offered, as shown in Figure 11.9.

Figure 11.7 Menu for bullets and numbering options

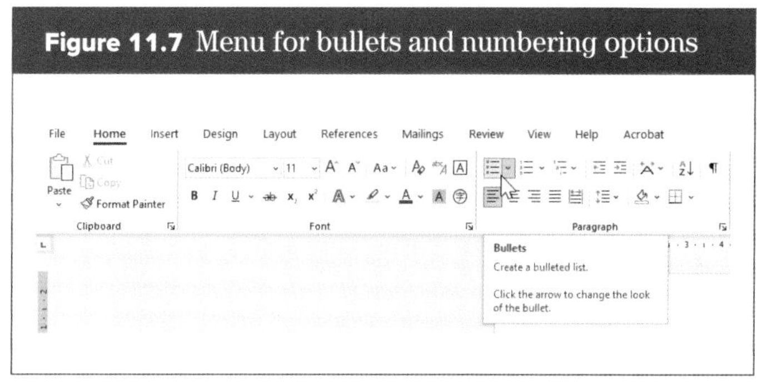

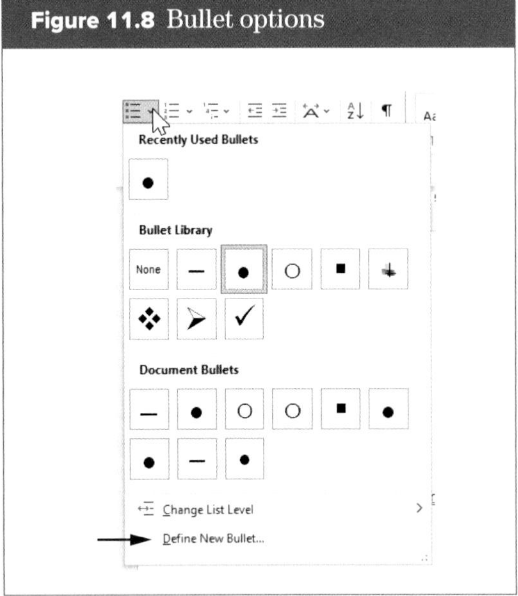

Figure 11.8 Bullet options

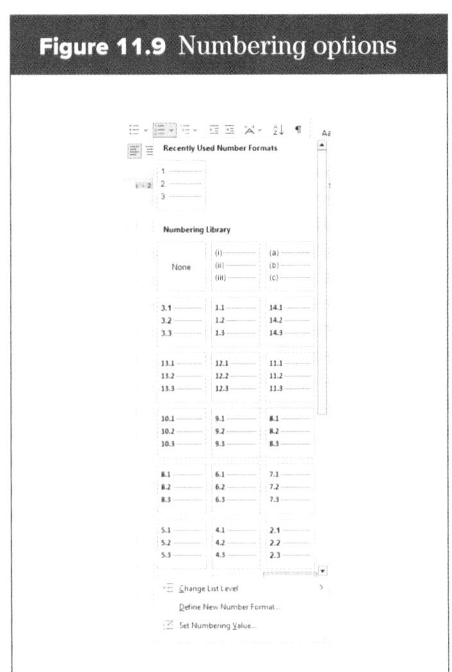

Figure 11.9 Numbering options

Sometimes a bulleted or numbered list will have various "levels". This means that a specific list item may have further items that are subordinate. For example:

- Main point one:
    - Subordinate point 1
    - Subordinate point 2
- Main point two:
    - Subordinate point 1 ... and so on.

Or

1. Main point one:
    a. Subordinate point 1
    b. Subordinate point 2
2. Main point two:
    a. Subordinate point 1 ... and so on.

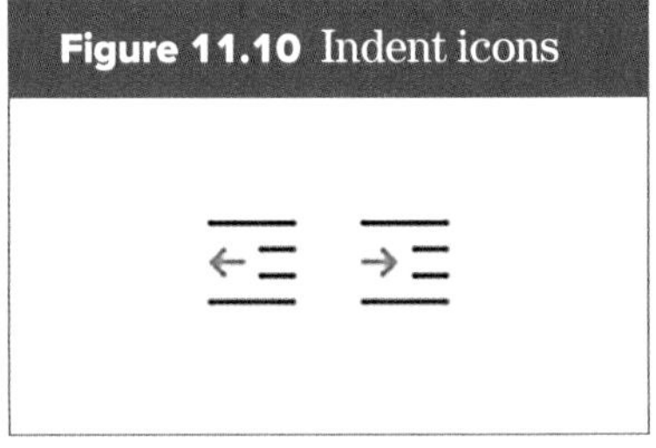

Figure 11.10 Indent icons

You can set the main or subordinate levels by highlighting the appropriate text and indenting it. Decreasing the indent (Figure 11.10, left) will promote the list item by one level, while increasing the indent will "demote" the list item by one level (Figure 11.10, right).

Further numbering functions will be covered in Chapter 12.

Try this now

2. Type a half-page of text and try some of these functions for yourself.

11.1.5 Choosing the most appropriate method of communication

Much of what we have covered so far relates to written letters or reports. Written communications, however, take many different forms. The following methods may be appropriate for different purposes:

- *Email*—when communication needs to be quick or to be sent to groups of people simultaneously.
- *Blog, newsletter or bulletin*—used for internal purposes to keep staff up to date on operational issues and general activities, or for external purposes to generate interest in your organisation's services or products.

- *Social media*—used to generate interest in your organisation and its products, services or community activities.
- *Form*—enables the organisation to present specific information.
- *Memo*—used to provide information to staff.
- *Agenda or minutes of meetings*—to prepare for or summarise decisions made at meetings.
- *Report*—used to provide information on various organisational activities.

The method you use will depend on your audience, the reason for the communication, and what will be done with the message once it is received. We will look at some of these individual aspects of communication in more detail shortly.

11.1.6 Establishing key points for inclusion

Having established who the communication is aimed at, what its purpose is and what format it should take, you need to establish the key points to be included. This might involve discussing what is to be communicated with relevant stakeholders—that is, those people who have an interest in the successful outcome of the communication or who will be responsible for authorising or following up on any key points. For example, if the correspondence is in response to a customer enquiring about a product or service, then the key points could include:

- basic information on the product
- how it should, or could, be used
- pricing options
- delivery times.

On the other hand, if the correspondence is in response to a letter of complaint from a customer, the key points might be an:

- acknowledgement of the nature of the complaint
- explanation of how (or if) the organisation intends to resolve the issue
- apology to the customer.

Depending on the purpose of the communication, establishing key points for inclusion means asking questions such as: What has been asked for? How am I going to address what has been asked for?

Try this now

3. Choose a brochure on any product. Write a letter to a customer about this product and include its key points.

Knowledge check

1. The intended audience for, and purpose of, a document will determine the appropriate style and tone to use. Explain why.
2. Describe what is meant by the term “house style”. What might it involve?
3. Describe the types of things that might determine a document’s format and structure.
4. Describe at least five formatting functions of a word processing program that you could use in a document.
5. Written communication can take place in a number of different ways. List at least five ways.

11.2 Drafting a simple document

Projecting a professional image means ensuring that any correspondence sent out by the organisation is well written, free of errors and neatly presented, regardless of whether it is a letter, a blog or an email. An initial draft of the correspondence will allow you to check that all the necessary key points have been included, that there are no errors and that the text fits neatly on the page. You may also need to discuss the correspondence with any relevant stakeholders, who may wish to add information or may have opinions as to what should be included, before you actually produce the document.

11.2.1 Developing a draft document to communicate key points

Given that a written document needs not only to deliver its intended message in its content but also to convey professionalism and high quality, it is useful to develop an initial draft of any document that is to be sent outside the organisation.

The first thing you need to do when drafting a document is to give thought to what it is you are writing. Consider the impression you want the recipient of your document to have of your organisation, keeping in mind the "image" it wishes to convey to outsiders and its organisational requirements. Make your intended points use clear, professional language. Bear in mind that any document you send out represents a *permanent* written record that can be produced at a later date as evidence of your organisation's intentions. A badly worded letter, with unclear intentions, could potentially result in a poor impression being given, or even in legal decisions being made against the organisation in the event of a later dispute.

Jot down bullet points of your ideas and thoughts, then develop them into short sentences and paragraphs using words that most people will understand. Of course, if the correspondence is of a complex nature (such as a legally binding contract or agreement), then the language and phrasing used may need to be very formal.

In order to make the document easy for the reader to follow, set out the information in a logical order. Begin at the beginning of the story or problem and go forward from there. Don't jump around from one subject to another and back again. This will confuse the reader, who will be unclear about what you are trying to tell them.

Basic business letter

In today's world of rapid communications, a traditional business letter is a less common way of communicating than it was in the past. It is generally only used now when a formal, written record of the communication is required. We will use Figure 11.11 as an example as we look at the components of a basic business letter.

Any business letter you write should conform to your organisation's requirements. These detailed requirements will vary from one organisation to another, but all such letters will have three main sections: the head, body and ending (or close). Further information may also sometimes be required.

Masthead

The masthead is the very top portion of the letter. There is usually a preprinted letterhead showing the organisation's logo, address and contact details. The letterhead is commonly found in the top right or top centre of the letter. The head section of the letter should contain the following:

- *Date*—in the top left-hand corner of the letter. If the organisation's logo and details are in this section, the date goes underneath them.
- *Recipient's details*—including contact name and title and address (placed below the date).
- *Subject line* or *reference* (if required).
- *Salutation*—using the correct form of address. For example, "Dear Andrew" for informal letters where the recipient is fairly well known; "Dear Mr Jones" where a more formal tone is appropriate; "Dear Dr Yu" when the recipient's title is known. This is most important, as people like to be addressed correctly. If you are unsure of how to address the recipient, always check.

Figure 11.11 A basic business letter

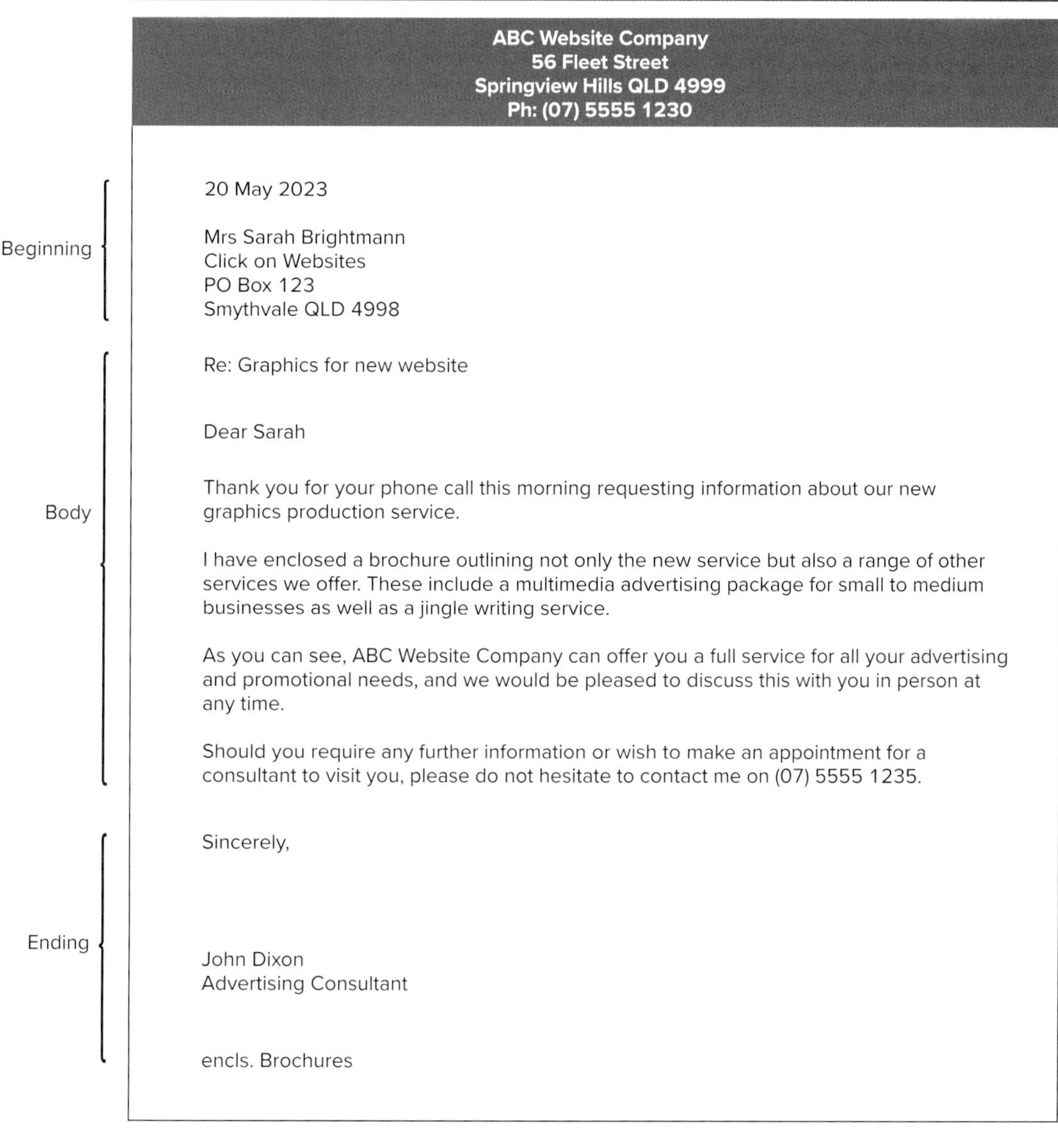

ABC Website Company
56 Fleet Street
Springview Hills QLD 4999
Ph: (07) 5555 1230

20 May 2023

Mrs Sarah Brightmann
Click on Websites
PO Box 123
Smythvale QLD 4998

Re: Graphics for new website

Dear Sarah

Thank you for your phone call this morning requesting information about our new graphics production service.

I have enclosed a brochure outlining not only the new service but also a range of other services we offer. These include a multimedia advertising package for small to medium businesses as well as a jingle writing service.

As you can see, ABC Website Company can offer you a full service for all your advertising and promotional needs, and we would be pleased to discuss this with you in person at any time.

Should you require any further information or wish to make an appointment for a consultant to visit you, please do not hesitate to contact me on (07) 5555 1235.

Sincerely,

John Dixon
Advertising Consultant

encls. Brochures

Body

The body of the letter is where you provide the required information. Ideally, a business letter should not be longer than one page. However, there are occasions when a letter may extend to many pages, such as if you are writing to a customer advising them of legal requirements or the terms and conditions of a contract. In general, though, it is best to keep letters short and succinct.

Bearing in mind the recipient of the letter and the reason you are writing it, set out your key points in two or three paragraphs. The body of your letter should begin with an acknowledgement or short statement to indicate what the letter is about. For example:

> Following our conversation this morning, I enclose the requested information and hope that it proves useful. Or
>
> Thank you for your phone call this morning requesting information about our new graphic imaging service. Or
>
> In celebration of our new graphic imaging service, we are offering our clients a free one-hour consultation!

Then, in two or three paragraphs, give the information required. For example:

> I have enclosed a brochure outlining not only the new service but also a range of other services we offer. These include multimedia advertising packages for small to medium businesses as well as a jingle writing service.

> As you can see, ABC Website Company can offer you a full service for all your advertising and promotional needs, and we would be pleased to discuss this with you in person at any time.

If your correspondence includes statistics, sales figures, product information or any other factual information, ensure that you have this to hand so that you can refer to it, and that it is up to date and accurate.

Ending, or close

The end of your letter should include a short sentence in closing. For example:

> Should you require any further information or wish to make an appointment for a consultant to visit you, please do not hesitate to contact me on ... 5555 1235.

Follow this with a greeting: "Sincerely", when writing to someone you don't know; "Regards" or "Best regards" when writing to someone you do know. Then add your name and title (if applicable).

Additional information

At the very bottom of the letter, after the signature line, you may sometimes have to include further information. If, for example, you have enclosed a separate document or a product brochure, you make a notation of this on the letter by writing "*encl.*" (abbreviation for "enclosure"). This lets the reader know that there should be something else included. Or perhaps you are copying the letter to another person (either to ensure that all the relevant people are aware of the communication, or as a courtesy to a third party who might be involved). In this case, add a notation on the bottom of the letter so that the main recipient is aware that a copy has been given to a third party. The notation is: *Copy: Mr Ian Smith* or *Cc: Mr Ian Smith*, where "Cc" is the abbreviation for "courtesy copy".

Email message

In today's busy world, more and more written communication is taking place via email. There are many internet service providers, and you will be familiar with some of them, such as Gmail, Hotmail and iCloud. Most businesses, however, will use more sophisticated networked systems such as Microsoft Outlook or Novell Groupwise. These systems give you more control over your email and can be linked to the organisation's website domain name—for example: AliceH@abcwebsitecompany.com

Email etiquette

When used in a work environment, email is a professional tool; therefore, the language and grammar used must be appropriate to the organisation's image and guidelines. There are several things to bear in mind when sending email messages.

- Don't use slang, abbreviations or industry jargon when writing to customers. For example, "The ETA of BA012 from LHR is 10:30 Zulu" uses a lot of travel industry jargon. In plain English, it would be written as: "The estimated time of arrival of British Airways flight 012 from London Heathrow is 10:30 am Greenwich Mean Time".
- Unless you know the person you are writing to very well, keep the language level formal.
- When copying your email to other people, make sure it really is necessary for them to have a copy. There is nothing more irritating than coming into work in the morning, opening your email and finding dozens of messages waiting for you—half of which you don't need to see. It takes time to read email messages and unnecessary ones waste time.
- If you advise in your email that you are attaching a file, make sure that you actually attach it before pressing send.
- There is a trend within the email community for sending jokes, thoughts for the day and chain emails. While these might be amusing, they are time wasters and can take up an enormous amount of memory if attachments are included. There is also the risk when opening an attachment that it is infected with a virus, which could potentially shut down and/or destroy your organisation's entire computer system.

When sending email broadcasts, particularly to a large number of addressees, you should put your own email address in the "To" address line and the remainder of the recipients in the "Bcc" (blind carbon copy) address line. There are two reasons for this.

- Email addresses shown in the "To" and "Cc" (carbon copy) address lines are visible to all recipients included in the email. An email with multiple addresses shown in the top section uses up a great deal of space unnecessarily.
- Just because a customer has given you their email address, it doesn't mean they want you to pass it on to other parties. They have entrusted their email address to you, and it becomes part of the company's confidential files (unless otherwise instructed by the customer). The "Bcc" address box is private—hence the name "blind carbon copy"—and addressees in this box cannot see the addresses of other recipients.

Figure 11.12 is an example of a new email message showing the To, Cc and Bcc options.

Figure 11.12 Email screenshot showing To, Cc and Bcc boxes

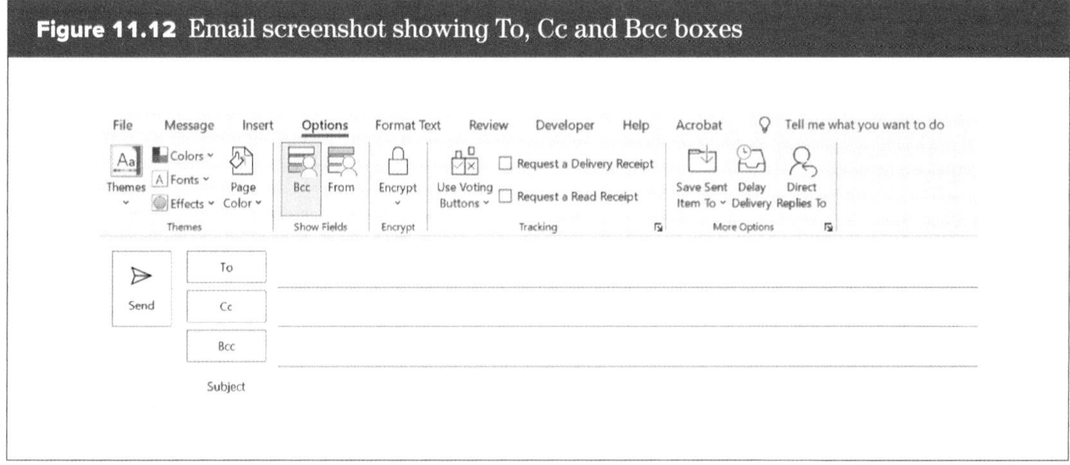

11.2.2 Checking that the draft meets the document's purposes and requirements

Before correspondence of any kind leaves the organisation, it should be thoroughly reviewed by not only yourself, but any relevant stakeholders, to ensure that it complies with organisational standards and requirements relevant to this specific type of document. Always remember: the reputation of an organisation rests upon the quality of its service and the ways in which it presents itself. We will cover this in more detail in the next section.

6. Explain why it is important to produce an initial draft of a document before finalising it and sending it out to the recipient.
7. Describe the purpose of the following written documents:
   a. internal memo
   b. agenda
   c. meeting minutes.
8. List at least four things you should check to ensure your draft is fit for its intended purpose.

11.3 Finalising a simple document

A written document will make a lasting impression on the recipient, who may save it and produce it later as evidence of what the organisation (or the customer) has agreed to do or not do or said or not said. Any document in which an agreement is reached that the organisation will supply certain services or products, or in which the customer has agreed to abide by certain terms and conditions, may represent a legally binding contract between the parties, so it is essential that the content is accurate. You may also be writing to win a new customer or to address a complaint you have received.

The final stages of producing professional correspondence therefore include proofreading the document to ensure the information it contains is correct and that there are no spelling or grammatical errors, and taking in any changes that need to be made.

11.3.1 Proofreading the draft

Proofreading will involve checking the following:

- The text addresses all the key points you want to make.
- It is accurate in terms of the information it provides.
- The language, tone and forms of address are appropriate for the target audience.
- The information is presented in a logical and efficient sequence.
- There are no spelling mistakes or grammatical errors.

You should also do a final check for words that are correctly spelled but have been misused. Grammatical errors are also unprofessional and can distract the reader from understanding the point you are trying to make. The following are some tools that can assist in the proofreading process.

- Use a *dictionary* to check the correct spelling and definition, and appropriate use, of words.
- Use a *thesaurus* or the *Synonyms* function in Word to find a word that best fits an idea that you are trying to convey. For example, when looking up the word "error" in a thesaurus, the following words are suggested: *mistake, fault, inaccuracy, miscalculation, blunder* (Figure 11.13). You can then choose the word that best suits what you are trying to say.

Figure 11.13 Drop-box showing synonyms/alternative wording

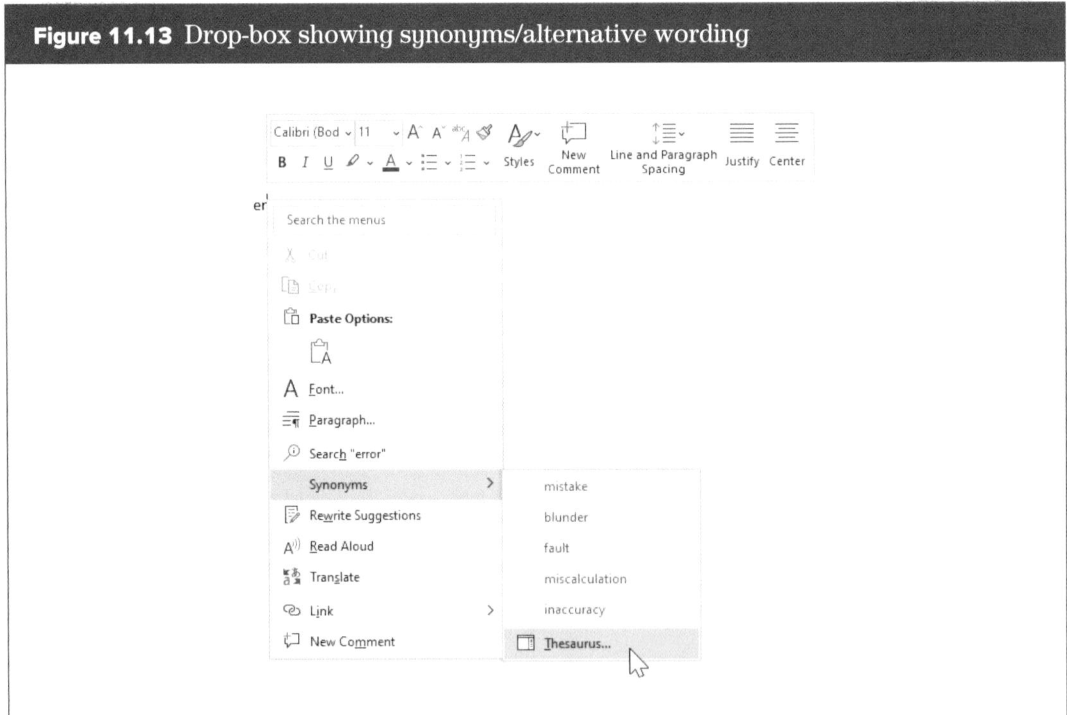

11.3.2 Making and checking any final necessary changes

Any errors or issues identified in the draft should now be amended to produce the final version of the document. The correspondence is now ready to be sent out after you have made one final check, as follows:

- *Ensure the correct letterhead paper is used,* in line with your organisation's requirements.
- *Ensure the address is correct.* Letters that are incorrectly addressed will normally be returned to the sender. This may take days or even weeks. If a communication (including an incorrectly addressed email) that you thought had been received by the recipient wasn't in fact received, this could cause embarrassment or even create a serious problem.

- *Ensure the name of the recipient is correct,* that it is spelled correctly and that you have used their correct title. Intended recipients may include:
  - the audience for the document—the person (or persons) who will ultimately be receiving the correspondence.
  - the signatory of the document—the person within your organisation who will be responsible for signing the correspondence (if that isn't you).
  - a supervisor or other staff member who may add to or forward the document to another recipient. Sometimes you may be preparing a document on behalf of another member of staff, who will forward it on when they have added personal information of their own or made adjustments to it.
- *Ensure the letter is signed by the appropriate person.* Letters should be signed personally.
- *Ensure the document is sent to the intended recipient.* There may be times when you will be sending letters to a large number of recipients and where names and addresses are included on all letters and envelopes. At these times, it is vitally important to ensure that you put letters in the correct envelopes. A letter misplaced in an envelope can cause serious problems for the organisation.

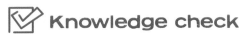

9. List at least five final checks that you should undertake to ensure a document represents the company image as laid out in its house style guide and conforms with document procedures.

Summary

The importance of writing well and concisely cannot be overstated. Well-written text will make it easier for the reader to follow what you are saying. The properties of such a text include:

- *It has a single main idea (unity).* When a composition contains one focused idea, the reader can easily understand what the message is about without having to reread it.
- *It is coherent and cohesive.* This means it is easy to understand the writing, and the ideas presented are logically connected, so that the reader is always clear about the point the writer is making.
- *It is well organised.* A well-organised piece of writing is clearly presented and easy on the eye for the reader.
- *It uses language well and appropriately.* It uses well-constructed sentences and appropriate vocabulary so that it is easily understood, uses pronouns consistently, and is concise, avoiding unnecessary wordiness.

Appendix

Using the right tools and technologies for the right job

During the course of a working day, you may be required to produce various documents and you will need to use a range of tools and technologies to do so. Choosing the right resource for the right job is a matter of determining what needs to be done and then deciding how best to accomplish that task with the resources at your disposal. Tools you can use in business communication may include:

- *email services,* such as Outlook, iCloud, Gmail or organisation-specific ones
- *professional networks,* such as LinkedIn (http://www.linkedin.com.au) and Flying Solo (https://www.flyingsolo.com.au), where you can join conversations on a range of business-related topics
- *presentation tools,* such as Microsoft PowerPoint and Canva
- *virtual meeting technologies,* such as Zoom (https://zoom.us) and Skype (https://www.skype.com/en), that allow you to hold video meetings with colleagues, suppliers or customers, no matter where they are located
- *office productivity software,* such as word processors or spreadsheet software.

Useful software

Software is the general term for **programs** and/or operating information used by a computer. It can be delivered via a digital file or subscription that is downloaded directly onto a device, or via a physical medium such as a disk or a game cartridge. **Hardware** refers to the physical system components used to run the software, such as a computer's disk drive or a gaming console.

Software has become an essential element in doing business. It is possible to predict business future trends using artificial intelligence software. Software is used in major stock markets, and to run fully automated factories. It is also used to store contact information, generate plans and schedule appointments and deadlines.

A program , sometimes also referred to as an "application", is a type of software that provides a set of "instructions" telling the computer what to do and how to behave. Just as there are thousands of movies you can buy to play on your DVD player, there are a great many programs you can buy to run on your computer.

When you buy a computer, you usually get some basic programs and applications pre-installed onto the device that are compatible with your **operating system**, such as an internet browser. You will then need to purchase and/or download any others you may need to perform specific tasks. For example, you might use a word processing program to write text documents, or a graphic design application to touch up photos and create visual displays. Other programs include:

- spreadsheet programs
- presentation software
- desktop publishing software
- database management software.

Word processing applications

Word processors are versatile software applications that allow you to create, manipulate or edit text files. In the absence of desktop publishing applications such as Adobe InDesign, word processors can also be used to create newsletters, promotional flyers and much more. Most word processors provide a range of useful functions that enable you to:

- edit and format a document to ensure a professional look
- create a range of documents, such as letters, reports, forms and so on
- check your spelling and grammar (to a certain degree, human input is still required in cases such as when words are spelled correctly but used in the wrong context)
- insert graphics, photos and tables alongside the text.

Some of the word processing programs available today include:

- *Microsoft Word.* This is one of the most widely used word processing programs and is part of the Microsoft Office suite of software.
- *WordPerfect.* Produced by Corel, this program offers much the same options as Microsoft Word and is also widely used.
- *iWork Pages (or AppleWorks).* This program has been specifically developed for use on Apple devices.
- *Google Docs.* This web-based word processing application integrates neatly with a range of other Google products and functions.

Graphic design applications

There are a variety of graphic design applications available to help you create, alter and enhance images. You can use this type of software to:

- create new images by merging several images together and manipulating their look
- animate images to provide movement and interest
- crop an image so that only a small portion of the original photo is used
- resize the image
- change the resolution of the image (i.e. increase or decrease the number of pixels that make up the image) to improve or reduce image quality: the larger the number of pixels, the better the quality of the image and the larger the file size—this is important when you are uploading an image to the internet or sending it via email, as large file sizes are often rejected by email carriers or websites
- change the colours and shapes of the original image, and much more.

Examples of graphic design software include Adobe Photoshop, Adobe Illustrator, CorelDRAW, Procreate and Affinity Designer.

Spreadsheet applications

Spreadsheet applications such as Microsoft Excel are used mainly for storing, organising and analysing data. The data is presented in tabular form and are organised into worksheets. Spreadsheets can be used for:

- tracking growth trends
- stock or inventory control
- tracking revenue and sales figures
- keeping track of customer details, in the absence of a specialised database
- maintaining the organisation's accounts, in the absence of specialised accounting software such as MYOB or QuickBooks.

Spreadsheets and their uses are covered in detail in Chapter 13.

Presentation software

Applications such as PowerPoint, Canva and Presenter Media are used to create professional presentations for a range of purposes such as meetings or lectures. These presentations can then be displayed on a large screen, by means of a computer/laptop and a data projector, or shared via a company intranet or website.

Each presentation can be themed with specific colours, fonts, graphics and animation to create a dynamic display of information. Online applications such as Canva also enable you to collaborate with others in real time, to produce presentations, tell stories or create albums.

Desktop publishing software

Desktop publishing software such as Adobe InDesign allow you to quickly and easily produce promotional materials such as flyers, newsletters, invitations, greeting cards, business forms, calendars, catalogues and much more. The program will usually include a large selection of themes, templates and graphics, which can save an organisation substantial sums on producing professional-looking promotional and other materials, if used effectively. Other desktop publishing software include:

- Canva for Enterprise
- Adobe InDesign
- Foxit PDF Editor
- Lucidpress
- QuarkXPress.

Database management software

Many organisations—in fact, whole industries—use purpose-built databases. Table 11.1 lists examples of database management systems and their uses in various industries. These databases contain thousands, perhaps millions, of details about customers and products. They are often written specifically for use in a particular industry and address needs unique to that industry.

Table 11.1 Examples of industry-based databases

Industry	Database management system(s)	Used for
Sales	Microsoft Access Salesforce Zendesk	Customer details Supplier details
Hotel	Fidelio/Micros	Reservations Customer details Stock control Account keeping Room inventory and allocation
Travel	Galileo Sabre Amadeus	Reservations Account keeping Printing airline tickets Customer details
Vocational Education	PowerPro WiseNet	Keeping student records Enrolment of new students Account keeping Staff details

There are other database management software available that not only allows you to keep accurate records of customers, products and projects, but also supports intelligent query processing. This means that, in a customer service or marketing sense, you can search your database for customers who regularly buy certain products. You can then alert them, by means of an email or brochure, that there will be a discount sale on those specific products coming up.

From an accounts point of view, on the other hand, you can ask the database to provide information about product sales broken down by product, price and quantity sold, or a list of creditors and debtors and how much money is owed ... and more.

Think about

1. **Think about the way in which you generally communicate in business. What hardware and software programs do you use? Why? How do you make use of mobile devices and apps?**

Knowledge check

10. Name three software programs that are typically used in a business environment. Briefly explain their functions.

CHAPTER 12

Design and produce business documents

Learning outcomes

12.1 Select and prepare resources

12.2 Design a document

12.3 Produce a document

12.4 Finalise a document

Basic letters are one thing, but sometimes you will need to produce more than just a simple document. Whether they are paper-based or in electronic format, the importance of business documents cannot be overestimated.

A company's image and reputation can rest on the quality of the products, services and information it provides and these are often associated with the documentation it produces. Documents can tell the story of a business: where it came from, what its aims are and the journey it has taken to achieve them. They can serve as a gateway through which a business can enter new markets and expand its reach. Documents, then, are important on many levels:

- They keep an organisation compliant. Meeting the compliance requirements of authorities is an essential aspect of good business practice and can ensure that penalties and fines for any breaches of regulations are avoided.
- Annual company reports can provide an insight into an organisation's corporate and financial standing.
- Documents protect the organisation's integrity. Keeping correct and accurate documentation allows an organisation to present itself in the best light.
- They project an image of the organisation and its professionalism, reflecting its brand.
- They provide written information on a range of topics to many different stakeholders.

12.1 Selecting and preparing resources

Workplace efficiency comes from understanding the tasks that need to be accomplished each day and knowing the right way to complete them. This means having a sound understanding of the technology and other resources that are at your disposal and using them to maximum benefit.

As discussed in Chapter 11, the business resources you choose will depend on the job you need to do. To recap, these could include computers and/or laptops, as well as internet access and software such as spreadsheets and word processing tools. You may also need to use mobile devices with a range of useful apps such as email, diaries, online surveys, presentation tools and more.

12.1.1 Selecting and using technology and software applications

Choosing the right resource for the right job is a matter of determining what needs to be done and then deciding how best to accomplish that task with the resources at your disposal. For example, you wouldn't use an ink jet printer to make 10 copies of a 200-page document if a photocopier was available. Equally, you would probably not use a computer, word processing software and a printer to write a short note to a colleague when a handwritten note or an email would do the job.

Technology

Technology is defined as the way in which we apply scientific knowledge for practical purposes. It includes machines such as computers, but also techniques and processes such as the way in which computer chips are produced. In an office environment, technology includes computers, printers, photocopiers and scanners, among other items.

A computer is an electronic device that executes software programs. A computer consists of two main components: hardware, which are the physical components of the device itself, and software, the programs that provide the computer with instructions to perform tasks. A computer *processes* information (or **input**) through input devices such as a mouse, touchscreen or keyboard. It *displays* information (**output**) through devices such as a **monitor** (where the information can be viewed on a screen) and/or a printer (where the information is viewed on a piece of paper). Computers have become indispensable in today's world and millions of people all over the world use them. Businesses also use them to calculate and pay their bills, prepare their accounts, pay their taxes online and perform many other functions.

Internet and mobile applications

In addition to the software outlined in Chapter 11, there are a range of online and mobile applications that can be useful in producing business documents. These are essential business resources as they connect a business to its customers, suppliers and other interested parties all over the world. They allow an organisation to quickly share information and collaborate on projects and documentation in real time. Some of these programs include:

- Canva (http://www.canva.com)
- Nintex.com (https://nintex.com)
- Xpertdoc.com (https://xpertdoc.com)
- Snapforms.com.au (https://snapforms.com.au).

Internet access is also essential for the following purposes:

- *Digital communications.* These may include resources such as:
  - email providers (e.g. iCloud, Gmail, Hotmail or those provided by your workplace)
  - messaging, using services such as WhatsApp and Facebook Messenger
  - mobile communication, such as mobile phones and tablets
  - videoconferencing, which is a convenient and cost-efficient way to hold meetings. It saves on the cost of travel and ensures that those attending such a meeting have all the necessary information at hand without having to transport files to external meeting venues.

Meeting platforms include Zoom (https://zoom.us), Google Meet (https://apps.google.com/meet) and Microsoft Teams (https://www.microsoft.com/en-au/microsoft-teams/group-chat-software), among others.

- *Online surveys.* Survey Monkey, Typeform, Google Forms and other online surveys are very useful tools. They allow an organisation to:
  - gain feedback on product or service performance
  - gather information about specific business issues they need clarification on
  - gain feedback on future plans and promotions to see whether the idea is worth spending time, effort and money on.

Try this now

1. Go to the Survey Monkey website (https://www.surveymonkey.com), or to a survey program of your choice, and familiarise yourself with its pages and navigation. You will need to use Survey Monkey for a later assessment (task 2).

What are business documents?

A document can represent a permanent record of a communication between the organisation and its customers, suppliers, industry authorities or government bodies. As such, documents should be accurate in terms of content and professional in appearance, as they may be called upon for review, audit or evidentiary purposes in the future. The following are examples of business documents.

- *Letters.* These are a relatively formal means of communication today. However, they are still used for a variety of purposes, such as formal communications regarding contracts or agreements, issues relating to human resources, or other matters that require a formal response. Letters are often sent electronically via software programs such as DocuSign, where recipients and senders can add their signature digitally. This removes the need for sending and receiving hand-signed documents via the postal system or by courier.
- *Forms and templates.*
  - **Forms** are used to gather information an organisation needs to complete a process or to help them make decisions. Forms are necessary to ensure that the information gathered is consistent. For example, if 100 people are asked for their opinions on a business's customer service, the way they write their responses might vary from person to person, making it impossible to meaningfully analyse the information they have provided. Forms avoid this problem by asking *specific* questions the organisation needs to have answered. One hundred people's answers to these questions will provide a consistent story that the organisation can build upon.
  - **Templates** are, in essence, the "master" version of a form: every form you fill out is based on that master template. Whenever a change needs to be made to an organisation's information requirements, it will amend the template, ensuring that all subsequent forms completed will be the latest version. A template can also revolve around specific document designs, showing what information should go into what space, what font must be used, where the logo should be placed, and so on.
- *Agenda.* Time is an important business tool and can easily be wasted during meetings when discussions move into areas that weren't anticipated or are irrelevant. This can be avoided by using an **agenda** to keep the meeting on track. An agenda will generally include:
  - a list of items to be discussed during a meeting
  - who will be speaking or addressing each item
  - the timeframes allocated to each topic, and so on.

- *Meeting minutes.* These work in conjunction with the agenda. **Minutes** are a detailed list of what was actually discussed during the meeting. They also note what action is to be taken as a result of the discussions, by whom and within what period of time.
- *Simple reports.* Most organisations will use **reports** on a range of subjects. They might be reports created by accountants that provide overviews or details of the company's financial situation, or reports that show what sales have been made over a given time period, or reports related to complaint handling and continuous improvement progress. Whatever their purpose, reports are a necessary tool for managers who need to make decisions on various aspects of the business. Accuracy is therefore important.
- *Spreadsheets.* As mentioned, these can be used for a variety of purposes—mostly dealing with calculations and analytics.
- *Newsletters and/or blogs.* These can be sent, via various means, to customers or staff with information or stories about the organisation.

We will look at software functions and different types of documents in more detail as we move through the chapter.

General organisational requirements

In addition to understanding what resources are available to produce documents, you also need to bear in mind any organisational policies and procedures related to these, as well as legislative requirements. These may include:

- *Internet usage and social media policies.* During work hours, staff should use the internet only for work purposes and shouldn't spend time chatting with friends on social media or browsing non-work-related websites. However, by posting information on the internet, a business can spread word about its activities rapidly and widely. To this end, most organisations will have policies that dictate such things as:
  - Who, within the organisation, is allowed access to the internet?
  - What types of websites are permitted to be visited, and which ones are not, when researching information?
  - How will social media and the internet be used to promote the organisation?
  - What information should be posted to the internet?
  - Who will be responsible for creating online content?
- *Industry codes of conduct.* These are generally rules or standards of conduct, set for an industry as a whole, that often include the relationships between industry participants and/or their customers. They provide the necessary regulatory support for a given industry and guard against misconduct and opportunistic behaviour, while encouraging long-term changes to business culture.
- *Budgets.* These may place restrictions on document production. In order to remain within a given budget, an organisation might, for example, decide to print fewer copies and to distribute the remainder by email, or to print the documents in black rather than in colour on a lower-quality paper, and so on.
- *Identifying the correct authorities for signing the correspondence/communications.* Letters should always be signed personally. An unsigned letter looks unprofessional and sends an impersonal message. Appropriate authorities for signature may be your supervisor or the company's manager or, depending on your role within the organisation, you may be permitted to sign specific types of correspondence.
- *Work health and safety (WHS) policies, procedures and programs.* Under the *Work Health and Safety Act 2011* (Cth), all employees (and employers) have rights and responsibilities while in the workplace. In terms of producing documents, this might relate to ensuring that:
  - equipment being used is in proper working order—for example, no frayed cables or loose electric sockets

- the area where you are working is well ventilated and well lit
- your desk area is set up correctly and you are able to sit comfortably while working.

An organisation may also have other requirements when producing documents. These may relate to:

- *Correct spelling and grammar.* Tools such as dictionaries and thesauruses are used to ensure that documents are created in a professional manner.
  - A **dictionary** is used to check the correct spelling of words. On a computer you would use spellcheck. You should use this with caution, however, as it doesn't recognise the incorrect use of correctly spelled words (dealt with a little later in the chapter).
  - A **thesaurus** lists words according to similar meaning. It allows you to find alternative ways to word things. For example, if you are looking up the word "document", a thesaurus will provide you with alternative words: *text, file, article* and *essay*. This is useful if the same word needs to occur throughout a document and you don't want to be repetitive.
- *Level of formality and tone used.* Depending on how well you know the person you are communicating with, the tone of a letter or message can either be:
  - formal, for people you don't know, or don't know well
  - informal and friendlier for people you are more familiar with.
- *Image of the organisation.* The organisation may have spent a great deal of money, time and effort on developing a corporate image. It will therefore have very specific requirements in terms of, for example, the colours used in letters, brochures and promotional materials. It will also have strict guidelines regarding its logo. For example, only certain staff may be allowed to specify its use, and how and where it is to be used.
- *Observing copyright legislation.* This means that any text you copy from another source (e.g. a textbook) must be properly referenced. Copyright infringement can lead to serious legal action being taken against not only the organisation but also the staff who produced the document.
- *Use of headers and footers.* These may be used in documents to show the organisation's name, time, date, document title, file name, etc.

Try this now

2. Highlight a word from a document you have created. Right-click on it and use the *Synonyms* function to find an alternative word.

Access and equity issues

As noted in Chapter 2, it is illegal to discriminate against any person because of their race, culture, religion, gender, age, or physical or mental ability. Therefore, any documents that you create for both internal and external use should be produced in such a way that they are easy for people of all backgrounds and abilities to read and understand, and should not contain any offensive language, images or suggestions. This means using simple terms and phrasing, or graphics and images, that help tell the story you are trying to convey. It may also mean producing materials in a variety of languages, if necessary.

12.1.2 Selecting the layout and style of publications

Any document you have sent out or prepared represents your organisation and must therefore project a professional image. In order to achieve this, many organisations will have set guidelines (or style guides) to ensure that all documents produced meet the required standards. **Style guides** are documents that outline the rules that staff must follow when producing documents. Style guides can be developed for both paper-based and online user documentation and may include information on such things as font and point size, placement of logos, images to be used, margins, and so on, as discussed in Chapter 11.

Basic principles of document design

Business documents are meant to engage readers and get a message across to them. To do this successfully requires an understanding of how to create the most effective layout. This, in turn, means having a basic knowledge of the key principles of design. These are:

- balance
- proportion
- order
- contrast
- unity.

Balance

Balance involves placing elements such as text and graphics so they appear to be either symmetrically (formally) or asymmetrically (informally) balanced.

Symmetrical balance refers to a page having a mirror-image balance—that is, when all the elements on one side of the page are reflected equally on the other side (Figure 12.1(a)). These elements don't necessarily need to be identical objects, but they should be similar in terms of numbers of objects, colours, size, and so on. The main consideration in using a formal balance is that readers don't have to work hard to see relationships between message elements. A document that has been produced in a symmetrical manner represents stability, security, authority and thoughtfulness. It can also, however, appear unexciting and unimaginative.

Asymmetrical balance is when items on one side of the page are obviously different from those on the other side (Figure 12.1(b)).

Most documents are designed in such a way as to be balanced asymmetrically, as this is generally considered more interesting and exciting. A message that is asymmetrically balanced is seen as dynamic, fresh, inviting, creative and friendly.

Figure 12.1 (a) Symmetrical design; (b) Asymmetrical design

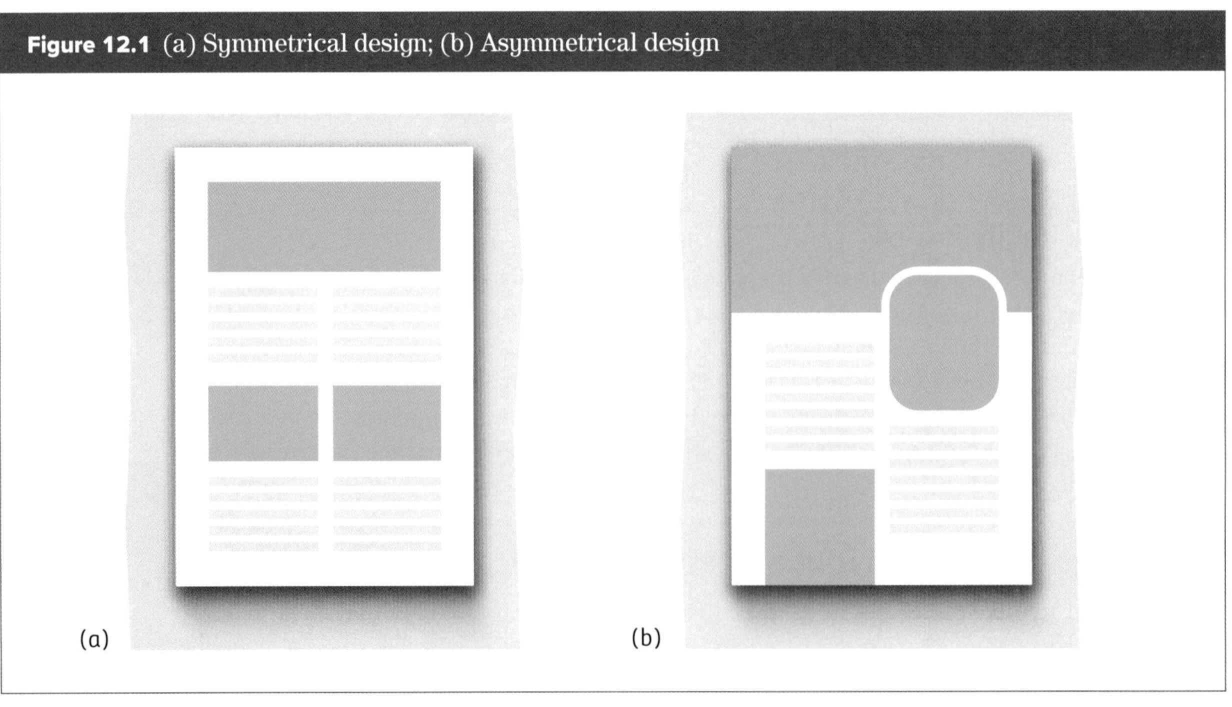

Proportion

Proportion relates to the relationships the eye detects between the elements on a page or in a document. This comparison determines whether the viewer finds the appearance of the page or document pleasing to the eye. A pleasing visual proportion can be created by dividing the page into thirds, with the middle section being the best place to put the most important elements. It should be in proportion to the rest of the page, creating a natural centre that will draw the eye when a person is viewing a document.

Order

This principle determines the sequence and importance of each section of the document. Information should be provided in a logical order so that the content flows naturally and is easy to understand.

Contrast

All good designs should have a focal point that stands out on the page, and this can be achieved through the use of shapes, sizing of objects, colours and so on, to emphasise specific texts or sections of the document. The use of contrast highlights differences and creates emphasis. For example, darker and larger visual elements stand out on a page; as the focus of the document design, they are therefore seen as more important or interesting than the other elements. Contrast can also be created through the use of headings.

Unity

This deals with how all the message elements tie together as a whole and complement each other. The pages in the document should hold a reader's attention, but they should be simple to follow. Each page should also have a similar structure so that they are consistent—or unified—throughout.

Page layout

The way information is presented can have as much, if not more, of an effect on the reader as the information itself. If the document is crowded or difficult to understand, readers will simply not take the time to read it.

Using white space

When a document is based solely on text, there is a risk that the information can become too crowded. Large, unbroken blocks of text can sometimes be difficult to read; imagine what a printed page would look like if there was no relief from the actual text. This is where white space comes in. "White space" refers to space on a page not covered by print or graphic matter. It is used to break up the blocks of text to make the printed page more pleasing to the eye. White space can be made up of wide margins and/or spaces between paragraphs.

Figure 12.2 Line spacing options

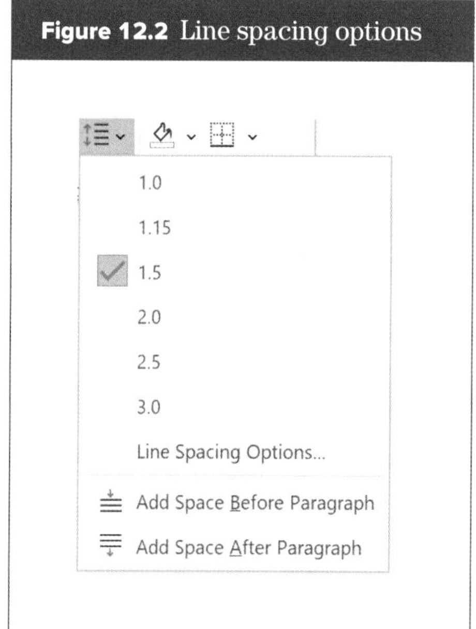

Line spacing

The amount of space between lines (let's say 1.5) can break up large amounts of text to make a page more "readable". The use of white space, even between text lines, can make a difference to the readability of a document.

Text spaced at say 1.0 is more difficult to read, as the lines are closer together. The more white space you have, therefore, the easier on the eye the text will be. Using the *Line and Paragraph Spacing* key (Figure 12.2) on the *Home* menu bar will bring up the drop-down box with a number of spacing options.

12.1.3 Discussing and clarifying format and style with required stakeholders

A final thing to bear in mind when preparing documents is the need to communicate with stakeholders who have an interest in the document, or who may have information you need to complete the work. For example, you may need to:

- clarify the format required for the document (e.g. should it be a printed report, a letter or an email?)
- confirm that it follows the organisation's style guide
- clarify the key points to be made in the document
- ensure that all the images to be used are appropriate to the message.

You may also need to determine:

- who will need to sign the document(s) when completed
- who will proofread it to ensure it is free of errors
- how it is to be formatted and designed
- how many copies should be produced
- how the document(s) should be distributed once they have been finalised.

Knowledge check

1. There are a number of different resources you can use to help you create business documents. List at least six resources.
2. Explain what a style guide is, why it is important and what it is used for. Give examples of what it might include.
3. When producing documents, an organisation may also have requirements that involve a range of other issues. List at least six issues.
4. Explain what is meant by the terms "access" and "equity", and discuss how they might impact on the creation of documents.
5. List the five basic principles of document design. Briefly describe what each one involves.
6. In designing your page layout, you should consider white space and line spacing. Explain what these terms mean.
7. Explain why it is important to discuss and clarify format and style of a document with relevant stakeholders.

12.2 Designing a document

The verb "design" means to decide upon the look and function of an object by making a detailed drawing, or plan, of it. When applied to a business document, this means planning the content of the document so you will know how it will look on the page, the order in which to place various text or graphic elements, and the placement of logos. You might also need to consider the use of headers and footers and what they should contain.

12.2.1 Identifying, opening and creating files

The way you work with files will vary greatly, depending on the platform or systems your organisation uses. For example, an organisation may choose to have its documents stored using one of the following methods:

- On a local computer drive that is not connected to any shared networks.
- On a shared drive where a number of computers are networked, either within a specific location or across multiple locations. Here, information may be stored on a company server where staff can access files according to their roles and levels of authority.

- In a cloud-based storage system, such as iCloud, Google Docs or OneDrive, where information is stored on the internet. This is a common way of storing information today and is the most collaborative method of working with files, as staff can access information stored here from wherever they are located.

Whichever is the case, when you produce a document, you are creating a file. This file will need to be stored and, at some point, retrieved and/or edited.

Files

When you *save* data to your computer, or to a cloud-based storage system, it is stored as a file. This file must be named. While it can be named in any way you wish, it should nevertheless be given a logical name so that it can be quickly and easily found again. Upon saving the document, the program used to create the file will automatically append a file extension to the end of the file name. This indicates the file type, which are associated with certain types of programs. For example, a document created in Microsoft Word would have the extension *.docx*, while a spreadsheet created in Excel would have the extension *.xlsx*.

When retrieving the file from a list of other files (as shown in Figure 12.3), the computer recognises the extension and runs the associated program installed onto your computer to read and edit the file.

Folders

The more documents you create and save, the harder it can become to find them later. Therefore, it will eventually be necessary to organise them into folders. The format these take will be governed by organisational requirements and can be based on subject, date, or numerical or alphabetical systems. In general, however, it is a good idea to give the folders logical names so they can be easily found. For example:

Figure 12.3 Example of folders and sub-folders

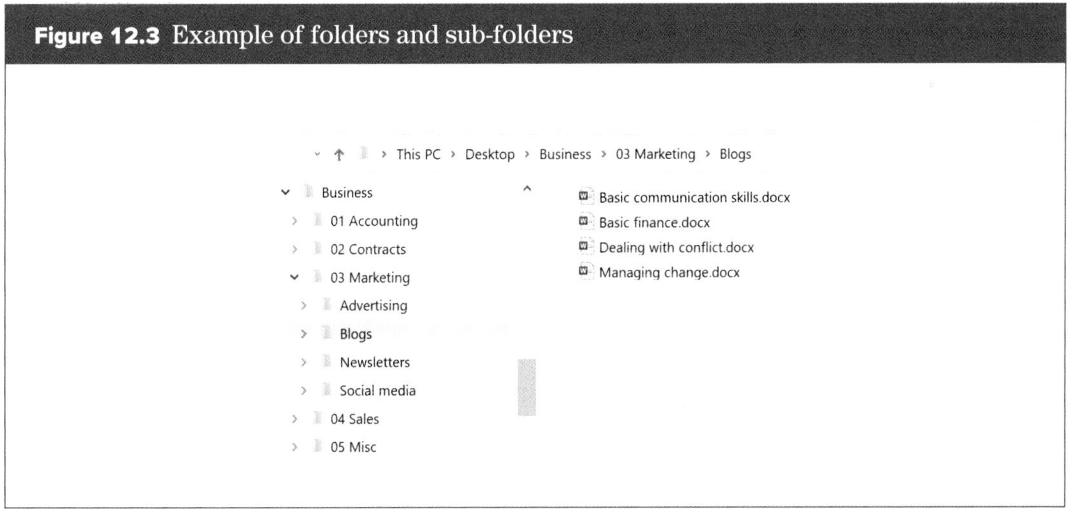

In the example in Figure 12.3, folder "03 Marketing" has a number of sub-folders for all marketing-related files. The sub-folder "Blogs", for example, contains all current blogs created by the marketing department. Likewise, the "Advertising" folder would contain all documents relating to the organisation's advertising campaigns. The folders you create should make it easy to store and to identify documents with a minimum of effort.

Alternatively, you can use the *Search* bar, located to the right of the window, beside the address bar, to look for a specific document or subject. The search shown in Figure 12.4 would find all files or sub-folders that include the word "marketing". If you search for a specific name or document title, it would look for any documents containing that specific name or title.

We will look at storing documents in more detail in the final section of this chapter.

Figure 12.4 Using the *Search* bar

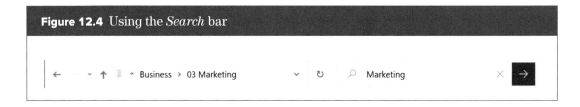

12.2.2 Designing documents and ensuring efficient entry of information

In the course of your working day, you may be called upon to create a range of different documents for a range of different purposes, including memos, meeting agendas and minutes, and reports. With this in mind, it is useful to understand the main elements and basic layouts of some of these documents.

Internal memos

Although largely replaced by email, a written memo (memorandum) is used exclusively for communication within your own organisation. A memo can be sent for a variety of reasons, including to:

- circulate monthly reports on workplace projects or other activities
- circulate new company information such as new policies, equipment, installations or procedures
- advise staff of hazards or risks
- address complaints
- share good-news stories.

A memo is a very simple document, with section headings as follows:

- *To:* Here you put the names of the main recipients of the document. There could be a number of them, so the names are normally listed individually in a column. This is done:
    - to keep the person informed of actions taken or decisions made that may have some bearing on their area of work
    - as a courtesy to a supervisor or manager
    - as proof to a supervisor or manager that a task allocated to you has been actioned.
- *From:* Your name goes here. Depending on the size of the organisation, you may need to include your title and department.
- *Re: (or Subject):* This advises recipients what the memo is about.

In the example shown in Figure 12.5, you might print five copies of the memo: one for each of the main recipients, one for the courtesy copy, and perhaps one for yourself. Ideally, however, and with sustainability in mind, it could be sent by email using a specific template the organisation uses for these types of messages.

Meeting agendas and minutes

Depending on the size and nature of the organisation, meetings can have varying degrees of formality. Smaller organisations may have informal meetings where staff simply meet on a regular basis to discuss any issues or areas of concern or to share information. They may not have a specific agenda of items they want to cover, and they may not keep a record of what is discussed. The whole process may take the form of a conversation, rather than a meeting. In other organisations, however, the process may be more formalised: a date is set for the meeting; a list of topics to be covered (agenda) is sent to those people who have been invited to participate in the meeting; and subsequently, a record is kept of what was discussed and what actions are to be taken (minutes of the meeting). The format these agendas and minutes will take will vary between organisations. In general, however, they will contain the same basic information.

Figure 12.5 Example of a memo

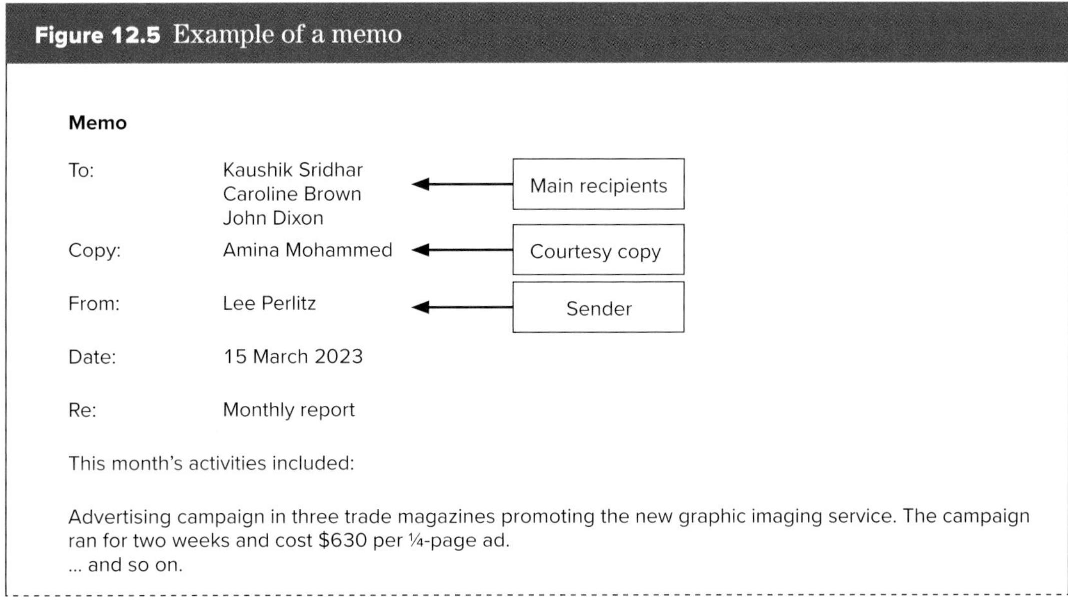
Memo

To: Kaushik Sridhar
Caroline Brown
John Dixon

Copy: Amina Mohammed

From: Lee Perlitz

Date: 15 March 2023

Re: Monthly report

This month's activities included:

Advertising campaign in three trade magazines promoting the new graphic imaging service. The campaign ran for two weeks and cost $630 per ¼-page ad.
... and so on.

Agenda

An agenda is used as a guideline in a meeting to ensure that all necessary points are covered, that discussions don't stray too far from these points, and that the meeting progresses in a timely manner. Each participant in the meeting will be sent a copy of the agenda in advance so that they know what will be discussed during the meeting and can be prepared. Agendas can be very simple, with just a bullet point list of topics, or they can be more complex, with information on who will be attending, where the meeting is being held, how long each presentation is expected to last and so on.

Figure 12.6 Example of a meeting agenda

Agenda		
Purpose: Department head monthly meeting		**Date:** 15/3/23
Venue: Boardroom		**Time:** 09:00
Participants: Joe Brown, Ying Cheung, Greg Appleton, Rae Huo, Sally Lee		
Time	**Item**	**Presenter**
09:00	Read minutes of last meeting and discuss any issues	Joe Brown
09:30	Results of customer service survey conducted last month	Rae Huo
10:00	Allocation of action points resulting from survey results	Joe Brown
10:30 ... and so on.	Marketing initiatives for the coming quarter	Ying Cheung & Greg Appleton

With the agenda from Figure 12.6 in hand, Rae Huo, for example, knows that she will need to prepare the results of a survey that was recently undertaken so they are ready for presentation at the meeting; make copies of the results for the other meeting participants; and be ready for any questions that are asked. Equally, Ying Cheung and Greg Appleton know that they need to provide details of the latest marketing program for the organisation and will also need to be able to answer questions. Each participant knows how much time has been allocated to them, to keep the meeting on track.

Minutes

During the meeting, someone will generally be required to take notes on what was discussed and of any action points that arise as a result of the meeting. These notes are called "minutes".

They can take a range of different formats but will generally include similar information. They will have details of what each person presented, any questions that were asked (and by whom), what action is to be taken and who is to take that action, as well as any time frames involved. Minutes will generally also include a date for any further meetings (Figure 12.7).

Figure 12.7 Example of meeting minutes

Meeting minutes			
Purpose: Department monthly meeting			**Date:** 15/3/23
Present: Joe Brown, Ying Cheung, Greg Appleton, Rae Huo, Sally Lee			
Item	**Action**	**Who**	**By when**
1. Customer survey. Rae presented information on survey results. The main points included: ◆ Customers unhappy with layout of store (difficult to find products). ◆ General dissatisfaction with service levels received. Joe, Rae and Sally discussed a variety of ways in which service levels could be improved.	Review store layout to determine how it could be improved. Customer service training to be undertaken by all staff.	Joe Brown—report at next meeting Sally Lee (HR)	20/7 31/8
2. Ying gave a presentation on the new advertising campaign. It was approved and agreed that new brochures will be produced in line with the new image and campaign. ... and so on.	New promotional materials to be produced.	Greg Appleton—ready for presentation at next meeting	20/7
Next meeting: 20/7/23			

Minutes can be used again at future meetings to discuss progress on action points that were previously allocated to participants. They also serve as a permanent record of items and action points that can be used by senior management and/or the board of directors who, for example, may need to make decisions based on progress being made.

Think about

1. How many different documents do you produce each day in your workplace? How do they differ from each other? Which ones do you create the most, and which ones do you create only occasionally?

Reports

The term “report” covers many types of written documents; the minutes of a meeting, the results of a research project, and a full-fledged business plan are just a few examples. Some reports will be short and to the point; others will be very detailed and require a great deal of research and collation of information. The following are examples of simple, short reports:

- *Stock reports*—listing each product, its code, price and number on hand.
- *Staff training reports*—listing training courses offered by the organisation, which staff members attended, dates of attendance and so on.
- *Enquiry survey reports*—detailing information about where customers heard about your organisation. This information is usually obtained by asking customers who phone you or visit your business premises and is useful in determining how effective your advertising and promotional activities are. Figure 12.8 is an example of an enquiry survey report. A report such

as this could include a graph that illustrates the statistics provided. Graphs are an excellent way to show a statistical analysis at a glance.

Figure 12.8 Example of an enquiry survey report that includes a graph

Enquiry survey report

Enquiry source information about where callers heard about ABC Website Company has been tracked since August 2004. The 2023 year to date results are as follows:

- Of the 203 enquiries received as at 25 August, word of mouth (WOM) remained the highest source, yielding 73 (44%) of enquiries. This was followed by people driving by and seeing the premises—32 (19%)—and then by people whose first contact with us was the website—28 (17%). The remaining 20% were spread across a variety of advertising media.
- May and June were the biggest months for enquiries to date, followed by March. It is believed that the high enquiry figures in June particularly are due to the major advertising campaign run in late May.

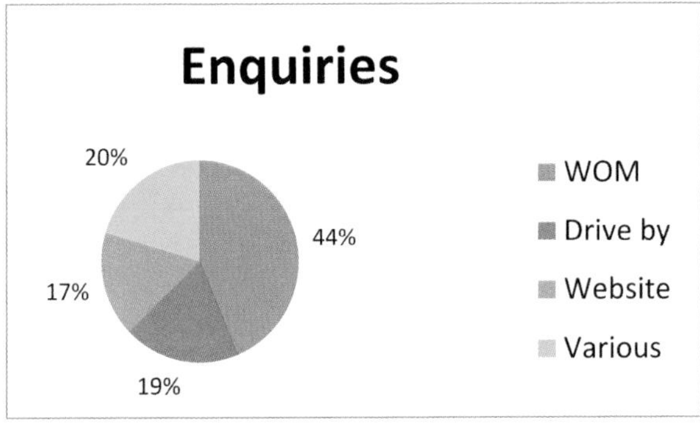

The format of a report will be governed by your organisation's particular house style and requirements. However, most of the more complex reports you may be required to compile will include the following main parts:

- *Title page.* This normally contains four main pieces of information:
  - the report title
  - the name of the organisation for whom the report is being written
  - the name of the person writing the report
  - the date of the report.
- *Executive summary.* Often, the people for whom the report is being written don't have the time to read an entire report immediately. It is a good idea, therefore, to include an executive summary of no more than one or two pages at the beginning of the report. This gives a brief overview of the main points in the report. It could include:
  - main purpose of the report
  - research done
  - conclusion reached
  - recommendations made.
- *Table of contents.* Most complex reports need a table at the beginning that lists the report's contents, making it easy for readers to find specific sections of interest. Word processing software allows you to create tables of contents fairly easily. Giving important sections of the report appropriate headings will allow the software to search through the document for these headings and create the table of contents.
- *Introduction.* The introduction to the report prepares the reader for the discussion that follows. It includes the report's purpose, scope and background.
  - Purpose states what prompted the need for the report, what research it is based on, what kind of problem or situation it addresses, and what this information will mean for the company.

- ◆ Scope refers to the ground covered by the report. For example:
  - how much detail was required
  - what, specifically, is covered in the report
  - whether the information relates to the whole of the organisation or only to specific sections of it.
- ◆ Background includes facts that the reader must know in order to understand what follows. These facts may include descriptions of events or conditions that caused the report to be generated.

- *Main body.* The main body of the report sets out, in detail, the research that has been undertaken on the particular subject the report addresses. It lists, point by point, what prompted the report, what research was undertaken, what information was gathered, where the information came from and how it relates to the subject, and what this information means for the organisation.
- *Conclusion.* This part of the report refines and condenses the information gathered and outlines the conclusions that were drawn from it. It may also outline the consequences of not acting on the conclusions reached.
- *Recommendations.* Recommendations are based on the conclusions of the research. They indicate how to move forward with the subject of the report. Because of the hard work that has gone before—all the research, the collating of the information and the conclusions drawn—these recommendations should have a solid basis in fact and result in informed decisions being made.
- *References.* When carrying out research, you will usually need to consult a variety of sources for your information. These should be listed at the end of the report, not only to validate your conclusions and recommendations, but also to assist anyone reading the report who wishes to obtain further information on the subject.
- *Appendices.* An **appendix** generally contains the facts that support your findings. It can include statistical analyses, research reports you assembled, testimonials—anything you used in your research that supports the report and is important or interesting enough that others might wish to read it.

Locating tools in the Ribbon

Creating a document means not only being able to input data, but also to amend and edit it until it is deemed satisfactory. There are a number of areas where editing tools can be found in a computer program. These may vary between specific programs, and between operating systems such as an Apple Mac and a PC. Figure 12.9 shows two main areas where editing tools can be found in Microsoft Word 365 for PC:

- The *Ribbon* organises the wide variety of tools needed to edit and format a document into tabs.
- *Tabs* group the individual tools into *Sections* by function and type to make them easier to find.

Figure 12.9 Microsoft Word Ribbon

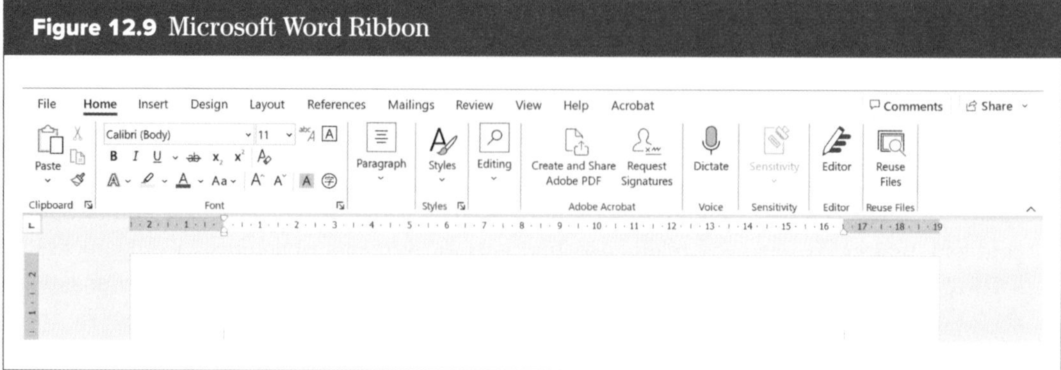

12.2.3 Using a range of tools to ensure consistency of design and layout

Most word processing software have a variety of tools that can help in producing professional documents. These include tools for:

- adding headers and footers
- editing the document text
- adding graphs and images
- adding tables
- tracking changes
- adding comments
- creating a table of contents.

Adding headers and footers

Often a document will require the use of headers and footers. A **header** is found at the top of a page, above the margins, while a **footer** is located at the bottom. The content contained inside a header or footer will appear on every page (or on selected pages) of the document. It is often used for displaying page numbers, the name of the document or the name of the company.

To insert headers or footers in Microsoft Word:

1. Click on the *Insert* tab on the Ribbon.
2. Click on *Header* or *Footer*, depending on where you want to insert information. This will present you with a range of options and styles to choose from.
3. Select the design that best suits your purpose and type in the relevant text.
4. You can also choose whether you want the text to show on all pages, only on odd or even pages, or to have a different first page (where such things as page numbers aren't necessary) (see Figure 12.10).

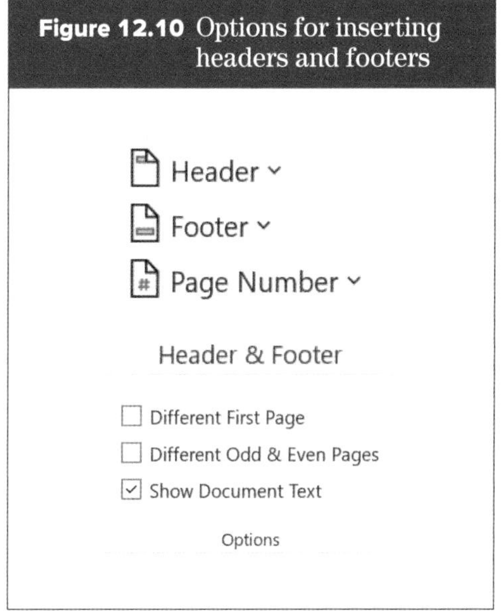

Figure 12.10 Options for inserting headers and footers

Editing the document text

The editing tools on a computer program allow you to control various aspects of document design. Figure 12.11 is taken from the Ribbon and shows the range of editing tools available to you.

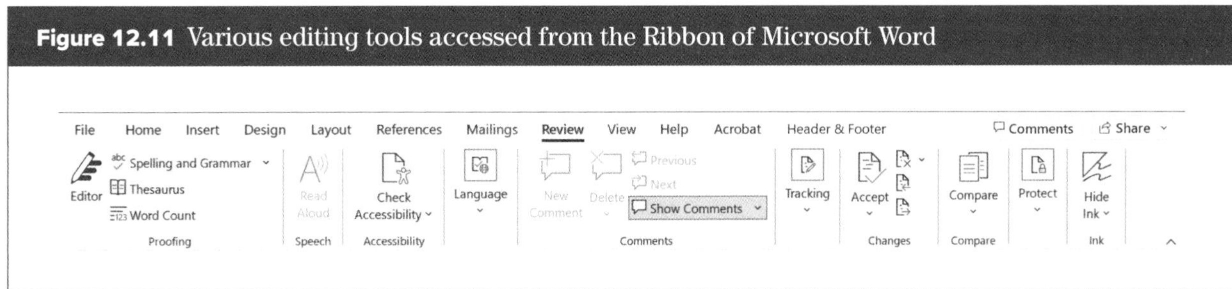

Figure 12.11 Various editing tools accessed from the Ribbon of Microsoft Word

The tools we will look at include:

- checking spelling and grammar
- cutting, pasting and copying text or objects
- inserting graphs and images
- inserting bullets and numbered lists
- tracking changes made to a document
- adding comments to a document.

There may also be times when you want to find, or replace, specific words within a document. The *Find and Replace* functions will let you search the document for these words. This can be particularly useful if you want to change one specific item in a document that may be mentioned a number of times. As shown in Figure 12.12, you can simply say that you want to replace BUSINESS with COMPANY (or whatever it is you want replaced) and the system will search through the entire document and make the necessary changes.

Figure 12.12 Editing using the *Find and Replace* tool to change words in a document

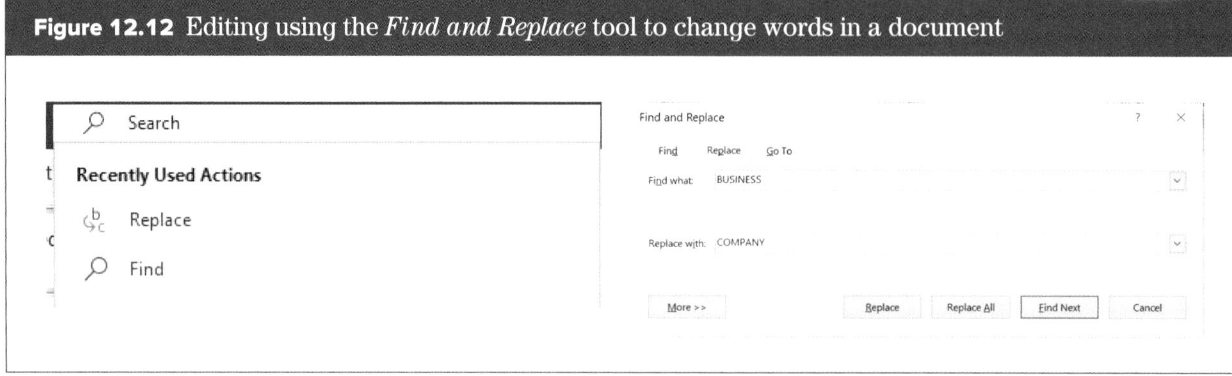

Figure 12.13 Cut and paste options

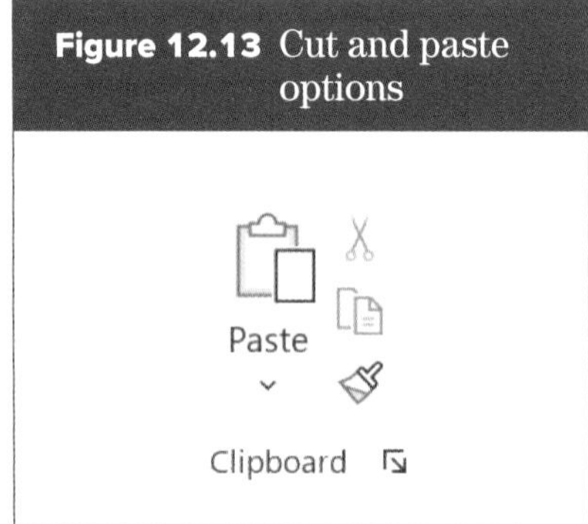

Spelling and grammar checking

Checking your spelling and grammar is another important function discussed in Chapter 11.

Cut, paste and copy content

There may be times when you have written a section of text and, on reflection, decide it isn't right for, or appropriate to, the document's purpose. The quickest method of deleting this section is to highlight the text to be removed and then press the *Backspace* key on the keyboard. This will remove it entirely. However, you may decide that the text could be used elsewhere in the document. In this case, you would highlight the text, use the *Cut* function (represented by the scissors) and *Paste* it into the new location (Figure 12.13).

Video: Cut, copy and paste in Word

This section of the *Home* tab also gives you the option to *Copy* (represented by two sheets of paper) highlighted items and to paste them into other section of the document, or into completely different documents.

Adding graphs and images

Sometimes it may be necessary to include a graph or some images in a document. The functions to accomplish this are found in the *Insert* tab (Figure 12.14). By clicking the appropriate tool, you will be given a range of options, including (but not limited to), inserting:

- tables
- pictures

Figure 12.14 *Insert* tab options

- shapes
- charts (among other options).

Each option will allow you to manipulate whatever it is you are inserting so that it conforms to your design specifications. When inserting a photo, for example, the image may not appear in the intended size or location on the page. By right-clicking the image you will see a list of options for adjusting the position of the image on the page (Figure 12.15). The figure shows an image sitting in line with the text so the surrounding text will not wrap around it. This leaves large areas of white space. Right-clicking the image produces a number of options, including the option to *Wrap text*. Clicking this displays further options to change how the inserted image interacts with the surrounding text.

Figure 12.15 Adjusting the text wrapping on an inserted image

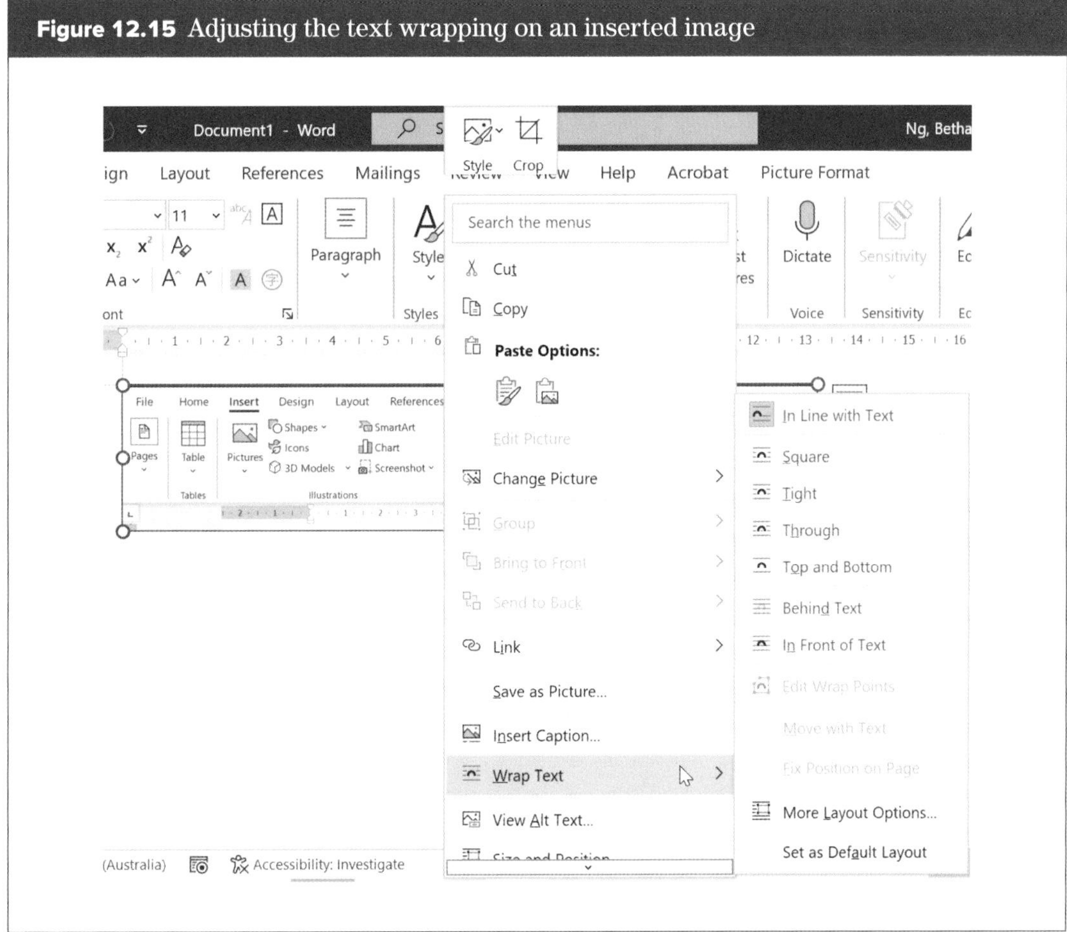

Try this now

3. Use a document you have created and try some of these options for yourself, seeing how an image interacts with the surrounding text with each one. You should also try to add a header, and page numbers in your footer.

Video: Inserting objects into Word: Part 2

Inserting tables

Tables can be an excellent way to present a large amount of information, particularly if they are lists of names or numbers. Not only do they allow you to highlight certain information, but they are easier to read on a page compared to a long list. For example, the list in Figure 12.16 has been set in

Figure 12.16 Example of a table to insert into a Word document

Vegetables

Vegetables can be served as a meal, or as an accompaniment to a meal, and may be cooked or uncooked. Popular vegetables used in salads and appetisers may include:

◆ Tomato	◆ Cucumber	◆ Cauliflower	◆ Capsicum
◆ Eggplant	◆ Artichoke	◆ Carrot	◆ Olives
◆ Broccoli	◆ Cabbage	◆ Onion	◆ Pumpkin
◆ Sweet potato	◆ Leek	◆ Spring onion	◆ Chives
◆ Garlic	◆ Celery		

a table of four columns, rather than being presented as a long bulleted list. The table provides the same information but is easier on the eye and takes up less of the page. The information was first typed into each of the columns and bullet points were added.

To insert a table into a word-processed document:

1. Click on the *Insert* tab on the Ribbon.
2. Click on *Table*. This will present you with a range of options. You can choose to simply highlight the number of rows and columns you want to insert (Figure 12.17), or you can choose to *Insert Table*, which will present you with a drop-down box where you can type in the number of columns and rows you want. (This option will also allow you to choose the width of the columns and/or the table.)

Figure 12.17 Choosing table options

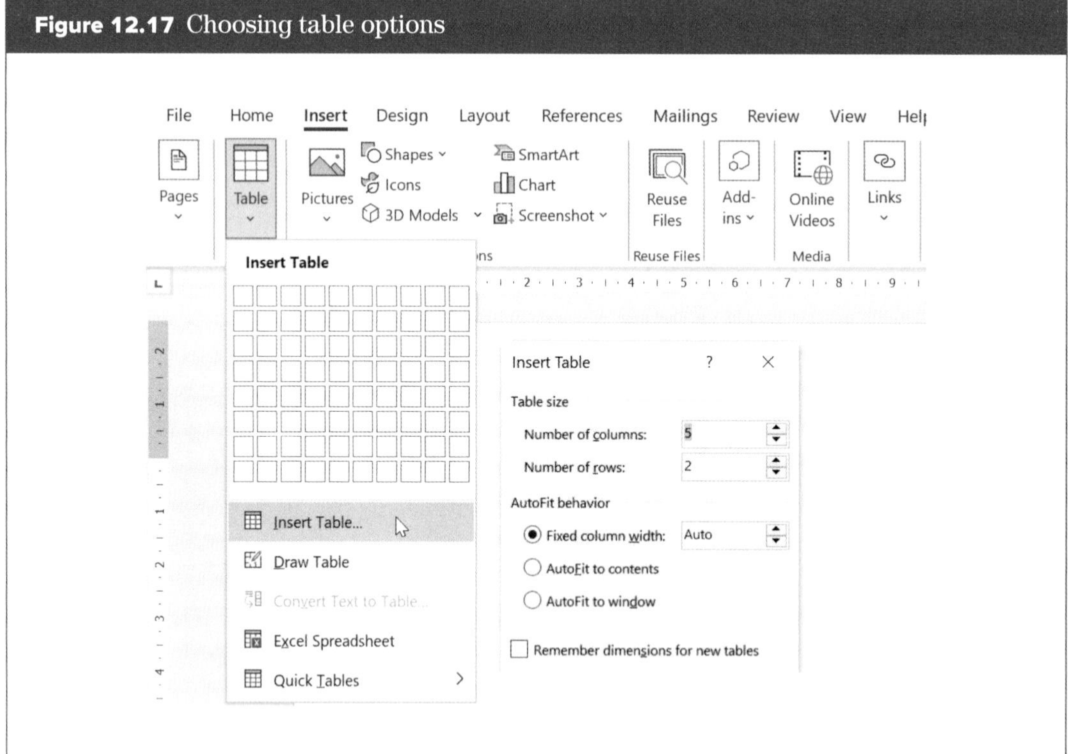

3. Once you have chosen the number of rows and columns you want, the table will appear in the document and you can then type information in to suit your needs.

You can also embed Excel worksheets into your document (Figure 12.18). This is very useful when you want calculations to be performed. An ordinary table will allow you to have columns of numbers, but it won't make any calculations. By copying a table in Excel and pasting it into your Word document with either the *Link & Keep Source Formatting* or *Link & Use Destination Styles* option, you can link the two files together and any subsequent amendments made to the spreadsheet will automatically update the table in the Word document and vice versa.

Figure 12.18 Embedding an Excel spreadsheet into Word

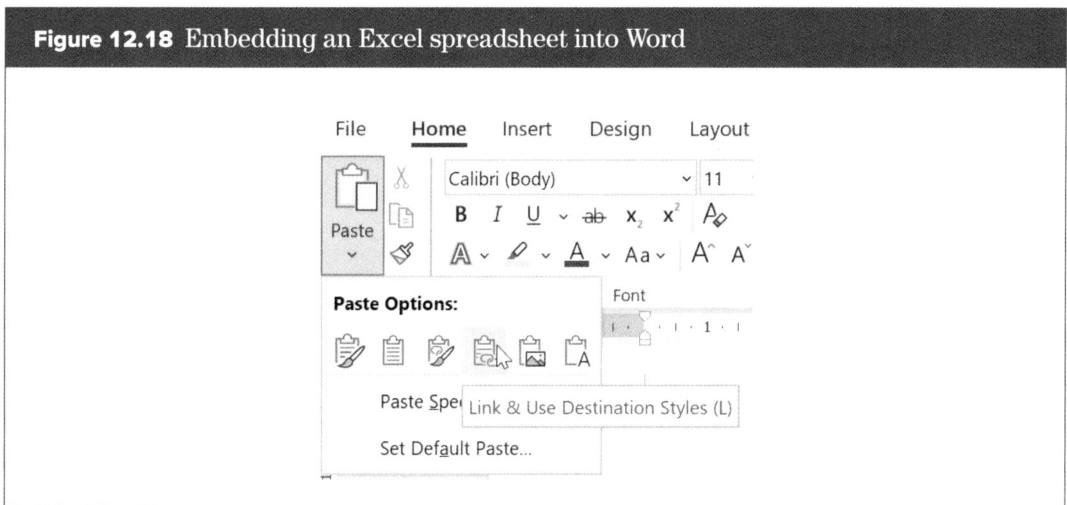

Tracking changes

There may be times when several people will be working on the production of a single document. They may all have their own sections to produce, or they may have been asked to review the document for content and accuracy.

Most word processing programs will give you the option to *Track* whatever changes other people have made to the document. Any alterations to the text, or to the format of the document, are marked and struck through in red (Figure 12.19), with the new text underlined in the same colour. (Figure 12.20).

Figure 12.19 Highlighting text to be changed

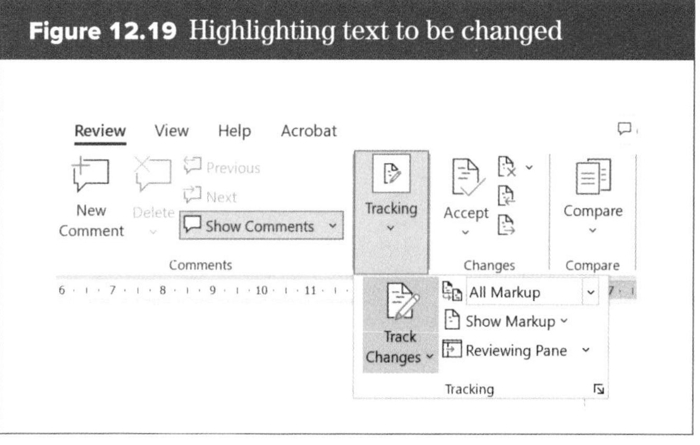

Figure 12.20 Tracking changes made to text in Word

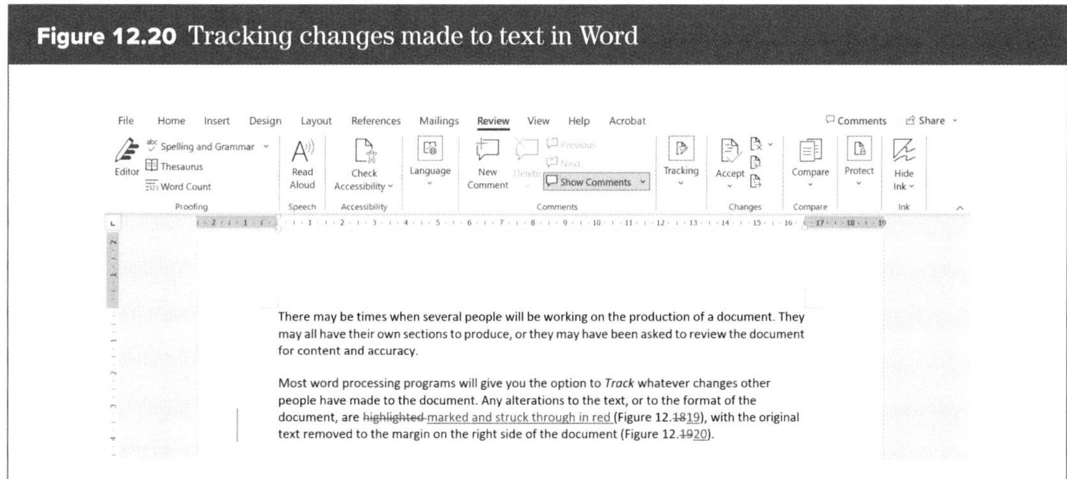

The main person responsible for the document, as a whole, can then either accept the changes others have made, in which case the original text will be deleted from the margin and the amendments incorporated into the document, or reject them, where the amended text is deleted and the original is reinstated.

The *Track Changes* tool can be accessed via the *Tracking* group of the *Review* tab.

Inserting comments

In the same way that a reviewer can make amendments to a document, they can also add comments for you to consider. By clicking the section you wish to comment on and selecting *New Comment* from the *Comments* section of the *Review* tab, you can make comments relevant to the text (Figure 12.21).

Figure 12.21 Inserting a comment into a document

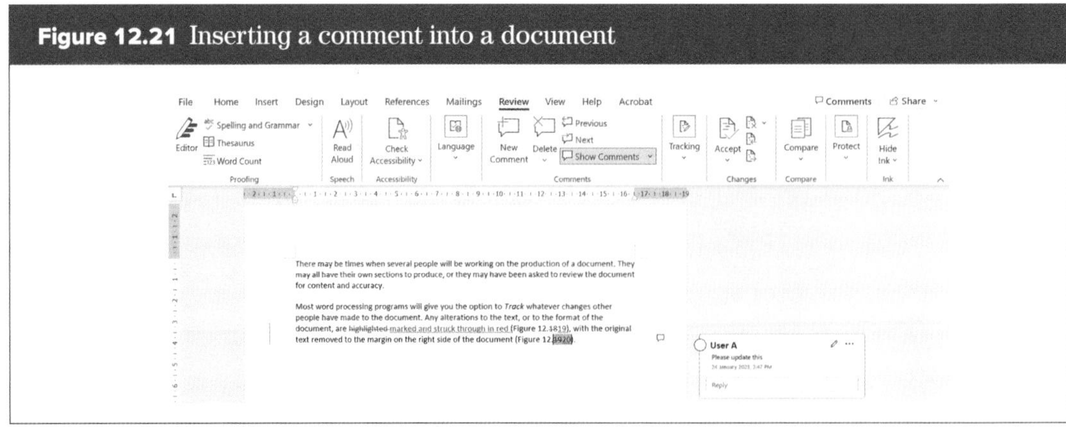

Figure 12.22 Heading and style options

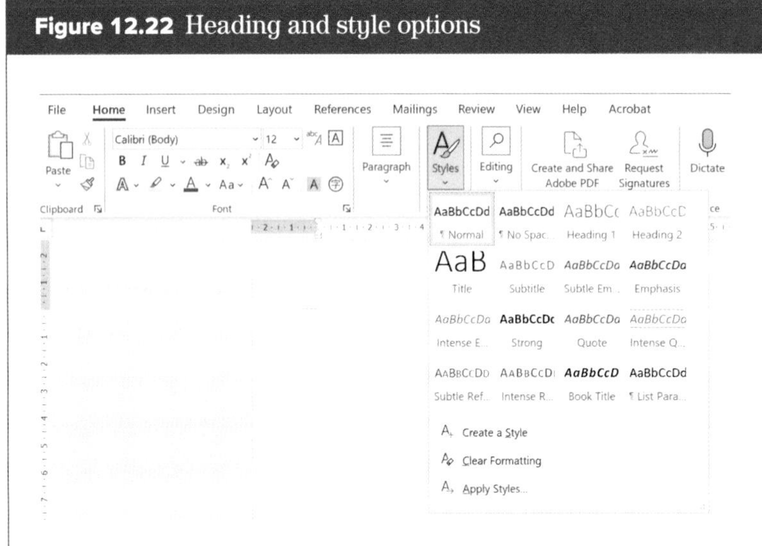

Figure 12.23 Table of contents options

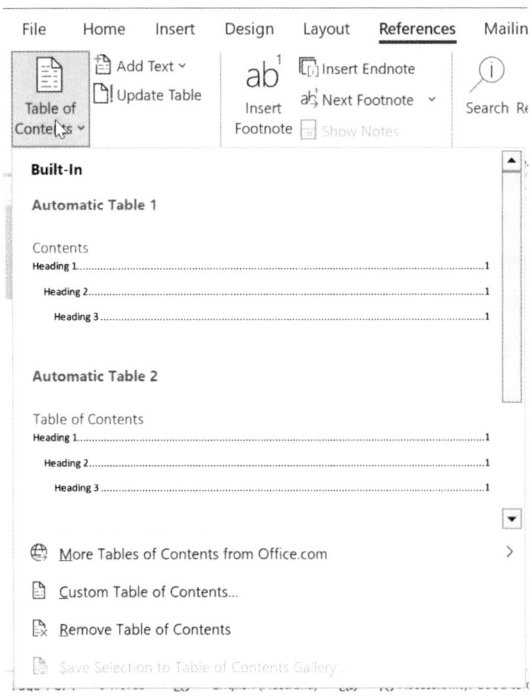

Once you have read and actioned the comments, you should delete them.

Creating a table of contents

Depending on the length of the document you are producing (e.g. a long, complex report), you may need to create a table of contents. Most word processing programs will allow you to create a table of contents automatically, provided that you have used the *Styles* tool to create headings. In the *Styles* section of the *Home* tab, you will see a variety of heading options: *Heading 1* is the main heading, with *Heading 2* subordinate to it, *Heading 3* subordinate to *Heading 2*, and so on (Figure 12.22). When typing your text, you therefore need to determine what will be a main heading and what will be subordinate to it. You then highlight the appropriate word or sentence and choose the level of heading you want it to be.

Once your document has been completed, you can return to the page where you want your table of contents to be shown: go to the *References* tab and choose *Table of Contents*. This will give you a range of style options to choose from (Figure 12.23), or you can customise your own.

Knowledge check

8. Name three storage methods you can use for your files and folders.
9. List at least four types of documents that you might need to create regularly.
10. Name four Word functions you can use to ensure the consistency of design and layout of a document.
11. When using the *Edit* function of a word processor, you will have access to a range of options. List at least five of these.

12.3 Producing a document

Your document has been written. Regardless of whether it will be in printed or electronic format, there are still a few things that need to happen before you can complete and distribute the final version.

12.3.1 Checking and completing document production

As we have previously stated, a document is produced to fulfil a specific purpose. As such, it is important to check that it actually does this before it is sent out to the intended recipients. Areas you should check can include the following:

- *Have the document reviewed by relevant stakeholders.* Any document you create and send out represents your organisation and the people in it. With this in mind, it is important that anyone involved with, or affected by, that document should be satisfied with it. This might take the form of simply skimming over it, or it may involve a thorough proofreading. Depending on the type of document, others may also need to sign off on it. This would be the case with business plans, marketing strategies, contracts and so on.
- *Ensure that it conforms with organisational standards.* The standards set by an organisation will vary a great deal and will be guided not only by the industry they are in, but also by their own code of conduct and ethics. To recap what we have previously discussed, the organisation will have developed specific policies and procedures that all staff must follow. In terms of producing documents these might relate to:
  - checking readability—does the document conform to set style guides?
  - checking that company logos, headers, footers and section headings are in place
  - ensuring the document is properly formatted and the final version is ready to be saved and stored.
- *Implement version control.* In an organisation where forms and documents are used on a regular basis or are subject to an external audit—by a government department, for example—you will almost always be required to show that the organisation is working with the latest version of specific documents. This is where version control is used. The method used will be determined by the individual organisation. For example, an organisation can ensure that only the latest version is being used by naming the file as follows:
  - the word "version" (or letter "V")
  - the version number
  - the date of amendment.

  A fully versioned document that has been changed three times might be named:

  V3 150423

  This means: version number 3 amended 15 April 2023. Any document with a version number lower than this would be an old, out-of-date document.

Think about

2. What form of version control, if any, does your organisation use? Does it help you in using the correct forms and templates? Why is this important?

12.3.2 Using *Word Help* to overcome basic difficulties

There may be times when you need to complete a specific task but are unsure of how to do it, or perhaps something isn't working properly and you don't know how to fix it. At these times, you will need some help. Most software programs come with such a feature. For example, on the top menu bar you will find a tab marked *Help*, as shown in Figure 12.24.

Figure 12.24 Available options under the *Help* tab

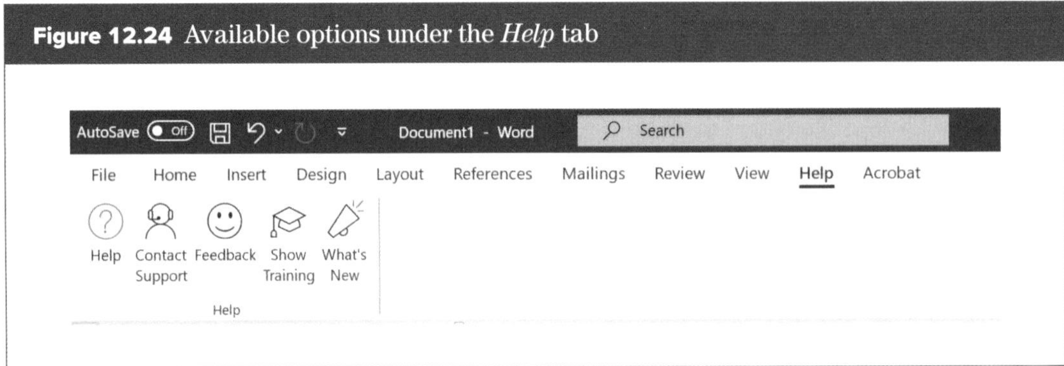

Figure 12.25 Result of a *Word Help* search

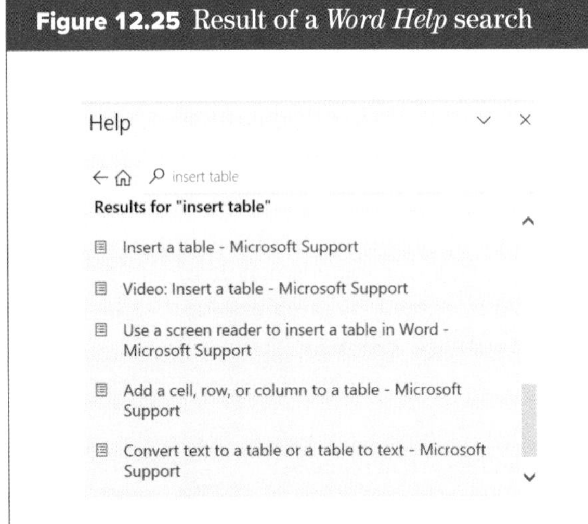

Clicking on the *Help* button will take you to *Word Help*, where you can search for solutions to your issue in Microsoft Support.

For example, if you were unsure of how to create a table, you could type "insert table" into the *Search* box and *Word Help* would provide you with some options, as shown in Figure 12.25. Clicking on the relevant options will provide you with guidance on how to work with tables—or whatever it was you asked about. If you aren't able to find a solution within Microsoft Support, you can search your query using the search bar at the top of the window, which will also search the internet for useful related articles.

Try this now

4. Using a document that you have created, search for a method of inserting an image, or any other search of your choice.

Knowledge check

12. Describe what checks you should make to a document before finalising it and preparing it for distribution.
13. Describe where you can find *Help* functions to overcome basic difficulties.

12.4 Finalising a document

12.4.1 Proofreading documents

Proofreading is a critical part of the writing process and should never be overlooked. It is the last chance that you have of finding and fixing any errors before a document is presented to readers. It eliminates mistakes in grammar, punctuation, capitalisation, spelling and formatting, and allows you to communicate your message accurately and effectively.

There can be many different methods used to proofread writing. For example:

- *Don't rely on spelling and grammar checkers.* These are excellent as a first step and can be useful in identifying major or obvious errors. Automated spelling and grammar checkers are severely limited, however, in that they cannot parse context or complex sentence structures. It is also important to remember (as previously discussed) that spellcheck functions can only identify misspelled words and overlook homonyms that are used incorrectly (e.g. "She did not *here* the instructions clearly", instead of "She did not *hear* the instructions clearly").
- *Read each sentence slowly or aloud.* A technique that many professional proofreaders use is to read the material out loud. This lets you voice every single word and so involves an additional sense—your auditory sense—in the process. Skim-reading can make your brain want to skip some words and to make unconscious corrections.
- *Divide the material into manageable chunks.* Dividing your work into smaller sections makes the task more manageable. Reading each smaller section carefully can prevent you from feeling overwhelmed by the task and will allow you to concentrate more effectively. This technique is especially useful if you are proofreading a very large document such as a company report or a contract.
- *Make a note of errors you make frequently.* Proofreading your writing on a regular basis can help you to identify your own strengths and weaknesses and understand where you commonly make mistakes. If you are aware of the errors you often make, you can learn to look for them during the writing process itself. Gradually, you will learn to avoid them altogether. Keep style guides and grammar rules at hand as you proofread. Look up any areas of which you are uncertain. Over time, you will develop your knowledge and your writing skills will improve.

Modifying a document according to task requirements

In proofreading your document, you are not only looking for spelling and grammatical errors, but also considering the flow of the text. During the review process, you may often find better ways of phrasing a sentence or paragraph. Once the review has been completed, have the relevant stakeholders give their final approvals.

12.4.2 Saving and storing documents appropriately

A very important task in producing business documents is ensuring that they are stored in such a way that they can be easily accessed and retrieved when necessary.

Saving files

In order for information to be easily accessible, it must be stored in a logical manner. How it is stored (or classified) will vary from one organisation to another. In most cases, however, information can be classified using one of the following methods:

- *By subject.* This method works very well if you intend to create sub-folders within that subject. For example, you might have a main folder labelled *Marketing* (Figure 12.26). Within this folder you could then have a number of sub-folders labelled: *Advertising, Blogs, Meetings, Newsletters, Promotions* and so on. A main folder labelled *Tax* might have sub-folders labelled: *Car Allowance, Expenses, Income,* etc.

Figure 12.26 Example of organising folders and files by subject

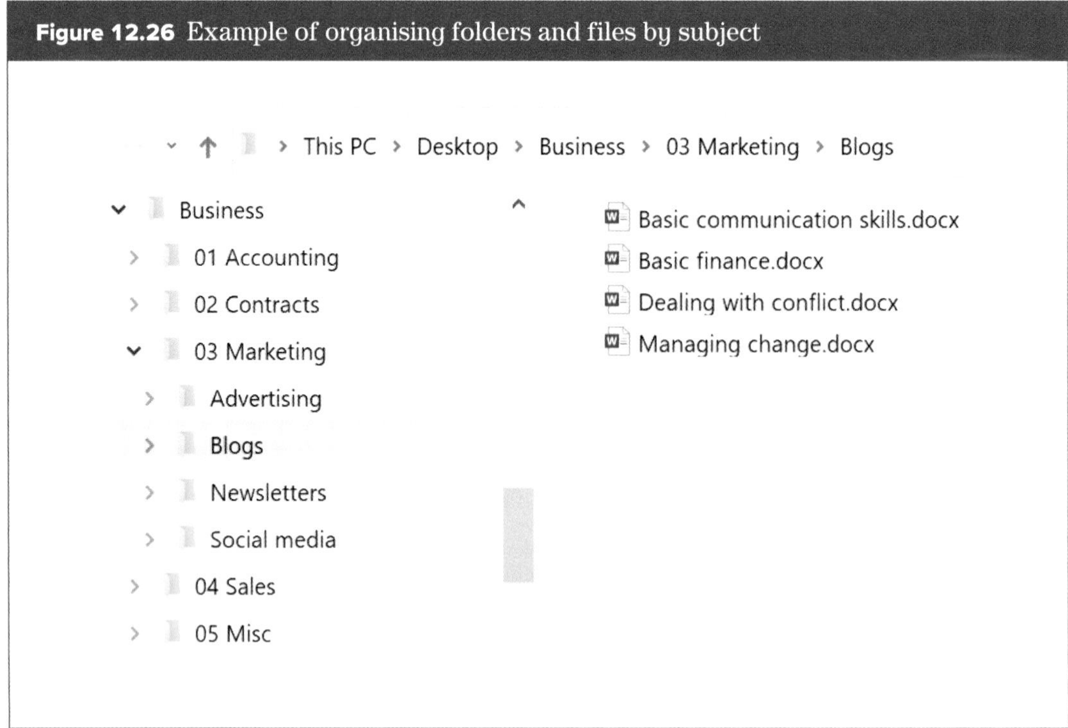

- *Alphabetically.* This method is excellent for file systems based on customer names, product lines, and so on.
- *Numerically.* A numeric system is a good choice when you need to arrange by the year of file creation. Numeric filing can also include the decimal numeric system. This system of filing arrangement is one of the most commonly used numeric filing methods. For example, each department within an organisation would have a numeric "parent" code, while sub-sections of that department will be given a specific decimal numeric "child" code. These child codes could then be further broken down by using a decimal point for each area within a given topic. In the example shown in Table 12.1, the human resources department has the parent code 200, while staff training has the child code 201. Any training courses within that area of the department will have their own unique code within "staff training". Documents dealing with professional development will all be filed under 201.1, documents dealing with WHS training will be filed under 201.2, and so on.

  The advantages of the decimal system include:

- virtually unlimited expansion of files, because of the fine divisions within each of the major codes
- rapid retrieval, because of the system's simplicity
- convenience of referencing and retrieval, because all related records are grouped together.

When coding within a decimal filing arrangement, an index system (like the one shown in Table 12.1) must be used to list the number codes assigned to each category of record or its divisions. This makes it easy for people to access the filing system and find what they are looking for.

Storage methods

File classification and naming are important factors in accessing documents. However, where and how these documents are stored are just as important. Methods for storing documents may include:

- *Cloud-based storage*, where files and folders are stored on the internet and are therefore accessible by relevant stakeholders no matter where they are located.

Table 12.1 Example of a decimal numeric filing system

Parent code	Department	Child code	Sub-group
100	Marketing	**101**	Demographic studies
		102	Customer surveys
		103	Competitor information
200	Human Resources	**201**	Staff training
		201.1	Professional development
		201.2	WHS training
		201.3	Skills gap training
		202	Position descriptions
		202.1	General manager
		202.2	GM personal assistant
		202.3	Sales manager
		202.4	Accounts manager
		203	Performance appraisals
		204	Pay scales
		205	Leave applications

- *Corporate electronic filing systems and network storage*, where files may be stored on the company server.
- *Portable storage*, such as external hard drives and flash drives.
- *Hard copy, paper-based filing.* This method is used less and less today as storage in cloud-based storage becomes more prevalent. However, filing hard copies of all computer-generated documents can still be done in filing cabinets or folders. Paper-based file storage systems include:
  - concertina files—for use in very small offices or the home. A concertina file can sit on your desk and be easily accessible. Separate pockets can be used to store files in the same way as indicated above: by subject, alphabetically, numerically, etc.
  - portable hanging indent files—this type of file system is basically a square stand on wheels with a space in the top where you can store hanging indent files. This system is also mostly used in small offices.
  - one- to four-drawer file cabinets—the most popular and widely used file system, file cabinets can be as small as one drawer or up to four drawers. Some larger organisations often have several cabinets in rows, offering vast amounts of storage space.
  - compactus—this is an excellent storage system where maximum storage capacity is needed in a limited space. The compactus shelves are on rollers and can be moved left and right to reveal the shelves inside.
  - specialist storage systems—these are normally industry-specific filing systems that can store maps, blueprints, etc.

12.4.3 Presenting documents

The way in which the final document is presented will depend largely on its intended purpose. For example:

- Will it be used for training purposes?
- Is it to be presented at a meeting or seminar?
- Will it be viewed on a screen (large or small)?
- Will it need to be printed?
- Will it be presented in electronic format?

Having thoroughly checked the document and considered these questions, the document can then be presented in line with its purpose and audience.

If the document is to be presented in electronic form, you might need to make decisions about the following:

- The equipment used to present it—for example, a laptop and projector for displaying the document against a wall or screen during a meeting.
- The online presentation methods used—for example the company's:
  - website, which can be accessed by the general public
  - internal intranet, which is accessible only by employees
  - social media platforms, which can be accessed either by the general public or by certain groups.

If the document is to be printed, this might mean making decisions about the following:

- The appropriate paper (e.g. plain white paper, company letterhead, or a heavier stock of paper for certificates or reports).
- Whether it needs to be printed in colour or black and white.
- Which office equipment to use to properly present the document. For example:
  - Reports can be spiral-bound so that they are presented as a booklet.
  - Individual pages can be inserted into a presentation folder.
  - Large documents may be printed professionally and bound in "saddle stitch" fashion.

Knowledge check

14. Describe the steps you would take in "proofreading" your document.

15. After proofreading a document, modifications and adjustments should be made. This means there is one final check to be made before distributing the document. What does this check entail?

16. List three methods you can use for saving files.

17. Name at least four things to consider when determining how the final document will be presented.

Summary

The importance of having well-written text cannot be overestimated. It makes it easier for the reader to follow what you are saying. Such a document has the following properties:

- *The writing has a unified focus (i.e. unity).* This is achieved when a composition contains one focused idea. Having unity in your writing helps the reader to easily understand what the message is about without having to re-read it.
- *It is coherent and cohesive (i.e. coherence and cohesion).* This refers to how easy it is to understand the writing and how well the ideas in the text are connected. When a piece of writing is coherent and cohesive, the reader won't "get lost" because the author has connected the ideas in the text.
- *It is organised (i.e. organisation).* An organised piece of writing is clear to read and appears well balanced to the reader's eye.
- *It uses appropriate language (i.e. language use).* A well-written text is clearly written with easily understood vocabulary, has subject–verb agreement, is consistent in its use of pronouns, and avoids redundancies and wordiness.

CHAPTER 13

Design and produce spreadsheets

Learning outcomes

13.1 Select and prepare resources

13.2 Plan spreadsheet design

13.3 Create a spreadsheet

13.4 Produce charts

13.5 Finalise and present spreadsheets

An organisation's success revolves around the quality of the information it uses as the basis for making its business decisions. Not all information, however, is presented in a useful format and the issue becomes one of how to achieve a sound understanding of the organisation, and of the knowledge it might need to stay successful.

As you learnt in Chapter 8, business knowledge is the culmination of a process involving the gathering of data, developing useful information from this data, and then using this information to gain an in-depth insight into, or knowledge of, a given subject. A spreadsheet can help you to sort out all the small bits of data and information and turn them into an understanding of how a business is actually performing. Spreadsheets are therefore important business tools.

13.1 Selecting and preparing resources

An organisation may have many bits of data which, when collated and analysed, will provide an actual story about how successful it is and what it might need to do to remain successful. Therefore, before creating a spreadsheet, you need to make sure you have access to all the necessary pieces of data that will create that story. You will also need to determine the most appropriate means of carrying out the task. Finally, you will need to have a clear idea of the spreadsheet's purpose and who it is being prepared for.

13.1.1 The primary purpose of spreadsheets

While they can vary in complexity, the primary purpose of a spreadsheet is to organise and categorise data into a useful and logical format. Their uses can include:

- *Business data storage.* Spreadsheets make it easy to process all kinds of data, such as:
  - financial data
  - customer details
  - product data
  - inventory tracking
  - work progress on a project.
- *Accounting and calculation.* In the absence of specialised accounting software or programs, many businesses still use spreadsheets to track their business accounts. You can enter **formulas** that can take care of a large range of calculations automatically, such as keeping track of money and inventory.
- *Budgeting.* Spreadsheets can help with:
  - keeping track of company expenditure
  - managing incomes
  - calculating percentages
  - calculating the differences between specific figures over given time periods.
- *Generating reports and charts.* Spreadsheets can be used to report on trends or make business forecasts. The information in these reports can then be turned into graphs that make it easy to compare different sets of data or to see, at a glance, how well the organisation is performing in a range of different business areas.
- *Administrative tasks.* You can use spreadsheets to generate receipts, invoices, price lists and other business documents.
- *Project management.* Spreadsheets help in tracking progress and milestones that need to be met.

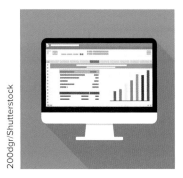

200dgr/Shutterstock

13.1.2 Identifying the audience for the spreadsheet

Audience is an important consideration when looking at spreadsheet design. Senior managers, for example, will seldom have the time to analyse lengthy columns and rows of data and might simply need an executive summary along with a graph that shows the important information they need. Accounts staff, on the other hand, will probably need very detailed information on the organisation's financial situation, while marketing staff would need details on what customers are saying about the organisation or where they heard about it. These details will provide them with important information upon which they can base their budgets and future decisions.

13.1.3 Identifying task requirements

You create a spreadsheet to perform a specific task, whether it is to keep an inventory of your organisation's products, to keep records of customer details, or to keep track of expenses or sales.

Whatever its purpose, you need to understand what the expected outcome should look like when setting up the spreadsheet.

Information is entered into a spreadsheet in columns and rows. What information you decide to put into columns and what you put into rows will affect how the data is presented. For example, entering information about *product sales* in rows and entering *month of sale* in columns (as shown in Table 13.1) produces the same total amount of sales ($5,929) as Table 13.2, where the *month of sale* information is entered into rows and the *product sales* information is entered into columns; however, any charts created from these will be different, as Figures 13.1 and 13.2 show. Therefore, you will need to set up your spreadsheet according to whether you are more interested in best performance by month or by product.

Figure 13.1 instantly identifies that the majority of sales were made in April. You can now ask questions about why this might be. Was it the result of a special promotional activity? Did something specific happen during that month that caused people to purchase more? The answers to these questions can then help the organisation to make plans to capitalise on that information and increase sales during other times of the year.

Table 13.1 Product sales: Month of sale in columns

Product	Jan ($)	Feb ($)	Mar ($)	Apr ($)	Total ($)
Pens	250	230	240	421	1,141
Paper	350	280	330	475	1,435
Folders	300	320	298	550	1,468
Pencils	450	425	395	615	1,885
Total	**1,350**	**1,255**	**1,263**	**2,061**	**5,929**

Figure 13.1 Sales by month

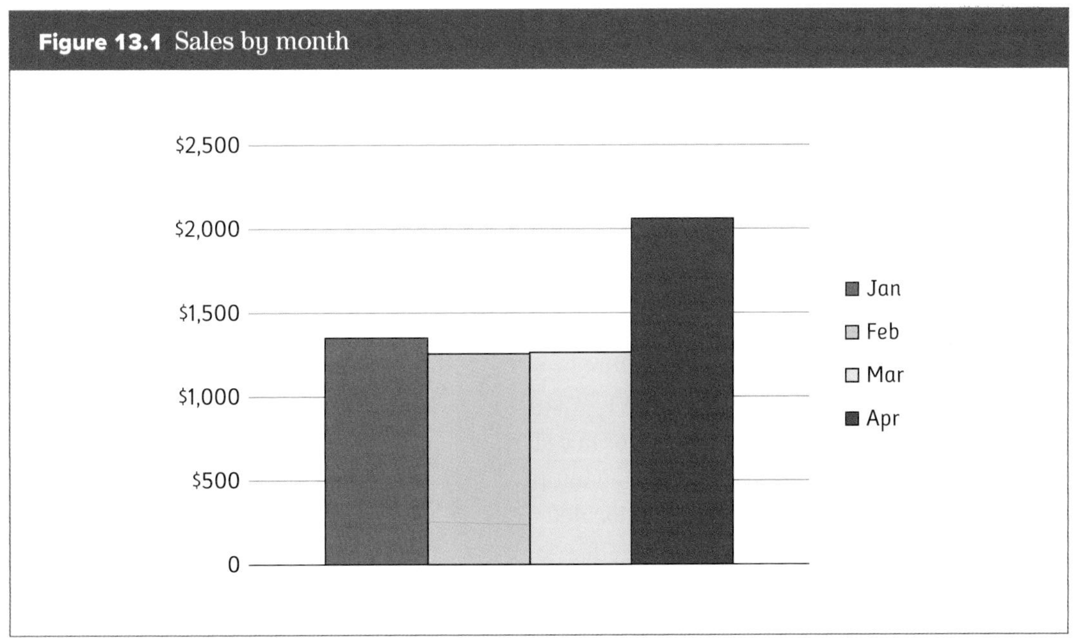

Table 13.2 Product sales: Month of sale in rows

Product	Pens ($)	Paper ($)	Folders ($)	Pencils ($)	Total ($)
Jan	250	350	300	450	1,350
Feb	230	280	320	425	1,255
Mar	240	330	298	395	1,263
Apr	421	475	550	615	2,061
Total	**1,141**	**1,435**	**1,468**	**1,885**	**5,929**

Figure 13.2 Sales by product

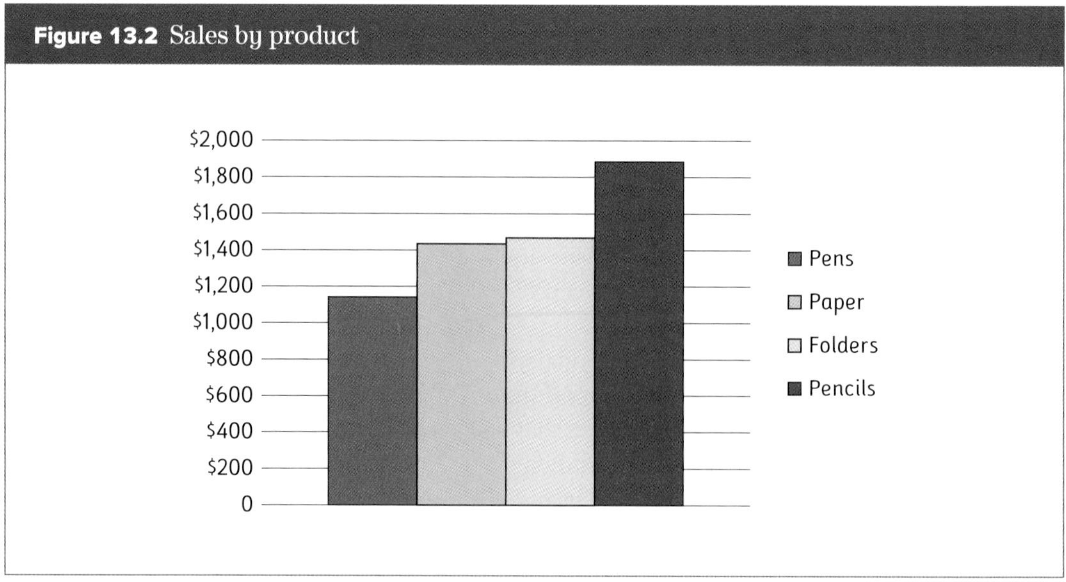

The information in Figure 13.2 shows that pencils were the highest-selling—and pens the lowest-selling—product over the period. This information is useful, as it can influence how many of each product the organisation should order and keep in stock, which allows for better budgeting and cash flow.

Before you set up your spreadsheet, it is also necessary to identify your organisation's requirements in relation to data entry, storage, output and reporting and presentation. For example:

- *Data entry.* When creating a spreadsheet, ask yourself:
  - How should the information be presented? Will you be required to produce charts? Which data should be highlighted? As you saw in Tables 13.1 and 13.2, data can be presented in a number of ways, depending on the needs of the organisation—are decision makers more interested in how well each product is selling (when deciding to buy more stock) or are they more interested in the number of sales made each month (for budgeting purposes)?
  - Does data need to be input into a new spreadsheet from "scratch"? Or can existing data be imported into this new spreadsheet?
- *Storage.* A spreadsheet contains data of varying importance to the organisation. The data is a resource the organisation can use for a variety of purposes such as business planning, budgeting or promotion. It must therefore be stored with care. Documents or files can be saved electronically in a number of different places and ways:
  - on the hard disk of your computer or in a shared location on your organisation's network
  - using cloud-based storage so that the information is accessible regardless of where you, or others who might need access, are located
  - as a hard copy or printout kept in folders and/or in file cabinets.

  Whether the data is saved on a disk, hard drive, in the cloud or as a paper document, it needs to be stored in a secure manner and in accordance with privacy and confidentiality requirements. The *Privacy Act 1988* (Cth) requires information to be handled and stored in such a way as to protect individuals' personal details. This includes the collection, use, storage and disclosure of such information.
- *Output.* Your spreadsheet may be:
  - included within the text of a report
  - added as an attachment at the end of a report
  - included in an electronic presentation, such as Microsoft PowerPoint
  - sent as part of an email.

Whichever form of output is used, you need to ensure that the spreadsheet can be read easily and will fit neatly onto a page or screen. If it extends over several pages, you should consider including a summary or graphs for ease of viewing and understanding.

- *Reporting and presentation requirements.* Every organisation will have standards with regard to the creation of documents. These could include: use of company details and logos, size and style of fonts, header and footer requirements, formats for numbers, paper sizes, standard margins and file naming conventions. We will cover some of these in more detail as we move through the chapter.

With a clear idea of where your data is coming from, how it is to be treated and the format it should take, you can begin to plan the design of the spreadsheet.

13.1.4 Selecting the most appropriate application to produce spreadsheets

Spreadsheet software is available from a range of providers, all offering many similar functions as well as some unique features (see Table 13.3). Microsoft Excel is one of the most popular programs used by businesses and is the one that will be featured in this text.

Table 13.3 Spreadsheet software

Software	Description
Microsoft Excel	This spreadsheet software contains a large range of functions and features, and is capable of handling large, complex spreadsheets. Graphs and charts are easy to insert and personalise, with almost every element clickable and customisable. There is a wide variety of styles or templates, and everything integrates with the rest of the Microsoft Office suite. Collaboration is simple and effective using Microsoft OneDrive or SharePoint. Changes update automatically across all devices, and the online chat feature and comment threads facilitate discussion between collaborators. The disadvantage with Excel is that the sheer number of features makes the software daunting for first-time, or inexperienced, users, for whom there is often a steep learning curve.
Google Sheets	Google Sheets is a highly collaborative application that can be integrated with other useful Google apps such as Analytics, Data Studio and Google Forms. As it is web-based, it can be easily shared with others wherever they are, and offers chat features, comments and real-time co-editing. With no software to download and everything stored in the cloud, Google Sheets makes collaboration very smooth. The major disadvantage is it doesn't offer as many advanced features as Excel.
Zoho Sheet	This spreadsheet software is completely web-based, so collaboration is smooth and intuitive, with real-time co-authoring, chat, individual cell versions and sharing permissions. It also offers multiple trend lines and aggregation. It is an incredibly powerful spreadsheet application with more than 350 tools. The layout is quite spartan, so you may need to dig through menus to find more advanced features. The ability to link external data, such as a CSV file or an RSS feed, is a handy feature for businesses. Charts and graphs are easy to create and customise, although there are fewer types and are overall less powerful than Excel.
Smartsheet	This spreadsheet software is best used for project management and other non-spreadsheet tasks, such as managing progress reports rather than analysing and visualing data.

Knowledge check

1. Give at least four examples of how a spreadsheet might be used.
2. Give an example of how a spreadsheet's intended audience could differ and how this may affect the spreadsheet's design.
3. Give at least three examples of factors to consider when identifying spreadsheet requirements.
4. There are a number of different programs and applications that can be used to create spreadsheets. Give at least three examples. Briefly explain each one.

13.2 Planning spreadsheet design

When creating a new spreadsheet, it is essential to have a very clear idea of what is required of it. Some spreadsheets can be very complex and there is little point in simply plugging bits of data in columns and rows without considering what you want the data to tell you. All of your efforts could be wasted if the resulting information isn't what was expected or asked for. The spreadsheet must be designed and formatted in such a way that the information it presents can be easily understood.

13.2.1 Designing a spreadsheet to suit its purpose, the audience and their information needs

When planning a spreadsheet design, there are a number of things to consider.

- *Parameters of the spreadsheet.* The **parameters** will provide exact details of what is to be included in—and accomplished by—the spreadsheet. For example:
  - What specific data must it cover?
  - How much data will be required to provide a useful outcome?
  - Will it be a quick, simple task, or will it be an ongoing project?
  - Who will need access to it?
  - Where should it be stored?
- *Appropriateness to required tasks.* Is a spreadsheet even required, or can you accomplish the same task using a different format or software? For example: if no calculations are required, then perhaps a table in a Word document will suffice.
- *Charts.* How will the information need to be configured? Is the data to be converted into charts?
- *Formatting.* What are the organisation's policies on the format of its documents or reports? Is there a specific style or design that must be incorporated (as discussed in Chapters 11 and 12)? Formatting may also refer to the way in which the spreadsheet is set out—for example, will the data be set out in rows or in columns?
- *Formulas and functions.* Will the spreadsheet need to incorporate any formulas or automated functions for undertaking calculations?
- *Headers and footers.* Will you be required to show specific information on each page? If so, what will this information include (e.g. document titles and page numbers)?
- *Headings and labels.* Will you need headings or labels to provide an easy overview of the information provided?
- *Import and export of data.* Will there be other documents that rely on the data from your spreadsheet or vice versa? If so, how will that data be transferred between the two?
- *Time frames.* How much time will you have to complete the work? Is there a deadline? Are there any milestone dates that you need to achieve?
- *Multi-sheet workbooks.* Will your spreadsheet be split over several worksheets to separate out information? (For example, in Figure 13.3, five separate sheets are used in the same workbook—one per state.) To add individual worksheets to a spreadsheet, you would click on the appropriate tab (represented by the "plus" sign on the worksheet tab at the bottom of the window). Other examples might include separate sheets for each product.

  Many of these issues will be discussed in more detail as we move through the chapter.

13.2.2 Designing a spreadsheet to enhance readability and appearance

As spreadsheets can be long and complicated documents, with figures covering many columns and rows, it is important that it is designed in a way that is logical, easy to read, and consistent with the organisation's image and reputation.

Figure 13.3 Worksheet tab in Excel showing multiple worksheets in the same workbook

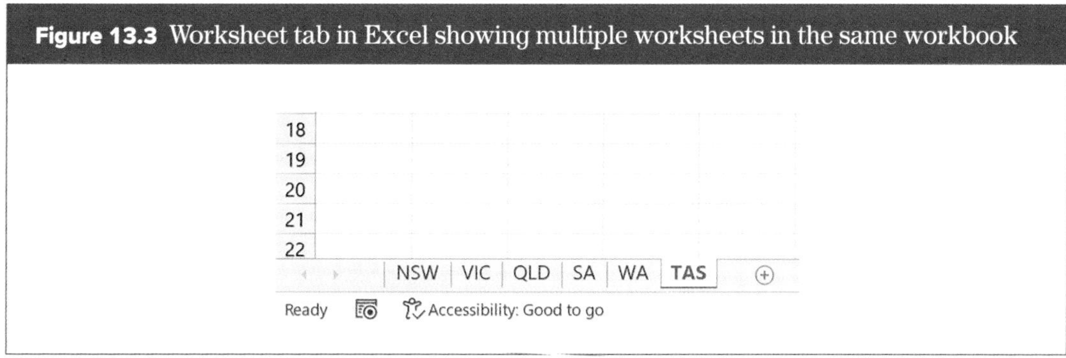

Consistency of design and layout

Many organisations will have spent considerable time, effort and money creating a specific image that presents a consistent image of professionalism and quality services or products to the public. If customers know they can rely on a business to offer the same level of service in the same manner every time, then they will put their trust in that organisation and continue to do business with it.

Consistency also means that all the documents the organisation produces have the same "look and feel" to them. Where spreadsheets are concerned, the design and layout may also include automated functions to ensure specific areas of information are always presented in the same way, making it easier to read large amounts of information and creating a uniform appearance.

Using available application tools to ensure consistency of design and layout

You can enhance the readability of your spreadsheet and ensure that it conforms with organisational requirements by using a range of automated functions to specify various formatting requirements, such as the way dates are set out, the alignment of text, the choice of fonts and borders and so on, to achieve a consistent design and layout. We will look at these functions in a later section of this chapter. Consistency of design and layout, however, may also mean ensuring the following:

- *Consistency with other business documents*. Spreadsheets that you create may need to be incorporated into other documents such as reports or strategic plans. It is important to liaise with any other staff involved in the development of these documents to ensure that your spreadsheet's design and layout are consistent with other documents of which it will form a part.
- *Design*. Spreadsheet software may allow you to create a number of different formats and designs, as shown in Figure 13.4. By highlighting the area in your spreadsheet that you wish to format and clicking on *Format as Table* in the *Formatting* section of the *Home* tab, you can choose from a range of styles and colours.

Figure 13.4 Format and design options

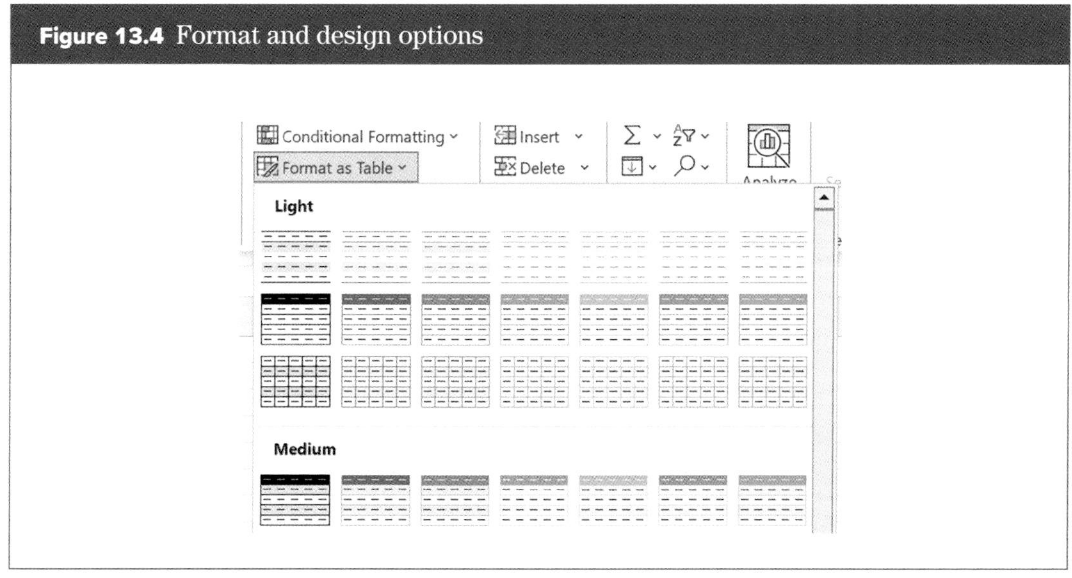

You can also change the entire appearance of the spreadsheet by using set themes or choosing your own colour scheme. These tools are available in the *Page Layout* tab, as shown in Figure 13.5.

Figure 13.5 *Page Layout* options

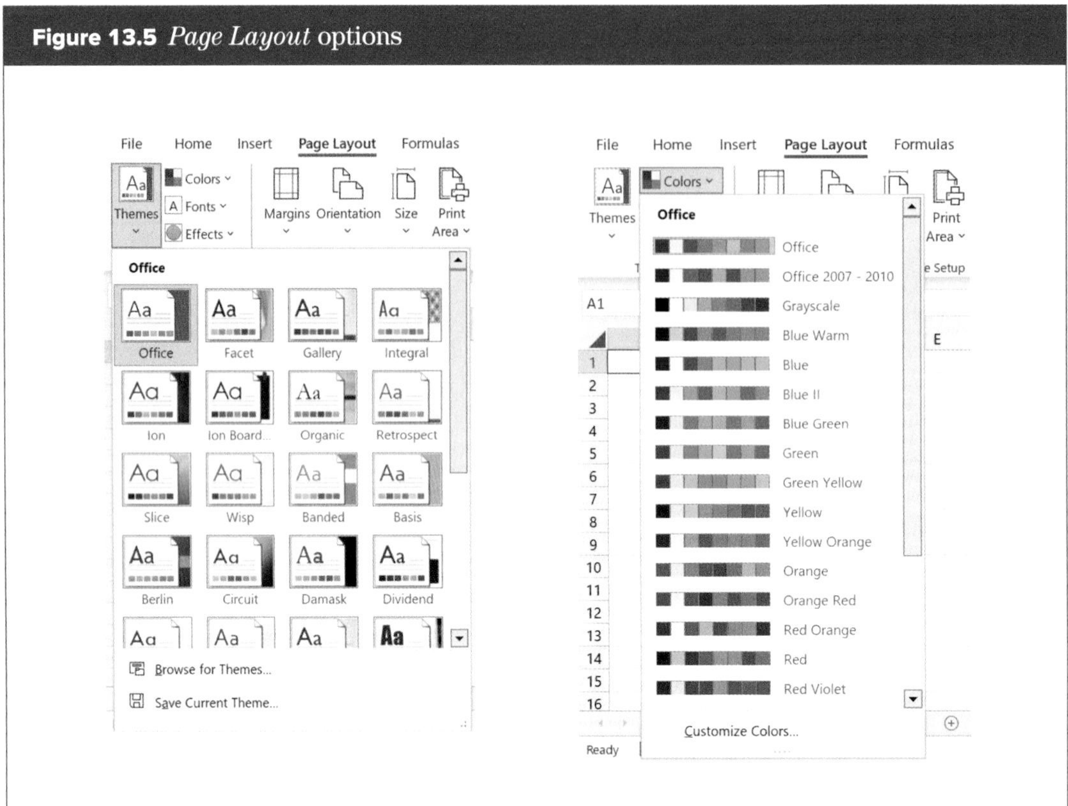

As we have seen, the main purpose of a spreadsheet is to make large amounts of data easy to understand. It must therefore be created with ease of readability in mind. When choosing the design and layout of your spreadsheet, ask yourself:

- Does it conform to organisational requirements?
- Is it laid out logically?
- Does it provide a quick and easy overview of the data?
- Does it allow the user to quickly draw useful conclusions?

Knowledge check

5. List and explain at least six things you need to consider when designing a spreadsheet to suit a specific purpose, audience and their information needs.
6. Explain what a *style guide* is and how it is used to ensure a consistent design and layout.
7. In addition to following the organisation's style guide, ensuring consistency of design and layout might also include a number of other things. Name two of these.

13.3 Creating a spreadsheet

Once you have all the resources you will need to prepare your spreadsheet and you know how it is to be set up and what functions can help you to do this, you can begin to enter your data.

13.3.1 Entering data, and maintaining consistency of design and layout

Depending on what your spreadsheet has been designed to achieve, entering your data will most likely mean that you will need to perform additions, subtractions, divisions or multiplications.

Let's begin with the basic components of the spreadsheet. Each sheet is made up of a vast number of **rows** and **columns** (Figure 13.6), which contain individual **cells** (Figure 13.7).

Figure 13.6 Rows and columns

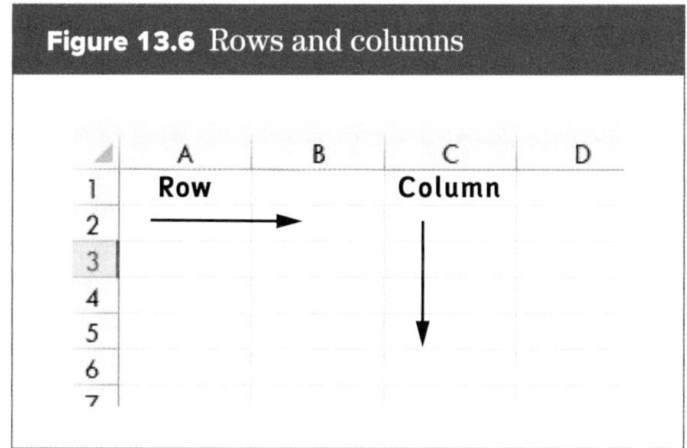

Figure 13.7 Individual cell

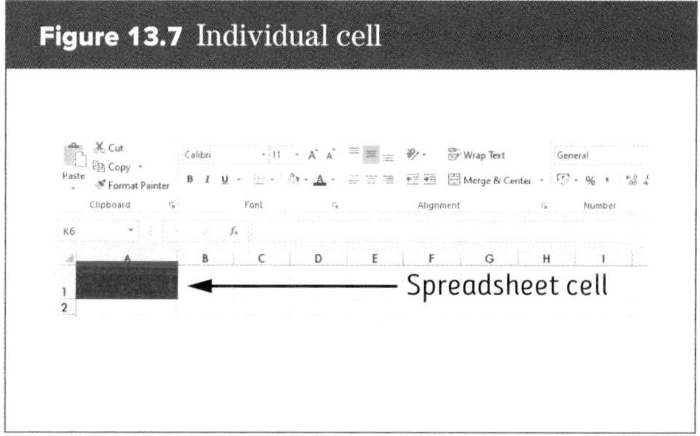

Each cell will contain data of some sort according to its purpose. This data can contain alphabetical and/or numerical as well as special characters.

Example

The marketing department of ABC Website Company has forecasted its expenses for 2022. This includes data about how much it has actually spent, as opposed to what it had originally forecast, as well as a percentage variation between the two—that is, by how much it has overspent or underspent. For example, it forecasted $500 would be spent on office expenses but only $252 was used, so it underspent by 49.6 per cent. On the other hand, it estimated it would spend $750 on phone bills but actually spent $1,113.33, so it overspent by 48.44 per cent. This is useful information as it allows the marketing department to analyse its expenses and make adjustments to ensure that it stays within budget if it is reviewed regularly throughout the year.

Figure 13.8 Example of an expenses spreadsheet

	A	B	C	D
1–2	**2021 Marketing (Expenses)**			
3–4	**Account**	**Forecast 2020**	**Actual 2020**	**%of Forecast**
5	Office expenses	$500.00	$252.00	49.60%
6	Printing	$10,000.00	$9,900.00	1.00%
7	Postage/mailouts	$2,500.00	$1,550.00	38.00%
8	Phones	$750.00	$1,113.33	-48.44%
9	Photocopying	$1,500.00	$1,400.00	6.67%
10	Advertising	$30,000.00	$20,000.00	33.33%
11	Promotion	$7,500.00	$4,500.00	40.00%
12	Website development	$6,000.00	$3,559.00	40.68%
13	International marketing	$1,500.00	$1,950.00	-30.00%
14	Subscriptions	$2,000.00	$1,394.00	30.30%
15	Catering	$500.00	$383.00	23.40%
16	**Totals:**	**$62,750.00**	**$46,001.33**	**26.69%**

Entering and sorting data

Data, whether in the form of numbers or text, is entered into spreadsheet cells. While you can put a large amount of data into a single cell, it is generally best practice to separate the data into separate cells where possible. An Excel spreadsheet, if set up properly, allows you to sort the data in a number of ways depending on the columns or rows you have chosen to sort by. For example, when creating a database of customer information, the input data can include name, address, suburb, city, postcode, phone number, email address and date of birth, along with the type of product the customer typically buys from you. While you can put all this data into a single cell, it renders the data fairly useless; if all the data is in one cell, there are no options to sort the data by. Conversely, if each piece of data is entered into separate cells, you can sort the customer list by postcode, suburb, state and any number of other options. Tables 13.4 to 13.6 show these different sorting possibilities.

The advantage of being able to sort data in this way is that it is easy to "interrogate" or query the database for specific purposes. For example, if you wanted to do a promotion *only* in specific suburbs or postcode areas, you can sort your data based on these criteria. If you wanted to send your customers birthday cards, you can sort your data based on date of birth and so on.

Spreadsheets can potentially be thousands of rows long and have a great many columns. The sorting option allows you to sort on a number of different levels. For example, you could sort first by state, then by the cities within that state, and then even by street name if you set up the database appropriately. In this way, you can identify and target thousands of customers according to the state, city and street they live in to create an effective promotional campaign.

Table 13.4 Data sorted alphabetically by customer's last name

Last name	First name	Address	Suburb	State	Postcode
Appleton	Drew	345 Arcadia Street	Broadbeach	Qld	4218
Chen	Naisi	15 Dunlop Circuit	Mermaid Waters	Qld	4218
Christiansen	Alan	2205 Gold Coast Highway	Miami	Qld	4220
Hollis	Jill	106 City Road	Beenleigh	Qld	4207
Matthews	Ricki	45/21 Wharf Street	Broadbeach	Qld	4218
Omar	Ibrahim	1 Moralla Avenue	Runaway Bay	Qld	4216
Powers	Jodie	34 Bayswater Avenue	Varsity Lakes	Qld	4227
Saleh	Lin	15 Classic Way	Burleigh Waters	Qld	4220
Smith	Jack	5 Barrow Court	Ashmore	Qld	4214
Wu	Lucy	123 Sample Road	Beenleigh	Qld	4207
Yakushev	Viktor	83 Surf Parade	Broadbeach	Qld	4218

Table 13.5 Data sorted by suburb

Last name	First name	Address	Suburb	State	Postcode
Smith	Jack	5 Barrow Court	Ashmore	Qld	4214
Hollis	Jill	106 City Road	Beenleigh	Qld	4207
Wu	Lucy	123 Sample Road	Beenleigh	Qld	4207
Appleton	Drew	345 Arcadia Street	Broadbeach	Qld	4218
Yakushev	Viktor	83 Surf Parade	Broadbeach	Qld	4218
Matthews	Ricki	45/21 Wharf Street	Broadbeach	Qld	4218
Saleh	Lin	15 Classic Way	Burleigh Waters	Qld	4220
Chen	Naisi	15 Dunlop Circuit	Mermaid Waters	Qld	4218
Christiansen	Alan	2205 Gold Coast Highway	Miami	Qld	4220
Omar	Ibrahim	1 Moralla Avenue	Runaway Bay	Qld	4216
Powers	Jodie	34 Bayswater Avenue	Varsity Lakes	Qld	4227

Table 13.6 Data sorted by postcode

Last name	First name	Address	Suburb	State	Postcode
Hollis	Jill	106 City Road	Beenleigh	Qld	4207
Wu	Lucy	123 Sample Road	Beenleigh	Qld	4207
Smith	Jack	5 Barrow Court	Ashmore	Qld	4214
Omar	Ibrahim	1 Moralla Avenue	Runaway Bay	Qld	4216
Appleton	Drew	345 Arcadia Street	Broadbeach	Qld	4218
Yakushev	Viktor	83 Surf Parade	Broadbeach	Qld	4218
Matthews	Ricki	45/21 Wharf Street	Broadbeach	Qld	4218
Chen	Naisi	15 Dunlop Circuit	Mermaid Waters	Qld	4218
Saleh	Lin	15 Classic Way	Burleigh Waters	Qld	4220
Christiansen	Alan	2205 Gold Coast Highway	Miami	Qld	4220
Powers	Jodie	34 Bayswater Avenue	Varsity Lakes	Qld	4227

Video: Sort and filter in Excel

You can access the *Sort* tool from the *Editing* section of the *Home* tab.

- Select the data you want to sort. Remember to always select the *entire* rows or columns so that all the data for each individual entry stays together. For example, if you only select the column with customer last names for sorting but leave their other details out of the sort, you would get an alphabetical list of customer surnames, but their address and other details will no longer be aligned as the data in the other columns were not included in the sort.
- Click on *Sort & Filter*. You can now choose to sort alphabetically A to Z, or Z to A, or you can choose a "custom" sort (as illustrated in Figure 13.9) to be more selective and specific about how you want to sort the data.
- Remember to tick the "My list has headers" box in the top right if your first row or column are headers; otherwise, Excel will think your headers are part of the data to be sorted.

Figure 13.9 Data sorting options

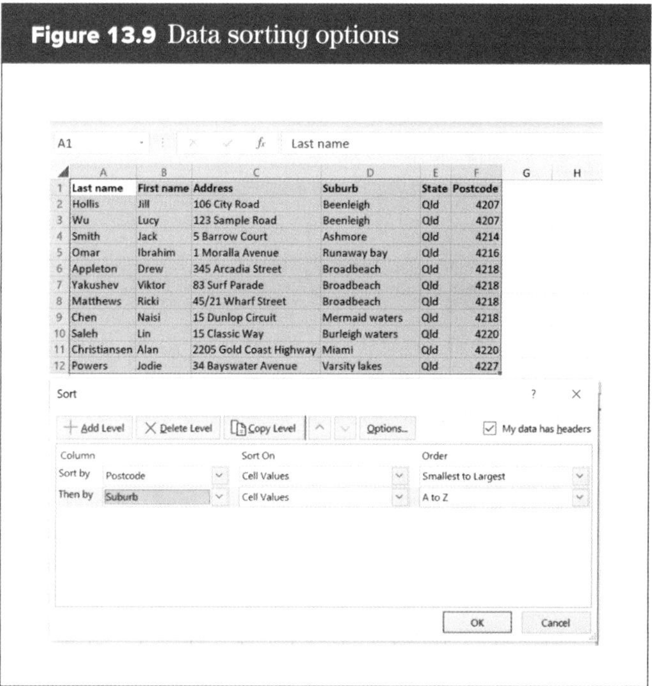

The same process applies to any other database that you want to create. You can keep a database of the organisation's products by product name, cost price, sales price, quantity sold, quantity in stock and so on. These bits of data can then be sorted in a number of ways that will allow the organisation to see different trends, including which items are selling better than others, which items need to be restocked and how much revenue each item generates. You therefore need to understand the desired outcome before you enter the data, and set up your spreadsheet in a way that will achieve this.

Working with formulas

Spreadsheet software such as Excel will allow you to make a number of calculations, return information and manipulate the contents of other cells according to specified conditions and parameters. Excel formulas, however, are written a little differently from mathematical formulas. In Excel formulas, the equation symbol (=) appears at the beginning, rather than in the middle, of the formula. Excel recognises any cell starting with an equation symbol to contain a formula rather than another piece of data.

Figure 13.10 Entering a formula into a single cell

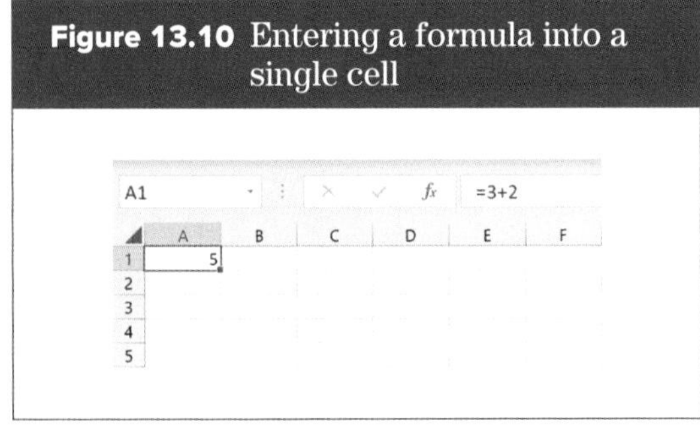

Excel formulas look like this: =3+2, rather than: 3+2 =

While entering the entire formula into a single cell (Figure 13.10) works, if you want to change the data being calculated, you need to edit or rewrite the formula, as you have specifically told the spreadsheet that the value in that cell is 3+2.

A better way to enter formulas would be to write them with reference to cells containing the relevant data so that you can change the result by changing the values in individual cells without having to change the formula itself. To do this, you need to tell Excel which cell(s) the relevant pieces of data are located in.

A cell's location in the spreadsheet is referred to as its **cell reference**. To find a cell reference, simply look at the column headings to find which column the cell is in, and across to find which row it is in. The cell reference is a combination of the column letter and row number—for example, A1 or B3. In Figure 13.10, the number 5 is located in cell A1. When writing cell references, the column letter always comes first. So, instead of writing the formula =3+2 in cell A1, do this instead:

1. Enter the required data components that make up the formula into the spreadsheet separately—for example, number *3* into cell A1, and number *2* into cell A2.
2. Into the cell where you want the result of the formula to show (e.g. A3), write: *=A1+A2* and press *Enter*. That cell will now show the result: 5.

By doing this, no matter what numbers you put into those two cells (A1 and A2), the formula will always display the summation of those two values in cell A3. For example, if you changed the number in cell A1 to 5 and the number in cell A2 to 6, the formula would calculate the value of 5+6, as you have instructed Excel to add the values of those specific cells rather than specific *numbers*. See Figure 13.11 for an example of how this looks in the spreadsheet. (*Note*: When you click on a cell containing a formula in Microsoft Excel, the formula always appears in the formula bar located above the column letters—circled in red in the example.)

Figure 13.11 Using Excel formulas with cell references

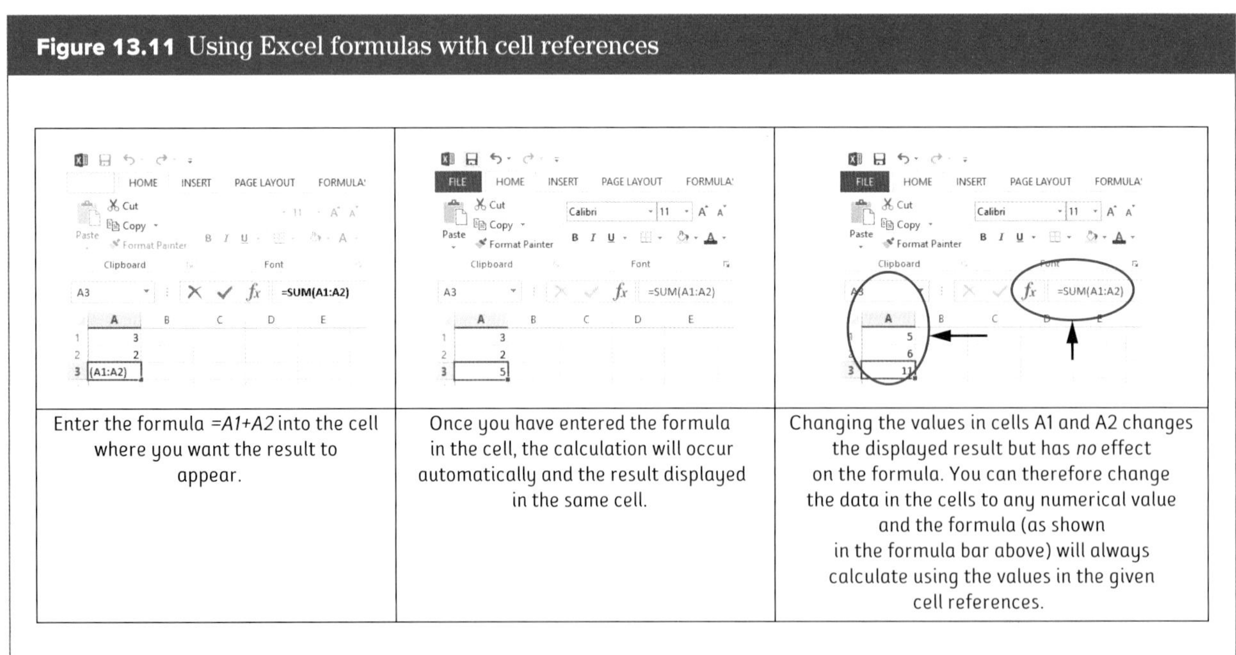

Enter the formula *=A1+A2* into the cell where you want the result to appear.

Once you have entered the formula in the cell, the calculation will occur automatically and the result displayed in the same cell.

Changing the values in cells A1 and A2 changes the displayed result but has *no* effect on the formula. You can therefore change the data in the cells to any numerical value and the formula (as shown in the formula bar above) will always calculate using the values in the given cell references.

If you were adding a row or column of numbers, you would include each cell to be added. There are a number of ways to do this. For example:

- Entering the cell references for each cell to be added, individually, into the formula bar. For example: *=A1+A2+A3+A4+A5*. This would then add all the numbers in cells A1 through to A5.

To save writing in each individual cell manually, you can enter the = sign into the cell where the result is to be shown, then click on each individual cell to be added and enter the + sign before clicking into the next cell (and so on) to achieve the same result.

- Entering the *range* of cell references to include in the addition. This formula is: =*SUM(A1:A5)*, where *SUM* means add the total range and the *colon* means A1 "*through to*" A5.
- Using the *AutoSum function*.

Figure 13.12 Using *AutoSum*

Using *AutoSum*

Sometimes the range of data you need to sum can be quite long. In these cases, the Excel *AutoSum* tool allows you to add all the numbers in a column or row by clicking the cell next to the row or column of numbers you want to sum and then clicking on *AutoSum* in the top right-hand corner of the *Home* tab (see Figure 13.12). This will then place a dotted border around the cells to include in the sum. If you are happy with the selected range of cells, press *Enter* and the result will be displayed, as shown in Figure 13.13.

You have the option to change the selected data range by "dragging" the edges of the dotted border to encompass the range of cells you wish to use. For example, you can drag the top border down so that the 5 isn't included in the sum. This is useful, as sometimes the header of a column might be a number itself (e.g. a year: 2022) and you don't want this number included in the sum.

Figure 13.13 Using *AutoSum* to calculate the sum of all numbers in a column

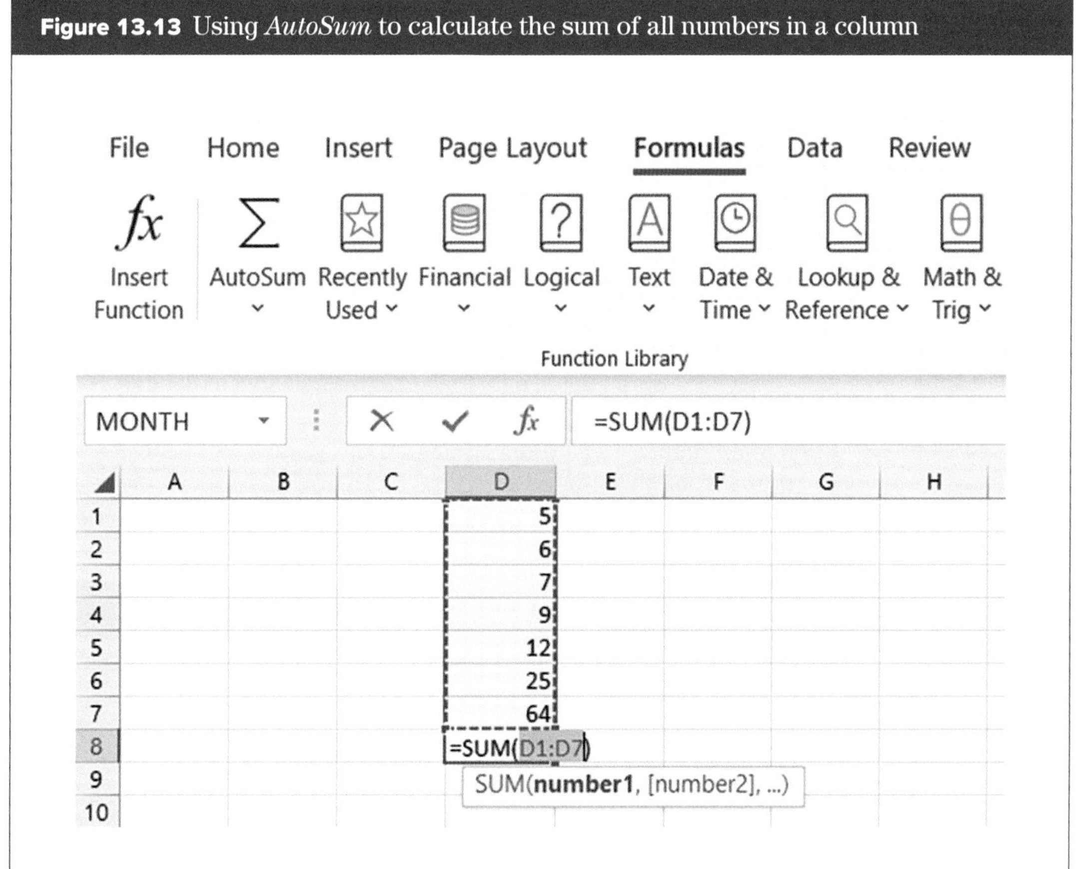

Try this now

1. Enter some data into a spreadsheet and try out the various tools we have covered so far.

Mathematical operators

Video: Formulas and functions in Excel

Creating basic formulas in Excel isn't difficult. It is a matter of combining the cell references of your data with the correct mathematical operator. **Mathematical operators** are instructions that specify what type of calculation you want to perform on the numbers: are you adding, subtracting, dividing or multiplying? The mathematical operators used in Excel formulas are similar to those used in mathematics:

- Subtraction: minus sign –
- Addition: plus sign +
- Division: forward slash /
- Multiplication: asterisk *

Figure 13.14 shows a few examples.

Figure 13.14 Examples of mathematical operators in Excel

Calculation:	Equation:	Formula:
(a) 20 divided by 5 is 4	20/5	A1/A2
(b) 20 multiplied by 5 is 100	20*5	A1*A2
(c) 20 minus 5 is 15	20–5	A1–A2

In this example, we have used cells A1 and A2 to demonstrate. These can be substituted with any cell references necessary for the calculation.

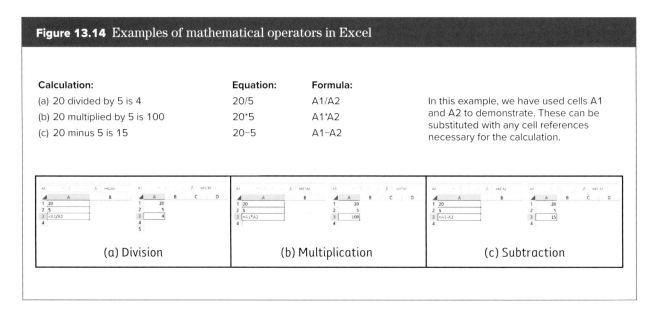

(a) Division

(b) Multiplication

(c) Subtraction

Calculations you make don't necessarily apply only to data in a single row or column as shown in Figure 13.14. You can add data from *any* cells within the spreadsheet. All you need to do is input each individual cell location into the cell where the result is to be shown, and press *Enter*. For example: =A1+B5+C6+D2 (see Figure 13.15).

Figure 13.15 Formula shown in the formula bar

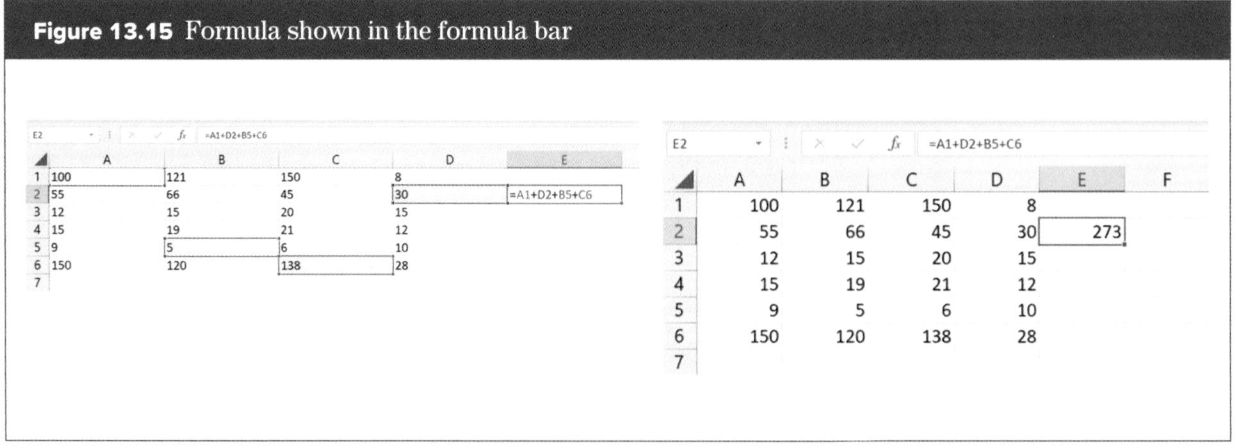

E2 =A1+D2+B5+C6

	A	B	C	D	E	F
1	100	121	150	8		
2	55	66	45	30	273	
3	12	15	20	15		
4	15	19	21	12		
5	9	5	6	10		
6	150	120	138	28		
7						

You have now learnt the basics of entering formulas into a spreadsheet. There are many complex calculations possible when using a spreadsheet, and you will learn these as you progress through your career.

Try this now

2. Using the data you previously entered into a spreadsheet, try some of these mathematical operators using formulas for yourself.

Calculating percentages

In a list of numbers, whether they are inventory figures or amounts of currency, you might need to know what percentage a certain figure represents—for example, what percentage of the whole a certain figure is, or what the average percentage of a range of data is.

In Figure 13.16, we have calculated the percentage of the total actuals for 2020 ($46,001.33) the figure in cell A3 represents. The calculation for this is the same as in maths: the individual figure we want to find the percentage for, divided by the whole. In this case: 252.00 divided by 46,001.33 = 0.54784178.

In cell B3, where we asked the results to be calculated, we instructed Excel to show the figure as a percentage to two decimal places, so the result is "0.55%".

The formula entered into Excel was = A3/A14, as shown in the formula bar.

Figure 13.16 Calculating the percentage of a sum

B3 | fx | =A3/A14

	A	B	C	D
1	Actual			
2	2020			
3	$ 252.00	0.55%		
4	$ 9,900.00			
5	$ 1,550.00			
6	$ 1,113.33			
7	$ 1,400.00			
8	$ 20,000.00			
9	$ 4,500.00			
10	$ 3,559.00			
11	$ 1,950.00			
12	$ 1,394.00			
13	$ 383.00			
14	$ 46,001.33			
15				

Averages, count of numbers and other features

To find out the *average* of a series of figures you need to add the data in each cell of a column of numbers and divide by the number of rows. Using *AutoSum*, we first add the data in column C, which gives us $12,815.33. We then enter the formula =C5/4 into the cell where we want the average to appear and press *Enter*. The result is an average of $3,203.83 across the four amounts queried (Figure 13.17).

There are, however, shortcut methods of completing these calculations. In the same way that Excel *AutoSum* lets you add a column or row of numbers quickly, it also provides shortcuts for determining averages and count of numbers. So, instead of manually calculating the column total and then dividing it by the number of rows, you can click into the cell at the end of a column or row where your data is listed, click on the arrow next to *AutoSum* and choose the *Average* option from the drop-down list (see Figure 13.18). This will then select the data to be averaged, so you can check the range to make sure it is what you want. Press *Enter*, and *AutoSum* will then provide you with the result.

This shortcut is also useful for determining the following for a row or column:

- *Count Numbers*—how many rows or columns contain numbers.
- *Maximum*—which number has the highest value.
- *Minimum*—which number has the lowest value.

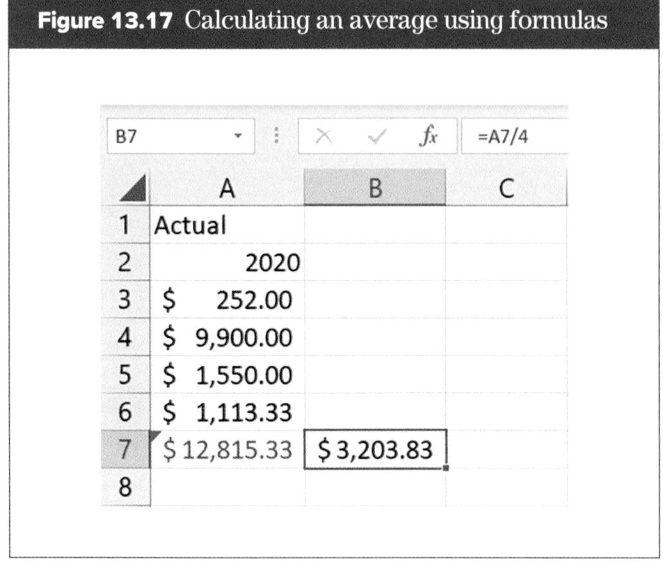

Figure 13.17 Calculating an average using formulas

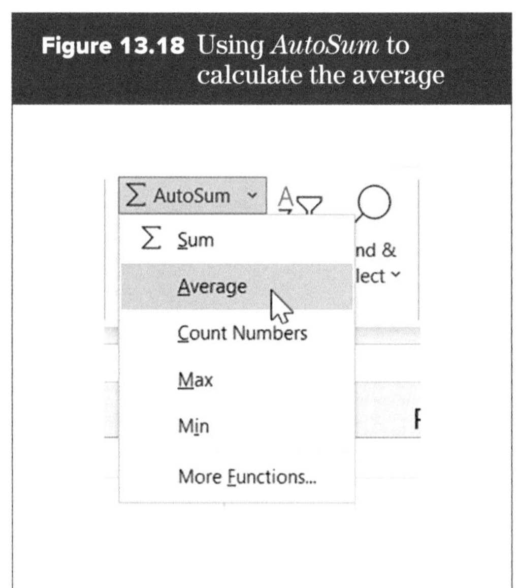

Figure 13.18 Using *AutoSum* to calculate the average

Order of operations and using brackets

In addition to the simple calculations discussed, you may sometimes need to make calculations that require a number of steps (e.g. when calculating *variations* between two sets of figures). This entails using round brackets (or parentheses).

Formulas indicate the order in which calculations are to be performed. In a series of calculations, the instructions *inside* the brackets will be carried out first, followed by the instructions *after* the brackets. The brackets are needed because the order in which calculations are performed can often affect the result. It is therefore important to understand how the order is determined and how you can change it to obtain the desired results.

As discussed, a formula in Excel always begins with an equation symbol, which tells Excel that the characters that follow constitute a formula. Following the equation symbol are the elements to be calculated (such as numbers or cell references), which are separated by mathematical operators (such as +, –, *, or /). For example: A1 is a cell reference and * is the mathematical operator for "multiply".

Excel actions the formula from left to right, according to a specific order for each operator in the formula. However, if you combine *several* operators in a single formula (e.g. =A1–A2*A6), Excel performs the operations in the order shown in Table 13.7 (note that this only an extract and not the full list of operators available in Excel).

Table 13.7 Excel order of operations

Operator	Description
: [colon] or , [comma]	Reference operator
–	Negation (as in –1) to show a negative figure
%	Per cent
* and /	Multiplication and division
+ and –	Addition and subtraction

Excel will therefore prioritise sections of the formula containing a colon or a percentage before it calculates multiplication and division, and it will calculate those before it calculates additions and subtractions. For example, the following formula produces a result of 11:

=5+2*3

It produces this result because Excel multiplies 2 by 3 to get 6, and then adds 5.

To change the order of operation, you need to enclose the part of the formula you want calculated *first* in brackets. For example:

=(5+2)*3

Excel now adds 5 and 2 together first to get 7, and then multiplies that result by 3 to produce 21.

A practical example of this is shown in Figure 13.19, where the variations between amounts budgeted in 2022 and 2023 are calculated. To calculate such a variance, you must first deduct the "new" number (2023) from the "old" number (2022) and then divide the result by the "old" number.

Because Excel calculates division before subtraction, this first step needs to be enclosed in brackets so that Excel knows to do this step first. The formula for this is shown in the formula bar in the figure: =(A2−B2)/A2.

Excel is then instructed to show the figures in column C as a percentage to two decimal points.

An excellent source of further information on calculating operators is the Microsoft Support Page (https://support.microsoft.com/en-us/office/the-order-in-which-excel-performs-operations-in-formulas-28eaf0d7-7058-4eff-a8ea-0a835fafadb8).

Figure 13.19 Calculating percentage variations

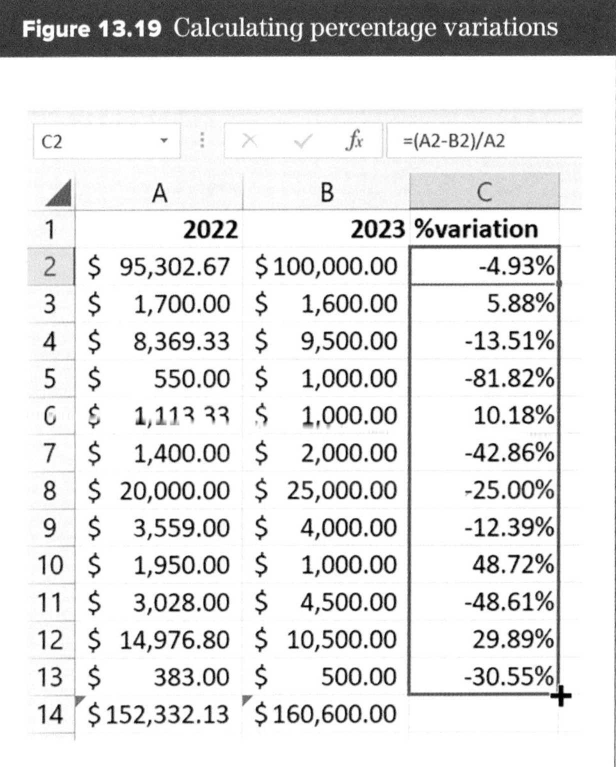

C2 | =(A2-B2)/A2

	A	B	C
1	2022	2023	%variation
2	$ 95,302.67	$ 100,000.00	-4.93%
3	$ 1,700.00	$ 1,600.00	5.88%
4	$ 8,369.33	$ 9,500.00	-13.51%
5	$ 550.00	$ 1,000.00	-81.82%
6	$ 1,113.33	$ 1,000.00	10.18%
7	$ 1,400.00	$ 2,000.00	-42.86%
8	$ 20,000.00	$ 25,000.00	-25.00%
9	$ 3,559.00	$ 4,000.00	-12.39%
10	$ 1,950.00	$ 1,000.00	48.72%
11	$ 3,028.00	$ 4,500.00	-48.61%
12	$ 14,976.80	$ 10,500.00	29.89%
13	$ 383.00	$ 500.00	-30.55%
14	$ 152,332.13	$ 160,600.00	

13.3.2 Formatting a spreadsheet

Consistency in formatting the documents an organisation produces is important. Too many different formats can make it difficult for internal staff and external contacts to review the information in spreadsheets and reports and can therefore result in poor decisions being made. For this reason, many organisations use Excel's various formatting tools to standardise the way in which their documents and spreadsheets are designed and presented. Some of these functions include:

- date formats
- alignment
- font
- border
- fill
- protection
- headers and footers.

Date formats

The *Number Format* tool group, where appropriate, can ensure consistency of information. For example, it would be confusing if a spreadsheet used a number of different date formats, such as 01JAN22, 01 January 2022 and 01/01/22. Specifying the date format for specific cells, or entire rows or columns ensures it will always be displayed in the specified format, no matter how you enter the date into the cell.

To ensure a consistent approach to date input, go to the *Number* section in the *Home* tab, where there are a number of quick number format options available, as shown in Figure 13.20. You can click the drop-down menu to see further more formatting options.

The example in Figure 13.21 offers two additional formats for dates: *Short Date* or *Long Date*. In this case, we have chosen *Long Date*. You will notice that the date in the formula bar (located above the columns) shows what you originally entered into cell A1.

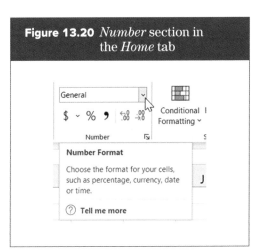

Figure 13.20 *Number* section in the *Home* tab

Figure 13.21 Selecting date format options

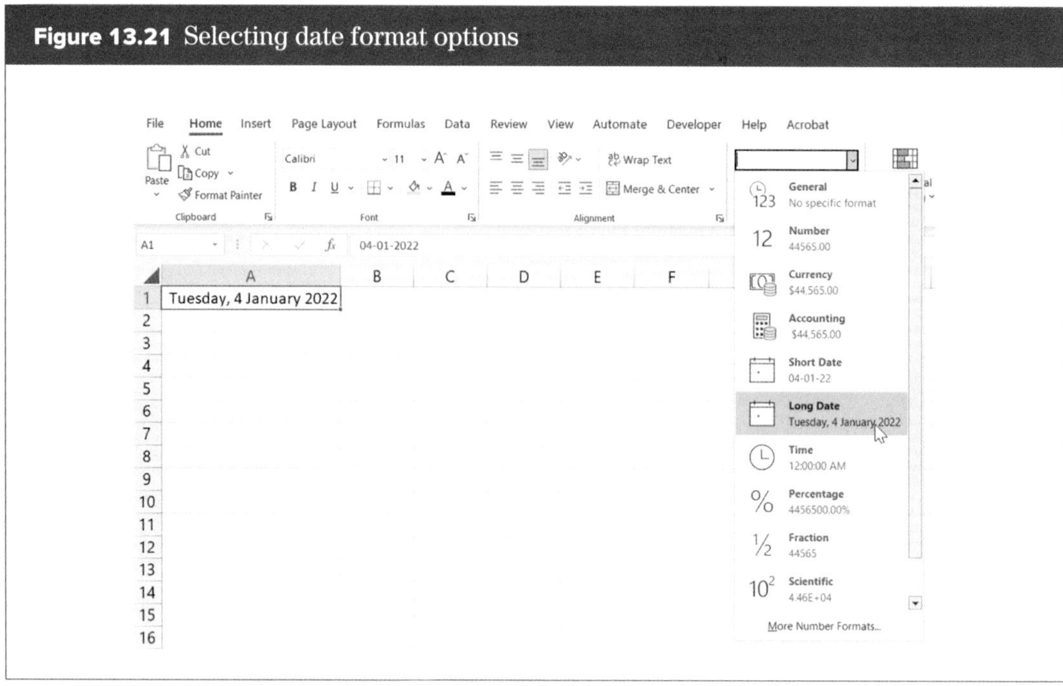

If neither of these options are suitable, there are further options available, as shown in Figure 13.22. At the bottom of the drop-down menu, there is an option for *More Number Formats*, where you can select from all the date format options available in Excel via the *Format Cells* dialogue box until you find one that best suits your needs.

Figure 13.22 More date format options in Excel

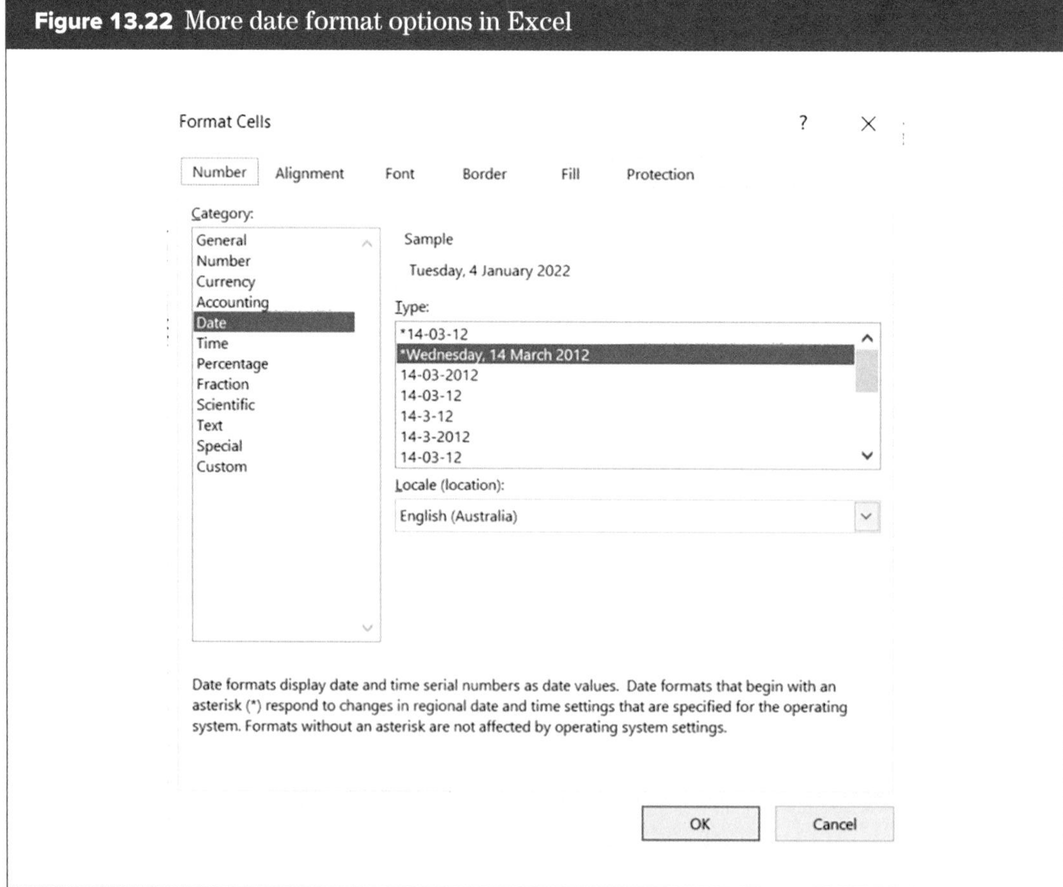

Alignment

You also have a range of choices when it comes to alignment. This tool dictates how an entry should be presented within each cell of the spreadsheet: that is, left, centred or right. In most cases, any text would be aligned to the left, whereas numbers such as currency figures would be aligned to the right (see Figure 13.23). You can also choose if the text should be aligned to the top, middle or bottom of a cell.

Font

The organisation may have a style guide that dictates what fonts (typefaces), styles (e.g. regular, bold, italic) and font sizes are to be used in all business documents, whether letters or spreadsheets (see Figure 13.24).

Figure 13.23 Words aligned to the left; numbers aligned to the right

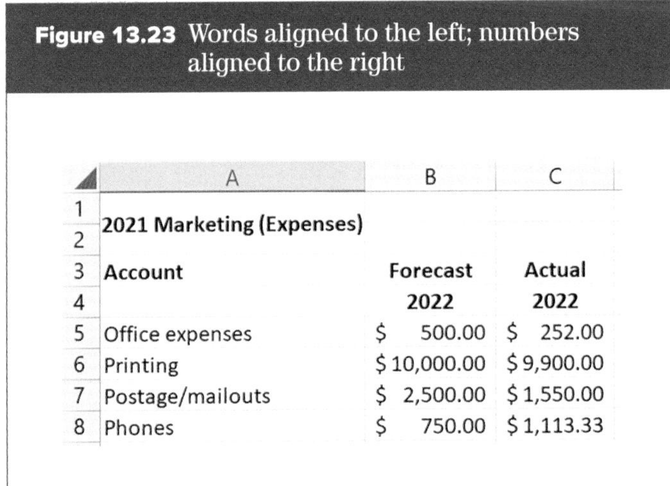

	A	B	C
1			
2	**2021 Marketing (Expenses)**		
3	**Account**	**Forecast**	**Actual**
4		**2022**	**2022**
5	Office expenses	$ 500.00	$ 252.00
6	Printing	$ 10,000.00	$ 9,900.00
7	Postage/mailouts	$ 2,500.00	$ 1,550.00
8	Phones	$ 750.00	$ 1,113.33

Figure 13.24 Font and alignment options

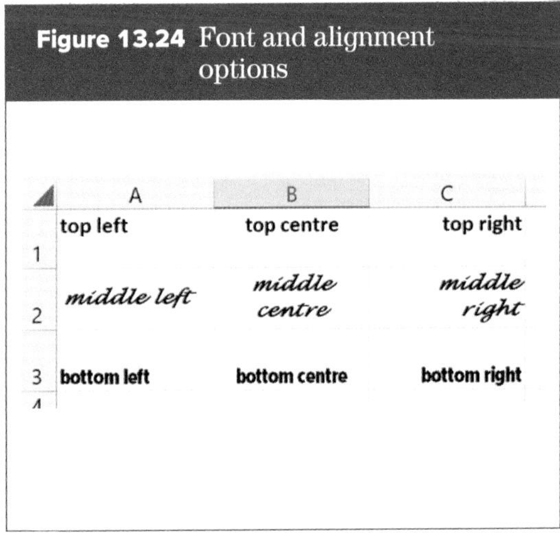

	A	B	C
1	**top left**	**top centre**	**top right**
2	*middle left*	*middle centre*	*middle right*
3	**bottom left**	**bottom centre**	**bottom right**
4			

The simplest way to access this tool is to click on the down arrows beside the *Font* or *Size* options in the *Font* tab on the *Home* tab (Figure 13.25).

You can also click on the arrow on the bottom right corner of the *Font* tab to launch the *Format Cells* dialogue box.

The *Font* tab in this dialogue box enables you to choose not only the font, but also the style (e.g. regular, bold, italic), as well as the size, as shown in Figure 13.26. It also gives you access to a number of other style options such as ~~strikethrough~~, superscript and subscript which might be useful depending on the data you are including.

Figure 13.25 Choosing font and size

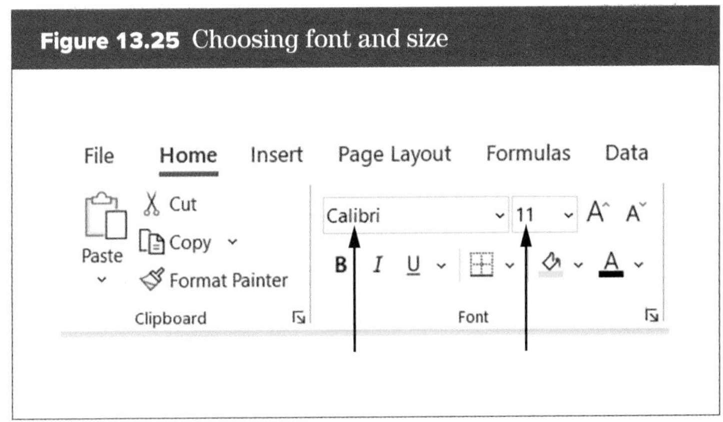

Border

There are times where you may want to highlight a specific cell or group of cells; adding borders is a good way to do so. The *Border* tab in the *Format Cells* dialogue box (see Figure 13.27) allows you to choose whether the selected cell (or group of cells) should have a border around them and, if so, what style the border should be.

Figure 13.26 Further font formatting options

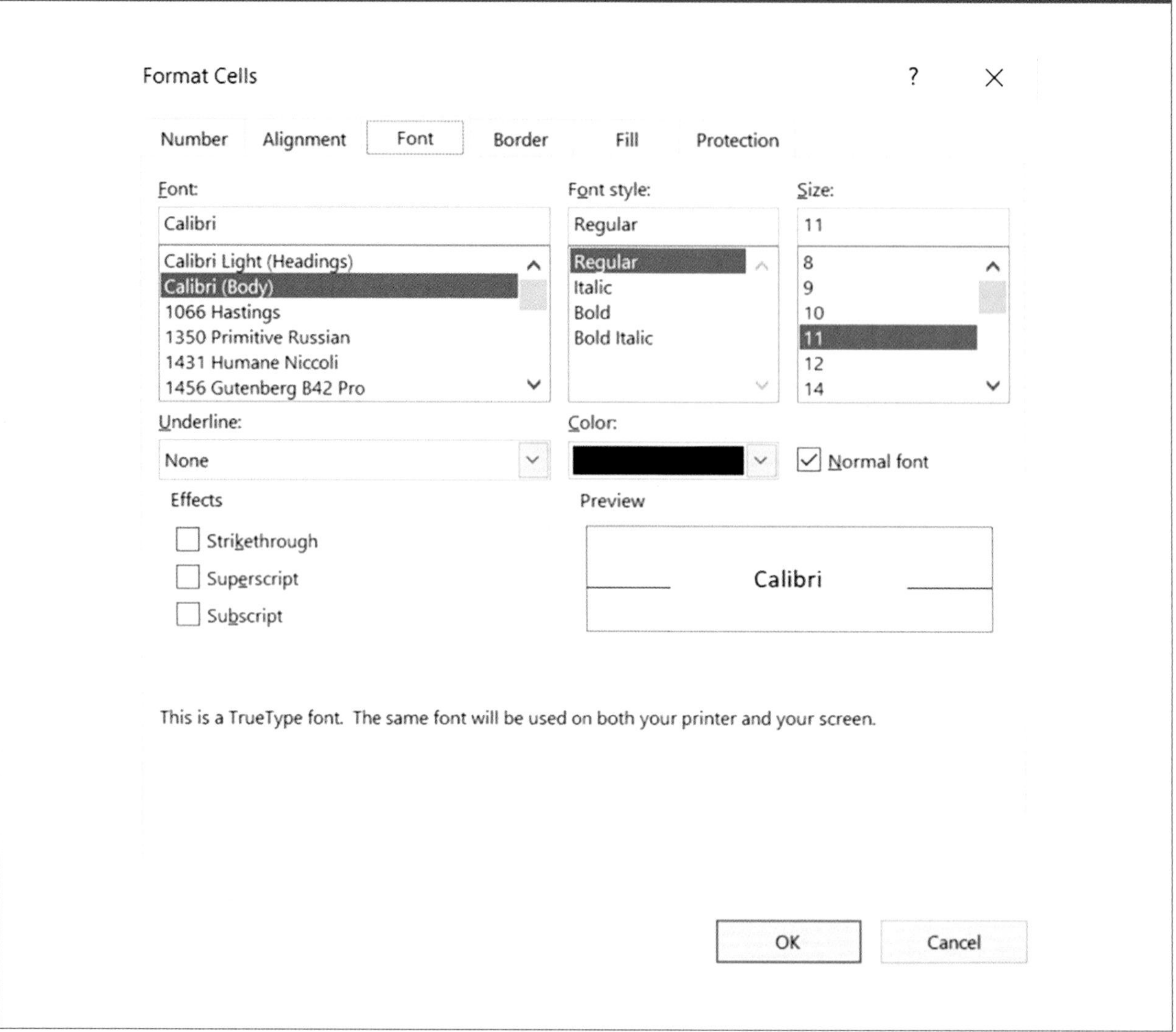

Format Cells
?
Number
Alignment
Font
Border
Fill
Protection
Font:
Calibri
Calibri Light (Headings)
Calibri (Body)
1066 Hastings
1350 Primitive Russian
1431 Humane Niccoli
1456 Gutenberg B42 Pro
Font style:
Regular
Regular
Italic
Bold
Bold Italic
Size:
11
8
9
10
11
12
14
Underline:
None
Color:
Normal font
Effects
Strikethrough
Superscript
Subscript
Preview
Calibri
This is a TrueType font. The same font will be used on both your printer and your screen.
OK
Cancel

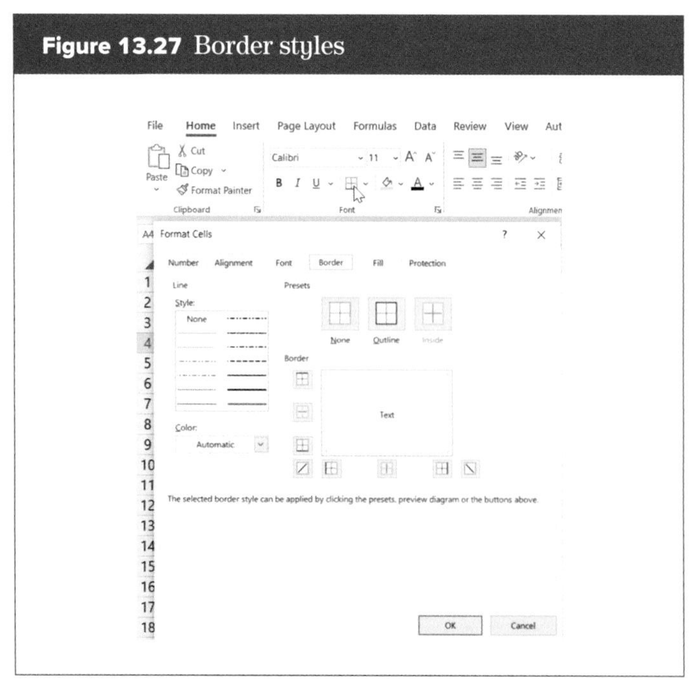

Figure 13.27 Border styles

File
Home
Insert
Page Layout
Formulas
Data
Review
View
Cut
Copy
Format Painter
Paste
Clipboard
Calibri
Font
Format Cells
Number
Alignment
Font
Border
Fill
Protection
Line
Style:
None
Presets
None
Outline
Inside
Border
Text
Color:
Automatic
The selected border style can be applied by clicking the presets, preview diagram or the buttons above.
OK
Cancel

Fill

This tab allows you to add a colour or pattern to a cell (or group of cells) to highlight them (see Figure 13.28).

Protection

This is a very useful tool, particularly if the spreadsheet contains a range of complex data and formulas. This tool (see Figure 13.29) allows you to lock cells so they cannot be changed, or to hide formulas in order to protect them from unauthorised access or from mistakes being made.

Headers and footers

Headers and footers are used to insert information you wish to display on every page, such as titles or page numbers. To access this tool go to the *Insert* tab on the menu Ribbon and

Figure 13.28 Filling cells with colour

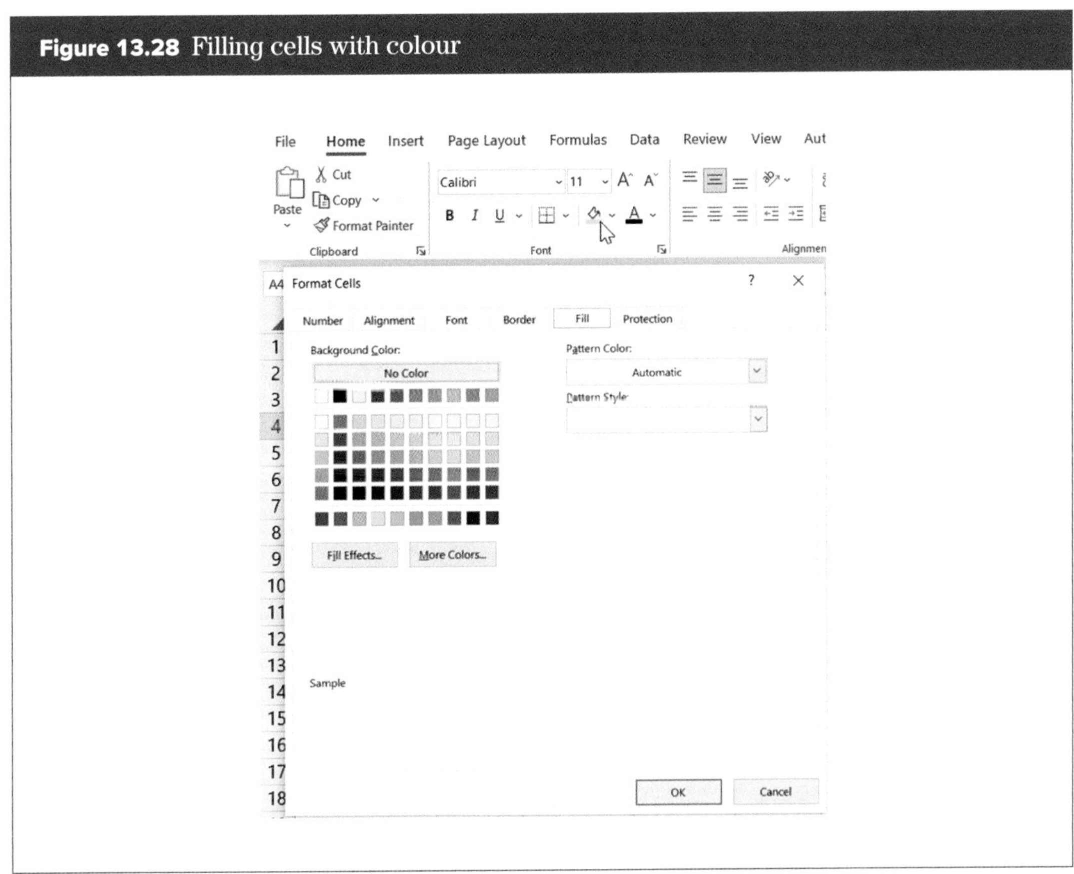

Figure 13.29 Protecting your spreadsheet

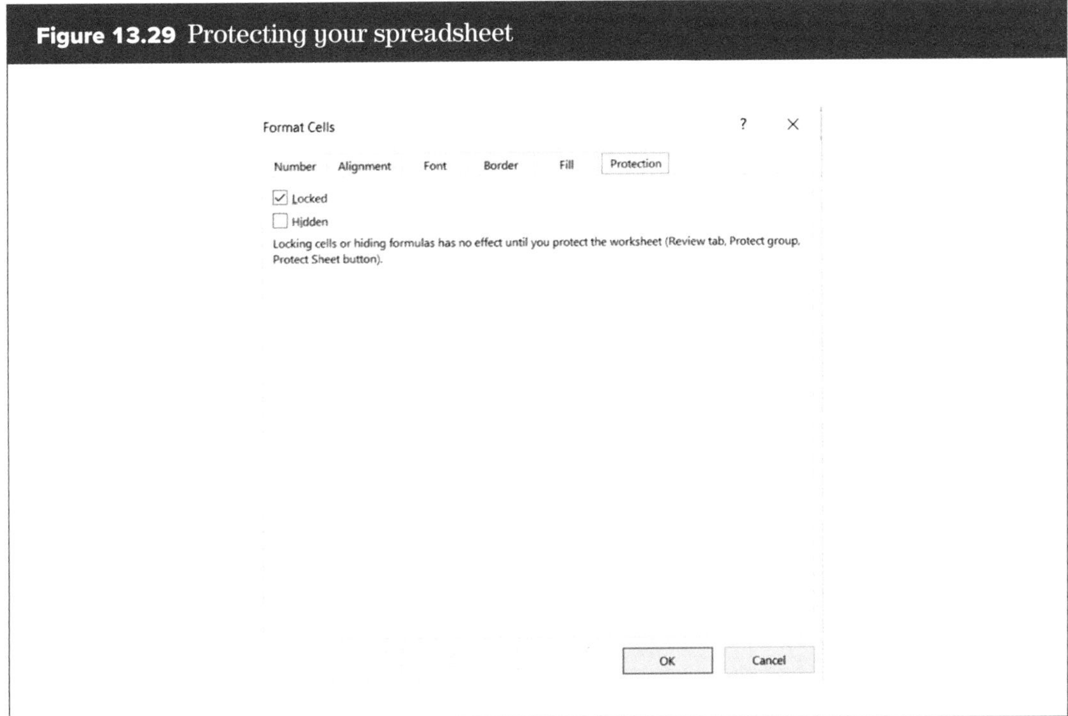

click on *Header & Footer* in the *Text* section. This will display a new *Design Tools* tab specifically for headers and footers (Figure 13.30) that allows you to:

- move between the header and footer of the document
- insert page numbers
- insert the current date and/or time

- include the file name and path
- choose to have information on only odd or even pages, and to have a different first page altogether.

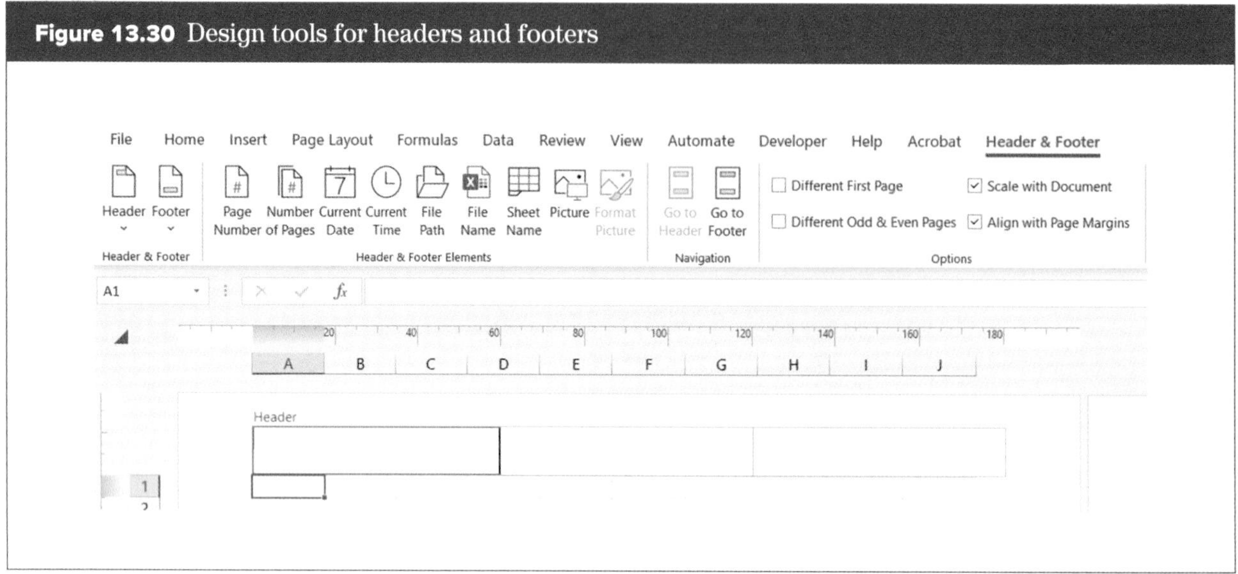

Figure 13.30 Design tools for headers and footers

Freeze panes

Sometimes a spreadsheet will have a large number of columns and rows. As you scroll through the data you will lose the headers at the top or sides of the spreadsheet, and it may become difficult to remember what you are actually looking at.

Excel offers the option to "freeze" certain rows or columns so that they will always be visible, no matter where on the spreadsheet you are. For example, you can be looking at row 2589 and be on column ZZ and still see the information in your header rows and columns. Figure 13.31 shows the options available to you in the *View* tab.

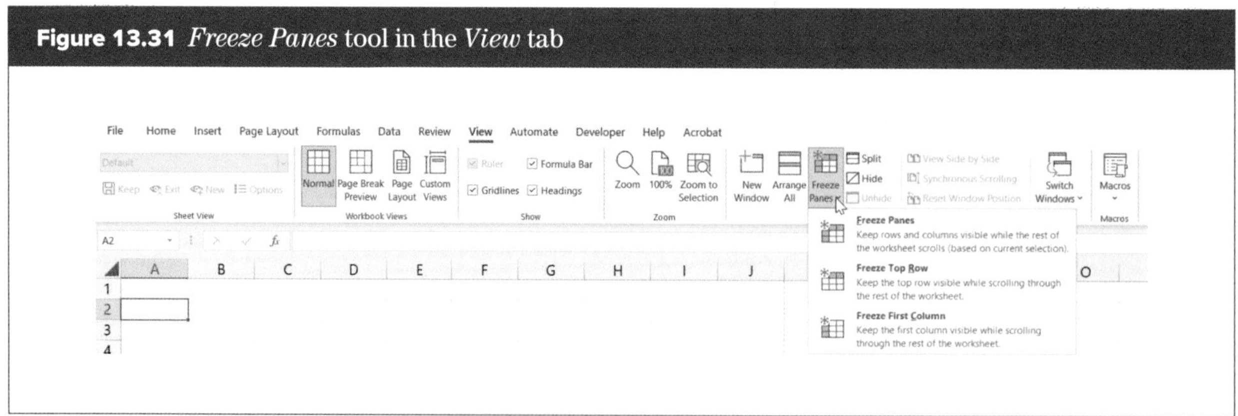

Figure 13.31 *Freeze Panes* tool in the *View* tab

Try this now

3. Try some of these tools for yourself.

13.3.3 Consulting with relevant stakeholders to test formulas

Spreadsheets represent a collation of data that can be used to make important decisions. As such, it is essential that the information they provide is correct and that formulas are working as they should. This means you should have the spreadsheet reviewed by relevant stakeholders—that is, those people who have special expertise in designing and creating them, or who will be basing decisions on them.

Stakeholders can include:

- *Accounting staff*, who need to work with the data to determine the organisation's financial position. This might involve:
  - keeping track of inventory items and the amount spent on them
  - keeping track of debtors and creditors (in the absence of specialised accounting software)
  - providing reports on cash flow and many other things.
- *Managers*, who rely on this information to make decisions about (among other things):
  - financial budgets for the organisation as a whole and/or for specific divisions within it
  - what products or services to continue to offer and which to discontinue
  - general financial health of the organisation and what direction to take in the future.
- *Supervisors*, who may need to keep track of progress on projects their departments are involved in, or who may use spreadsheets to report on performance levels within their divisions.
- *Colleagues*, who may use spreadsheets to record sales they make, or the hours they work, or any number of other things they want to keep a personal record of.
- *Spreadsheet experts*, who can review the spreadsheet to assess the following:
  - Does the information flow logically?
  - Will it work? Is the data arranged in such a way that it produces the required results?
  - Do all the formulas work as they should?

13.3.4 Using *Excel Help* and actioning issues as required

There may be times when you need to complete a specific spreadsheet task but are unsure of how to do it, or something may not be working properly and you don't know how to fix it. At such times, you will need assistance. Most software programs, including Microsoft Excel, come with a *Help* tool.

The *Excel Help* tool is located in the *Help* tab on the Ribbon. (Figure 13.32). Here you can either type in keywords related to your issue in the search bar, which will look for solutions in *Microsoft Support*. You can also use the search bar at the very top of the window, which also looks for solutions on the internet.

Figure 13.32 Accessing *Excel Help* from the Ribbon

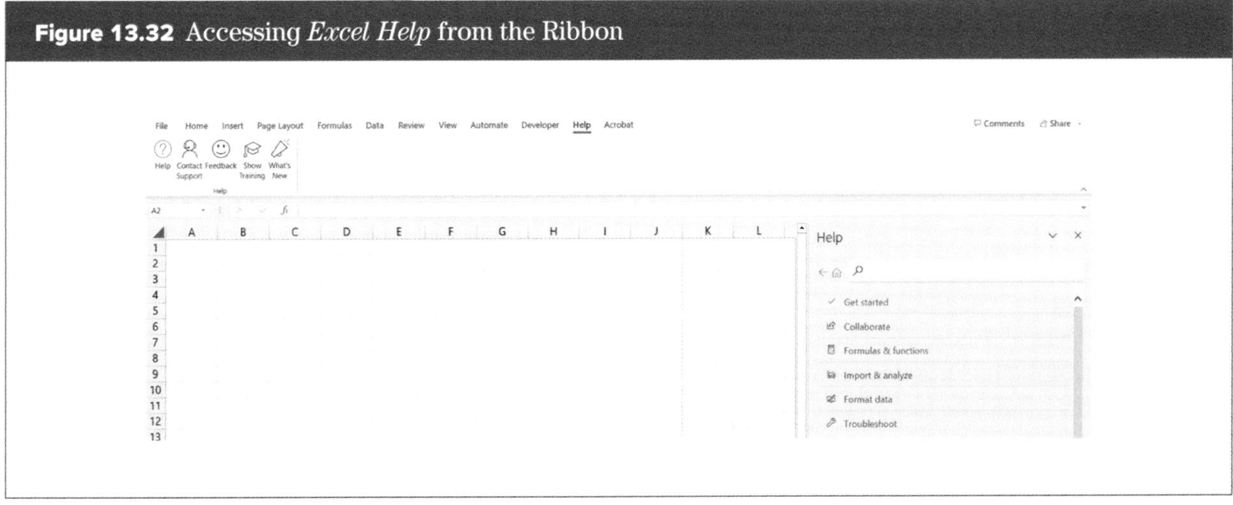

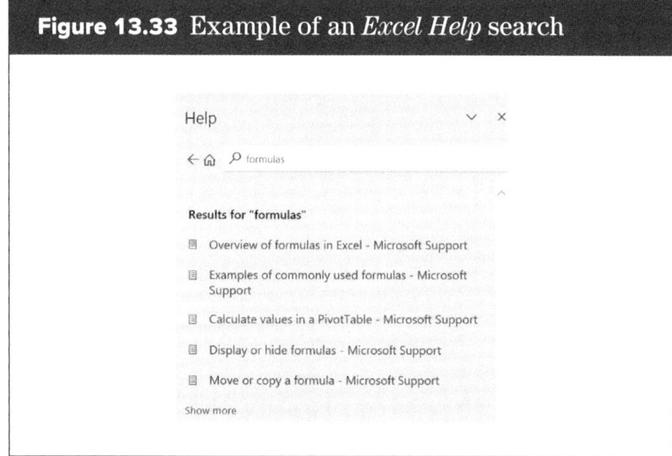

Figure 13.33 Example of an *Excel Help* search

For example, if you were unsure of how to set up a formula, you could type "formulas" into the *Excel Help* search box and *Excel Help* will return a list of possible solutions, as shown in Figure 13.33. By clicking on the relevant options, you will then be given guidance on how to work with formulas—or whatever it was you asked about. This is the quickest way to find help with Excel features and tools.

Knowledge check

8. Explain why it is important to enter data into separate and specific columns.
9. You can use a number of methods to sum columns or rows of numerical data. Describe three of these.
10. There are four basic mathematical operators. What are they?
11. Describe the inbuilt Excel function you can use to calculate averages, count of numbers, minimums and maximums.
12. Explain why it is necessary in to use brackets in some formulas.
13. List at least five functions that you can use to format a spreadsheet for a consistent look and presentation.
14. Spreadsheets are created for stakeholders from different areas of an organisation and for different purposes. List at least four different types of stakeholders. Briefly discuss why each of them might need the information.
15. Describe where you can find help when you need assistance.

13.4 Producing charts

Spreadsheets are often long and complex, with multiple rows and columns of numbers. These can be difficult to work with—especially for busy managers and senior staff who don't always have time to read them thoroughly. To this end, graphs and charts can be very useful, as they will turn hundreds of rows and columns into one (or a small series) of visual pictures that give an excellent overview of the data.

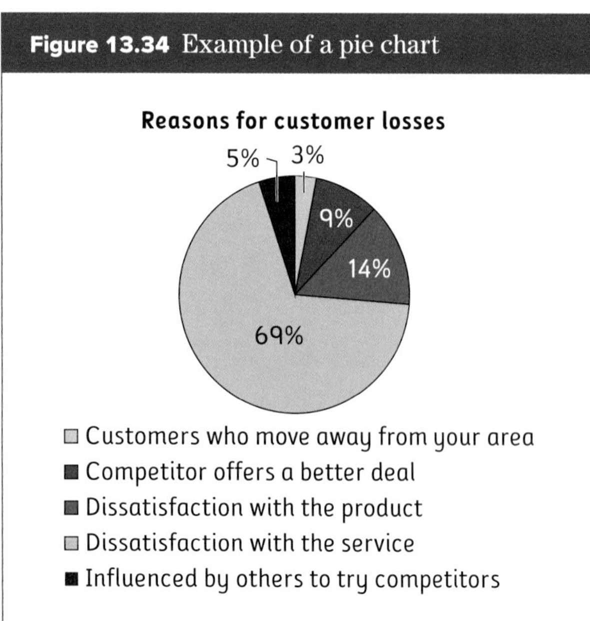

Figure 13.34 Example of a pie chart

13.4.1 Selecting chart type and design

Excel offers a range of options when creating charts, the most popular of which are pie, bar and line charts. Each of these will have specific uses: *pie charts* are useful for gaining a quick overview of information, whereas *bar charts* and *line charts* can be used to show trends and comparisons. For example, if you want to view total performance over a specific time frame or how different product sales have performed over time, then bars or lines are the best format.

In the pie chart shown in Figure 13.34, you can see *at a glance* that the majority of customers (69 per cent) are lost to the business due to dissatisfaction with the service. You don't have to read through pages and pages of data or survey forms to come to this realisation.

Graphs and charts can also show trends. In the line graph in Figure 13.35, information on the same subject has been carried out over a number of years. This will provide information on how trends have changed. We can see that while customer dissatisfaction with the service is still the main reason why the organisation is losing customers, it also shows that this has steadily declined over the past few years—an indication that the service levels are improving.

Figure 13.35 Example of a line graph

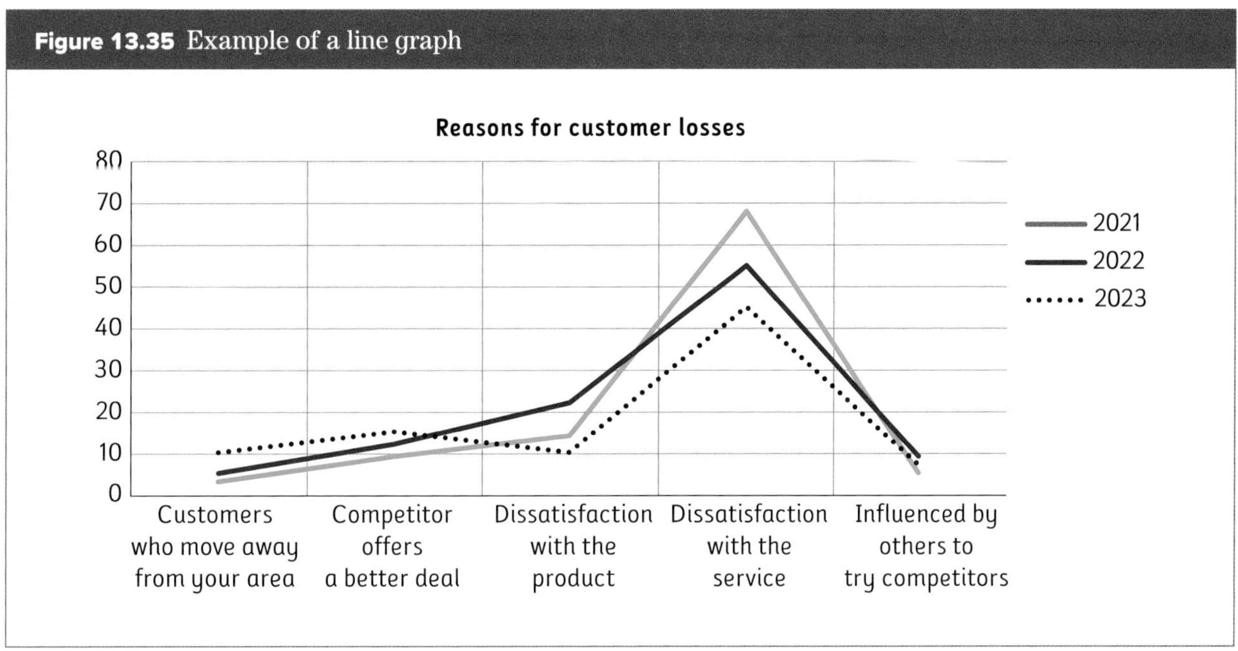

13.4.2 Creating charts using a selected data range in a spreadsheet

Pie charts

A **pie chart** is used when you want to visually represent percentages of a whole. It allows you to show individual items and what part of the whole they represent. For example, if you collected information on the reasons why the organisation is losing customers, you could represent the results visually in a pie chart such as Figure 13.34, which showed that the main reason why customers are choosing not to do business with this organisation is dissatisfaction with the service levels (69 per cent).

Video: Inserting charts in Excel

To create a pie chart:

1. Enter the required data into your spreadsheet, as shown in Table 13.8.
2. Select the cells to be represented in the pie chart. In this case, you would highlight cells A1 through to B6 (rows 1–6 and columns A and B).
3. Click on the *Insert* tab and choose the arrow next to the *Insert Pie or Doughnut Chart* option, grouped under *Charts*. A drop-down box will appear, giving pie chart options (Figure 13.36).

Table 13.8 Example of data entered into a spreadsheet

	A	B
1	**Reasons for customer losses**	
2	Customers who move away from area	3
3	Competitors offer better deal	9
4	Dissatisfaction with product	14
5	Dissatisfaction with service	69
6	Influenced by others to try competitor	5

4. Choose the option that best suits your needs.
5. Upon choosing the best option, the pie chart will be generated using the selected data and will appear in the body of the spreadsheet.

Line graphs and bar charts

A **line graph** or **bar chart** is used to show comparisons and trends between selected categories. For example, the line graph in Figure 13.35 relates to the customer losses pie chart, but where

Figure 13.36 Inserting a pie chart

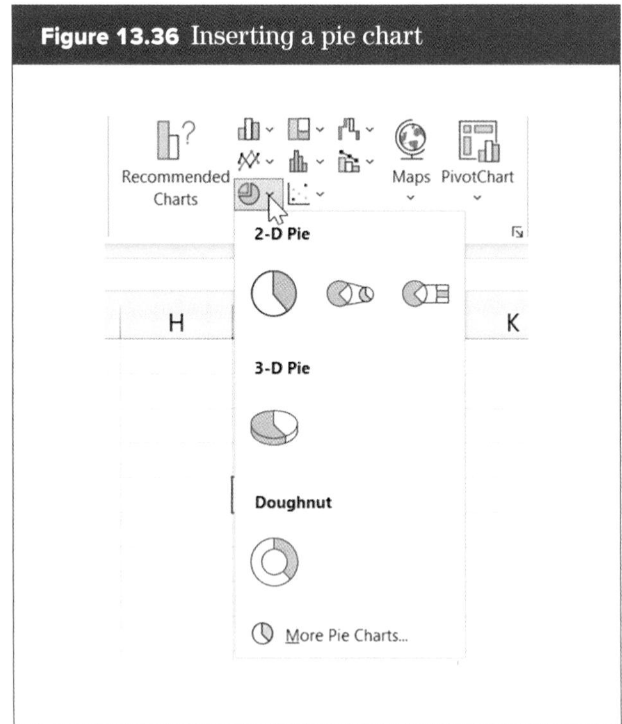

the pie chart only shows the percentage allocated to reasons why customers are being lost, the line graph shows trends in customer losses over a number of years. This is extremely useful information, because if the same problems persist over a number of years, the organisation can clearly see that action must be taken to address the situation.

A line graph or bar chart can therefore be used for more complex visual representations, while a pie chart can generally only be used to show one stream of information.

Example

The marketing department of ABC Website Company is looking at its expenditure on office stationery over the years, in order to cut its costs. To help them assess their expenditure, they follow this procedure to create a line graph or bar chart:

1. Enter the required data into a spreadsheet, as shown in Figure 13.37(a).
2. Select the columns and rows to be represented in the graph. In this case, these are cells A2 to D12.
3. Click on the *Insert* tab and then on the arrow beside *Insert Column or Bar Charts*. A drop-down box will appear (Figure 13.38).
5. Choose the option that best suits their needs (e.g. *Clustered Column*).
6. The bar chart is now created and appears in the body of the spreadsheet. You can then enter a title for the chart, as shown in Figure 13.37(b).

The resulting chart (Figure 13.37(b)) shows ABC Website Company's marketing department that their most-used stationery item was manila folders, followed by photocopy paper. With this information in hand, they can now decide how to change office procedures in order to minimise

Figure 13.37 (a) Spreadsheet with marketing information for creating (b) a bar chart

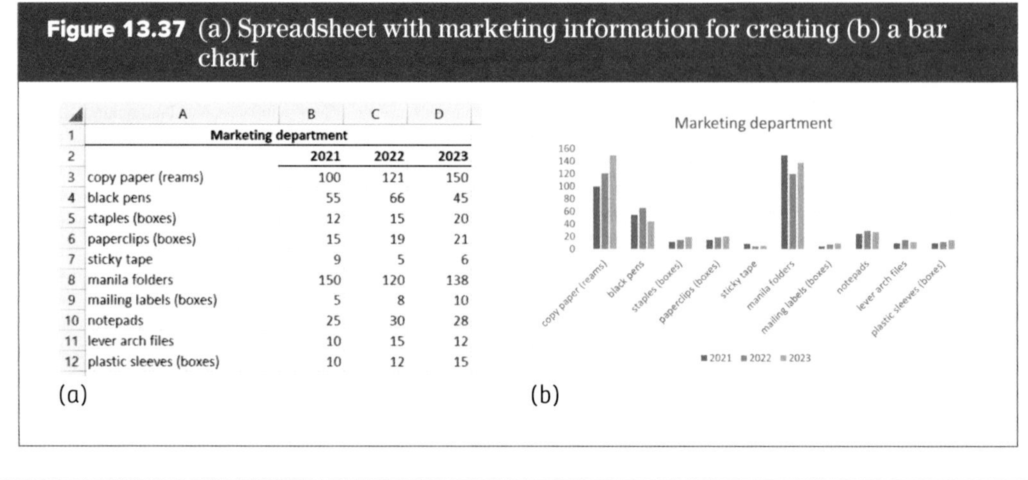

	A	B	C	D
1	Marketing department			
2		2021	2022	2023
3	copy paper (reams)	100	121	150
4	black pens	55	66	45
5	staples (boxes)	12	15	20
6	paperclips (boxes)	15	19	21
7	sticky tape	9	5	6
8	manila folders	150	120	138
9	mailing labels (boxes)	5	8	10
10	notepads	25	30	28
11	lever arch files	10	15	12
12	plastic sleeves (boxes)	10	12	15

(a)

(b)

the use of paper-based products, thereby cutting the organisation's costs while also contributing to sustainability in the workplace.

Figure 13.38 Selecting the most suitable column chart style

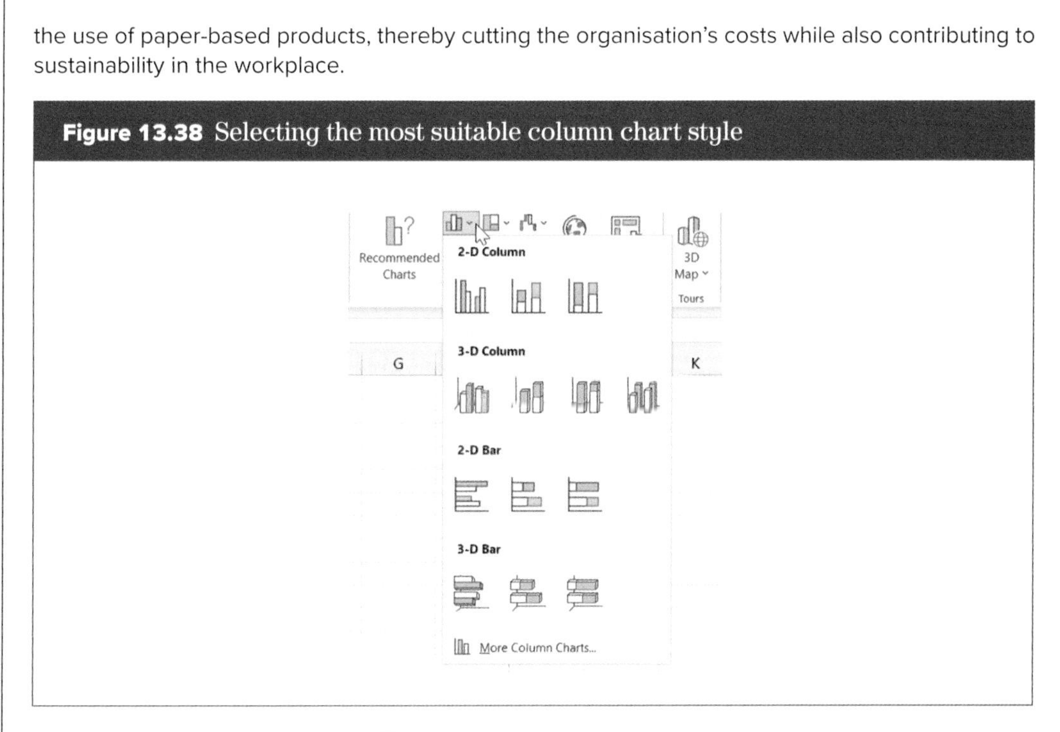

Formatting the chart

You have created a chart, but it may not look or perform exactly as you wish it to, or it may need to be adjusted to provide additional information. In the same way that you can format a spreadsheet itself to look and behave the way you want it to, you can ensure that your charts follow the format you require. You can add:

- *data labels*—such as percentages or numeric data relating to the chart
- *legends*—to show what each data stream relates to
- *titles*—to clarify the chart's purpose.

To add any of these elements to your chart, first click into the chart to open additional tools specifically related to charts. Now click on *Add Chart Element* under *Chart Design*. You will be presented with a drop-down box offering a range of options, as shown in Figure 13.39. Click on the element you wish to add to your chart, choose the option that best suits your needs and then follow the prompts.

Figure 13.39 Adding a legend to a chart

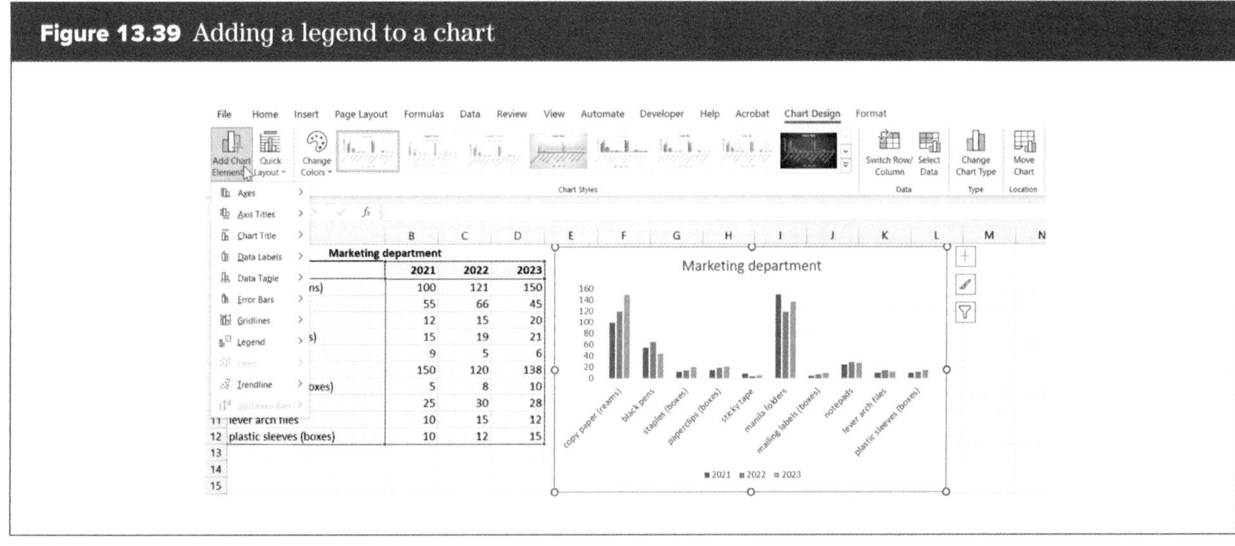

Adding this information can make a difference to the readability of the graph. Using our previous pie chart as an example, the chart (a) in Figure 13.40 has no labels or titles, while chart (b) does, making it easier to understand what the chart is telling you.

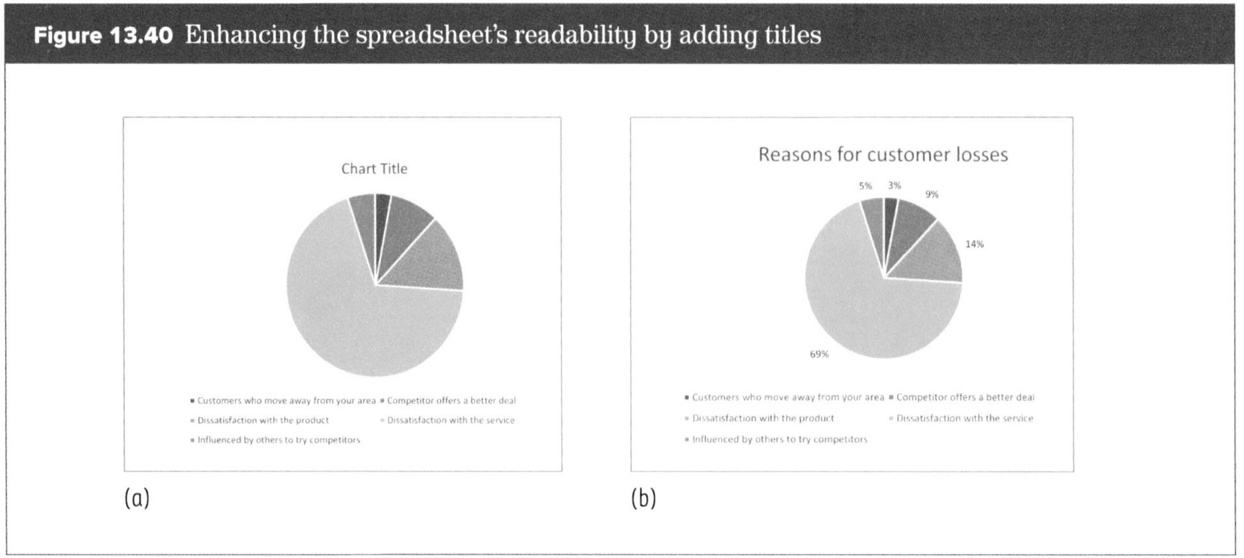

Figure 13.40 Enhancing the spreadsheet's readability by adding titles

Modifying chart type and layout

Sometimes, having created a chart, you may decide that the format chosen isn't quite what you were after. Excel allows you to change the chart type as follows:

1. Right-click your chart.
2. Select *Change Chart Type* from the context menu.
3. The *Change Chart Type* dialogue box will appear with all available chart types for you to browse (Figure 13.41).
4. Choose the one you want to change to, and click OK (or press *Enter*).

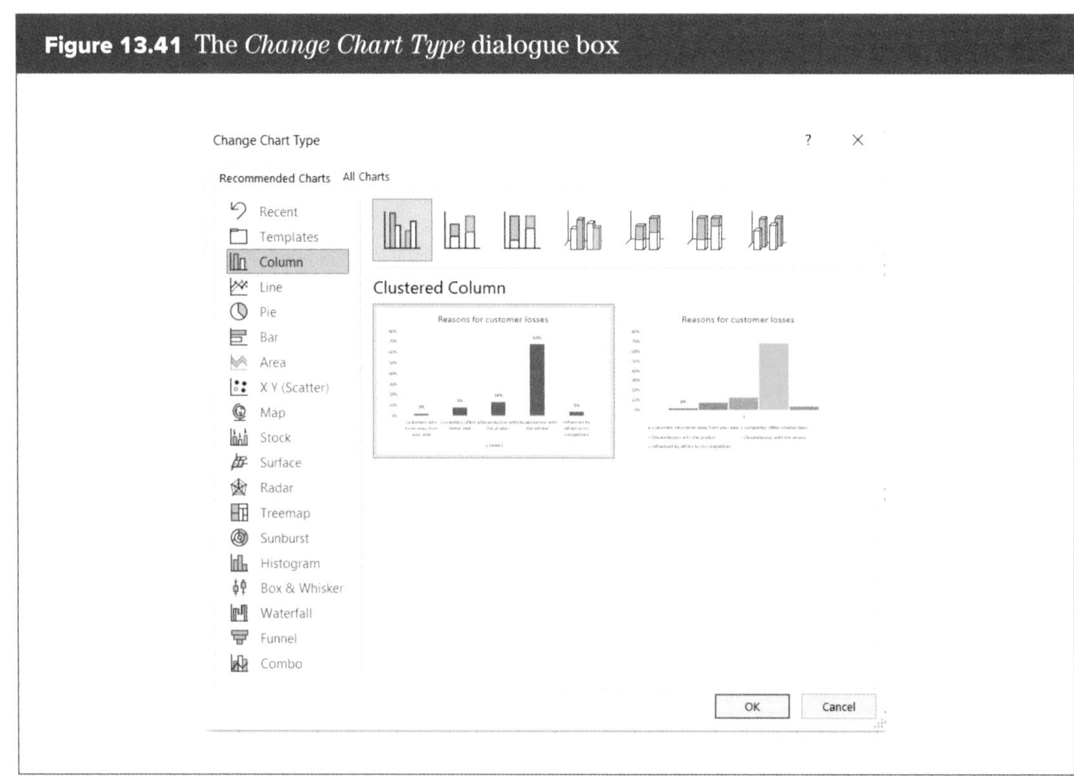

Figure 13.41 The *Change Chart Type* dialogue box

Example

The management of ACME Financial Planning is in the process of putting together its financial budgets for the coming year. As part of this process, they review the expenditure of each department within the organisation to determine how much it has spent and how much it will be allocated in the new budget. In past years, the organisation has spent considerable sums on advertising but didn't always know if this money was spent effectively, in terms of attracting clients. This year, fortunately, the administration staff began keeping enquiry statistics (Table 13.9). They asked each caller where they heard about the company and kept a record of their responses.

These responses were then tallied to provide the results shown in Table 13.9 and Figure 13.42. From this information, management could clearly see that promotion via the company's website was the main source of enquiries—and also the least expensive in terms of cost per enquiry. The decision was therefore made to spend less on television and national newspaper advertising (the most expensive method per enquiry) and to invest more in the website.

Table 13.9 Tracking statistics can help with budgeting

Source	Expenditure ($)	Enquiries	Cost per enquiry ($)
TV	50,000.00	1,000	50.00
National newspaper	25,500.00	2,500	10.20
Local paper	15,500.00	1,893	8.19
Radio	5,500.00	985	5.58
Website	35,000.00	10,965	3.19
Trade show	6,500.00	1,002	6.49
Total	**138,000.00**	**18,345**	**7.52**

Figure 13.42 Graph created from the spreadsheet in Table 13.9

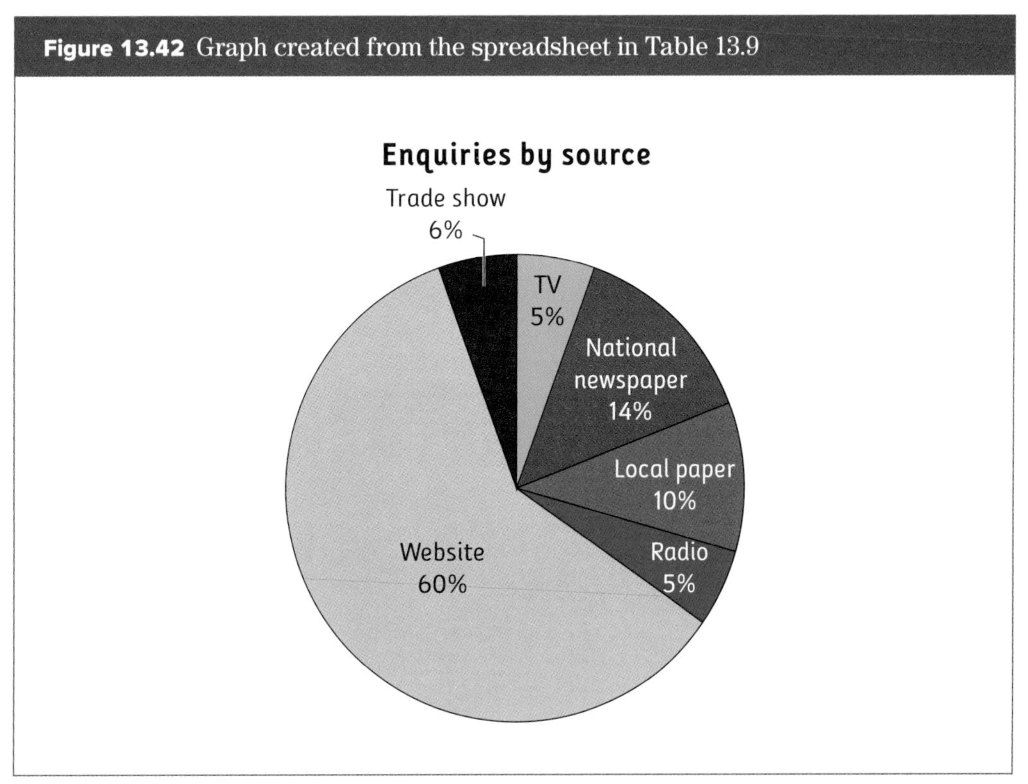

Try this now

4. Using the information you have already produced, or using a new spreadsheet, try some of these tools for yourself.

Knowledge check

16. Give an overview of how a chart can be used to enhance a spreadsheet.
17. Describe what a pie chart is best used for.
18. Describe how a bar or line chart is best used.
19. There are a number of options for formatting and modifying a chart to make it more easily understood. List three of these.

13.5 Finalising and presenting spreadsheets

As with all important documents, a final check should be made of all data and formatting requirements. Important decisions may be made based on information you provide, so it is important to check it for accuracy.

13.5.1 Reviewing and editing final spreadsheet and accompanying charts

Before the spreadsheet can be finalised and distributed to stakeholders, it needs to be reviewed to ensure it is accurate and relevant to organisational needs. A review can show areas that may need improving, sections that aren't functioning as they should, or results that don't address the issue as they are meant to.

Check the following:

- Is the spreadsheet design fit for its purpose? Is it fit for its intended audience?
- Do the formulas all work and show correct information?
- Does the spreadsheet fulfil its intended purpose?
- Will it provide the information sought?
- Have you included all the necessary data?
- Does it conform with organisational style guides?
- Is it easy to read and understand?
- Are there any spelling mistakes?

These questions, among others, will need to be asked and answered before you can distribute the spreadsheet and its results to other stakeholders. You will also need to check any charts you are including in your report. For example:

- Have you used the right kind of chart?
- Does it represent the purpose of the spreadsheet accurately?
- Does it show, at a glance, the main points for which the spreadsheet was designed?
- Is it consistent in features and style of presentation with organisational guidelines?

13.5.2 Delivering the document to required stakeholders

Once completed, the spreadsheet needs to be presented to the relevant stakeholders. They may include:

- *External stakeholders*, such as:
  - suppliers, who may need information on what inventory of theirs you have in stock
  - government authorities, who may need information on a range of different aspects of the organisation's business dealings, for legal or audit purposes

  - industry bodies and associations, which may have need of statistics relating to your specific industry, which information may then be used to help change industry conditions, gain government benefits and so on.
- *Internal stakeholders.* Managers, supervisors and other internal staff will have need of the information provided by spreadsheets for a variety of reasons as outlined in section 13.3.3.

You may also need to consider the method of delivery. Depending on the type of information the spreadsheet contains, how confidential it is, and the forum in which it will be presented, methods of delivery can include:

- an email to those people who are entitled to see the information
- a presentation to a group during a meeting or at a conference
- a written report for wider circulation
- online—depending on the confidentiality of the information, it might be made freely available on the company website for anyone to see, or it may be available only on the company intranet for use by internal employees.

Organisational policies and procedures

A final check must also be made to ensure that the information presented is in line not only with the organisation's policies and procedures, but also with any legislative requirements that, if breached, could cause legal or ethical problems. Therefore, when delivering your spreadsheet, you may also need to consider the following:

- *Access and equity.* Ensure that the spreadsheet is presented in such a way that stakeholders from various backgrounds can access it easily and understand the material.
- *Anti-discrimination legislation.* Ensure that information in a presentation isn't in breach of anti-discrimination laws. In Australia, it is against the law to discriminate against people because of their:
  - race
  - religious beliefs
  - gender
  - family status
  - cultural background.

  You must ensure that materials you produce are in no way offensive to others and have no racial or bias overtones.
- *Version control.* This is an important consideration. It is unlikely that any document created by an organisation will always stay the same. Changes happen, and for a variety of reasons. This may mean that forms, templates and other documents produced by an organisation will also need to change. This can become a problem when several versions of a document are stored within the organisation's files and staff use whatever version they locate first. This can lead to necessary information not being included in a form, or to outdated information being used. For this reason, version control should be used to ensure that only the latest, updated, version of a document is being used by ALL staff. An organisation will determine its own preferred version control method, which may be a complicated series of letters and/or numbers or a simple method using a version number and the date the document was updated—for example: V01/18MAR23.

Name and store spreadsheet

Storing the work you have completed is an important step. You must be able to work with and retrieve the spreadsheet easily and quickly. Every organisation will have its own specific policies and procedures for storing information. In general, however, a number of things should be observed:

- Follow naming protocols set by the organisation. These can vary greatly between companies, but may be based on the subject matter, name of the project, geographic location or the date of creation.

- Close down the spreadsheet (and any other work you have open) when you have finished working on it to:
  - maintain confidentiality, privacy and security
  - avoid unauthorised staff seeing the work
  - avoid loss of information should the system fail.
- Save the document you are working on regularly, to ensure that you don't lose any information should the system suddenly go down.
- Store the document in line with the organisation's policies and procedures. These may relate to:
  - access
  - filing locations
  - backing up of files
  - filing of hard copies
  - file security
  - file storage methods (e.g. folders or sub-folders, physical disks, portable drives (e.g. USBs, external hard drives) on the company server or in a cloud-based storage area).

A significant amount of work may go into the creation of a spreadsheet, so the correct storage of these materials is essential.

Knowledge check

20. Describe the things you should review in both the spreadsheet and chart before finalising and distributing them.
21. Describe what methods you could use to distribute the spreadsheet to relevant stakeholders.
22. There are a number of organisational policies and procedures to observe when finalising your spreadsheet. Describe three of these.
23. List at least three things that you need to consider when naming and storing your spreadsheet.

Summary

Most organisations will have enormous amounts of information that needs to be sorted and analysed. Conclusions must then be drawn from this information, and far-reaching decisions may be made on the basis of it. Without the use of spreadsheets, this would be a difficult and complex task. There are therefore significant advantages to using spreadsheets. For example, they improve the way in which the organisation handles its data and make it easier to collaborate on its collection and review. They enable dynamic calculations through the use of built-in formulas and preset functions. Spreadsheets also provide the option for including graphs and visual aids, making complex information easier to understand. In short, spreadsheets help to turn long, complex lists of numbers into understandable stories about what is happening within your organisation.

CHAPTER 14

Create electronic presentations

Learning outcomes

14.1 Prepare to create a presentation

14.2 Create a presentation

14.3 Finalise a presentation

Communicating with a group of people can be complex and can take place in a variety of ways. The more important the message, the clearer you want the communication to be; and the larger the audience, the easier the message must be to understand. You also need to consider the diversity of your audience: what is the most effective way of presenting the message so that everyone is engaged? Sometimes an **electronic presentation** is the best choice for communicating information to groups of people, for the following reasons:

- It can provide a visual explanation of what you are trying to say.
- It can be used to reinforce important information.
- It can link complex ideas and themes.
- It can summarise information.
- You can make changes right up to the last minute.
- Slide transitions and animations provide more control over pacing.
- Text and graphic animations capture the audience's attention and help to illustrate your points.
- You can use multimedia effects such as sound and video to best advantage.

As the saying goes, "A picture is worth a thousand words". This is certainly true of an electronic presentation, where you can provide information in both visual and audio formats, making your message clear to even the most diverse audience.

14.1 Preparing to create a presentation

A well-prepared presentation can have a significant impact on an audience and influence the way they think about the topic in question. You may be hoping your audience will buy a product you are presenting, or be enabled to make important decisions based on your information, or will learn new work skills and procedures. It is important, therefore, to get the groundwork right for any presentation you are preparing.

14.1.1 The right work environment

Before beginning work on your presentation, it is essential to ensure that your workspace is properly set up. We looked briefly at this topic in the introduction to this text. To recap: a well set-up work area allows easy access to the resources and equipment that you need in the course of your normal working day. Whenever possible, place your computer monitor and keyboard directly in front of you, rather than off to one side. This set-up avoids your needing to twist in your seat, which could injure your spine over time. You should also ensure that your work area is well lit and ventilated and there is no excessive noise. In the workplace set-up, ensure that items such as in/out trays, paper, letterheads, envelopes, pens and files are within easy reach, making the area an efficient and productive place to work.

peart.ru/Shutterstock

It is a good idea, at this point, to review the information in the Introduction as you will need it to answer the knowledge questions at the end of this section.

14.1.2 Purpose, audience and mode of presentation

There may be any number of reasons why a presentation is needed, just as there will be a variety of appropriate presentation modes, so you should never simply use a "cookie-cutter" version of the last one you did. Why and how you present your material will depend on the audience it is aimed at, as well as on the facilities and venue available.

Audience and purpose

Who you are presenting to will determine how formal the presentation should be, how much detail you will need to include and the level of confidentiality that may apply to the information you are presenting. For example, a presentation may be designed for the following purposes:

- *Discussing business planning with the board of directors of a large firm.* This type of presentation will probably be aimed at a relatively serious-minded group of people and refer to relatively serious subjects. It would therefore be straightforward and to the point, with clearly presented facts and figures, and will involve a high degree of confidentiality.
- *Teaching the alphabet to a group of children.* This type of presentation should be fun, in order to capture (and retain) the audience's attention. It should be colourful and include lots of pictures and movement.
- *Presenting a new household product to a group of potential customers.* Such a presentation will need to show the advantages of the product for the customer. Therefore, you would need to demonstrate the product being used in a normal household environment, showing how easy it is to use, clean and store. In addition to the actual demonstration, you might include testimonials from people who have used it.
- *Delivering a training session to staff.* Here you will need to incorporate both serious issues (the subject they need to learn about) and fun or engaging activities and demonstrations to encourage them to apply this new knowledge in their work.

Therefore, before you begin to plan a presentation, you must first be very clear about *why* the information needs to be presented and *who* it is being presented to.

Mode of presentation

Once you are clear about the presentation's purpose and audience, you will need to consider *how* you are going to present it. For example:

- *Local presentation*—where content is saved on a computer or shared network for individuals to access at a convenient time.
- *Online presentation*—where content is made available to the intended audience via the internet or internal organisational intranet.
- *Conference presentation*—where a speaker, on stage, presents their subject to the conference audience.
- *Self-running (automated) presentation*—often used at trade fairs, where a monitor and laptop are set up to showcase the company's products and services on a continuous loop until it is switched off.

Think about

1. Think about a presentation you would like to make. It can be work-related or personal. Who is your audience? What method of presentation will you use? Why would you choose this method?

14.1.3 Identifying organisational and task requirements

In creating a presentation, you will be placing your organisation in full view of an audience—whether internal, or out in the wider community. How the presentation is designed, and the information it includes, will therefore have an impact on your organisation's reputation and standing in the business and wider community and so must be created with the requirements both of your organisation and the task in mind.

Organisational requirements might relate to:

- Adhering to your organisation's house style and company image (as discussed in Chapter 11).
- Meeting inclusivity needs, such as:
    - language considerations
    - adjusting the presentation for audience members who may have visual or hearing impairments.
- Meeting legal and legislative requirements, such as:
    - industry codes and regulations (when presenting information about issues specific to your industry)
    - work health and safety (WHS) issues.

Task requirements might include:

- Understanding the objective of the presentation and ensuring this is adequately covered.
- Sequencing the information so that it flows logically and can be easily understood.
- When including activities for audience members to participate in, providing:
    - break-out spaces for them to undertake these activities
    - worksheets that provide information on what they need to do
    - assessments, if applicable, to test the audience's retention of the material.
- Keeping the audience engaged by:
    - scheduling exercise breaks into conference or meeting agendas to ensure the audience is fully alert during presentations

  - providing a mix of repetitive and other activities—again, to keep the audience engaged and alert
  - providing rest periods so that participants have time to absorb new information, discuss implications of the information with colleagues, and just simply rest their brains.
- Reviewing the presentation to determine if it achieved its purpose.

Additional considerations

You will also need to consider the resources that will be required. For example:

- *Venue.* Where will the presentation be held?
  - Is there enough seating for the expected audience?
  - How will the seating be arranged? You will need to ensure that all audience members can see the presentation clearly.
  - Have access issues been considered so that all audience members can participate equally?
- *Computer equipment and peripherals for on-screen presentation.* You will generally need:
  - a computer (or laptop) to run your presentation
  - a data projector to project the images from your computer or laptop onto a screen (or white wall).
- *Equipment.* For example:
  - digital pointer
  - annotation pen—a device that can help you highlight certain areas of a slide during a PowerPoint presentation.
- *Hard copies of documents.* For example:
  - handouts
  - speaker notes (including copies of important slide slow images).
- *Internet and network access.*

14.1.4 Selecting the required application to produce the presentation

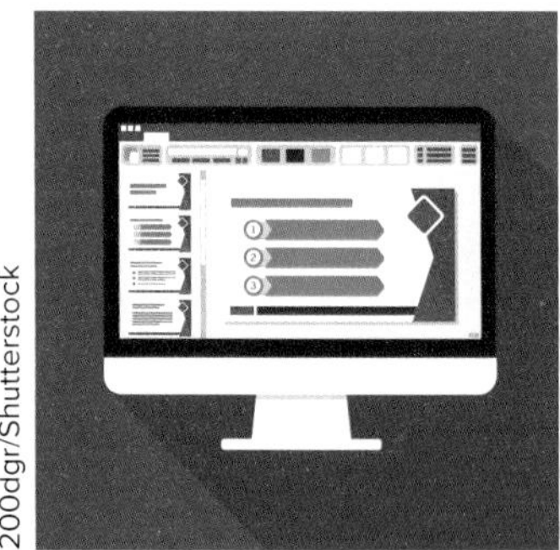
200dgr/Shutterstock

The most commonly used presentation software is PowerPoint, which comes as part of the Microsoft Office suite. We will focus mainly on this software in this chapter. Other presentation software include:

- Prezi: https://prezi.com
- Google Slides: https://www.google.com.au/slides/about.

Both of these are similar to Microsoft PowerPoint, and each has advantages and disadvantages. Google Slides, for example, has the advantage of integrating seamlessly with other Google applications online, while PowerPoint gives you the ability to embed audio files and draw your own animations.

Using Canva to create content

While not an actual presentation program in itself, Canva offers professional content creation tools. Once the content is designed, it can then be exported to PowerPoint format. Canva offers more than 50,000 templates and hundreds of thousands of stock photos, videos and graphics from which to choose.

Canva also allows you to:

- manipulate templates to suit your specific needs
- upload your own photos as well as choose from a vast library of stock photos

- edit and enhance images by:
  - cropping and straightening
  - adding textures
  - adding text and creating memes
  - adding frames
- create and edit short videos
- collaborate with up to 10 other people (in the office or working remotely) in creating content.

Figure 14.1 shows a few of the options available.

Figure 14.1 Canva account home page

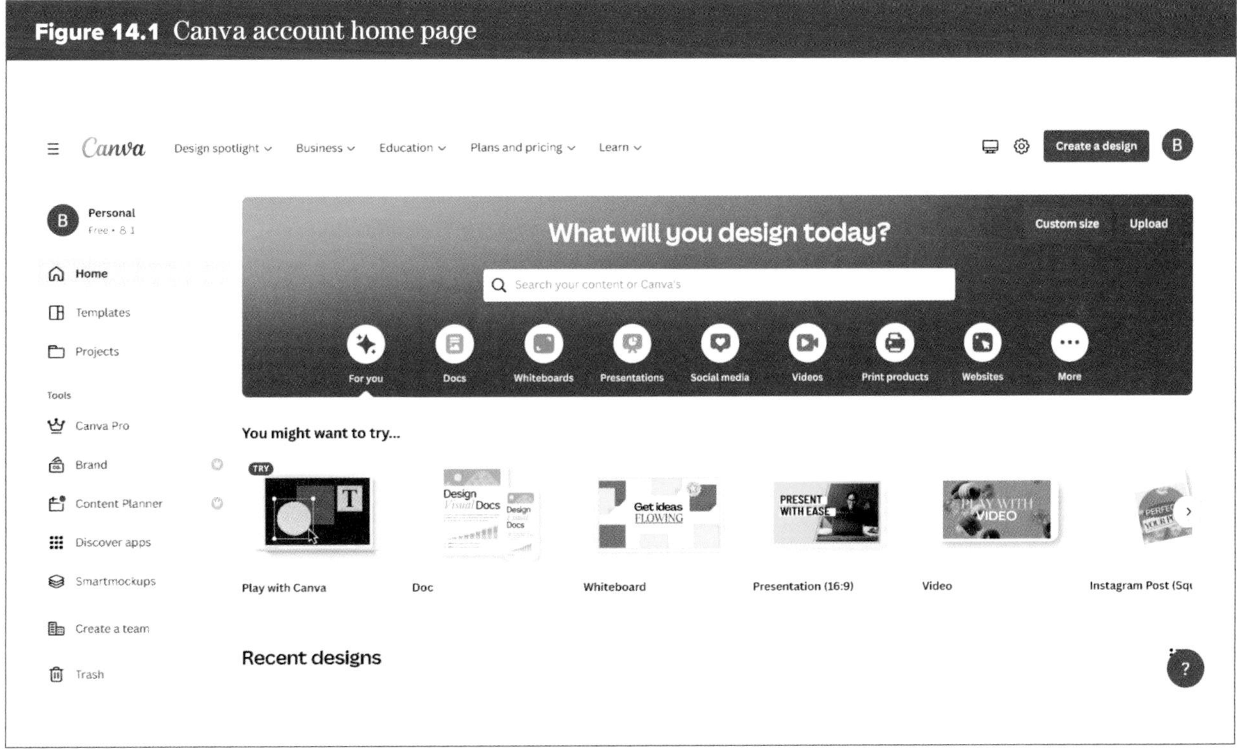

Source: Canva, https://www.canva.com/en_au

Once you are satisfied with the design of your content, you can export it as a PPTX file and import it into PowerPoint as follows:

1. Log into your Canva account and select the design you want to export.
2. Click the *Download* button in the top-right corner of the design.
3. In the drop-down menu, select *PowerPoint*.
4. Your design will download as a PowerPoint file. You should now be able to open the file in PowerPoint and present your designs.

Try this now

1. Go to Prezi, Google Slides and Canva and explore their various options.

For the remainder of this chapter, our examples will be focused on Microsoft PowerPoint.

Knowledge check

1. Before beginning work, ensure that your workplace is properly set up. Explain what this might entail.
2. Name at least three reasons why you might need to create a presentation.
3. Describe at least four modes in which a presentation might take place.
4. When delivering a presentation, there are a range of resources you may need access to. Name at least four of these and give examples of what they might include.

14.2 Creating a presentation

Creating the presentation means looking at the information you need to include, how you will best present it, and what graphs, photos or other items you will need to include. You will then need to sort this information into a logical sequence and develop a design that best suits the presentation's purpose and audience.

14.2.1 Planning and preparing the presentation to organisational requirements

The main purpose of an electronic presentation will *always* be to get a specific message across. In the planning phase, you should therefore ask questions such as:

- Does it send the right message?
- Is it aimed at the right audience?
- Will this information influence the audience in a positive way?
- Do we need to include information about:
  - organisational policies and procedures?
  - legal obligations?
- Will we need to consider the correct use of the organisation's style guide and keep its image in mind in relation to:
  - colour schemes?
  - logo?
  - audio visual materials used?

Answers to these questions, among others, will give you the foundations upon which to base your presentation.

In planning and preparing the design of your presentation, it is also important not to clutter the message with too many distractions. For example:

- Heavy use of colour can overwhelm the text or graphics.
- Insufficient colour separation (background to text), such as a grey background with a darker grey text, can make slides difficult to understand.
- Irrelevant animation or photos may serve no real purpose other than to distract.
- Multiple transition or animations can be distracting. It is possible to animate each slide—for example, on a slide with five bullet points you can set it up so that each bullet point line appears on the slide separately as or before the speaker discusses that point. However, too many of these on a slide may lose the interest of the audience by taking a considerable amount of time to present in this manner.

- Overly busy backgrounds can also be a distraction.
- Overuse of sounds such as transition noises can be off-putting and may get in the way of the speaker's presentation.
- Too many words or pictures per slide, as well as fonts that are too small, can make the information difficult to read.

14.2.2 Using application tools to ensure consistency

As we have previously discussed, many organisations have specific requirements relating to materials they produce, and this applies to presentations just as much as it does to letters or other printed materials. A presentation is a window into the organisation and its vision, so it must be designed and prepared in line with the organisation's reputation, image and preferred style.

Most presentation applications will have functions that can be used to ensure a consistent and professional look across the entire presentation. Before we move on to specific software functions, however, we will take a brief look at the tabs of PowerPoint's Ribbon (Figure 14.2).

Figure 14.2 PowerPoint Ribbon

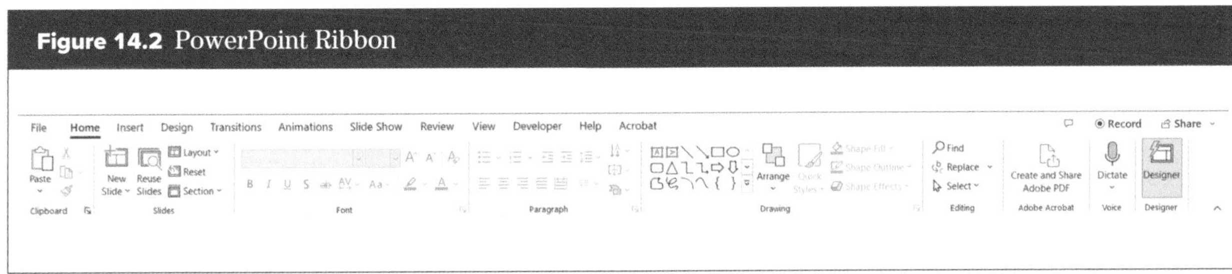

The Ribbon includes the following tabs:

- *File.* This tab allows you to open, save and print your presentations.
- *Home.* This tab contains the following sections (or control groups):
    - *Clipboard*—allows you to cut, paste and copy items.
    - *Slide*—allows you to add or delete slides, choose the appropriate layout for the slide, and reset any changes you made to the "default" or original settings.
    - *Font*—allows you choose the font, style and size, and how it should be displayed.
    - *Paragraph*—allows you to insert bullets or numbered lists, set the alignment of the text and so on.
    - *Drawing*—allows you to insert different shapes, lines and effects, as well as to work with colours.
    - *Editing*—allows you to find and/or replace information within the presentation without having to go looking for it.
- *Insert.* This tab enables you to insert tables, pictures, clip art, screenshots, shapes, charts, headers, footers, dates, times and videos.
- *Design.* This tab lets you choose from a variety of themes for your presentation. You can use the pre-set themes or make up ones of your own by changing colours, fonts and effects to suit your needs.
- *Transitions.* These dictate how slides change from one to the next. They can simply change without any effects, or you can set a special animation effect to happen when changing to the next slide (*Fade*, *Wipe* and *Dissolve* are only a few of the options). In this tab, you will also be able to select *Timing* settings:
    - sounds for the presentation
    - how long each slide will be shown for (in an automated slideshow)

- whether slides should change automatically or will be controlled by the presenter (by mouse click).

- *Animations.* This tab enables you to choose how text appears on the slide. You can set how the text will "enter" the slide, how it should behave on the slide, and how it should "exit" it.
- *Slide show.* This tab allows you to rehearse the slide show as a final presentation, including:
  - setting the slide show on a continuous loop (if necessary for a trade show or similar)
  - determining if an electronic pen or laser pointer can be used and what colours they should be
  - options for rehearsing the timing of the presentation
- *Review.* This tab provides options for spelling and grammar checks, inserting comments and other editing functions.

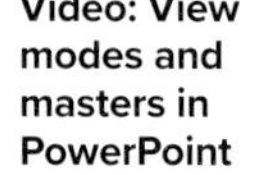
Video: View modes and masters in PowerPoint

- *View.* This tab provides options for how you view your slides while you work (Figure 14.3).
  - *Normal*—the editing mode most frequently used to create and edit individual slides.
  - *Slide sorter*—lays out all slides in your presentation as a sequence of thumbnails and allows you to rearrange the order of slides.
  - *Notes page*—shows each slide individually and provides a space for speaker notes to be included.

Figure 14.3 PowerPoint *View* tab

Try this now

2. Spend some time looking at the menu sections of PowerPoint, Canva and Google Slides. Open a new presentation and try out the various options each of them provides.

Using application tools to customise the presentation

Presentations are created to fulfil specific purposes, but that doesn't mean they all have to look the same. There are a range of features and tools that allow you to customise the look of your presentation, ensuring not only that it fulfils its purpose but also engages the audience and presents the organisation in the best possible light.

Some of these tools may include:

- *Backgrounds.* You can choose from a range of backgrounds, such as:
  - solid colours
  - graded backgrounds (where the colour fades in a manner selected by you)
  - patterned backgrounds
  - photo backgrounds.
- *Colour schemes.* These can be chosen according to pre-set themes, or you can create your own.
- *Importing images and graphics.*
- *Master Views.* These allow you to gain an overview of your presentation, rather than sorting through slides one by one.

- *Slide Master.* Slide masters are templates that control universal design aspects of a presentation, including the background, colour, fonts, effects, placeholder sizes and positioning (see Figure 14.4). They can be customised for every presentation. The key benefit of modifying and using slide masters is that you can make universal style changes to every slide in your presentation, including ones added later to the presentation, which saves time because you don't have to type the same information on more than one slide. Because of this, slide masters come in especially handy when you have extremely long presentations with lots of slides. You create and edit a slide master or corresponding layouts in the *Slide Master* view, which is separate from the working slides. You can move between slides more easily by simply clicking on the "thumbnail" of the slide you wish to work with and change the order of the slides by dragging the thumbnail of the slide you want to move into a new position. **Thumbnails** are small versions of a slide and are shown in list format down the left-hand side of the screen.
- *Handout Master.* If handouts are to be given to audience members, the handout master can be used to determine how these handouts will look, how many slides will appear per handout page (up to nine), how they will be oriented on the page, and so on.
- *Notes Master.* This is primarily used for versions of the presentation that the presenter prints out for their own use. The presenter can add notes to the bottom of each slide that won't show on the presentation screen, which they can use to help guide them through their presentation to ensure they have covered all the key points.

Figure 14.4 The *Slide Master* view

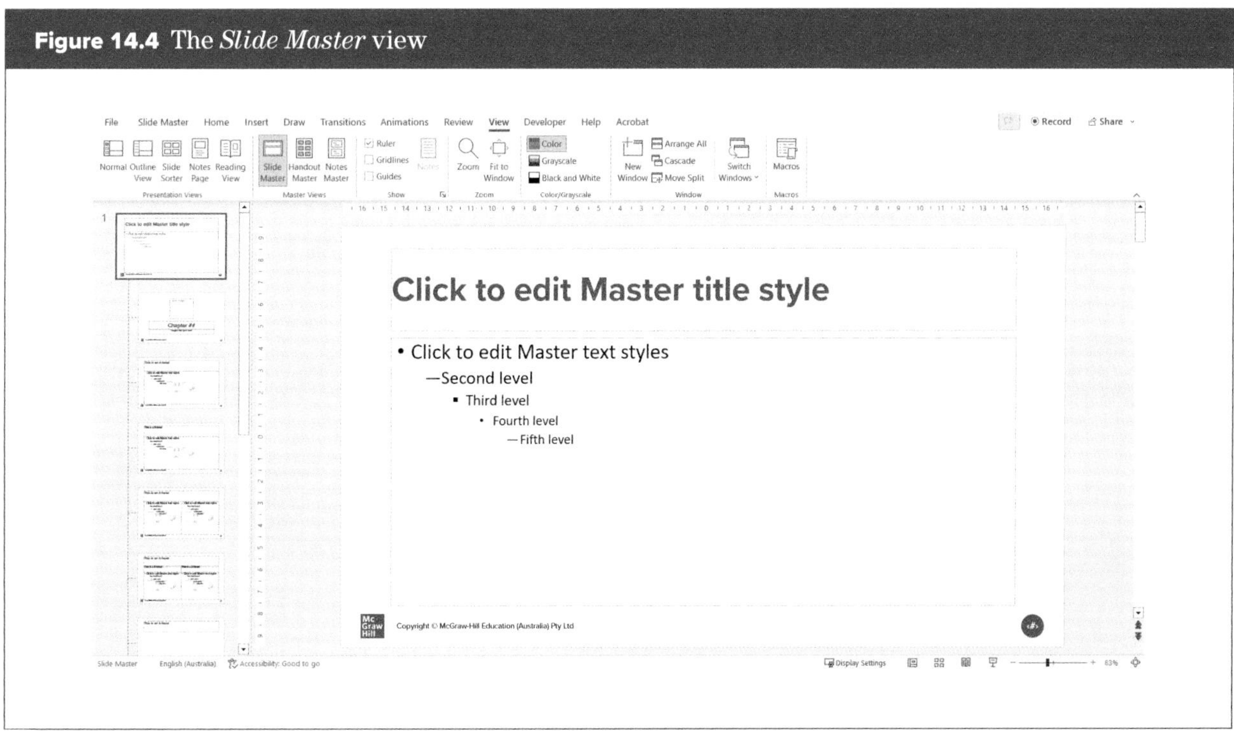

Choosing a template or theme

When you first open PowerPoint (or any other presentation application), you will be shown a range of template/theme options (as seen in Figure 14.5). A **theme** determines the look and colours of the slides, including the slide background, bullet and font styles, font colour and size, placeholder positions and various other design accents.

You can apply or change a theme at any stage of creating the presentation. If you decide later that you would rather use a different theme, you can apply a different one from the *Themes* group in the *Design* tab.

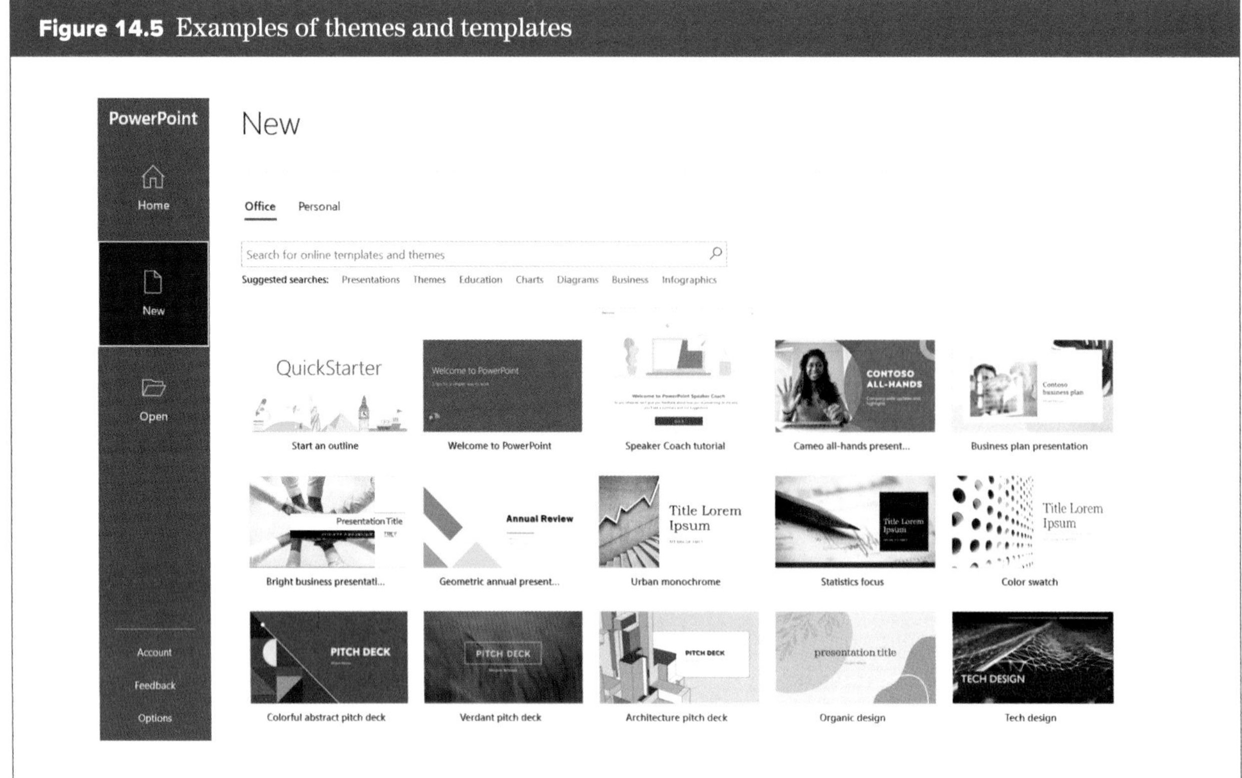

Figure 14.5 Examples of themes and templates

Having chosen your template and/or theme, you will have a large work space in the middle of the screen, with a panel on the left that contains your thumbnails. That middle space is the **slide window** (Figure 14.6). Alternatively, you can work on and export a presentation from programs such as Canva and import the file into your PowerPoint presentation.

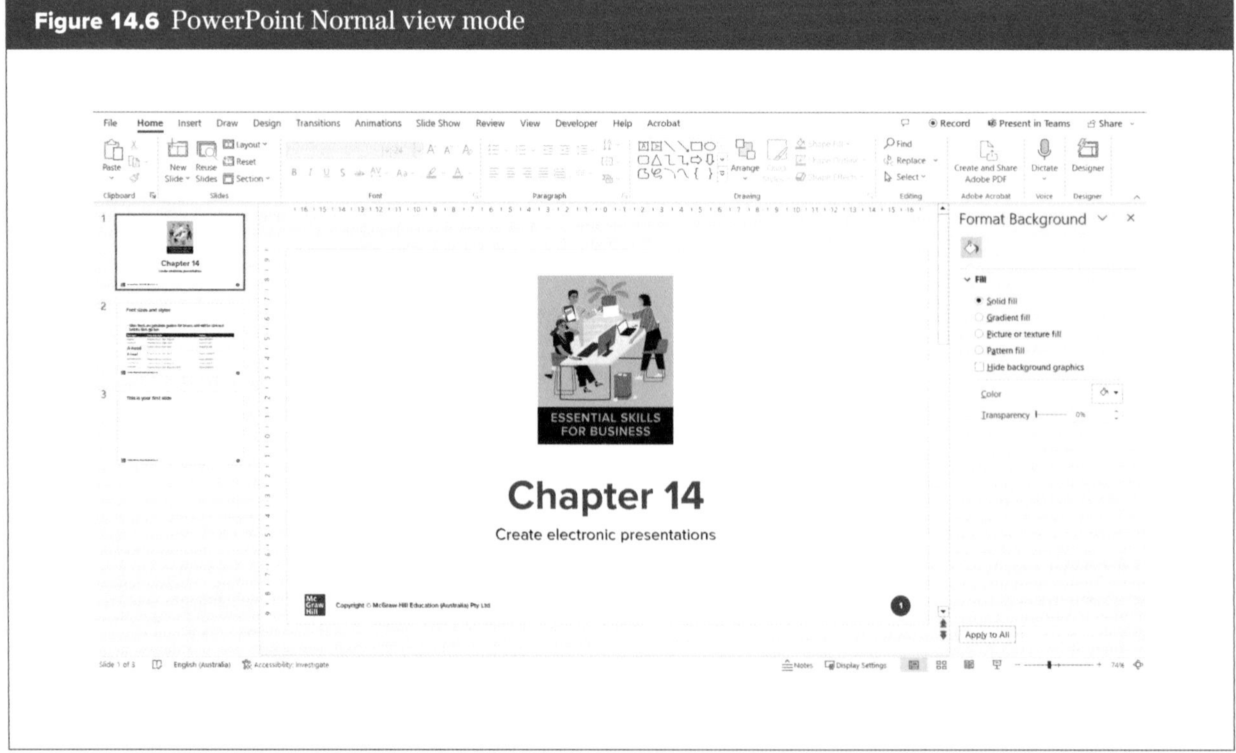

Figure 14.6 PowerPoint Normal view mode

Think about

2. Imagine you had to create a presentation for the following two groups. What type of template and theme would you choose?
   - Teaching a group of six-year-olds the "ABC" song.
   - Presenting an idea for improving a work process to your team at a staff meeting.

Adding text

Working Normal view, you will see a box with a dashed border called a **placeholder**. These mark out where different objects such as textboxes and images will sit on the slide. Most slide layouts include one or more placeholders for titles, body text such as lists all text in PPT is default formatted as lists unless you delete the bullets, and other content such as pictures, graphics or tables.

To add text, click on the placeholder text box where you want the text to show and start typing (see Figure 14.7). Remember not to make your slides too "busy"; too much text will turn your audience off, so keep to bullet points or short sentences.

PowerPoint also allows you to choose how text fits into a text box from the *Text Options* tab in the *Format Shape* pane, where you can choose to fit the text automatically to the shape, shrink the text to fit the shape or resize the shape to fit the text.

Figure 14.7 Adding text to a slide

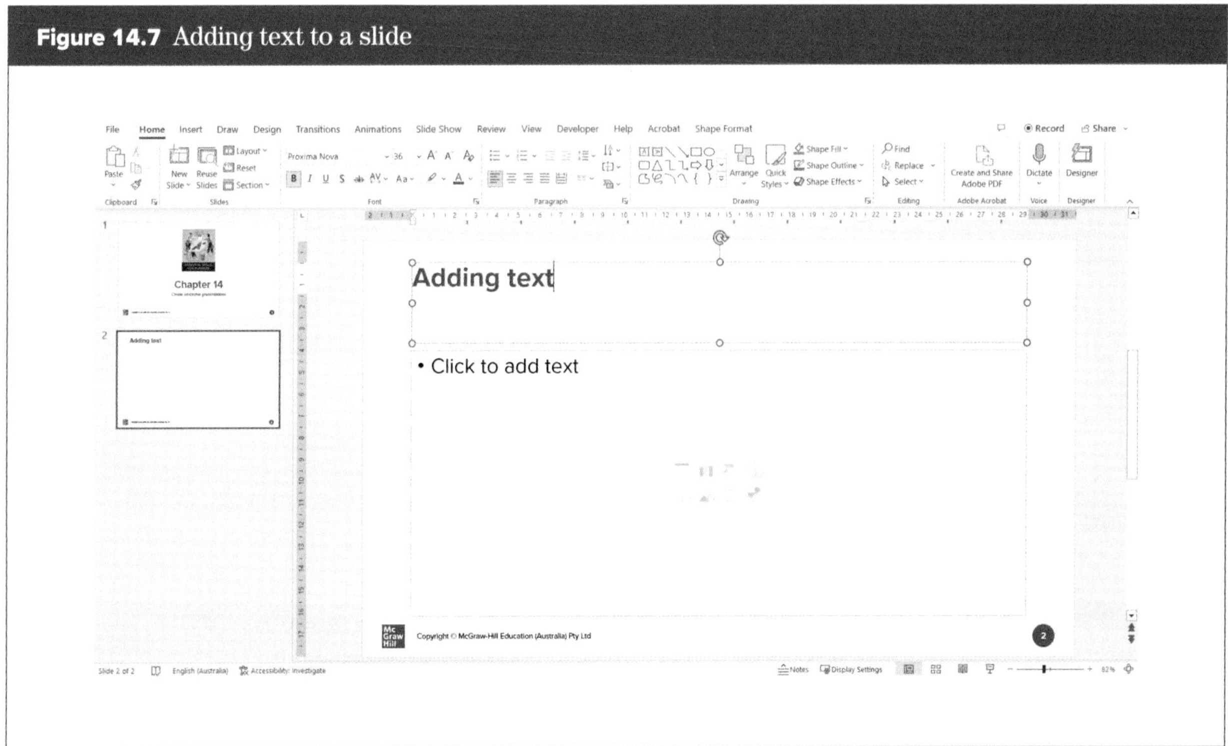

Applying a layout

Some slides may only require bullet point text on them, while others may need a combination of text, graphics and/or video. As you create slides, you will need to consider where to place the things you want on them. You can choose how these different components will look on the slide using slide layouts that provide a specific combination of placeholders arranged on the slide. For example, if you know you'll have text on the slide and you also want a picture or graphic of some kind, choose a layout that supplies the placeholder types and arrangement that you want.

You can select slide layouts from the *Layout* drop-down menu located in the *Slides* group on the *Home* tab. From here, you can then decide which option best suits your needs for that particular slide. Figure 14.8 shows some of the default layouts available in the *Slide Layout* tool.

Figure 14.8 Examples of default slide layouts

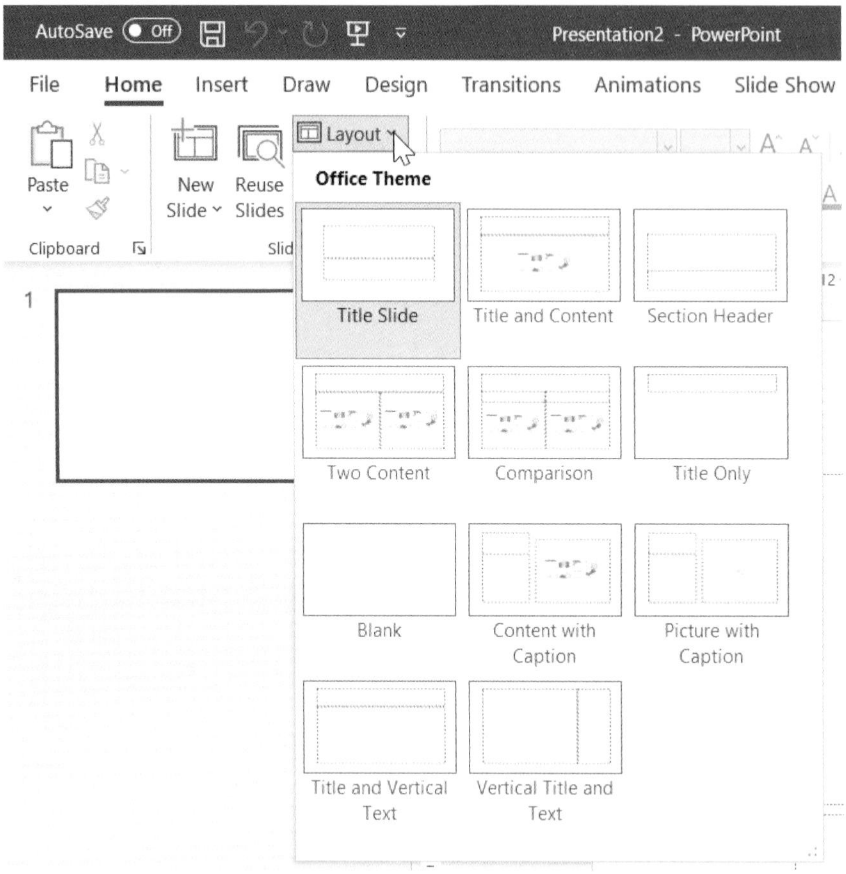

Inserting objects

To insert an object such as an image or chart, use the *Insert* tab. If you click on the placeholder where you want the object to appear first, it will then be placed in that area of the layout. Otherwise the object will be placed in the middle of the slide by default. Figure 14.9 shows options in the *Insert* tab.

Figure 14.9 Options in the *Insert* tab

Adding additional slides

When you first create a new PowerPoint presentation, there is only one slide in the deck. It is up to you to add the rest. Add them as you go, or several at a time, as you prefer. There are multiple ways to insert a new slide. The easiest method is to use the *Slides* group in the *Home* tab, as shown in Figure 14.10; you can choose from the list of slide layouts available in the presentation.

A new slide can be added:

- after each consecutive slide
- at any place within the presentation, by going to the thumbnail panel, clicking on the space between two existing slides where you want to insert a new one, and selecting the slide layout for the new slide from the *Slides* group. Clicking on *New Slide* without selecting a layout will create a slide using the default layout for the presentation.

Figure 14.10 Adding new slides to a presentation

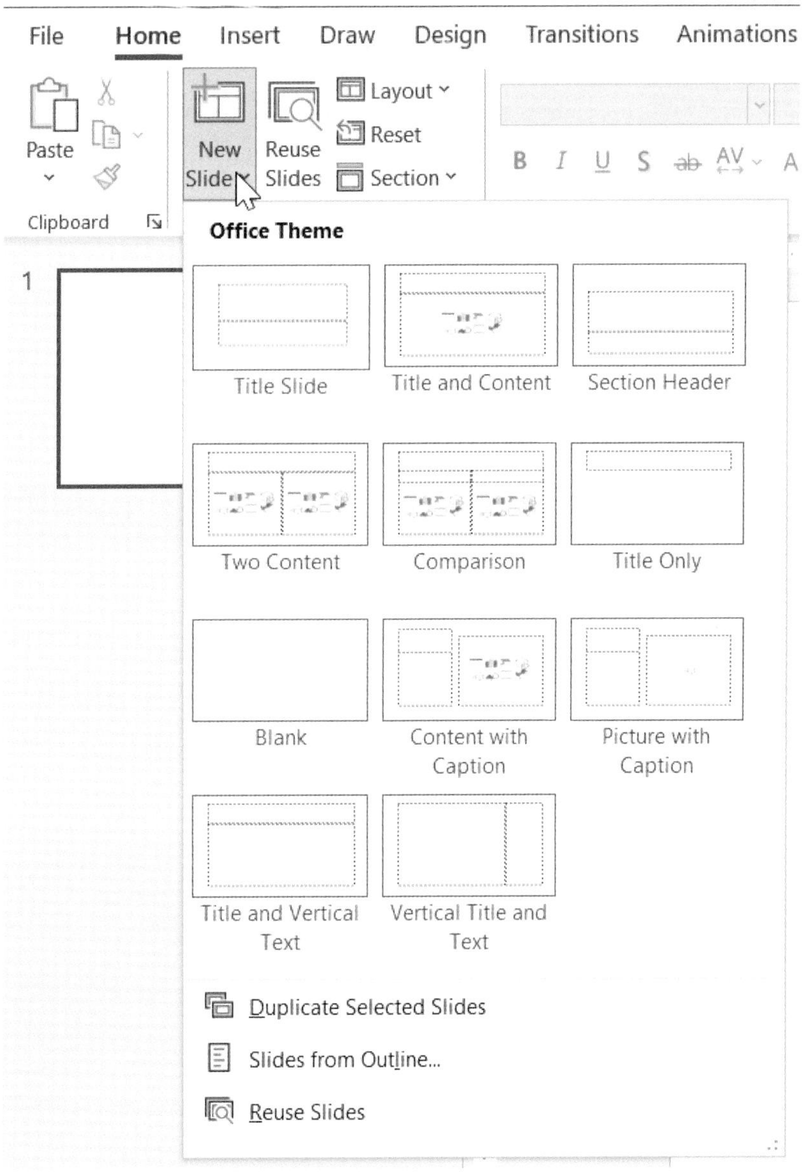

Try this now

3. Create a presentation based on your idea from a previous task. Add at least four pages to the presentation. Try some of the options discussed so far (e.g. change your layout and template).

Balancing presentation features for visual impact and emphasis

If your main purpose in developing an electronic presentation is to capture people's attention, you can really only do that if your presentation offers information that is of interest to them *and* has been designed for visual impact. You have to not only catch their attention, but also keep it. The following features can help you to achieve this:

- Animations and images.
- Charts, rather than lots of tables of data.
- Graphics such as photos, logos, video clips or illustrations.
- Headlines or titles that highlight the text.
- Music or sound—this should be used with care, as if it is too loud or inappropriate it could drown out or distract from the speaker. If, on the other hand, the presentation was meant to be shown without dialogue (e.g. as a continuous loop showing products and services at a trade fair), then well-chosen music could greatly enhance the presentation.
- Pacing and timing—an audience is likely to be turned off if too much time is spent on any one subject. The pace of the presentation is important. Each slide should not be too busy (offering too much information) and should have only enough information on it to prompt the speaker or capture the audience's attention before moving on to the next slide.
- Text content—keep the content of each slide simple and uncluttered to ensure that the audience's attention doesn't waver.
- Transitions—the way one slide transitions to the next can make the presentation more dynamic. Figure 14.11 shows some of the transition options available.

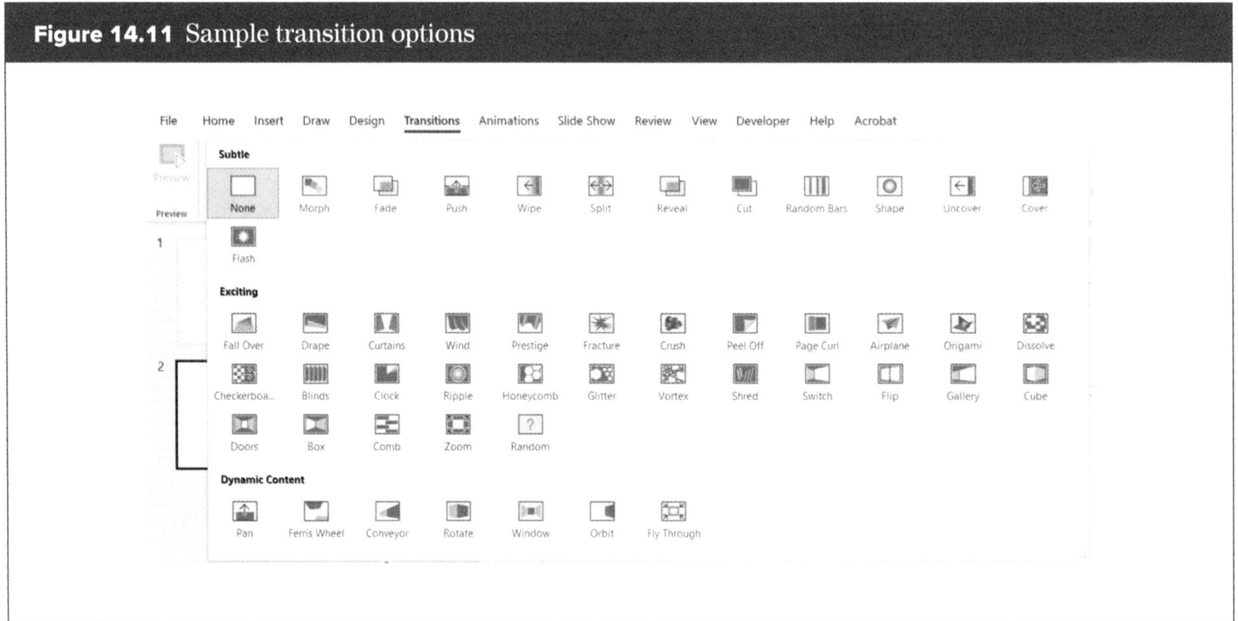

Figure 14.11 Sample transition options

Complex presentations

Video: Custom shows and agenda slides

Some presentations will be simple, requiring only one deck of slides to cover the topic. Others, however, may be very complex—for example, during a large conference or meeting with more than one presenter and more than one topic. You can combine an agenda slide with custom shows to make a complex presentation look more professional.

Agenda slides and custom shows

An **agenda slide** is a slide consisting of a simple list of topics that are linked to groups of slides (called "subsets"). These subsets are called **custom shows** and can be either part of the same presentation file (basic) or saved as a separate file (hyperlinked). When you click one of the hyperlinks on the agenda slide during a presentation, PowerPoint displays the linked custom show and then automatically returns to the agenda slide afterwards. Agenda slides and custom shows are useful for dividing your presentation into logical areas and for keeping your audience tuned in to where you are in the presentation.

The procedure for creating a hyperlinked custom show on an agenda slide (Figure 14.12) is as follows:

1. Highlight the item on the agenda that will link to the new presentation.
2. Right-click on the highlighted text and click *Link*.
3. Select from a list of recently opened files or click *Insert Link* at the bottom of the drop-down menu.
4. Find the folder or file that contains the required presentation.
5. Click on the required file and then OK. The item on your agenda slide will now be hyperlinked to that specific presentation.

Figure 14.12 Hyperlinking an agenda item to an external presentation file

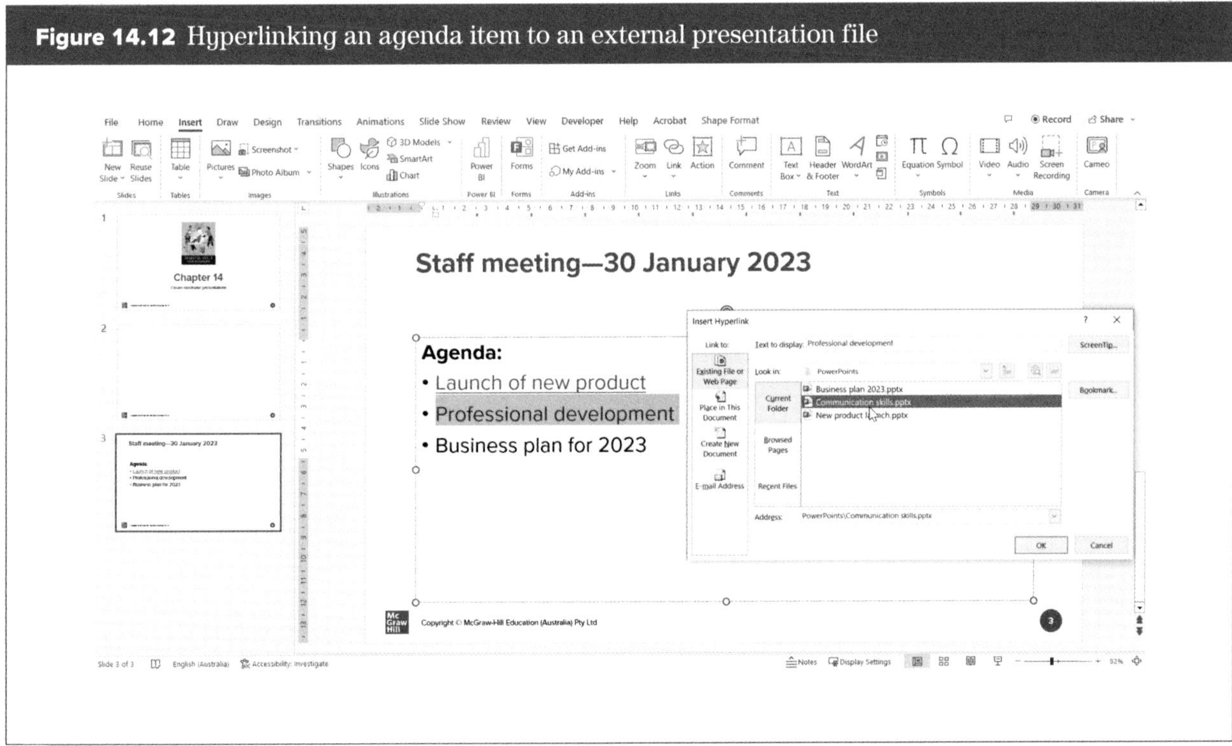

Inserting slides from another presentation

During a conference or seminar, you will often have a range of people each presenting a topic in turn. You can, of course, have each presenter close their presentation after they have finished, and have the next presenter open theirs. This, however, takes time and can lead to a range of issues.

Instead, you can set up basic custom shows within presentations by inserting each presenter's slideshow into the larger conference presentation in the order in which they will each speak.

Using this type of feature is helpful in keeping control of the conference; you don't run the risk or losing presentations as they are all linked together.

To set up this type of presentation:

1. Click the space between two slides in the thumbnail pane where you want to insert the new slides
2. Click *Reuse Slides* from the *Slides* group in the *Insert* tab (Figure 14.13).

3. Browse for the relevant PowerPoint file in the *Reuse Slides* panel on the right, or select from the list of recommended files.
4. Click *Choose Content.*
5. Select the slides you want to insert, or click *Insert All.*
6. The selected slides from the other presentation file should now be inserted into the specified location of the currently open presentation.

Figure 14.13 Inserting slides from an existing PowerPoint file

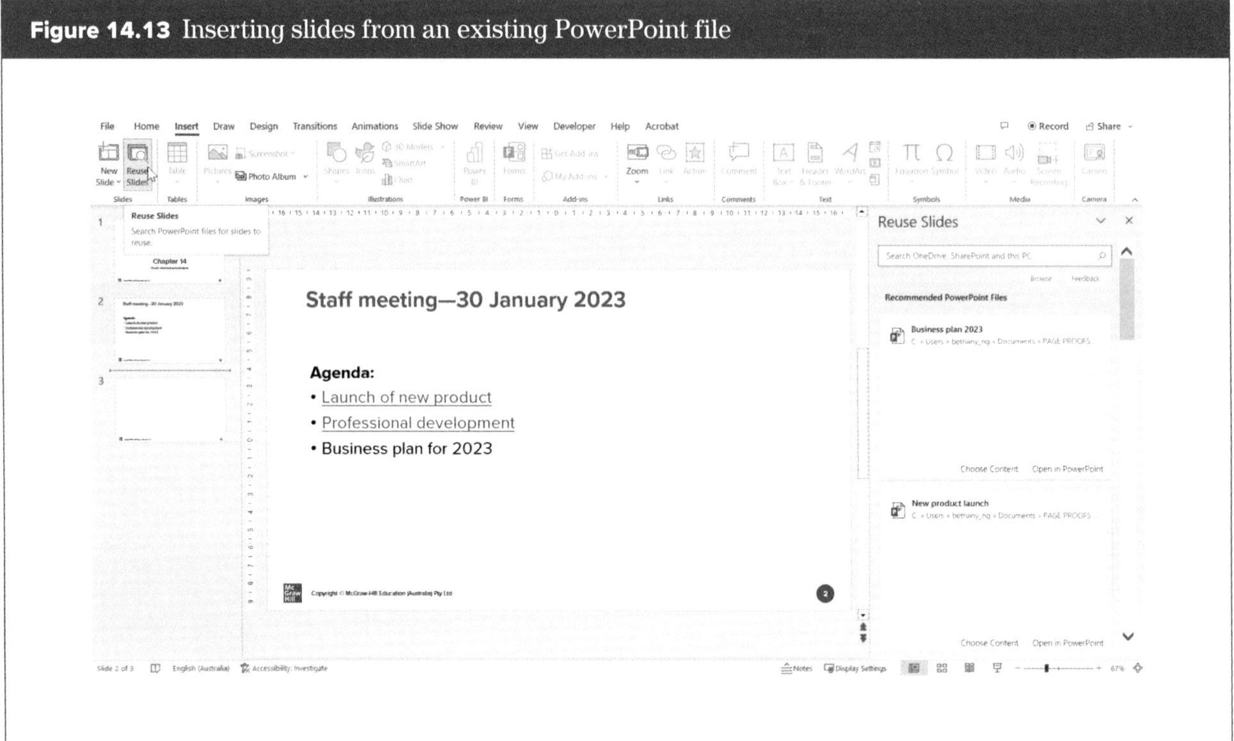

Preparing presentations within designated timelines

Time is a very important consideration in any work situation. This is also true for presentations, which are usually prepared for a very specific reason, purpose or event. This means that you will need to have to hand all the required information and resources needed to create the presentation within the designated timelines. These may include:

- organisational timeline (e.g. conference deadline requirements)
- timeline agreed with internal or external client
- timeline agreed with supervisor or person requiring the presentation.

Other people will be relying on you to complete your tasks on time. Any delay could cause significant problems, with deadlines missed and opportunities lost.

Your designated timelines will also refer to how long the actual presentation must last. This means that it is important to factor in the time required to present each slide, and to set up its transitions (Figure 14.14).

You can choose the type of transition you would like to create between each slide and the duration for each transition. Figure 14.14 shows that the transition between slides is set at two seconds. You can also decide how long each slide should be visible on the screen before it advances onto the next slide. There are two options to *Advance Slide:*

- *On mouse click.* This means that the slide will stay on the screen until you click your mouse or remote control.

Figure 14.14 Customising transitions and timing using the *Transitions* tab

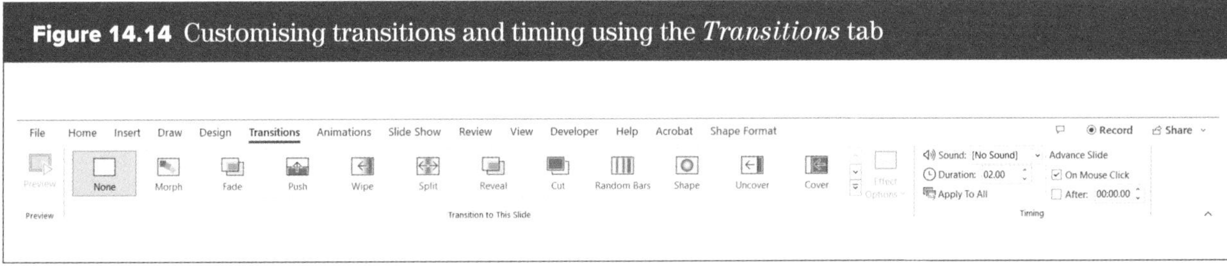

- *After*: This option is useful for automatic or self-running presentations that are not led by a presenter. You can choose how many seconds each slide remains on the screen.

Depending on the number of slides in a presentation, you may need to adjust the transitions, or the viewing time, in order to fit all the slides into the time frame allocated to the whole show.

Try this now

4. Using the presentation you created, allocate a total time frame for the entire show and apply transitions and timings accordingly.

14.2.3 Using *Help* tools to overcome issues relating to presentation creation

Things don't necessarily always go as planned when you are creating a presentation. You may have to overcome problems with the design of the slides, or the presentation may not be coming together quite as you would like it to. In these cases, there are some help options available to you. The quickest way to find help is to use the actual *Help* tool of the software program.

At the right-hand end of the PowerPoint Ribbon you will see the *Help* tab (Figure 14.15). By clicking on this option, you will be taken to *PowerPoint Help*, powered by Microsoft Support. Here you can type in the problem you are having, which will bring up a number of Microsoft Support articles relating to your problem. For example, if you were unsure of how to set up an agenda slide, you could type "set up an agenda slide" (Figure 14.16) into the search box and the help facility would provide you with some options.

This is probably the quickest way to find useful information. In some cases, however, you can perform a wider search of your computer, network and/or internet using the search bar at the top of the window.

Figure 14.15 Finding the *Help* menu

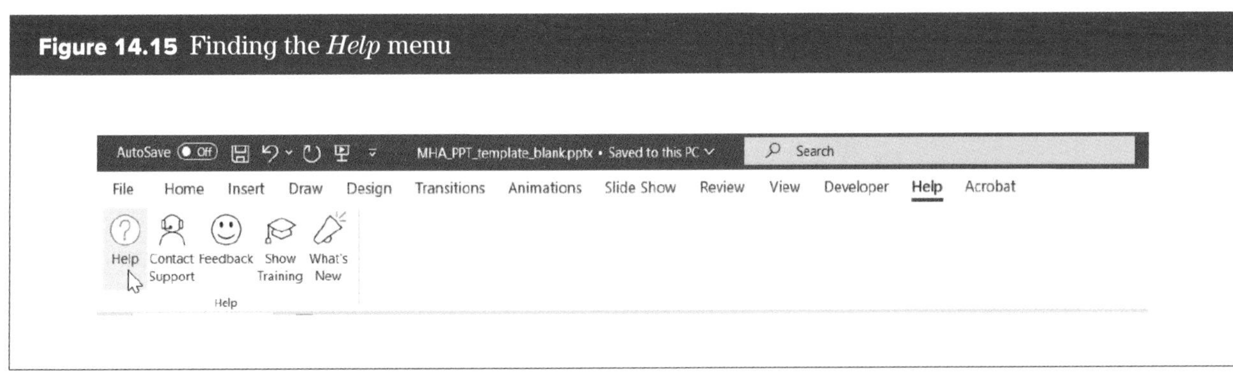

Figure 14.16 Searching *PowerPoint Help* for "set up an agenda slide"

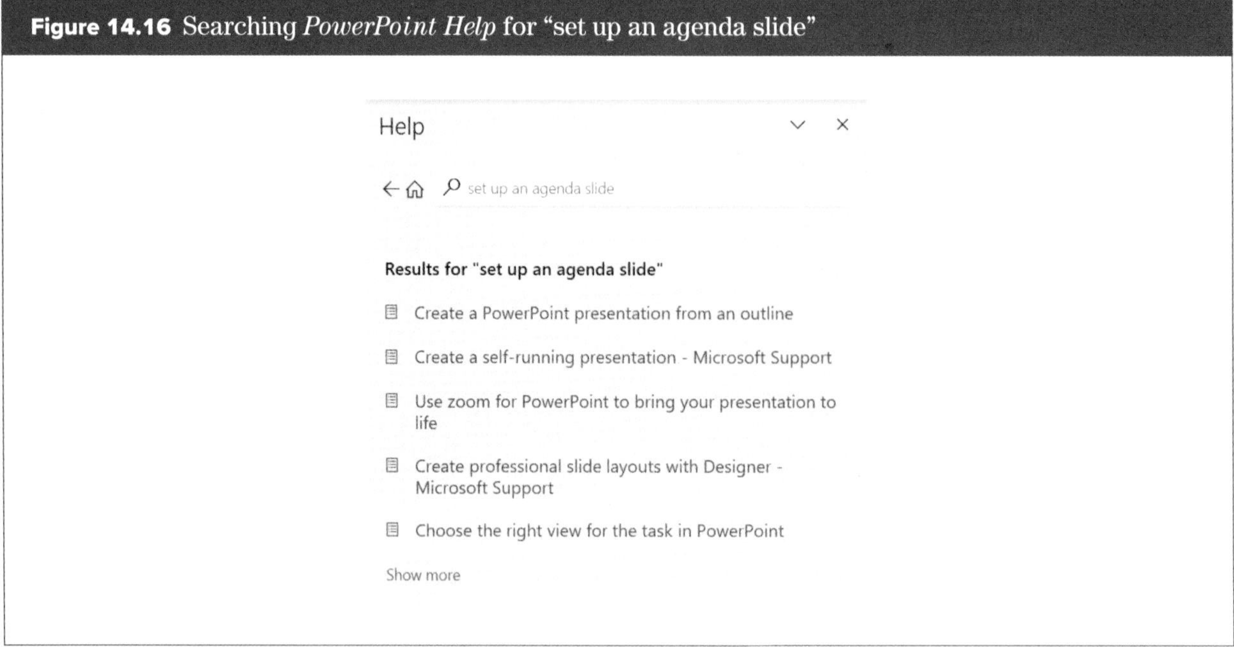

Knowledge check

5. Describe the benefits of using a content creation platform such as Canva.
6. Explain the purpose of the following tools on the PowerPoint menu:
   a. Insert
   b. Transitions
   c. Animations
7. Describe at least three application features that you can use to work with, and customise, your presentation.
8. Explain the purpose of the slide master.
9. Balancing your presentation for visual impact and emphasis is important. List at least four features that can help you to achieve this.
10. Explain the purpose of an agenda slide.
11. Describe the tools you would use to ensure that your presentation fits within the designated time frame.

14.3 Finalising a presentation

Your presentation may be viewed by a great many people. As your organisation's reputation can rest on the quality of the presentation you have created, it is important that you make a final check to ensure that everything is correct and in line with your organisation's requirements.

14.3.1 Checking your presentation

Before using your presentation in a public forum, check the following:

- Is the information you are presenting up to date and accurate?
- Are there any spelling mistakes? There is nothing worse than running a presentation in front of hundreds of guests only to have spelling mistakes show up on the screen. As discussed elsewhere, be careful when using the spellcheck facility of the software program, which will check for correct spelling but not for context. (In different contexts, different spellings are correct, such as: *here/hear, see/sea, there/their, to/too/two.*) Use the spellchecker, by all means, but also check the presentation yourself.

- Are there any grammatical errors?
- Is the presentation consistent in features and style? Ensure that each slide fits in, visually, with the next and that there are no inconsistencies in the way the material is presented.

Think about

3. Imagine you were presenting a business proposal to a group of senior managers in your organisation. Consider the impact it would have on your own reputation if your presentation included information that was incorrect or had many spelling errors.

14.3.2 Preparing the presentation materials for delivery

While an electronic presentation is meant to be viewed electronically, it may nevertheless be necessary to print out some materials. Whether this is necessary, and what needs to be printed, will depend on the presenter and/or audience requirements. For example:

- Will audience members need to take notes during the presentation?
- Does the presenter wish to give the audience copies of the slides for later reference?
- Will there be handouts (e.g. paper printouts of the slide show itself)? These may also be used to facilitate activities for break-out groups or quizzes.
- Do you need outlines of the presentation that will guide staff assisting in the presentation on what will have to happen and when?
- Are speaker notes required? Each slide shown will have bullet points (or short sentences or illustrations) of a given topic. The speaker, however, may need a great deal more information in order to cover the topic properly. To this end, they may have speaker's notes that provide them with all the necessary information on each slide. These need to be printed out in line with the speaker's requirements.

14.3.3 Saving the presentation

Saving the presentation is an important step. You must be able to work with and retrieve the presentation easily and quickly prior to the actual presentation. Organisations will have their own specific policies and procedures for storing information. In general, however, a number of things should be observed:

- Save the document you are working on regularly to ensure that you don't lose any information should something go wrong with the application or computer.
- Store the documents in line with your organisation's policies and procedures. This may include:
  - giving authorised access only to those staff who need to work with the document(s)
  - saving to locations in line with organisational requirements
  - following organisational policy for backing up files
  - following organisational policy for filing hard copies
  - ensuring security of the files (e.g. password-protecting them so they can't be altered by unauthorised staff)
  - saving documents to folders or sub-folders, on disk drives, servers or to cloud-based facilities.

A significant amount of work may go into the creation of a presentation, so it is essential that the files are saved correctly.

Knowledge check

12. Describe the types of things you need to check when finalising your presentation.

13. Explain what handouts might be used for.

14. Describe at least three methods of storing your presentation.

Summary

You don't create a presentation for no reason. A great deal may rest on the quality of your presentation, so it must make its point quickly and effectively while keeping your audience fully engaged. The message you are trying to convey may be aimed at selling a product, teaching a skill, presenting a business idea, or any number of other things.

Whatever its purpose, and whoever its intended audience, your presentation should take full advantage of the many features available to create a professional message.

CHAPTER 15
Maintain financial records

Learning outcomes

15.1 Recognise the key components of organisational accounting systems and procedures

15.2 Prepare journals required for posting to the general ledger

15.3 Post journal entries and reconcile discrepancies

15.4 Maintain the general ledger

15.5 Understand legislation, codes of practice and national standards

Financial transactions are a vitally important area of any business operation and great care must be taken when dealing with finances—both incoming (money customers pay you) and outgoing (money you pay to suppliers)—to ensure the organisation's continued financial success.

Maintaining accurate financial records is important not only for the effective management of a business, but also as a basis for planning and making sound business decisions. In addition, you may need to present financial and performance records to banks and other financial institutions, as well as to potential investors, in order to provide a snapshot of the business. Keeping and maintaining up-to-date financial records in an orderly manner is therefore essential to managing a business.

Accounting is a complex subject—much more complex than we can realistically cover in this chapter. Instead, this chapter aims to give you the accounting tools and skills you will need to successfully maintain *basic* business finances and to understand the terms used. If you enjoy working through this chapter, you might use it as a stepping stone to further your studies!

15.1 Recognising the key components of organisational accounting systems and procedures

GoodStudio/Shutterstock

To begin to understand this process of keeping accurate financial records, you need to be familiar with their key components. Let's look first at the difference between the bookkeeping and accounting components. *Bookkeeping* is the recording of financial transactions. Most people can do bookkeeping with a small amount of training. It is generally about being accurate in your findings and knowledgeable about certain financial topics. *Accounting*, on the other hand, is the process of interpreting, classifying, analysing, reporting and summarising financial data.

15.1.1 The key components

Many of the following terms will be explained in detail as we work through the chapter.

Accounting system

An **accounting system** is the set of manual or computerised procedures an organisation uses to identify relevant transactions or events and to record them accurately. The term covers such things as:

- preparing financial source documents (to be discussed further)
- entering financial data into the accounting records
- processing financial transactions
- updating master files
- generating financial documents and reports.

Account customer

Many organisations will offer their regular or large customers an account. These account customers can buy products from you on their account, take the products with them immediately, and pay for them at a later date. This date will be individually negotiated and can be anywhere from 7 to 30 days from the date of purchase.

Accounts receivable

Accounts receivable is the official name given to credit accounts an organisation extends to its customers. They are classed as current assets, representing money the organisation expects to be paid for services performed or merchandise sold on credit.

Accounts payable

In the same way that your organisation offers regular customers credit accounts, a supplier might offer you a credit account. **Accounts payable** represent your obligations to pay within a given time frame for goods and services you have already received.

Balance sheet

Also known as the "accounting equation", the **balance sheet** reports on the organisation's assets and liabilities, and its owner's or shareholders' equity, at a specific point in time. It provides the basis for calculating the rate of return on the owner's investment and evaluates the company's financial—capital—structure. The balance sheet provides an overall picture of what the organisation owns and owes, and the amount invested by its shareholders. We will look at assets, liabilities and equity in more detail a little later in the chapter.

Credit and debit

In accounting terms, a **credit (CR)** is a record of all money flowing *out* of an organisation's account. **Debit (DR)** is a record of all money flowing *into* the organisation's account. Debits and credits are bookkeeping entries that balance each other out. Consider that, for accounting purposes, every transaction must be exchanged for something else of the exact same value. (The terms "credit" and "debit" can be confusing. They will be explained in greater detail later in the chapter in the section entitled "The rules".)

Double-entry accounting

Double-entry accounting is a system of recording financial transactions in a way that maintains the *balance* of the organisation's accounts. Each transaction is recorded as a *credit* in one business account and as a *debit* in a *connected* account. For example, when you sell a product, you receive an income from that sale; however, at the same time you have decreased the stock of the product you have on hand. Therefore, your business bank account has an increased amount of money, but the connected stock inventory account has a decreased value. For this type of accounting, every transaction must have at least one debit and one credit and they must be equal. (We will look at this in more detail later under the heading "The double-entry system".)

General ledger

The **general ledger** is the "book" that contains all the individual financial accounts of a business. At the end of a given business period (week, month, etc.), entries from the various journals or accounts are summarised and entered into the general ledger. For example, financial accounts within a general ledger can include the following, along with many others as determined by the individual organisation:

- *Accounts receivable*—the account where all money that customers owe you is recorded.
- *Accounts payable*—the account where all money that you owe your suppliers is recorded.
- *Inventory*—the account where movement in your stock levels is recorded, such as when new stock has been ordered to supplement your supply or when stock has been sold to customers.
- *Sales*—the account where the details of any sales you have made within a given period is recorded.
- *Cash at bank*—the account where the banked income from sales made is recorded.

Journal (account book)

In accounting transactions, a **journal** (or an **account book**) is where individual transactions are recorded as they occur, within their specific groups of accounts. Journals can be of different types, such as:

- **Purchase journals**—where any purchases you make on account are recorded. (You purchase the item but won't pay for it yet.)
- **Cash payment journals**—where any purchases you make, and pay for immediately, are recorded.
- **Sales journals**—where sales made to account customers are recorded. (They have taken the goods but haven't paid for them yet.)
- **Cash receipts journals**—where all cash sales made to customers who pay immediately are recorded.

Profit and loss statement

Often also referred to as an **income statement**, the **profit and loss statement** is a financial report that summarises the revenue, costs and expenses incurred by the organisation during a specific period of time (usually a financial year) ("for the period ..."). The report provides information about the organisation's success (or lack of) in generating a profit by increasing its revenue and/or reducing its costs.

Source and accountable documents

The Australian Taxation Office (ATO) requires every business to keep records of all its financial transactions so that they can show their exact income and expenses for each year. In order to ensure that this is done correctly, most of the financial forms and documents you need to complete are what are known as **source documents** or **accountable documents**. They will have *sequential* numbers pre-printed on them. In this way, each document issued by the organisation is accounted for. You can't, for example, report a list of receipts issued to customers numbered 2110, 2111, 2112, 2114, 2115 and 2116 without having to explain why receipt number 2113 is missing. You must be able to show each receipt issued. If number 2113 was cancelled because it wasn't filled in correctly, or the customer changed their mind about making the purchase, then the receipt should still be accounted for, showing that it was cancelled and why.

Source and accountable documents can include:

- **receipts**—a customer's proof of purchase
- **purchase orders**—an organisation's formal request to buy from a supplier
- **tax invoices**—a supplier's demand for payment
- **credit notes**—a supplier's approval of a refund on returned goods
- **bank statements**—a bank's summary of transactions related to an organisation's bank account
- **tax returns**—a document that must be submitted to the ATO each year
- **business activity statements (BAS)**—ongoing reports supplied to the ATO related to an organisation's financial transactions.

Trial balance

The **trial balance** is a list of all the accounts in the general ledger and their balances as of a specified date. A trial balance is usually prepared at the end of an accounting period and is used to check for any errors in the accounting process. We will look at this in more detail later in the chapter.

It should be noted that the trial balance is different from the balance sheet. The trial balance is an internal report that stays in the accounting department. The balance sheet, on the other hand, is a financial statement that can be accessed by other departments, investors and lenders.

Eventually, the information in the trial balance is used to prepare the financial statements for the period. In contrast, the balance sheet pulls together multiple accounts, summarising the assets, liabilities and shareholders' equity in the accounting records at a specific time ("as at" a certain date). The balance sheet includes outstanding expenses, accrued income, and the value of the closing inventory, whereas the trial balance does not.

15.1.2 Main classifications of bookkeeping transactions

Financial transactions take place every day, whether you are making or receiving a payment. Money being paid to you is classified as an income, while money you must pay someone else is classified as an expense. It is important to ensure that all financial transactions are recorded correctly, so we will spend some time here exploring these aspects of bookkeeping.

In bookkeeping terms, it is necessary to accurately classify and describe what transactions have taken place. There are five main classifications of transactions: assets, liabilities and owner's (or owners') equity (shown in the balance sheet), and income and expenses (shown in the profit and loss statement).

The **accounting equation** is the basic principle of accounting and is described as follows:

Assets = liabilities + owner's equity

This equation sets the foundation of double-entry accounting, which we will look at shortly, and highlights the structure of the balance sheet.

Assets

An **asset** is anything owned by an individual or a business that has commercial or exchange value. For example, assets may consist of:

- specific property, such as buildings
- machinery and equipment
- money in the bank
- money owed to it by account customers.

Assets have an economic value to a business and can be converted into cash. Assets can be either current (short term) or non-current (long term).

- **Current assets** are any assets that can easily and quickly be converted into cash (generally within a 12-month period). Examples of current assets include:
  - *Cash.* This is money that is available immediately, such as in bank accounts. Cash is the most liquid of all short-term assets.
  - *Accounts receivable (a general ledger account).* This is money that is owed to the business for purchases made by customers, suppliers and other vendors, who have an account with the organisation. This money is generally due to be paid within a short time frame.
  - *Stock.* The organisation's product inventory represents a monetary value that can be quickly sold and turned into cash if necessary.
- **Non-current assets** are those assets that cannot be converted quickly into cash. In particular, **fixed assets** are often classified as non-current assets. Fixed assets can include:
  - *Land.* Unlike other fixed assets, land isn't depreciated, because it is considered an asset that will never wear out.
  - *Buildings.* These are categorised as fixed assets and are depreciated over time.
  - *Office equipment.* This includes office furniture and equipment such as computers, printers and photocopiers used in your business.
  - *Machinery.* This represents machines and equipment used in your plant to produce your product. Examples of machinery might include lathes, conveyor belts and a printing press.
  - *Vehicles.* This would include any vehicles used in your business.
  - *Goodwill.* This reflects a business's loyal customer base.

All of these non-current assets represent a monetary value but may take considerable time to liquidate.

Example 1

Greyson's Imports currently has the following current and fixed assets:

- $350,000 in its bank account—*current asset*
- an office building that includes normal office furniture and equipment (total value of $1.5 million)—*fixed asset*
- a showroom to showcase its products (total value $2.5 million)—*fixed asset*
- two company vehicles leased at $35,000 each—*fixed asset*
- outstanding customer accounts valued at a total of $124,500—*current asset.*

Think about

1. Which items and/or equipment in your organisation would be classified as current or non-current assets?

Liabilities

In accounting terms, **liabilities** are amounts of money that an organisation owes to other parties. Examples include:

- a bank loan
- an operational expense, such as the cost of purchasing new stock for the shop (an expense has been incurred but not yet paid)
- any other form of claim on the organisation's assets that must be paid or otherwise honoured.

As with assets, liabilities can be either current or non-current.

- **Current liabilities** are amounts of money owed to suppliers with whom the organisation holds short-term credit accounts and involve day-to-day business expenses. In accounting terms, these liabilities are known as "accounts payable". Current liabilities also include bank overdrafts and any other kind of credit payments to be made within a defined time frame.
- **Non-current liabilities** are items that will not be paid off in the short term. They include items such as bank loans, mortgage payments or hire purchase payments.

Example 2

Greyson's Imports has ordered a supply of decorative items to properly showcase its products in a home-like setting. When ordering these items, Greyson used its credit account with the supplier, Nifty Designs. It will need to pay the invoice for these goods within a short time frame. Greyson's Imports' current liabilities include:

- a bank loan for construction of building extensions valued at $500,000—*non-current liability*
- purchase (on account) of decorating supplies from Nifty Designs valued at $6,595. Payment must be made within 30 days—*current liability*
- lease on two company vehicles valued at $70,000. Payments amount to $2,000 per month—*current liability*.

Owner's equity

Owner's equity (or share) in a business is what is left over after the business's income has been used to pay its outstanding debts. In other words, it is the difference between its assets and its liabilities owed to the owner(s). Hopefully, its assets exceed its liabilities and there is a positive owner's equity. Owner's equity reflects the overall state or situation of the business at a given point in time. For example, if the total assets of the business are $100,000 and the liabilities are $20,000, the net worth of the business is $80,000 ($100,000 less $20,000). Therefore, $80,000 represents the owner's investment in the business.

Revenue (income) accounts

Revenue (income) is the amount of money an organisation earns or generates. Typical revenue accounts may include:

- sales revenue from each product the business offers, to be tracked individually
- income from interest earned
- income from consulting services offered
- rent received from leasing out its premises to other organisations
- income from fundraising or donations.

Most organisations restrict the number of income accounts they have. For example, an organisation such as Bunnings Hardware, with many thousands of product items, won't have an income account for *every single* product it sells; instead, it will group similar items into one income category.

Too many accounts can be very hard to control accurately and may not tell management what it wants to know. Nevertheless, if there's a source of income the organisation wants to track, they can create an account for it.

Expenses

An organisation will likely also have a separate account for each type of **expense** it incurs. Much the same expenses are generally incurred each month, so once established the expense accounts won't vary much from month to month. Typical expense accounts include:

- salaries and wages
- telephone
- electricity
- repairs and maintenance
- depreciation
- interest
- raw material purchases
- vehicle maintenance
- promotional activities.

In summary: the bookkeeping process follows a set of logical steps (see Figure 15.1). This ensures that an organisation always knows exactly how much money it has, in order to be able to determine its financial position. This process includes:

1. The transaction
2. Source documents
3. Journal entries
4. Posting to ledger
5. Trial balance.

Figure 15.1 The financial process

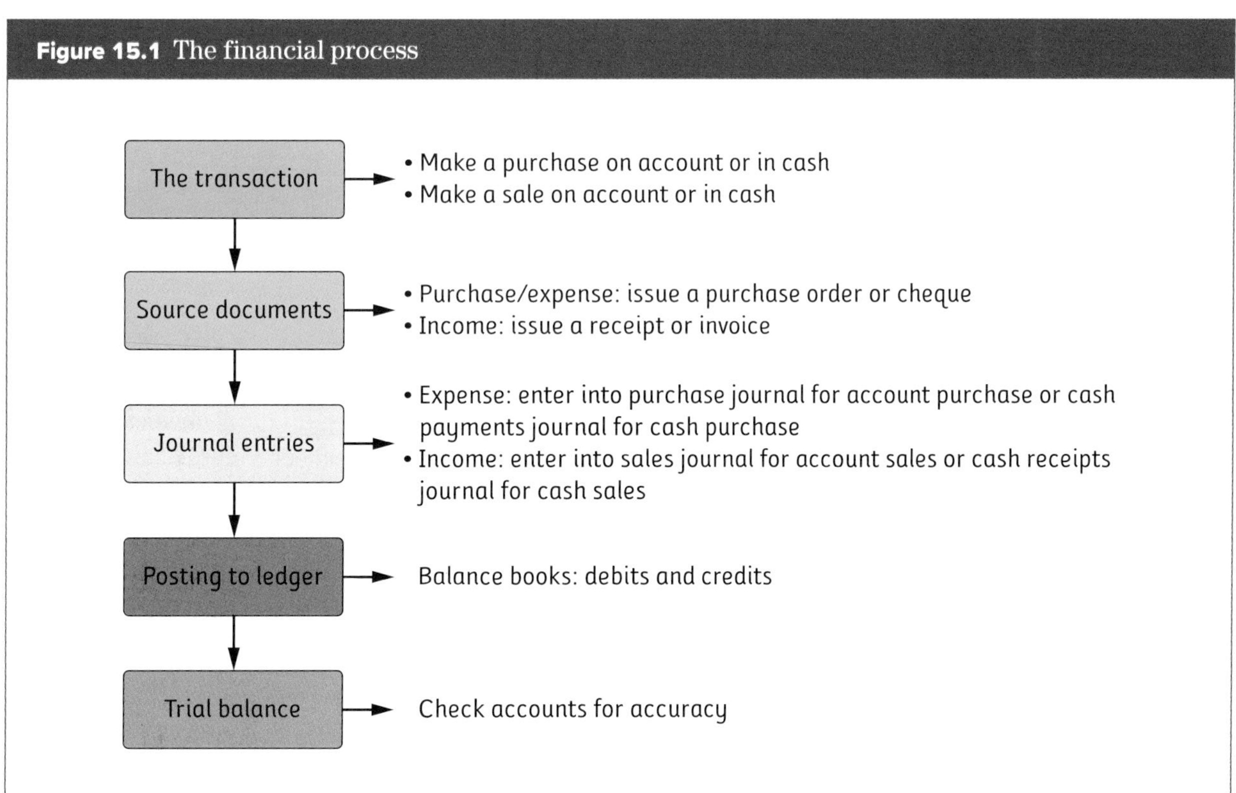

15.1.3 Accounting software used for maintaining financial records

Most organisations today use software programs to maintain their financial records. Such software is generally capable of recording and categorising financial transactions, sending invoices to customers, managing payrolls, paying bills and much more. There are many advantages to using software-based accounting systems. For example:

- It saves time. Entering each transaction into the system as it is made saves on time-consuming manual entry.
- Key financial reports can be generated instantly.
- All financial data is synced. For example, financial data stored across multiple business areas (bank accounts and payroll services) can be synced so that you don't have to switch between accounts to produce specific reports.
- It produces professional-looking financial statements.
- It can simplify payroll by automating payments to employees, and correctly calculating superannuation contributions and payroll tax.
- Streamlining tax reports and filings.

While some larger organisations will have customised software, there are a variety of off-the-shelf accounting programs to choose from, such as QuickBooks, MYOB, POS Accounting and Xero. While these programs can fulfil most bookkeeping and accounting functions, it is nevertheless useful to understand the basic principles of the process, which will be covered in the next section.

Think about

2. What software programs or systems does your organisation use to keep track of sales and other financial transactions?

15.2 Preparing journals required for posting to the general ledger

Every transaction undertaken by an organisation that involves money must be recorded, whether it is incoming or outgoing. There are two main reasons for this:

- It is a legal requirement to maintain accurate financial records. The ATO can choose to audit a business's finances at any time. Failure to provide the necessary records could result in penalties and/or legal action being taken against you or your organisation. Compliance with your legal obligations is therefore essential.
- The organisation can maintain control over its financial health if it knows how much income it has to work with, and how much money it owes suppliers or others. Future plans often cost money, and it is essential that the organisation has a sound understanding of its financial footing.

15.2.1 Identifying, preparing and documenting journal entries

Each day when sales are made, you will either issue a receipt to a customer who has paid you in cash, or you will issue an invoice for customers who are purchasing goods on their account. Whenever you pay a supplier (having received an invoice), you will make a payment via electronic funds transfer (EFT) or by writing a cheque. These transactions must be recorded. In basic terms, this is done by keeping a set of account books (or journals), as shown in Figure 15.2.

For outgoing money, the transactions will be recorded using the following journals:

- *Purchase journal.* This is used when making purchases on account, which you won't pay for immediately.
- *Cash payments book.* This is used for making purchases that you are paying for immediately (by cash or cheque) and for when you subsequently pay an account invoice you previously entered into the purchase journal.

For sales and incoming money, the transactions will be recorded using the following journals:

- *Sales journal.* This is used when customers buy goods from you on account; that is, they order and receive their goods but don't pay for them immediately.
- *Cash receipts book.* This is used when you make cash sales, or when an account customer pays against an invoice you sent them (having previously been recorded in the sales journal).

Figure 15.2 Processing income and expenses into the correct journals

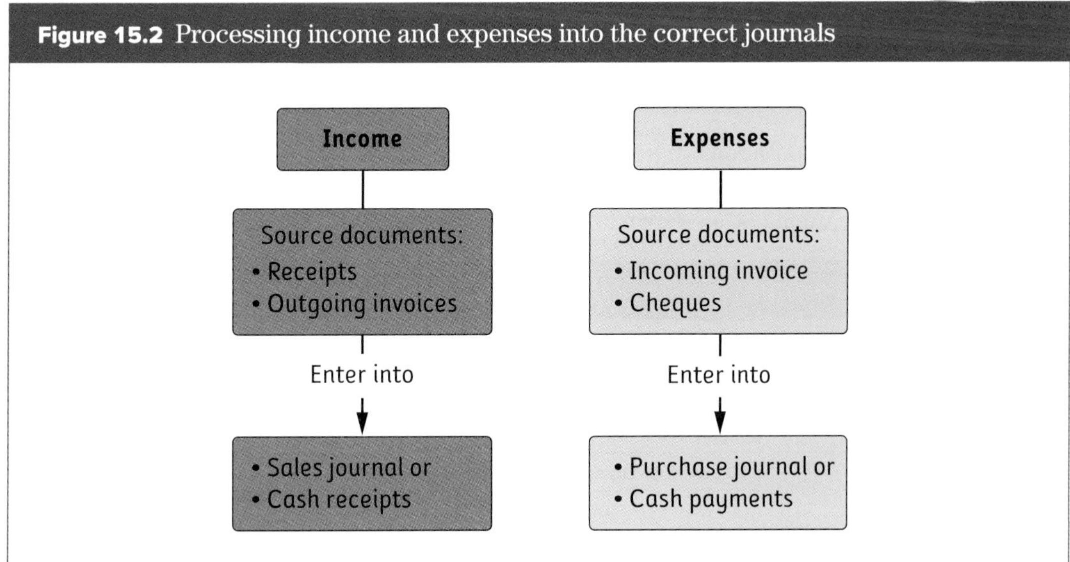

Journals—or account books—can have as many columns of information as required by an individual organisation. The financial transactions that are recorded will be based on the nature of the industry. For example, standard columns used by most organisations might include telephone, electricity, rent, maintenance and advertising, while industry-specific transactions to be recorded might include:

- tuition fees (for education)
- installation fees (for computer or electrical work)
- government fees (if the business deals frequently with government departments), and so on.

Purchase journal

The purchase journal is used for *outgoing* expenses—in this case, it is money that has been committed but not yet actually spent. This would be the case if you were purchasing goods or services on account. For example, you might need to get your local printer to print some new brochures or business cards, or you may need to buy additional raw materials in order to manufacture your product. The organisation would have accounts with many of the companies that it deals with on a regular basis. In these cases, you would issue a purchase order for the goods or services, place the order and check it is correct when it is delivered. Your money has been committed to this supplier, but you haven't yet paid for the goods. The transaction is recorded in the purchase journal to indicate the financial commitment to that supplier.

At some point in the following week(s), the supplier will send you an invoice for the goods and at this point, payment would then be made against the invoice. When invoices are received and payments are made against them, they would then be entered into the *cash payments book* to show that the financial commitment has been honoured.

For example, let's say you made the following purchases on account this week:

- 9 March—from Accent Press: 10 boxes of envelopes. The cost is $150.00 plus GST. You issue purchase order (PO) 15893.
- 11 March—you place an advertisement in the *Bulletin News* newspaper. You issue PO15894. Cost: $1,500.00 plus GST.

These payments would be recorded in your purchase journal, as shown in Figure 15.3.

Figure 15.3 Extract from purchase journal

Date	Reference number	Details	Supplier	Amount ($)	GST ($)	Total amount ($)
9/3	PO15893	10 boxes of DL envelopes with logo	Accent Press	150.00	15.00	165.00
11/3	PO15894	½-page ad in newspaper: new product	*Bulletin News*	1,500.00	150.00	1,650.00

Like most large organisations, you have separate pages for each main supplier you have accounts with, so you split the above purchases into individual accounts and add them to previous purchases from these suppliers, as shown in Figure 15.4.

Figure 15.4 Extracts from purchase journal for individual suppliers

Account: Accent Press					
Date	**Reference number**	**Details**	**Amount ($)**	**GST ($)**	**Total ($)**
3/3	33123	5 reams of letterhead paper	100.00	10.00	110.00
9/3	**15893**	**10 boxes of DL envelopes with logo**	**150.00**	**15.00**	**165.00**

Account: *Bulletin News*					
Date	**Reference number**	**Details**	**Amount ($)**	**GST ($)**	**Total ($)**
1/3	3092	Positions vacant ad: PR officer	800.00	80.00	880.00
6/3	3177	Newspaper subscription for February	25.00	2.50	27.50
11/3	**15894**	**½-page ad in newspaper: new product**	**1,500.00**	**150.00**	**1,650.00**

Note: In journals, the **goods and services tax (GST)** is shown in the entries you make for sales or purchases. When posting to the general ledger, however, GST becomes a separate account in its own right and the amounts posted against various accounts such as accounts receivable, accounts payable, sales, cash at bank and so on, don't include GST. The GST amounts are separated out and shown in their own specific accounts, such as:

- GST incurred on expenditure—for purchases made
- GST collected on revenue—for sales made.

At the end of each month, these accounts are posted to the general ledger.

Cash payments book

The cash payments book is where you record any transactions that involve payments you have made, whether by:

- cash
- cheque
- EFT, etc.

For example, let's say you paid the following bills for your organisation today (15 March):

- Telstra's February telephone bill: $550.00 plus GST of $55.00.
- The deposit for exhibition space at a local trade show: $500.00 plus GST of $50.00.
- AB Catering's bill for food supplied for a boardroom lunch on 10 March: $150.00 plus GST of $15.00.

Plus, you paid for the following purchases previously made on account:

- Accent Press sent in invoice number 33421 for 10 boxes of envelopes: $150.00 plus GST.
- Invoice 3429 from *Bulletin News* for an advertisement you placed: $1,500.00 plus GST.

Entries into the cash payments journal would be as shown in Figure 15.5.

Figure 15.5 Example of cash payments journal

Date	Details	Reference number	Payment type	Total payments ($)	GST ($)	Phone ($)	Advertising ($)	Rent ($)	Sundry ($)
15/3	Telstra: Feb phone bill		BPAY	605.00	55.00	550.00			
15/3	Events Unlimited/trade show deposit		Chq: 089	550.00	50.00				500.00
15/3	AB Catering/ boardroom lunch 10/3	INV4285	Chq: 090	165.00	15.00				150.00
15/3	**Accent Press**	**INV33421**	**Chq: 091**	**165.00**	**15.00**				**150.00**
15/3	***Bulletin News***	**INV3429**	**EFT**	**1,650.00**	**150.00**		**1,500.00**		
	Total			**5,885.00**	**535.00**	**550.00**	**1,500.00**	**2,500.00**	**800.00**

The total of these columns is $5,885.00 (same as in the "Total payments" column).

The last two entries shown in Figure 15.5 relate to amounts previously entered into the purchase journal and which have now been paid.

Note: The term "sundry" (as used in Figure 15.5) relates to miscellaneous items for which the organisation has no particular or separate account. For example, catering for a luncheon, dry cleaning the office curtains, or providing milk and coffee supplies for the office kitchen might all fall under the category of sundry expenses.

You will notice that the total of GST plus the other individual account columns adds up to the same amount shown in the "Total payments" column. This is a check for you to ensure that the amounts in each area have been recorded correctly.

As with the purchase journal example, large organisations generally have separate pages, or spreadsheets, for each different account type. This makes it easier for them to keep track of how much of their budget is spent on specific areas over a period of years. When it is time to calculate the next year's budgets, it is then a fairly easy matter to see what was spent over the previous years on each account and to forecast what will need to be spent in the coming year. For example, in Figure 15.6 you can easily see how much was spent on telephone charges for the period.

The reference number normally refers to the source document being processed, such as a receipt number, invoice number, purchase order number, account number, and so on. In the case of the telephone account, this would be the monthly phone bill. "Payment type" refers to the method by which payment was made: cheque, EFT, etc. In the case of a cheque, you should put the cheque number in this space.

Depending on organisational procedures, these entries can be made into the relevant accounts as they occur during the day, or at the end of the day, using source documents as your reference.

Figure 15.6 Extract from cash payments journal individual account

Account: Telephones							
Date	**Reference number**	**Payment type**	**Details**	**Supplier**	**Amount ($)**	**GST ($)**	**Total ($)**
12/1	B23759	BPAY	December phone bill	Telstra	698.34	69.83	768.17
16/2	8700029CD	BPAY	January phone bill	Telstra	499.14	49.91	549.05
15/3	B24899	BPAY	February phone bill	Telstra	550.00	55.00	605.00
			Total		**1,747.48**	**174.74**	**1,922.22**

Sales journal

The sales journal is the account where all sales made on credit are recorded. This would be the case if a customer who had an account with you purchased goods from your organisation. The goods have been delivered to them but haven't yet been paid for. The source document for these sales is normally an invoice. For example, the following sales were made by account customers on 12 March, as outlined in Figure 15.7.

- Jill Samson, from Barrington & Lyle Lawyers, purchased a desk for a new law partner. The price of the desk is $895.00 plus GST, and you issued them invoice number 10263.
- Simon Morrison, from the local City Council office, picked up the new boardroom table he ordered. The cost is $3,500.00 plus GST and you gave him invoice number 10264.

Figure 15.7 Extract from sales journal

Date	Description	Customer	Ref	Amount ($)	GST ($)	Total ($)
12/3	Cherrywood desk	Barrington & Lyle	10263	895.00	89.50	984.50
12/3	Boardroom table	City Council	10264	3,500.00	350.00	3,850.00

Cash receipts book

The cash receipts journal is where all cash sales are recorded (Figure 15.8). This would be the case if a customer came in, purchased and paid for goods immediately. Payments from account customers are also recorded here *once they have paid their invoice*. For example, the following sales were made this week:

- On 19 March, Miso Sugimoto came in and purchased a pair of teak side tables @ $295.00 each. You issued receipt number T2236.
- On 21 March, Christine James bought a table lamp for $355.95. You issued receipt number T2237.
- Account customers Barrington & Lyle and the City Council have also paid their accounts with you.

Figure 15.8 Extract from cash receipts journal

Date	Details	Invoice/receipt number	Amount ($)	GST ($)	Total ($)
19/3	Teak side tables/Miso Sugimoto	T2236	590.00	59.00	649.00
21/3	Table lamp/Christine James	T2237	355.95	35.60	391.55
22/3	Barrington & Lyle	INV10263	895.00	89.50	984.50
24/3	City Council	INV10264	3,500.00	350.00	3,850.00

Once again, separate accounts can be kept for either the product line or the account customer in order to see clearly what is selling or to whom, as shown in Figure 15.9.

Figure 15.9 Extract from journal for individual accounts

Date	Account: Barrington & Lyle	Reference	Amount ($)	GST ($)	Total ($)
12/1	Replacement boardroom chair	INV9845	258.00	25.80	283.80
22/3	**Cherrywood desk—D112**	**INV10263**	**895.00**	**89.50**	**984.50**

Date	Account: City Council	Reference	Amount ($)	GST ($)	Total ($)
8/1	Oak credenza	INV9811	1,500.00	150.00	1,650.00
28/1	Storeroom bookshelf unit	INV9869	2,550.00	255.00	2,805.00
24/3	**Boardroom table—special order**	**INV10264**	**3,500.00**	**350.00**	**3,850.00**

To this point in the process, the necessary steps have been relatively simple: a transaction has taken place and has been recorded in the appropriate journal to show where and when money was spent or received.

15.2.2 Assessing and identifying general ledger accounts affected

As we move through this chapter, we will look in greater detail at identifying ledger accounts and how they work. Briefly, however, whenever you deal with a financial transaction, an entry into a specific journal will be required.

Where journal entries are relatively simple, you enter the date, source document, account name, amount involved, and so on. In the general ledger, entries are much more complex. These are generally entered (or posted) using the double-entry system in order to correctly balance the organisation's accounts in a series of debits and credits. Debits and credits follow specific rules in that if you are increasing an amount in one account, then you must decrease another, different, account by that same amount. Before you can post a transaction from a journal to the general ledger, then, you need to know and understand what ledger account the transaction belongs in, and whether it will increase or decrease that account.

To assess and identify the transactions to be made:

1. Determine what ledger accounts will be affected by the transaction. For example, when purchasing office stationery supplies, the accounts likely to be affected are the expense account and the cash account because you are purchasing goods (expense) and paying for it with money (cash).
2. Determine what type of account each of these is (asset, liability, revenue, expenses or owner's equity).
3. Assess whether the account is increasing or decreasing; that is, is the transaction a debit or a credit to the account?

We will examine debits, credits and the double-entry system in detail in the next section.

Maintaining accuracy in financial records

All organisations need money to sustain them. They need to pay for rent, wages, utilities, supplies and many other things. They can only do this successfully if they are in command of their financial stability—and this means keeping accurate financial records.

Correct financial information is important for a range of reasons, including to:

- make it easier to complete tax returns
- monitor the health of the organisation in financial terms
- assist in making plans for the organisation's future
- demonstrate the organisation's financial position when taking out bank loans, and much more.

Think about

3. What other reasons can you think of why it is vital to maintain accurate financial records?

Knowledge check

1. Briefly describe each of the following accounting terms:
   - accounts receivable
   - accounts payable
   - balance sheet
   - credit
   - debit
   - double-entry accounting
   - general ledger
   - profit and loss statement
   - trial balance.
2. Bookkeeping has five main aspects. Describe each aspect briefly (giving examples) and explain how they relate to the accounting equation.
3. Explain the advantages of using accounting software. Give at least three examples of current software.
4. Explain what each of the following journals is used for:
   - purchase journal
   - cash payments journal
   - sales journal
   - cash receipts journal.
5. Explain the process of assessing and identifying transactions that affect the general ledger.

15.3 Posting journal entries and reconciling discrepancies

To "post a transaction" means to transpose (or transfer) financial information from individual accounts and journals to the general ledger. The general ledger is the "book" where all the organisation's financial assets, liabilities, owner's equity, revenue and expenses come together to form a whole picture of its financial standing. Accuracy in transferring this information is therefore extremely important, as far-reaching business decisions may be made based on the organisation's financial status.

As mentioned previously, each organisation will have its own policies and procedures for undertaking these tasks; they may have a simple manual bookkeeping system, or they may use sophisticated software that takes care of all these tasks automatically. In general, however, the principles of working with general ledgers will apply to all forms of accounting and it is the *basic* principles that we will be addressing here.

15.3.1 Posting journal entries into the general ledger system

In the previous section, you learnt how to make simple entries into account books (or journals). While these might be an accurate reflection of the organisation's day-to-day financial dealings, they result in endless rows and columns of information that are disjointed and don't give an easily understood overview of the organisation's entire financial position. A further process will turn this information into a useful and valuable resource, and this is where actual *bookkeeping,* in the true accounting sense, starts to happen.

Whenever a payment is made in one of the areas we have previously discussed, the correct amount must be entered in the correct manner. *Accounting* is concerned with *balancing* the organisation's financial accounts and therefore involves debiting one account and crediting another account in equal amounts. As we saw above, this is known as the double-entry system. If one account is affected, then it will have an equal (balancing) effect on another account. For example, if I purchased $1,500 worth of stock for my shop on 30 March, I have increased my inventory—but I have also decreased the amount of money I have in my bank account by $1,500, so two entries will be required.

15.3.2 The chart of accounts

Before we explain and illustrate the debits and credits in accounting, we will discuss the accounts in which the debits and credits will be entered or posted. To keep a company's financial data organised, a system was developed that sorts transactions into records called *accounts.* When an organisation's bookkeeping system is set up, the accounts most likely to be affected by the organisation's transactions are identified and listed. These could include any of the income and expense accounts previously discussed, such as:

- advertising
- salary and wages
- rent
- phone
- sale of products (or each product could have a separate account).

In addition to these, other commonly used general ledger accounts include:

- *Accounts payable,* which is a transaction record of all **creditors**—those who have extended credit to your organisation. For example, these would be the major supplies your organisation has purchase accounts with and to whom you owe money.
- *Accounts receivable,* which is a transaction record of all **debtors**—for example, customers who have accounts with your organisation and who owe you money.
- *Cash at bank account,* which is where you record all banking transactions—for example, when a cash sale is made and money is banked.

This list of accounts is referred to as the organisation's **chart of accounts**. Depending on the size of the organisation and the complexity of its business operations, the chart of accounts could list a few or hundreds of accounts.

Each organisation will design its chart of accounts to best meet its needs. Accounts might be given code numbers, as shown in Table 15.1.

As you know, in the normal course of daily business, a document is produced each time a financial transaction occurs. Sales and purchases usually involve invoices, purchase orders or receipts. Deposit slips are produced when lodgements are made to a bank account. Cheques are written to pay money out of the account, and so on. Bookkeeping involves recording the details of all these source documents and transactions into one of the accounts, as outlined in the previous section.

Table 15.1 Example of a chart of accounts

Account	Code	Sub-account
Revenue	101	Product sales
	102	Fundraising
	103	Incoming interest
	104	Consulting fees
Expenses	201	Office rent
	202	Telephones
	203	Electricity
	204	Wages
	205	Superannuation
	206	Advertising
	207	Stock purchases
... and so on.		

At the end of a given period (e.g. end of the week or month), these transactions are then summarised and transferred to the general ledger.

The double-entry system

For the accounts to remain in balance, a change in one account must be matched with a change in another account, as you saw earlier. General ledger accounts are set up as **T-accounts**, so called because they resemble the letter "T" when the account is empty (Figure 15.10). Historically, debit entries have been recorded on the left-hand side of the accounts book or ledger and credit values on the right-hand side.

Figure 15.10 Example of a T-account

Account 206: Advertising	Debit	Credit

Under the double-entry system, every business transaction is recorded in at least two accounts. One account will receive a "debit" entry, meaning the amount will be entered on the *left* side of that account. Another account will receive a "credit" entry, meaning the amount will be entered on the *right* side of that account. The initial challenge with double entry is to know which account should be debited and which should be credited.

Table 15.2 Rules of credit and debit

	Increase	Decrease
Income	Credit (CR)	Debit (DR)
Expense	DR	CR
Assets	DR	CR
Liabilities	CR	DR
Owner's equity	CR	DR

The rules

In bookkeeping, the terms "credits" and "debits" don't have the same meaning as in general language and the subject of what is a debit and what is a credit can be extremely confusing. Table 15.2 might help in clarifying the issue, and it is best not to try to make this information fit into what you would normally believe to be correct! Until you become familiar with this rule, it is a good idea to keep a copy of the grid handy to help guide you through the maze of what goes in the debit (or left side) of the accounts and what goes in the credit (or right side) of the accounts.

If I have:

- an increase in income, it is a credit (CR).
- an increase in assets, it is a debit (DR).
- a decrease in liabilities, it is a debit (DR).
- a decrease in expenses, it is a credit (CR).

While some of this may not make sense initially, in accounting terms it does actually work—so, persevere!

Double-entry accounting in practice

In this section, we see how double-entry accounting works in practice. For example, if I purchase stock for my shop, this means I:

- increase my inventory (an asset) by $1,500 (a debit entry).
- decrease the cash in my bank account (an asset) by $1,500 (a credit entry).

The ledger entry would look like Figure 15.11. The debit and credit columns both total to $1,500.00, so the accounts are balanced.

In another example, a business borrows $1,000 from a bank. The transaction will affect its cash at bank account and its loan account (Figure 15.12).

Figure 15.11 Example of entries into inventory and cash at bank accounts

	Debit ($)	Credit ($)
Account: Inventory 30/3 Purchase new stock	1,500.00	1,500.00
Account: Cash at bank 30/3 Payment for new stock		
Total	**1,500.00**	**1,500.00**

Figure 15.12 Further T-account entries

	Debit ($)	Credit ($)
Account: Cash at bank Income from bank loan	1,000.00	
Account: Loan Loan proceeds		1,000.00

The proceeds of the loan from the bank are an asset and, according to the rules, an increase in assets is a debit entry. At the same time, it is an increase in liabilities (it is an amount that will have to be repaid to the bank) and is therefore posted, in accordance with the rules, to the loan account as a credit.

In a further example, Rose Allenby purchases four sofa cushions from your business for $100.00 cash. The transaction affects your sales and cash at bank accounts (see Figure 15.13). Remember the rules:

- Making a sale is an increase in income and is therefore a credit entry.
- Depositing the proceeds from the sale into your bank account is an increase in assets and is therefore a debit entry.

Figure 15.13 Further example of T-account entries

Account: Sales	**Debit ($)**	**Credit ($)**
29/3 Sale of four cushions to Rose Allenby		100.00
Account: Cash at bank		
29/3 Sale of four cushions to Rose Allenby	100.00	

Let's now assume that Rose purchases the sofa cushions on account, which makes the entries a little more complex as she has received the goods but won't pay for them until later. This will require two lots of entries, as follows.

- Initially the sales account will be affected because your business has made a sale. This is an increase in income (credit). The money, however, hasn't been paid yet, so the accounts receivable account is also affected. Accounts receivable are an asset, so this is a debit entry.
- When Rose eventually pays for the goods, the amount of money in the accounts receivable account is decreased—and a decrease in an asset is a credit entry. The cash at bank account is also affected, as you have now banked the money. This is an increase in assets, so it is a debit entry (Figure 15.14).

To recap, within the general ledger system there are a number of accounts that serve to balance the organisation's expenses and revenue. In addition to those already mentioned, these accounts may include the following:

- *Accounts payable ledger.* This account gives details of the money owing to suppliers (or creditors) with whom you have accounts during that particular month.

Figure 15.14 A range of T-account entries

Account: Sales	Debit ($)	Credit ($)
29/3 Sale of four cushions to Rose Allenby		100.00
Account: Accounts receivable		
29/3 Sale of four cushions to Rose Allenby	100.00	
2/4 Payment from Rose Allenby		100.00
Account: Cash at bank		
2/4 Payment from Rose Allenby	100.00	

- *Accounts receivable ledger.* This account is a detailed list of all monies received from account customers (or debtors) during that month.
- *Individual accounts.* These can be any number of accounts dealing with cash-type accounts.

Let's look at some further examples. In the previous section, we looked at the purchases shown here as Figures 15.15 and 15.16.

Figure 15.15 Example of a purchase journal entry

Date	Reference number	Details	Supplier	Amount ($)	GST ($)	Total ($)
9/3	INV33421	10 boxes of DL envelopes with logo	Accent Press	150.00	15.00	165.00
11/3	INV3429	½-page ad in newspaper: new product	*Bulletin News*	1,500.00	150.00	1,650.00

Figure 15.16 Example of a cash payments book entry

Date	Details	Ref number	Payment type	Total payment ($)	GST ($)	Phone ($)	Advertising ($)	Rent ($)	Sundry ($)
15/3	Telstra—Feb phone bill		BPAY	605.00	55.00	550.00			
15/3	Events Unlimited—trade show deposit		Chq: 089	550.00	50.00				500.00
15/3	AB Catering—boardroom lunch 10/3	INV4285	Chq: 090	165.00	15.00				150.00
15/3	**Accent Press**	**INV33421**	**Chq: 091**	**165.00**	**15.00**				**150.00**
15/3	***Bulletin News***	**INV3429**	**EFT**	**1,650.00**	**150.00**		**1,500.00**		

These are amounts of money the organisation has paid or owes its suppliers and would be entered into the general ledger as shown in Figure 15.17. Columns show each account in the chart of accounts listed individually, a description of the transaction undertaken, and then the debit and credit columns.

In the previous journal examples, the purchase of envelopes from Accent Press was made on account and was an *increase* in *expenses*. According to the rules, this is therefore entered into the purchase account as a *debit*. As this was a purchase made but not yet paid for, it is also an *increase* in the company's *liability* and must therefore (in accordance with the rules) be entered into the *accounts payable* account as a *credit*. The entries for this are shown in the general ledger figure as a *solid line* and arrows. When the company paid the account on 15 March, it represented a *decrease* in the *liability* (*debit* entry) and a *decrease* in the amount of cash the company has in the bank (an *asset*) and is therefore entered as a *credit*. The entries for this are shown in the figure as a *dotted line* and arrows.

Figure 15.17 Example of a general ledger showing individual accounts

Account	Description	Debit ($)	Credit ($)
Accounts payable	**09/3 Accent Press—Envelopes**		**165.00**
	09/3 ACME—Office rent February		2,750.00
	11/3 *Bulletin News*—Advertising		1,650.00
	15/3 Accent Press—Envelopes	**165.00**	
	15/3 ACME—Office rent February	2,750.00	
	15/3 *Bulletin News*—Advertising	1,650.00	
Advertising	11/3 ½-page ad *Bulletin News*	1,650.00	
Cash at bank	15/3 BPAY Telstra phone bill February		605.00
	15/3 Cheque 089 Deposit trade show		550.00
	15/3 Cheque 090 Catering/AB Catering		165.00
	15/3 Accent Press—Envelopes		**165.00**
	15/3 ACME—Office rent February		2,750.00
	15/3 *Bulletin News* advertising		1,650.00
Purchases	**09/3 Accent Press—Envelopes**	**165.00**	
Rent	09/3 ACME—Office rent February	2,750.00	
Telephones	15/3 Feb phone account	605.00	
Sundry	**15/3 Deposit Trade Show Catering**	**550.00**	
	15/3 Catering for boardroom lunch/AB Catering	165.00	

The same applies to the *Bulletin News* account for advertising. In the case of purchases made on account, two separate entries are required: once when the goods are ordered and received, and once when they have eventually been paid for. In contrast, the cash payments only have one entry when the actual purchase was made and paid for—the caterer provided lunch for a function and presented an invoice for $550.00. This was paid for by cheque immediately. In this case, the cost of the lunch was an *increase* in *expense* and is entered as a *debit*. Equally, it *decreases* the amount of *cash in the bank* (an *asset*), so it is entered as a *credit* in the cash at bank account. Spend a few minutes looking at the general ledger in Figure 15.17 to see how the accounts balance.

Revenue, or income, is treated in much the same way as purchases. In the previous section, we looked at the income shown here as Figures 15.18 and 15.19.

Figure 15.18 Example of a sales journal entry

Date	Description	Customer	Ref	Amount ($)	GST ($)	Total ($)
12/3	Cherrywood desk	Barrington & Lyle	10263	895.00	89.50	984.50
12/3	Boardroom table	City Council	10264	3,500.00	350.00	3,850.00

Figure 15.19 Example of a cash receipts book entry

Date	Details	Invoice/receipt nr.	Amount ($)	GST ($)	Total ($)
19/3	Teak side tables/Yuki Sugimoto	T2236	590.00	59.00	649.00
21/3	Table lamp/Christine James	T2237	355.95	35.60	391.55
22/3	Barrington & Lyle	INV10263	895.00	89.50	984.50
24/3	City Council	INV10264	3,500.00	350.00	3,850.00

On 12 March, Barrington & Lyle purchased a desk on account. According to the rules, this represents an *increase* in *income* and is entered as a *credit* in the sales accounts of the ledger shown in Figure 15.20. At the same time, it is an *increase* in current *assets*, as it is money that we can expect to receive in the future and is entered into the *accounts payable* account as a *debit*.

When Barrington & Lyle subsequently pay for the desk, it *decreases* that current *asset* (in accounts payable) and is entered as a *credit*. It also *increases* the cash in bank account (an *asset*) and is therefore entered as a *debit*. Again, where the entries involve an account customer there are two entries: once when the goods were purchased and delivered, and again when they were eventually paid for. With cash sales, only one set of entries is necessary: when Yuki Sugimoto purchased her side tables, an entry was made in the sales account (income) and balanced out in the cash at bank account (asset). These transactions would be entered into the general ledger as shown in Figure 15.20.

Figure 15.20 Further example showing individual accounts within the ledger

Account	Description	Debit ($)	Credit ($)
Accounts payable	9/3 Accent Press—Envelopes		165.00
	9/3 ACME—Office rent February		2,750.00
	11/3 *Bulletin News*—Advertising		1,650.00
	15/3 Payment Accent Press—cheque 091	165.00	
	15/3 Payment ACME—EFT	2,750.00	
	15/3 Payment *Bulletin News*—EFT	1,650.00	
Accounts receivable	**12/3 Sale to Barrington & Lyle**	**984.50**	
	12/3 Sale to City Council	**3,850.00**	
	15/3 Payment Barrington & Lyle		**984.50**
	15/3 Payment City Council		**3,850.00**
Advertising	11/3 ½-page ad *Bulletin News*	1,650.00	
Cash at bank	15/3 BPAY Telstra phone bill February		605.00
	15/3 Cheque 089 Deposit trade show		550.00
	15/3 Cheque 090 Catering/AB Catering		165.00
	15/3 Accent Press—Envelopes		165.00
	15/3 ACME—Office rent February		2750.00
	15/3 *Bulletin News*—Advertising		1,650.00
	15/3 Barrington & Lyle—Desk	**984.50**	
	15/3 City Council—Boardroom table	**3,850.00**	
	19/3 Teak side tables/Yuki Sugimoto	**649.00**	
	21/3 Table lamp/Christine James	**391.55**	
Purchases	9/3 Accent Press—Envelopes	165.00	
Rent	9/3 ACME—Office rent February	2750.00	
Telephones	15/3 February phone account	605.00	
Sales	**12/3 Barrington & Lyle—Desk**		**984.50**
	12/3 City Council—Boardroom table		**3,850.00**
	19/3 Teak side tables/Yuki Sugimoto		**649.00**
	21/3 Table lamp/Christine James		**391.55**
Sundry	15/3 Deposit trade show/Events Unlimited	550.00	
	15/3 Catering for boardroom lunch/ AB Catering	165.00	

At the end of a given period of time, usually monthly, the individual accounts in the ledger are totalled and balanced, as shown in the general ledger example in section 15.4 (Figure 15.21). The information from that ledger will then be transferred to a trial balance which closes the accounts, reducing them to zero balance, ready for the next accounting period.

15.3.3 Rectifying any discrepancies

Given that bookkeeping can be fairly complex, it is important to ensure that entries are accurate. Errors and discrepancies could have a snowball effect, with a small mistake in a journal entry repeating itself through the various stages of bookkeeping. This can trigger countless hours of searching for the reason why accounts don't balance.

Rectifying discrepancies uses up valuable staff time and causes delays in producing reports needed for important decision making and future planning. Missing zeros or decimal points in the wrong place can have an enormous impact on an organisation's financial statements.

Consider:

- Missing zero: 100 instead of 1,000, or 1,000 instead of 100
- Wrong decimal: $1,000.00 instead of $10.00, or $10.00 instead of $1,000.00

Discrepancies could occur in the following ways:

- *Bank charges*—where fees imposed are too high or not appropriate.
- *Interest*—an incorrect amount of interest is calculated.
- *Dishonoured cheques*—occurs when a person has issued a cheque to you but doesn't have sufficient funds in their account to cover the amount it is made out for. Fees for this are charged by the bank but not transposed to accounts.
- *Errors in transposing*—when an amount is copied incorrectly when copying amounts from one account to another (e.g. writing 678 instead of 687).
- *Incorrect issue of documents*—receipts, invoices and so on that are not completed correctly (e.g. wrong amount or wrong product code).

Errors can also be found in financial documentation such as purchase credit notes, purchase invoices, sales credit notes and sales invoices.

The ATO requires all business records to be kept for five years after they are prepared or the transactions involved have been completed. By law, an organisation is also obliged to present its financial records to the ATO upon request. This means that, at any time, the ATO can request an audit of an organisation's financial dealings and the organisation must be able to show accurate records for as far back as five years if necessary. You can see, then, why it is so important to ensure that financial transactions are dealt with correctly and are free of errors.

Wherever an error or discrepancy is found, it is important to trace it back to its root. For example, if you are totalling the accounts for the past month and they don't balance, you should:

- add the total again to ensure it wasn't a simple addition error
- if the total is still wrong, ask someone else to check the addition
- check obvious areas where the error might have occurred (e.g. subtotals)
- check for errors in transposing data from source documents or account books to the general ledger.

Think about

4. What might be the consequences for a business if errors are made in its financial accounts and aren't identified or rectified?

Escalating discrepancies

If, after taking these steps, the error still exists, then you will need to bring the matter to the attention of designated staff who may have more experience or whose role includes working with such issues. Designated persons may include:

- bank staff, who can assist in tracking errors from their side
- a supervisor or manager, who may have more experience and will have greater authority
- your organisation's accounts department, which is generally responsible for all bookkeeping tasks
- a statutory body; for major or suspicious discrepancies, it may be necessary to call for assistance from an external source such as the ATO, an industry governing body or even the police.

When undertaking a financial transaction, whether it is as simple as issuing a receipt for a small sale or as complex as producing a profit and loss statement, don't allow yourself to be distracted. If you have to put the task aside when midway through it, check, when you return to it, what you have already done before you continue the task, to ensure you haven't missed anything. Take the time to check that all financial source documents issued by you, or received by you from other parties, are correct.

15.3.4 Preparing adjusted journal entries

Because the financial health of an organisation is of extreme importance, it is essential that all its financial transactions are checked for correctness at regular intervals. This might mean adjusting and closing journal and ledger entries and preparing a trial balance before a profit and loss statement can be prepared for distribution to the organisation's various stakeholders.

Adjusted entries are used to update previously recorded journal entries. They ensure that those initial entries line up to the correct accounting periods. This doesn't mean, however, that those transactions are deleted or erased; adjusted entries are new transactions that keep business finances up to date. They are usually made at the end of an accounting period that often coincides with the business fiscal year.

There are four main types of adjusting entries:

- **Prepaid expenses** are payments in cash for assets that haven't yet been used. For example, the company's *insurance* protects the business from possible losses, such as by fire or theft. The insurance is paid for, but these events haven't happened and no claim has been made.
- **Unearned revenue** is cash received before the product or service is provided. For example, when you pay annual business networking membership fees or subscriptions, you are paying in advance for future service.
- **Accrued revenue** is money that has been earned by providing goods or services, but for which no cash has yet been received. These are recorded as "receivables" on the general ledger to reflect the amount of money customers owe you for goods or services they have purchased.
- **Accrued expenses** are expenses that are recognised on your books before they have been paid for (i.e. the expense is recorded during the accounting period in which it is incurred). An example of an accrued expense might be when you purchase goods from a supplier but haven't yet received an invoice for the purchase. It might also involve interest payments on loans, warranties on products or services received, as well as tax payments—all of which have been incurred, or obtained, but for which no demand for payment has yet been made.

Here is an example of how this would work. On 1 May, you sell a service worth $3,000 to a client. You receive the payment for the provided service; however, you forget to make a journal entry to note this. At the end of October, you compare your actual cash reserve with the cash reserve shown on your balance sheet. Since the two sums won't match, it means there is a missing transaction somewhere. At this point, you need to make a journal entry adjustment.

Knowledge check

6. Explain the rules of credits and debits in the double-entry system.
7. Explain what is meant by "posting to the general ledger". Describe why this process is important.
8. Give at least four examples of where discrepancies could occur in bookkeeping.
9. Explain the process you would use to identify discrepancies.
10. Describe the four main types of adjusting entries in bookkeeping.

15.4 Maintaining the general ledger

Before you move on to the next step—the trial balance—it is important, once again, to check the entries that you have made. Checking and double-checking how much money the organisation owes its suppliers, and how much money is owed by customers, is very important. Being overcharged by a supplier, or not being paid in a timely manner by a customer, can have a dramatic effect on the organisation's financial position.

To ensure that all entries are accurate, it is necessary to reconcile the accounts payable and accounts receivable with the general ledger. This can be done by checking:

- invoices sent out to debtors, as well as individual debtor account balances in the cash receipts journal, sales journal and general ledger entries
- invoices received from creditors, as well as individual creditor account balances in the cash payments journal or purchases journals, as well as general ledger entries
- cash payments and receipt journals against the bank statement.

Once this has been done, the general ledger can be balanced and closed for that financial period and the final steps in the process can then be made.

15.4.1 Preparing the closing and post-closing trial balance from the general ledger system

At the end of a given time period, the figures in the general ledger are totalled and a final check for accuracy is made. This process is known as a "trial balance". When it has been established that the trial balance is correct and that the accounts are properly balanced, then final statements such as the profit and loss statement can be produced.

At this point, certain accounts are balanced so that they have a zero balance at the beginning of the new accounting period. The act of zeroing these accounts is called **closing entries** and is the last step in the accounting cycle. This process is, in fact, a fairly complicated one and requires a deeper understanding of the accounting process than we will cover in this chapter. Briefly, however, it involves:

- *Closing the revenue accounts*—that is, debiting the revenue account by the amount of its balance at the end of the accounting period to reduce it to zero. This means crediting the income summary account by the same amount. The income summary is an account used specifically for the closing process. For example, in closing the general ledger you find that the business has $100,000 in revenue, so you would debit $100,000 to the revenue account and credit $100,000 to the income summary account.
- *Closing the expense accounts*—that is, crediting each expense account by the amount of its balance to reduce each account's balance to zero. For example, if you have balances of $30,000, $12,000 and $18,000 in the wages, utilities and advertising expense accounts, respectively, you would credit $30,000 to the wages expense account, $12,000 to the utilities account and $18,000 to the advertising expense account.

- *Closing the income summary account*—that is, debiting the amount of net income to the income summary account and crediting the same amount to the retained earnings account. Alternatively, credit a net loss to the income summary account and debit the same amount to the retained earnings account. These entries reduce the income summary account to zero and either add net income to or subtract a net loss from retained earnings. For example, debit $40,000 in net income to income summary and credit $40,000 to retained earnings
- *Closing the dividend account*—that is, debiting the retained earnings account by the amount of the dividend account's balance and crediting the dividend account by the same amount. This reduces the dividend account to zero and reduces the retained earnings account by the amount of dividends paid during the period. For example, if your dividend account has a $5,000 balance, you would debit retained earnings $5,000 and credit dividends by $5,000.

For students who are interested in the more complex nature of accounting, there are several excellent courses you can take, or you might wish to research various subjects on closing procedures. Some examples:

- Michael Allison, "How Do I Close a General Ledger?" (https://youtu.be/J2_b_Q6carg)
- Investopedia, "The Accounting Equation" (https://www.investopedia.com/terms/a/accounting-equation.asp)
- Small Business, "Primary Components of a Trial Balance Sheet" (https://smallbusiness.chron.com/primary-components-trial-balance-sheet-53682.html)
- Corporate Finance Institute, "Closing Entry" (https://corporatefinanceinstitute.com/resources/knowledge/accounting/closing-entry/).

15.4.2 Preparing the trial balance and checking it meets the accounting equation

A trial balance is prepared in each financial period as a summary of the general ledger. The total of the debit side should always be equal to the total of the credit side, which proves the arithmetic accuracy of the ledger entry. The trial balance is also therefore a tool for detecting any errors that may have occurred during the process of recording double-entry transactions in the ledger.

We will now look at the general ledger we have worked on earlier and use the information to prepare a trial balance. (This simpler approach better reflects day-to-day entry-level administrative roles.)

- Closing the general ledger shows the balance of each account, as shown in Figure 15.21.
- Transferring the **closing balance** of each account gives us the trial balance, as shown in Figure 15.22.
- Each side of the ledger is equal, so the accounts are closed and the next financial period can begin with a zero balance. If, however, the debit and credit columns don't balance, then an error has occurred somewhere in the process and must be rectified before the organisation's books can be finalised for that period.

In the final analysis, all this accounting serves one purpose: to report on and keep track of the organisation's financial status. This information is important for reporting on:

- the organisation's profit and loss for taxation purposes
- its financial health and viability to its stakeholders by ensuring it meets the accounting equation (as previously discussed).

Stakeholders involved in all of this may include:

- the organisation's accountants, who will be responsible for overseeing the maintenance of the journals and ledgers and producing the reports
- board members, who will need an accurate view of the organisation's financial state so that they can make decisions about its future dealings and projects

Figure 15.21 General ledger

Account	Description	Debit ($)	Credit ($)	Balance ($)
Accounts payable	9/3 Accent Press—Envelopes		165.00	
	9/3 ACME—Office rent February		2,750.00	
	11/3 *Bulletin News*—Advertising		1650.00	
	15/3 Payment Accent Press—cheque 091	165.00		
	15/3 Payment ACME—EFT	2,750.00		
	153 Payment *Bulletin News*—EFT	1,650.00		
	Closing balance	**4,565.00**	**4,565.00**	**0.00**
Accounts receivable	12/3 Sale to Barrington & Lyle	984.50		
	12/3 Sale to City Council	3,850.00		
	15/3 Payment Barrington & Lyle		984.50	
	15/3 Payment City Council		3,850.00	
	Closing balance	**4,834.50**	**4,834.50**	**0.00**
Advertising	11/3 ½-page ad *Bulletin News*	1,650.00		
	Closing balance	**1,650.00**		**1,650.00 (DR)**
Cash at bank	15/3 BPAY Telstra phone bill February		605.00	
	15/3 Cheque 089 Deposit trade show		550.00	
	15/3 Cheque 090 Catering/AB Catering		165.00	
	15/3 Accent Press—Envelopes		165.00	
	15/3 ACME—Office rent February		2,750.00	
	15/3 *Bulletin News*—Advertising		1,650.00	
	15/3 Barrington & Lyle—D112 desk	984.50		
	15/3 City Council—Special/boardroom table	3,850.00		
	19/3 Teak side tables/Yuki Sugimoto	649.00		
	21/3 Table lamp/Christine James	391.55		
	Closing balance	**5,875.05**	**5,885.00**	**9.95 (CR)**
Purchases	9/3 Accent Press—Envelopes	165.00		
	Closing balance	**165.00**		**165.00 (DR)**
Rent	9/3 ACME—Office rent February	2,750.00		
	Closing balance	**2,750.00**		**2,750.00 (DR)**
Telephones	15/3 February phone account	605.00		
	Closing balance	**605.00**		**605.00 (DR)**
Sales	12/3 Barrington & Lyle—D112 desk		984.50	
	12/3 City Council—Special/boardroom table		3,850.00	
	19/3 Teak side tables/Yuki Sugimoto		649.00	
	21/3 Table lamp/Christine James		391.55	
	Closing balance		**5,875.05**	**5,875.05 (CR)**
Sundry	15/3 Deposit trade show/Events Unlimited	550.00		
	15/3 Catering for boardroom lunch/AB Catering	165.00		
	Closing balance	**715.00**		**715.00 (DR)**
	Total	**21,159.55**	**21,159.55**	

Figure 15.22 The final trial balance

Account	Debit ($)	Credit ($)
Accounts payable	4,565.00	4,565.00
Accounts receivable	4,834.50	4,834.50
Advertising	1,650.00	
Cash at bank	5,875.05	5,885.00
Purchases	165.00	
Rent	2,750.00	
Telephones	605.00	
Sales		5,875.05
Sundry	715.00	
Total	**21,159.55**	**21,159.55**

- project managers, who will need to be allocated budgets, and work within them, to achieve the organisation's vision
- managers of various divisions within the organisation, who will have specific tasks and budgets allocated to them.

Knowledge check

11. Explain what a trial balance is.

12. Give a brief description of what is involved in closing and post-closing the trial balance from the general ledger.

13. In the final analysis, all this accounting serves one purpose: to report on and keep track of the organisation's financial status. Explain why this is important to the organisation.

15.5 Understanding legislation, codes of practice and national standards

There are legal requirements, codes of practice and national standards that may affect both financial record keeping and certain aspects of financial operations. These may relate to:

- tax records required to be kept by businesses
- accounting
- ethical principles
- GST legislation
- local, state and territory work health and safety (WHS).

15.5.1 Tax records required to be kept by businesses

The ATO requires every business to keep records of all its financial transactions for five years from the date it lodges a tax return. It must be able to show its exact income and expenses for each year for taxation purposes. Examples of records that need to be kept include:

- income statements or payment summaries from the employer
- bank and other financial institutions' statements showing interest earned during the fiscal year
- dividend statements
- summaries from managed investment funds

- receipts or invoices for equipment or asset purchases and sales
- receipts or invoices for expense claims and repairs
- contracts
- tenant and rental records.

Other matters to keep in mind include:

- If a business acquires a capital asset, such as an investment property, shares or managed fund investment, it must start keeping records immediately because it may have to pay capital gains tax if it sells the asset in the future. Keeping records from the start will ensure the organisation doesn't pay more tax than necessary.
- If the organisation is claiming the cost of a depreciating asset an employee has used for work, such as a laptop, it must keep records for five years following its final claim, including either:
  - purchase receipts and a depreciation schedule
  - details of how it calculated the claim for decline in value.

Such records can be kept in paper or digital format and must be a true and clear copy of the original (Australian Taxation Office 2022).

15.5.2 **Accounting**

As we have seen in this chapter, accounting is the act of recording financial transactions carried out by a business. It involves summarising, analysing and reporting these transactions to relevant stakeholders such as oversight committees, industry regulators and tax agencies.

In order to ensure a uniform and ethical approach to the accounting process, the Australian Accounting Standards Board (AASB) developed a set of Accounting Standards. These are policy documents that outline how financial statements are to be structured. They ensure that transparent, credible and consistent standards are maintained by all business holdings. The standards have four main elements:

- *Recognising financial events.* This involves keeping a steady record of everyday transactions within a business.
- *Measuring said economic events.* This point deals with the calculative aspect of financial transactions: accurately recording the date, time and money involved in each transaction and posting these details to the correct account or journal.
- *Presenting financial records in a fair manner.* At this stage, the data will need to be distributed to the final organisational accounts where the "books" are balanced.
- *Disclosing organisational requirements.* This is a necessary step to maintaining transparency between investors, auditors and any other party involved in the organisation's finances.

15.5.3 **Ethical principles**

Ethical behaviour in business is essential. This is particularly true when clients are trusting you with private information and their money. Therefore, in addition to the normal ethical behaviour expected of anyone in a business environment, a specific code of ethics applies to the accounting profession: the APES 110 Code of Ethics for Professional Accountants. There are five fundamental principles of ethics to observe:

1. *Integrity*—be straightforward and honest in all professional and business relationships.
2. *Objectivity*—do not compromise professional or business judgements because of bias, conflict of interest or undue influence of others.
3. *Professional competence and due care:*
   a. Attain and maintain professional knowledge and skill at the level required to ensure that a client or employing organisation receives competent professional activities, based on current technical and professional standards and relevant legislation; and
   b. Act diligently and in accordance with applicable technical and professional standards.

4. *Confidentiality*—respect the confidentiality of information acquired as a result of professional and business relationships.
5. *Professional behaviour*—comply with relevant laws and regulations and avoid any conduct that might discredit the profession. (CPA Australia 2014)

15.5.4 GST legislation

Goods and services tax is a consumption tax which is charged at the rate of 10 per cent of the sales price of most goods and services in Australia. Organisations that turn over more than $75,000 in revenue a year must be registered with the ATO for GST.

If an organisation is registered, then GST is normally included in the price of most goods or services it sells to others in the course of its business. These sales are called **taxable sales**. There are other types of sales where GST is not included in the price. These are known as either input-taxed sales or GST-free sales. For example, basic food items such as bread, milk, eggs, fruit and vegetables fall into this category. Takeaway food and restaurant meals, however, are not GST-free.

Organisations that are registered for GST can generally claim a credit for any GST included in the price they pay for products or services required for their business. This is called a GST credit. When a taxable sale is made to a GST-registered customer, they will generally need a tax invoice so that they can claim their GST credits for purchases of more than $82.50. The tax invoice you issue or receive for goods sold or purchased must include certain information. The information will vary depending on the amount of the sale. For amounts less than $1,000, you need to include:

- the words "tax invoice" in a prominent position
- the seller's name
- the seller's Australian business number (ABN)
- the date the tax invoice was issued
- a brief description of the goods sold
- the GST-inclusive price
- the GST amount (should also be shown separately).

In the case of invoices for more than $1,000, you should also include the buyer's name, address and ABN. All GST-registered organisations are required to pay to the ATO the GST they collect on a regular basis. The total amount that must be paid to the ATO is reduced by the amount of GST credits the organisation can claim for things purchased for its business. GST obligations are accounted for on the business activity statement by the organisation's accountant at the end of each tax period. For taxation reporting reasons, it is important to account for GST sales and purchases separately when recording financial transactions. For guidelines on dealing with GST, see: http://www.ato.gov.au/content/downloads/bus20724nat3014.pdf

15.5.5 Local, state and territory work health and safety (WHS)

The *Work Health and Safety Act 2011* (Cth) sets out the laws about health and safety requirements affecting most workplaces, work activities and specified high-risk plants. The main objective of this Act is to provide for a balanced and nationally consistent framework to secure the health and safety of workers. There are, nevertheless, local, state and territory regulations that may apply to WHS issues and you will need to be aware of the ones that apply in your location and for your specific industry (see Table 5.2 in Chapter 5 for examples).

In addition to the issues mentioned, most organisations will also have internally developed policies and procedures. These may relate to the following:

- *Audit requirements*. Most organisations will undergo both internal and external audits at some stage. External audits are conducted by entities such as government bodies and the ATO, while internal audits may be conducted on behalf of the board of directors of an organisation, or as a means of continuous improvement. Audit requirements may determine:

- how often an audit should take place
- the scope of the audit (whether it will be company-wide or will focus only on specific business areas)
- who will conduct the audit
- the purpose of the audit
- what actions will be taken as a result of the audit, and so on.

- *Data and finance management.* The organisation may have guidelines and preferred methods for working with its financial information. This could include specifying who is responsible for working with financial records, and the systems or software programs that are used to record this information.
- *Distinguishing between individual transactions and summary transactions.* The organisation may have procedures and policies for identifying income, expenses, journals, ledgers and trial balances and how they should be recorded and reported.
- *Storage and security of, and access to, information.*
- *Resolution procedures.* When discrepancies (or errors) are found in financial documentation, there must be a set procedure for rectifying it so that all financial transactions can be accurately traced and recorded, even when mistakes are made.
- *Aging debts.* Essentially, this is a measurement of the total amount of money that customers of the business owe. An aged debtors report can be produced that shows a complete list of all the invoices that haven't yet been paid, minus any credit notes that have been issued to customers and are not yet refunded.
- *Bad and doubtful debts.* A bad debt occurs when you know a customer isn't going to pay their invoice, whereas a doubtful debt is one where the debt hasn't yet become a bad one and there is still a chance of receiving payment.
- *Time considerations—working within, or to, designated timelines.* There may be time constraints in working with specific financial documents; for example, business activity statements that report income generated by an organisation *must* be submitted to the ATO on or by specific dates. This means that all transactions that occurred within a given reporting period must be up to date, correct and completed.

Every organisation will have set guidelines on how issues such as these are to be dealt with. They set these guidelines and standards so that all staff are aware of what they need to do and of the standards to which they must perform. The primary reasons for doing this are so that:

- *The organisation can offer a consistent level of service.* This is important in building an organisational reputation for quality. If all staff are working to the same standards and levels of service, then quality levels should remain consistently high.
- *Any legislative or regulatory obligations will be met.* Ensuring your organisation's compliance with legislative and regulatory conditions is an essential part of your role and a legal obligation. Breaches of these compliance issues could result in fines, penalties or legal action being taken against you or your organisation.

Think about

5. What policies and procedures does your organisation have in place to safeguard the security of its financial information and processes?

Knowledge check

14. Provide at least eight examples of the types of tax records every business must keep.

15. Give a brief overview of GST legislation.

Summary

Dealing with an organisation's finances is a serious and often complex business. The health and success of an organisation revolves around how well it manages and accounts for its money.

Accurate record keeping is a large part of keeping the organisation moving forward. While you may not be directly involved in any of the tasks outlined in this chapter, it is essential for you to understand how important it is to ensure accuracy in all aspects of financial transactions.

References

Australian Taxation Office, 2022. "Records you need to keep", updated 8 July 2022,

https://www.ato.gov.au/individuals/income-and-deductions/records-you-need-to-keep, accessed September 2022.

CPA Australia Ltd, 2014. "An overview of APES 110 code of ethics for professional accountants", https://apesb.org.au/uploads/meeting/board_meeting/01102014094104_26_8_14paper17.pdf, accessed September 2022.

3

PART 3

Working with customers and

CHAPTER 16

Deliver and monitor a service to customers

Learning outcomes

16.1 Identify customer needs

16.2 Deliver a service to customers

16.3 Evaluate customer service delivery

The delivery of quality customer service is, without question, the most important aspect of any business that wants to be successful. While a good location, product range and well-trained staff are also important, none of these things matter if customers won't do business with you.

16.1 Identifying customer needs

The cornerstone of any successful business is knowing and understanding its customers' needs—that is, knowing what, when and how to provide the products and services they expect. Ever-increasing competition for customers' disposable incomes means that if *you* can't provide what customers want, then there are many other organisations that can. It is essential, therefore, to the success of your organisation that you are continually aware of what your customers' needs and expectations of your organisation might be.

16.1.1 Who is the customer?

Before we look at identifying customer needs and expectations, however, it is useful to have a better idea of who customers are, as they aren't all the same and shouldn't all be approached in the same way. Customers can be of many types. For example:

- *Corporate/account customers*. These are individuals or organisations that do business with you often enough to have an account. This means they can order products or services and will pay for them at a later date—against an invoice that you send them. These types of customers are an excellent, ongoing source of income.
- *Customers from other organisations*. This type of business is commonly referred to as B2B (business-to-business). Customers of this type could be:
  - suppliers to your organisation who provide you with the raw materials, products or services you need in order to produce or provide your own services and products
  - other organisations that need your products or services in order to produce or provide their own services and products.
- *External customers*. The external customer is someone who pays your organisation money in exchange for products or services (and who therefore ultimately makes your pay cheque possible). External customers have choice; if they don't like your product or service, they can take their business elsewhere. Great (external) customer service creates customer satisfaction, customer loyalty and customer retention.
- *Internal customers*. An internal customer can be anyone within your organisation, such as a co-worker or another department. To create positive internal customer service, all departments work together cooperatively, agree on processes and procedures, and negotiate expectations. Like gears meshing in sync, interdependent business units within the organisation meet each other's needs, work productively together to meet common goals, and deliver high-quality products and services to the external customer. The focus on developing effective internal customer service helps organisations to cut costs, increase productivity and improve interdepartmental communication and cooperation. Excellent service to the external customer is dependent upon healthy internal customer service practices.

Viktoria Kazakova/Shutterstock

Customer types

Meeting the needs and expectations of customers will also depend on the *type of customer* you are dealing with. People aren't all the same and therefore won't need or expect the same things. To a certain degree, customers can be categorised according to a variety of factors, as listed. However, don't make generalisations about any type of customer—these groupings are a guideline only!

- *Social and economic background*. Each group of customers can be divided into a number of sub-groups. This category of customers could range from the upper levels of society, who are used to getting the best of everything, to people of more modest upbringing and background. What these groups need and expect when travelling, for example, will vary to an enormous degree and will depend not only on cost but also on the lifestyle they are used to. When choosing a hotel, wealthier clients may require luxury accommodations such as suites or penthouses in five-star hotels in the best locations. More budget-conscious clients, on the other hand, may look for accommodation that represents value for money while also being of good quality and may be happy to stay in hotels a little outside of the main tourist areas.

- *Cultural background.* This category of customers will include a variety of religious beliefs and customs, depending on their country of origin. Their needs and expectations will depend entirely on cultural considerations; for example, Muslims require food to be prepared in a strictly controlled way, so their needs in this respect are very different from those of other belief systems.
- *Age.* This group of customers can also be broken down into a number of sub-groups, such as children, teenagers, young adults, mature adults and senior citizens. Each of these sub-groups will have very clear ideas on their needs and expectations in regard to your services.
- *Special interests.* These customers usually have a specific purpose in mind when approaching your organisation. For example, in the travel industry, they might travel in special-interest groups, such as golfers wanting a "golfing holiday" or hikers interested in "mountain trekking". Their requirements can be very specific.
- *Special needs.* Customers who have special needs may include:
  - elderly people
  - parents with young children
  - pregnant women
  - people with a disability
  - those with special cultural or language needs
  - unaccompanied children.
- *Physical abilities.* Within this group of customers, you may have people with a degree of physical or mental limitation whose needs and expectations could be very different from other customer groups. Considerations might include the need for wheelchair access, Braille menus or information pages, and so on.

In order to meet the needs of all these different types of customers, you will have to:

- ask them relevant questions—and then actively listen to their answers
- have a sound knowledge of your products and services, such as:
  - terms and conditions of various aspects of tourism products and services
  - waiting times (if any)
  - prices, fees and charges, as well as payment options
- identify and anticipate any potential operational issues and take action to minimise their effect on the customers—for example, issues such as:
  - unavailability of services on the dates customers have specified
  - delays in receiving or generating any necessary documentation (such as application forms for a service)
  - delays in delivering the goods or services.

16.1.2 Identifying and clarifying customer needs and expectations

Along with understanding basic customer types, it is also important to know that people buy products and services for two very basic reasons: they have a *need* or they have a *desire*. The motivations for the two are very different and you should understand this difference:

- A **need** is something that is necessary to a person's physical or mental comfort—for example, they may need to buy food or to pay rent.

- A *desire* (or *want*) is something we don't actually need but wish to have anyway. Impulse buys, for example, are driven by desire. You may not need a new jacket, but you want a particular one, so you buy it. You don't need the latest surround-sound system, but watching movies is your hobby so you spend the money to buy the best system.

GoodStudio/Shutterstock

Regardless of whether a purchase is made to satisfy a need or a desire, the customer will also have certain expectations of the products or services they are buying. You must therefore not only address what they need (or want) when they are buying a product or service, but also ensure that the product or service meets their expectations. An expectation can be either a great hope that something will happen, or anticipation of success or fulfilment.

In summary, the way in which you approach a customer will depend on a number of things: the type of customer, their reasons for buying, and their specific needs and expectations. As you have learnt, they can be of different ages, come from different cultures, and have different social needs and more; therefore, when you are providing a service you need to take all these issues into consideration. Understanding customer needs and expectations will help you to make the most of each sales opportunity while providing quality customer service.

Let's take a closer look at one of these factors and see how the requirements can vary. For example, how will customers' needs and expectations differ among the various age groups? Do you think that a teenager will have the same needs and expectations as a family with children, or the elderly, when looking for a car to buy?

- Teenagers may be thinking of their image and will *expect* their car to have a variety of features and gadgets that they can show off to their friends. The colour, style and speed of the car will also influence their choice.
- A couple with small children will need to consider safety and security when choosing a car and they may *expect* the safety features to be of a high standard. While the humble cup-holder may produce a snicker from teenagers, it may be an important point for this family. Other features such as size, comfort and boot space will all be important issues in the decision-making process.
- Elderly people may need to consider comfort and reliability. They will *expect* to be able to get into and out of their seats easily, so they will need a car that is relatively high off the ground. They may not be very interested in speed or gadgets.

Do remember, however, that these are all presumptions. An elderly couple may well want to drive a Porsche; and just because a person is wealthy, it doesn't mean they don't want value for their money.

Think about

1. **Think about your own expectations of a holiday. How do they differ from someone 10 years older or younger than you?**

Additionally, customers may expect certain things from an organisation they are dealing with. For example:

- *The information it provides is accurate.* Just as it is important to describe the characteristics of a product or service it is equally important to explain the proper use, terms and conditions and safety requirements of a product. Selling a product or service is one thing, but once the customer has made the purchase you have a duty of care to make sure they know how to correctly use or access it and what contractual obligations they may be entering into with the supplier of that product. This may extend itself to a simple description of washing instructions for a new item of clothing, to a full consultation about how to operate a new piece of technology. The customer must be in a position to make an informed decision as to what they will or will not purchase. They can only do this if provided with accurate information. It should also be remembered that incorrect or misleading information can, in some cases, lead to legal action being taken against you and/or your organisation.

- *The information it provides is relevant.* They will expect the salesperson to provide advice or information on how the product or service can be applied or adapted to meet their needs.
- *They will be treated with respect and courtesy.* Good customer service policies must ensure that customers' basic human rights are observed (e.g. they will be treated with courtesy and respect) and equal opportunity principles are followed.
- *After-sales assistance is provided.* An appointment will be made for them with specialists should a demonstration, or a presentation of a recommendation, or business proposal, be necessary.
- *Prices are competitive.* The customer receives value for their money.
- *Returns/refund policies are in place.* Customers expect to be able to return or get a refund on the organisation's products and services if they don't meet their needs.

This all means that, in order to identify and clarify their needs and expectations, you will need to ask customers questions. For example:

- What are they looking for exactly?
- What will they be using the product or service for?
- Under what conditions will they be using it?
- How long will they need it for?
- What are their expectations of the product or service?
- How soon do they need it?

The customer's answers to these questions will enable you to provide information tailored exactly to their requirements.

16.1.3 Evaluating customer needs and determining priorities

Busy customers will always appreciate prompt and courteous service. If you are talking with another customer, smile at the new customer and say, "I'll be with you shortly". They will usually then be happy to wait until you can attend to them.

Not all products and services can be delivered instantly, however. For example, in the travel industry a person might book a flight interstate or overseas but not actually travel for many months. On the other hand, they may have an emergency and need to fly that very day. The customer's reason for travelling, and the degree of urgency involved, will therefore influence the priority you give them. With the first customer you can take your time in organising all the necessary bookings, whereas with the second customer you will need to see to their arrangements immediately so that they can get to the airport on time and make their flight.

There may also be varying degrees of urgency involved in other industries. Depending on your industry, you may need to assess how urgently a product or service is required in order to be able to prioritise your work. Your organisation may have policies around this. For example:

- *First come, first served.* When no other policy exists, this is the easiest way to prioritise customers. This doesn't mean that you have to answer low-priority requests before urgent, troubleshooting requests, but it gives you a place to start.

- *Customers set their own level of urgency.* While they may use different criteria from your organisation for determining the importance of their enquiry, letting them explain their need is a great way to establish trust. You can then determine whether to deal with their request immediately or ask them to be patient until you can work with them.
- *Priority is given to electronic requests.* Depending on the type of business you are in, electronic requests (such as website contact forms) can be prioritised by including enquiry categories such as "sales", "general enquiries", "complaints" or "troubleshooting". This then allows you to sort requests for service according to the organisation's own priorities. For example: troubleshooting or complaints would take priority over general enquiries.
- *Priority is given to regular customers.* You could categorise customers into groups based on the amount of business they have done with your organisation in the past. For example, regular customers could be classed as "A"-level customers and might take priority over a first-time customer who might be categorised initially as level "B" or "C".

Regardless of these methods of determining priorities when dealing with customers' requests, it is always important to answer requests for service as quickly as possible—even if it is simply to say that a response might take a while. This at least acknowledges the customer, who will then normally be happy to wait for a reasonable time.

16.1.4 **Informing customers about available choices**

Customers are relying on your expertise to provide them with information about a product or service that will fulfil their requirements. They may well be spending a substantial amount of money based on your recommendation, so they are putting a great deal of faith in you. It is important for your organisation, and for your own reputation, that any recommendation you make has a solid foundation. Finding the right product or service for the right customer is a matter of having an in-depth knowledge of your organisation's products and services and then presenting customers with options suited to their specific needs.

robuart/Shutterstock

No two people are alike, and the products or services that may suit one person may not suit another. For example, customers buying home entertainment equipment will have very different needs. Someone who simply wants to watch television may not require complex equipment with a lot of features they will never use. Conversely, someone who loves watching movies and playing video games may want a very sophisticated home entertainment system with many options and features. The type and complexity of the equipment being recommended will, of course, also have an impact on the price—which must also be taken into consideration.

Assisting customers with their selection

It is your job to determine exactly what your customer wants and then to find the right product for them. If you listen carefully to what the customer is saying, ask them questions to gain further information, clarify your understanding where necessary and watch the customer's body language, you should have all the information you need to provide them with exactly what they want.

Suggesting products and services to customers can be a serious business, so you must ensure that any recommendation you make can be backed up by verifiable evidence and is presented in a suitable format. In other words, you must be able to show that any claims you make in your recommendation are backed up by facts. Evidence supporting your recommendation could include:

- product brochures or manuals provided by the manufacturer
- articles from newspapers or magazines highlighting the value or uses of the product or service
- personal experience in using the product or service—this might be your own experience with the product, or comments received from other customers who have purchased it
- allowing the customer to try the product or service for themselves before purchasing—subject, of course, to the industry or organisation's policies
- explaining in detail to the customer the product's or service's features and benefits.

A customer may have already seen a similar product elsewhere—on television, or in a newspaper ad, or in a competitor's store. You must therefore also be able to make comparisons with other products. This might be between products or services offered by your *own* organisation, or between your products and services and those of competitors. Comparing products might mean looking at such issues as:

- similarities between the two products
- features and benefits of the two products and how they compare
- price difference between the products
- ease of access and availability of the products
- determining which of the products being compared is a better match to the customer's needs and expectations.

From an organisational point of view, the main objective when making comparisons is to place your own product in a more favourable light. Serving customers and ensuring that they are satisfied is extremely important to any organisation, but so is earning maximum revenue for the organisation. This must be done, however, without resorting to dishonesty or any kind of unethical behaviour.

Your organisation may have a selection of **preferred products**. These are products or services supplied by companies you deal with, or order from, who will pay your organisation an incentive, or bonus, for high volume sales. This means that the more of this particular product or service your organisations sells, the higher the amount of incentive it will receive.

For obvious reasons, it will be your organisation's policy to sell these preferred products ahead of others that will only pay (or charge) standard rates. It is therefore essential that you know these products very well. You need to be able to point out the positive advantages of using this particular product, as opposed to a non-preferred one, quickly, clearly and convincingly. You want your customer to be happy with their purchase—but you also want to earn the maximum revenue that you can from the sale.

Try this now

1. Find two products that are similar, but are different brands. Compare the two products. List the differences between them and what you do and don't like about them.

Identifying limitations, and seeking assistance, in addressing customer needs

Sometimes customers will have requests that you are unable to deal with yourself. For example:

- The service they have requested, or the issue they have raised, is *outside your area of expertise*. You simply don't have enough knowledge, yet, to answer their query.
- The request they have made is *outside your area of responsibility*. You don't have the authority to supply or approve the required service.

At such times, rather than try to deal with a request that is beyond your scope, it is better to call in assistance from the right person on staff. This could be:

- a service expert or specialist in that specific service field, who will be able to answer complex questions the customer might have
- a supervisor or manager who has the authority to approve requests or to call in any necessary experts
- an external source of assistance, whereby you may need to refer the customer to experts outside of your organisation.

Knowledge check

1. Explain the differences between a need, a desire and an expectation.
2. Give an example of how expectations might differ between various customer types, such as people:
    - of different ages
    - with different economic and social backgrounds
    - from different cultural backgrounds.
3. List at least five areas where a customer might have specific expectations of an organisation.
4. Give at least two examples of methods you could use to evaluate customer needs and determine priorities.
5. Explain why it is important to provide customers with information about available choices.
6. Customers may sometimes have requests that you are unable to deal with yourself. Explain why this might happen and who you might need to call for assistance.

16.2 Delivering a service to customers

Any organisation that wants to be successful must deliver the highest standard of customer service. But what is a standard and how do you measure it? And what does "deliver a service" actually mean? Service can take place in a number of ways. You might be serving customers in a shop or in an office; or you might be dealing with them online, or within a specific industry such as transport or hospitality. Then, too, delivering service might take the form of selling products or services to them, dealing with their requests, or simply providing them with information. Whatever the case, the delivery of service should be aimed at providing customer satisfaction.

Delivery of *excellent* customer service, however, is more than simply having staff smile, say hello, and be courteous and friendly to customers. It is a matter of having well-planned policies and strategies. Without these, service may be subject to fluctuation; it may be great one day and sub-standard the next. Organisational *standards*, then, are an essential aspect of a *consistently high level* of customer service delivery.

What are standards?

> In the absence of any clearly defined, communicated and understood standard of performance, whatever the worker does is right.

Look at the above statement: in the absence of any clearly defined, communicated and understood standard of performance, a worker won't know what is expected of them and so their work may fall far below an acceptable level. Who is at fault here if the worker doesn't know exactly how to perform their job? You can't really place blame on the worker *if there is no procedure or standard for them to follow.*

The development of a standard can be a complex and lengthy process involving government agencies and industry bodies and associations. For purely *internal organisational purposes*, however, and at its very simplest, a **standard** is a statement that describes the level of performance that staff must work to in order to be competent in a given task or work aspect. Workplace standards will guide staff on how they are to behave, and the benchmarks to be achieved, at all times. This will then lead to a consistently high level of service—one that customers can come to expect and rely on and that will enhance the organisation's reputation for quality. Standards ensure that:

- the organisation's products or services are of a consistently high quality
- workers know exactly what they have to do in order to perform their duties correctly
- there is no confusion in the workplace, at any level, about what needs to be done and how it is to be done.

Standards can relate to the following:

- time
- length
- number (correct)
- texture
- taste
- weight
- shape
- number (e.g. of rings)
- angle
- attitude
- height
- smell
- temperature
- colour
- volume.

For example:

- Number of rings: telephones must be answered *within three rings*.
- Time: customers must be attended to *within five minutes* of them entering the store or office.
- Weight: each chocolate brownie dessert served must weigh *250 g*.
- Volume: each serving of wine must be *exactly 200 mL*.

These standards are very specific; they leave no doubt as to what needs to be done to satisfy the organisation's requirements and leave no room for error.

The benefits of a sound customer service strategy and measurable standards include:

- *It builds trust.* These days, people will stay loyal to an organisation only if they have a very good reason for doing so. If you don't provide the service they expect, they could choose to take their business to a competitor. As a result, you have to work even harder to keep customers and to build their trust in your brand. By providing excellent customer service, you will increase trust, and that could make the difference between loyal customers and customers who leave.
- *Customer service often matters more than price.* Various studies have shown that, for many consumers, receiving good service is much more important than price. To get the right level of service, they are often willing to pay a premium.

- *It builds brand awareness.* Word of mouth is one of the most powerful methods of generating loyalty and gaining new customers. What your existing customers say to others could make or break your business. When you provide excellent customer service, people will remember your brand, talk about you, and recommend your products or services to others. And the best part of this is it doesn't cost anything other than offering the best service possible.
- *It will reduce problems.* Problems are always going to arise for any business, no matter how hard you try to avoid them. While you can't run a perfect business with perfect customers, you can ensure that conflict doesn't become an issue. If customers know they can voice complaints and that those issues will be handled quickly and efficiently, they will feel more comfortable about doing business with you.

16.2.1 Developing good communication skills

The delivery of excellent customer service starts with developing good communication skills. You can do this by:

- asking questions effectively to identify and understand the customer's needs
- listening actively to what they are saying, so that there are no misunderstandings
- understanding the nature of non-verbal communication, so that you can better gauge the customer's reaction to what you are saying.

We looked at workplace communication in detail in Chapter 1, so you can refresh your knowledge by reviewing that chapter. To recap the main points, however:

- *Ask effective questions.* A customer may be unsure of what they are looking for, which could make it difficult for you to know what information to provide. Effective questions can help the customer clarify in their own mind what they are seeking, which will then assist you to provide them with information that they will find useful. We looked in Chapter 1 at the different types of questions—open, clarifying, leading and closed—and at how and when to use them.
- *Really focus on and listen to what they are saying.* This is just as important as asking the customer effective questions, as is the ability to focus on a person and *really* listen to what they are saying. If you are not paying close attention, this can lead to a misunderstanding or even to a possible conflict, because they may feel you haven't taken them seriously.
- *Understand non-verbal language.* Non-verbal language is made up body movements, gestures and subconscious signals (e.g. eye contact, voice tone, language level used and culture-specific mannerisms) that could potentially undermine what you are saying if they make it appear you are being dishonest or are hiding something.

It is also important to be aware of your surroundings when talking to customers or colleagues. It is unprofessional to joke and banter overly much with other staff or long-term customers when you are within earshot or view of new visitors to your organisation.

16.2.2 Providing service to meet customer needs in line with direction

It is always essential to keep service standards and procedures in mind. As mentioned, an organisation invests time, effort and money in developing standards aimed at ensuring a consistently high quality of service. All staff must therefore ensure that they comply with these standards.

Organisational requirements

Depending on the industry you work in, organisational requirements may vary a great deal. When working in a *service industry* such as tourism or hospitality, for example, where service is extremely important, the following requirements might apply:

- *Professional service standards and protocols for service industry personnel.* For example:
  - how customers should be greeted
  - general customer service procedures

  - professional presentation and hygiene codes
  - workplace ethics
  - duty of care to colleagues and customers
  - compliance with all legislative requirements.
- *Attitudes and attributes expected by your organisation when serving customers.* For example, as tourism and hospitality are classed as an intangible service (you can't actually pick up what you have paid for and take it home), the attitude towards customers should be to make the process of acquiring the service as enjoyable for them as possible. As a service industry professional, you may therefore need specific attributes. For example:
  - an open and friendly nature
  - a genuine liking for people
  - an understanding that different types of people will have different needs and expectations
  - a desire to help customers meet their needs and wants.
- *Types of customer loyalty programs.* Most industries today will have loyalty programs that are designed to attract customers and to encourage them to come again. Usually, they are based on points earned for purchases made. You will need to be familiar with the terms and conditions of your organisation's loyalty program so that you can provide customers with correct and current advice.
- *Essential features and uses of the customer databases maintained by your organisation.* Databases fulfil an important role in any business. They store information about customers that can be used for a range of purposes and assist when new purchases are being made as all relevant contact details are already on file. Databases can be used to:
  - store a customer's general details such as name, address, phone and email
  - store information about a customer's preferences—for example, it might advise that the customer prefers one brand over another
  - keep track of previous purchases for promotional purposes—for example, if you are offering a special deal on a specific type of product or service, you can search the database for customers who have previously purchased the product or service and might be interested in such a promotion and send them an offer.
- *Payment and delivery options.* Not all customers will want to pay for their purchase outright (particularly if it is expensive), and not all products or services will be available for immediate delivery. To advise the customer, you may need to know about the following available options:
  - Payment plans. These allow customers to pay for their goods over a specified period of time. With the layby system, customers must pay for the items in full before they can access them; using the hire purchase system (or similar), they have immediate access to the items.
  - Delivery options. How, when and where products and services are delivered will be governed by a number of factors, including:
    - availability of stock on hand
    - availability of transport to deliver the goods to the customer
    - preferred dates/times according to customer availability.

  In determining which of these options to offer the customer, you need to identify the urgency of their needs and help them make a decision that best suits those needs.
- *Replacements and refunds.* In accordance with the *Australian Consumer Law*, customers have the right to ask for goods they have bought but which they find unsatisfactory to be repaired or replaced, or to request a refund of the purchase amount. This being the case, all businesses must have policies and procedures relating to exchanges and refunds. This might involve giving customers a:
  - refund of all monies paid
  - refund less an administration fee
  - credit note for future use.

- *Quality and continuous improvement processes and standards.* Feedback received from customers should always be seen as an opportunity to improve the service offered them. This is an issue that should be looked at on a regular and continual basis so the organisation can grow and increase its business and improve its reputation. We will look at this subject in more detail later in the chapter.
- *Privacy, confidentiality and security requirements.* These are very important issues and, in this context, mainly concern the security of information within an organisation. Information about customers should always be kept confidential and never be given out to people outside the organisation—possibly not even outside your department. The customer trusts your organisation with their personal details and expects that trust to be honoured. Equally, information stored in the organisation's filing systems and databases should be kept confidential. It is important to keep files secure and out of sight when not being used. When your computer is not in use, you should also log out to ensure that no one has access to your files while you are away from your desk.

Think about

2. What are your organisation's policies on customer service? How do you, as a customer, expect to be treated?

Legislative requirements

Legal requirements are an extremely important aspect of every business and it is essential that you are familiar with your organisation's legal and regulatory obligations. Breaches of any compliance issues may result in fines, penalties or legal action being taken against the organisation and/or the person who caused the breach. Issues to be aware of, in addition to those covered in the Preface of this text, can include things such as understanding the *Competition and Consumer Act 2010* (Cth) as well as the codes of practice relevant to your industry.

Competition and Consumer Act 2010 (Cth)

The *Competition and Consumer Act 2010* (Cth) is a national law that regulates fair trading in Australia and governs how all businesses must deal with their customers, competitors and suppliers. The Act promotes fair trading between competitors while also ensuring that consumers are treated fairly. The Australian Competition and Consumer Commission (ACCC) administers and enforces the Act along with state and territory regulators. It covers:

- unfair market practices
- industry codes
- mergers and acquisitions of companies
- product safety
- collective bargaining
- product labelling
- price monitoring
- industry regulation—airports, electricity, gas, telecommunications.

This law sets out consumer rights, called "consumer guarantees". These include a customer's rights to a repair, replacement or refund, as well as compensation for damages and loss and being able to cancel a faulty service.

Fair trading laws ensure that trading is fair for your business and your customers. For example:

- When you sell a product or service, you must comply with fair trading regulations.
- When you buy a product or service, you have consumer rights and guarantees.

Australian federal and state laws protect you, your business and your customers from unfair trading practices. These laws, together with industry codes of practice, help your business to operate fairly and competitively, and ensure that your customers are properly informed and protected. See https://business.gov.au/products-and-services/fair-trading/fair-trading-laws for more information.

Industry codes of practice

Industry codes of practice are regulations and practices developed by individual industries in order to provide a consistency of service and policies across the industry as a whole. For example:

- The airline industry is regulated to a large extent by the International Air Transport Association (www.iata.org), which outlines regulations covering safety, financial arrangements between travel agents and airlines, quality assurance, and more.
- The insurance industry is regulated by a number of associations, including the National Insurance Brokers Association (www.niba.com.au) and the Insurance Advisors Association of Australia (www.iaaa.com.au).
- The industry bodies responsible for the advertising industry include the Advertising Federation of Australia (www.afa.org.au) and the Advertising Standards Bureau (www.adstandards.com.au).

These associations are an excellent source of information about their specific industries and the regulations that apply to them.

Try this now

2. Look up the industry codes of practice relevant to your organisation and familiarise yourself with them.

16.2.3 Establishing and maintaining a rapport with customers

Repeat customers are an excellent source of steady income and word-of-mouth referrals to other potential customers. It is important, therefore, to establish a rapport with customers so that they are happy to return to your organisation on a regular basis. "Establishing a rapport" means taking the time to create a harmonious relationship that makes customers feel comfortable before getting down to business. No matter who the customer is, they should all be treated with care, courtesy and respect.

Here are some simple tips for creating a harmonious relationship with others.

- *Use communication skills effectively.* Establishing a positive rapport with customers depends to a large extent on how well you communicate with them. For example:
  - How interested are you in what they are saying?
  - Does your body language reflect that interest?
  - Are you genuinely interested in assisting them?
  - Are you actively seeking open communication?
- *Be aware of your body language.* Remember that people don't only listen to what you are saying but will also watch your gestures and other mannerisms, so keep them—and your tone of voice—positive and friendly.
- *"Match and mirror" the other person's gestures.* Mirroring the customer's gestures and tone of voice will make them feel more comfortable. For example:
  - If they are soft spoken, then don't speak to them in a loud voice—match their pitch.
  - If they appear to prefer a certain amount of personal space as a buffer, then don't crowd them.
  - If they speak slowly, then don't chatter away at a rapid pace—slow your speech pace down to match theirs.

By matching their behaviour, you are offering them a comfort zone—an atmosphere in which they can feel confident in their dealings with you. Opposing behaviour (speaking loudly and quickly, if they seem shy and softly spoken) will turn a customer off and you may lose not only a sale but the opportunity to build a long-term relationship with them. They simply won't like dealing with you.

robuart/Shutterstock

Try this now

3. Try matching and mirroring your behaviour with a colleague or friend. Ask them for feedback on how they felt while talking to you.

The most important thing to remember is that the customer is the *sole provider* of every business. They represent the revenue stream that pays for everything: your wages, rent for the premises, phone bills, stock, security, insurance and more. You can have the very best products or services, and great accountants and managers to look after the business, but that all means nothing without a steady revenue stream. This revenue stream is directly linked to sales made, and nothing happens until something is sold to a customer. Therefore, ensuring that the customer is happy with your products and services is vital to the success of the business.

16.2.4 Managing customer complaints

A complaint, no matter how trivial it might sound to you, is legitimate in the eyes of the customer and *must* be taken seriously. Customers come into your organisation to do business. They have a need, and they believe (or hope) that you will be able to fulfil that need. They are willing to pay for your time, effort and service, and they expect your full and undivided attention. If they don't receive this attention or a satisfactory product or service, they are not receiving value for their money and have every right to complain.

Customers may complain for any number of reasons, including:

- dissatisfaction with service quality
- damaged goods
- delivery errors—for example, the wrong product was delivered, or the product wasn't delivered in full or on time
- service errors—for example, incorrect information may have been provided, or mistakes made with product orders
- administrative errors, such as incorrect invoices sent or wrong prices charged
- customer's expectations of products and services aren't met—for example, the product or service isn't performing as promised
- prices or quotes were incorrect and they are now being asked for additional funds
- customer special requests aren't being processed or provided as agreed
- misunderstandings or communication barriers have occured during the course of a conversation or consultation.

These are all matters that don't take much time to do correctly in the initial customer contact. However, it takes a lot of time, effort and (possibly) money to fix the relationship between the customer and the organisation if such errors and problems arise.

Complaint resolution

There will be many instances during your working life when you will have to deal with difficult people or need to resolve a problem. When problems or complaints arise, it is important to define and clarify exactly what the problem is. Only when you fully understand the issues can you find a mutually acceptable solution.

In dealing with such issues, it is important to acknowledge the customer and their right to complain. Ignoring them, or hoping that if you don't acknowledge the problem it will go away, will often do just the opposite. Complaints are often mishandled because conflict has arisen, and conflict arises due to misunderstandings. It also arises when it seems more important to determine who is right and who is wrong. In the initial instance, who is right or wrong is irrelevant—it's not a contest. The customer has bought a product or service in good faith and, for some reason, feels that they haven't received what they paid for.

The first step in resolving the conflict, therefore, shouldn't be to have an argument with the customer. You need to foster good relations with them, and calm them if they are upset, by being understanding and showing empathy, by staying calm yourself, and by listening to what they want to say without interrupting them. Once this has been achieved, two-way communication can proceed. Figure 16.1 sets out the steps to follow in finding a mutually acceptable solution to a customer complaint.

Documenting complaints and resolutions

Information about how a problem occurred and what was done to resolve it can be used to make improvements to procedures and policies. This might mean acknowledging receipt of the customer's complaint, with details of the complaint and when it was lodged. Understanding the way in which a complaint was made, and the time involved in its resolution, can be important for developing better policies and procedures in future. Methods of documenting the process can include:

- letters written to acknowledge the customer's complaint, and to advise what action has been, or will be, taken on their behalf
- internal forms that outline the complaint in terms of:
  - the exact nature of the complaint
  - where and when it occurred
  - how the issue was (or will be) resolved

- resources needed to resolve the issue
- cost to the organisation of the resolution
- logging the incident into the organisation's continuous improvement register (which we will cover shortly).

Figure 16.1 Steps in finding mutually acceptable solutions to customer complaints

1. Listen intently	**2. Thank them**	**3. Apologise**	**4. Seek the best solution**
Listen to the customer without interrupting them. They need to tell their story and to feel that they have been heard.	Thank the customer for bringing the problem to your attention. You can't resolve something you aren't completely aware of or about which you may be making faulty assumptions.	Sincerely apologise for the way the situation has made them feel. This isn't the time for justifications or excuses; you must apologise.	Ask the customer what they are looking for as a solution. They may surprise you by asking for less than you initially thought you'd have to give.
5. Reach an agreement	**6. Take quick action**	**7. Follow up**	**8. Document the process and the outcome**
Work towards reaching an agreement on a solution that will resolve the situation to their satisfaction. Your best intentions can miss the mark completely if you still fail to deliver what the customer wants.	Act on the solution without delay. Customers will often respond more positively to your intention to help them immediately than to the solution itself.	Follow up to ensure the customer is completely satisfied, especially when you have had to enlist the help of others for the solution delivery. Everything up to this point, will be for nothing if the customer feels that "out of sight is out of mind".	

Think about

3. When was the last time you had reason to complain about a service? What was the complaint about? Was it resolved to your satisfaction? If not, how would you have handled the issue?

16.2.5 Providing assistance and responding to customers with specific needs

Quite aside from the fact that there are all types of customers with different needs and expectations, you may also have to deal with those who need extra assistance from you. Their needs might relate to:

- *Language needs.* The global nature of our world means that you may frequently be dealing with customers from other countries. Their English language levels might not be sufficient for them to make themselves clearly understood. In such cases, you need to be patient and try, through gestures and signs, to determine what they are after. In some cases, you may need to contact an interpreter service.
- *Information needs.* Aside from general information, customers might need more details on specific products or services. For example, they might need a detailed price breakdown rather than a "package" price. They might need to be made aware of any *terms and conditions* that

apply to a service they are requesting, as this may mean they are entering into a contract of sorts and will therefore need very specific details. Whatever the information needs, it is important to make sure the details you are providing are accurate and up to date.

- *Industry-specific needs.* These might be requests that are unique to your specific industry. In hospitality, for example, this might relate to specific food-related needs, such as vegetarian food, or specific dietary requirements of different religious groups. You may also need to be aware of food ingredients, as some customers may have severe allergies (such as to nuts) which can be life-threatening if they eat these foods.
- *Access needs of people with physical or mental impairments.* We will look at these needs separately.

Assisting customers with access needs

These customers have the same needs and expectations as everyone else, but may need special assistance to help them make their choices or to access the premises. Here are some tips for assisting such customers.

- *Customers who use a wheelchair or other mobility device.* When greeting a person in a wheelchair, bend slightly so that you are at that person's eye level to facilitate conversation. Be mindful to look at, and speak directly to, the person rather than to a companion who may be accompanying them.
- *Customers with a visual impairment.* When greeting a person with a visual impairment, always identify yourself and introduce anyone else who might be present. If offering them assistance (e.g. to sit), allow them to take your arm (at or about the elbow). This will enable you to guide rather than propel or lead the person. Let the person know in advance if you will be moving from one place to another. (Don't leave them on their own without saying so.) Let them know when you need to end the conversation. Guide dogs should always be allowed to enter the facility; they are highly trained and should never be petted, fed, talked to or called without permission from the owner.
- *Customers with a hearing impairment.* When talking with a person who is deaf or hearing impaired, look directly at them and speak clearly, naturally and at a normal pace. Only raise your voice if requested to do so. Place yourself facing the light source and keep your hands away from your mouth when speaking. To get the attention of a person with a hearing impairment, tap them lightly on the shoulder or wave your hand. Make sure that the person has understood what you wish to communicate. Brief, concise written notes may be helpful.

There may be a range of other special needs and requests that you receive from customers. The main thing is to remember that the customer is paying you for your service and you should provide it in a friendly and courteous manner.

16.2.6 General opportunities to promote and enhance services and products

Every day, with each and every customer, there will be several opportunities to make a positive impact. Recognising these opportunities should become second nature as you interact with customers.

- *Acknowledge the customer on arrival.* Customers need to feel that they are important, so ignoring them when they come into your shop or office isn't going to make them feel good. Greeting the customer immediately is an opportunity to excel. This can be done by giving them a friendly smile or nod, or by saying a few welcoming words when they walk in. If you are currently tied up with another customer, give a friendly acknowledgement to the newcomer and let them know you will attend to them as soon as possible.
- *If you know the customer's name, use it.* Whether you believe it or not, your name is one of the most important things to you and you will immediately tune into the sound of it. Have you ever been in a crowded room, talking to a group of people, the other sounds just a distant

buzz—when someone on the other side of the room mentions your name? Your ears suddenly become antennae and you zoom straight into what is being said about you! Using a customer's name gives them the feeling that they matter to you. It makes the service they are getting much more personal for them.

- *Focus your attention on the customer.* Chatting with colleagues, or allowing yourself to be constantly interrupted or distracted by other staff or by phone calls when you have a customer to deal with, is rude and unprofessional. As already stated, the customer is paying for your time, so it is only common courtesy that you give it to them.

GoodStudio/Shutterstock

From an administrative point of view, an organisation can introduce opportunities to enhance the customer's service experience. For example:

- *Extended payment terms.* Customers may be given an extended time to pay off their products or services.
- *Review of packaging procedures.* The organisation can minimise breakages or other damage to goods by ensuring that they are securely packaged for transportation. This might also extend to ensuring that the packaging of products is in line with sustainability practices. Many customers are very aware of environmental issues and will appreciate an organisation that has given some thought to sustainability.
- *Review of procedures for delivery of goods.* One of the most annoying experiences for a customer is being told: "The delivery driver will be there between 7 am and 5 pm." While deliveries are often subject to traffic conditions and may be a little later or earlier than expected, giving a 10-hour time frame is unacceptable and indicates unsound time management practices. If customers are asked to wait all day for a delivery, they may be unable to attend to other tasks or to do their own work. Options should be provided to ensure the customer isn't inconvenienced in this way.
- *Returns policy.* Customer-friendly policies and procedures in this regard will also be appreciated. As mentioned earlier, according to fair trading laws in Australia a customer has the right to return goods to the place of purchase if they are unsatisfied with them. Making this process difficult for the customer does nothing to enhance service quality and, in some cases, can lead to the customer making a formal complaint and spreading negative comments about the organisation—exactly the opposite of what you need to happen to create a loyal customer.

- *Review of the organisation's customer service charter.* Make sure you are delivering the best possible service by:
  - continually looking at the services offered
  - responding to customer feedback
  - keeping in touch with market trends and customer needs and expectations.

To recap, delivering good-quality customer service is a matter of understanding what the customer wants and providing the required products or services in a prompt and friendly manner. It also includes dealing with any problems or complaints in a courteous and helpful manner and working towards creating a loyal base of customers.

Knowledge check

7. Explain the benefits of a sound customer service strategy.
8. Most organisations will have specific requirements of staff when delivering a service to customers. List at least five of these.
9. In addition to internal policies and procedures for staff to follow, an organisation will be subject to government legislation. List at least five of these legal obligations.
10. Explain why it is essential to comply with legislative requirements.
11. Describe the steps you could take in establishing a good rapport with your customers.
12. Describe the steps you would take to resolve a customer's complaint.
13. List at least five examples of general opportunities to promote and enhance service.
14. You may sometimes be required to provide assistance to customers with specific needs. Describe at least four instances in which special assistance might be needed.

16.3 Evaluating customer service delivery

A very important aspect of service excellence is making sure that the required standards are actually being met at all times. Any good business will be continually looking for ways to improve its service by reviewing staff performance and the way in which the organisation operates. This means gathering feedback and evaluating the results. Feedback is the process by which a person or organisation can get information on how their products or services are performing. It takes the form of sharing observations, suggestions or issues of concern that affect an organisation at every level.

16.3.1 Why is feedback important?

One of the main purposes of gathering such information is to provide a foundation for improvement. If an organisation never looks for ways to improve the products and services it offers, it will soon stagnate and get left behind by more market-conscious competitors. Feedback can be used to:

- *track the success of a promotional activity or advertising campaign.* Many organisations spend substantial sums on promotion and advertising. Feedback allows them to determine if the campaigns were successful or whether they need to be amended to better suit the market.
- *ensure customer satisfaction and repeat business.* This is one of the most important aspects of customer service delivery. Repeat business and ensuring customers are happy are the backbone of any successful organisation.
- *maintain the organisation's reputation.* This is also very important. It takes very little for a negative comment about an organisation to become widespread. Once a reputation has been damaged or lost, it takes a great deal of effort to re-establish it.

- *learn from errors or mistakes.* Feedback can point out where the organisation is going wrong. By knowing where things aren't working as they should, they can make appropriate changes for the better.
- *improve productivity and efficiency.* Sometimes an organisation's processes and procedures can be outdated or inefficient. Feedback can also point out these areas and allow the organisation to improve.

As you have learnt, every business needs to have satisfied customers if it is to stay successful. You need to listen to what they are saying about you, and then use that information constructively to stay successful. Even complaints should be welcomed—if your organisation doesn't know where it has gone wrong, how can it be fixed?

Think about

4. Why do you think feedback is important? How could it help not only your organisation improve, but also your own service levels?

16.3.2 Reviewing customer satisfaction with service delivery

Feedback about customer satisfaction levels can be gained in a number of ways. It can be unsolicited feedback, or deliberately sought. Unsolicited feedback is normally gained simply by listening to casual customer (or staff) comments during a conversation or complaint. While these comments may be made in passing, they should nevertheless be taken seriously and passed on to relevant supervisors or managers for possible action. Feedback that is deliberately sought, on the other hand, is the product of a planned and structured process and is based on verifiable sources.

GoodStudio/Shutterstock

16.3.3 Seeking and responding to customer feedback

When looking at how effective your organisation's customer service strategies are, or how effective the solution to a complaint or other feedback was, some of the questions that should be asked could include:

- What did we do well?
- What did customers like about dealing with us?
- What products sold well?
- What promotional activities worked?
- How can we capitalise on these issues and improve upon them?

In looking at negative situations, there are some further questions that can help to initiate improvement. For example:

- *Why did this situation happen in the first place?* A close examination of the circumstances surrounding a complaint or negative feedback from both the customer's and the organisation's perspective can show up problems in procedure, policy, or product or service delivery. Issues to look at could include:
  - Was there a breakdown in communication?
  - Is the service delivery as good as it could be?
  - Are the organisation's policies and procedures as effective as they could be?
  - Was the service/product faulty in some way?
- *Did we resolve the issue effectively?* This is a very important question from both the customer's and the organisation's point of view.
  - *For the customer*—resolving the problem effectively could mean that they are satisfied, that they have received value for their money and, most importantly, that they will probably continue to do business with you.
  - *For the organisation*—resolving the problem effectively could mean that they have retained a customer and kept within organisational guidelines and budgets.
- When looking at how the problem was resolved:
  - *Ask critical questions about the outcome.* Was it the best possible option for everyone concerned? Did it cost your organisation money? Too much money? Was the outcome worth the cost?
  - *Evaluate the customer's reaction to your proposal.* Were they happy with it? Were they prepared to be reasonable? Will they continue to do business with you?
  - *Compare the situation to any previous incidents of this nature.* How was it handled last time? Is there a pattern emerging that should be addressed?
- *What can we do to prevent it happening in the future?* By looking at how the problem occurred in the first place and how effectively you resolved it, you can then take any necessary steps to prevent the same thing happening again. This might mean:
  - changing a policy or procedure
  - changing a product or service
  - training staff in customer service skills
  - training staff in conflict and complaint handling.

By asking these and other relevant questions, you can make improvements to the organisation. This could lead to greater customer and staff satisfaction, which will have a positive impact on the organisation's continued success and prosperity.

Verifiable feedback sources

As mentioned, feedback should be sought on a regular basis as a **benchmark** of the organisation's performance levels and as an indicator of what needs to be improved. Acting on such feedback, however, could potentially be time-consuming and expensive. Any changes to be made as a result of feedback should therefore be based on accurate and verifiable information sources. Some of these might include:

- *Surveys and questionnaires.* These are an outstanding way of gathering feedback on customers' feelings about your organisation. They can include the following:
  - Preprinted questionnaires that customers can complete while they are on your premises, or they can be completed online as part of a feedback/survey campaign (Figure 16.2).
  - Customer forums, or focus sessions, where customers are invited to come in and talk to you in small groups. These are better, in some ways, than a preprinted questionnaire, as they allow you to dig deeper into the answers given. For example, in a preprinted questionnaire you can only get one answer to the question: "How often do you shop here?" where options might be (a) often, (b) occasionally and (c) never. When asking that question in a forum or focus session, however, if the customer answered "often", you could then ask follow-up questions such as: "Exactly how often would that be?" or "Do you shop here on specific days?", and so on.

- *Discussions with colleagues and customers.* As previously mentioned, direct conversations with colleagues and customers can give you information about:
  - the positive and negative aspects of a product or service
  - what promotions or initiatives are working well, and which are not
  - what is currently popular
  - what is no longer popular, and much more.

  This type of feedback is invaluable, as it is first-hand information—the person has actually experienced the product or service and can give you a detailed account of it.

- *Returned goods and/or complaints.* Instances where goods are returned, or complaints are made, aren't always negative. They represent opportunities for an organisation to take a close look at the issues surrounding the incident and to review its service and general operations. This, in turn, should then lead to opportunities to make improvements.
- *Audit documentation and sales reports.* A "formal" review can also involve an actual audit being conducted within the organisation. This might include looking at each of the organisation's standards and procedures, and measuring staff (or sales) performance against them. Areas where performance is below the expected level represent areas for improvement.

A regular review of customer satisfaction levels should be second nature to any business and need not be complicated or take a lot of effort. Service standards and policies should also be monitored on a regular basis to ensure that the organisation's requirements are being complied with and staff are following procedures correctly.

Figure 16.2 Typical customer survey form

The Very Useful Product Company

Customer survey form

How often do you shop with us?

- ☐ Often
- ☐ Never
- ☐ Occasionally

When did you last come into the store?

- ☐ This week
- ☐ This month
- ☐ In the last 6 months
- ☐ In the last 12 months

How did you hear about us?

- ☐ Newspaper
- ☐ Magazine
- ☐ TV
- ☐ Radio
- ☐ From a friend
- ☐ Internet
- ☐ Other: ____________________

What products do you normally buy? (please tick as many boxes as you need)

☐ [product A]	☐ [product D]	☐ [product G]
☐ [product B]	☐ [product E]	☐ [product H]
☐ [product C]	☐ [product F]	☐ [product I]

How do we compare with our competitors? (1 being the highest—5 being the lowest)

Please score us in terms of:	1	2	3	4	5
Our product range					
Our efficiency in dealing with your needs					
Our location and accessibility					
Our pricing					
Our staff					

16.3.4 Acting on feedback to enhance the quality of customer service

Collecting feedback and monitoring customer service delivery is only useful if your organisation actually does something with the information received. Comments and survey results are an excellent tool that can be used by an organisation's management to improve its service and products wherever feasible. Questions resulting from a review of feedback received might include:

- Are customer comments positive? If not, what can we do to improve?
- What are the main issues facing the organisation? How can we deal with or improve them?
- Are we supplying the right products or services at the right price?
- Do our customers feel it is easy to deal with us?
- Are we creating a friendly and courteous environment for customers?
- What are our competitors doing that we aren't? Should we be doing this, too?

16.3.5 Documenting and submitting recommendations for customer service improvements

All feedback received should be documented and discussed with relevant personnel, as it forms the basis for improvement programs. Only by working together as a team, using documented and verifiable feedback, can the organisation develop better policies, procedures and strategies for improvement. The relevant stakeholders in the development process might include:

- *supervisors or team leaders*, who can assist with information on how new procedures will affect their work areas
- *the organisation's manager or owner*, who will be responsible for the overall improvement project
- *human resources staff*, who may need to design and deliver staff training programs around the new procedures
- *suppliers*, who might be providing you with new or improved products or services and who will be able to advise on whether what you have planned is feasible.

Documenting the information can be accomplished in a number of ways, including by:

- passing customers' complimentary or complaint letters on to management once they have been dealt with
- collating information from survey forms and reporting on the results
- writing a report on the outcome of a customer forum
- filing documents relating to customer complaints (and the solutions found) in a manner easily accessible by relevant staff
- listening to and recording relevant details of customer comments (good and bad)
- keeping an eye on the local business community for avenues where you could improve your business.

It is important to ensure that any reports submitted are clear, detailed and contain recommendations focused on improving service delivery. Improvements made to an organisation's procedures should always be documented in a continuous improvement log, as shown in Table 16.1. This log can then be used to:

- keep track of the types of issues raised by staff and customers
- over time, show trends in service levels (both positive and negative) that may need to be addressed at a more fundamental level
- provide information on what action is to be taken about an issue
- show when that action was undertaken, and by whom, so you can check that the improvement has actually been made.

Table 16.1 Example of a continuous improvement log (for a restaurant)

Date	Issue	Action taken	By whom	Completed
25 June	Client complained food was cold by the time it got to them	Service timings and methods reviewed to ensure meals were delivered promptly	Alex Brinkman	1 July
28 June	Position of table 6 is very close to the washroom facilities. Customers complain about the noise ... and smell.	Table moved to alcove—well away from the washroom.	Gabriella Yu	28 June
	... and so on.			

Knowledge check

15. Explain why it is important to gather customer feedback on your organisation's performance.

16. List at least six questions your organisation should ask when seeking and responding to customer feedback.

17. Explain what "verifiable" feedback is and give at least three examples.

18. Having received feedback from your customers, there are a number of further questions you should ask in order to act on this feedback and improve your service. List at least five such questions.

19. List at least five methods you could use to document and pass on feedback information and suggestions.

20. Feedback information and suggestions for improvement should always be submitted to relevant personnel. Explain who these people might be and why they would need this information.

21. Describe the advantages of keeping a continuous improvement register.

Summary

Good customer service is said to be like a swan gliding serenely over the surface of a body of water. The customer sees only the part of the swan that is above the water, looking calm, elegant and gracious; not the feet that are paddling furiously beneath the surface. And this is as it should be. Excellence in customer service means giving the customer gracious service while putting in every effort behind the scenes to ensure a smooth and seamless operation.

Delivering good customer service requires a combination of many things. It's more than just teaching your staff to say, "Hi, how are you?" to customers but then neglecting to teach them that at the same time they should be smiling and maintaining eye contact! It's more than just mouthing words to get the customer to pay up and then get them out of your shop or office as quickly as possible.

Good customer service depends on the customer's perception of ease and contentment. You must show a solid front in all aspects of your customer dealings. Like bricks in a wall, this front should be underpinned by such things as a well-planned customer service policy (of which staff are aware), as well as the staff's:

- ability to communicate effectively
- general attitude
- ability to deal with conflicts and complaints
- willingness to be helpful
- genuine interest in helping the customer
- understanding of the customer's needs and expectations, and awareness of how to go about satisfying them
- sound product knowledge.

The success of any business depends on its ability to keep customers happy, and to keep them coming back time after time. Moreover, for a business to stay successful, it needs its customers to tell others how good the service is.

How do we achieve such a thing? We learn to appreciate the value of a customer to our business. To treat them with courtesy and respect—after all, if you didn't have customers, you wouldn't have a business.

CHAPTER 17

Advise on products and services

Learning outcomes

17.1 Develop product and service knowledge

17.2 Respond to customer requests

17.3 Enhance the information provided

Customers are the mainstay of any business; without them there would be no reason for the business to exist. A large component of an organisation's success, then, comes from dealing with its customers effectively and not only providing them with the products or services they require but doing so in a way that ensures they come back time after time. Every employee of an organisation is therefore responsible, in part, for ensuring that the organisation is successful. By listening to customers, and doing your best to provide them with what they want, you establish a trusting relationship with them that can last for years. This requires you to:

- know what products or services your organisation offers
- provide accurate, detailed and honest advice
- understand the characteristics of your products or services
- maximise every opportunity to promote your products or services effectively
- listen to customers' feedback to identify ways to improve your products or services.

17.1 Developing product and service knowledge

Product knowledge is a key element in business success. In order to advise customers effectively on products and services, you must first have a sound understanding and knowledge of them. Why is this important?

- The success of any business depends on making sales.
- Customers deserve to receive value for their hard-earned money.
- Keeping customers happy ensures that they come back again (and tell their friends about you), thereby building a solid and loyal customer base.
- It avoids complaints (or returned goods) about products or services that don't perform as the customer expected.
- It fulfils your duty of care towards the customer—giving them the best and most professional advice possible.

17.1.1 Identifying and accessing sources of information

Your knowledge about the products offered by your organisation—or indeed, your industry—will build up over time. As you gain more experience in your job and in your industry, you will know where to look for product or service information. Where you find this information will vary from industry to industry, but there are a few avenues that are consistent across most.

When researching information about products and services, bear in mind that customers will be relying on you to provide them with up-to-date and accurate information. It is very important, therefore, that you use authoritative sources—that is, those sources that have genuine expertise in or knowledge of the particular subject.

Sources of information could include:

- *Authorised suppliers.* An authorised supplier or the manufacturer of the product is perhaps the most reliable source, as their information can be trusted to be accurate.
- *The internet.* A great deal of information is available via the internet. Most companies will have a website, and products supplied by them will generally have a web address printed on them. It is a good idea to browse the websites of the main suppliers on a regular basis, as these sites will provide you with the most up-to-date information about a particular product or service. It is also fairly simple to find information online via search engines.

However, when using the internet for research, always be careful to ensure the information you download is from an "authorised" or expert site—that is, an official website that has been developed by the product or service principal, wholesaler or other official source (government, industry body, and so on). Anyone can upload or post information on any subject they choose. They don't need to be an expert on the subject or even to know anything about it at all. For every opinion you find on a subject, you will find just as many opposing ones, so the information on a website may not be accurate or even true. Be sure to verify any information before passing it on to customers or colleagues.

- *Relevant staff members.* Asking other staff members about a product or service is an excellent way of learning about it. Other staff often:
  - have first-hand experience of using the product
  - have sold the product before
  - are product specialists.
- *Organisational or supplier product manuals.* Depending on the complexity of the product or service, there may be manuals available containing full details of the product characteristics.
- *Product labels.* Labels will often give a description of a product's selling features, ingredients or components, care and handling instructions, and so on.

GoodStudio/Shutterstock

- *Taking a tour.* Taking a good look at what your store or office has available, and where items are located, allows you to answer customer questions quickly and efficiently. There is nothing more unprofessional than not knowing if your organisation offers a particular item or where to find it.
- *Government or council websites.* These provide up-to-date information about legal and legislative issues that all organisations and their staff should be aware of. They are also a source of formal, legal application forms such as licences for various industries, Blue Card application forms for the childcare industry, business grant applications, and many others.
- *Lifestyle programs.* Lifestyle programs on television can provide in-depth information about countless industries, products and services. Whole programs are devoted to interest areas such as:
    - fashion
    - technology
    - home improvement
    - arts and crafts
    - health and fitness.

  These sources can also keep you up to date on the latest trends and emerging technologies.
- *Trade magazines.* There are a variety of trade or special-interest magazines, such as *Retail World* and *Hospitality* magazines, that are filled with articles about their industry. Trade magazines are an important source of information about future trends, innovations and competitors, and can also be used effectively when recommending products to customers.

- *General media.* In addition to the trade magazines mentioned, there are a great variety of off-the-shelf magazines devoted to certain interest groups that can provide good information relating to your industry—for example, magazines about:
  - information technology
  - gardening
  - home improvement
  - fashion
  - photography
  - arts and crafts.

  Referring to articles published in reputable magazines can help with establishing credibility, especially if you can actually show the customer an article outlining the product or service you are offering them.
- *Trade associations and/or industry bodies.* These organisations will provide the latest information about new innovations within an industry, information about new government legislation, information on insurance and human resource issues, and much more. Examples of just some of the associations/industry bodies in Australia are:
  - Council of Textile and Fashion Industry of Australia: www.tfia.com.au
  - Australian Information Industry Association: www.aiia.com.au
  - Mortgage & Finance Association of Australia: www.mfaa.com.au
  - Restaurant & Catering Australia: www.restaurantcaterer.asn.au
  - Internet Industry Association: www.iia.net.au
  - Retail Traders Association: www.retail.org.au
  - Advertising Federation of Australia: www.afa.org.au
- *Wholesaler/principal product launches.* Wholesalers and principals often hold functions, to which you may be invited, to launch new products.
  - **Principals** are the companies that manufacture, provide or produce the products that your organisation sells. For example, a computer store might sell Microsoft products—the products are manufactured by Microsoft (the principal). As principals don't *usually* have shops or offices, they will tend to distribute their products to the wider market via wholesalers or retailers.
  - Wholesalers are companies that act as an *intermediary* between principals and retailers. For example, in the food distribution industry:
    - The farmer will grow crops and is the principal (or primary producer).
    - The farmer's crop would be sold to a wholesaler (the local fruit and vegetable wholesale market).
    - The grocery shop/supermarket (the retailer) would then buy the produce from the wholesale markets for its stores to sell to its customers (consumers).
- *Wholesaler/principal sales representatives.* The sales representatives of the companies you do business with can also be a valuable source of product knowledge, as they work for the principal (or the wholesaler). They have very detailed knowledge of the particular products they supply and can tell you a great deal about them. They will also be able to advise you of product availability, product uses, and the suitability (or unsuitability) of the product in certain conditions. They may also be of help when your customers have requirements that are outside of your personal knowledge base.

It is important to keep yourself up to date on new products, trends, and legal or legislative issues to ensure that your customers are getting the very best available advice on the products and services your organisation offers.

Try this now

1. Research a product of your choice using at least three sources of information. Which one was the most reliable and/or useful?

17.1.2 Interpreting information about availability, features and benefits of products and services

Developing product knowledge means knowing not only what products and services your organisation offers, but also how those products work, how they can be used, whether they can be adapted to suit specific needs, and so on. Product knowledge, then, includes in-depth knowledge about the **characteristics of a product** or service, including:

- what the product is used for
- how many different functions it can perform
- whether it comes in different sizes (or colours)
- how long the product or service will last
- the conditions under which it must be used
- whether there are any special handling and storage requirements
- whether the product has a limited shelf life, or a "use by" date, the customer should be made aware of
- whether the item is currently available or needs to be ordered, and, if the latter, what the expected delivery time is
- what the product's safety features are
- whether the product includes a warranty which guarantees its quality and outlines the conditions under which it can be returned, repaired or replaced by the manufacturer
- ingredients or materials contained in the product that some people may have an allergic reaction to, which could raise potential issues.

You should also be aware of, and be able to answer questions on, the following:

- *Pricing issues.* What is the basic cost of the item? Are there any optional extras? If so, how much do they cost? What payment options are available? These may include:
  - cash payment
  - electronic funds transfer at point of sale **(EFTPOS)**
  - credit card
  - online payments, such as **PayPal**
  - payment plans, such as **Afterpay**.
- *Competition.* How does your product compare to your competitors' products in terms of price, service, features, brands?
- *Sales trends.* What are people buying from you? How often are they buying? How much are they paying?
- *Problems with products.* Are there any inherent issues with particular products that you need to be aware of in order to advise the customer (e.g. the product doesn't respond well to heat or to some other climatic condition).
- *Innovations.* Are new, emerging technologies or trends influencing the products you offer?
- *Complementary products and services.* (This topic is covered a little later in the chapter.)
- Features and benefits of a product or service (covered next).

Understanding features and benefits

A customer doesn't buy a food processor because it has a "six-speed setting"; they buy it because they like to cook, and a food processor with six speed settings will allow them to *save time* and prepare foods in different ways, helping them to *prepare gourmet meals*.

While these two things amount to the same thing, it's the *perception* that will make the difference between making a sale to a customer, and not making it. One of these descriptions is a feature, and the other describes the benefit that this feature represents. Six speed settings (a *feature* of the food processor) will mean very little unless you explain how these settings will impact on the budding chef's ability to prepare dishes "quickly, easily, with a greater variety of ingredients and with perfect precision" (a *benefit* of the food processor having that particular feature).

In a further example, it's not enough to tell a customer that your hotel is rated as "five stars", has six restaurants, in-room temperature controls and 24-hour room service. These are *features*. You need to tell them what this means to *them*—that is, why it's a good thing that it's a five-star hotel with many restaurants.

- It is a five-star hotel (feature). This means they will be staying at one of the best, most luxurious and most comfortable hotels around (benefit). This, in turn, appeals to their emotions, making them feel good about themselves—another benefit.
- It has six restaurants (feature), so they'll have a lot of variety and will be able to choose whatever suits their mood and appetite without having to leave the hotel (benefit).
- The in-room temperature controls (feature) will maintain the room at a temperature they personally find most comfortable (benefit).
- The 24-hour room service (feature) will allow them to indulge themselves any time they please (benefit).

Therefore, while it is very important to know the features of a product or service, it is even more important to explain how these features will *benefit the customer*. The customer's main interest in making a purchase will always be their comfort and enjoyment. Features don't address these needs, but benefits do, so when describing the features of a particular product or service always be sure to involve the customer's emotions by explaining what the features mean in terms of comfort, status and entertainment value.

In a final example, Figure 17.1 shows a description of a computer from a computer retailer's website. It is filled with features. The question here is: as a layperson (non-expert) in computers, would you buy this product without first understanding how these features might *benefit* you, and how they would be of value in your work or hobby? For example:

- Why is it good to have 8GB of RAM?
- What is so good about having 512GB SSD storage, or 1.5TB total storage?
- What does it mean that the computer has one HDMI port, one USB 2.0 port and four USB 3.0 ports?

Explaining what benefits these features represent can make the difference between selling the customer a computer, or not.

Figure 17.1 Product specifications showing only features

Computer type	Desktop all-in-one
Display size (inches)	23.8
Screen size range (inches)	23 to 26.9
Resolution (pixels)	1920 x 1080
Screen resolution	Full HD
Display type	LED LCD
Processor type	AMD Ryzen 7
Processor model number	3700U
Processor cores	Quad core
Processor memory cache	2MB
Processor clock speed (GHz)	2.3
Processor max. clock speed (GHz)	4
RAM (GB)	8
HDD storage	1TB
SSD storage	512GB
Total storage	1.5TB
Graphics processor	Radeon™ Vega 10 Graphics
HDMI ports	1
USB 2.0 ports	1
USB 3.0 ports	4
Ethernet/LAN ports	1
Bluetooth	v4.2

17.1.3 Comparing products and services based on product information

Sometimes a customer will have already seen a similar product elsewhere—in a television or newspaper ad, say, or in a competitor's business—so you must also be able to compare your products and services with other products and services. Comparing products might mean looking at things like:

- similarities between the two products
- features and benefits of the two products and how they compare
- price difference between the products
- ease of access and availability of the products
- determining which of the products being compared is a better match to the customer's needs and expectations.

The main objective when making comparisons is to place your own product in a more favourable light, but without being dishonest or unethical.

17.1.4 Identifying and using opportunities to update knowledge

Day by day, the world we live in changes rapidly. Over the past few years, customers' expectations of the products and services they buy have changed, as have their methods of accessing and purchasing them. As a result, many organisations have not only changed the way they distribute information and deliver products, but have also realised that the marketplace has changed to a degree that allows for bigger, better and more expansive product ranges. This means that you need to take every opportunity to update your knowledge and skills. There are a number of ways in which you can do this:

- Subscribe to trade magazines or journals.
- Join industry associations—local, state and national—to gain a perspective on what is happening in your industry and what are current and upcoming trends.
- Attend industry-based seminars or conferences to hear speakers discuss issues relating to your industry.
- Attend business networking events in your area, where you can discuss general business trends and make contact with people who may be of benefit to your or your organisation—for example, by making referrals to you or putting you in touch with suppliers.
- Subscribe to website newsletters of sites that are of interest to you.
- Take part in training courses or professional development opportunities. These may take the form of formal qualifications (gained through a college, for example) or training days/afternoons offered by your organisation or your networking partners.

Knowledge check

1. List at least six sources of information on products and services.
2. List at least six issues you need to consider when interpreting information about products and services.
3. Explain why it is important to understand both the features and the benefits of a product or service.
4. Describe the areas of a product or service you might address when making comparisons between them.
5. List at least five opportunities you could take advantage of to update your product knowledge.

17.2 Responding to customer requests

Interacting with customers means communicating with them. This means you will need to answer their questions, and respond to their requests, in a friendly, courteous and professional manner. In these interactions, it is important to remember that the customer may be making long-term, expensive purchases based on the information and advice you provide them, so ensure it is accurate, detailed and up to date.

Depending on the nature of the product or service the customer is enquiring about, you may also need to describe its correct use, as well as any specific safety requirements. This is particularly true of products or services that have the potential to cause harm or injury, or that could be damaged if not operated correctly. For example, if the customer has purchased a complicated power tool, you might need to show them how to turn it on, use it, turn it off, and store it correctly and safely.

Describing product use and safety requirements isn't only good customer service; it may also be an organisational and legislative necessity. The consequences of not abiding by this requirement could range from a minor inconvenience to customers—say, when products break or don't work the way they are supposed to—to a catastrophe, where customers are injured or even killed if they aren't made fully aware of how to use a product safely. In extreme cases, your organisation (or you) could be subject to legal action. Care must therefore be taken when discussing these aspects of any product or service that you are selling.

17.2.1 Answering customer questions about products and services

Customers' questions will depend on the industry you are in, and the nature of the product or service you are providing. Let's use the tourism industry as an example (Table 17.1).

Table 17.1 Examples of questions customers might ask

Sector/product	Typical questions
Airline tickets	■ How far in advance must tickets be booked and paid for? ■ Are there any minimum stay requirements at the destination point? ■ What luggage restrictions are there at their class of travel? ■ How much tax must be paid on their travel itinerary? ■ How far in advance of departure time must they check in? ■ Can the booking be cancelled or changed, and what penalties apply for doing so?
Hotels and restaurants	■ When are guests allowed to check into their rooms? ■ At what time must they check out? ■ What facilities does the hotel offer? ■ Are there any special conditions attached to promotional hotel rates? ■ What are the restaurant opening hours? ■ Is room service available? ■ Are there peanut-based products in any of the menu items?
Tour companies	■ When must deposits be paid? ■ When are final payments for the tour due to be paid? ■ Are there any charges for amendments or cancellations to bookings? ■ What is and isn't included in the cost of the tour?

It is *essential* that you answer customers' questions honestly and in as much detail as possible. They may be making major purchases, or deciding on product or service options that will have a far-reaching impact on them, so the information you give them must be:

- *accurate*—that is, true and based on actual facts
- *up to date*—to avoid causing problems for the customer that might lead to them taking legal action
- *relevant*—that is, useful and not likely to cause confusion.

If the customer is required to enter into a contract with the supplier of a product or service, they must be fully aware of what they are agreeing to in the event that they wish to cancel or amend the contract.

Try this now

2. Using a product that you previously researched, write a list of questions that customers could potentially ask you about it. How would you respond to these questions?

17.2.2 Using communication skills to clarify customer needs

Communication is without doubt one of the most important skills in a business environment. Whether you are communicating with your team on work task issues, with supervisors or managers, or with customers, it is essential that you have good communication skills. Having a clear understanding of what your customer wants starts with asking them effective questions and listening attentively to their responses. Only then can you truly provide them with advice that is useful and relevant to their needs.

You have learnt that asking the right kinds of questions will get you the information you need in order to provide the best possible advice on the products and services you offer. To gather initial information and clarify your understanding, ask questions such as:

- "What do you have in mind?"
- "How will you be using the product/service?"
- "What else can you tell me about your specific needs?"
- "If I have understood you correctly, then ... Is that right?"

By listening attentively to what your customer is saying, you will pick up clues as to the products or services you can provide them that might suit their needs. At the same time, watch for their non-verbal signals: are they actually interested in what you are suggesting, or will you need more information from them before you are able to make an appropriate suggestion?

Explaining product and service details

Explaining product and service details to a potential customer means providing information on the following:

- *How to operate a product*—particularly if it is a complicated piece of equipment.
- *The conditions under which it should be used, or how to take care of it*—for example, how to wash a pure-wool jumper without shrinking it, or what the effect of humidity will be on a given product.
- *Inclusions that come with the product*—for example, along with their main purchase of a hotel room, does the customer also get breakfast and entry to the hotel's gym, or does a bus tour also include accommodation, meals and sightseeing, or does the customer need to budget for these separately?
- *Terms and conditions of purchasing certain items*—for example, if the purchase of a product means that the customer is entering into a contract with the supplier and must abide by the terms of that contract, the customer *must* be informed of those terms and conditions before the purchase is finalised.
- *Ingredients in, or components of, a product*—for example, when there may be health risks involved for a customer who has food allergies, or where harmful chemicals are involved.

17.2.3 Sourcing additional information when the answer to a request is unknown

There may be times when a customer asks a question that you don't know the answer to. There is nothing wrong with admitting that you don't know, so *never* make up an answer. Instead, tell the customer that you will find out and get back to them.

GoodStudio/Shutterstock

Sources of additional information don't really differ from those that were outlined earlier in this chapter. However, to obtain further, more detailed information, the following may be useful sources:

- *Product manufacturers*, who will have an in-depth knowledge of the product and can advise you on different aspects of its use, how it could be adapted to suit specific needs, and so on.
- *Product or service manuals and operating instructions*, which provide detailed descriptions of how products or services should be used.
- *Online research*, which can provide:
  - product reviews by other users, identifying what is good, bad or indifferent about the product
  - information on different ways the product or service was used, and the results
  - information on the compatibility of the product or service with others that might be complementary and thus enhance the original product.
- *Colleagues or supervisors*, who may have more experience or knowledge of the product or service.
- *Industry associations or networks*, which can provide more detailed information about the product or service.
- *Customers who you know have used the product or service*, and who can provide information on how they use it, how easy it is to work with, and so on.

17.2.4 Interacting with customers in accordance with store or organisational policies and legislative requirements

Dealing with customer enquiries can be very simple: they may enter your business, browse for a while, choose a product and then pay for it. Sometimes, the customer may ask questions about a product or service they are interested in or request a demonstration of how it works. This is where solid product knowledge is essential; you should be able to confidently answer questions and show the customer how the product(s) can be used.

In doing this, however, you need to be mindful not just of organisational policies about the way you interact with customers, but also of any legislative issues or obligations. These policies and procedures might relate to the following matters:

- the manner in which you should greet customers
- how much time to spend with any one customer (so as to avoid spending a long time with a customer who ends up buying nothing, or something of only minor value, when other customers are waiting for service)
- offering preferred products over others (dealt with later in the chapter)
- obtaining customer contact details for marketing purposes
- levels of authority for negotiating deals with customers, so that you know who you can turn to for assistance should a customer request a special deal or something outside of the norm
- distribution of duties and responsibilities among staff for certain products or specific areas of service
- pricing policies for products and services, such as discounting, credit arrangements, and so on.

Anyone dealing with the public will also need to be aware of, and observe, any legislative requirements associated with the industry you are in. To refresh your memory, these include:

- *Australian Consumer Law* (ACL) (https://consumer.gov.au). The ACL provides Australian consumers with a set of guarantees relating to the products or services they buy. These guarantees are that the goods are of an "acceptable quality, that they will be safe to use, that they will do what they are meant to do, and that they will be reasonably durable". The ACL also guarantees that if a product or service fails to meet these guarantees, then the consumer has a right to repair, replacement or refund. See also the *Competition and Consumer Act 2010* (Cth) (previously known as the *Trade Practices Act 1974*) (https://consumer.gov.au/australian-consumer-law/legislation).
- *Industry codes of practice* (https://www.accc.gov.au/business/industry-codes). Most industries have an association, or governing body, that provides advice and guidelines on legal issues of relevance to that industry, best-practice policies and procedures, guidelines for dealing with human resource or customer-related issues, and so on. In some cases, they may have specific requirements for licensing or registration purposes. These must be kept in mind when dealing with customer requests.
- *Product or service-specific legislation*. Some industries will also have specific legal obligations that must be met. For example:
  - hospitality businesses that deal with the preparation and sale of food must meet with very strict hygiene regulations, as set out in the Food Standards Australia New Zealand
  - stores that sell tobacco products are subject to the smoking and tobacco laws
  - venues and businesses that serve and sell alcoholic beverages are subject to state alcohol laws.

A professional person is one who not only takes the time to learn about the products and services their organisation offers, but keeps in touch with new and emerging trends and offers the best possible advice to their customers.

Knowledge check

6. Explain the purpose of the following legislative, or industry, authorities:
   a. Australian Consumer Law (ACL)
   b. industry codes of practice.
7. When communicating with others, there are four basic types of questions. Give a brief description of each type.
8. List at least four things about a product or service that customers might need advice on.
9. Sometimes you may not know the answer to a question the customer has asked. List at least five sources of additional product/service information.
10. Whatever a customer enquiry or need entails, it is essential that you answer their questions honestly and in as much detail as possible. What three things must you make sure of in your answers?

17.3 Enhancing the information provided

Advising customers on products and services has a specific purpose: to make a sale. There may be times when the information you initially provide may not be enough to satisfy the customer, leaving them unimpressed or needing more of a reason to make a decision. You may therefore need to improve on the information you have provided in order to make the product or service more attractive to them or to influence them in favour of making a decision.

17.3.1 Identifying situations where additional information may assist the customer

Sometimes plain, basic facts might not be enough to help the customer make up their mind. This might be the case when, for example, they are comparing one product with another similar one and want to know:

- why one product is more expensive than the other
- what the actual differences are between the products that warrant them paying more for your product.

An example of this is explaining to a customer the differences in the various classes of air travel. There is an enormous difference between the cost of an economy class ticket and a business or first class ticket. You would need to explain clearly the enhanced service the customer would get in business class or first class, as opposed to in economy class (e.g. bigger seats that fold down into beds, as opposed to small seats with restricted leg room), and how these differences influence the cost. In other words, you would describe not just the features, but also the benefits.

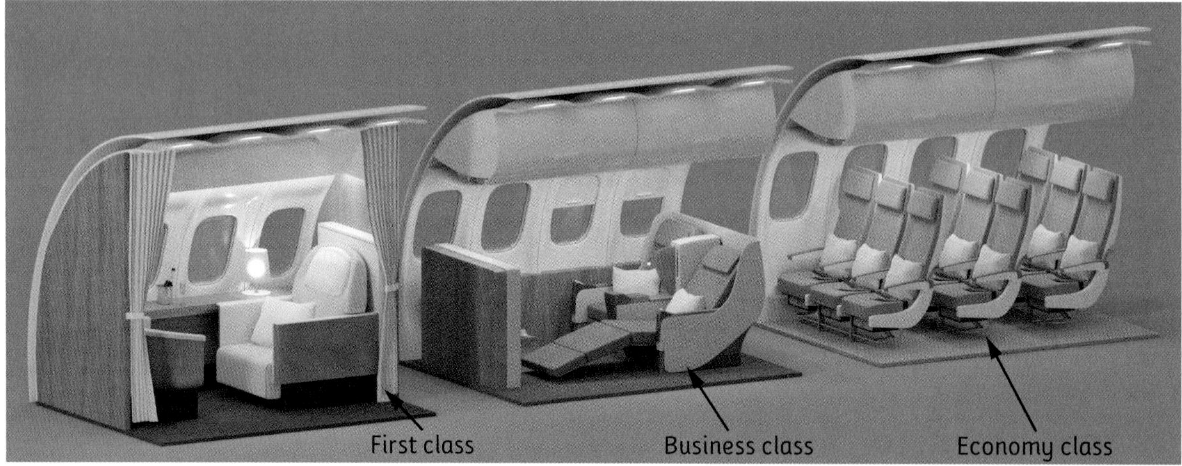

tele52/Shutterstock

The same principle can be applied in any situation where customers need to make a choice between different products or services or, indeed, at all. As mentioned above, the object of providing advice is to give the customer the information they need to make a purchase. If selling to customers is part of your role, then it will also be part of your role to make the products and services your organisation offers as attractive as possible.

Think about

1. Think about the difference between “brand name” products and plain, generic products of the same type. How would you go about justifying to a customer the difference in price between these products?

17.3.2 Advising on alternative products or services

There will be times when the specific products or services your customers have asked for are simply not available. Let's continue with the travel industry example: travelling to Europe during the summer season (or anytime around the Christmas holiday period) is often difficult, as airline seats are booked out many months in advance. When this happens, you can often find alternative means of transport, or different routes, that will get your customer to their destination or provide them the service they are seeking. For example:

- Travel via a different route (e.g. via the United States or Africa, rather than via Asia, if the customer's ultimate destination is Europe).
- Use a different fare type (which might be more expensive but still has seats available).
- Use alternative means of transport if travel is domestic (e.g. coach or rail instead of flying).
- Consider different types of rooms in the customer's preferred hotel or check the availability of their preferred room type in a hotel that is close to their first choice.

This strategy of suggesting alternative products or services is useful, and often effective, in *all* business situations; if the product or service the customer wants isn't available, do the following:

- Offer them a different, but similar, product or service.
- Offer them a different brand.
- Order in the product and advise the customer when it is expected to be delivered.
- Make a booking for the service at the next available time or date.
- Contact a competitor to enquire if they have that specific product or service immediately available and offer to get it in for your customer.

As a last resort, and in the spirit of goodwill and cooperation with the customer, refer them to a competitor.

Regardless of the options available, it is an important component in building customer trust and loyalty that you do your best to accommodate your customers' needs wherever possible.

17.3.3 Recommending complementary products, specials, new lines and promotions

Serving customers and ensuring that they are satisfied is extremely important to any organisation. However, earning maximum revenue for the organisation is just as important. It is part of a salesperson's role to take advantage of every opportunity to increase sales while at the same time keeping customers happy. This can be done in a number of ways, including by:

- selling preferred products
- offering complementary products
- holding promotions.

Preferred products

Depending on the type of industry you work in, and the organisation you work for, there may be a range of **preferred products**. These are products you get from your regular suppliers who will pay your company an incentive, or bonus, for high volume sales. This means that the more of this particular product you sell, the more incentive they will pay your organisation.

For example, a company that supplies you with stock for your shop may normally charge you $9.95 per item that you order from them. As an incentive for you to make more sales and place larger orders with them, they may give you a discount for higher volume sales: if you order 1,000 items, they will give you a discount of 10 per cent; if you order 2,000 items, they will give you a discount of 15 per cent; and so on.

For obvious reasons, it will be your organisation's policy to sell these preferred products ahead of others that are not. It is essential, therefore, that you know these products very well. You must be able to point out the positive advantages of using a particular product, as opposed to a non-preferred product, quickly, clearly and convincingly. If a customer asks for a non-preferred product, then you must provide them with it—but offer it together with the preferred product, explaining its features and benefits for comparison.

Complementary products and services

Another method of maximising sales is to offer **complementary products**. These are items, products or services that "complement" the main product that is being purchased. Have you ever bought a pair of leather shoes, and the shop attendant asked if you needed leather polish to keep them clean and in good shape? They were offering a complementary product. Equally, when buying a hamburger the attendant may ask, "*Do you want fries with that?*" Along with increasing revenue for the organisation, it also enhances the customer's enjoyment of the product or service they initially purchased.

Promotions

From time to time, an organisation may enter into promotional activities for a variety of reasons. A promotion enables them to:

- announce the addition of a new line of products or services
- let customers know that the organisation is moving to a new location
- announce a sale of specific products or services
- make a public announcement about an activity they may be involved in.

GoodStudio/Shutterstock

There are a number of ways in which you can let the consumer know that something new is happening, or that you have something special to offer. These methods can include:

- *Social media platforms.* For example, TikTok, Facebook and Instagram.
- *Media announcements/releases.* These are stories that you submit to local media outlets such as newspapers, radio and television. They outline what your organisation is doing that might be of public interest and are of a "non-advertising" nature. These announcements are published at the discretion of the media outlet and are free of charge.
- *Media advertising.* These are paid advertisements that are placed in the newspaper, on the radio or on television.
- *Staff functions—product inductions.* These could be meetings or get-togethers where staff are informed of new products or services.
- *Customer functions—product launches.* Product launches can be small gatherings or could be very elaborate—such as breakfasts or dinners to which clients or customers are invited and at which the new product/service is presented.

- *Websites*. This is an effective way to promote products and services. Depending on the nature of the website, it can be fairly easy and quick to update with all the latest information about special offers.
- *Flyers and promotional literature*. This is the most used form of promotional activity. You can design the flyer yourself on your computer and then print as many as you need to distribute.

Whichever medium you use, you should always ensure that the information provided is clear, accurate and supported by evidence.

Knowledge check

11. Sometimes plain, basic facts might not be enough to help the customer make up their mind. Describe situations in which additional information might be needed to assist them to make a decision.
12. Describe what alternatives you could offer a customer if the product or service they are after isn't available.
13. Describe what is meant by "complementary products and services".
14. List at least five policies or procedures an organisation might have in place in relation to interacting with customers.
15. Describe the skills you could display when listening attentively to a customer.
16. Describe the types of things customers might need to know about product or service pricing.

Summary

Organisations that provide customers with accurate information and advice will earn their trust. This trust is invaluable: customers who trust an organisation will be much more likely to refer their friends and family to it. It is vital, therefore, that all team members are able to communicate effectively with customers, and work together to provide an efficient, complete experience for them.

CHAPTER 18

Process customer complaints

Learning outcomes

18.1 Receive complaints

18.2 Process complaints

18.3 Resolve complaints

Dealing with complaints or difficult customers is part of every staff member's role—one that should be accomplished with tact and a graciousness that leaves the customer feeling valued. A complaint, no matter how trivial it might sound to you, is legitimate in the eyes of the customer and must be taken seriously. Customers come into your organisation to do business. They have a need, and they believe (or hope) that you will be able to fulfil that need. They are willing to pay for your time, effort and service, and they expect your full and undivided attention. If they don't receive this attention or a satisfactory product or service, then they are not receiving value for their money and have every right to complain.

In dealing with complaints and problems, in the first instance, it is important to acknowledge the customer and their right to complain. Ignoring them, or hoping that if you don't pay attention to the problem it will go away, will often do just the opposite. When problems or complaints arise, define and clarify exactly what the problem is. Only when you fully understand the issues will you be able to find a mutually acceptable solution. By using effective communication skills, you can gain the understanding you need and show the customer that you have taken them seriously.

We will look at the processes involved in this as we move through this chapter.

18.1 Receiving complaints

No business, however well its staff are trained or however good its products and services, will entirely avoid receiving customer complaints. Some of these complaints may be easy to deal with, while others may involve complex issues that need to be negotiated and carefully considered. How you receive and handle these complaints will depend on which category they fall into.

Types of complaints, and issues you may need to deal with in resolving them, will vary. They can include the following:

- *Product-related complaints*. Some of the most common complaints are related to the products or services offered by an organisation. They may involve:
  - poor quality of the product or service
  - high price compared to products or services offered by competitors
  - missing pieces or difficulties in assembly
  - damaged goods
  - the product being the wrong size or colour, and so on.
- *Service-related complaints*. These might be connected to:
  - the time customers have to wait for a service to be delivered or an enquiry answered
  - issues with the staff providing the service
  - incorrect information given by staff
  - shipping or delivery problems
  - poor user experience in general.
- *Public complaints*. These could, arguably, be considered the worst type of complaint. In today's world of instant communication, some of the most damaging complaints are those made on social media platforms. It isn't uncommon for customers to air their grievances about a company online, where the word can be spread far and wide in a very short space of time.
- *Complaints due to misunderstandings*. Good communication skills will often avoid misunderstandings, such as where a customer is expecting a specific type of product or service and hasn't fully understood the nature of what they are purchasing. Equally, if the terms and conditions of a sale weren't fully explained or disclosed, then the customer may not be satisfied.
- *Loyal customer complaints*. These types of complaints should be taken very seriously, as loyal customers represent repeat business. They trust your organisation, which is why they continue to do business with you. If you lose this trust, it may take considerable effort to win it back.

Think about

1. When was the last time you had cause to complain? What was the complaint about? How did it make you feel as a customer?

18.1.1 Acknowledging a complaint

Complaints, no matter what type, should always be taken seriously. With a whole world of choices and options available to the consumer today, it is important to make sure your customers are happy and continue to do business with you; after all, if you can't provide the service they are after there are many other organisations that can and will.

When you receive a complaint, you need to engage with the customer in a calm and professional manner. Any engagement you have with them should be in line with the organisation's policies and procedures. These have been put in place so that staff know what is expected of them—and how they are to behave—in any given situation, so following these directions is important, especially

GoodStudio/Shutterstock

when receiving complaints. Customer engagement can happen in a number of ways, including:

- *In writing.* If the complaint was sent to you via the post, then you should acknowledge it in the same way (unless the customer's letter invites you to phone or email them). Any letters sent out should be produced in line with the organisation's style guide, using the correct letterhead, typeface and level of formality.
- *In person.* If the customer has entered your premises to lodge their complaint, you can offer an apology and discuss the issue with them there and then. It is important, when dealing with a complaint in person, to use communication skills effectively.
- *Over the phone.* This also allows you to address an issue straight away. Many organisations may have specific protocols for customer contacts via the phone.
- *Email and online contact.* Many company websites have "contact us" forms. If a complaint or query comes in such a form, or in an email, it's important to answer it within 24 hours.
- *Social media.* Comments made on the organisation's social media sites, such as Facebook or Instagram, should be answered in a friendly, reassuring and non-aggressive manner. Entering into an argument with someone via social media can do significant damage to the organisation. As "trolls" join the conversation, the thread loses its intended purpose, and word is spread far and wide to the amusement of people who have nothing to do with the initial issue.

In any event, and depending on the complexity of the complaint, an acknowledgement, along with an apology, might be all that is needed to satisfy the customer. We will look at some of these issues in more detail later in the chapter.

If the matter is complicated and requires discussion, however, then the *acknowledgement* should be no more than that: an acknowledgement that the person's complaint has been received, an apology for any inconvenience caused, and a statement that the matter will be investigated.

When considering what to do with a complaint, you may also need to be aware of your organisation's policies and procedures relating to the following:

- *Escalation processes.* These involve understanding your own role and responsibilities.
  - What authority do you have to make decisions?
  - What issues must you hand over to more senior staff for action or approval?
  - What information will you need to gather before handing the matter over?
- *Stock-handling processes.* These involve managing the organisation's inventory of products or services. In many cases, the resolution to a complaint is to provide a replacement product or service. This is a *cost* to the organisation in that an item has been supplied but not paid for. This must be recorded in the stock list so that the inventory balances correctly during an audit or stocktake.

18.1.2 Assessing a complaint

Once a complaint has been acknowledged, you will need to assess it properly to determine what to do about it. This might involve defining the nature of the actual complaint in detail and deciding what outcome you want to achieve.

Defining the complaint

Everyone involved in the complaint needs to agree on exactly what the problem is before it can be solved. This could mean describing it in terms of each person's needs and understanding of the issue at hand. Questions to consider might include those shown in Figure 18.1.

Figure 18.1 Define the problem by asking questions

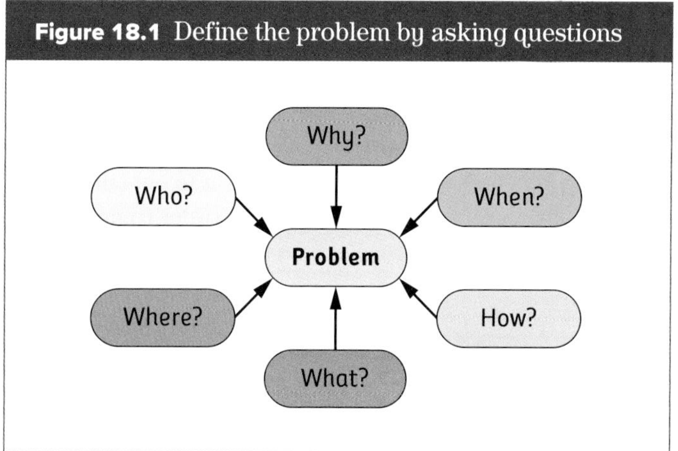

- What is the exact nature of the problem?
  - Is it my problem to deal with?
  - Who else needs to be involved?
  - Should I escalate it to the next level of authority?
  - Is it a matter of an actual faulty product or service, or is it simply a misunderstanding?
- Can I solve it?
  - What resources will I need?
  - What will it cost to solve the issue?
  - Is it worth solving?
- Is this the real problem, or is it a symptom of a much larger one?
  - If it is the latter, who needs to know about it?
- Does it need an immediate solution or can it wait?
- Does the problem have ethical dimensions?
- Are there any legal implications?
- Will the solution affect something that must remain unchanged?
- Will I need help?

Asking these types of questions will outline what all the issues are from various perspectives and give you a firm foundation for exploring options.

Depending on the nature of the problem and what will be required to resolve it, it might (in an extreme case) be better to let the matter go. It is certainly important to keep a customer satisfied, *but not at all costs.* If a customer is being completely unreasonable and demanding, and if the resolution is too costly in terms of time, effort and resources, then sometimes it is the better option to lose that customer. This, of course, will be determined by your organisation's policies in regard to customer service and its marketing and financial strategies, and should only be considered when all else has failed.

Think about

2. Look back at the complaint you thought about earlier. Apply these questions to the situation you encountered then to see how you would have resolved it.

Determining the expected outcome

You also need to develop a clear understanding of the expected outcome of dealing with the complaint. This could be:

- a mutually acceptable solution to the issue
- an agreement on acceptable compensation for faulty products or service

- a better relationship with the customer
- the other person to respect your opinion.

With an understanding of what would be an acceptable outcome in mind, you can determine the next steps. These would begin by informing the relevant staff within the organisation who might need to be involved or to give their approval. You will also need to document the process you have undertaken so far in order to maintain a record of what has—and hasn't—been agreed to at this point.

18.1.3 Informing relevant stakeholders that a complaint has been received

Complex complaints will almost certainly involve other stakeholders, both external and internal.

- *External stakeholders* include:
  - suppliers or contractors, from whom you obtain the products you sell, or who were involved in the sale of the product or service. These stakeholders can provide information and advice, or they may need to become involved if it was found that their product was faulty or service was substandard. They may be required to provide a replacement or to repair the product, depending on their own policies in this regard.
  - customers, whose complaint you will need to acknowledge receiving so that the customer knows that something is being done to resolve their issue.
- *Internal stakeholders* include:
  - supervisors, who have a higher degree of decision-making power and may be able to help with keeping the customer calm or to advise on possible solutions.
  - managers, who may need to approve the use of resources needed to resolve the issue or any costs involved.
  - sales and marketing staff, whose role it is to engage in a positive way with existing and potential customers and who will need to find ways to mitigate any negative media comments.

18.1.4 Documenting customer complaints

The reasons for recording business information, including complaints, are many. It is important, particularly where solutions to a complaint are being negotiated, to keep a record of what has been said and not said; of what was agreed to and what wasn't. Occasionally, a complaint may escalate and legal action may be taken. In such cases, keeping detailed records can provide evidence of all actions that have been taken up to that point.

Documenting interactions with customers is also an extremely useful tool in ensuring the continuous improvement of any successful business. Continuous improvement means looking at how effective your organisation's customer service strategies are, or at how effectively it solves complaints or handles other negative feedback. By documenting information or complaints received from customers, you can examine your organisation's responses by asking the following types of questions:

- *How did this complaint come about?* Looking objectively at the complaint from both the customer's and the organisation's point of view could identify potential problems in procedure, policy, or product or service delivery. Issues to look at could include:
  - Is the service delivery as good as it could be?
  - Did we provide the customer with all the information they needed?
  - Are the organisation's policies and procedures as effective as they could be?
  - Was the service/product faulty in some way?

- *Did we solve the complaint effectively*? This is a very important question from both the customer's and the organisation's point of view.
  - For the customer, resolving the problem effectively could mean they are satisfied that they have received value for their money and, most importantly, that they will probably continue to do business with you.
  - For the organisation, resolving the problem effectively could mean that it has retained a customer and kept within its organisational guidelines and budgets.

  When looking at how the complaint was resolved:
  - take an in-depth look at the outcome—was it the best possible solution for everyone concerned? Did it cost your organisation money? Was the solution worth the money it cost?
  - evaluate the customer's reaction to your proposal—were they happy with it? Will they continue to do business with you?
  - compare the situation to any previous incidents of this nature—how was it handled last time? Is there a pattern emerging that should be addressed?
- *How do we avoid similar complaints in future*? By gaining an understanding of how the complaint occurred in the first place and how effectively you resolved it, you can take the necessary steps to prevent it happening again. This might mean:
  - making changes to policies or procedures
  - making changes to a product or in service delivery
  - training staff in customer service skills
  - training staff in conflict and complaint handling.

By asking relevant questions, and documenting your responses, you can make improvements to the organisation. This could lead to greater customer and staff satisfaction, which will have a positive impact on the organisation's continued success and prosperity.

Knowledge check

1. There are a number of reasons why customers complain. List at least four reasons and briefly explain each one.
2. List four ways of engaging with customers who make a complaint. Briefly describe each of them.
3. Describe the communication skills you might use when dealing with a complaining customer.
4. Identify the external and internal stakeholders you may need to inform about incoming complaints.
5. Explain why it is important to document customer complaints.

18.2 Processing complaints

Having taken steps to define a problem, to inform the necessary stakeholders and to document the initial acceptance of a complaint, you now need to begin the process of finding a solution that is acceptable to all parties. You will likely be able to deal with less complex issues yourself, with very little input from other stakeholders. You may simply need to apologise to the customer and, having determined that a product was indeed faulty, offer to replace or repair it.

18.2.1 Identifying complaints that require escalation

There may be times when a complaint will need to be handed on (or escalated) to a supervisor or manager. An escalation can happen where a customer isn't pleased with an employee interaction and wants someone at a higher level within the company to resolve the complaint. Escalations should be taken seriously, because they often mean you have an irate or agitated customer on

GoodStudio/Shutterstock

your hands. If you fail to handle an escalation effectively, the organisation may not only lose that customer but may even find itself involved in a serious confrontation.

There are a number of reasons why customer complaints may need to be escalated. They include:

- The customer is angry.
- The customer is being verbally abusive.
- The customer's behaviour is physically threatening or abusive.
- The staff may not be able to answer the customer's questions.
- The staff lack knowledge of the product or service.
- The staff lack confidence to resolve the issue.
- The staff have a negative or disagreeable attitude.
- The customer hasn't received an apology.
- The customer thinks staff aren't communicating clearly or quickly enough.

Whatever the reason for the escalation, you should hand over the matter to a supervisor or manager, giving them as much information about the complaint as possible. (Asking a dissatisfied customer to repeat their story again will rarely make them any happier or calmer.)

18.2.2 Using communication skills to identify additional information requirements

When a customer makes a complaint, they may feel anxious about doing so and want to voice their complaint as quickly as possible. This can sometimes mean that the information they are giving you is incomplete, or they may not have expressed themselves as clearly as they would normally. By listening calmly and attentively to them, without interruption, you will make it easier for them to make their point and express their feelings, after which they will generally calm down. At this point, you can discuss the matter with them in detail and ask further questions, all while acting in a professional manner.

If the customer has entered your premises to lodge their complaint, you should do the following:

- *Act and speak calmly.* Arguing with a customer or colleague could result in a full-blown confrontation. Pause before responding to them. This will give you time to collect yourself, to calm any irritation you might feel, and work out how to phrase your response in the most appropriate way.
- *Try to put yourself in the other person's place.* Empathise with them. Use expressions such as "I can understand why you would feel that way" and encourage them to share their point of view.
- *Listen carefully to what they are saying.* Hear them out without interrupting them. Show you are interested through adopting a positive listening attitude and ask clarifying questions to make sure you have understood them correctly.
- *Be patient and understanding.* Again, don't interrupt them. Once they have had their say, they will generally be a lot calmer and easier to reason with. The problem can then often be resolved in a civilised manner.
- *Ask what they would like to happen to resolve the issue and then determine whether this is feasible.* When asked for their opinions and about their needs, customers will generally be very reasonable.

In the event that a complaint is made by phone, most organisations will have specific protocols, such as:

- Answer the phone within a certain number of rings (usually three).
- Introduce yourself immediately, so the caller knows who they are talking to.
- Speak clearly, so that you can be easily understood.
- Listen actively and take notes.
- Use proper language—don't use slang or industry jargon.
- Remain friendly.
- Tell the caller if it's necessary to transfer their call and tell them the name of the person you are transferring them to.
- Be honest if you don't know the answer to a question.

Regardless of whether the complaint is made in person, or via the phone, open questions you can ask to get a clear idea of what the person's complaint is include:

- What were your expectations of the product or service?
- In what way did the product or service fail?
  - How was the product or service used?
  - Under what conditions was it used?
  - Was it used or operated correctly?
  - Was this done in accordance with the manufacturer's or supplier's instructions?
- Was there any damage or harm to property or persons because of the product failure?
- What outcome are you expecting from this situation?

Such questions provide an exact picture of the issue at hand and can determine if a product or service was, indeed, faulty or whether there might have been some mistake in the way the customer used it. This information will help you to determine to what extent the complaint is valid, and then what you need to do to progress the matter. It will also give you an idea of what the customer wants to happen.

Think about

3. In thinking back on the complaint you have been examining, how did the person you made the complaint to handle the situation? Were they professional in their attitude? Were you satisfied with the results? Do you still do business with that company?

18.2.3 Preparing information for resolving complaints

Regardless of whether you are engaging with the customer to resolve the complaint on your own or will be handing it on to someone else, some information will be needed to finalise the negotiation process. This might mean you need to prepare, or gather, the following:

- *Documented report.* This is a written report on the discussions held with the customer and details what was agreed to during those conversations.
- *Product warranties.* These provide information about how the manufacturer or supplier of a product will handle faults. If there is a fault with the actual product a customer purchased, your organisation will usually refer the customer to the manufacturer for repair or replacement under the product's warranty.
- *Product or service brochures.* These give detailed descriptions of the product or service and its functions, limitations and general uses. They can be used to determine if the customer used the product or service correctly.

- *Operating manuals.* These are provided by the organisation or product manufacturer and include exact instructions on how, when and where a product must be operated.
- *Forms to be completed.* These might include warranty forms, refund requests, and so on.

All of this information can then be used to decide on what action needs to be taken to resolve a complex complaint.

Knowledge check

6. Asking effective questions can help you to understand the exact nature of a complaint. List four types of questions you might ask.
7. List at least six reasons why customers might complain.
8. Explain why it might be necessary to get additional information from a customer, and what questions you should ask to get it.
9. Describe the type of information you should prepare for resolving complaints.

18.3 Resolving complaints

When problems occur, businesses are often reluctant to look back on their performance in order to understand what happened and why. But this is an essential part of achieving business success, so it is important to properly manage complaints to make it easier to identify their root causes.

Complaints are often a valid indication that some part of an organisation isn't functioning as well as it should. Listening to what customers have to say is an important means of identifying such areas and of helping to resolve not only their complaints but also the underlying operational issues that may have caused them.

18.3.1 Identifying the implications of a complaint for the customer and the organisation

Complaints will always impact on the business in some way, be it minor or major. Reputations are made or lost on the word of customers, so complaints are often viewed in a negative way. On the positive side, however, customer complaints can be viewed as a business improvement opportunity, as they allow you to do the following:

- *Identify vital areas for service improvement.* Highlight key areas where your organisation needs work or systems need updating.
- *Identify improvements that may be needed in policies and procedures that are no longer working.* Legislation regarding things such as privacy and consumer law is constantly evolving, and the organisation will need to stay current and compliant with all relevant legal requirements.
- *Improve communication with customers.* Communication protocols have changed considerably over the past years. Sending letters to clients is no longer an efficient means of contacting them, so protocols that include emails, social media and website contact forms should be introduced to keep pace with modern communication methods as and when they change.
- *Keep senior management informed about what is happening "on the floor" of the organisation.* This can trigger conversations that can lead to improvements.
- *Use complaints received as a method of improving staff training.* Complaints illustrate what can happen if standards aren't met and offer opportunities to train staff in how to respond appropriately.

Complaints received in any of these—or other—areas can trigger organisational improvements. However, a business's success rests on the quality of the service it offers. When its customers are dissatisfied, an organisation will lose business and its reputation. Figure 18.2 outlines the results of surveys conducted on consumer shopping habits, which show how poor service is reflected in customers' shopping choices.

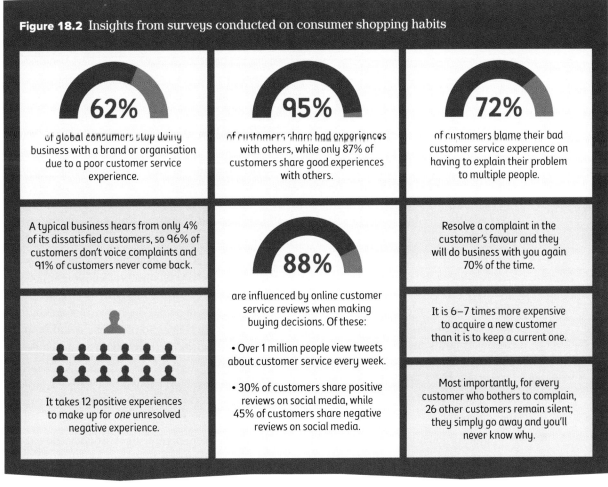

Figure 18.2 Insights from surveys conducted on consumer shopping habits

62%

of global consumers stop doing business with a brand or organisation due to a poor customer service experience.

95%

of customers share bad experiences with others, while only 87% of customers share good experiences with others.

72%

of customers blame their bad customer service experience on having to explain their problem to multiple people.

A typical business hears from only 4% of its dissatisfied customers, so 96% of customers don't voice complaints and 91% of customers never come back.

88%

are influenced by online customer service reviews when making buying decisions. Of these:

- Over 1 million people view tweets about customer service every week.
- 30% of customers share positive reviews on social media, while 45% of customers share negative reviews on social media.

Resolve a complaint in the customer's favour and they will do business with you again 70% of the time.

It takes 12 positive experiences to make up for *one* unresolved negative experience.

It is 6–7 times more expensive to acquire a new customer than it is to keep a current one.

Most importantly, for every customer who bothers to complain, 26 other customers remain silent; they simply go away and you'll never know why.

Source: CX Central, 2019. "Useful facts and figures about customer experience", updated 29 December, https://cxcentral.com.au/useful-facts-and-figures, accessed 23 August 2022

With these figures in mind, it becomes clear that providing excellent customer service should be at the forefront of every organisation's plans for a successful future and that complaints should be resolved quickly and effectively.

Think about

4. **Looking at the statistics in Figure 18.2, think about the implications of bad feedback and how it would affect your organisation.**

Organisational and legislative issues to consider

The ideal solution to a complaint is to ensure that the customer goes away satisfied with the result and is happy to continue doing business with your organisation. This should not, however, be achieved at all costs. There are a number of things to consider.

- *Costs issues.* Often, a conflict with a customer will be centred on dissatisfaction with a product or service. If the product or service was actually found to be faulty, then the simplest solution to the problem is a straightforward replacement. Sometimes, however, the situation isn't that simple and the customer will demand further compensation. In these cases, a replacement may not be enough, and something extra may need to be done. When determining the extent of compensation, if any, to be offered to the customer, issues to consider include:

- customer goodwill and repeat business. If your organisation is dependent on customers coming back again, then this is an important consideration.
- the organisation's reputation. Dissatisfied customers can do a great deal of damage to an organisation. Consider the statistics shared in Figure 18.2.
- direct cost. Compensation to a client can be in the form of cash, additional products or services, or an upgrade from the product or service they have purchased. If compensation is to be of a monetary nature, then the cost to the organisation must be considered.

- *Organisational policy on refunds or exchange.* Most organisations will have policies on giving refunds. Some companies refund money, while others will give credit for products or services they provide. In some industries, you must also consider the refund policies of the principals you deal with. Organisations that act as agents for the actual suppliers of the products or services (principals), such as insurance or mortgage brokers or travel agents, also need to consider the refund policies or penalty clauses of these principals. It should be noted, however, that in line with consumer law, a customer can insist on a refund under the right circumstances.
- *Resource implications.* The amount of time you spend with a customer in trying to solve a problem is a cost factor. Your time is worth money to the organisation and while you are spending time with them, you are not dealing with other customers or tasks. Anything you may give away in order to solve the problem also costs money, whether it is a discount, a "free" giveaway product or an exchange product. Before agreeing to provide a solution to the customer, you must therefore first determine if it is financially viable to do so and take the organisation's policies and procedures into account.
- *Legislative issues.* In making a judgement on complaint resolution, you may also be required to bear in mind the legal implications that may be involved. These might include being aware of the following:
  - Anti-discrimination issues when dealing with people from diverse backgrounds. Be careful not to cause offence. There are a number of legal obligations that you must bear in mind involving the following legislation:
    - *Age Discrimination Act 2004* (Cth)
    - *Disability Discrimination Act 1992* (Cth)
    - *Racial Discrimination Act 1975* (Cth)
    - *Sex Discrimination Act 1984* (Cth).
  - Ethical principles of business. These may include applying your organisation's or industry's *code of practice*, observing duty of care rules, and being open and honest in all your dealings with the customer. Misleading information provided to a customer can be a breach of these codes of practice and could result in penalties or, in extreme cases, in the loss of a business license or registration.
  - The *Privacy Act 1988* (Cth). This Act dictates how the information you gather must be handled, what you can and cannot share with others, and how the information is stored.
  - Work health and safety (WHS) issues. These may be involved in the return of products or services, or may be the result of an aggressive and escalating grievance situation.
  - Other key provisions of legislation relating to customers. These may include the Australian Consumer Law (https://consumer.gov.au) and consumer guarantees, which offer advice on consumer rights regarding such things as conditions under which refunds may be requested and what recourse a customer may have if they remain dissatisfied with complaint resolution.

18.3.2 Analysing options for resolving customer complaints

In any situation where a negotiation is possible (particularly in complex matters), you may need to have a range of options to put forward for discussion, each of which should have high and low outcome levels (see Figure 18.3). These could be:

- *Ideal outcome.* This represents the high level: "This is what I would really like to achieve in the negotiation process".
- *Realistic outcome.* It is usually unlikely that you will achieve your ideal outcome, so this is a realistic expectation of what you will end up with: "I would really like to achieve ... but I'm happy to compromise on ...".
- *Fallback parameters.* This is the minimum that you will settle for: "I won't accept anything less than ...".
- *Unacceptable outcome.* At this point, the negotiation has failed to achieve a reasonable outcome and may need to be escalated.

Figure 18.3 Negotiating options to resolve a complaint

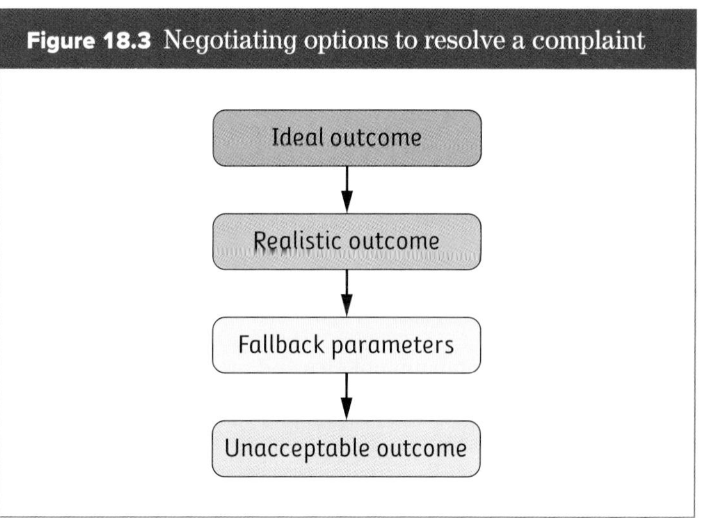

Brainstorming for options

With your own level of expectation decided, you can brainstorm for different ideas and suggestions. There might be a number of solutions to the problem that could work for everyone involved, so don't get stuck on one option just because it's the first one you find. Be creative about the possibilities available to you and look for common ground.

Evaluating the solutions

In deciding the best result from the options available, you should weigh up the pros and cons of each one based on your organisation's policies and procedures, cost or budgetary constraints, the legal ramifications, and the mutual benefit for both the organisation and the customer. Questions you might ask in the analysis process could include:

- Is this the best possible solution for both parties?
- What will we do if the customer doesn't accept this option?
- What concessions are we willing to make to satisfy the customer's expectations?
- What concessions are we not willing to make?
- If we don't make the concessions asked for, how will this impact on our organisation?
- What are the resource and cost implications of offering this solution?

18.3.3 Proposing options

When a viable solution has been agreed on within the organisation, the customer (if not directly involved in the resolution) needs to be informed of the outcome. With your own position clear, you can present the best option to your customer, outlining:

- what you are offering to do to resolve their complaint
- any constraints on, or terms and conditions for, accepting the offer
- their required input or consent to the proposal
- any concessions needed, as per your outcome expectations
- any alternative options if the first option is unacceptable or if negotiations fail.

In presenting the proposed solution, you should always come back to the positive aspects of the option being put forward and how it fits the customer's need—in the process, leading them gently towards agreement.

During any **negotiation** process, you should be open to good arguments rather than pressure or manipulation from the other party. Be open to reason but closed to threats. In difficult situations, however, it might be necessary to bring in another person to mediate or take over the presentation of the proposal.

18.3.4 Escalating matters for which a solution cannot be determined

In most cases, a customer will be fairly reasonable about the resolution you offer to their complaint; as long as you refund the money they paid, or exchange the product, then they will generally go away happy. Problems can and do arise, however, when the customer's needs cannot be satisfied. This might be the case, for example, when:

- company policies and procedures prevent a simple refund or exchange of goods
- the customer's request is reasonable, but you don't have the knowledge (or the authority) to grant it
- the customer may have unreasonable expectations about what should happen to resolve their complaint
- negotiations have stalled and you cannot move forward without assistance.

In such cases, you may need to call in, or refer the customer to, other people. Escalating the matter to appropriate personnel may involve the following:

- Relevant superiors within the organisation who may have more knowledge or authority. For example a:
    - direct supervisor. If the issue is relatively minor and can be handled within your own department, then your direct supervisor can normally be called upon for help. For example, if a product or service was purchased that wasn't satisfactory and a straight exchange isn't possible, then the supervisor could authorise an upgrade of product or service if this is the best way to solve the problem.
    - senior manager. Where a supervisor isn't able to solve a problem because the issue at hand is outside their sphere of authority, a senior manager may need to be called in. This could happen if a customer isn't being reasonable about the solutions offered or if the issue has turned into an argument or a shouting match.
- External bodies, such as the following:
    - Government authorities. As a last resort, when the problem cannot be resolved internally, then outside sources may need to be involved. This could mean referring the issue to external bodies such as the Commonwealth Ombudsman, the relevant government department or an industry body responsible for the industry to which the organisation belongs. These outside authorities would investigate the matter and make an unbiased judgement when all parties have put forward their case.
    - Police. On rare occasions a situation may escalate to the point where it can become dangerous, where arguments and shouting turn to swearing or shoving. If a situation cannot be resolved peacefully and becomes threatening, then security or the police may need to be called.
    - Suppliers. At times, you may not be able to supply what a customer has asked for. In these cases, calling the supplier (or principal) of a product directly can sometimes help and is good customer service.

Wherever there is any doubt, it is always advisable to refer a matter to a supervisor or other relevant team member. Never promise something that you aren't sure you will be able to deliver just so that you can solve the problem quickly. This may, in the end, lead to much bigger problems if the organisation is unable to fulfil the promise you made and can cause a further deterioration of the organisation's reputation in the customer's eyes.

Knowledge check

10. Receiving a complaint from a customer isn't necessarily always a negative thing. List at least four reasons why complaints can have positive implications for an organisation.

11. When determining how to resolve a complaint, you need to take organisational issues into consideration. Describe at least three such issues.

12. You also need to consider legislative implications in resolving a complaint. List four of these.

13. Describe the steps you would take when analysing options for resolving customer complaints.

14. Explain the things you need to outline to the customer when presenting your proposed solution.

15. There may be times when you have to escalate a complaint to a higher authority. List at least three reasons why this might happen.

16. Give at least three examples of stakeholders to whom you might escalate a problem.

Summary

In today's internet-driven world, customers have more power than ever. If they have a positive experience, they will share this with friends, family and connections, which in turn can lead to new business for your organisation, all at zero cost. But if you fail to provide a positive customer experience, your customers will complain.

A customer's complaint highlights a problem, whether it's a problem with a product, a staff member or an internal process. By hearing these problems directly from customers, you can investigate and make improvements in order to prevent further complaints in the future.

Research has also found that customers whose complaints are handled quickly can often turn into loyal customers—and even brand advocates.

CHAPTER 19

Organise personal work priorities

Learning outcomes

19.1 Organise and complete your own work schedule

19.2 Evaluate your own work performance

19.3 Coordinate personal skills development and learning

Wherever you work, you will have certain tasks to perform. There will often be standards to which these tasks must be performed in order to maintain the highest possible quality of service and/or product, and there may be time frames in which they must be achieved. No one in an organisation, however, works in complete isolation. You will work with colleagues and supervisors in your own department. You may work with other departments as a member of a committee or team. Whatever the case, it is important to understand how your role fits into the departmental and/or organisational picture. The duties you perform may represent an important step in an organisation's procedures or processes, or they may be part of a larger task or project working with others—all contributing toward getting a specific task done. You may all be working on the task or project simultaneously, or each person may need to complete their part so that the next person can complete theirs. You must therefore be aware of who relies on you to get your work done so that they can complete their own tasks.

It is also important to be aware of the time frames in which you need to complete your specific tasks, since holding up the workflow could cost the company its customers, revenue and/or reputation. A successful organisation should run like a well-oiled machine, with each cog turning in sync with the others so that it meshes with the machinery as a whole (Figure 19.1). Broken cogs can damage the machinery, just as inefficient work practices and poor teamwork can damage the organisation.

Finally, it is important to learn and grow in your work role by taking advantage of all opportunities to improve your skills and knowledge. Using opportunities to learn will enhance your value to the organisation but will also give you greater job satisfaction and may lead to more responsibility or a promotion.

Figure 19.1 An organisation should run like a well-oiled machine

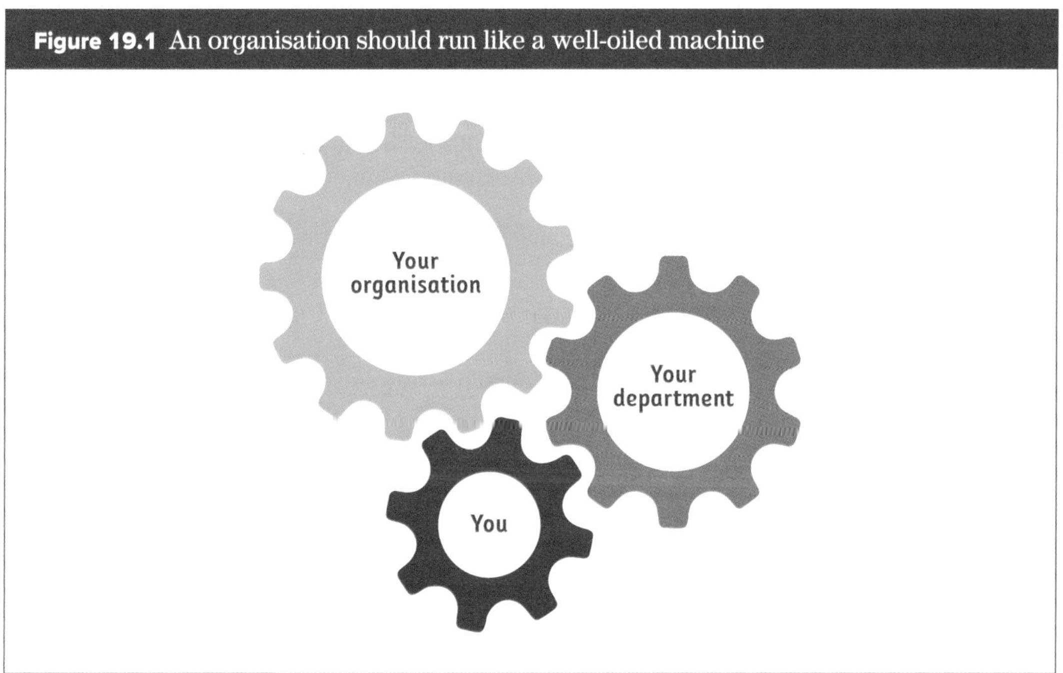

19.1 Organising and completing your own work schedule

After you've completed an initial induction period, most employers will expect you to get on with your job. During the first few weeks you may be somewhat hesitant in your actions, so it may be useful to organise a schedule of what you need to do. As you become more proficient in your role, the schedule can still be useful in helping you to keep on track so that all your work is done and is done on time.

As mentioned, the work that you do will have an impact on others within your organisation. Using a marketing coordinator's role as an example, you might be responsible for the following:

- *Preparing and placing advertisements for staff vacancies.* Other departments within the organisation will be waiting on these ads to be placed so that they can employ people they need either for specific short-term projects or as full-time staff. In either case, a hold-up in your part of the recruitment process means that the work the new employees are required to do will also be delayed.
- *Preparing advertisements for promoting the organisation.* This is a very important task, and organisations usually plan the placement of their promotional advertisements very precisely. For example, they may be introducing a new product line and have organised a major launch campaign—with sales, celebrities, prizes and many other things to entice customers to buy the new product. In this case, ads promoting the launch campaign must be placed to an exact time schedule to ensure maximum exposure. Forgetting to place the ads for this event could lead to embarrassment for the organisation and a serious loss of sales.
- *Undertaking specific project work.* This often involves a team effort, with each person on the team being allocated a task to complete within a given time frame. If a team member is behind on their particular task, it can hold up the entire project and cause serious problems.

This all means that you need to be organised and know what to do, and when. A well-planned and thorough schedule (or work plan) is an excellent tool to help you keep on top of all the things you need to do.

19.1.1 Developing work goals and key performance indicators

Many organisations have clearly defined business plans and work towards specific goals. In order for them to achieve these goals, every staff member must play their part. In fact, they may be given specific targets, or **key performance indicators (KPIs)**, to achieve. For example, if one of the organisation's main objectives is to increase its profitability, it might do the following:

GoodStudio/Shutterstock

- Give each *individual salesperson* a specific sales target that they must meet.
- Set targets for *administrative staff* to minimise wasteful use of resources (e.g. paper products and copier toner), which will reduce office expenses.
- Give *operational staff* KPIs tailored to their individual roles. For example, production staff may need to produce a specific number of products per day, all of which must meet organisational standards.
- Identify KPIs for *marketing and PR staff* based around media exposure.

All these KPIs are designed to decrease costs, and increase sales and profitability, with each team member contributing.

Think about

1. Do you have KPIs in your job role? If not, what might they be? Can you set some for yourself?

As you know, most organisations will also have operational plans determining how the organisation will actually function. In terms of your specific work role, these might include issues discussed in the Preface of this text, such as:

- compliance with legal obligations, including:
  - anti-discrimination legislation
  - privacy and confidentiality laws
  - work health and safety (WHS) obligations
- customer service standards, providing staff with guidance on how they are to interact with customers
- the manner in which work tasks are to be undertaken and completed, with specific steps and standards to ensure these tasks are carried out efficiently and effectively.

Standards set by the organisation (covered in Chapter 16) are essential in supporting a consistently high level of work efficiency. They ensure the following:

- The company's products or services are consistently of a high quality.
- Workers know exactly what they have to do in order to perform their duties correctly.
- There is no confusion in the workplace at any level about *what* needs to be done and *how* it is to be done.

Principles and techniques of goal setting and measuring performance

When organising your personal work priorities, it is useful to understand how to develop your goals in such a way that you can measure them.

Goal setting

In most instances, an overall goal will be set by your organisation's management. You will then, in consultation with your supervisor, develop your own goals specific to your role but based on the organisation-wide one. In this way, everyone will be heading in the same direction.

Any goal, whether it is personal or business-related, needs three basic elements to be achievable, with the possible addition of a fourth (see "Measuring performance"):

1. *The goal itself.* This is the "what". What is it the organisation, or the individual, wants to achieve?
2. *The strategy (or steps to be taken).* This is the "how". How will the organisation, or the individual, achieve their goal?
3. *The time frame.* This is the "when". When does this need to be achieved by, and what are the various time milestones that need to be reached in order to stay on track?

Developing your goal begins with understanding what it is your organisation wants to achieve and looking at how your role and responsibilities might be able to contribute. For example, if the organisation's overall goal for the year is to decrease expenditure by 15 per cent compared to last year, as a marketing coordinator your strategies to help achieve this goal might include the following:

- Conduct customer surveys to find out how they heard about your organisation. This will help you to determine which advertising media you are paying for are working and which aren't, so that you can eliminate unproductive media and thereby reduce your costs.
- Look for free or low-cost methods of marketing the organisation, again helping to reduce costs.
- Renegotiate contracts with suppliers, such as printers, to get lower rates.

Any proposed goal should follow the **SMART principle**:

- *S—Specific.* What exactly are you trying to achieve?
- *M—Measurable.* How will you know if you have achieved, or are on track to achieve, your goal? A measure should ideally be numerically based. For example:
  - You will reduce advertising costs by 5 per cent over the year.
  - You will reduce printing undertaken by outside organisations by 10 per cent and, instead, produce any posters or other marketing materials needed in-house.
- *A—Achievable.* Is the goal realistic? Can you actually get it done in the time allotted and with the resources available to you?
- *R—Relevant.* Does your goal actually contribute to the organisation's overall objective?
- *T—Time-bound.* When will the goal be accomplished? How will you manage each part of your goal to ensure it is achieved on time and in line with the organisation's stated time frames?

The Studio/Shutterstock

Measuring performance

To support your plan for achieving a goal, it is useful to add a fourth element:

4. *The means you use to measure your performance.*

You must be able to measure if the goal or objective has been achieved, or that it is on track to be completed successfully. For example, the role of office receptionist involves a great many tasks, not all of them efficient or even necessary. You may spend several hours each day working on non-essential things that could be delegated to others or done away with altogether. If one of your KPIs was to reduce the amount of time wasted on this non-essential work by one hour per day, you would need to be able to answer the question: “Have I reduced my workload, and by how much?” The “by how much” will be the gauge against which you can measure whether you have successfully achieved your KPI.

Here is a further example. As a salesperson, you may have to make a specific number of sales calls per week or achieve a specific dollar figure in sales. You could measure your progress by keeping track of how many calls, or sales, you make. By regularly monitoring your progress, you can identify issues that might be preventing you from your meeting your goal and can then take corrective action.

Methods you could use to record your progress in meeting goals might include:

- Use of a *spreadsheet or organisational database* that records each task and/or goal and provides a quick overview of progress.
- Regular *face-to-face meetings* with the other people involved in achieving the overall goal, where each person updates the group on their progress.
- *Sales or financial reports* that measure whether goals have been met, are on track, or are falling behind.

Table 19.1 Measuring performance against KPIs

Salesperson	Target	Actual	% var
James	$20,000.00	$19,800.00	−1.0%
Franken	$20,000.00	$21,500.00	7.0%
Daria	$20,000.00	$15,400.00	−29.9%
Joe	$25,000.00	$26,700.00	6.4%
Haley	$25,000.00	$27,000.00	7.4%
Totals	$110,000.00	$110,400.00	0.4%

As you can see from Table 19.1, all sales staff at this organisation have been given specific targets to achieve. We can see that both James and Daria didn’t achieve their targets, and while James is only a little below his KPI, Daria has fallen short by 29.9 per cent. It will be important to both Daria and the organisation’s management to find out why this shortfall happened so that improvements can be made or assistance given where necessary.

Try this now

1. Set yourself some goals (work or personal) and develop a system to help you measure your performance. Check regularly to see if you are on track.

19.1.2 Prioritising your workload according to task time frames

You may have a number of tasks to complete and you can’t do them all at once. How should you prioritise them? Consider the next example.

Example: Competing tasks

You have three tasks to perform.

1. File the notes from this morning’s staff meeting.
2. Meet a 12 pm deadline for an advertisement you are placing in tomorrow’s newspaper.
3. Print out a report for the general manager who is in the process, right now, of negotiating a multimillion-dollar contract.

In which order should you complete these tasks?

You will need to sort out what to do, in what order, and determine when it needs to be done by. You can do this by managing your time effectively and determining the urgency and importance of tasks. Not all the tasks you need to complete will have the same degree of importance or urgency.

You need to determine which tasks are more important or more urgent than others. The terms "urgent" and "important" can be defined as follows:

- *Urgent*—compelling immediate action or attention.
- *Important*—strongly affecting the course of events.

You will therefore need to look at your workload in these terms:

- How soon does the task need to be completed?
  - Is anyone else in your organisation waiting for it or depending on this task being done? (Consider the domino factor: if one task falls over, will it cause others to fall behind?)
  - Is there a deadline that has to be met?
- How important is the outcome of this task to the organisation?
  - How will it impact on any current work being done?
  - Will it influence a customer's decision about buying from your organisation?
  - How will it affect the organisation's plans and objectives?
  - How will it affect the organisation's reputation?

Some tasks will have a high urgency factor and be very important to the organisation. Others will have a low urgency factor but still be very important. The importance of a task to the organisation will normally always take precedence over issues that might be urgent but not all that important. Therefore, when deciding what to do first, look at each task in those terms: What is urgent? How important is it? Figure 19.2 illustrates this process of determining urgency and importance.

Figure 19.2 Determining the urgency and importance of tasks is a crucial aspect of time management

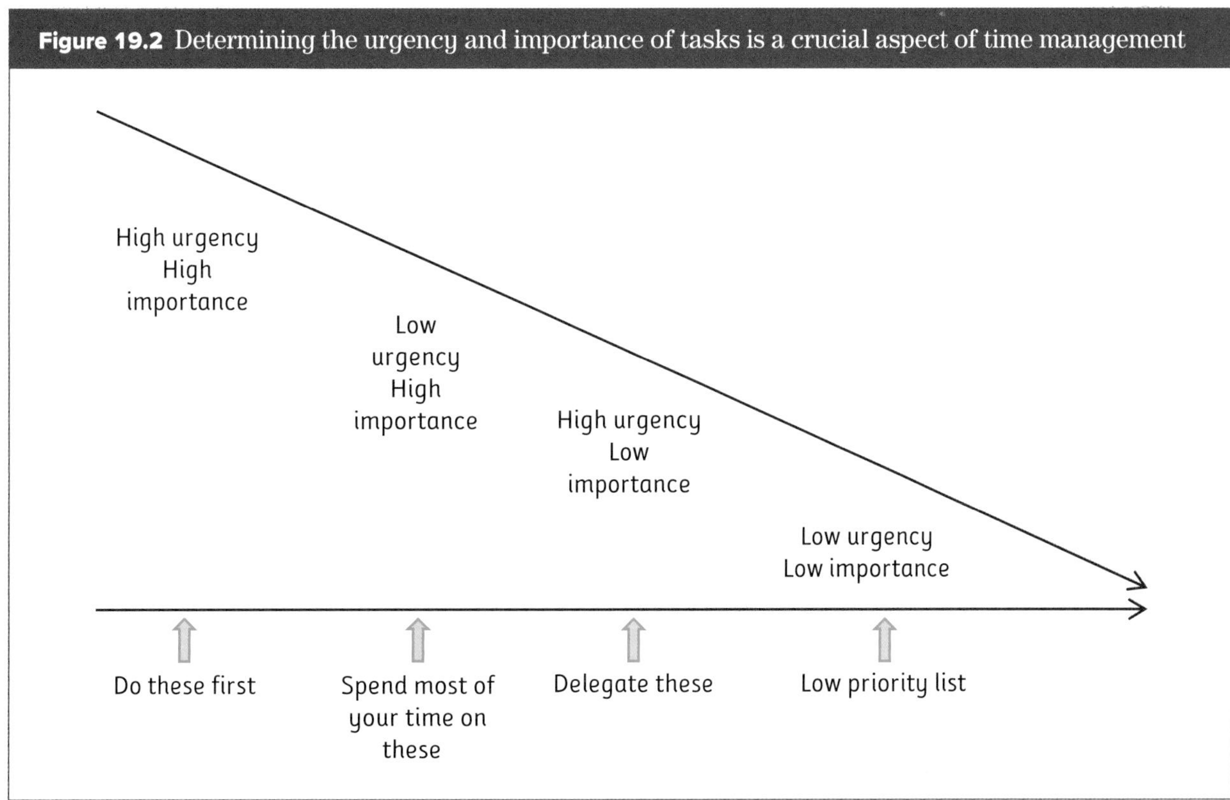

Example: Is it urgent? Is it important?

Going back to the earlier Example, which task do you think is the most important?

1. *Filing the notes from this morning's staff meeting.* This is certainly an important task, as it is a record of what was discussed and agreed to at the meeting and people may want to refer to it at some point. But is this task:
   - urgent? Will other people be unable to do their job properly if they can't access this information immediately? If it isn't available immediately, what is the worst thing that can happen?
   - important? Are other people depending on this information being available right away? Can they call you for information contained in the notes if they need it to get on with their work?
2. *Meeting a 12 pm deadline for an advertisement you are placing in tomorrow's newspaper.* This is definitely a task of some urgency as well as importance, but consider:
   - How much work is involved in getting the advertisement ready?
   - Can someone else do part or all of the work?
   - When is the absolute latest you can stretch the deadline to? Sometimes, a phone call to the newspaper will gain you some extra time.
   - What would happen if the advertisement didn't appear in the newspaper tomorrow? How much did it cost? What was it for? How will it impact on other departments if it doesn't appear tomorrow (the domino factor)?
3. *Printing a report for the general manager who is in the process of negotiating a multimillion-dollar contract.* The fact that a big contract is being negotiated right now in the general manager's office is going to put this task at the head of the list. However:
   - The report doesn't need to be written, just printed. Can someone else do that task?
   - If it must be you, can you hand anything else on your "To Do" list to someone else?

Once you have established the priorities for the day, number the tasks in order of priority, then start at number one and steadily work your way down the list. Some jobs may be boring or distasteful, and some you just don't want to do. Don't be tempted to put these off or to move them down the list—they won't go away. If the task is next on the list, then do it. Take action and get if off your desk; the sooner you deal with issues, the better chance you will have of completing all the work you are meant to do that day. And the sooner you deal with it, the sooner you can return to other more pleasant jobs.

19.1.3 Identifying factors affecting achievement of work objectives

You have written a "To Do" list, you've put it in order of priority, you are working your way through it—then something unexpected comes up that has to be dealt with immediately and stops you from doing what you had planned to do. These are circumstances that we may have to deal with on a daily basis. Some examples are given below.

- *Competing work demands.* In an administrative role, for example, you may do work for a number of different departments in the organisation. Each department will believe its tasks are more important or urgent than another department's tasks. If necessary, you may need to get your supervisor to determine whose work gets priority.
- *Technical/equipment breakdowns.* There are times when the equipment you need in order to complete a task simply fails: the photocopier breaks down or the computer system crashes. These are things that cannot be altered and must be accepted as a normal part of working life. Make a phone call to the person who is relying on you for the work to be completed to inform them of the problem and seek alternative means of getting it done if necessary.
- *Environmental factors.* Factors such as weather or traffic can also impact on your planned workday. Arriving late at work because of traffic jams or bad weather can put you behind in your work before you've even started.

- *Resource issues.* Sometimes you might not have access to equipment or other resources you will need to complete the work. For example:
  - The supplier is out of stock of the particular type of paper you need for a promotional flyer.
  - The photocopier is being used by another department to do a large copying job.
  - You forgot to book the data projector you need for this afternoon's presentation and it is being used out of the office by a sales representative.
- *Extenuating circumstances.* These might be of a personal nature, such as family issues that you need to deal with, or they can be work-related and of an unforeseen nature.
- *Staff shortages.* Depending on the nature of their job role, the absence of a staff member could place a burden on others to do their job, thereby putting them behind in their own schedule.
- *Changes in procedure.* This may mean work has to stop while you are brought up to date or trained in new work methods.

These are issues that are avoidable to a large degree. If you know you are going to need resources in advance, make sure that you book or order what you need to ensure the work gets done on time.

19.1.4 Developing personal work plans

Understanding the tasks that must be performed as part of a given role is one thing, but, as we have seen, you cannot do all of these things at once. There will be certain tasks that need to be performed each day. There will also be tasks that are assigned to you for a specific purpose or project that must be completed in addition to your normal daily routine, and these will generally need to be completed within a given time frame. For example, the daily tasks for an office receptionist might include:

- dealing with daily telephone enquiries and emails
- reading newspapers, trade magazines or online articles of interest to the organisation
- updating database systems
- placing newspaper, magazine or online advertisements
- dealing with enquiries from other departments
- producing simple product flyers for use by sales staff.

Special projects they work on might include assisting with:

- organising a special event such as a conference
- producing a company prospectus
- producing special reports
- organising shoots for corporate videos or professional photos.

To ensure that you can meet your goals, not only today but on an ongoing basis, you can develop a work plan. A work plan is a formally set out list of tasks that detail the steps required to accomplish your goals. It breaks down all the work tasks assigned to your role and provides you with individual timelines. Steps in developing a work plan can include:

1. *Identify the goal for your work plan.* The first thing you should do is to determine your goal, in order to be prepared properly. Discuss with your supervisor your general duties, as well as any specific projects, to refine what you need to do each day or within given time frames. Your work plan may include such things as:
   - daily duties (and the standard to which they should be completed)
   - special project work you are doing as part of a team
   - personal development goals.
2. *Write a background or introduction.* A background, or introduction, is usually written for professional business work plans. It can help to put your work plan into context. It should be short and engaging, setting out your reasons for creating it.

3. *Define the objectives of the plan.* Goals point to things you want to accomplish through your work plan. Goals are usually focused on the big picture of your project and include individual strategies for achieving them. You should be able to check each strategy off your list as you accomplish it. Using the SMART concept for setting the right goals can be helpful.
4. *Break down the task.* Write down all the tasks you have to complete. If there are some very large tasks, break them down into component elements so that they can be more easily achieved. For example, organising a cocktail function for clients is a major task, but it can be broken down into manageable components, as follows:
   - obtain quotes for venue
   - check menus and costs
   - obtain guest list from supervisor
   - send out invitations
   - accept RSVPs.

   Do this until you have listed everything that you have committed to do. Once you have done this, prioritise the tasks in order of urgency and importance.
5. *Create a list of your resources.* This list should include anything that will be necessary for you to achieve your goals and objectives.
6. *Think about constraints.* Here you can identify any obstacles that may get in the way of achieving your goals and objectives. For example:
   - Risks. These may apply to any project you are working on. They are the things that could potentially go wrong. For example, during 2020 and 2021, COVID-19 posed a serious health risk and meant that many public meetings and travel plans were severely disrupted. This, in turn, had a dramatic effect on how business was conducted. Not every risk is as dramatic and far reaching as this example, but whatever risk is identified in your business must be evaluated and eliminated (where possible) or its effect reduced.
   - Contingencies. Wherever a risk exists, you should think about contingencies. These are your "Plan B"—that is, how you can still achieve your goal or complete your task if something goes wrong. For example, during a sudden airline strike, what contingencies could you have in place for staff who are meant to be coming from across the country to a national sales conference? Or if, during a formal presentation, your electronic equipment suddenly failed, how would you continue your talk?
7. *Define accountability.* Who do you report to in your work area, and within the organisation as a whole? How does your work impact on them, and how does their work impact on what you do?
8. *Manage your time.* Look over your work plan and decide how you will reach your goals and objectives by overcoming all the constraints. Identify an appropriate time management software or use a personal calendar to keep this information organised.

Schedule every step in your work plan. Keep in mind that unexpected things can happen and that you need to build flexibility into your schedule to prevent falling behind. It is important to monitor project performance and to periodically review progress against the objectives you have set out in your work plan. Figure 19.3 shows a very simple work plan for an office receptionist.

Try this now

2. With your organisation and job role in mind, draw up a work plan for the next couple of weeks.

Figure 19.3 Example of a work plan

Time	Task	Frequency
Office receptionist Role/purpose: To ensure the smooth and efficient functioning of the reception area and to provide assistance to customers (walk-ins, on the telephone and via the company website) **Goal:** To improve reception efficiency by replacing paper-based work with automated systems by the end of 2023		
Reports to: Office Administration Manager		
	Work plan	
	General duties	
On arrival		
08:00	Open office and turn off alarm	Daily
	Turn on air conditioner (set to 21°)	Daily
	Listen to overnight telephone messages: **1.** Fill out message slips (include date and time of call). **2.** Distribute messages to specific call recipients as soon as possible. **3.** Return calls as needed and record in phone log.	
	Check office has been properly cleaned: **1.** Floor vacuumed. **2.** All office surfaces dusted. **3.** Reception area windows cleaned ... and so on	Daily
08:30	Open doors to customers.	Daily
	Deal with phone and walk-in customer enquiries as required and in line with organisation's customer service policy and procedures.	Daily
... and so on.		
	Work plan goal strategies	
	Research IT systems for: **1.** dealing with and filing marketing and product information **2.** client contact information.	**By 15 June**
... and so on.		
	Personal development	
	Enrol in Diploma of Management course	**By 10 May**
	Attend monthly administrator networking breakfast	**First Tuesday of each month**
... and so on.		

Using business technology effectively

There is a great deal of technology available today to help you keep track of tasks that must be completed and thereby to control your work plan. These technologies can be used to consolidate all your tasks in one place and give you a precise plan of action.

A work plan is an essential tool when you need to carry out several different tasks or have made a number of commitments. Storing the relevant information electronically will allow you greater access and flexibility.

Electronic "To Do" lists

"To Do" lists can function as a work plan and can be electronic or paper based. Most corporate electronic mail programs such as Outlook and GroupWise have sections for inputting "tasks", and you can work your way down the list via your computer screen (as shown in Figure 19.4). Most databases also offer task list functions to help you keep control of your day. Later, you can print out an activity report to show what you have achieved over a given period of time. This can be a useful tool during staff review sessions with your supervisor.

Figure 19.4 Example of an electronic "To Do" list

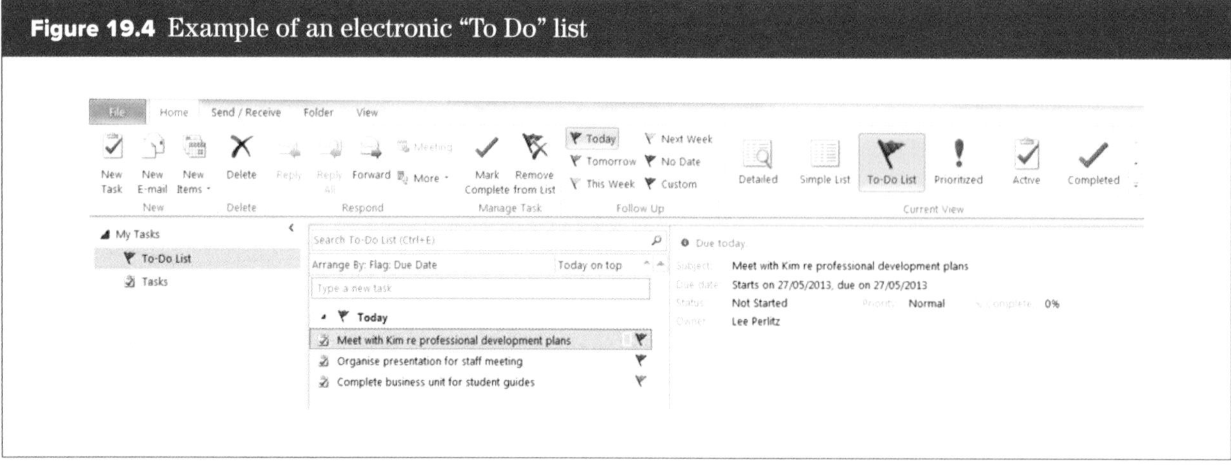

"To Do" list apps

Today's mobile technology makes it possible to have instant access to your "To Do" list or work plan, regardless of where you actually happen to be. There are numerous apps available for phones and tablets that allow you to:

- keep a list of appointments and meetings
- keep a list of things you need to do today
- determine if you are on track to completing all the items on that day's list
- determine (from project milestones) if you are on track to completing longer work processes.

Knowledge check

1. When organising your personal work priorities, there are a number of policies and procedures you may have to consider in your work. List at least three of these and give a brief description of each.
2. List the three main elements used in setting goals.
3. Describe the first steps in goal setting and give examples of how you could determine your work goals.
4. Explain what is meant by SMART goal setting.
5. Explain why it is important to measure goal performance. List at least three measurement methods.
6. Prioritising your workload means determining the urgency and importance of each task you do. List some of the questions you might need to ask in doing this.
7. List at least five factors that could affect the achievement of your work objectives.
8. Describe the purpose of a work plan.
9. Explain the steps involved in developing a work plan.

19.2 Evaluating your own work performance

Simply keeping a work plan may not be all that is required to ensure that work gets done correctly and on time. You will need to check your own performance levels against the required organisational standards on a regular basis to ensure that you are working to your very best ability. You should also monitor your own performance with an eye to improving your skills, which is important from a career progression point of view.

19.2.1 Identifying variations between expected and actual work performance

The standards that organisations require completed work to achieve might revolve around issues such as how customers are served, the quality of products manufactured, and the time frames in which tasks must be completed. Any variations between these standards and the way the work is carried out in practice can seriously damage the organisation's reputation and may even expose it to the risk of a law suit if products don't meet customer expectations. **Quality control** is therefore a critical factor in many organisations. To monitor the quality of work being produced, a regular review should be conducted against, for example, a checklist of the required standards. For example:

- Is the work being carried out in compliance with legislation and/or organisational requirements?
- What variations have been identified? What issues have been identified? How often are they happening?
- How are these variations being reported and to whom?
- What immediate action can be taken to correct the variation?

In your own work role, your performance is measured against organisational requirements. Any gaps or training needs in your performance that are identified can then be discussed and acted upon as necessary.

Reporting variations in work practices

Having assessed actual work performance against the expected standards, you might find there is a gap between what the organisation's standards require and the way work is actually being done. This could happen for a number of reasons:

- You may not have received sufficient training in a particular task or role.
- Changes to standards or procedures have been made but not passed on to staff.
- Stress levels cause a lapse of concentration. (We will look at this subject shortly.)
- Work quality isn't regularly reviewed and monitored, so standards are slipping.

Sometimes the quality of the service or products provided may have nothing to do with staff or their performance levels. Areas of non-performance may, in fact, be related to the products or services themselves. Problems in this regard could include:

- *Product faults.* The product itself may be faulty, which must be addressed in order for it to meet market and customer demands.
- *Infrastructure.* An organisation's premises or equipment may no longer be able to provide service to the required levels.
- *Policies and procedures.* These may no longer meet or be in line with market demands and may need to be reviewed and brought up to date.

Areas where negative variations are identified are important matters, as they affect the quality of the work output and, therefore, the organisation's reputation.

Think about

2. Do you and others in your organisation always follow procedures correctly? What do you think might happen to an organisation's reputation, and to the quality of its output, if staff continually fail to work to the required standards?

Whatever the reason, variations in work practices should be reported to the relevant personnel so that corrective action can be taken. Also, this will give you the opportunity to learn and grow into your role more effectively. Relevant personnel could include the following:

- *Your direct supervisor*—who is in charge of your specific area and has some authority to make alterations or recommendations within the scope of their own role.
- *The company manager*—who has responsibility for the organisation as a whole and will need to authorise any major changes.
- *Colleagues you work with*—who may not be doing a task correctly themselves, or whom you can ask to check that your work performance is in line with organisational standards. A casual conversation with others on your team may be all that's needed to sort out any variations in work practices quickly.
- *Human resources staff*—who may need to arrange gap training so that staff can continue to work to the desired standards.
- *WHS officers*—where the variation poses a health and safety hazard, WHS officers need to be informed so that any risks can be eliminated.

19.2.2 Seeking feedback

As part of the self-development process, you should endeavour to seek regular feedback on your work performance. This is important for reasons such as to:

- ensure that you are doing the job correctly
- identify any performance gaps you may have
- identify any training needs you may have
- develop a plan for progressing in your role.

Feedback on performance levels can be sought in a variety of ways, including:

- *Formal performance appraisals.* These are normally annual interviews, where your performance is reviewed and discussed together with your supervisor or manager, and actions for improvement are determined (if necessary). Many job roles include KPIs (i.e. the personal targets you are required to reach), which may be the measure of how well you have performed in your job.
- *Getting feedback from clients, supervisors and colleagues.* Feedback from these sources might include praise or compliments that let you know you are doing a good job, or complaints that let you know there is room for improvement.
- *Routine organisational methods for monitoring service standards.* These could include results of internal or external audits, customer surveys on the organisation's overall performance, and so on.

19.2.3 Researching sources of stress and accessing appropriate support

Not all stress is necessarily negative. Stress can sometimes be positive and is normal and necessary for performing work in a satisfactory manner. However, if stress is intense and continuous, if a person is unable to cope with their stress levels, or if support isn't available or forthcoming, then stress can have very negative effects that sometimes lead to physical illness and psychological disorders.

An extremely important part of monitoring your progress and performance is making sure that your personal wellbeing isn't neglected. Stress in the workplace is a major source of concern. According to the Australia and New Zealand Anatomy of Work Index 2021, work stress is costing the Australian economy $10.9 billion a year. The top burnout factors, according to workers, are:

- being overworked (50 per cent)
- not being able to switch off or disconnect after they finish work for the day (34 per cent)
- not feeling connected to or supported by the team (31 per cent).

In contrast, 49 per cent of workers surveyed stated that having work that is enjoyable would motivate and refresh them, 44 per cent believed that knowing their work was valued would be a motivating factor, and 41 per cent stated that knowing their work will support their career progression would keep them satisfied (ASANA 2021).

Work stress can be caused by a range of different things, including work factors, the physical environment in which you work, the organisation's practices, changes to the workplace itself and/or working relationships (see Table 19.2).

Table 19.2 Examples of different stress factors

Types of stressors	Examples
Work factors	Excessive work hours Unreasonable performance demands
Physical environment	Noise and overcrowding Health and safety risks Ergonomic problems
Organisational practices	Lack of autonomy Poor communication Unclear roles and responsibilities
Workplace change	Insecurity in the job Poor chances for promotion High staff turnover
Relationships	Office politics, competition or conflicts Poor relationships with supervisors

Symptoms of stress

When people are unable to cope with the stress in their lives, it can present in a number of different ways, including:

- **absenteeism** (absence from work, sometimes for many weeks) as a result of illness caused by work stress
- abuse of alcohol or other substances
- conflict with other staff members when tempers flare or patience is tested
- **presenteeism** (poor work performance on the job, such as when an employee comes to work but, due to an illness or other medical condition, is unable to function properly).

GoodStudio/Shutterstock

Symptoms of stress can also manifest as physical and psychological conditions, such as:

- frequent headaches
- backaches and other muscular aches and pains
- cramps in the neck, shoulders or arms
- poor memory, trouble concentrating
- feeling frustrated, irritable or angry
- feeling weepy or tearful
- loss of energy and motivation
- feeling anxious, helpless or afraid
- apathy and hopelessness
- changes in appetite and weight
- sleep difficulties
- continual tiredness, even exhaustion
- generally feeling worn out or run down.

Some of these symptoms can be relieved relatively easily if they are recognised early. However, others may become serious or even life-threatening, so it is important to ask for help and advice if you feel that you are under too much pressure to get your job done.

Think about

3. Think about a time at your own workplace when you felt stressed. How did these feelings manifest? How did you cope? Were you offered any support?

Policies and methods for preventing and alleviating the effects of work-related stress

Every organisation should have a stress prevention policy. Ideally, it should be developed together with employers and workers and their representatives. Such policies should focus on the development of good work processes and ensure that work-related stress is approached in the same way as any other health and safety factor. For example, WHS policies require that hazards should be eliminated, or minimised if they can't be eliminated. Similarly, better ways of organising work should be found that eliminate or reduce the causes of work-related stress.

Some basic steps that can be taken to eliminate or reduce work-related stress include:

- Structure work hours, including shift schedules, rest breaks and overtime arrangements, to ensure that adequate time is provided for rest and recuperation from the physical and mental effects of work.
- Distribute workloads fairly and ensure that targets are realistic.
- Examine the work plan to determine if any changes can be made to ensure a better workflow.
- Ensure that leave provisions, including annual, family and sick leave, are adequate.
- Ensure the work environment is safe and comfortable, with adequate facilities provided for staff.
- Eliminate or control all health and safety hazards.
- Ensure that staff are aware of the stress management policies and steps the organisation has taken to assist them.
- Organise group activities such as team-building days (or weekends) to allow staff to interact in a less formal environment and get to know and trust one another.
- Schedule training for staff in a range of areas to ensure that they are competent in their own roles as well as being familiar with the organisation's policies, standards and procedures.
- Set up **employee assistance programs (EAPs)** to enhance the emotional, mental and general psychological wellbeing of all employees. These programs also include services for immediate family members of employees. The aim of an EAP is to provide methods for the early detection, identification and/or resolution of both work and personal problems that may negatively affect a person's performance and wellbeing. The problems EAPs can assist with may include:
  - relationships
  - health
  - trauma
  - substance abuse
  - gambling and other addictions
  - financial problems
  - depression
  - anxiety disorders
  - psychiatric disorders
  - communication problems
  - legal issues
  - coping with change.

- Eat regularly and well. Stressful working environments may mean that people skip breaks at work, including lunch and other meal breaks. Furthermore, workers exposed to stress may gain weight by eating to relieve their feelings, or lose weight due to a stress-related loss of appetite.
- Take regular exercise. Regular exercise is important for maintaining good health. Exercise and maintaining physical fitness can reduce the severity of our response to stressful events. Aerobic exercise has been shown to increase sleep length and decrease general fatigue. Regular exercise can also reduce musculoskeletal and psychological symptoms associated with stress. When people feel stressed, it may be difficult to maintain motivation for an exercise program, but the benefits are worth the effort.
- Use relaxation techniques. If practised regularly, relaxation and meditation techniques have also been shown to mitigate stress response. To be successful, daily practice may be needed for six to twelve months followed by regular practice two to three times a week.
- Get a good night's sleep. One block of seven to eight hours of uninterrupted sleep per day is preferable. Avoid strenuous exercise in the last one to two hours before bedtime, as it raises the heart rate and makes sleep more difficult. Avoid caffeine and other stimulants close to bedtime.
- Attend to family and social life. Feeling too tired and/or having a lack of interest in social and/or family life is frequently reported as a consequence of work-related stress. Irritability and/or difficulty in "switching off" from work may also negatively affect personal and social relationships. Additional effort and planning to spend time with family and friends and to make time for hobbies and other non-work related activities may be necessary to overcome these risks.
- Limit the use of tobacco, alcohol and other drugs. Alcohol within one to two hours of bedtime can lead to disrupted sleep patterns, as can caffeine, found in high concentrations in coffee and many soft drinks. The use of sleeping pills is hazardous—some are highly addictive and they may cause a person to remain sleepy when it is time to wake up. While over-the-counter painkillers can alleviate headaches and other pain in the short term, prolonged use of these substances can have a range of negative health effects. If you feel you are overusing either alcohol or other drugs as a result of work-related stress, or for any other reason, you should seek medical advice.

Knowledge check

10. List at least three types of technology you could use in goal development, measurement and monitoring.
11. Explain why it is important to identify variations between expected and actual work performance. Give examples of how variations could be monitored.
12. List at least three reasons why variations in work performance might occur.
13. Explain why it is important to get feedback on your work performance. List three methods of gaining it.
14. Explain why it is important to monitor work stress levels. List at least four work factors that can cause stress.

19.3 Coordinating personal skills development and learning

A very important aspect of organising your personal work priorities and development is to continually look for opportunities to improve your skills and knowledge. In order to do this, you need to be aware of your current capabilities in relation to the organisational standards for completing tasks and then determine if you need to improve or update your skills.

19.3.1 Identifying personal and professional development needs for your job role

Identifying whether you need to develop and improve your skills is, in simple terms, a matter of looking at the standards to which your organisation expects a task to be completed and comparing that to your own performance in that task. This process of undertaking a comparison—known as a **training needs analysis**—is shown in Figure 19.5. If there is a discrepancy between the two, then it means you may need some training.

Figure 19.5 Determining the gap between organisational requirements and your own skills

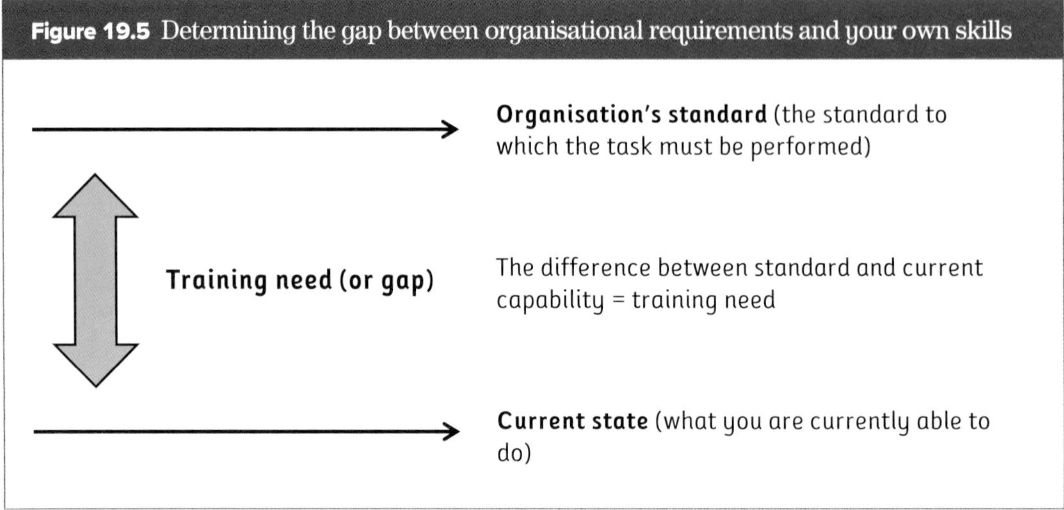

Try this now

3. Apply Figure 19.5 to your own workplace tasks. Do your skill levels match the organisational requirements? In thinking of the future, and positions you might like to apply for, what training could you undertake to improve your skills?

19.3.2 Identifying opportunities to undertake and access personal skill development activities

During the course of your working life, there will be many opportunities to develop your skill levels. Some of these activities may be of short duration (e.g. attending an industry conference), while others might address long-term goals, such as when you undertake a course or develop a **career plan**.

A successful career rests on foundations built in its early stages. A good work ethic and a career development plan will take you a long way in building a successful and effective work life. In looking at your future career, however, you should (together with your supervisor or HR staff) develop a specific plan to ensure that you achieve your career objectives.

Like a business plan, a career plan has three elements:

1. *Determining the goal.* You must have a clear idea of what it is you want to achieve, and your goal should be achievable. There is little point in setting a goal to be an astronaut with NASA if you aren't interested in fields such as engineering or physics.
2. *Determining the steps to be taken.* Having determined what your goal is, you should break it down into manageable "chunks". This is important as, depending on the nature of the goal, it may be a little overwhelming and take considerable time to achieve. By breaking the goal down into individual steps, you can work your way through the list of steps to be accomplished and feel like you are getting somewhere. For example, if you were working as

a junior administration assistant and your goal was to one day be the general manager, your development plan might look like the one shown in Figure 19.6.

Figure 19.6 Example of a simple career progression plan

Goal: To become general manager
Steps:
1. Complete Diploma of Management qualification
2. Undertake work experience in all departments of the organisation
3. Career progression planning:
a. Supervisor of administration area
b. Sales coordinator in sales and marketing department
c. Sales representative in sales and marketing department
d. Sales manager
4. Join business networks

3. *Determining the time frame.* The final part of the planning process is to actually have time frames in place to ensure that each step of the progression plan happens in a timely manner, as shown in Figure 19.7. Without a realistic time frame in which to complete each stage of the plan, you may end up not doing any of these things. The time allocated to achieve each step should be realistic and based on levels of experience and expertise gained to move on to the next step.

Figure 19.7 Career progression plan with timelines

Goal: To become general manager	
Steps/Time:	
Completed by end 2023	1. Complete Diploma of Management qualification
Completed by end 2023	2. Undertake work experience in all departments of the organisation:
11 February	a. Operations
15 March	b. Marketing department
21 April	c. Accounts department
22 June	d. Sales department
Achieve by:	3. Career progression planning:
2024	a. Supervisor of administration area
2025	b. Sales coordinator in sales and marketing department
2026	c. Sales representative in sales and marketing department
2028	d. Sales manager
2032	e. General manager
By end of this month	4. Join business networks

Each of the career progression stages must then also include plans on what you will need to do to achieve each career goal. For example, to move from administration assistant to the administration supervisor, you may need to ensure that you:

- are familiar with all tasks involved in both the assistant and supervisor roles
- work closely with the supervisor to assist them in their role
- ask the supervisor to mentor you in relation to gaining more management experience
- work in cooperation with all departments and with management levels so that you are well regarded within the company as a whole.

A career progression plan such as the one outlined above doesn't necessarily mean that you must follow it exactly. For example, if, while you are still an administration assistant, an opportunity presents itself to move into the sales department as a coordinator or sales representative, then you should by all means apply for the position. It is important to remain flexible in your approach and to take opportunities to improve your skills and expertise whenever they are presented.

Think about

4. Where would you like to be, in your career, in the next five years? Ten years? What steps might you need to take to get there?

While a training needs analysis can identify a skills gap and outline any training you need to complete in order to fulfil your current role successfully, you should also look for opportunities to improve your skills over and above the normal requirements of your job if you wish to grow and gain greater responsibilities. Opportunities for you to improve your skills can include:

- *Coaching and mentoring.* Getting assistance from a more experienced work colleague or supervisor can help you to improve your existing skills and learn new ones.
- *Formal study (both internal and external).* They could include:
  - attending work training courses that are designed to improve performance or offer new skills
  - undertaking a course outside of normal working hours—for example, getting a certificate or diploma at TAFE, or studying for a university degree in order to improve your employability
  - gaining formal recognition for current skills by way of "Recognition of Prior Learning" (RPL). This is a service offered by training organisations and colleges, which provide formal certificates or diplomas to people with existing, current skills.
- *Professional development (PD) opportunities.* Personal development can also be undertaken by taking advantage of PD activities in and around your organisation. PD activities can include:
  - subscriptions to trade/industry journals, magazines and newsletters that can keep you up to date on the latest developments within your industry
  - industry networking functions, where others from your industry meet in an informal way to chat and discuss industry issues
  - seminars, workshops or conferences that provide a more formal setting for networking with industry colleagues.

In looking at career opportunities, it is important to develop your plan in a logical and timely manner. For example, if you were working as a receptionist in a marketing company, it might seem fun to learn about graphic art or the process of producing a video for a client, but it would be more relevant to your current role to improve your skills in using business technology and developing a better understanding of customer service delivery. These types of skills would be a high priority in your development plan, whereas learning about graphic art or video development would be something you could undertake in non-work hours or when your current skills match (or exceed) organisational expectations.

19.3.3 Recording and incorporating feedback and professional development

The success of your work life depends on your ability to recognise and act upon any areas for self-improvement. During the course of your performance appraisals, feedback received may have highlighted areas in which you could either improve your current work practices or take advantage of opportunities to move up in your career. Such feedback (both positive and negative) should always be acted upon. For example, if, during your appraisal, your supervisor asks why you haven't met your KPIs, you should discuss the reasons why and what you could do to improve your performance. On a more positive note, they may talk to you about potential job openings that will give you the opportunity to grow. In such cases, you might discuss what you need to do to apply for that position and, possibly, make amendments to your career plan. Remember: you must be flexible.

Whatever the case, any PD activities you undertake should be recorded in your personnel file to show that you have taken steps to continuously improve your skills. A professional development log could look like the one shown in Table 19.3.

Table 19.3 Example of tracking your professional development activities

Date	Event or activity	Evidence attached
25/5	Subscribed to *Marketing Today* industry newsletter	Subscription receipt
30/5	Attended Chamber of Commerce breakfast	Receipt for ticket
16/7	Participated in "customer service excellence" half-day training workshop	Payment receipt
2023	Undertook Diploma of Business course	Diploma

Knowledge check

15. Describe the method by which you could determine any gaps in your work performance that might require you to undergo training.

16. Describe the steps you would take to develop a career goal.

17. Describe three opportunities you could access to improve your skills and knowledge.

18. Explain why it is important to incorporate feedback into your professional development plan.

19. Explain why it is important to record any professional development activities you undertake. Give an example of how you could record these activities.

20. List at least five symptoms of work stress.

Summary

Career development matters because a career means a great deal more than just getting paid each week. A career affects what you can become and contribute, and who you impact in the pursuit of your work. To speak about "career development" is to speak about what your career means over your entire lifetime. It is a process that continues indefinitely. A sense of purpose, meaning, gratification and passion is found not only in the result but in the pursuit of work itself. Understanding this can mean the difference between simply having a job and embarking on a lifelong career. It can mean making sacrifices in the short term in order to gain long-term advantages and satisfaction.

Reference

ASANA, 2021. Australia and New Zealand Anatomy of Work Index 2021: *Overcoming Disruption in a Distributed World,* https://resources.asana.com/rs/784-XZD-582/images/PDF-FY21-APAC-EN%20ANZ-Anatomy%20of%20Work%20Report.pdf?alild=eyJpljoic1BBYzhadVdBK045dHhWOSlslnQiOiJFbEdNNDdjcHJteDBtWFcxRmJ5NjhnPT0ifQ%253D%253D, accessed 26 August 2022.

CHAPTER 20
Work in a team

Learning outcomes

20.1 Identify individual work tasks within a team

20.2 Contribute effectively to team goals

20.3 Work effectively with team members

20.4 Communicate effectively with the team

Working for any organisation, no matter what size or in what industry, means working with people. You will work with colleagues and supervisors in your own department; you may work with other departments as a member of a committee or team; and you will work with customers, suppliers and networks from across a number of industries. No one works in complete isolation. Whatever the case, it is important to understand that working relationships can be fragile, especially in the workplace where they are often built and can be destroyed by the actions we take. Cooperation between work colleagues is an essential element in any workplace if it is to function effectively, so it stands to reason that building effective relationships is necessary for a number of reasons.

The health and wellbeing of the team depends on what happens within the organisation and the way it operates. Overwork, stress, or being subjected to harassment or bullying all impact on a person's health and therefore on their ability to fulfil their role within the organisation.

An organisation can only function with the cooperation of its individual team members. Staff are at the coalface of the organisation, fulfilling all the functions necessary to ensure its success. If there is disharmony in the workplace, this can impact negatively on that success.

An organisation can also have a profound effect on the wider community. People may be dependent on it for the necessities of life, such as food, household products and/or other goods that the organisation might supply. Well-run organisations are generally stable, and therefore also offer a stable environment for their staff and other people who depend on them.

Society is, in essence, a web of relationships that require all parties to work together in order to create something that functions effectively and efficiently. But a society works even better when those relationships are positive, cooperative and respectful.

20.1 Identifying individual work tasks within a team

Every business has goals and objectives, mostly to provide services and/or make sales to customers. In order for this to happen as effectively and efficiently as possible, a range of different tasks need to be undertaken. It is the responsibility of individual team members to carry these out.

20.1.1 Identifying your own responsibilities

Wherever you work, you will be allocated a range of these tasks to perform. There will be standards to which these tasks must be performed in order to maintain the highest possible quality of service, and there will be time frames in which they must be achieved. In order for you to do your job as efficiently as possible, you need to know what those standards and time frames are.

In most organisations, the human resources department (or department manager) will have drawn up a work plan or a **position description** for each role within the organisation—from general manager or managing director through to reception or administrative assistant roles. Position descriptions clearly identify everyone's role within the organisation and set out:

- the position title
- who this role reports to
- the position's objectives—the reason why the position exists
- the selection criteria—the qualities and qualifications the person in the role needs to have
- the position's duties and responsibilities—the actual tasks the person in that role must perform.

A position description (a brief example is shown in Figure 20.1) enables each person in a given role to fully understand what is expected of them. While your own individual tasks might seem narrow in focus and limited to your particular work area, they nevertheless are a part of the wider picture of what your organisation is trying to achieve. The position description can therefore give you an understanding of how your role impacts on, and contributes to, the organisation as a whole.

Figure 20.1 Example of a position description

Position description

Position title: Marketing coordinator

Reports to: Director of marketing

Objectives: The position of marketing coordinator was established to administer the marketing and promotion of the organisation and carry out administration of the database. The marketing coordinator supports the director of marketing.

Key selection criteria

- Demonstrated experience, skills and knowledge in marketing activities
- Ability to successfully organise promotional events and activities
- High-level communications skills, with the ability to interact effectively with staff and the wider community
- Computer skills relating to word processing, desktop publishing and working with social media
- Well-developed organisational and administrative skills, including the ability to manage the organisation's database
- Ability to demonstrate tact and discretion, and to maintain privacy and confidentiality

Specific duties and responsibilities

- Prepare and place advertisements for staff vacancies and promotion of the organisation.
- Prepare editorial material for promotional publications.
- Stay in touch with current trends and news items.
- Maintain regular updates of organisation's prospectus and other publications.
- Maintain a social media presence.
- Update the organisation's website.
- Develop and coordinate production of marketing materials.
- Assist with the planning and organisation of promotional functions and events.
- Ensure events and activities are planned and implemented efficiently.
- Provide administrative support for the director of marketing.
- Provide clerical support for marketing meetings.

Think about

1. Does your job have a position description? How detailed is it? Does it give you all the information you need to do your job effectively?

20.1.2 Identifying your own role and task requirements within a team

As an individual within an organisation, you will be part of a larger team and will be working in line with, and towards, the overall team purposes, goals, plans and objectives. These may include the following:

- *Goals for individuals*. Within your organisation or department, you may be given specific goals that you will need to reach. These are often referred to as "key performance indicators" (KPIs) and may form part of your daily work plan. For example, you might need to complete tasks to a given standard; you might need to make a certain number of sales per day; or you might need to have your part of a team project completed by a given deadline.
- *Goals for work teams*. Similar to individual goals, these will be related to an overall team effort. In the same way that your individual work and performance has an impact on the organisation, so too does the performance of a team, either from the same department or work area, or a group working on a joint project. Goals (or team KPIs) will be set for the team to achieve specific tasks and/or revenue targets, to the required standards and within given time frames.
- *Expected outcomes and outputs*. These are generally the standards that goals are expected to meet.
  - Outcomes are the end result of a process or project that has been successfully achieved within the required parameters. For example, the outcome of a marketing campaign might be to increase the company's income by 10 per cent over the same period last year.
  - Outputs involve calculating and recording the results of any activity that can be measured in numbers. For example, the expected output for a marketing campaign might be to make *30* telephone calls per day to customers, or to post *three* items on social media each day.

The impact of your role in the workplace

During a normal working day, you will work with colleagues and supervisors in your own department, or you may work with other departments as a member of a committee or team. Depending on your role within the organisation, these people will depend on you to get your work done on time and to the required standards. Going back to the marketing coordinator's role from Chapter 19, you could look at your role and its impact as set out in Table 20.1.

It is important, therefore, to understand how the work you do fits into the departmental and/or organisational picture. The duties you perform may represent an important step in an organisation's procedures or processes, or they may be part of a larger task or project working with others—all contributing towards getting a specific job done. Every member of the team needs to take responsibility for the work allocated to them, and should be encouraged to do so. This encouragement could take the form of:

- talking to team members who are having problems and helping them to take control
- ensuring that adequate resources are available for all staff to do their work effectively
- communicating roles, responsibilities and objectives clearly so that everyone knows what is expected of them
- giving praise where it is due; we are very good at pointing out others' faults and mistakes but often forget to offer praise when someone has done a good job.

Table 20.1 Potential impact of a marketing coordinator's role on the business

Your role	Impact
Preparing and placing advertisements for staff vacancies.	Other departments within the organisation will be waiting on these ads to be placed so that they can employ people they need either for specific short-term projects or as full-time staff. In either case, a hold-up in your part of the recruitment process means that the work the new employees are required to do will also be delayed.
Preparing advertisements for promoting the organisation.	This is a very important task, and organisations usually plan the placement of their promotional advertisements very precisely. For example, they may be introducing a new product line and have organised a major launch campaign—with sales, celebrities, prizes and all manner of other things to entice customers to buy the new product. Ads promoting the launch campaign must therefore be placed according to an exact time schedule to ensure maximum exposure. Forgetting to place the ads for this event could lead to embarrassment for the organisation and a serious loss of sales
Undertaking specific project work—often involves a team effort, with each person on the team being allocated a task to complete within a given time frame.	If a team member is behind on their particular task, it can hold up the entire project and cause serious problems.

Organisational policies and procedures

Roles and responsibilities within an organisation will vary greatly, depending on the industry you are in and your level of authority. An organisation's policies and procedures are intended to ensure that the work a team does is in line with any relevant standards and the organisation's legal obligations. Therefore, in performing your tasks and working in teams, you need to be aware of, and comply with, these policies and procedures. They might include:

- *Taking part in the organisation's* **induction** *and* **orientation programs**. For example:
  - receiving the necessary training in work health and safety (WHS) issues specific to that workplace
  - understanding your role and the tasks you will be expected to perform
  - taking an orientation tour of the premises so that you know where everything is
  - being introduced to key organisational staff and to the team in the area where you will be working, which may include being briefed on team structures and hierarchies, and who to report to for specific issues
  - learning about the organisation's mission and values, its work culture and reputation, so that your work reflects well on the organisation and conforms with its standards and values.
- *Abiding by organisational and industry codes of conduct.* A code of practice (or code of conduct) is based on the organisation's principles, values and behaviours. It applies to all staff and contractors, their employees and representatives. Visitors engaging in any activity related to the business are expected to conduct themselves in a manner consistent with this code. Regardless of industry, the objectives of such a code might be to:
  - provide direction to staff around expected conduct while affiliated with the organisation
  - assist staff in dealing with ethical issues in ways that reflect the organisation's values and standards
  - promote professionalism and excellence
  - express shared assumptions and organisational values
  - provide staff with direction in ethically ambiguous situations
  - detail the organisation's social responsibilities
  - in some instances, provide a statement on public accountability and corporate governance.

  It is important to remember that for every organisation the code of practice will vary. Then, too, some industries offer national codes of practice that provide standards of behaviour for their specific industries.
- *Observing environmentally sustainable working practices*, such as recycling and using energy efficiently and responsibly.

- *Observing policies that reflect legal issues*, such as:
  - supporting diversity and inclusion to provide all team members with support.
  - proactively minimising bullying and harassment. Bullying can be psychological, physical or even indirect (e.g. when a person is deliberately excluded from work-related activities). Organisations can establish procedures for early identification of any unreasonable behaviours or situations likely to increase the risk of workplace bullying and implement control measures to manage these risks.
- *Being aware of WHS responsibilities*. Regardless of whether you are working on your own or as part of a team, you must always do so with WHS responsibilities in mind. While employers provide you with valuable opportunities to gain experience in your profession, it is important to understand that they have responsibilities towards you—and that you have responsibilities towards them—while in the workplace.

20.1.3 Articulating the team structure and the roles of other team members

Working in a team is most successful when everyone fully understands the purpose of the team, who is part of that team, and what is expected of each individual. Without these expectations, members can't develop mutual accountability or trust in the group. When expectations are clear and members meet (or exceed) them, trust and an increased sense of "harmony" are natural by-products.

Most teams should have a designated team leader—someone who is responsible for, and accountable for, the team's results. This person will often act as a spokesperson for the group when dealing with management or other departments. Depending on the size of the organisation and/or group, a team might also have a "facilitator". This is a role that exists to help guide the team's progress and may also include setting agendas for, and running, team meetings.

Types of teams

Teams can generally be divided into groups such as project, virtual and operational teams. The type of team that needs to be formed will depend on its purpose, location and the organisational structure.

- *Project teams* are groups of employees who work together towards achieving a shared and specific goal. This type of team works in a highly structured, measurable and time-constrained way. Clear roles, responsibilities and deadlines can be assigned. Experienced team members may often be able to act as informal coaches or mentors to other, less experienced, staff.
- *Virtual teams* are made up of people who work in different physical locations and who will be relying on collaboration tools such as Zoom and Canva to get things done together. Virtual teams provide members with a better work–life balance and allow business owners to employ the best experts in the field, regardless of where they may be physically located.
- *Operational teams* are formed in order to support and underpin the work of other types of teams. They help to make sure that all back-office processes go smoothly and are often seen as the "face" of the organisation by people who use their services. They may work directly with people, provide services or produce goods. In any case, they perform the primary tasks within the organisation while implementing its policies and displaying its standards.

Typical compositions of work teams

Whatever the purpose of the team, each member should have something to contribute to the group. An effective and innovative team is one that has a broad range of talents, interests and expertise that can be used to generate new ideas, help create processes and procedures, and keep the team grounded in reality. It takes all different types of people to ensure that work is carried out not only creatively, but efficiently as well.

GoodStudio/Shutterstock

Establishing teams that work well together, that cooperate on projects, and that consistently look for ways to improve their own work performance as well as the organisation as a whole, requires bringing people into the team based on what needs to be achieved and how each member can contribute. The potential contributions of team members could, for example, relate to:

- special interests that they have that could prove useful in working on particular projects
- past jobs in which they have gathered experience and expertise that can be useful to the group
- technical strengths that allow them to work with specific equipment or ideas
- work preferences and styles that dictate how, where and when people like to work
- how the individuals "fit" into the team, ensuring that personality, work ethics and vision are compatible with the group as a whole. Having said this, it is necessary for groups to include different personality types to ensure that differing viewpoints are available and considered. If, for example, all the members of the team were creative and hyper-enthusiastic, with no one in the group to keep their ideas grounded in reality, it could lead to wildly imaginative ideas being developed that are impractical, expensive and out of line with the organisation's vision.

Think about

2. Think about a team that you were part of (work or personal). What contributions did each team member make? How valuable were these contributions?

20.1.4 Planning and prioritising your own tasks

While ensuring that project- or team-related tasks get done on time is important, so is getting your own work done. As discussed in Chapter 19, this is a matter of looking at the things that need to be achieved by the end of the day, week or month and determining the order in which you complete them.

Figure 20.1 showed a job description for a marketing coordinator who had the following duties and responsibilities:

- Prepare and place advertisements for staff vacancies and promotion of the organisation.
- Prepare editorial material for promotional publications.

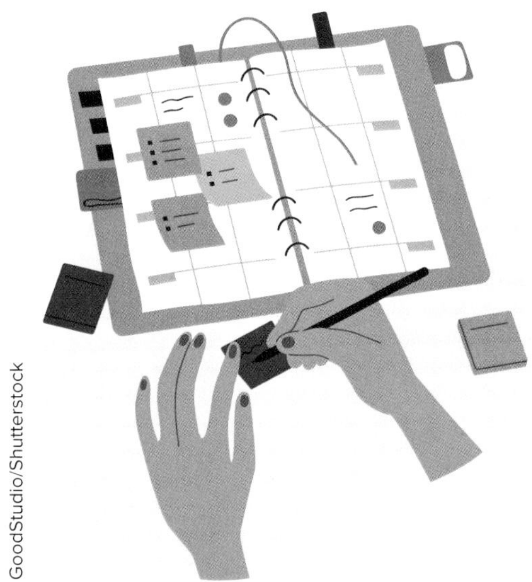

GoodStudio/Shutterstock

- Stay in touch with current trends and news items.
- Maintain regular updates of organisation's prospectus and other publications.
- Maintain a social media presence.
- Update the organisation's website.
- Develop and coordinate production of marketing materials.
- Assist with the planning and organisation of promotional functions and events.
- Ensure events and activities are planned and implemented efficiently.
- Provide administrative support for the director of marketing.
- Provide clerical support for marketing meetings.

Some of these tasks might seem more important than others. For example, providing administrative support for the director of marketing would certainly be among the marketing coordinator's top priorities, as these duties would involve top-level management activities, while assisting with the organisation of events might only happen occasionally. How you prioritise will be a question of what work you have to accomplish on any given day, who is depending on that work being done, and what impact it will have on the organisation when it is completed (or not completed). We looked at determining importance and urgency in Chapter 19.

Knowledge check

1. Explain why it is important for you to understand your own responsibilities within your workplace.
2. Describe a document that can give you the information you need to understand your role within the company.
3. Describe three different organisational goals that might help you identify your own task requirements within a team environment.
4. Working in line with both organisational and legislative requirements is an essential part of any work you do. Give at least four examples of these requirements.
5. Describe the typical composition of a work team and the potential contributions they can make to the workplace.
6. Explain what questions you would ask when planning and prioritising your workload.

20.2 Contributing effectively to team goals

No two people are alike; we are all the result of how we were brought up and educated, of the life experience we have gained, and of our belief and cultural systems. This means that there is potential for conflict in the workplace—but it also means that there is great potential for sharing information, experience and expertise, and for creating a dynamic work environment in which team members can contribute and thrive. The important factor in establishing such an environment is to acknowledge others' talents and build an atmosphere in which everyone can contribute equally.

20.2.1 Identifying team goals and your responsibilities relevant to achieving them

Everyone within the workforce has something to contribute—the important thing is to learn what your colleagues' strengths are and to use these, in conjunction with your own, to build a dynamic team of people and an agreeable work environment. However, the team also needs to know what its objectives are so that everyone is moving in the same direction, working towards those goals and objectives as a cohesive whole.

Team goals may relate to:

- addressing particular customer feedback where product or service issues need to be resolved
- conceiving and implementing a particular project that will improve or change work conditions or fulfil some other purpose
- developing new services or products for the organisation
- generating ongoing ideas within the work unit to continually improve conditions and keep staff motivated and refreshed
- improving budgetary performance by looking at ways to better use resources and/or reduce costs
- encouraging new ideas that impact beyond the workplace—for example, projects that have a broader social or community impact, such as fundraising for charities or community organisations.

When working towards a goal in a team environment, there are a number of steps that should be followed to ensure success. These include:

1. *Identify the individual tasks that need to be completed.* These will be the steps the team needs to take to achieve its overall goal. Sometimes, goals might be too big to handle all at once and must be broken down into individual tasks that are easier to manage and achieve. This is often referred to as "chunking". There may be a number of tasks that need to be completed in order to achieve a specific goal, so it is important to prioritise them early in the project so that things are done in the correct order. For example, when developing a national advertising campaign for management's approval, there is no point in producing a proposal for them until all the advertising components have been sourced, costed and put into place. The order in which things are done is very important as, often, one task cannot be started or completed until the previous one is in place.
2. *Determine the time frame in which these tasks need to be completed.* There will always be a deadline by which the overall goal needs to be completed, so each individual task also needs a time frame in order for all the pieces to fall into place according to the required standard and on time. Once again, the order in which tasks are completed is important. If step 1 in the process isn't completed on time, it will hold up the next steps and the whole project is then in danger of not being completed by the deadline. However, time should be allowed for thinking through, challenging and collaborating on tasks and ideas to ensure that schedules for the work are realistic and achievable.
3. *Designate tasks to individual members of the team according to their strengths.* Each member of the team will have strengths and talents; make use of them and delegate tasks that they have experience and expertise in. Each team member will be responsible for ensuring their specific work is done in line with organisational standards and within given time frames.
4. *Monitor the work progress.* This is very important. Time frames need to be kept to so that the work to be completed doesn't fall behind schedule or below the required standards. To avoid this, the team should meet at regular intervals to check on progress.
5. *Seek and offer assistance when required.* If a member of the team is having difficulty, help them! Equally, if you, as a team member, are having difficulty, ask for help. The team goal is to complete the work or project as quickly, efficiently and cost-effectively as possible and assistance should be given where needed. Often other team members will have personal knowledge that can help you, or they may have within their network of contacts someone who can assist with the task. If it becomes necessary to initiate a change in tasks, this can be discussed with individual team members who are unable to complete their assigned tasks.

6. *Provide feedback on the task progress.* Meetings should be held at regular intervals to let other team members know how the work is progressing. Questions to ask include:
    - Is the work on track?
    - Does anyone need assistance?
    - Are there any problems that need to be dealt with?
    - How are the individual tasks or components fitting together?
    - What, if any, adjustments need to be made?

    These steps are summarised in Figure 20.2.

Figure 20.2 Steps in working successfully in teams

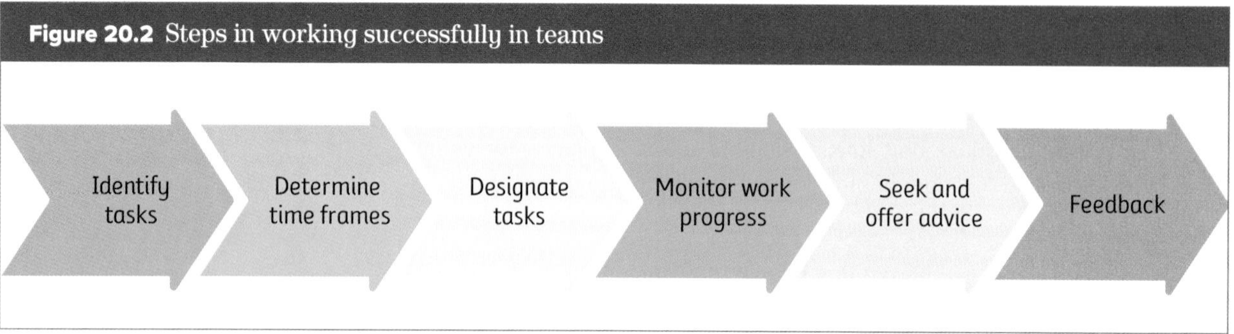

Having a clear understanding of the job that needs to be done, how it is to be done, and by when, is essential to a team successfully meeting its objectives and organisational goals. It is also essential in helping you make your own contributions to the team effort by spelling out exactly what part you play in achieving the overall goal and how your specific role fits into it.

Think about

3. Think about a project that could help make the workplace more efficient. Who would you choose to be on your project team? Why would you choose them?

20.2.2 Contributing ideas and information in team planning discussions

Another important part of working in a team is sharing information and discussing ideas and work progress. Contributing ideas and information can be done in a number of ways. For example:

- *Share information, knowledge and experiences about new trends and recent product or service experiences with other staff members.* This enriches the pool of information the entire staff has to draw from, thereby supporting the whole-of-team effort. You cannot always know everything about organisational operations and plans, so synergy within the workplace can often reveal "just the thing" you need to move your work forward. **Synergy**, in simple terms, means that the whole is greater than the sum of the individual parts. In a business sense, this means that teamwork will produce a much better result than if each person in the organisation was working towards the same goal individually.
- *Use brainstorming sessions and "what if" scenarios.* This means coming up with as many ideas about how the goal is to be achieved as possible, no matter how trivial or silly they may initially sound, and testing to see if they work by applying the question "What if?" to these ideas and possibilities. The "What if?" question could be applied to scenarios in a positive or negative way. For example, if an idea sounded plausible but there were a number of issues standing in its way, asking "What if we did this ...?" or "What if we tried it that way ...?" could help in finding solutions to a viable idea by thinking outside the box in a positive way. On the other hand, in

the same situation, the devil's advocate position would be to ask: "What if this happened ...?" or "What if this went wrong ...?" While someone who takes this position could be seen as being negative, they are merely pointing out areas that could go wrong and prompting discussion on how to address the issue or to make the idea work.

- *Discuss ideas proactively*. Having an understanding of the tasks that the team needs to complete in order to reach a goal may only be the first and most basic step towards actually accomplishing that goal. Wherever groups of individuals come together to form a team, there will be a range of different ideas and opinions on how to achieve their objectives. This may lead to conflict if the team as a whole doesn't allow for open discussion on how to move forward with the work. Promote positive interaction by methods such as the following:
  - Select a project supervisor or leader (if one hasn't been appointed by management). These people are also very important in the development of an idea or innovation. They help keep team discussions under control and make sure the work remains on track.
  - Ask questions and openly discuss the various suggestions:
    - Does the suggestion under discussion have merit?
    - Does this particular idea solve the issue under discussion?
    - Will the plan being discussed help achieve the overall goal?
    - Do we have the resources required to put this plan into action?
    - Do organisational policies and/or procedures need to be adjusted in order to introduce this plan? If so, what adjustments need to be made and who will need to approve them?
    - Will there be a need to train staff when introducing new procedures? Who will conduct the training and where will it be held?
    - Will this plan require any new or updated technology to implement it? Who will provide the technical knowledge or expertise to do this?
    - Who will resource the ideas going forward? People from other departments or from outside the organisation may need to be involved to provide such things as staffing, departmental resources and agreement in principle to ensure the idea can move forward.
    - What are the budgetary implications? Plans and ideas for innovation can often mean spending money, or they might raise other monetary issues that need to be considered. People who have a financial background, or a stake in the change to be made, can offer advice on how much the change might cost or give an estimate of how much revenue it might generate.
    - Can this idea be further improved upon?
    - What alternatives are there?
    - What objections might there be to the idea?
    - What do we need to do to overcome objections?

By encouraging and supporting team members to contribute, an organisation can build a creative, innovative and highly productive workforce, one where all staff take responsibility for their own work and are supportive of the organisation as a whole.

20.2.3 Enabling effective teamwork

You have a team of people around you from a range of backgrounds, and with a range of talents and expertise—everything you need to ensure that work is carried out efficiently. This doesn't mean, however, that work team dynamics will automatically be harmonious or even cooperative. Wherever groups of people work together, there will be differences of opinion and different ways of viewing and solving problems. It is important, therefore, to establish ways for the team to work together in the most effective manner.

Developing effective workplace relationships means building and maintaining trust among colleagues and having the confidence that they will support you in the performance of your tasks. Effective teams have the following characteristics:

- *Integrity*. This is the quality of being honest and having strong moral principles. It means being open with the people you work with (whether they are colleagues, customers or suppliers) and living up to any workplace commitments you have made. It also means completing tasks allocated to you conscientiously, to the required standard and within the required time frame, so that people know they can trust you.

- *Respect*. This is the quality of admiring someone for their abilities, qualities or achievements. It can mean:
    - sharing your knowledge and abilities freely with colleagues and helping them wherever you can
    - acknowledging others' achievements, abilities and qualities and tapping into these skills. The fact that they have these attributes and are prepared to share them for the good of the organisation is the important factor here, and they should be respected for what they contribute.
- *Empathy*. This is the ability to understand and share the feelings of others. No two people are alike and they won't view or react to given situations in the same way that you, perhaps, might. This doesn't mean that your views are right and theirs are wrong; it just means that they see things from a different perspective. Understanding this and showing empathy with their ideas and feelings will allow them to feel confident in contributing to the workplace without fear of rejection or ridicule.
- *Open communication*. Most colleagues will communicate with one another on an ongoing basis throughout the day. It is important, however, that teams have regular contact to discuss work issues and progress on work that is being done, and to monitor the team's performance and offer assistance where needed. The timing of these meetings is something the team should agree on as a whole. Ways of communicating should also be agreed upon. Will informal conversations with colleagues be enough to monitor work progress, or will regular meetings be needed? Will face-to-face meetings in a boardroom be required, or will emails sent out to all team members be sufficient to cover everything?

Working as an effective team means that individuals within that team take responsibility for their own work. However, it also means that individual team members work in harmony and cooperation with others to achieve organisational goals and objectives.

Knowledge check

7. Teams may be formed to undertake specific goals. In order to achieve them, you must first be able to identify their purpose. List at least four different reasons a team might be brought together.
8. There are six steps to follow when working on a team project. What are they? Briefly describe what each step involves.
9. Describe three methods for contributing ideas and information during team discussions.
10. Effective teamwork includes having *integrity*, being *respectful*, showing *empathy* and *communicating openly*. Explain what these terms mean and how they enable effective teamwork.

20.3 Working effectively with team members

Teams, whatever their purpose, are expected to produce results, so all team members need to be working towards their common goals and objectives. A team environment is one in which brainstorming, collaboration and joint projects are the norms and work best if everyone communicates effectively and "pulls their weight". Working effectively in a team environment, then, requires tact, patience and a willingness to work in concert with your colleagues. A team that works well together has the potential to produce exceptional results, as well as providing dynamic and interesting work experiences.

20.3.1 Communicating clearly and respectfully with team members

No matter what industry you work in, and whatever your role, you will need to communicate with other team members every day. Doing so effectively can mean the difference between a good working environment and a less-than-pleasant one. There are a number of ways in which communication between teams can occur (as Figure 20.3 shows). For example:

- *Open meetings.* These are an excellent way to share information and discuss work projects with large numbers of people. They give team members the opportunity to voice their opinions and to make suggestions that can be openly discussed among the group.
- *Emails.* These are a quick and easy way to distribute information. They also form a written record of the information exchange.
- *One-on-one conversations.* Sometimes you need to communicate face-to-face with a single person, especially when confidentiality is a consideration. Such conversations promote faster decision making than a meeting where some of the participants might not be involved or interested in the subject under discussion.
- *Visual presentations to the team.* There may be occasions when you, or the team, need to present information to larger groups of people, or where diagrams, statistics or images are required in order for others to fully understand the information.

Figure 20.3 Communication between team members can occur in a number of ways

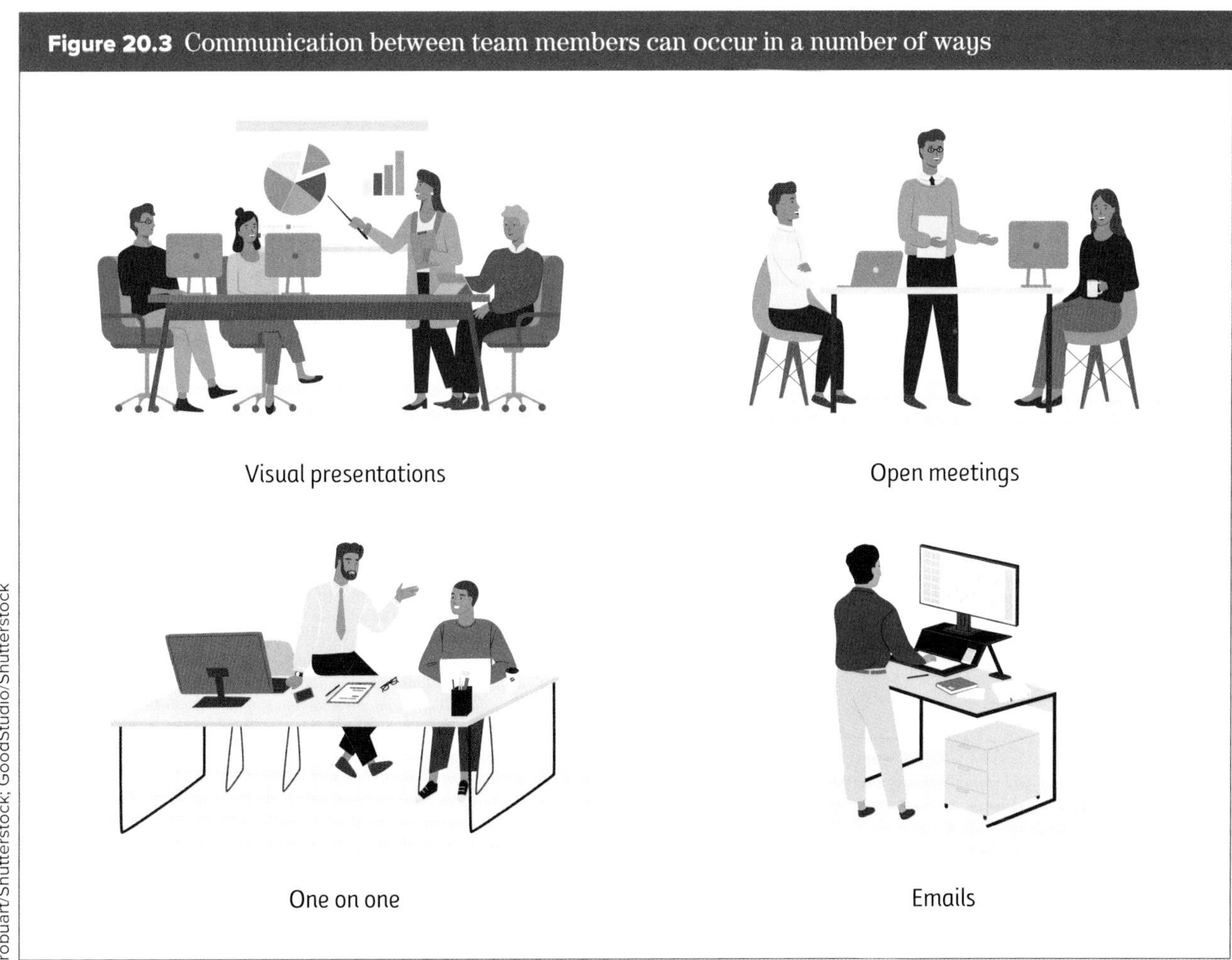

robuart/Shutterstock; GoodStudio/Shutterstock

Whatever method you use when interacting with team members, it is important to sound confident and professional when talking to others. Speak in a clear voice and resist the urge to use jargon, slang or unnecessarily complicated words or phrasing. Above all, it is important to listen to what others are saying. Listening attentively shows others that you are taking them seriously; it also builds trust and encourages participation.

Key principles of cross-cultural communication

The key principles of cross-cultural communication add a further dimension to the communication methods already outlined. You can adjust your communication style to accommodate colleagues from different cultures by:

- remaining flexible about the way in which work is completed, allowing for the diverse nature of the work team
- providing a variety of methods for distributing information—face-to-face discussions, short videos for people to watch, memos, emails—whatever is needed to ensure that all staff can understand what is needed
- being self-aware and ensuring that you treat all people in your workplace equally and with respect
- being self-motivated—for example, if you identify areas of communication that aren't working for the whole team, report the problem to your supervisor and/or take action to fix it
- speaking slowly and avoiding using slang or euphemisms
- providing staff with alternative methods of completing work tasks if they have problems with reading, writing or calculations.

It is important to acknowledge and accept that different cultures communicate in different ways. These differences are apparent in how people greet others, how they take turns when speaking, how they address each other, how they express their feelings and how they react to others' expressions of their feelings. To work effectively with colleagues and clients from other cultures, we need to learn to do the following:

- *Interpret non-verbal communication across different cultures.* Gestures, movements, tone of voice, eye contact and facial expressions vary in meaning across cultures. In India, for example, shaking the head from side to side is an indication of agreement rather than disagreement, which is how we understand it in Australia.
- *Respect people's personal space.* Different cultures interpret personal space differently. In one culture, for example, maintaining a certain distance from another person might be misinterpreted as being unfriendly, while standing close to them might be thought inappropriately intimate or pushy. The genders of the people communicating face to face are also an important consideration when determining what amount of personal space is appropriate.

Other cultural accommodations could include:

- allowing staff members time off work to attend religious events
- encouraging staff from other cultures to share their customs and practices with members of their work group
- providing workplace procedures and guidelines in languages other than English, or in graphic format
- providing handicapped access to and through your office or store, such as by ensuring that passageways are wide enough to accommodate wheelchairs or people who have difficulty walking
- using **augmentative and alternative communication** (AAC), in addition to the spoken word, when communicating with a colleague who has a visual or hearing impairment—for example, by making use of:
  - sign language
  - photographs, drawings, pictures and diagrams
  - written materials
  - specially designed apps on tablets or computers
- clarifying the preferred method(s) of communication with the person so you can accommodate them

- using inclusive language and "person-first" expressions that acknowledge diversity and convey respect to all people by focusing on them and not on their difference or disability—for example, say: "She *has* a visual impairment", not "She *is* blind".

In making these adjustments, you are ensuring that all colleagues feel comfortable dealing with you and can confidently contribute to the work.

Think about

4. Think about colleagues or friends who are from backgrounds different from yours. Have you needed to adjust your communication style when talking with them? How did you make these accommodations? What impact do you think making such adjustments has on team spirit?

20.3.2 Collaborating effectively with team members

In today's working world, both technology and global health issues have changed the way people interact with each other and do business. Even as the world recovers from COVID-19, many people still work from home and go into their actual place of business on an irregular basis. Then, too, technological advancements in the way we communicate have made it possible for us to work with colleagues, customers and suppliers from all around the world. Team members could therefore be in a variety of situations. For example:

- *Working in an office*—where everyone can gather, in the normal manner, and have face-to-face discussions of what needs to be done.
- *Working remotely*—for example, out on fieldwork, where services need attention, or covering a territory as a sales representative. These people need to be in touch with other staff in order to report back on issues and information they have gathered, as well as to receive information and instructions on what they are meant to do.
- *Working in a different part of the city, state or country—or in another part of the world entirely*—people working remotely must have access to all the information they require to do their work and will need to liaise with other team members in order to be effective in their roles.
- *Working from home*—it is not unusual, today, for staff to work from their homes. This type of arrangement is cost effective and has proven to be very productive. People working from home need access to information, programs and other team members if they are to do their job properly.

GoodStudio/Shutterstock

Collaborating with other team members, then, has taken on whole new aspects. We don't necessarily have face-to-face and personal interaction with others, but we all still need to work together effectively. This can be achieved in a number of ways. For example:

- *By using mobile devices.* Phones and mobile devices that don't depend on fixed communication methods (such as those that require a person to be bound to a desk or an office) allow for communication to take place wherever a colleague is operating from.
- *By videoconferencing.* Software and applications such as Skype, Zoom and Canva allow you to conduct meetings, collaborate with team members in other locations, hold conferences and webinars, and a good deal more, thus allowing all team members to feel part of the company and to contribute.

- *By employing other digital tools or software.* For example:
  - tablets and laptops that allow you to stay in touch with the office and to make contact with customers
  - industry- or organisation-specific software programs that allow you to file reports and to receive information.

Whatever method is used, all of the principles of teamwork discussed so far still apply. In addition, you need to consider any constraints others might be working under. For example:

- *Time of day.* Team members in other cities or countries may be working in different time zones and this will need to be taken into consideration when setting up meetings or requesting information.
- *Technical delays.* Even though telecommunications today are relatively fast and reliable, there may be times when networks break down, causing delays or disruptions to communication.
- *Language barriers.* While colleagues in other parts of the world may be able to speak the same language as you, they may not be 100 per cent proficient, so you will need to take this into account when communicating and make any necessary adjustments.

It is important to remember that, regardless of where each team member is located or what method they use to stay in touch, they are still members of the team and need to feel included and valued.

20.3.3 Seeking and providing assistance

Establishing an effective and innovative team environment also means ensuring not only that you have the support you need to get your work done, but that you offer your support and guidance to colleagues as and when they need it.

Workloads can sometimes become overwhelming and team members may struggle to complete their work. This can cause unnecessary stress as staff try to cope. At these times, a simple offer to help or a gesture of support can help them to get back on track. However, providing support and guidance to colleagues also means offering encouragement to them when they have ideas or suggestions for improvements. You may also offer colleagues opportunities to contribute by involving them in your own projects and ideas. Feeding ideas and suggestions back and forth will help all team members to improve their own skills while also finding better ways of achieving organisational goals.

In many cases today, staff pay is based on performance: the more you sell or the better you perform, the more you will be paid. This brings with it a culture of competition with your colleagues, which may not be a bad thing. It can be detrimental, however, if it is taken too far and help is denied a colleague due to jealousy and competitiveness. Everyone needs support at some time, and the welfare of the whole team should always be considered.

You can provide support by:

- explaining or clarifying tasks, procedures and structures to new team members
- helping colleagues when they have too much to do or they have special projects to complete and you happen to have some spare time

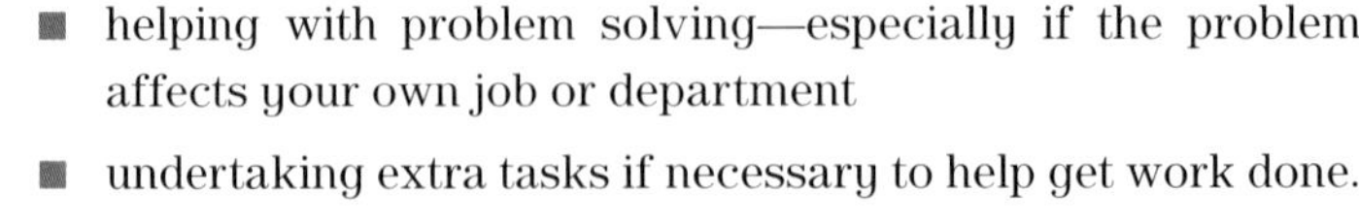

- helping with problem solving—especially if the problem affects your own job or department
- undertaking extra tasks if necessary to help get work done.

BRO.vector/Shutterstock

One of the best ways of encouraging a supportive environment is to be a role model for others in the workplace. A role model reflects the qualities that the organisation values in its employees and is someone for others to emulate and look up to. This might mean being:

- *collaborative*—asking others for their opinions and suggestions as well as encouraging them to put forward ideas of their own

- *equitable*—this means being fair and impartial in your dealings with colleagues
- *fun*—keeping the workplace fun and interesting (without impacting on productivity)
- *hard-working*—modelling a strong work ethic means ensuring that you get all your work done to the required standards and on time, and possibly taking on extra tasks and/or helping and supporting team members to ensure that all their necessary work gets done
- *reflective*—thinking about problems or issues and looking for the best way to solve them
- *responsible*—acting within the organisation's guidelines, doing nothing to harm the organisation, its staff or customers, and being sympathetic to and supporting colleagues who need assistance in some way.

Knowledge check

11. Communicating clearly and respectfully means using the appropriate language, listening attentively, understanding non-verbal language and asking effective questions. Give a brief description of each of the following:
    - appropriate language
    - positive listening attitude
    - non-verbal language
    - effective questioning.
12. List, and explain, three principles of communication with individuals with special needs or disabilities.
13. List at least six ways in which you can adjust your communication method, or style, to accommodate team members from different cultures.
14. Collaborating with team members in remote locations can be achieved in a number of ways. List three methods.
15. Explain what constraints might be involved in communicating with team members who work remotely.
16. List at least five ways in which you can assist and support team members.

20.4 Communicating effectively with the team

The one message that should have become clear in the course of this chapter is that effective communication is essential to a good team environment. This applies as much to communication between colleagues as it does to communication with a team leader appointed temporarily to lead a specific, short-term project team, or with a permanent supervisor responsible for an entire work team and/or area.

20.4.1 Receiving and confirming your understanding of task instructions or directions

Regardless of whether the team leader is temporary or permanent, they will guide you in how to complete your work efficiently. Most organisations have set standards as to how work is to be carried out, and in order to maintain this quality it is important that you understand the instructions given to you. Don't simply nod and say "Okay", and then try to work it out on your own if you don't understand. Misunderstanding what you need to do can lead to mistakes that could be costly in terms of work health and safety, resources and money spent on rectifying the mistake.

When receiving information, then, you should confirm that you have fully understood it. You can do this by using positive listening, being aware of non-verbal communication (as discussed previously) and by asking relevant questions, such as open or clarifying ones.

- *Open questions*. For example, when asking your supervisor about your part in a project or work role, ask: "How would you like this done?" or "When does it need to be done by?", which require detailed answers, instead of: "Do you want me to do this?", where they might simply answer "Yes". Equally, when communicating with a colleague to offer your support, you could get a better idea of what is bothering them by asking: "How can I be of help?" rather than "Are you okay?"

- *Clarifying questions*. For example, in summarising your understanding of instructions you have been given, ask: "So, what you're saying is that you would like [repeat your understanding of the instructions you received]. Is that correct?" They will either confirm your understanding or correct you.

Communicating personal commitments

The importance of effective communication in organisational commitment and employee behaviour cannot be overestimated. Organisational commitment is a measure of your own attachment to the organisation and is closely related to job satisfaction and employee retention. It is also associated with high job performance, as well as with active involvement and motivation to work with the team and the organisation.

Your personal commitment to the organisation and the team, then, can be communicated by:

- supporting other team members
- showing loyalty to the team and to the organisation
- treating all employees equally and with respect
- building trust and showing you can be relied upon to complete your work correctly and on time.

Think about

5. Think about your own commitment to your organisation. Do you relate to the points made so far?

20.4.2 Identifying and reporting any issues that might prevent the completion of workplace tasks

Working effectively also means taking workplace constraints into consideration. You may not always have sufficient time and resources to complete a given task or project. To work effectively, and to avoid delays and issues, you may need to:

- keep an eye on workplace resources—if stores are getting low, ensure that these are reordered or replaced regularly so that productivity isn't affected and projects aren't delayed.
- minimise waste of resources—wherever possible and appropriate, reuse or recycle materials.
- estimate the amount of time a task or project may take and ensure that you work to this schedule.
- let people know if you're running behind schedule so that they can adjust their own tasks and time frames accordingly.

Issues that may impact team performance and outcomes

You know what work you have to do, and you have prioritised it to make sure it is done on time. However, there is always the possibility that issues will crop up unexpectedly that will impact on the team's performance and their work outcomes. Such issues might include:

- a lack of clarity about what, exactly, is expected of an individual or the team
- trust issues, where trust hasn't yet been established and it is affecting team productivity

- personal conflicts with others, which can have a very negative affect on the team and need to be dealt with
- team members withholding important information from the group
- lack of communication when the team members are busy with their own tasks or haven't established team trust
- competition between individuals, where competitiveness stands in the way of the team working collaboratively.

Where these sorts of issues arise in the course of a working day, try to discuss them with the team members and find solutions or alternatives.

20.4.3 Seeking and acting upon feedback

Feedback is a vital part of any team member's skill set; not just giving feedback, but also receiving it, is essential for efficiently sharing information within teams and groups. Constructive feedback is a powerful tool for creating a healthy environment, boosting productivity and engagement, and achieving better results. It positively influences communication, team members' interaction and teamwork results in different fields. Why, exactly, is feedback so important?

- Feedback keeps everyone on track, which is beneficial for everyone involved in any type of activity, such as working on a project, preparing for an event and studying.
- By creating a clear and honest communication flow during any kind of teamwork, it saves you the time of correcting someone's work, minimises errors caused by miscommunication and prevents regrets of those who feel like they have failed.
- Feedback helps you to form better relationships. It promotes honesty and trust. It often involves criticism, which is something most people aren't comfortable with; however, when given in the right way, it can help them to evolve.
- Constructive feedback motivates people. It helps others see where they may be going wrong by giving advice rather than judging them.
- Feedback promotes personal and professional growth. It involves listening actively, taking the time to understand a problem, and then thinking of how to perform better. It brings people together and creates a healthy communication flow.
- Feedback helps to create a friendly work environment. It isn't uncommon that the best ideas come from someone on the team who simply mentions a possible solution to a problem or points out an issue that others haven't noticed yet.
- Feedback produces some direct, business-related benefits, such as business growth, reduced costs, higher sales, timely completion of projects, and other positive changes in finance, relationships with customers and the organisation's market position.
- It plays a crucial role in education and learning by helping the team to adopt new knowledge sooner and to avoid repeating mistakes.

Techniques for giving and receiving feedback in a constructive manner

The first step in evaluating the success of team performance is to gather feedback and to generate discussion and debate on the issues at hand. Feedback can be gained by way of:

- formal and/or informal performance appraisals with supervisors and managers
- formal and/or informal discussions and evaluation sessions (of a positive and constructive nature) with colleagues about work-related issues
- personal reflection, that is, thinking about the way you or a colleague handled a situation or particular work methods and ways of improving these
- routine organisational methods for monitoring service delivery, such as:
  - surveys conducted with staff, usually done using forms with a number of set questions to which the organisation requires answers

- focus sessions with staff, which produce better results for an organisation than written questionnaires because they are conducted face to face and staff can be asked follow-up questions to obtain more detailed information.

Knowledge check

17. Explain why it is important to ensure you understand, and confirm, any instructions or directions you receive from your team leader.
18. List four ways in which you can communicate your personal commitment to the organisation and the team.
19. List four ways in which the team can avoid issues that prevent them from completing their work.
20. List at least five issues that impact on team performance and outcomes.
21. Explain why giving and receiving feedback is important.
22. List four techniques for giving and receiving feedback.

Summary

Working in a team can sometimes be difficult, as everyone is different, with many different points of view or ways of doing things. But it can also be extremely rewarding. Sharing knowledge and experience with colleagues, and learning from them in return, can open doors and create opportunities for personal growth that you might not otherwise have access to. Understanding your own role within the organisation and the part you play in its success, as well as how everyone else fits into the overall plan, will allow you to contribute, communicate and work in the most effective way.

CHAPTER 21

Support effective workplace relationships

Learning outcomes

21.1 Gather information and ideas

21.2 Develop team relationships and networks

21.3 Contribute to positive team outcomes

A good location and good-quality products and services are all invaluable assets to any organisation. However, none of these things matter very much if workplace relations between colleagues, suppliers and customers aren't built on solid foundations (Figure 21.1). Distrust and dishonesty among staff, bad relationships with suppliers, and service staff who are indifferent to the needs of customers can all seriously damage an organisation's reputation and standing in the community.

Relationships can be fragile, especially in the workplace where they are often built and destroyed by the actions we take. Building healthy, secure and harmonious relationships is important not only to us personally, but also to underpin the success of the organisation you work for. You need to build effective relationships for a number of reasons:

- People's health is affected by what happens in their organisations and by what they do. Overwork, stress, being subjected to harassment or bullying all impact on a person's health and therefore on their ability to fulfil their role within the organisation. Staff who are stressed make mistakes, which can cost the organisation time, effort and money and damage its reputation.
- Organisations only function with the cooperation of people who work with them. Staff are at the coal-face of any business, fulfilling all the functions necessary to ensure success. If there is disharmony in the workforce, this can impact negatively on the organisation's success.
- Organisations can have a profound effect on people who don't work for them but who depend on them to produce the necessities of life (e.g. food, housing and clean water). Well-run organisations are normally stable and therefore also offer a stable environment to their staff and others who rely on them.

Figure 21.1 Elements in a successful team

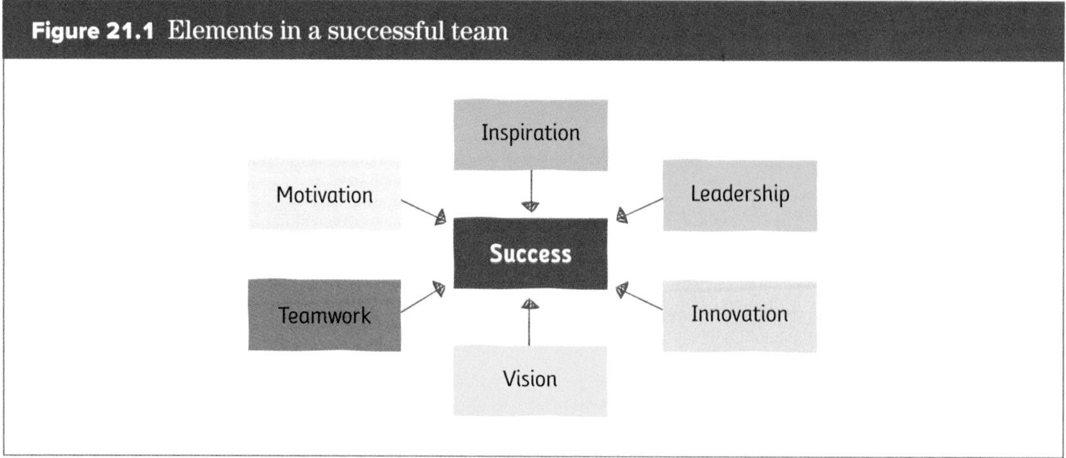

21.1 Gathering information and ideas

Having an in-depth knowledge and understanding of your organisation's products and services is essential to delivering a consistently high level of customer service. Equally, sharing knowledge, and understanding the role that each person plays within an organisation, is essential to building and maintaining effective workplace relationships.

21.1.1 Identifying information on work roles and objectives of work teams

The term "work role" refers to a person's position on a team, while "objectives" refer to the goals and/or duties of their particular role. Each member of the team is responsible for specific tasks within an organisation, and the more clearly a supervisor outlines how those tasks are to be completed, the better the chance that this will happen.

For a supervisor or team leader to effectively delegate specific work tasks, however, they must understand the individual roles within the organisation, defining each person's job, their responsibilities and the success criteria within the team. This will ensure the following:

- *Everyone knows what they are doing.* When roles are clear, people know what is expected of them, how they are to behave and what they need to achieve. Then, too, if they can see the importance of their contribution to the team's overall efforts, they often feel more motivated to succeed in their role.
- *Everything gets done.* In high-pressure environments, or under tight deadlines, tasks can slip through the cracks. This is especially true of the tasks no one wants to do. When everyone knows their responsibilities, as well as those of others, there is greater accountability, which ensures that tasks aren't forgotten.
- *People cooperate more effectively.* There is less conflict among the team members when interesting and agreeable tasks are equally distributed. Individuals also have far more respect for colleagues when they can see the vital part they play in the team's overall success. A respectful environment is more positive, collaborative and creative.
- *Productivity increases.* When teams understand what is expected of them, they know what they need to work on. Having a clear definition of their individual responsibilities will increase the team's overall productivity, which will create momentum and ensure success in the long run.

The benefits of role definition are clear: understanding the work role of those people you work with will give you an insight into how their work fits in with, and impacts on, your own work and on the organisation as a whole. But how do we reach this understanding of an efficient, focused workforce? Every position within an organisation should have detailed criteria defining the given role. Such criteria can be found in documents and descriptions such as work plans (also called a "job description", as discussed in Chapter 20).

Work plans are more than just an official title or designation of a role; they sum up everything that is required of whoever holds the position. For example:

- *Roles or responsibilities.* These are the expected results associated with the position.
- *Tasks or functions.* This part provides a detailed and specific list of the employee's activities and the standards to which these tasks must be completed.
- *Competencies.* These are the skills, capabilities and capacity necessary to fulfil the responsibilities of the role. For example, in the role of a marketing coordinator, the competencies might include the ability to produce creative designs for posters or blogs, or time management skills needed to work to strict deadlines.
- *Experience and education.* This addresses the educational background required to gain the competencies of the position in the first place. For example, the position of company accountant will almost certainly require a formal qualification in accounting. It may also require a given number of years working in that field if the position is a senior one.
- *Performance management and indicators.* This part of the work plan explains how the employee will be evaluated with respect to their performance. For example, how have they performed against the key performance targets allotted to them?

The role attributes outlined in a work plan will ensure that each team member knows exactly what to do, when they need to have tasks done by, and to what standard. Working to such a plan makes them far more likely to deliver not only the expected organisational outcome, but also to reach their own potential within the team.

Think about

1. How much information about your job does your work plan include? Could it be more detailed?

As other team members will be depending on you to get your work done on time and to the required standard, it is important to bear in mind how your role fits into the departmental and/or organisational picture. You will need to be aware of who is relying on you and the time frames in which you need to achieve the work allocated to you. To ensure this happens as effectively and efficiently as possible, you should develop, with your supervisor, a work plan that outlines the scope of your own role by addressing the following questions:

- What is the purpose of your role?
- How does your work contribute to the organisation as a whole?
- What are your exact duties and to what standard must they be completed?
- What are your responsibilities to your team, your department and the organisation as a whole?
- How do your duties impact on other roles, and what happens if you fail to fulfil your tasks?

Looking back at the marketing coordinator's role from Chapter 20, for example, we can answer some of these questions as follows:

- *What is the purpose of your role?* Broadly, the purpose of the role is to support the marketing manager in the promotion of the organisation and to carry out the tasks required to produce promotional materials and plan events.
- *How does your work contribute to the organisation as a whole?* The role helps to spread a positive image of the organisation to the wider community via a range of traditional and social media platforms.

- *What are your exact duties and to what standard must they be completed?* These include:
  - Prepare and place advertisements for staff vacancies and promotion of the organisation. All ads must include the organisation's logo and correct colours and be approved by the marketing manager before placement.
  - Prepare editorial material for promotional publications. This must be done in line with the organisation's style guides.
  - Stay in touch with current trends and news items. Enter information of interest into the ideas and improvement log on the organisation's intranet.
  - Maintain a social media presence, and post at least once each day on all social media platforms the organisation subscribes to.

Identifying team objectives

Whatever the purpose for forming a team, when working towards a goal in a team environment, there are a number of things that need to happen to ensure success. One of these is to develop team cohesion. Team goals can only be achieved successfully if all members work together as a *whole unit*, rather than all pulling in different directions. Cohesive teams have a clear understanding of what needs to be accomplished and the roles and responsibilities of each member of the team.

Team members brought together for a given project should be chosen according to their abilities and the contributions they can make to the team. In addition, they should be able to to work in harmony with the rest of the team and be willing to offer constructive comments and critiques when necessary.

In the initial stages of a team, the members may not yet know each other well and can fall into the trap of "going along to get along"—even if they don't agree with the suggestions being made. This is known as the Abilene paradox. Named by J.B. Harvey in the early 1970s, the Abilene paradox describes a situation in which team members inwardly disagree with a collective, unanimous decision but outwardly support it in order to avoid conflict or being seen as a "spoiler". Such situations can potentially cause a breakdown in team cohesion and can lead to outcomes that are less than successful because nobody actually liked the idea. It makes sense, then, to ensure there are members of the team who can speak up and disagree when necessary.

Having said that, once the team members have been chosen and the goal to be achieved has been defined in detail, the next steps are to identify the individual tasks that need to be completed and to determine the time frames and the order in which these tasks need to be done. With the order of tasks determined, you can then assign tasks to individual members of the team according to their skills and expertise.

It is always important to monitor work progress as the project moves along to ensure that everything is on track to be completed by the stated deadline. Monitoring also offers the opportunity to look for or offer help where necessary.

21.1.2 Locating and communicating organisational processes

Working in teams doesn't mean you *only* work together when there are specific projects to be completed. You are a work team every day in every situation and must always work together, sharing knowledge and information for your own wellbeing and for the benefit of the organisation.

All teams need information on organisational policies and procedures in order to work efficiently. Information and ideas, however, are only as good as the use to which they are put. Gathering all the right kind of up-to-date information is of little use if it is then stored away in a folder somewhere and never used. To be truly useful, information needs to be shared with colleagues to ensure that all staff are working towards the same goal.

Sources of information

Information about job roles and company policies and procedures can come from a number of sources, both external and internal. *External* sources can include the following:

- *Government websites.* These offer information on pay scales, awards and working conditions. For example, see Fair Work (http://www.fairwork.gov.au/pay/minimum-wages/pay-guides).

- *Other web-based resources.* These could also be government departments that oversee specific industries. For example, the Australian Competition and Consumer Commission provides information on marketing via social media (https://www.accc.gov.au/business/advertising-promoting-your-business/social-media). They could also be industry associations and governing bodies that provide organisations within that industry with a range of supports. They may also offer guidance on compliance and legislative requirements within their specific industries, as well as work role information. For example:
  - Accommodation Association of Australia (www.aaoa.com.au)
  - Australasian Legal Practice Management Association (http://alpma.com.au)
  - Australian Marketing Institute (https://ami.org.au).

Internal sources can include the following:

- *Supervisors, managers and colleagues* who have experience and expertise in specific areas and the manner in which tasks need to be completed.
- *Organisational policies and procedures.* Most organisations will have policies and procedures that provide staff with guidance on how to behave in, or deal with, given situations. In most cases, these policies and procedures will have been created with a great deal of thought and care and will set the standards to which tasks are to be performed each and every time in order to offer a consistently high level of service. The setting of these policies and procedures may be internally driven (e.g. the organisation has developed a set of standards that it believes reflects the image it wants to achieve) or externally driven (e.g. the policies and procedures are based on legislative requirements in which case they are a matter of law). In either case, all staff must comply with them. Organisational policies and procedures might, then, revolve around things such as:
  - work health and safety (WHS) and security procedures
  - equal opportunity and anti-discrimination policies
  - customer service policies and standards
  - staffing policies and procedures
  - privacy laws.
- *Product or service brochures* that provide information you will need in order to promote and/or sell to the organisation's customers.
- *Internal newsletter or intranet* that provides up-to-date news on what is new within the company or any activities that it is currently engaged in.

Organisational goals and processes

As an individual within the organisation, you will be part of a larger team. In addition to achieving the required work standards, you will also need to be aware of and work in line with the organisation's overall plans. These may include the following:

- *Organisational goals, objectives and plans.* You should have an understanding of the direction the organisation is heading in and how it intends to get there so that you, together with your team, can contribute in the best possible way. This information might be communicated in a number of ways, including:
  - project plans that outline the purpose of a specific work goal or objective and how the organisation intends to achieve it.
  - overall business plans that detail all areas of the business operation and what it needs to do to remain successful into the future.
  - sales and marketing strategies that provide information on how the organisation will connect with customers and increase its sales.
  - staff handbooks that provide employees with all the information they need about working in that specific organisation.
- *Organisational structure.* Having an understanding of the organisation's hierarchy, its reporting channels and its procedures means you will know who to contact for any particular reason

and the correct protocols to follow. "Going over someone's head" and bypassing the chain of command can often have a very negative effect on team cooperation. Make sure you have a copy of the company's organisational chart and that you understand who you need to report to.

- *WHS responsibilities*. Regardless of whether you are working on your own or as part of a team, you must always do so with your WHS responsibilities in mind.
- *Legislative or industry-based regulations and codes*. Depending on the industry you work in, you may also be subject to legal frameworks and/or industry standards, regulations and codes of practice. For example:
  - Staff who work in a bar that serves alcohol must have a Responsible Service of Alcohol qualification.
  - Kitchen staff must be fully aware of food safety standards and follow strict hygiene regulations.
  - Childcare workers must be fully qualified to deal with issues and the education of young children and infants in their charge.
  - Marketing and advertising businesses must abide by ethical standards when promoting products and services, whether this is on television, in a magazine or on a social media platform.
- *Environmental issues*. Depending on the industry you are in, you may have legal obligations to follow environmental procedures, such as when disposing of toxic or hazardous substances and materials. Aside from these considerations, it makes sense, both from a business and a community perspective, to use resources such as energy and water responsibly and to recycle products wherever possible.
- *Equal opportunity and anti-discrimination*. It is against the law in Australia to discriminate against people because of their race, religion, age, culture, gender, or physical or mental abilities. Any work environment must therefore take these laws seriously and endeavour to treat all people with equal respect and courtesy.

Methods and techniques for communicating information and ideas

When sharing information about organisational processes with the team, there are a number of things to consider. For example:

- *Is the information of a confidential nature*? You need to be aware of whom certain information can be shared with. The type of information you share, and the methods you use, will depend on the stakeholders involved. They may include:
  - external stakeholders—for example, contractors, customers or suppliers. Your communication here might be via telephone or email—perhaps even by letter (depending on the nature and formality of the communication). You would also need to be mindful of privacy and confidentiality issues when sharing information with stakeholders outside of your own organisation.
  - internal stakeholders—for example, colleagues, other organisation departments, supervisors and team leaders. Communication here might also be via telephone or email; however, it is more likely to be by face-to-face discussions or meetings.
- *What is the best method of distributing information so that all staff can access it*? Methods and techniques can include:
  - regular staff meetings—where issues and general information can be discussed.
  - meetings held specifically to share information—these might include progress reports on specific projects or brainstorming for ideas on a given work activity.
  - training sessions—these can be used to share in-depth information about new products or services, or to provide refresher information about roles and responsibilities.
  - emails or memos to staff—that can be sent and accessed instantly.
  - reading distribution lists—where staff are required to read certain materials and to check off that they have read and understood it.

- *the organisation's intranet*—which can be used to update the team on news and activities.
- *Push, pull and interactive communication techniques.*
  - Push communication is a method of communication that is controlled by you and that is used when you want to send information to *specific* stakeholders. It broadcasts a message for the recipients to read and respond to. Examples of push communication include memos, letters, voicemails and emails.
  - Pull communication is used when your message is of a more general nature. You want people to know about this, but you don't necessarily expect a response and they can read the information at their leisure. Examples of pull communication include blogs, intranet, online training databases and bulletin boards.
  - Interactive communications, unlike push or pull communication methods, is a multidirectional communication method: you send out your message and you expect an immediate response. Interactive communication most often means meeting with, or talking to, stakeholders and discussing a particular issue, conveying information face to face and getting feedback instantly. This is best used when the information is sensitive or when urgent feedback is necessary. Examples include meetings, workshops, videoconferencing and training sessions.

Think about

2. Looking at your own industry, or one you would like to work in, are there any specific legal obligations or processes that you must meet? How did you learn about these?

21.1.3 Seeking contributions for refining ideas and approaches to teamwork

The success of any organisation rests, to a large degree, on how well people work together. Contributing ideas, or looking for contributions from others, is a well-rounded approach to assessing organisational requirements as it considers all points of view and takes advantage of the total pool of knowledge.

When working together in an organisation, never forget that you are all working to achieve the same goal. To this end, it is desirable to achieve a sense of harmony and team spirit by developing a rapport with other members. You can contribute to developing this spirit by:

- discussing with other team members how best to accomplish large or complex tasks
- breaking projects down into individual tasks to refine ideas, which can lead to better management of the process
- helping to solve problems
- identifying the talents of individual staff and looking for ways to best harness these
- looking for alternative means of getting work done and ways in which work processes could be improved.

robuart/Shutterstock

Everyone within the workforce has talents or areas of expertise in their field that they can contribute. The important thing is to identify those strengths and to use them, in conjunction with your own, to build a dynamic team of people who understand where they are going and what is required of them.

When team members work together to accomplish a goal, it can be rewarding for them personally but also very productive. A team that using a **proactive**, rather than a **reactive**, approach contributes to this productivity by finding creative ways to move forward, rather than waiting for something to happen and then reacting to it.

21.1.4 Identifying and consulting with team members on potential work-related issues

Despite having policies and procedures for staff to follow, a workplace doesn't always function as well as it should: mistakes happen, systems become outdated, and former methods of completing a task no longer work efficiently. Additionally, newly introduced legislation or industry codes of practice might mean changes in usual policies and procedures, or WHS hazards or risks may have become apparent, or sometimes changes just happen. These, among many other things, can potentially cause problems for the organisation and will need to be assessed and dealt with. Discussing these issues with other members of the team can produce a range of ideas and suggestions. Each team member will have different levels of experience and can contribute their knowledge to the pool of information needed to solve any potential problems.

Problems can be solved using a variety of methods, including:

- *Brainstorming*. This is a method used by teams to generate ideas to solve clearly defined problems. Brainstorming encourages the team to throw out ideas and suggestions regardless of how practical they might seem initially. The process of brainstorming might include the following:
  - Setting a time limit. This will depend on the complexity of the problem but shouldn't be too long.
  - Starting with a brief on the problem. A brief will outline the issue and how it affects the organisation or the team.
  - Refraining from judging or criticising anyone's suggestions. Everyone should be free to express their opinions freely in this initial phase of generating ideas.
  - Building on ideas. Brainstorming is a process of *association*, where team members should expand on others' notions and reach new insights, allowing these to trigger further ideas. Once all ideas have been put forward, it then becomes a matter of sifting through each one and discussing their practicality and viability in relation to the actual problem and the resources available to solve it.
- *Discussing the problems*. Sometimes a simple discussion with the colleagues involved in a given situation, looking at the pros and cons of possible solutions, might be enough to address or solve it.

Try this now

1. Together with a group of your colleagues or friends, identify a problem and brainstorm for ideas on how to solve it. Write them all down, then discuss which one/s might be the most practical.

The plan-do-check-act (PDCA) cycle

In simple terms, a PDCA check is a model for carrying out major changes. It involves a simple four-stage method that enables a team to avoid making mistakes in improving its processes (Figure 21.2). The four stages are as follows:

1. *Plan*. In this stage, the team will simply plan what actually needs to be done by asking the following questions:
   a. What is the core problem we need to solve?
   b. What resources will be needed and what resources do we actually have?

c. What is the best solution for fixing the problem with the available resources?
d. What are our goals in this, and how will we measure their successful accomplishment?

Figure 21.2 The PDCA cycle

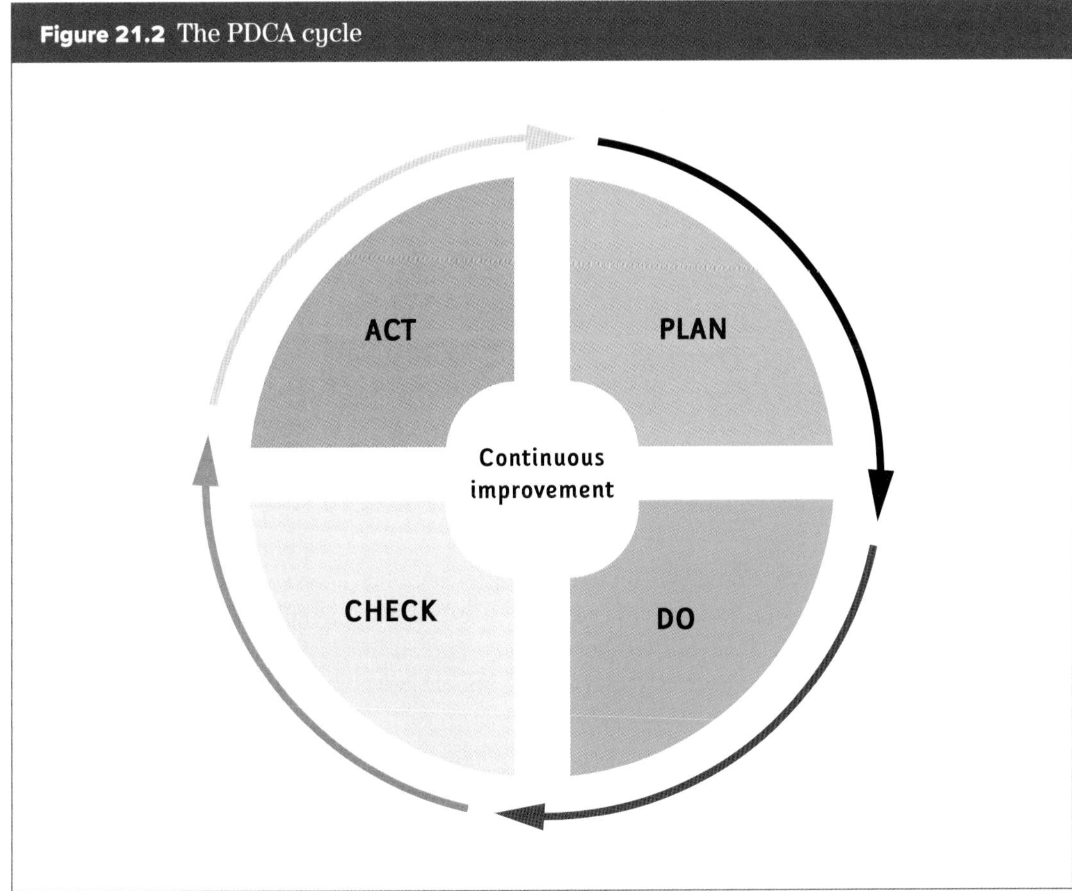

2. *Do*. After the plan has been agreed upon, action must take place, applying everything the team outlined in stage one.
3. *Check*. At this point, the team should "audit" the plan's execution to see if the initial intent has actually worked. This is also an opportunity to identify any problems with the current process and to eliminate them in future plans.
4. *Act*. This is the final stage. If all unanticipated issues have been considered and resolved, you should now be able to adopt the entire plan for change.

Knowledge check

1. Explain why it is important to identify information on the roles and objectives of the work team.
2. Describe what things should be included in a job description.
3. What questions should you ask when defining the scope of your own role within an organisation?
4. When forming a team to complete a work project, there are a number of steps to take. Identify and briefly describe them.
5. Give at least four examples of external and internal sources of information.
6. Describe at least five methods and techniques for communicating information and ideas.
7. Explain why it is important to seek contributions from the team in refining ideas and approaches to teamwork.

21.2 Developing team relationships and networks

Effective workplace relationships can only be built and maintained when there is trust, respect and empathy among colleagues and the confidence that they will support you in the performance of your tasks. This doesn't mean that you have to be best friends with all of the people you work with, but you must be able to work with them in a professional and courteous manner. Disharmony in the workplace can, in extreme cases, bring an organisation to its knees. Such an atmosphere must be dealt with and avoided at all costs if the business is to be successful.

In looking at how to establish a trusting and confident relationship with colleagues, we need to understand the key aspects of building and maintaining such relationships. These are: integrity, respect and empathy, and were discussed in Chapter 20. Such relationships develop from consistent actions that show colleagues you are reliable, cooperative and committed to team success.

21.2.1 Encouraging communication within teams

Effective relationships should be developed within the framework of the organisation's social, ethical and business standards. Some of these have already been covered. Standards may relate to:

- *Diversity and inclusion.* All people should be treated equally regardless of their background. It is, in fact, illegal to discriminate against a person because of their race, religion, culture, gender, age, or physical or mental abilities. Every person on the work team has something to contribute and the organisation you work for should have strategies in place to ensure it embraces diversity.
- *The organisation's vision, mission and value statements.*
    - **Mission statement** defines the company's current business, its objectives and its approach to reaching those objectives.
    - **Vision statement** describes the future position the company wishes to take and how it intends to get there.
    - **Value statement** defines how it expects people to behave with each other within the organisation.

  Some excellent examples of mission and vision statements can be found at ClearVoice (https://www.clearvoice.com/blog/difference-between-mission-vision-statement-examples/).
- *Psychological safety.* This means looking after your own, and your team's, wellbeing and reducing stress wherever possible.
- *Communication protocols.* Some organisations will have specific methods and policies about communication, both with internal and external people. For example:
    - rules about communicating with the media—what you can and can't say about the company and its staff.
    - appropriate use of any communication channels and their uses—for example, when, where and how to use email, newsletters, telephone calls, meetings or social media platforms.
    - meeting protocols—for example, how will meetings be conducted—boardroom-style or casual? Will they be held online or face-to-face? Will there be a minimum number of participants required in order to make decisions? Who will be responsible for preparing agendas and taking the minutes of the meeting?
- *Rewards and recognition for high-performing staff.* While this might generate competition among staff, it is also a way to encourage the desired behaviour.
- *Standards expressed in legislation and regulations*, such as anti-discrimination legislation—ensuring that all team members are aware of not only their obligations under legislation, but also their rights. Policies and procedures should be developed to ensure these issues are addressed and followed by all staff.

With these and other standards in mind, team members should be encouraged to:

- discuss and solve problems before they become critical issues that will affect not only the workplace but also team relationships
- share knowledge with each other to improve work conditions or capabilities
- offer or ask for help when it is needed
- understand each other better so that they know who to rely on or call on when needed.

A team that communicates openly will be more engaged with the organisation, understanding that what they do matters to its success as a whole.

Think about

3. Think about times, either at work or at home, when you have been supported by those around you or when you have supported someone else. How has this helped you?

21.2.2 Adjusting interpersonal styles and methods

In your everyday working life, you will often interact with people from many different backgrounds. They may come from different countries or cultures, so that English isn't their main language, or they may have physical or mental disabilities. Whatever the case, you may need to adjust your style and method of communication to accommodate them. This might mean:

- remaining flexible about the way in which work is completed, allowing for and considering the differences in culture and physical or mental abilities
- providing a variety of methods for distributing information, such as face-to-face discussions, short videos for people to watch, memos, emails—whatever is needed to ensure that all staff can understand what is needed
- being self-aware and ensuring that you treat all people in your workplace with respect and equality
- being self-motivated; if you identify areas of communication that aren't working for the whole team, you should report it to your supervisor and/or take action to fix the problem.

In making these adjustments, you are ensuring that all colleagues are comfortable dealing with you and can feel confident about contributing to the workplace.

21.2.3 Identifying and using workplace networks to help build relationships

Networking is perhaps one of the most valuable skills in building a successful organisation. Business networks, if used effectively, have the capacity to grow and expand a business's reach exponentially. This means that if you know 10 people and tell them good things about your organisation, and they each tell another 10 people good things about it, then within a relatively short time 100 people have heard good things about your organisation. This number will continue to grow as these contacts pass on positive comments.

A workplace network doesn't need to be complicated. It may simply be a matter of knowing someone who knows someone else. This is what networking is all about. No organisation can work in complete isolation. Networks enable it to access people and resources that can help it to achieve its goals or objectives.

An effective workplace network can be made up of the following:

- *Customers*—who can give you access to additional potential customers via their friends and family.

- *Suppliers*—who provide you with a range of services as well as access to their own networks should you need additional services.
- *Staff*—who can give you access to their own networks of friends and family. This may be useful if you are looking to recruit new staff and they have relevant contacts, or you may wish to have specific jobs done for the organisation and they have friends or relatives who can undertake these tasks.
- *Other businesses in the area*—who can provide services to you, or referrals to potential customers.

Workplace networks can be formal or informal, internal or external.

- *Formal networks* are properly structured, with a database containing information about the network such as contact details, the industry they are in, how that industry might benefit your organisation, any agreements between network members, ways in which members have worked together or contributed to the organisation in the past, and any other useful information.
- *Informal networks* are far less structured and may consist of nothing more than a collection of business cards.
- *Internal networks* might be a simple list of people within your own organisation, including supplier connections and their connections.
- *External networks* may be made up of people you connect with outside of your own organisation, such as through membership of the local chamber of commerce, business networks such as BNI (https://www.bni.com.au) or other business groups, or internet-based networks such as LinkedIn (https://www.linkedin.com) or 100AM (https://www.100am.co/).

21.2.4 The value of networks and other work relationships

A business network is only as good as the use to which it is put. There isn't much point in having hundreds of contact names in your database if you never contact them or make use of them. Business networking is an effective low-cost marketing method for developing business opportunities based on referrals and introductions. This can happen either face-to-face at meetings and gatherings, or by other contact methods such as phone, email, and (increasingly) social and business networking websites.

robuart/Shutterstock

A business network is both a pathway to the market for you, and a marketing method in itself. It offers a way to reach decision makers who might otherwise be very difficult to engage with using conventional advertising and promotional methods, as well as personal introductions, which are always helpful in developing business opportunities.

21.2.5 Benefits of establishing networks and relationships

Networking helps an organisation to expand its reach, enhance its reputation and generate additional revenue. Benefits include:

- *Generating referrals to increase business.* This is probably the most obvious benefit and the reason most business owners participate in networking activities and join networking groups. Referrals received from networking contacts are normally of a high quality and may even be pre-qualified for you. This means that the contact referring them to you has already asked them basic questions about what they are after and has then, based on their response, recommended your organisation.

- *Helping to identify opportunities.* A motivated group of businesspeople who network regularly can be a source of opportunities such as joint ventures, client leads, partnerships, speaking and writing opportunities, and business or asset sales. The opportunities offered by networking are almost limitless.
- *Expanding connections.* "It's not *what* you know, but *who* you know." This is very true in a business sense. Success in business often rests on the connections in your network that you can call on when you need them. Networking provides you with these sources and could give you access to influential people that you wouldn't otherwise be able to meet.
- *Being a source of advice.* Meeting with like-minded businesspeople provides the opportunity for you to get advice from them on a range of issues related to your business.
- *Raising the organisation's profile.* Being visible and getting noticed is a major benefit of networking, so it is important to regularly attend business and social events that will help get your organisation known.
- *Being a positive influence and increasing your confidence.* The people that you associate with and talk to influence who you are and what you do, so it is important to surround yourself with positive, uplifting people who can help you to grow and thrive in business. The more you network and talk with people you don't know, the more your confidence will increase.

Think about

4. Think about the networks that you have established. Have they proven valuable to you? How? How could you take better advantage of them?

Not only is networking one of the best resources for building a successful organisation, it is also useful for career development and professional success. A good network can provide job leads, possibilities for advancement and opportunities for personal improvement. If you hope to grow your career and increase your chances of professional success, you need to understand the importance of a network.

A good network has the potential to provide you with insight into different fields, information on what potential employers are looking for and advice on how you can improve professionally. If you are willing to form and maintain the relationship, a single contact could get you into meetings or interviews with several organisations without you having to work to form connections at each one.

Using technology to best advantage

Networking successfully will expand your knowledge base and increase both your business potential and your personal potential. It can also help to build better relationships between team members as they share their knowledge and expertise.

All of the information gathered, both in terms of organisational processes and its networks, however, will need to be processed and properly stored so that it is available as and when needed. Technology can help an organisation to keep track of all the information it needs to operate successfully, as well as its business contacts. It can help in reaching out to customers, suppliers and network partners in order to maintain a presence in the ever-expanding global market.

Most business databases will allow you to "interrogate" them for a range of useful information. For example:

- What contacts do you have in your network who can refer you to a specific source of information or other contacts?

- Which products and/or services are selling well—and which are not?
- What are customers buying, how much are they paying, and are there specific times of the year when they are making purchases? All this information is useful for inventory management.
- How can you reach a greater audience?

Information such as this will not only enable you to track the success of your business but will also help you to make informed decisions based on known facts.

Technology you can use in the workplace includes:

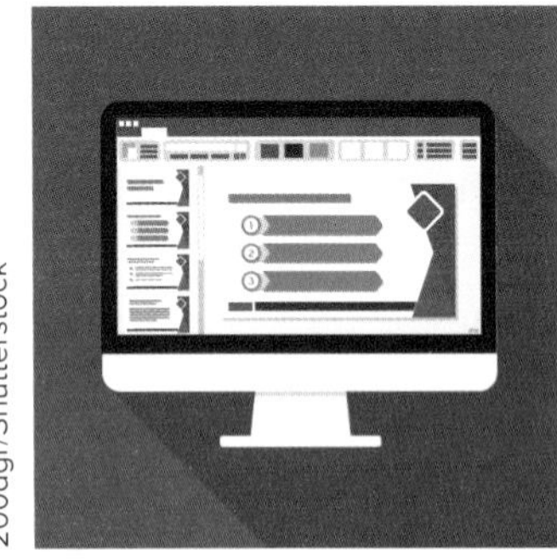
200dgr/Shutterstock

- **Cloud-based systems**. An organisation can store its data on the internet through a cloud computing provider such as Apple, Microsoft or Google. This data is then available for any organisation member with password access to work with, no matter where they are located.
- **Shared drives**. In a similar way to a cloud-based system, information is stored and available to a team of people. However, the data is stored internally on an organisational server.
- **Customer management systems**. A CMS allows an organisation to manage all its relationships and interactions with existing and potential customers. It helps it to stay connected to its business networks and customers, streamline its processes and improve its profitability.
- *Email services*. Most organisations today use email to communicate with customers, suppliers and staff. There are two types of email services: email client and webmail:
    - Email client is an application for the desktop and allows the user to configure single or multiple email addresses—composing, sending, receiving and reading emails from your computer. An example of an email client is Microsoft Outlook.
    - Webmail is an application for accessing emails via a browser. This means that you can access your email from any device that can be connected to the internet. Examples of webmail include Gmail and Yahoo.

    Often, an organisation will have a company website that will allow for a certain number of email accounts. Depending on how their systems are set up, email on these accounts can also be accessed on mobile devices. You can recognise such email accounts as they include the name of the organisation. For example, the email account bertha@abcwebsiteco.com belongs to Bertha at the ABC Website Company.
- *Spreadsheets*. In the absence of any specific database software, spreadsheets are a useful tool in managing a range of information. You can create spreadsheets to store client information, keep track of inventory, manage your finances and a great deal more.
- *Virtual meeting technology*. Depending on the nature of a meeting, **virtual meetings** often prove a better alternative than actually travelling to one. A virtual meeting can take place at a moment's notice and allows the participants to access all the documents or other resources they may need to carry on a negotiation or conversation. While a personal meeting still offers a range of benefits, the various factors involved in arranging face-to-face, personal meetings make them less cost effective. Travel time, venue hire for the meeting and other expenses are all issues that need to be considered. Examples of virtual meeting technology include Zoom and Skype.

Technology allows you to network and interact with staff, customers and business partners in a range of different ways that will keep them up to date on your organisation's activities, projects and promotions, and helps build stronger links and networks.

Knowledge check

8. Describe at least three methods you can use to solve problems.
9. What do the terms "integrity", "respect" and "empathy" mean? Why are they important in workplace relationships?
10. Encouraging communication within a team is important, but it should be done within the framework of the organisation's social, ethical and business standards. List at least four issues that you would need to consider in this regard.
11. In your everyday working life, you may be interacting with people from all walks of life and from many different backgrounds. Describe methods you could use to adjust your communication style to accommodate them.
12. An effective workplace network can be made up of a range of different stakeholders. List at least three of these.
13. Workplace networks can be formal or informal, internal or external. Give a brief description of each type.
14. Business networks provide a number of benefits. List at least five benefits. Briefly describe each one.

21.3 Contributing to positive team outcomes

Effective and cohesive workplace relationships don't simply happen; they take cooperation and the will to get along with other people. Positive teams are those that support each other, trust each other, and work hard to achieve team and organisational goals. With positive teams, work takes place in a more relaxed atmosphere, with less stress and is measurably more productive. However, there will be times when conflict or difficulties arise. These need to be dealt with quickly and efficiently so that the situation doesn't disrupt the workplace.

21.3.1 Identifying issues to be rectified within your own level of responsibility

You know now that you can contribute to a positive team environment by ensuring your work is carried out well, on time and to the organisation's required standards. However, for your own sake and for the benefit of your team, you should also be aware of areas where your performance falls short of your own and others' expectations and could be improved. Improving your performance will increase your value to your organisation as well as your own level of job satisfaction.

Rectifying issues you identify in your performance levels might involve:

- discussing your work role with your supervisor or human resources staff to clarify your understanding of what is required of you and to identify the options available for improvement
- taking part in training to improve or upgrade your skills
- attending seminars or business networking activities that will give you greater business insights, as well as access to more experienced people who can help you improve your knowledge and understanding
- coaching and mentoring by a supervisor or more experienced colleague to develop your skills.

Think about

5. Are there any areas of your workplace that could be improved upon? What can you do about them? Who would you need to speak to, or involve, in order to get them rectified?

21.3.2 Supporting colleagues in resolving work difficulties

In today's workplaces, where staff pay is often based on performance—that is, the more you sell or the better you perform, the more you will be paid—a culture of competition can prevail. This isn't altogether a bad thing, but it is important that competitiveness and jealousy don't prevent colleagues from supporting each other. You can support your fellow team members by:

- providing advice or expertise to help them accomplish their work tasks
- explaining procedures and policies to them when necessary
- helping to solve work problems as they crop up
- providing them with encouragement and positive reinforcement
- sharing feedback about performance or customer comments with them.

Providing assistance and support not only ensures that work gets done on time, but also strengthens the team as a whole. Having the confidence that team members are there for one another creates an agreeable work atmosphere.

21.3.3 Reviewing team outcomes and implementing improvements

Every business needs to have goals for it to be productive. Setting specific goals for the team to achieve, and ensuring that each member understands their role in helping the organisation to meet its objectives, is motivating and can lead to improved work performance. Regularly updating the team on goal progress can enhance team cohesion and maintain motivation. Reviewing team outcomes with key stakeholders on a regular basis is therefore critical in meeting goals.

Carry out the review process by asking:

- Is the work being carried out in compliance with legislation and/or organisational requirements?
- What issues have been identified?
- How often are they occurring?
- What immediate corrective action can be taken?
- Are we choosing the right people, with the right skills, to work on team projects?
- How can we improve on our team-building processes?
- Are we communicating with the team in the most effective way?
- Are we using our networks to advantage?
- Was the objective of a specific project achieved? If not, why not? What could we do better next time?
- Does the current process of developing project plans work?
- How could the process be improved?
- Did we have sufficient resources?
- What did we do well?
- Were there any unanticipated problems?

Processes for monitoring and analysing team outcomes

In reviewing team outcomes, it is important to remember that the world is changing at a rapid pace and work conditions and procedures should keep pace with these changes. Processes for monitoring and analysing team outcomes may include the following:

- *Coaching and mentoring*. This involves analysing the team's current performance levels and then providing training for any gaps identified.
- *Conducting organisational health checks*. This may mean discussing current work practices with relevant team members to see if any issues have arisen. It may also mean conducting a full

workplace "audit", where each work process is rigorously checked to ensure it is still viable, and is in line with organisational policies and, importantly, legal requirements.

- *Conducting performance appraisals and reviews.* These are generally in the form of personal, one-on-one discussions with each member of the team to discuss their performance, their future career options, and any training or other relevant issues. Performance appraisals are traditionally carried out yearly; however, ideally, they should be done on an ongoing basis as and when needed.
- *Observing teamwork.* Supervisors have a duty to the organisation to ensure that work gets done properly and on time. The best way to gauge whether this is actually happening is to observe how the work is carried out, take corrective action if necessary, and give praise where a good job was done.

By monitoring team outcomes, an organisation can track work progress and identify where things are going well or where issues may need to be addressed. For example, if a project was being held up by inefficient team cooperation, steps could be taken either to discuss the matter with the staff members concerned and find a solution, or to change the team members. Or if the issue is a lack of resources, steps could be taken to address this so that the work can continue to move forward.

To do this effectively and to ensure that all aspects of processes and procedures are reviewed realistically, you may need to involve a range of stakeholders from within the organisation. While the organisation's management may have developed the procedures that are in place, it is the staff who have to carry them out who may be better judges of whether those procedures actually work and if improvements could be made. Consultation with relevant staff is therefore important.

Relevant personnel may include:

- *team members* from across different areas of the organisation, who, collectively, can take a broad view of the issues under discussion
- *human resources staff*, who are responsible for the organisation's staff members as a whole and look after the interests of both the business and the staff
- *finance staff*, who may need to be consulted about budgets and resource acquisitions
- *supervisors*, who will be directly responsible for the staff in their department
- *managers*, who will have the ultimate approval of any plans or changes that need to be made.

Think about

6. **How often does your organisation or work team get together to review processes? How are gaps in processes identified? Who gets involved in the review process?**

Introducing ways to improve work relationships

The review process may have identified areas of work processes or workplace relationships that need improving. How improvements are implemented will depend to a large degree on the level of complexity involved. For example, it may be a relatively simple matter to change a minor procedure within a specific department, without infringing on any organisational policies. However, making major changes to the way in which departments work with each other, or changing the organisation's human resources policies, would require a great deal of

GoocStudio/Shutterstock

consultation between departments, and a detailed plan outlining the shortcomings of the current policies, the benefits of making the changes, and the steps needed to transition from the old to new procedures. This could all take a great deal of time and would involve different stakeholders providing feedback on their experience with given work processes or relationships and making suggestions on how these might be improved.

New processes, once approved by all the stakeholders concerned, could then be introduced, using methods such as:

- Communicate with staff about the changes that are to be made and, importantly, why they are necessary. This will help to overcome any resistance and improve the chances that staff will accept the need for new procedures and will carry them out efficiently.
- Produce written guidelines for staff to follow (keeping diversity considerations in mind).
- Provide training for staff in the new procedures so that they are fully aware of what is expected of them.

Workplace relationships themselves can be improved by:

- organising and/or participating in external events such as team sports days or similar team-building activities
- organising professional development seminars or training sessions that may include team-related games
- holding regular team meetings at which "burning issues" (i.e. things that may not be task-related but which have become a problem for staff for some reason) can be discussed.

Think about

7. What other activities could you do, in the workplace, to improve relationships?

Encouraging and acknowledging feedback

Feedback should always be actively sought. Everyone wants to do the best they can and to improve their skills. Part of the path to self-improvement is to listen to the people around you who have more experience, or who have a different approach that might be useful. Supportive relationships within the workplace also mean that you offer feedback to your colleagues—let them know when they are doing a good job, or gently point out where they could improve their performance.

Feedback therefore involves sharing information with others and discussing opportunities to improve work efficiency and team dynamics. It can include:

- formal and/or informal performance appraisals with supervisors and managers
- formal and/or informal discussions with colleagues about work-related issues, conducted in a manner that is positive and constructive
- personal reflection, that is, thinking about the way you or a colleague handled a situation or particular work methods, and ways of improving
- routine organisational methods for monitoring service delivery, such as surveys and focus sessions.

In whatever way the feedback is provided, it should be viewed as an opportunity to make improvements to your work habits, to learn lessons and to grow in your career.

21.3.4 Contributing constructively to conflict resolution

Differences of opinion occur in any team environment, but such differences should never be allowed to evolve into conflict. Conflict between colleagues has the potential to damage "team spirit" and completely disrupt the workplace. It is corrosive; if left unchecked it can weaken, and perhaps even destroy, an organisation. To prevent a relatively minor issue from escalating into a major one, conflict situations need to be identified and dealt with quickly.

Work conflict can arise among staff when:

- someone's performance is below normal levels or doesn't meet required standards
- they are disengaged from work and colleagues, and show little interest in their work
- they take more sick leave than normal
- they break rules or don't follow procedures
- they fail to share information or to involve others in decision making
- they use negative non-verbal language such as a clipped tone of voice, roll their eyes or turn away while others are talking
- they spread negative or malicious gossip about other staff members or management
- communication is poor and there is a lack of information
- practices and procedures change
- there are cultural misunderstandings
- colleagues are vying for power
- staff are dissatisfied with management
- there is weak leadership or a change of leadership
- colleagues or supervisors lack empathy
- there are general complaints that aren't dealt with.

GoodStudio/Shutterstock

All of these issues can cause dissatisfaction and a lowering of team morale. If acted upon sensitively and quickly, such issues can be resolved without disrupting work. If they are ignored, they can de-motivate the workforce, which can affect the organisation's productivity. Poor productivity affects the organisation's revenue earnings, which, in an extreme case, could destroy business.

Here are some suggested ways to resolve conflict:

- *Avoid jumping to conclusions.* Let each person have their say, without interrupting them or imposing your own thoughts or ideas on them.
- *Find some common ground with the other person.* Look for something you can agree on. This will keep the process on a positive footing.
- *Keep to the facts and don't let emotions get in the way.* Allowing emotions to surface can often break down the communication process, as tempers heat up and people become agitated.
- *Avoid placing blame.* Determining who is right or wrong, or who is at fault, isn't your goal when resolving a conflict. A problem exists; what you are trying to do is to find a solution to the problem that will be satisfactory to everyone concerned. Blaming someone isn't going to resolve the situation.
- *Consider cultural differences.* Perhaps the conflict has arisen due to a misunderstanding over different beliefs or customs. In this case, an effort could be made to gain this understanding and perhaps even to learn something new.
- *Check to see if anything has been left unsaid.* Issues, even minor ones, that haven't been dealt with, or that haven't been resolved satisfactorily, can fester and spring up again without warning. A situation that you thought was resolved may not be! Ask questions to ensure that the other person is satisfied with the resolution, or if there are issues that still need to be addressed.
- *Be courteous and respectful.* Allow the other person to state their case without interruption or interference.
- *Consult a third party* (e.g. a supervisor or manager) if you cannot resolve the situation.

Knowledge check

15. Explain the advantages of using database technology to store business information.

16. In identifying areas of your work performance that need improving, you can use a training needs analysis. Describe this process.

17. List at least five ways in which you can support colleagues in resolving work difficulties.

18. Reviewing team outcomes is essential for ensuring business and team relationship success. List at least eight questions you could ask when reviewing the team's performance.

19. List at least three processes for monitoring and analysing team outcomes.

20. Describe the steps you might need to take when introducing ways to improve work relationships.

21. List at least three ways in which you can gather feedback.

22. List at least five steps you can take to resolve work conflict.

23. Explain why it is important to identify and consult with team members on potential issues.

Summary

Healthy working relationships are founded on open and honest communication, acceptance of diversity, mindfulness in words and actions, mutual respect and trust.

A final word

Circling back to the Preface of this textbook, regardless of what industry a company represents, they all *do* business. So, undertaking a qualification in a business field will set you on a path that can lead to many different job roles in many different industries. In completing your training, you have learnt how to deal with a range of situations—from customer complaints, to working on team projects, developing your career, dealing with finances, producing a range of business documents, and much more. All of these new, or expanded, skills will stand you in good stead for the career ahead of you.

Congratulations!

Glossary

absenteeism the practice of regularly staying away from work without good reason.

access in terms of inclusivity, it refers to the manner in which companies provide equal opportunities and amenities to individuals with difficulties or challenges, thereby ensuring all employees are treated the same.

account a record or a statement of financial transactions.

accountability the fact of being responsible for something.

accountable documents documents that contain financial information that must be accounted for (such as receipts, invoices and purchase orders).

accounting equation the basic principle of accounting which shows that an organisation's total assets are equal to the sum of its liabilities and its owner's equity.

accounting system the system an organisation uses to record transactions so that financial statements can be created and checked by stakeholders.

accounts payable the amount of money owed by an organisation to its creditors.

accounts receivable the amount of money customers/other businesses owe to an organisation.

accrued expenses expenses that have been recorded in the accounts but that have not yet been paid.

accrued revenue the money that has been earned by providing goods/services, but for which no payment has yet been received.

adjusted entries accounting journal entries that are made at the end of an accounting period after a trial balance has been prepared.

Afterpay a "buy now, play later" (BNPL) platform that allows shoppers to receive goods immediately and pay them off later in fortnightly instalments.

agenda a list of items to be discussed or actioned during a meeting.

agenda slide the first slide of a PowerPoint presentation; also called the "table of contents".

agreement a formally negotiated, and often legally binding, arrangement between parties.

anti-discrimination practices aimed at preventing people from being treated unfairly because of their race, gender, age, religion, sexuality, etc.

appendix a collection of supplementary materials, usually at the end of a book or report, that provides additional (non-essential) information.

appointment a previously arranged meeting with an individual or a group.

apps short for "applications"; these are types of software that fulfils a range of useful functions when installed and run on a computer, tablet or smartphone.

asset anything that is owned by an individual or a business that has commercial or exchange value.

asset management system a formal process of listing and managing the assets owned by an organisation.

balance sheet a statement of the assets, liabilities and owner's equity of a business at a given point in time, i.e. its net worth.

bank statement a list, provided by a bank, detailing all financial transactions completed within a given period.

bar chart a graph that presents numerical data with rectangular bars that are different heights/lengths.

benchmark a point of reference detailing how a given standard is to be achieved.

benefits advantages that can be gained.

brand a type of product/service/company operating under a particular name.

business activity statement (BAS) companies registered for GST must submit this form to the Australian Taxation Office (ATO), detailing all financial transactions made within a specified time frame.

business environment all the internal and external factors that influence business operations.

business strategies sets of guidelines and action plans designed to ensure that business objectives are met.

capital resources any resources used by a business in the production of goods or services.

carbon footprint the amount of carbon dioxide released into the atmosphere as a consequence of individual, community or organisational activities.

career plan a formalised plan to help you achieve your career goals.

cash payment journal a record of all cash payments made by an organisation.

cash receipts journal a record of all cash sales received by an organisation.

cell an individual box in a spreadsheet that may contain data.

cell reference a cell's location in a spreadsheet.

characteristics features/qualities that are typical of a product/person.

characteristics of a product the features of a product (e.g. size, shape, weight, colour and quality).

chart of accounts a list of all the different financial accounts held in the general ledger of an organisation.

clarifying question a question that is asked to gain a better understanding and to eliminate confusion.

closed question a question that can be answered with a short or one-word answer, e.g. 'Yes' or 'Red'.

closing balance the debit or credit balance of a general ledger account at the end of an accounting period.

closing entries the act of balancing accounts at the end of an accounting period, so that they have a zero balance at the beginning of a new accounting period.

cloud computing facilities that store and process data via the internet.

cloud-based system a method of working and storing information on the internet so that it is accessible to authorised individuals regardless of their location.

codes of practice sets of guidelines instigated by organisations (or whole industries) to ensure workers comply with ethical and health standards.

communication the exchange of information through verbal or non-verbal means.

communication barrier anything that prevents a message from being received or understood.

communication skills the ability to convey and understand messages clearly.

complementary product a product that enhances and/or adds value to another product.

conflict a disagreement between two or more people.

conflict resolution the process of resolving a disagreement between two or more parties.

consumable resources day-to-day items (e.g. paper) used in business that need to be replaced frequently.

contextualisation altering a practice or guideline to better suit specific organisational or individual needs.

continuous improvement a business strategy implemented by organisations to ensure the ongoing betterment of processes and services.

credit (CR) a record of all money flowing into an organisation's account.

creditor an individual, or company, who is owed money because they have provided goods or services.

critical thinking the objective evaluation of information to make an informed decision.

current asset cash or any other asset that is expected to be converted to cash within a year.

current liabilities all outstanding amounts owed that will be paid or settled within the financial year.

custom show a series of PowerPoint presentation slides that have been modified to suit a specific purpose.

customer contact database a list of customers who do business with an organisation.

customer management system (CMS) a system for storing, accessing and using customer information to manage all existing and potential customer relationships.

debit (DR) a record of all money flowing out of an organisation's account.

debtor an individual, or company, who owes money for goods or services that have been provided to them.

dictionary a resource, in either print or electronic format, that lists words alphabetically with their meanings.

disposable income the amount of money you have left over after deduction of taxes.

double-entry accounting an accounting system that ensures all transactions have an equal and opposite effect in at least two different accounts; a decrease in one account equals an increase in another.

EFTPOS electronic funds transfer at point of sale is a method of paying electronically (via debit/credit card) for goods at payment terminals.

electronic document management systems software systems used for storing and organising documents.

electronic presentation a method of promoting or presenting information in a variety of formats, using technology and appropriate presentation software.

employee assistance programs (AEPs) off-site work programs designed to give employees access to professional assistance.

employee assistance schemes (EASs) free, confidential work services that provide employees with counselling and support during difficult times.

environmental audit an evaluation of a company's environmental impact, which measures risk and suggests corrective actions.

environmental hazard any substance or event that has the potential to negatively affect the health of humans and the natural environment.

equal employment opportunity a legal obligation that relates to equal access to employment opportunities.

ethical relating to the principles of morality.

etiquette a code of polite and appropriate behaviour.

expense any money an organisation needs to pay for goods or services.

fair work legislation Australian law that governs the relationship between employers and employees.

features details about a product or service's capabilities or attributes.

feedback culture a business culture where every employee in an organisation (regardless of their role) can give feedback to fellow employees.

financial budget a prediction of an organisation's income and expenses for a certain period.

fixed asset any asset that is purchased for the long term and is not expected to be converted to cash quickly (e.g. land, buildings, equipment or vehicles).

footer the area at the bottom of a page that contains information that is common to the other pages in the document.

forecasting a technique of making informed and educated estimates of future needs based on historical data.

forms documents with blank spaces that are used to obtain information.

formula a type of equation that is entered into a cell in a spreadsheet that returns a specific result.

general ledger a set of numbered accounts that are used to keep track of financial transactions and to prepare financial reports.

goods and services tax (GST) a 10% tax levied on most goods, services and other items sold or consumed in Australia.

greenhouse gases gases, such as carbon dioxide and methane, that contribute to the greenhouse effect by trapping the heat from the sun in the atmosphere.

hardware the physical system components used to run software, e.g. a disk drive or a gaming console.

hazard anything that is a potential danger and that can cause injury or harm.

hazardous substances/dangerous goods any agent or item that can cause harm to people, animals and the environment.

header the area at the top of a page that contains information that is common to the other pages in the document.

health and safety representatives (HSRs) individuals who have been elected to monitor the health and safety procedures within their organisation.

hierarchy a tiered system in which individuals or items are ranked based on authority or importance.

hierarchy of control the system used to reduce and control risks in a workplace.

house style the prescribed way in which documents should be created and presented within a business to standardise its written communications.

inclusive practices approaches that recognise people's differences and use these in a positive way to ensure that all individuals are treated equally.

income see *revenue*; the amount of money a business earns or generates.

income statement a statement showing an organisation's revenue, expenses and profitability over a given period of time; also called a "profit and loss statement".

induction a workplace program offered to new staff to familiarise them with the company processes and their colleagues.

information management the process of collecting, storing, managing and maintaining data.

input the data that is sent to a computer by way of a keyboard, mouse click or tapping a touchpad.

Internet of Things (IoT) the concept of devices connecting and exchanging information with other connected devices and systems via the internet.

intranet a local, private communications network internal to an organisation.

inventory number a serial number given to each item in an organisation's inventory/stock.

journal an account book of specific financial transactions which, at given periods, are then transferred to the general ledger.

key performance indicators (KPIs) a set of goals/targets given to individual workers, or groups, that must be achieved.

key stakeholders the individuals who are most crucial in the execution of a project or an idea.

leading question a question that is asked to prompt a person in providing a desired answer.

liabilities the organisation's financial obligations (e.g. the money that it owes its suppliers and staff, and any outstanding loans).

line graph a graph that connects individual data points with lines.

mathematical operator the element that specifies the type of calculation a person wants to perform, e.g. addition and subtraction.

minutes an official report of what was discussed during a meeting.

mission statement a short paragraph that outlines an organisation's vision or reason for existing.

monitor a computer screen on which to view information.

multimedia a form of communication combining text, audio, images and video in one presentation.

needs in business terms, this is something a person *must* purchase in order to fulfil basic human needs (e.g. food, housing and healthcare).

negotiation a strategic discussion that aims to ensure agreement between parties.

networking the interaction between individuals or groups of like-minded people who can benefit each other in business.

non-current asset an asset owned by a business that is not expected to be converted to cash quickly.

non-current liabilities debts that an organisation owes, but that are not due for payment for at least 12 months.

non-verbal communication communication that happens without using spoken or written words, i.e. using visual cues like hand and facial gestures.

open question a question asked when a long answer is sought.

operation system (OS) software that acts as an intermediary between computer hardware and users.

organisational culture a collection of values, expectations and practices that create the environment (vibe) of an organisation.

orientation programs see "induction".

output any information that is sent out by an electronic device, e.g. text viewed on a computer monitor.

owner's equity the amount of money that would be returned to investors if all the assets were liquidated and all debts were paid off.

parameters a set of factors or limits that affects how something can be done.

PayPal one of the original online payment platforms that allow you to shop without having to enter your debit/credit card details.

peak in a business sense, it represents times of high usage or sales.

performance review a formal, structured assessment of work abilities (and discussion of development opportunities) between a manager and an employee.

person conducting a business or undertaking (PCBU) a broad term used in health and safety legislation to describe the "person" (whether it be a public company or a sole trader) responsible for ensuring the health and safety of workers and visitors.

pie chart a graph that uses a circle which is divided into sections (slices) to represent parts of a whole (e.g. a percentage).

placeholder an area where information can be entered.

position description a formal document that provides an employee with all the information on their role, e.g. title, who the role reports to, and the duties and responsibilities.

positive listening skills the ability to truly listen to what a person is saying.

preferred product a product (or service) that provides the organisation with additional revenue, commission or an incentive to sell it.

presenteeism the practice of being at work for more hours than required, especially as a result of insecurity about one's job.

principal in business terms, the owner of a business or manufacturer of a product.

proactive working with, creating or controlling a work-based element *before* it becomes an issue.

procurement in business terms, this the process of sourcing, acquiring and paying for goods and services.

productivity a measure of how efficiently work is accomplished.

profit and loss statement a summary of the revenue, costs and expenses incurred by an organisation during a specific period of time (usually a "financial year").

programs a series of instructions in programming language that instructs a computer to execute specific tasks.

protocols established rules within an organisation that explain the correct procedures to be followed.

purchase journals records of all purchasing transactions made by an organisation.

purchase order a document that is issued to a vendor/supplier when placing an order.

purchase specification the guide used for the procurement of goods/services, ensuring businesses buy the correct items under appropriate circumstances.

purchasing strategy the set process a business puts in place to make buying decisions.

quality control the process of monitoring the quality of work being produced.

reactive responding to an issue that has occurred, as opposed to being proactive and controlling it before it happens.

receipt a customer's proof of purchase.

recurring appointments appointments that occur at regular intervals, such as monthly staff meetings.

reports business documents which contain important information about a business and its performance (e.g. an analysis of a project or task).

resources sources of supply or support needed to complete a task or project.

revenue the income generated by an organisation through the sale of goods or services.

risk the potential of a hazard to do damage or cause harm.

safety data sheets documents containing information on the properties of hazardous substances, how they affect health and safety in the workplace, and how to minimise risk.

safety share when a worker shares safety information and lessons learned from personal experience to create awareness and prevent accidents.

sales journal a record of all sales transactions made by an organisation.

schedule a list of activities that take place over a given time frame.

shared drive online folders that a work team can use to store, search and access files.

slide window the PowerPoint slide currently on your screen.

SMART principle a method of monitoring goals; they should be specific, measurable, achievable, relevant and time-bound.

social diversity the differences (in cultures, belief systems and background) observed in a particular group of people.

software a set of programs instructing a computer to perform specific tasks.

source documents see also "accountable documents"; the financial forms and documents that need to be kept as required by the Australian Taxation Office (ATO).

standard the level of quality to be achieved in completing specific tasks.

stereotypes a fixed, and often unfair, belief or judgement about a group of people.

style guide a manual containing a set of standards that need to be followed when writing and/or designing documents to ensure consistency across multiple documents within an organisation.

sustainable policies and procedures standards on how staff are to ensure their organisation meets its legal and environmental obligations.

synergy the successful interaction or cooperation between parties that, combined, has a greater effect than individual efforts.

systemic relates to something that affects an entire system (or organisation).

T-accounts a set of financial records using the double-entry bookkeeping system.

tax invoice a formal document used as a demand for payment of goods or services provided, indicating taxable items.

tax return a compulsory submission to the Australian Taxation Office (ATO) detailing all income and expenses during a financial year.

taxable sales sales where GST is payable.

template an established document format that needs to be copied to ensure uniformity in presentation when creating similar documents.

tender an invitation to suppliers to bid for a contract.

theme a specific design that can be applied to all PowerPoint slides within a presentation.

thesaurus a resource, similar to a dictionary, that orders words according to similar meanings.

thumbnail a list on the left margin of the presentation window in PowerPoint that shows small versions of each slide in their correct order.

toolbox talk a brief and informal safety meeting before the start of a shift to promote safe work practices.

tradeoffs giving things of value in exchange for other things (e.g. in negotiation).

training gap the difference between the standard at which an employee is expected to perform and the actual standard at which the employee performs.

training needs analysis a method of comparing an employee's performance with the organisation's expectations; if a discrepancy exists between the two, training is required.

training schedule (lesson plan) a plan detailing how and when training/a lesson will be delivered.

trends general directions in which things are developing.

trial balance a list of all the accounts in a general ledger and their balances as of a specified date.

troughs in business terms, it represents times of low usage or where sales might be lower than usual.

unearned revenue money received by the organisation for goods or services that have yet to be provided.

value statement see "mission statement".

verbal communication when spoken words are used to convey a message or an idea.

virtual meetings a form of communication that enables people in different locations to use technology to conduct meetings.

vision statement the standard that defines an organisation's current business, objectives and its approach to meeting its objectives.

wellbeing the feeling of wellness—physically, mentally and emotionally.

wellbeing program a program aimed at promoting and maintaining a healthy lifestyle.

WHS policies and procedures a formal set of guidelines and work practices that set out how to secure the health and safety of individuals within a workplace.

workplace culture the principles, values and behaviours that collectively create the environment and atmosphere at work.

Index

A

absenteeism 379
access 33
accountability 122, 175, 374
accountable documents 284
account book *see* journals
account customer 282
accounting 282, 295, 307
accounting equation 284
accounting system 283
accounts payable 282, 283, 286, 295, 300
accounts payable ledger 297
accounts receivable 282, 283, 285, 295
accounts receivable ledger 298
accrued expenses 302
accrued revenue 302
acquisition of resources 124–128
  contracted supplier ordering 127–128
  internal approvals 128
  non-tendered processes 128
  reviewing 127–128
  tendered processes 128
acquisition processes 148–150
active listening 11, 16–21
adjusted entries 302
administrative staff 86, 368
administrative tasks 230
advertisements
  for promoting the organisation 367
  for staff vacancies 367
Afterpay 341
aged care services 56
Age Discrimination Act 2004, 362
agenda 162, 193, 205, 213
agenda slide 274–275
aggressive communication style 8, 49
aging debts 309
Agreed Issue Resolution procedures 97
agreement 178
Allison, Michael 304
analysis skills 65
annual reports 138
anti-discrimination 410
  issues 362
  law 28
  legislation 168, 259
appendix 216
appointment, defined 152
appointment schedules
  development and priorities 163–164
  procedures for 160–162
  timelines and diary commitments 165–167
apps 6
assertive communication style 8, 49
asset management system 181
assets
  consist of 285
  current 285
  facilitating registration of 181
  financial 179
  fixed 285
  non-current 285
  record-keeping systems for 173
asymmetrical balance 208
attitude 33
audit documentation 333
audit requirements 308–309
augmentative and alternative communication (AAC) 398
Australia 25
  Australian Human Rights Commission 26
  environmental authorities in 108–109
  religion in 28
Australia and New Zealand Anatomy of Work Index 2021, 378
Australian Accounting Standards Board (AASB) 307
Australian Bureau of Statistics 25
Australian Consumer Law (ACL) 322, 347, 362
Australian HR Institute (AHRI) 55
Australian Human Rights Commission 26
Australian Public Service Commission 27
authorised supplier 338
automated presentation 263
AutoSum 241

B

baby boomers 29
Bacon, Sir Francis 38
balance sheet 282–283
bank charges 301
bank statements 284
bar charts 252, 253–254
benchmark 332
benefits 68
benefits-based incentives 57
body language 324
bonding 75
bookkeeping 282
  transactions 284–287
brainstorming 66, 363, 412
brand 10
budgeting 230
budgets 125–126, 186, 206
business activity statements (BAS) 284
business data storage, in spreadsheets 230
business documents 203–228, 235
  access and equity issues 207
  adding headers and footers 217
  agenda 205
  asymmetrical balance 208
  checking and completing production 223
  contrast 209
  design and layout tools 216–222
  designing 210–223
  editing text 217–218
  finalising 225–228
  format and style with required stakeholders 209–210
  forms 205
  graphs and images 218–219
  inserting comments 221–222
  internal memos 212
  layout and style of publications 207–210
  letters 205
  meeting agendas 212–214
  meeting minutes 206, 212–214
  newsletters and/or blogs 206
  order 209
  organisational requirements 206–207
  page layout 209
  presentation 227–228
  principles of document design 208–209
  production 223–224
  proofreading 225
  proportion 209

business documents (*continued*)
reports 214–216
saving files 225–226
selecting and preparing resources 204–210
simple reports 206
spreadsheets 206
storage methods 226–227
symmetrical balance 208
table of contents, creation 222
tables, insertion 219–221
technology for 204–205
templates 205
tools, locating in Ribbon 216
tracking changes 221–222
unity 209
Word Help 223–224
business environment 9
business equipment 119, 120, 181
business letter 194–196
business networking 416
business resources
acquiring resources 124–128
business equipment 119, 120
capital resources 119, 120
consumables 119, 120
current and future requirements calculation 119–123
effective decision making 131
equipment needs and supplier selection 123
handling resources in line with organisational requirements 128–130
human resources 119, 120
legal requirements 121–123
monitoring effective resource usage 130
monitoring resource usage and maintenance 128–133
obtaining and storing 124–126
organisational acquisition considerations 125–126
organisational requirements 121–123
requirements 119–123
resource analysis sheet, usage and costs 120
reviewing acquisition process 127–128
shortages, impact of 123
types of 120
business strategies 122
business-to-business (B2B) 313

C

Canva 264–266
capital resources 119, 120, 173, 181
carbon footprint 102
career plan 382, 383
cash at bank account 295
cash payment journals 283
cash payments book 289–292, 298
cash receipts book 289, 292–293, 299
cash receipts journals 283
cell reference 240
cells, in spreadsheet 237
characteristics 74
and composition of work team 74–75
of good team 74–75
of product 341
chart of accounts 295–300
charts 252–257, 258
bar charts 253–254
creation 253–257
formatting 255–256
line graph 253–254
modifying type and layout 256
pie chart 252, 253
types and design selection 252–253
child protection services 56
clarifying questions 16
clients 146
closed questions 16–17
closing balance 304
closing entries 303
cloud-based storage system 211, 226, 418
cloud digital platforms 143
code of conduct 139
code of ethics 139
codes of conduct 186, 206, 389
codes of ethics 25
codes of practice 4, 77, 78, 108–109, 168, 306–309, 324, 347
colleagues 127, 140, 146, 251, 346, 378
supporting, in resolving work difficulties 420
columns, in spreadsheet 237
committee members 146
Commonwealth Department of Agriculture, Water and the Environment 108
communicating information and ideas 410–411
communication 2, 33 *see also* personal wellbeing; simple documents; written communication
active listening 16–21
adjusting for diverse backgrounds/special needs 11–12
aggressive style 8
appropriate approach 48–50
appropriate language and levels of formality 21
arranging to communicate with supervisor 52
assertive style 8
audience and purpose of 3–4
challenges, identifying and reporting 13–15
content of message planning 9
contributing clear ideas and information to workplace discussions 21–22
with customers 360
developed plan 52–53
digital 7
effectiveness of 22–23, 53–54
establishing and selecting methods of 5–7
information needs and communication requirements 4–5
Internet of Things (IoT) 6–7
in legal issues 184
message/information 9–12
method of 185
model 19
non-verbal 16, 17, 18
open 75, 396
participating in 15–23
passive-aggressive style 8
passive style 8
planning 3–9, 50–51
planning with supervisor 48–52
positive listening 17
potential risks/safety hazards 14
purpose of 184
questioning techniques 16–21
receiving and responding to workplace information and instruction 12
reviewing the effectiveness 53–54
seeking feedback from others 22–23
style guides and templates 10
with supervisor 52–54
supporting others to communicate in workplace discussions 22

techniques to resolve challenges 14–15
types of 17
unethical/inappropriate 14
verbal 5–6
written 6
communication barrier 37
cultural barriers 37
defined 37
language barriers 37
strategies to overcome 37–38
communication protocols 414
communication skills 52, 65
to clarify customer needs 345
complaints 358–359
communication styles
advantages of 48
aggressive 8, 49
assertive 8, 49
disadvantages of 48
guides and templates 10
passive 8, 49
passive-aggressive 8, 49
rapport creation 49
compactus 145, 227
competencies 407
Competition and Consumer Act 2010 (Cth), 323–324, 347
competitor information 137
complaints 352
acknowledging 353–354
assessment of 354–356
defining 355
documentation 326–327, 356–357
due to misunderstandings 353
escalating matters 364–365
escalation 357–358
expected outcome determination 355–356
fallback parameters 363
ideal outcome 363
implications, for customer and organisation 360–362
informing relevant stakeholders 356
loyal customer complaints 353
management of 325–327
organisational and legislative issues 361–362
preparing information for resolving 359–360
processing 357–360
product-related complaints 353
proposing options 363–364
public complaints 353
realistic outcome 363
receiving 355–357
resolution 326
resolving 360–365
service-related complaints 353
unacceptable outcome 363
using communication skills, additional information requirements 358–359
complementary products and services 350
computers 142–143, 204
concertina files 145, 227
conference 160
presentation 263
program 160, 161
confidentiality 308
issues 122
conflict resolution 14, 35, 422–423
conflicts 34, 35, 326, 379
with clients/team members 13–14
consumables 119, 120
resources 181
contextualisation 75
contingencies 374
continuous improvement 22
log 42
register 94
contracted supplier ordering 127–128
Cook, Thomas 24
copyright legislation 207
corporate/account customers 313
corporate electronic filing systems 227
correct log-on procedures 186
costs
direct 362
issues 361–362
COVID-19, 6, 374, 399
credit (CR) 283
rules of 296
credit notes 284
creditors 295
criteria-based method 67
critical thinker, skills of 65
critical thinking
application of 65
apply to individual and team situations 71
defined 64
evaluating with team members 69–71
skills of critical thinker 65
steps in 64
in team environment 60–72
workplace problems, solution for 64–65
cross-cultural communication 12
cross-cultural training 11
cultural barriers 37
cultural differences 15, 423
cultural diversity 11, 24
in Australia 26
value of 34
culture 27, 57
personal factor 45
workplace factors 46
current assets 285
current liabilities 286
customer contact database 158
customer databases 322
customer forums 333
customer loyalty programs 322
customers 337
age 314
alternative products or services 349
answering customer questions 344–345
communication skills to clarify customer needs 345
complaints *see* complaints
complementary products and services 350
corporate/account 313
cultural background 314
delivery of service 320–330
effective workplace network 415
evaluating needs and determining priorities 316–317
external 313
identifying limitations and seeking assistance 319
information 348
informing, about available choices 317–319
internal 313
needs and expectations, identifying and clarifying 314–316
needs identification 313–319
organisational policies and legislative requirements 346–347
from other organisations 313
physical abilities 314
preferred products 349–350
promotions 350–351
responding to customer requests 344–348
social and economic background 313–314
sourcing additional information 345–346

customers (*continued*)
special interests 314
special needs 314
survey form 334
types 313–314
customer service delivery 320–330
acting on feedback to enhance quality of 334
assisting customers with access needs 328
benefits of 320–321
complaint resolution 326
customer satisfaction with 331
documenting and submitting recommendations for 335
documenting complaints and resolutions 326–327
establishing and maintaining rapport with 324–325
evaluation 330–335
feedback 330–331
good communication skills development 321
legislative requirements 323–324
managing customer complaints 325–327
opportunities to promote and enhance services and products 328–330
organisational requirements 321–323
providing assistance and responding to needs 327–328
seeking and responding to customer feedback 332–334
verifiable feedback sources 332–334
custom shows 274–275

D

dangerous goods 96
data 135
entering and sorting, in spreadsheets 238–239
database management software 201
databases 144
data entry 232
data management 309
deadlines 162
debit (DR) 283
rules of 296
debtors 295
decimal numeric filing system 227
decision-making
effective 131
information useful in 150
degree of decision-making 356
delivery of goods, procedure for 329
designing documents 210–223
and ensuring efficient entry of information 212–216
identifying, opening and creating files 210–212
range of tools 216–222
desire 315
desk diaries 154
desktop publishing software 201
diaries and planning tools 154–159
dictionary 207
digital communications 7, 204–205
digital tools 400
direct cost 362
direct supervisor 364
Disability Discrimination Act 1992 (Cth), 362
disability services 56
dishonoured cheques 301
disposable income 45
diversity 414
advantages of 36
on personal wellbeing 46
dividend account, closing 304
documentation 38, 52, 97
business documents 203–228
customer complaints 356–357
customer's complaints and resolutions 326–327
methods for accessing wellbeing resources 57–58
simple documents 183–202
documenting feedback 42
document retrieval systems 144, 145
document specifications 188–189
double-entry accounting 283, 295–300
drafting, simple document 194–197
to communicate key points 194–197
proofreading 197–198
purposes and requirements 197

E

economic wellbeing 45
education, on personal wellbeing 45
effective communication skills 324, 352
effective decision making 131
effectiveness of communication 22–23, 53–54
effective workplace relationships 405–424
adjusting interpersonal styles and methods 415
communicating information and ideas 410–411
conflict resolution 422–423
elements in team 406
encouraging and acknowledging feedback 422
encouraging communication within teams 414–415
external sources 408–409
gathering information and ideas 406–413
information on work roles 406–408
internal sources 409
locating and communicating organisational processes 408–411
monitoring and analysing team outcomes 420–421
objectives of work teams 406–408
organisational goals and processes 409–410
positive team outcomes 419–423
potential work-related issues, identifying and consulting with team members on 412–413
rectifying issues within your own level of responsibility 419
reviewing team outcomes and implementing improvements 420–422
seeking contributions, teamwork 411–412
sources of information 408–409
supporting colleagues in resolving work difficulties 420
team objectives identification 408
team relationships 414–418
workplace networks, for build relationships 415–416
Eisenhower matrix 61, 63
electronic document management systems 144–145, 182
electronic filing systems 144
electronic funds transfer (EFT) 288
electronic funds transfer at point of sale (EFTPOS) 341
electronic presentations 261
adding text to slide 271
additional slides adding 272–273
application tools 267–277
applying layout 271–272
audience and purpose 262
Canva 264–266
checking 278–279
complex presentations 274–276

computer equipment and peripherals for on-screen presentation 264
creation 266–277
designated timelines, presentations within 276–277
equipment 264
finalising 278–279
hard copies of documents 264
inserting slides from another presentation 275–276
internet and network access 264
materials for delivery 279
mode of presentation 263
objects insertion 272
organisational requirements 263–264, 266–267
PowerPoint Help 277–278
preparation 262–266
right work environment 262
saving 279
task requirements 263–264
template/theme, choosing 269–270
venue 264
visual impact and emphasis 274
electronic tools 155–157
elements in team 406
emails 6, 192, 195–197, 354, 397, 418
embezzlement 14
emotional wellbeing 45
empathy 35, 396
Employee Assistance Professional Association of Australasia (EAPAA) 55–56
employee assistance programs (EAP) 57, 380
employee assistance schemes (EAS) 57
employee responsibilities in workplace 74–80
employer responsibilities in workplace 74–80
employment services 56
empowerment 46
energy-saving tips at work 103–104
enquiry survey reports 214–215
environmental audit 106–107
environmental factors 372
environmental hazard 109–111
hazardous waste regulations 109–110
types of 109
waste disposal 110–111
environmental issues 410
environmentally sustainable working practices 389
environmental management framework 114
Environmental Protection Acts 108–109
Environment Protection and Biodiversity Conservation (EPBC) Act 1999, 108–110
environment, on personal wellbeing 45
Environment Protection Authority (EPA) 108
equal employment opportunity 62
equal opportunity 410
equipment consumables 119, 181
escalation processes 354
ethical 14
ethical principles 168, 307–308
of business 362
ethnic groups 26
ethnicity 24
etiquette 11
Excel formulas 239–240
Excel Help 251–252
expense accounts, closing 303
expenses 287, 298
experience sharing 39
external agencies 146
external customers 313
external networks 416
external stakeholders 258–259, 356, 410

F

face-to-face communication 5
face-to-face discussions 22
face-to-face meetings 370
facial expressions 20
fair work legislation 62
family structure, inclusive practices 28–29
family support services 56
features 68
feedback 69
customer 5
customer service delivery 330–334
encouraging and acknowledging 422
to enhance quality of customer service 334
evaluating and identifying opportunities for improvement 40–41
identifying and implementing, to WHS 84
incorporating to make improvements 41–42
seeking feedback from others on effectiveness of communication 22–23
seeking feedback, from supervisor 40
on task progress 394
verifiable sources 332–334
feedback culture 40
files 211
finance management 309
finance staff 421
financial assets 179
financial budget 172
financial information 137
financial records maintaining 281–310
account customer 282
accounting 307
accounting software used for 288
accounting system 282
accounts payable 282, 283
accounts receivable 282, 283
accuracy maintenance 284
adjusted entries 302
assessing and identifying general ledger accounts affected 293
balance sheet 282–283
bookkeeping transactions, classifications of 284–287
chart of accounts 295–300
codes of practice 306–309
credit (CR) 283
debit (DR) 283
double-entry accounting 283, 296–300
escalating discrepancies 302
ethical principles 307–308
general ledger 283, 303–306
GST legislation 308
journal 283
key components 282–284
legislation 306–309
local, state and territory work health and safety 308–309
national standards 306–309
organisational accounting systems and procedures 282–288
posting journal entries into general ledger system 294–295
preparing journals, for posting to general ledger 288–294
profit and loss statement, 283–284
rectifying any discrepancies 301–302
source and accountable documents 284
tax records 306–307
trial balance 284

financial reports 370
5 Rs (refuse, reduce, reuse, repurpose and recycle) 114–115
fixed assets 285
folders 211–212
font style 10
footer 217
forecasting 119
formality level 207
formal networks 416
formal performance appraisals 378
formal studies 384
formatting documents 189–192
- bullets and numbered lists 191–192
- spelling and grammar checking 189, 191
- styles 191
- text boxes 189, 190

G

gender
- defined 30
- inclusive practices 30–31
- non-binary people 30–31
- stereotypes 30
- transgender 30–31

general ledger 283
- assessing and identifying 293
- closing and post-closing trial balance 303–304
- maintenance 303–306
- posting journal entries into 294–295
- preparing journals for posting to 288–294
- trial balance and checking 304–306

general media 340
generation alpha 29
generation gap 29
generations
- categorised, by their birth years 29
- characteristics of 29

generation X 29
generation Y 29
generation Z 29
gestures 20
goal setting 369
good communication skills 21, 49, 353
- development 321

goods and services tax (GST) 290
- legislation 308

Google Calendar 155–157
government authorities 258, 364
government organisations 146
government payments 56
graphic design applications 200
graphs 253
greenhouse gases 102–103
Green Office program 114–116

H

Handout Master 269
hard copy 227
hardware 200
hazard identification 79–80
- conducting 90–92
- form 97
- in work area 88–90

hazard/incident report 99
hazardous substances 96
hazardous waste 110
- regulations 109–110

hazards 14
- to appropriate personnel 111
- identification 79–80

header 217
health and safety committees 81–82
health and safety representatives (HSRs) 81
health behaviours 57
health-care costs 57
hearing impairment 328
hierarchy 115
hierarchy of control 92, 93
homelessness services 56
house style 10, 187
human resources 119, 120
human resources staff 47, 86, 335, 378, 421
hyperlinked custom show 275

I

important tasks 61, 371
incentives, benefits-based 57
incident investigation form 98
inclusion and diversity 46, 414
inclusive practices 24
- age 29–30
- assessment 39–42
- benefits 25
- cultural background 27
- developing plans for incorporating 32–33
- evaluating feedback and identifying opportunities for improvement 40–41
- family structure 28–29
- gender 30–31
- identifying and implementing 36–37
- identifying individual differences in colleagues, clients and customers 25–32
- incorporating feedback to make improvements 41–42
- intellectual/physical ability 31–32
- modifying verbal and non-verbal communication, individual differences 37–38
- organisational policies and procedures 32
- religious background 27–28
- seeking feedback, from a supervisor 40
- sharing and documenting knowledge, skills and experience 38–39
- social diversity 27
- stereotypes 27
- support individual differences in workplace 25–33
- supporting colleagues and sharing skills 34–36
- treat people with integrity, respect and empathy 35–36
- working effectively with individual differences 34–39

inclusivity policies
- examples of 33
- issues 33

income accounts 286–287
income statement 283
income summary account, closing 304
individual accounts 298–300
individual differences 25–33
- age 29–30
- in colleagues, clients and customers 25–32
- cultural background 27
- cultural diversity, value of 34
- family structure 28–29
- gender 30–31
- intellectual/physical ability 31–32
- modifying verbal and non-verbal communication in 37–38
- religious background 27–28
- social diversity 27, 34
- stereotypes 27
- working effectively with 34–39

individual salesperson 368
induction 389
industry-based databases 201
industry bodies 108–109, 259, 340
industry codes of conduct 186, 206, 389
industry codes of practice 168, 324, 347

industry-relevant strategies 51
industry-specific needs 328
inference skills 65
informal networks 416
information 348 *see also* customers; organise workplace information
of confidential nature 410
management 139
needs 327–328
sessions 87
sources of 338–340, 408–409
on work roles and objectives of work teams 406–408
innovation 8, 341
cycle of 41, 42
input 204
insurance 302
integrity 35, 307, 395–396
intellectual wellbeing 45
interactive communications 411
internal approvals 128
internal customers 313
internal memos 212, 213
internal networks 416
internal stakeholders 259, 356, 410
internet 137, 186, 204–208, 206, 338
Internet of Things (IoT) 6–7
intranet 6
inventory 283
levels 176
number 181
register 129, 179
invoice 179
tax 179, 284, 308

J

job description 406
journals 283
cash payments book 289–292
cash receipts book 289, 292–293
identifying, preparing and documenting entries 288–293
income and expenses into 289
posting entries into general ledger 294–295
preparing for posting to general ledger 288–294
purchase journal 289–293
sales journal 289, 292
justification 10

K

key performance indicators 368–370
key stakeholders 63
knowledge 135

L

language barriers 11, 37, 400
language needs 327
leadership 46–47
leading question 16
legal and organisational policies, guidelines and requirements 122
legal obligation 73
legislation information 146
legislative issues 362
lesson plan 86, 87
liabilities 286, 298
lifestyle programs 339
line charts 252
line graph 253–254
line management 146
local presentation 263
loyal customer complaints 353

M

managers 85, 127, 140, 251, 356, 378, 421
manufacturers' guidelines 186
margins 10
marketing coordinator's role on the business 389
market research 138
material safety data sheets 110
mathematical operators 242–243
measuring performance 369–370
meeting minutes 206, 212–214
memo 212
mental impairments 328
Microsoft Excel *see also* spreadsheets
date format options in 246
formulas 239, 240
mathematical operators in 242
order of operations 244
Microsoft Outlook 155, 196, 418
Microsoft PowerPoint 87, 232, 264–272, 275–278
Microsoft Word 191, 211, 216, 217
minutes 205, 213–214
mission statement 414
mobile devices, for communication 6
monitor 204
multimedia 69

N

need 314
negotiation 364
networking 415
benefits of 416–418
for build relationships 415–416
external 416
formal 416
informal 416
internal 416
using technology 417–418
value of 416
newsletters 50
non-binary people 30–31
non-current assets 285
non-current liabilities 286
non-tendered processes 128
non-verbal communication 16–18
across different cultures 398
culturally specific communications and customs 20
eye contact 20
facial expressions 20
gestures 20
handshakes 20
in individual differences 37–38
physical presentation 20
rate of speech 20
tone and pitch of voice 20
non-verbal language 17–20, 321
notes master 269
notifiable incident 94–96

O

objectivity 307
observation skills 65
office productivity software 199
one-on-one conversations 397
one-on-one meetings with peers and supervisors 50
one-size-fits-all approach 57
one- to four-drawer file cabinets 145, 227
online assessments 50
online presentation 263
online research 346
online surveys 205
open communication 75, 396
open meetings 397
open questions 16
operating system 200
operational procedures 135
operational staff 368
operational teams 390
opportunities 33
order form 178
organisational acquisition considerations 125–126
budgets 125–126
storing resources 126
time frames 126
organisational culture 10
defined 10
qualities 10

organisational database 370
organisational goals and processes 409–410
organisational methods
 for monitoring service delivery 403–404
 for monitoring service standards 378
organisational policies and procedures 9, 14, 48, 73, 168, 169, 186
 effective workplace relationships 409
 inclusive practices 32
 monitoring and modifying information 146
 to receiving and acquiring information 138–139
 spreadsheet 259
organisational product manuals 338
organisational protocols 172
organisational reputation 10, 362
organisational requirements
 business documents 206–207
 customer service delivery 321–323
 disclosure of 307
 electronic presentations 263–264, 266–267
 and legal requirements 121–123
 and protocols for planning tools 153–164
 simple documents 185–188
 and your own skills 382
organisational structure 409–410
organisation needs resources 118
organisation's customer service charter 330
organise schedules *see* schedules
organise workplace information 134–151
 about competitors 135
 additional required information 140
 analysis and interpretation 141–142
 clear, accurate, current and relevant 139–140
 commonly needed across all industries 136
 distributing information to relevant stakeholders 146–148
 external sources 137–138
 forms and templates 135
 identifying and documenting future needs 150
 internal sources 137–138
 issues identification 147
 monitoring and modifying information 146
 operational procedures 135
 organisational policies and procedures 138–139
 product 136
 receiving and acquiring 137–139
 reviewing feedback and suggesting updating 148–150
 reviewing information needs 148–150
 seeking feedback 148
 sources of 135
 storage, using relevant systems and technology 142–145
 in suitable format for analysis 141–146
orientation programs 389
output 204
owner's equity 286

P

packaging procedures 329
paper-based file storage systems 145, 227
paper-based methods 154
paper trail 6
parameters 234
 fallback 363
passive-aggressive communication style 8, 49
passive communication style 8, 49
payment and delivery options 322
payment type 291
peaks 131
peer/buddy systems 88
performance appraisals 421
performance management and indicators 407
performance review 40
personal factors, on personal wellbeing 45–46
 culture 45
 education 45
 environment 45
 family life 45
 financial state 45
 psychological state 45
personal organisers 158–159
personal skills development
 career plan 382, 383
 and learning 381–385
 need for your job role 382
 opportunities for 381–384
personal wellbeing 44 *see also* communication
 appropriate communication approach 48–50
 factors that impact 45–48
 personal factors on 45–46
 planning communication with supervisor 48–52
 planning relevant content for communication 50–51
 resources 54–58
 workplace factors on 46–48
personal work priorities 366–385
 business technology 375–376
 developing personal work plans 373–376
 evaluating your own work performance 376–381
 expected and actual work performance 377–378
 factors affecting achievement of work objectives 372–373
 goal setting 369
 measuring performance 369–370
 organising and completing your own work schedule 367–376
 personal and professional development needs for your job role 381–382
 personal skills development and learning 381–385
 reporting variations in work practices 377–378
 seeking feedback 378
 sources of stress and accessing appropriate support 378–381
 work goals and key performance indicators 368–370
 workload according to task time frames 370–372
person conducting a business or undertaking (PCBU) 81, 82
physical impairments 328
physical presentation 20
physical wellbeing 45
pie charts 252, 253
placeholder 271
plan-do-check-act (PDCA) cycle 412–413
planning wall chart 154
portable hanging indent files 145, 227
portable storage 227
position description 387
positive listening 17
positive listening skills 52
positive team outcomes 419–423
PowerPoint 264–272, 276, 277
practical demonstrations 88
practical problem solving 75

preferred products 318, 349–350
prepaid expenses 302
preprinted questionnaires 333
presentation software 199, 201
presenteeism 379
principals 340
Privacy Act 1988 (Cth), 232, 362
privacy laws 168
proactive 412
probity 175
problem-solving skills 65
process-oriented thinking 41
procurement 175
product and service knowledge
  based on product information 343
  characteristics of a product 341
  development of 338–343
  features and benefits 342
  identifying and using opportunities to 343
  sources of information 338–340
product information 136
productivity 3, 126
product labels 338
product manufacturers 346
product-related complaints 353
professional behaviour 308
professional boundaries 66
professional competence 307
professional development 382
  needs for your job role 381
  opportunities 384
  recording and incorporating feedback and 384–385
professional networks 199
profit and loss statement 283–284
programs 200
project management 230
project teams 390
proofreading 225
protocols 121
psychological safety 46, 414
psychological state, on personal wellbeing 45
psychological wellbeing 45
pull communication 411
purchase goods and services 172–182
  action to resolve non-compliance with specifications 181
  approval for 177
  determining your own role and limits of your authority 174–175
  facilitating registration of new assets 181
  filing and storing records 181–182
  making purchases 175–180
  methods 177
  place an order 178–180
  purchase specifications from relevant personnel 176
  quotations from suppliers 177–178
  receiving goods, checking for compliance with specifications 180
  record-keeping systems for purchases and assets 173
  understanding and clarifying, organisation's purchasing strategies 173–174
purchase journals 283, 289–293, 298
purchase order 124, 125, 178, 179, 284
purchase specifications 176
purchasing process, steps in 174
purchasing strategies 173
  understanding and clarifying 173–174
push communication 411

Q

quality control 377
questioning techniques 16–21

R

Racial Discrimination Act 1975 (Cth), 362
rate of speech 20
raw materials, stocks and supplies 119
reactive 412
receipts 284
Recognition of Prior Learning (RPL) 384
record-keeping systems, for purchases and assets 173
recurring appointments 164–167
recycle 115
reference retrieval systems 144
refuse 114
relaxation techniques 381
relevant staff members 338
religion 27–28
religious practices 28
repetitive strain injury (RSI) 89
reports 205, 214–216
repurpose 115
resolution procedures 309
resource acquisition processes 127–128
  contracted supplier ordering 127–128
  internal approvals 128
  non-tendered processes 128
  tendered processes 128
resource issues 373
resource parameters 122
resource shortages, impact of 123
respect 396
  people's personal space 398
  treat people with 35–36
returns policy 329–330
reuse 115
revenue 286–287, 299
revenue accounts, closing 303
risk 79, 90–93, 374
  control measures 93–94
  evaluation 92
  identifying and assessing 91
  implementing control methods 92–93
  levels and actions 93
risk assessment 73, 79–80, 90, 97
  chart 92
risk/hazard identification and action form 112
risk management 176
rows, in spreadsheet 237

S

safety committees 88
safety data sheet (SDS) 110, 111
safety share 50
sales journal 283, 289, 292, 299
sales reports 333, 370
sales representatives 340
scepticism 53
schedules 152
  appointments, timelines and diary commitments 165–167
  areas of improvement 170–171
  customer contact database 158
  developing appointment schedules and priorities 163–164
  diaries and planning tools 154–159
  effectiveness of 169–171
  electronic tools 155–157
  legislative requirements, codes and standards 168–169
  management 164–169
  management requirements 162–164
  management software programs 159
  manual tools 154
  negotiating alternative arrangements 165–167
  organisational requirements and protocols for planning tools 153–164

schedules (*continued*)
  personal organisers 158–159
  procedures for appointments and 160–162
  recording and managing 167–168
  recurring appointments 164–165
  requirements 153–164
  seeking feedback 169–171
scheduling resource usage 129
seeking feedback 22–23
  on clarity, accuracy, relevancy and sufficiency of information 148
  effectiveness of schedules 169–171
  from others on effectiveness of communication 22–23
  personal work priorities 378
  from supervisor 40
segregation of duties 173
self-development process 378
self-running (automated) presentation 263
senior manager 364
service-related complaints 353
service-specific legislation 347
Sex Discrimination Act 1984 (Cth), 362
sexual harassment 14
shared drives 418
sharing information 36, 39, 147, 394, 410, 422
simple documents 183–202
  budgets 186
  communication methods 192–193
  document's audience and purpose 184–185
  drafting 194–197
  file usage and storage 186
  finalising 197–199
  format, style and structure 188–189
  formatting, using software functions and features 189–192
  house style 187
  key points for inclusion 193
  making and checking any final necessary changes 198–199
  organisational and legislative policies, guidelines and requirements 186
  organisational requirements 185–188
  planning 184–193
  response times 186
  use of templates and forms 185–186
single-parent families 28
skill sharing 38
slide masters 269
slide window 270
SMART principle 369, 374
SMS (Short Message Service) 6
social diversity 11, 27
  defined 27
  value of 34
social housing 56
social media 6, 137, 186, 193, 206, 354
social wellbeing 45
software 144, 200
source documents 284
specialist storage systems 145, 227
spiritual wellbeing 45
spreadsheets 144, 206, 370, 418
  alignment 247
  application tools 201, 235
  audience and their information needs 234
  audience for 230
  AutoSum 241
  averages 243, 244
  border 247, 248
  charts 252–257, 258
  consistency of design and layout 235, 237–245
  count of numbers 243
  creation 236–252
  date formats 245–246
  delivering 258–260
  designing 234–236
  entering and sorting data 238–239
  Excel Help 251–252
  features 243
  filling 248, 249
  finalising and presenting 258–260
  font 247
  format and design options 235
  formatting 245–250
  freeze panes 250
  headers and footers 248–250
  mathematical operators 242–243
  name and store 259–260
  order of operations and using brackets 244–245
  page layout options 236
  parameters of 234
  percentage calculation 243
  primary purpose of 230
  protection 248, 249
  readability and appearance 234–236
  reviewing and editing 258
  selecting and preparing resources 230–233
  software 233
  stakeholders to test formulas 251
  task requirements 230–233
  working with formulas 239–241
staff rosters 130
staff shortages 373
stakeholders 223, 304
  business documents, format and style with 209–210
  consultation with, WHS 81
  distributing information to 146–148
  external 258–259, 356, 410
  internal 259, 356, 410
  receiving complaints 356
  responding to challenges and questions from 68
  solution to relevant 68
  spreadsheet needs 258–260
  test formulas, in spreadsheets 251
  in WHS training 85–86
standard 320
standard contracting arrangements and templates 173
state/territory environment protection authority 108
stationery inventory register 105
stationery items 119, 181
stationery order form 124
statutory bodies 146
stereotypes 30
  defined 27
  gender 30
stock-handling processes 354
stock reports 214
stress 378–381, 405
  absenteeism 379
  factors 379
  policies and methods for preventing and alleviating of 380–381
  presenteeism 379
  sources of 378–381
  symptoms of 379
style guides 207–208
supervisor, communication with 52–54
  arrangement 52
  developed plan 52–53
  planning 48–52
  reviewing the effectiveness 53–54
supervisors 127, 140, 251, 335, 356, 378, 409, 421
  feedback from 378
supplier product manuals 338
suppliers 129, 258, 356, 364
  authorised 338
  effective workplace network 416
  obtaining quotations from 177–178
  selection 123, 178

supply chain program, for purchasing alternative products 114
survey forms/questionnaires 22
sustainability policies and procedures 104
sustainability practices 129
sustainable work practices 101
  benefits of 113
  environmental hazard 109–111
  Green Office program 114–116
  identification 103–104
  measurement 102–107
  recording and measuring resource usage 105–106
  reporting breaches to appropriate personnel 111–112
  reporting hazards to appropriate personnel 111
  resource deficiencies identification 106–107
  resources identification 104–105
  seeking opportunities for improvement 113–116
  supporting 107–112
  sustainability procedures, identifying and complying with 108–109
  working with colleagues to identify and assess potential improvements 113–114
symmetrical balance 208
synergy 35
systemic problems 61

T

T-accounts 296–298
task items identification, 163–164
taxable sales 308
taxes
  invoices 284, 308
  records 306–307
  returns 284
team goals and your responsibilities relevant to achieving them 392–394
team leader 390, 406
team meetings 50, 169
team members 421
  collaborating effectively with 399–400
  communicating clearly and respectfully with 397
  evaluating critical thinking processes with 69–71
  key principles of cross-cultural communication 396–399
  knowledge and experience of 65–66
  potential work-related issues, identifying and consulting on 412–413
  seeking and providing assistance 403–404
team relationships and networks development 414–418
teams, type of 390
teamwork
  effective 395–396
  effective workplace relationships 421
  goals for 388
  impact of your role in workplace 388–389
  individual work tasks within a team 387–392
  organisational policies and procedures 389, 390
  planning and prioritising your own tasks 391–392
  potential contributions of 391
  seeking contributions 411–412
  team goals and your responsibilities relevant to achieving them 392–394
  working effectively with team members 396–401
  your own responsibilities 387
  your own role and task requirements within team, identification 388–390
technical delays 400
technical/equipment breakdowns 372
technology 142–145, 164, 417–418
  for business documents 204–205
  defined 204
  internet and mobile applications 204–208
templates 10–11, 135, 173, 185–186, 205, 269, 270
tendered processes 128
themes 269, 270
thesaurus 207
thumbnails 269
time frames 126
time management software programs 159
toolbox talks 50, 88
toxic chemicals 126
trade associations 340
trade magazine 339
tradeoffs 67
Trade Practices Act 1974, 347
training gap 84
training needs analysis (TNA) 84, 382, 384
training schedule 86
training, work health and safety
  arrangements for 85–87
  competence development, strategies and opportunities for 85–88
  methods 87–88
  needs of work team 84–85
transgender 30–31
transparency 175
transport/travel policies 130
trend information 146
trends 131
trial balance 284, 303
  and checking 304–306
  closing and post-closing, 303–304
troughs 131

U

unearned revenue 302
upcycling 115
urgent tasks 61, 371

V

value statement 414
verbal communication 5–6
  in individual differences 37–38
verbal harassment/abuse 14
version control method 259
videoconferencing 6, 399
violence 14
virtual meeting technology 199, 418
virtual teams 390
vision statement 414
visual impairment 328

W

waste disposal 110–111
welfare services 56
wellbeing 386 *see also* communication; personal wellbeing
  defined 44
  initiatives in workplace 54, 55
wellbeing programs 51, 57–58
wellbeing resources 54–58
  documenting methods 57–58
  external sources 55, 56
  identifying and reviewing 55–57
  internal sources 55–57
  online resources 55–56
  selection 57
white space, defined 209
word processing 144, 200

work health and safety (WHS) 62, 176, 263
- aware of responsibilities 390
- checklists 105
- legislation 168
- local, state and territory 308–309
- managing schedules 168
- officers 378
- policies, procedures and programs 122, 186, 206–207
- requirements 130
- responsibilities 410
- team structure and other team members role 390–391

Work Health and Safety Act 2011, 76–79, 186, 206, 308

workloads 47

workplace communication *see* communication

workplace culture 46

workplace factors, on personal wellbeing 46–48

work health and safety (WHS) 47, 73
- completing and maintaining incident records in work area 94–99
- consultative arrangements for management 80–84
- encouraging others to participate in arrangements 83
- feedback, identifying and implementing improvements to 84
- health and safety committees 81–82
- health and safety representatives (HSRs) 81
- implementing consultative processes 82
- issues 4, 83, 362
- legal obligations in reporting 94–99
- policies and procedures 74–80
- training 84–88
- wardens and officers 56

work health and safety (WHS) policies and procedures 74–80
- characteristics and composition of work team 74–75
- explaining 75–76
- hazard identification and risk assessment outcomes 79–80
- health and safety requirements of work team 75
- legislative requirements 75–76
- ramifications of failing to comply with legal obligations 76–79

workplace problems
- critically evaluating and selecting solutions 66–67
- critical thinking 64–65, 71
- cross-functional process map 70
- evaluating critical thinking processes with team members 69–71
- finalising and reviewing solution development 68–71
- identifying and selecting 61
- key stakeholders 63
- knowledge and experience of team members 65–66
- mapping process 69
- organisational and legislative frameworks 62
- preparing to address 60–64
- process analysis 69, 71
- questions to identify key issues and challenges 62–63
- redesigning, implementing and communicating the new process 71
- single-purpose process map 70
- solutions for 64–67
- stakeholders, solution to relevant 68

workplace relationships *see* effective workplace relationships

work-related injuries 78

work role, defined 406

workshops 87

work stress *see* stress

World Health Organization (WHO) 25

written communication 6, 184
- methods 192–193

Y

youth justice services 56

Notes